Rubens's Massacre of the Innocents

THE THOMSON COLLECTION
AT THE ART GALLERY OF ONTARIO

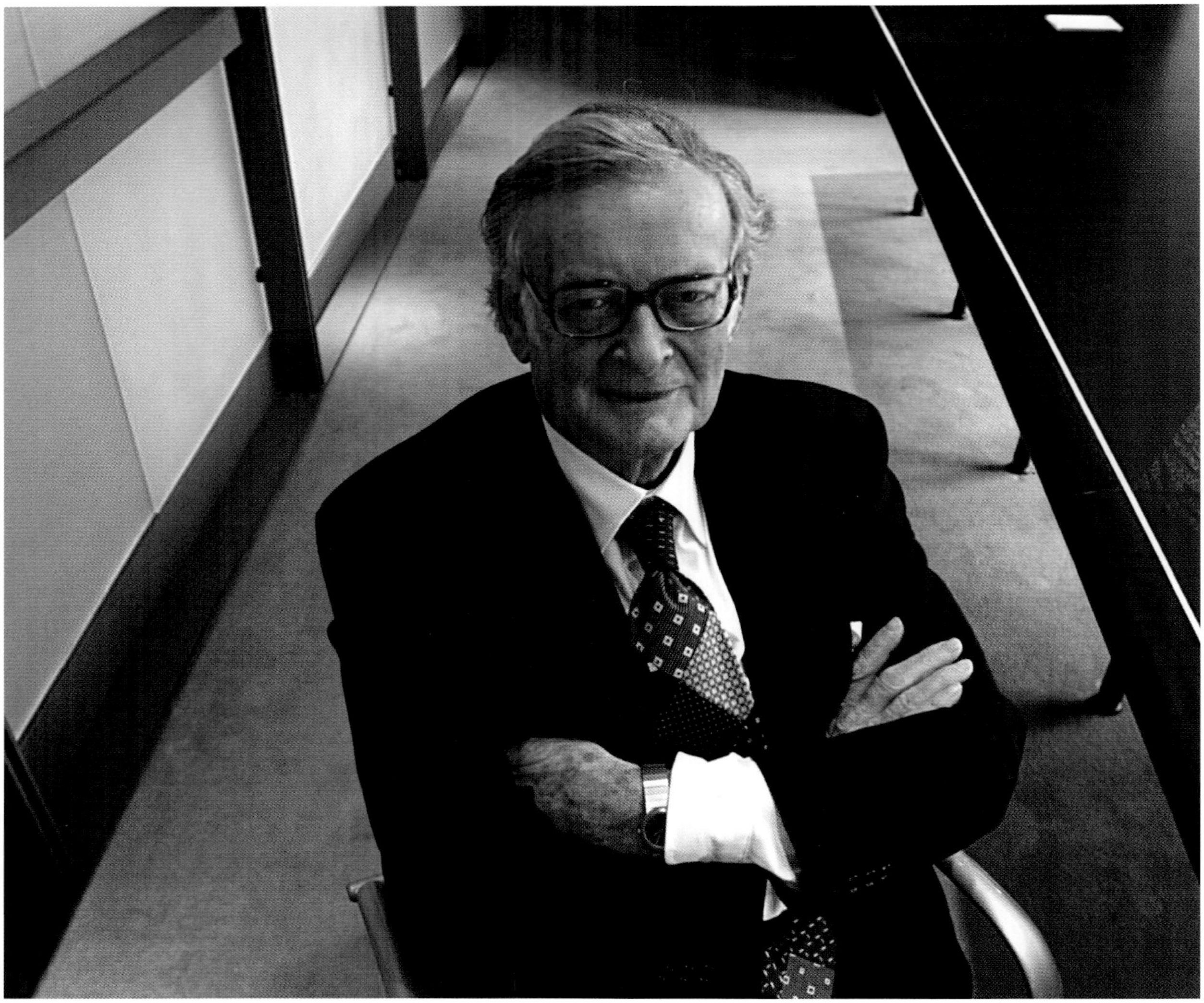

Rubens's Massacre of the Innocents

THE THOMSON COLLECTION
AT THE ART GALLERY OF ONTARIO

David Jaffé
with a contribution by
Giovanna Tonelli

SKYLET PUBLISHING /
THE ART GALLERY OF ONTARIO

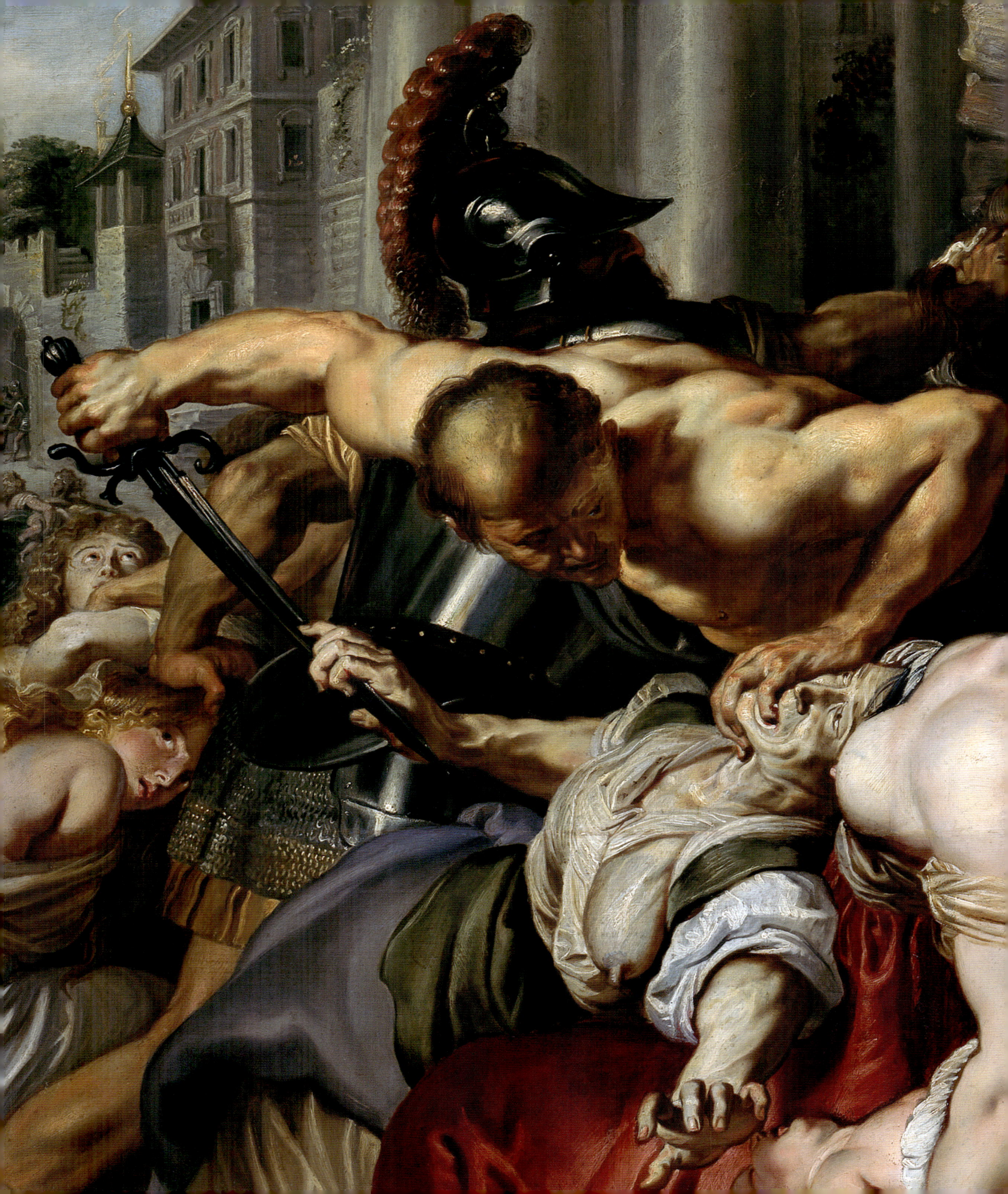

Contents

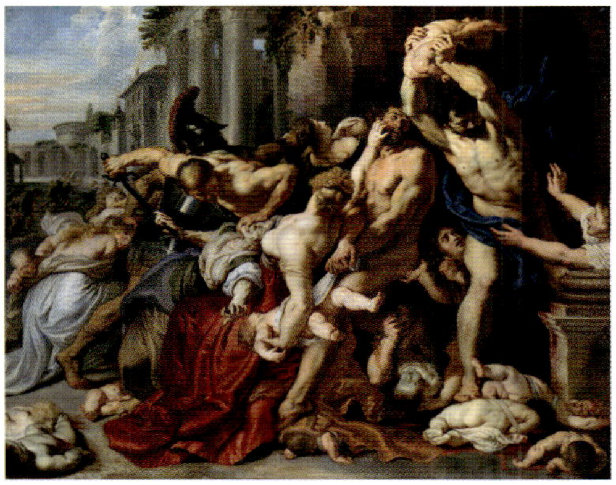

A double-page reproduction of *The Massacre of the Innocents* folds out at the end of the book

Foreword

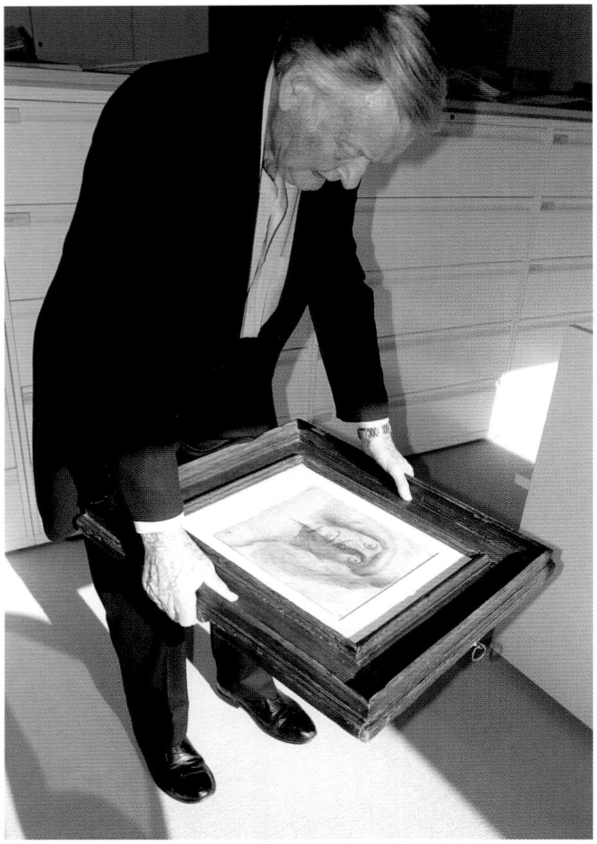

KENNETH ROY THOMSON, 2nd Baron Thomson of Fleet, or Ken as we all knew him, was an extraordinary human being. He built upon his father's legacy to construct one of the most successful global business empires. He amassed with an ever-growing passion what is undoubtedly the finest collection of art ever in private hands in Canada. He was the catalyst for and the enabler of Transformation AGO, and he still retained the common touch. Ken derived great joy from his interaction with people from all walks of life – whether pointing out to total strangers intriguing bargains at the local Loblaws, or sending a photograph (perhaps not of museum quality) he had taken of you with his basic camera at an event the night before.

At a lunch following a TD board meeting after Ken flipped one of his brightly coloured signature ties over his shoulder to avoid attracting the soup of the day, I asked him how he became interested in art. He began seriously collecting in 1953 when he spotted two miniature ivory busts in a Bournemouth antique shop. Shortly thereafter, Ken became excited by the prospect of acquiring an exquisite boxwood figure and was admonished by his advising dealer: "You must not look like that when you see it. You must control yourself and look very solemn. You will put the price up with enthusiasm like that." Ken took the advice to heart, but it was an enduring struggle to restrain his natural enthusiasm for marvellous works of art.

Over the years, Ken developed an ever more discerning and refined eye, but his guiding rule in acquiring art was, "If your heart is beating, you know it was made for you." I remember Ken confessing that, while assembling his collection, he viewed the Art Gallery of Ontario as a competitor but, as time passed, he came to envisage the AGO as the ideal vehicle for keeping the collection intact and exhibiting it to the people of Canada so that they could experience the same pleasure as he did from his art. "It might make people see and enjoy objects previously unfamiliar to them. . . . It might open up their horizons. I do not see how you can walk past these beautiful objects, look at them, and not see the glory of art and its creation." Accordingly, Ken determined to donate his unsurpassed collection and to work with Matthew Teitelbaum and Frank Gehry to transform the Art Gallery of Ontario.

Ken wanted the works displayed in an atmosphere where the viewer could feel "at home." At one time, he contemplated music in the galleries, and he liked the idea of a series of rooms that led one into the other so that people could walk through "chapters" of his collection.

Ken remained intimately engaged in the Gehry project to the end. He continued to purchase works of art to enhance the quality of the Thomson Collection and with exceeding generosity took steps time after time to encourage the realization of Transformation AGO at the highest level. I remember Ken leaning over at a curatorial discussion of the David Milne exhibition in 2005 and saying, "I don't want to jinx it, Charlie, but I think our project is going to be the best." That seemed appropriate, because everything about Ken Thomson was the best.

A. CHARLES BAILLIE, O.C.
PRESIDENT, ART GALLERY OF ONTARIO

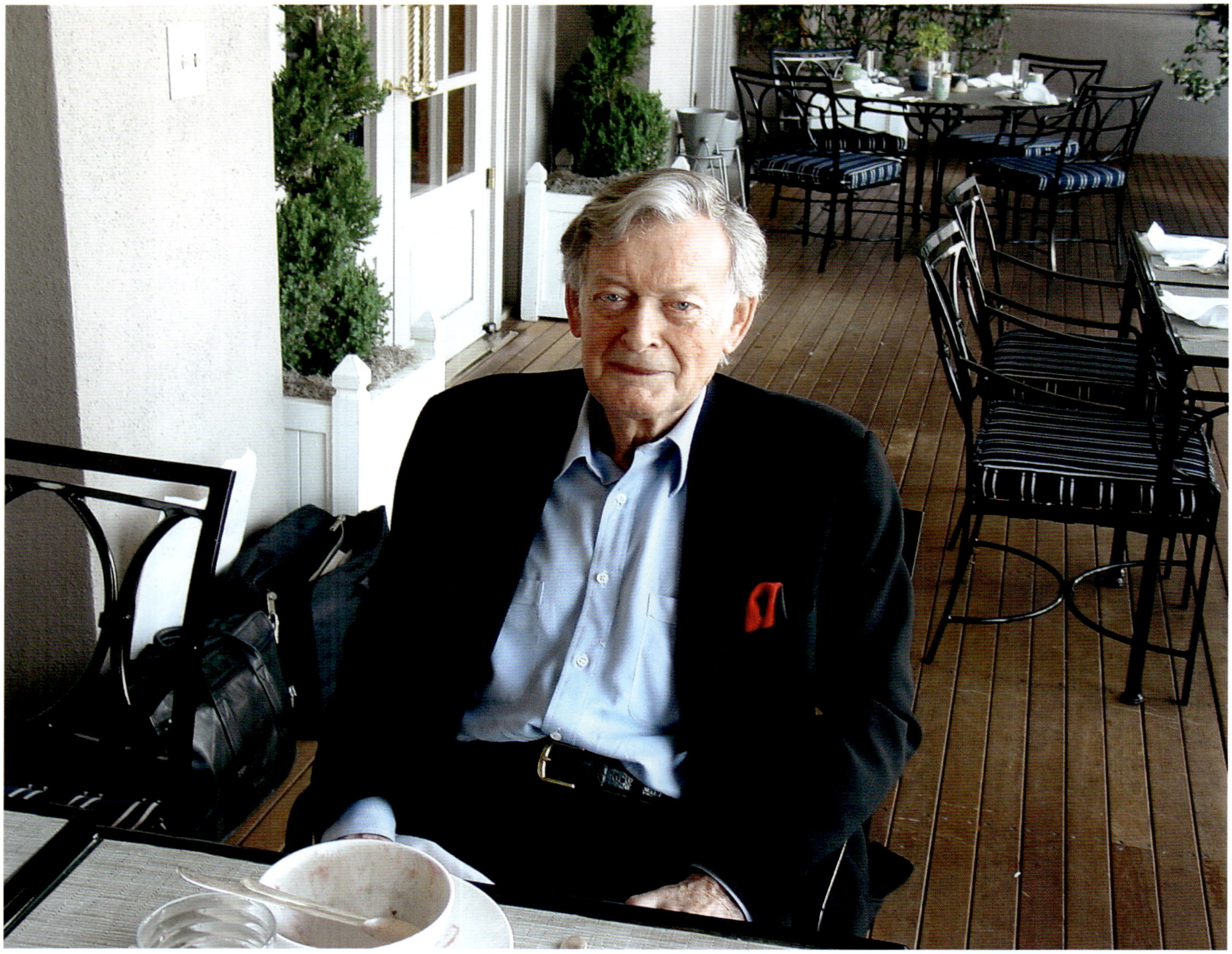

Introduction

MY FATHER COMMUNED WITH OBJECTS. The journey lasted a lifetime. The pursuit was manic and often solitary. My father channelled his energies and unravelled passions that allowed him a solace few could possibly comprehend. Deep friendships developed around this journey of perception and discovery. The facets seemed endless and were reflected. The legacy was a collection of objects that defied linear logic.

Some collectors derive pleasure from the status of ownership; others sustain interest through economic motives. The inherent value of an artwork is gauged by the heart. Experience is often visceral and radiates to one's core. The journey of an art collector is compelled by complex internal forces, from melancholy to wonderment.

My father's course evolved over the years and interactions around art became the barometer of life. He would extract the deepest pleasure from human companionship; artists, collectors, dealers, researchers and any soul with whom he might share his enthusiasm were enlisted for their visceral response to Group of Seven sketches or a Gothic diptych. My father's letters attest to the profound role of communication in his daily life. The art often turned out to be incidental to the friendships that lasted a lifetime. In all spheres the essence of my father's spirit was immersed within the act of consideration, rather than the prospect of possession. The formations of these collections represent a lifetime's journey inspired by the human condition.

The objects within the various collections remain tangible evidence of an immense ambition around the visual experience. My father followed his innermost convictions and had the courage to press his feelings. In some instances, he stood alone as a precursor to the subject or established new thresholds of value. The dogged determination drew the admiration of friends and foes alike, as primal competitive instincts emerged from this gentle soul. My life with father in this realm created a unique bond between us. The human spirit was constantly engaged in all its myriad of shapes and forms. The imprint was quite extraordinary, as the journey became an exploration of the human condition. Father's curiosity seemed insatiable and the objects were conductors through which the widest spectrum of human spirit coursed. The pursuit of art allowed father to make sense of the world and celebrate life in all its resplendent forms.

DAVID THOMSON

Author's Introduction to the *Massacre*

Rubens's *Massacre of the Innocents* is one of his most revealing works. It allows so many insights into his artistic development, ambition and inspiration, that studying the work and its provenance is much like discovering and delving into the artist's own diary.

Rubens painted the *Massacre* in about 1610 on his return home to Antwerp after eight years in Italy, at a time we now recognize as a key moment in his career. In Italy Rubens had studied the art of ancient Rome as well as absorbing the lessons of modern painters such as Elsheimer, Tintoretto, Michelangelo, Raphael, the Carracci and Caravaggio. These antique and modern sources are visually 'mentioned' in the *Massacre*, as are works by the artists who had dominated the Antwerp scene in the previous years, such as Frans Floris, Martin de Vos, Willem van Tetrode and Otto van Veen.

The biblical story of the Massacre of the Innocents was a subject much valued by artists for its expressive and dramatic possibilities, and it was widely illustrated and distributed through engravings after Raphael, Bandinelli, Floris, Tintoretto and Goltzius. So in painting his version Rubens was consciously competing with his Northern and Italian predecessors, as well as more recent practitioners such as the Genoese painter Giovanni Battista Paggi, whose *Massacre* caught his attention in 1606.

Around the same period as he was painting his *Massacre* Rubens was involved with major biblical and mythological works such as *Judith and Holofernes* (lost, but known from an engraving), *Samson and Delilah* (National Gallery, London; fig. 45), *Ecce Homo* (Hermitage, St Petersburg), *Tarquin and Lucretia* (private collection; fig. 38), *Juno and Argus* (Wallraf-Richartz Museum, Cologne; fig. 31), *The Beheading of Saint John the Baptist* (private collection; fig. 15) as well as the great triptych of *The Raising of the Cross* in Antwerp Cathedral (fig. 17). Rubens must have relished the pictorial challenge that the subject of the Massacre represented, as he could draw on his profound knowledge of ancient and modern literature to enrich the work, tempering the graphic violence of the scene with references to earlier expressions of anguish, grief and loss.

It is as yet uncertain whether Rubens had a particular patron or location in mind when he made his picture, but important evidence about the seventeenth-century provenance of the *Massacre* has recently been revealed. It tells us a great deal about the context in which Rubens worked and the market in which his paintings were commissioned and collected in the Southern Netherlands.

The first known owner, Giacomo Antonio Carenna, arrived in Antwerp in the first decade of the seventeenth century to make his reputation and fortune just as Rubens was embarking on his own career. We are not sure when this Milanese merchant-financier acquired the painting but it may have been around the time of his ennoblement in 1655. In his will drawn up in 1669 Carenna records the work as by a fellow knight and as a chimney-piece, something which indicates that the work had been hung high above head height. The *Massacre* next appears in the possession of another leading citizen of Antwerp, the Imperial Postmaster of the Netherlands Jan-Baptista Anthoine, and was then exported to the Viennese collection of the Prince of Liechtenstein, one of the German Catholic winners from the Thirty Years' War. The migration of the *Massacre* from Antwerp was paralleled by a large exodus of other Rubens paintings at the end of the seventeenth century to destinations across Europe, a dispersal that had already begun with the sale of the painter's estate in 1641. Ironically, as Antwerp's fortunes declined, the work of the city's greatest painter became more widely distributed and prized, even if his authorship was sometimes confused with that of his pupils, at least in the case of his relatively early works.

In 1610 Antwerp, and the Southern Netherlands, was trying with limited success to reinvent itself during a pause in its own violent history. Rubens by contrast brilliantly succeeded in creating a new international style, and the manner in which the *Massacre of the Innocents* became a trophy in the three prestigious collections through which it passed in the next hundred years is a measure of his achievement.

Rubens's letters show he was curious about the new worlds of the Americas and Australia, so that he might not have been surprised to find his painting's final destination would be the Thomson Collection at the Art Gallery of Ontario, Toronto. There it joins a group of anatomical drawings by the artist (figs. 91, 96, 99, 100, 102) which were crucial to its inception, and a late record of his 1610–11 *Raising of the Cross* (fig. 18). The replica was made by his workshop, then repainted by his own hand for engraving, in order to celebrate, at the end of his career, his first public triumph on his return to Antwerp. The proximity of the *Massacre of the Innocents*, now the feature painting of the Thomson Collection, and a re-jigged recollection of another masterpiece from the same date is a happy conclusion to the painting's long journey.

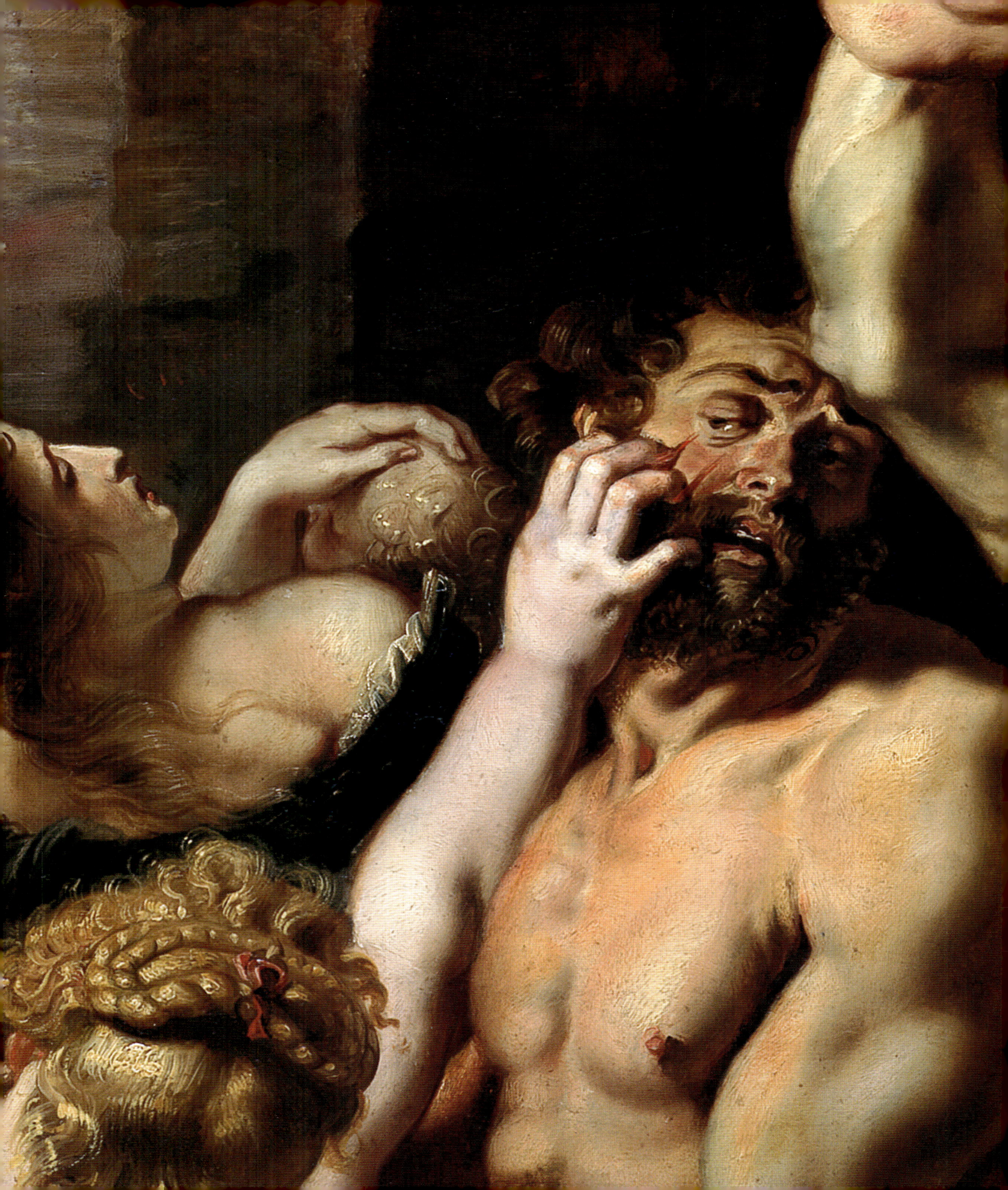

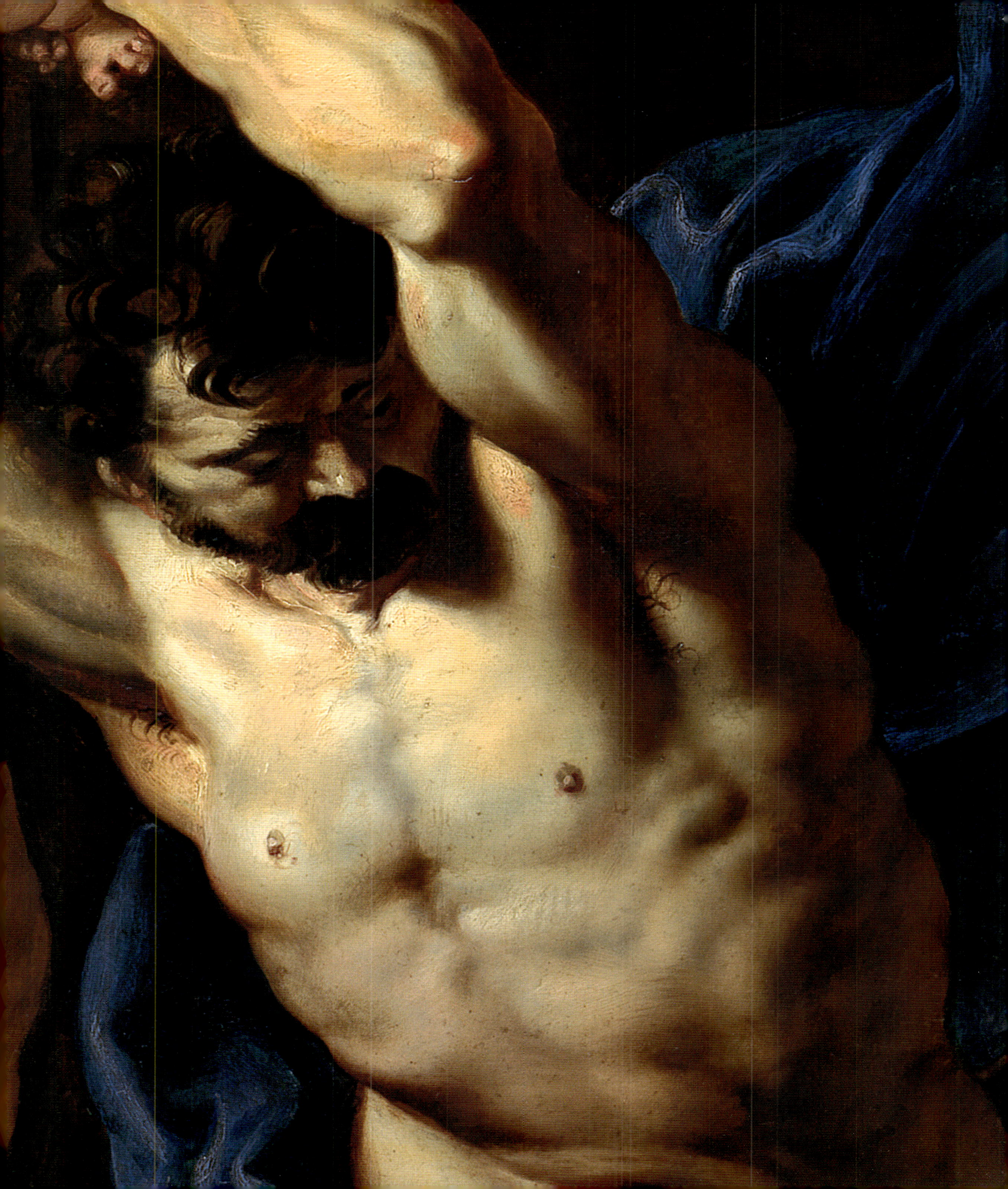

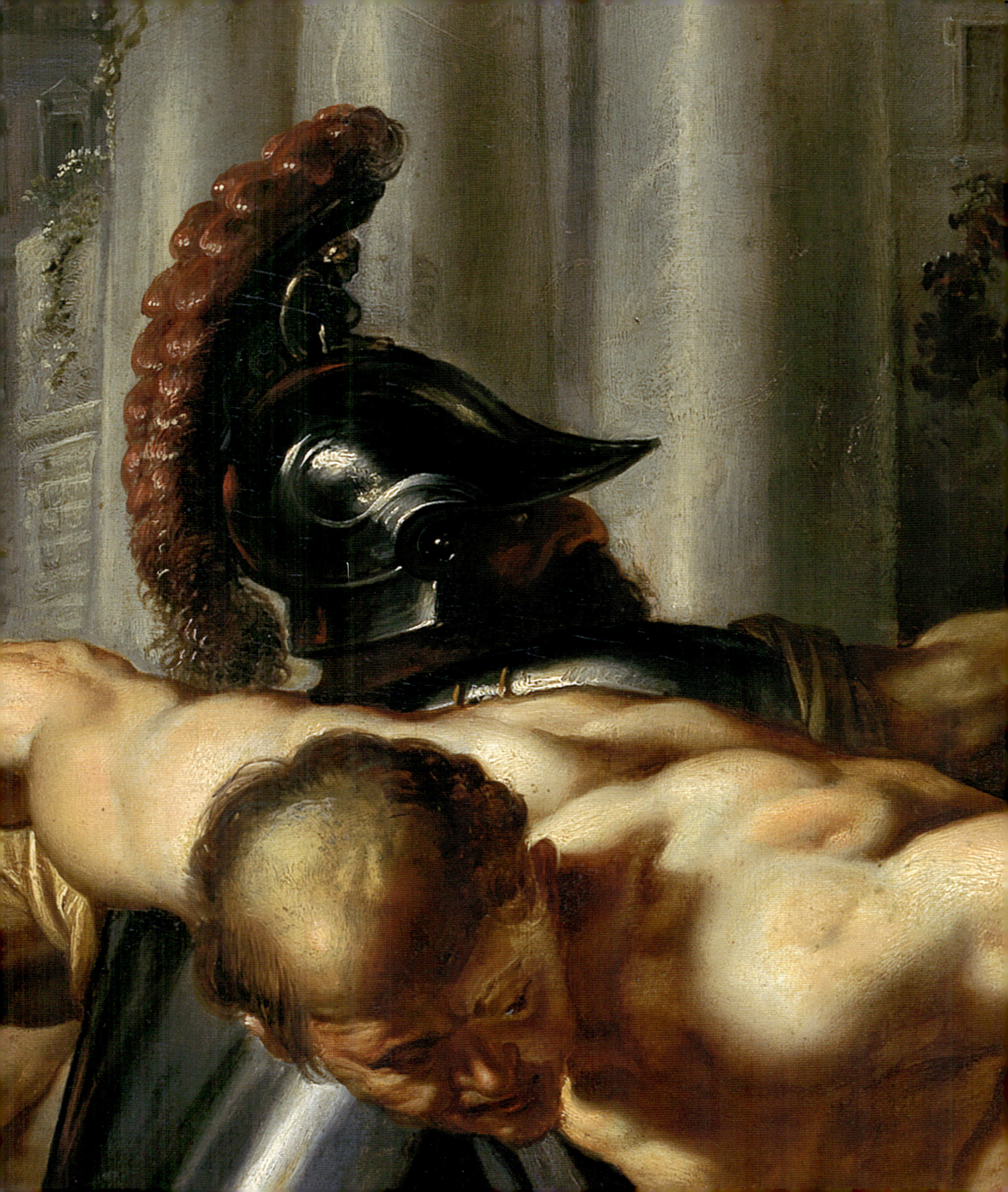

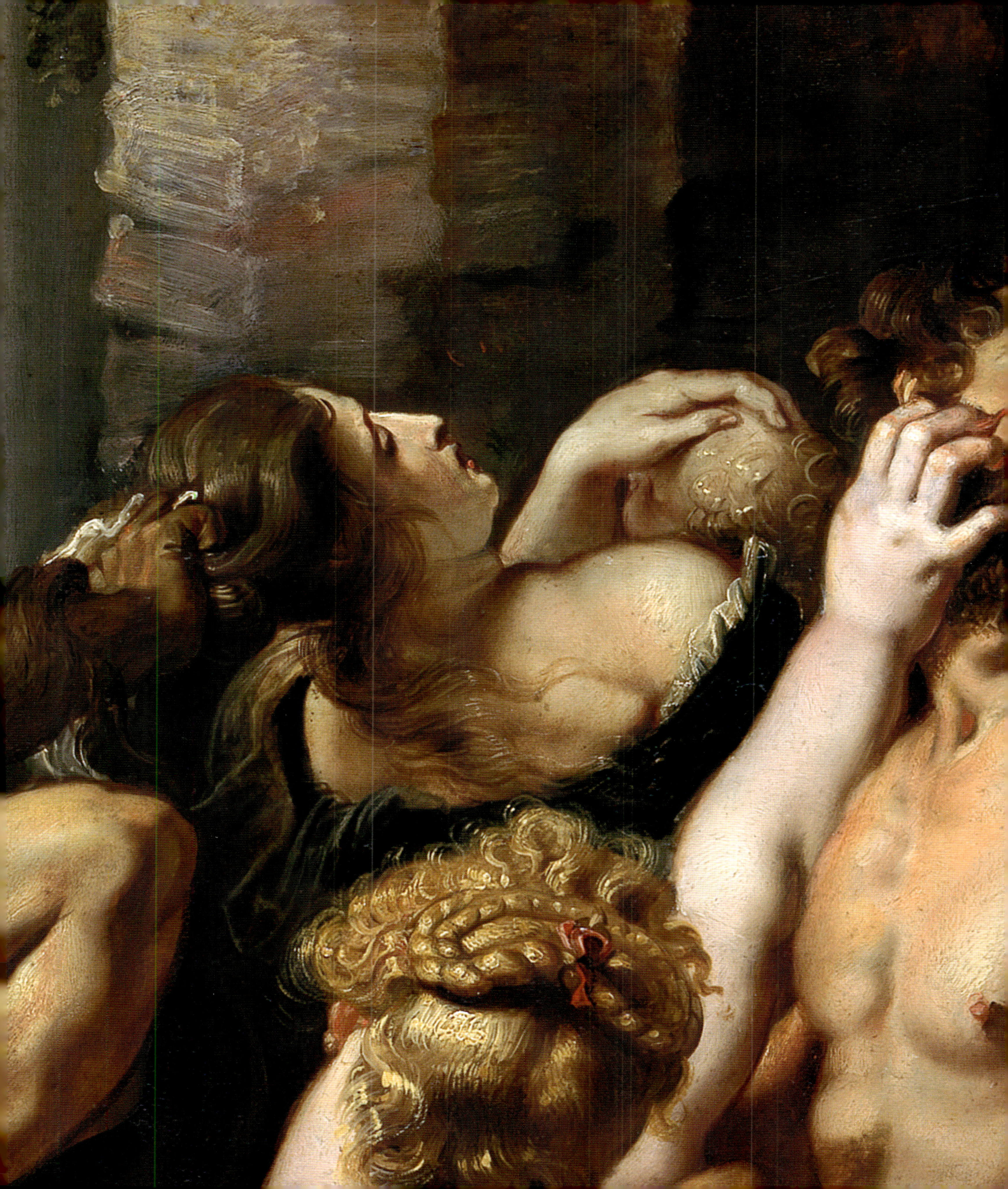

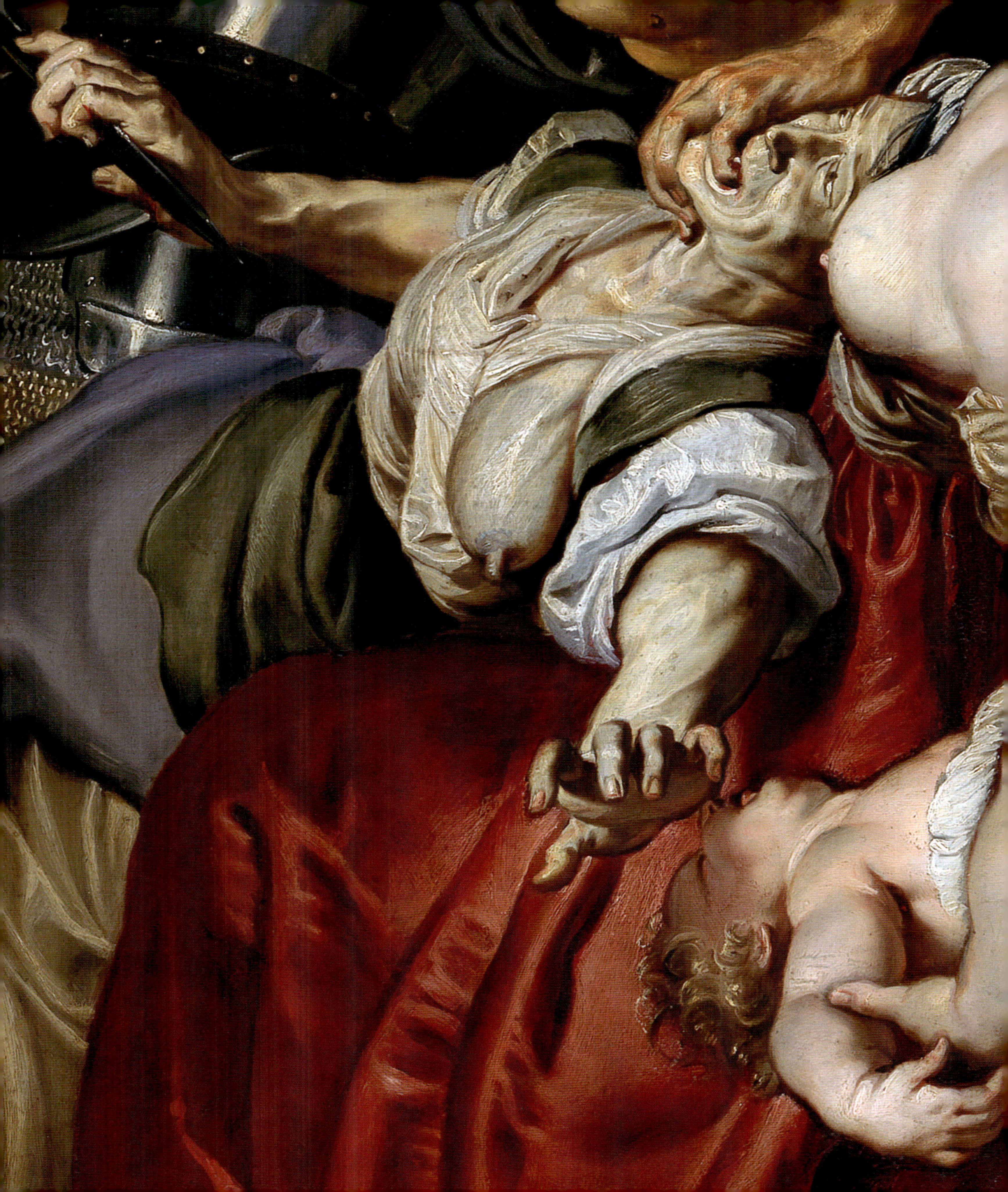

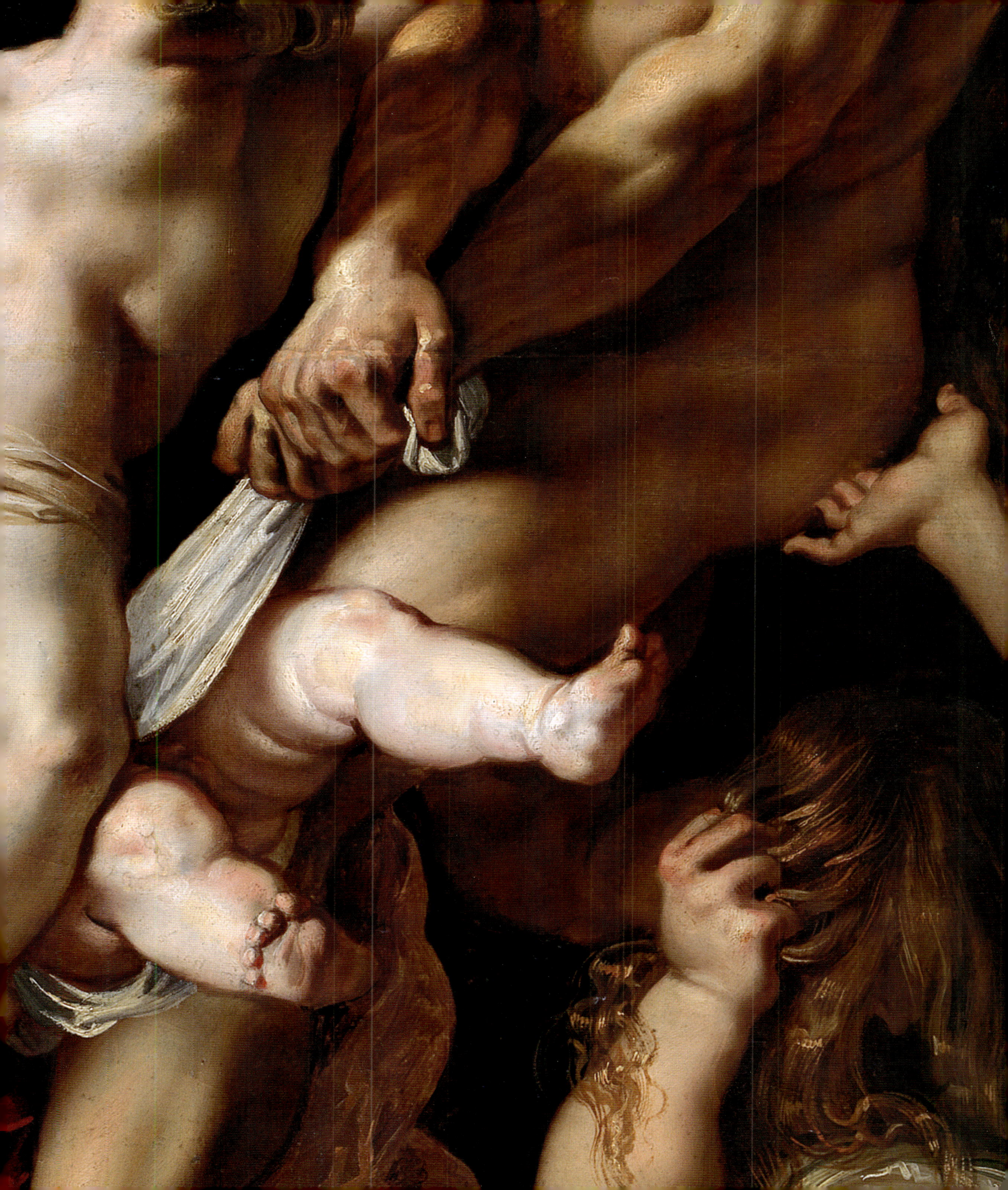

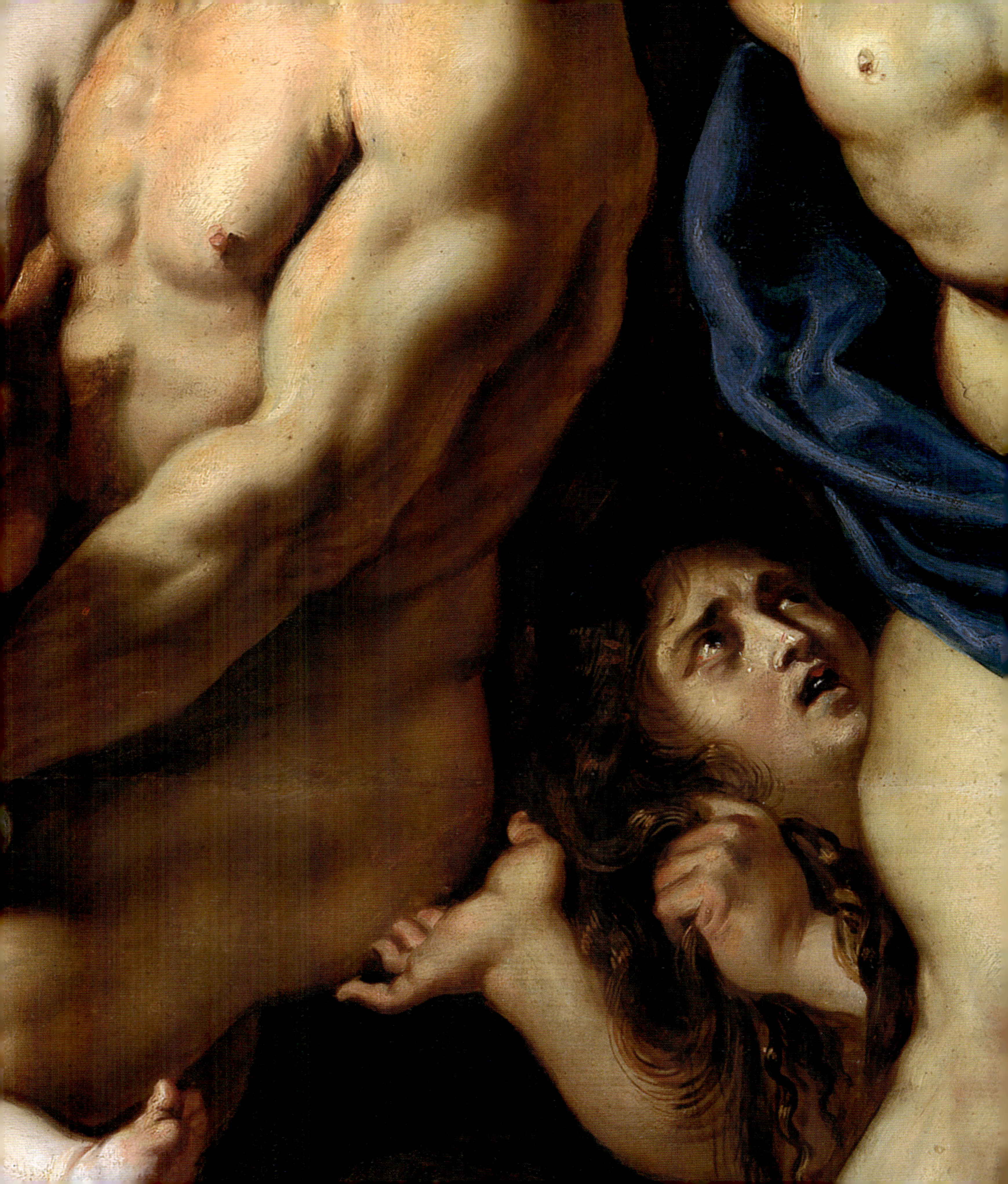

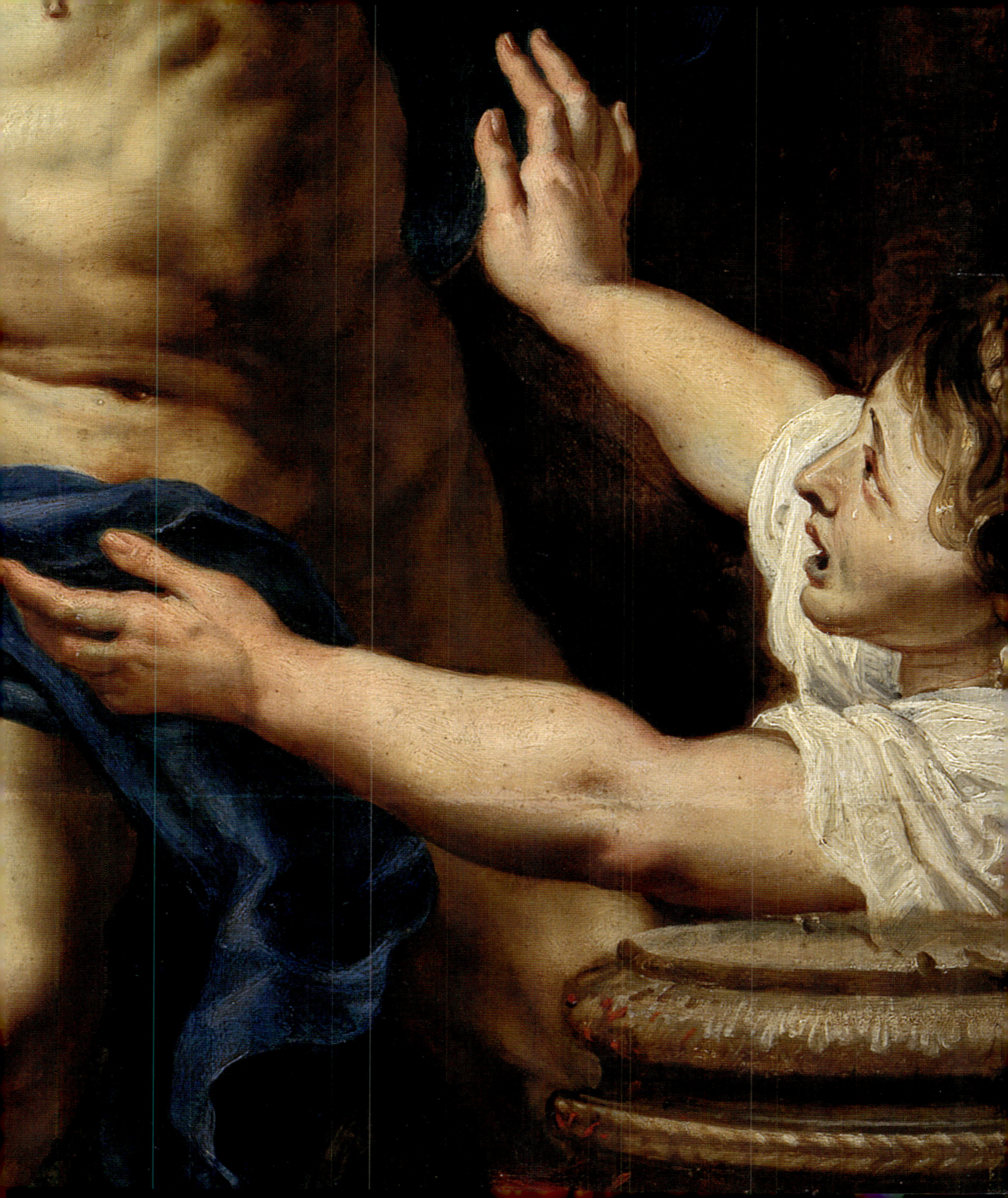

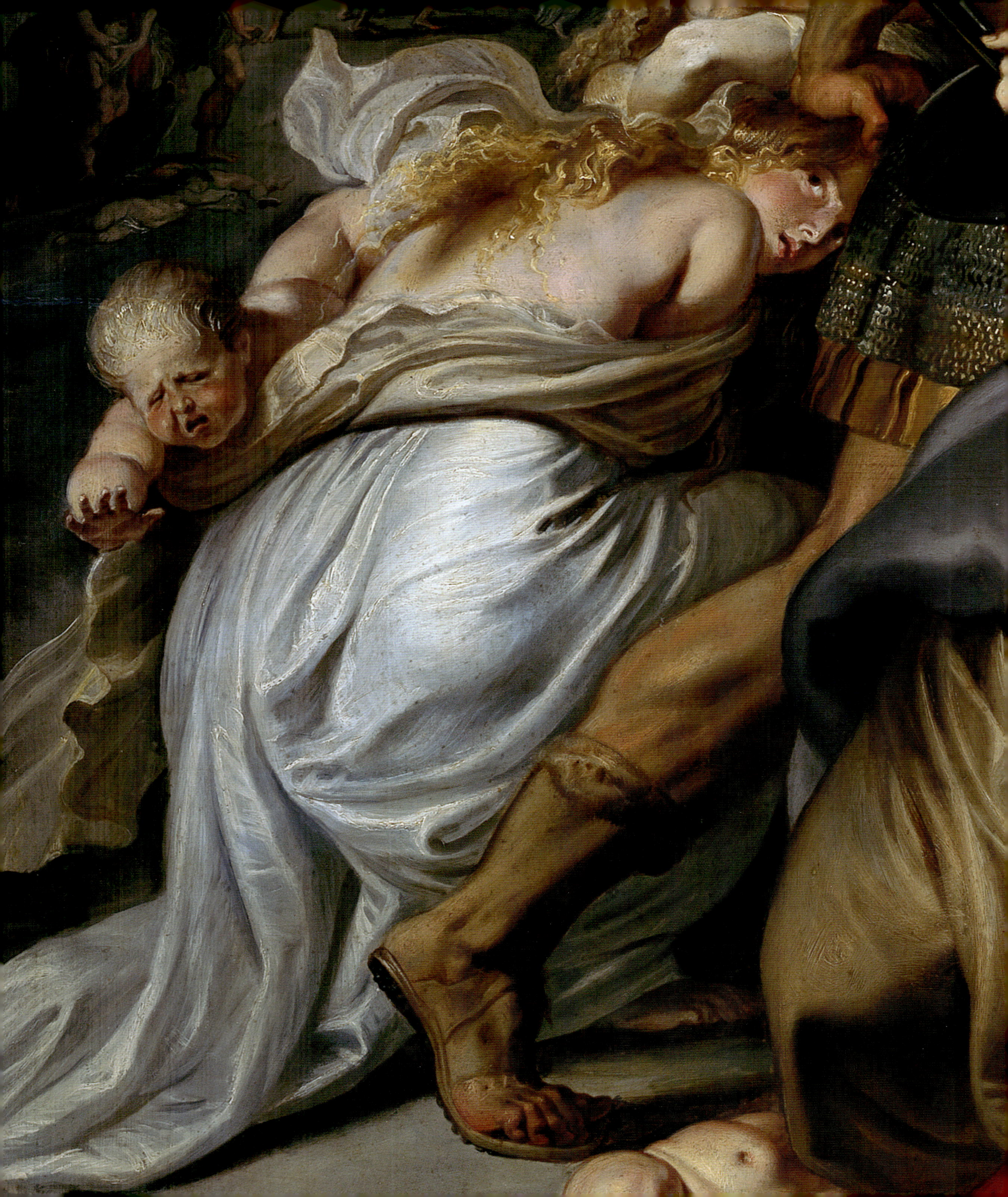

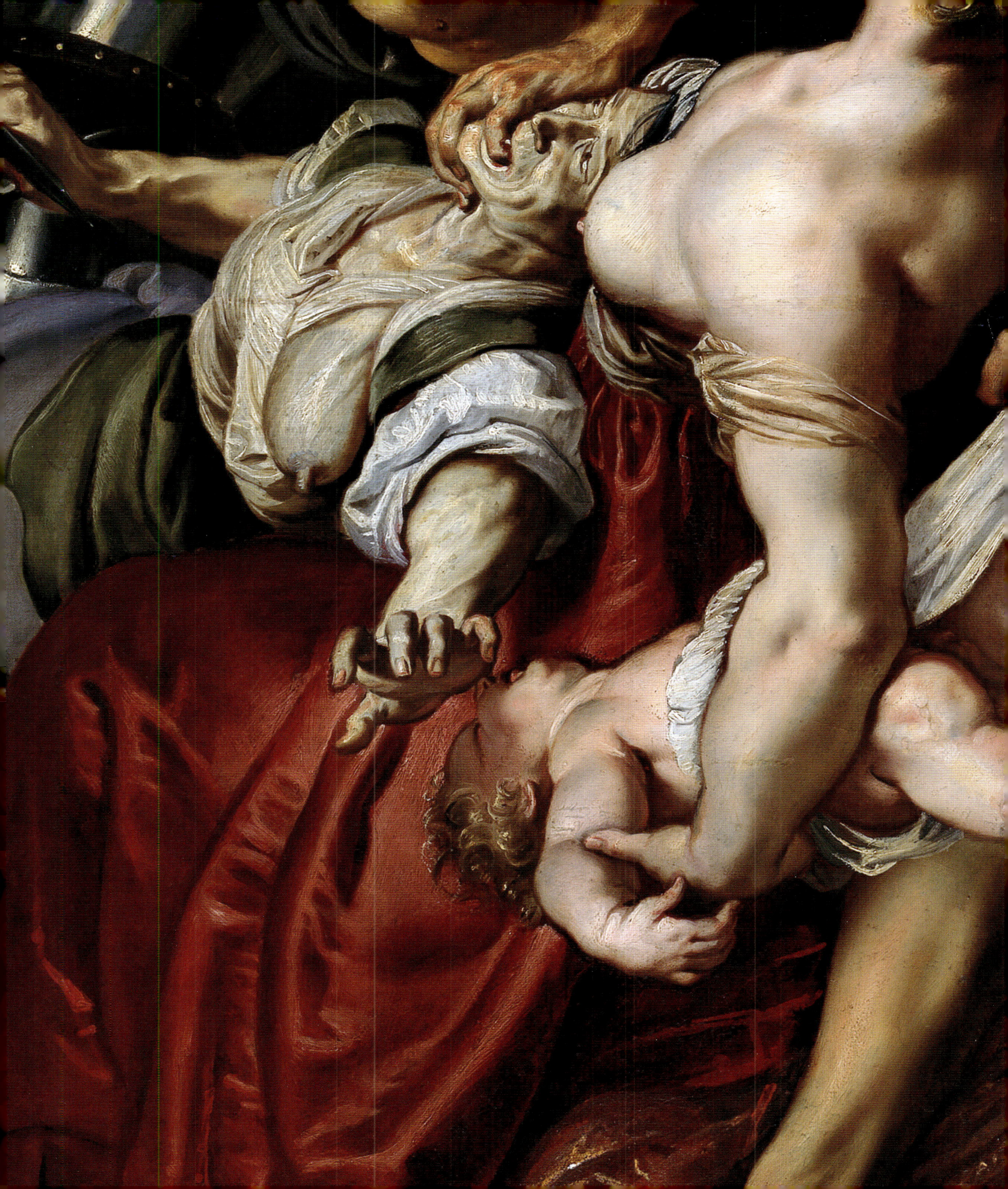

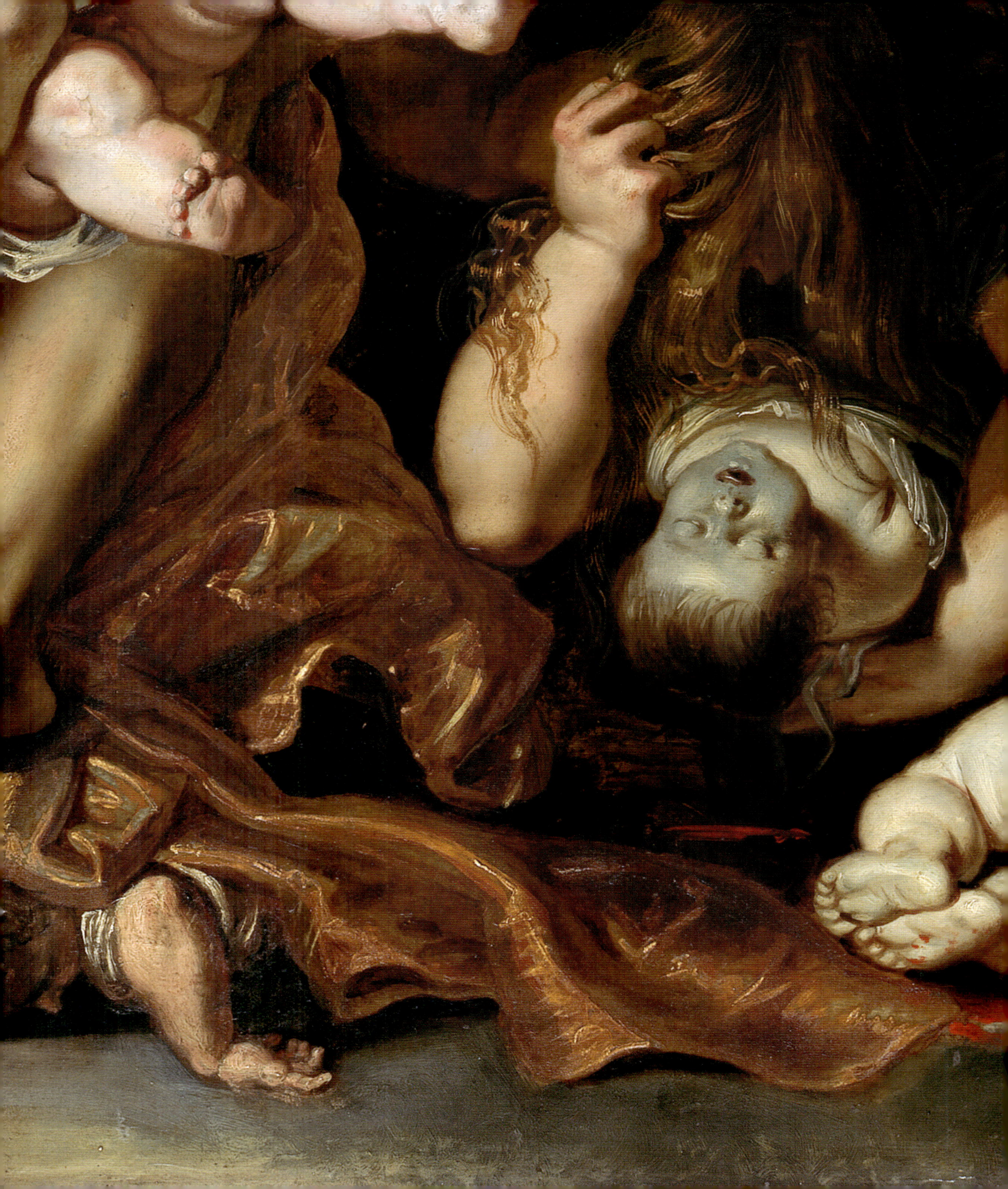

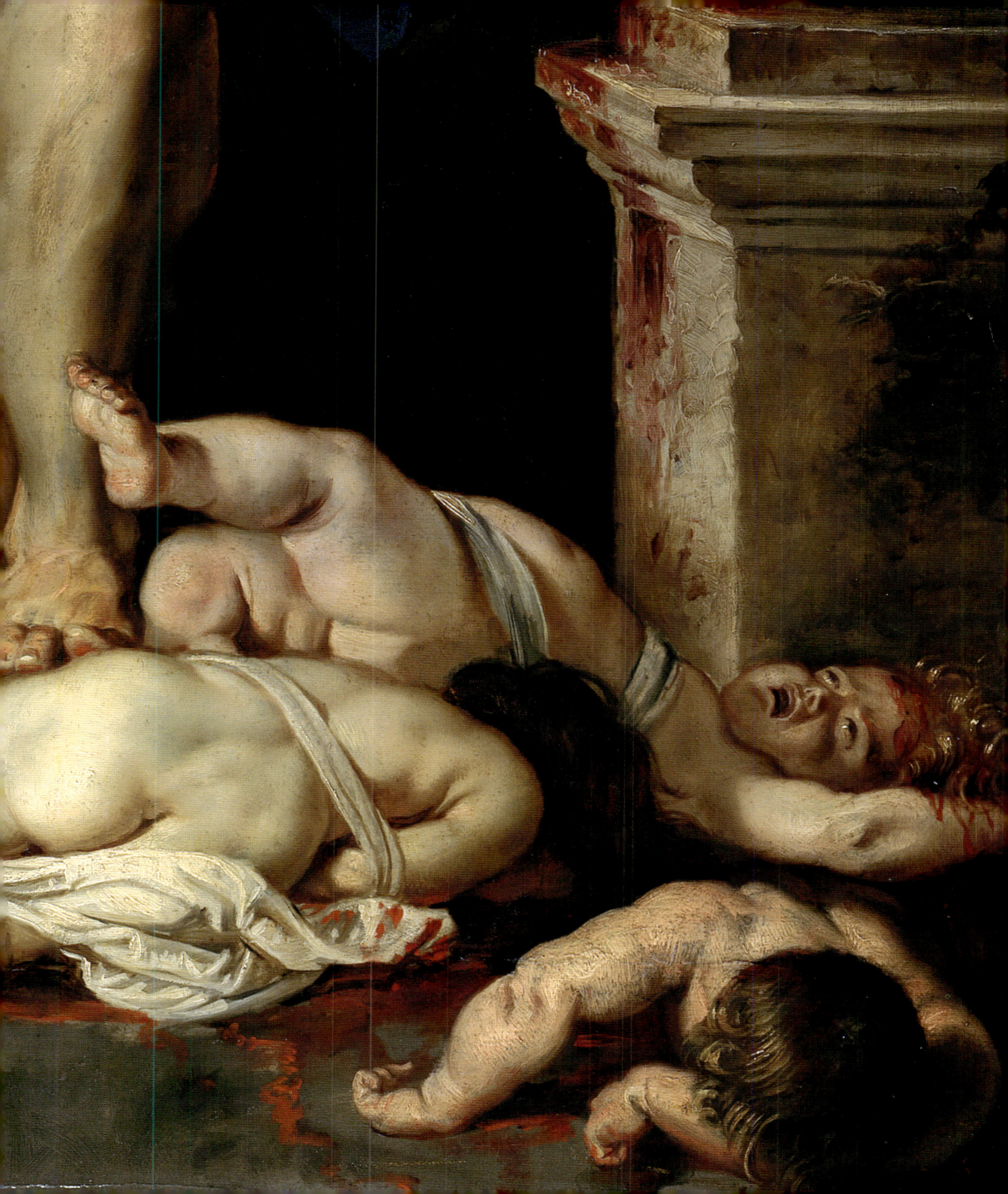

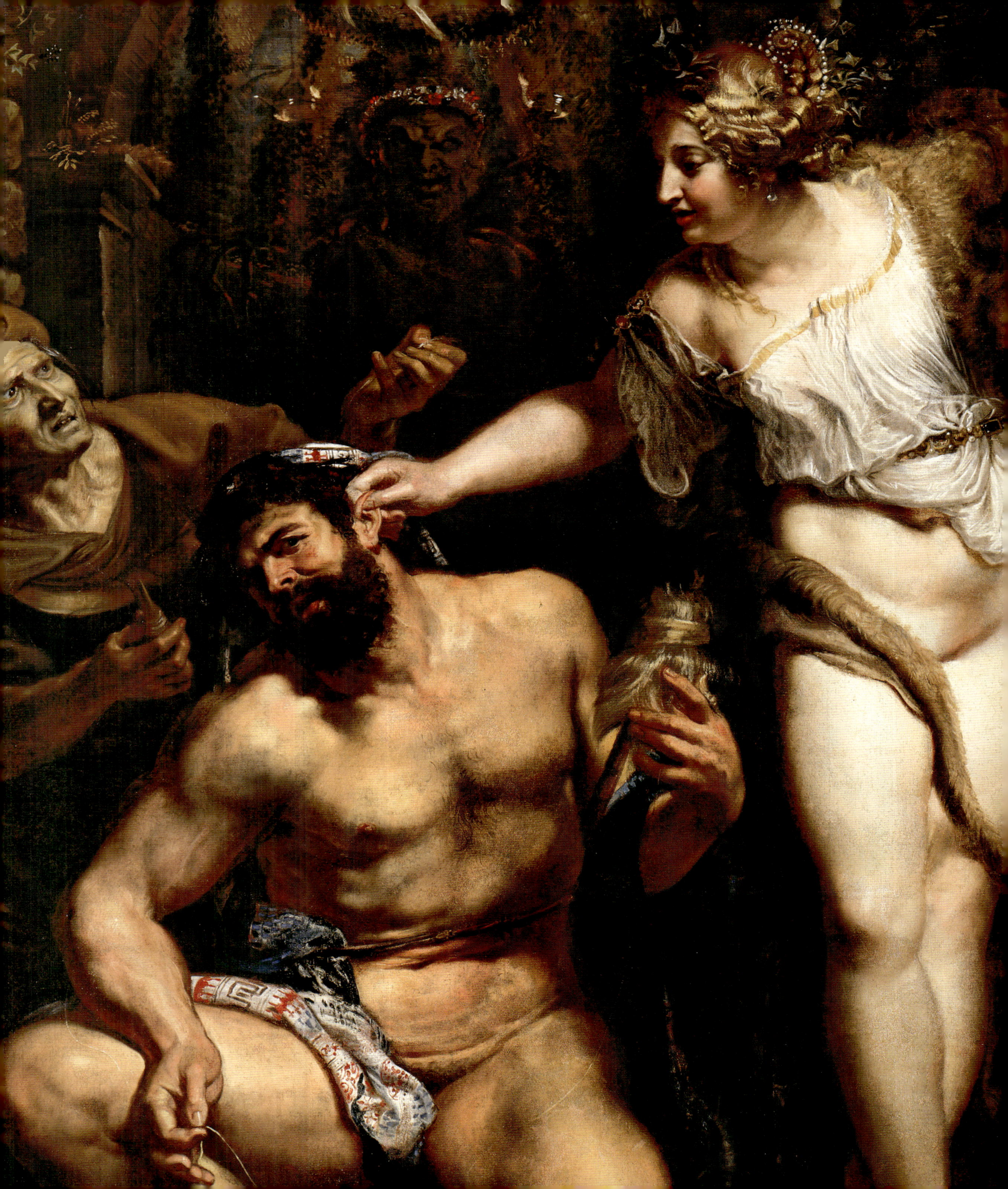

The *Massacre* in context, 1: Rubens's early life and artistic development

Peter Paul Rubens was born in Siegen, Westphalia, on June 28, 1577 to Jan Rubens, an Antwerp lawyer and alderman, and Maria Pypelincx.[1] They had left Antwerp for Germany, fleeing from religious war, but personal as well as political reasons forced them to move again in 1578, this time to Cologne, to suit Jan Rubens's Calvinist sympathies. His death in 1589 enabled the family, reconverted to Catholicism, to return to Antwerp. Peter Paul was soon enrolled at the highly esteemed 'Latin school' of Rombout Verdonck, where he must have laid the foundations for his life-long engagement with antiquity. He left at the age of thirteen and spent some time serving as a page to Marguerite, comtesse de Lalaing, which may or may not have given him a taste for court life.

Rubens's artistic training began in the 1590s, when he was apprenticed to the landscape painter Tobias Verhaecht and then to Adam van Noort, but it was Otto van Veen, whose studio he entered around 1594, who was the most important influence on Rubens in these early years. Van Veen was not only an important and successful artist but also a scholar and humanist. Although there is no definite proof, it seems likely that during his apprenticeship with Van Veen Rubens met his lifelong friend and future patron Nicolaas Rockox.[2] It was while Rockox was its Senior Treasurer that Van Veen was commissioned by the city of Antwerp to design a series of tapestries depicting the campaigns of Archduke Albert in the Netherlands. Rockox was accountable not only for the funding of the scheme but also for the supervision of its execution, and he must have paid numerous visits to Van Veen's studio during Rubens's internship. Rubens left Van Veen's studio in 1598 but ties remained. He was probably called back, a year later, to assist in decorating the triumphal arches his former master was painting to celebrate the entry of the new Habsburg governors of the Netherlands into Antwerp. During the entry, when the tapestries were presented, Rockox was knighted.

A handful of works dating from the 1590s can be attributed to the young Rubens. They show the pronounced influence of Van Veen and of Renaissance prints, as for example in *The Judgement of Paris* in the National Gallery, London (fig. 1), which is based on a print by Marcantonio Raimondi. Distinguishing between the hand of Rubens and that of Van Veen is sometimes difficult and it was not until he reached Italy that Rubens found his own artistic identity. Van Veen had studied in Italy, too, and he may have encouraged his young pupil to visit the country himself rather than relying (as was common) on prints, casts and bronzes as artistic aids. The prolonged encounter with Italian art over the eight years that Rubens stayed in Italy transformed him as an artist.

On May 9, 1600, aged just twenty-two, Rubens left Flanders for Italy. Within a year he had joined the portraitist Frans Pourbus as a court painter to Vincenzo I Gonzaga, Duke of Mantua, a position he held for seven years. It is possible that a recommendation had come from Van Veen, who,

Hercules and Omphale
(detail of fig. 6)

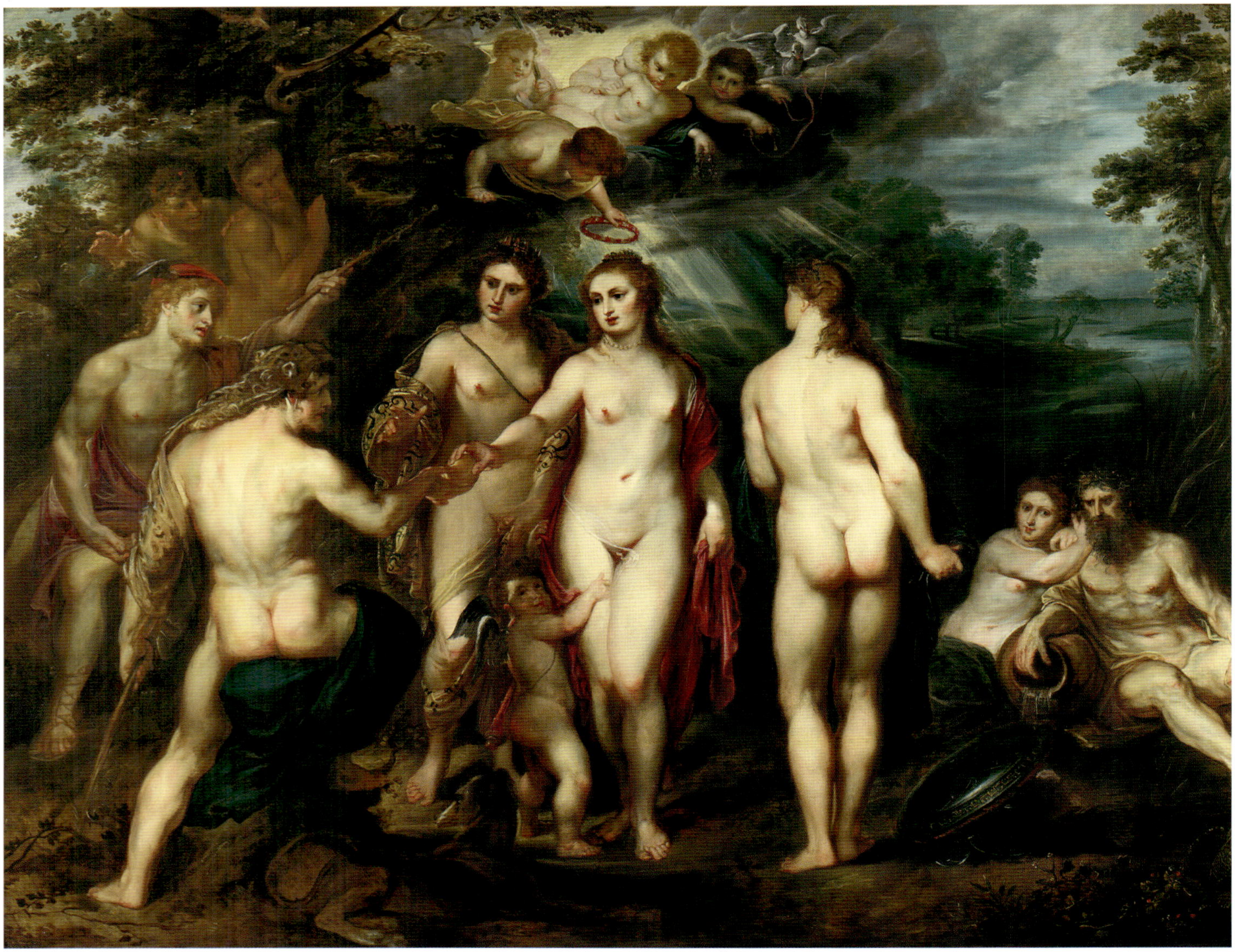

1
PETER PAUL RUBENS
(1577–1640)
The Judgement of Paris, *c.* 1597–99
Oil on oak
133.9 × 174.5 cm
The National Gallery,
London, NG 6379

as court painter to the joint governors of the Southern Netherlands, Archduke Albert and the Infanta Isabella, had met Vincenzo during his state visit to the Netherlands in 1599. As court painter at Mantua Rubens may have been involved chiefly in the rather mundane production of copies and small portraits, but the appointment provided unparalleled opportunities to travel and to meet other patrons (whose commissions Vincenzo permitted him to accept). Rubens was in fact given only one major commission by Vincenzo, the decoration of the principal chapel of the church of the Santissima Trinità in Mantua, where *The Baptism of Christ* (now Koninklijk Museum voor Schone Kunsten, Antwerp) and *The Transfiguration* (now Musée des Beaux-Arts, Nancy) hung on the side walls flanking *The Adoration of the Trinity* (now Palazzo Ducale, Mantua).

From Mantua in Lombardy Rubens would have been able to visit Venice relatively frequently. The monumental works there in the various *scuole* (charitable religious confraternities), churches and palaces, and especially the Palazzo Ducale, were important for Rubens's own method, which, as he famously claimed when pitching for the commission to decorate the Banqueting House in London in the 1620s, "was better fitted to execute very large works than small curiosities."[3] The influence of Tintoretto and Titian was particularly important. Possibly the first full-scale copy Rubens made in Italy was after Titian's *Portrait of Isabella d'Este in Red*, the original of which is now lost, but which was in Mantua at the time of his stay.

There were more works by Titian in Madrid than in Venice, thanks to Charles V and Philip II's liberal patronage of the artist. Rubens would have seen some of Titian's works when he travelled to Spain in March 1603 in order to deliver diplomatic gifts from Vincenzo to Philip III; he wrote that he had visited the Escorial and "the king's palace," probably the Alcázar at Madrid, where Titian's famous *poesie*, or series of mythological scenes painted between 1554 and 1562 for Philip II, were kept. It was not until 1628 that, during another diplomatic visit, Rubens managed to paint copies of Titian's pictures there, and these were amongst the thirty-three copies after Titian recorded in his estate on his death in 1640.[4]

In 1606, while still in the employment of Vincenzo I, Rubens visited Genoa and worked for various families of its aristocracy. His portraits of *Marchesa Maria Grimaldi* and *Marchesa Serra Pallavicino* (National Trust, Kingston Lacy) and *Marchesa Brigida Spinola Doria* (fig. 4) set grand new standards for female portraiture. One precedent for these impressive images is perhaps Veronese's treatment of sumptuously dressed Venetian ladies. Rubens came to own portraits and other works, including oil-sketches, by Titian, Tintoretto and Veronese;[5] they included a portrait of a Venetian lady attributed to Veronese (fig. 3). The more reflective surfaces of his *Brigida Spinola* also recall the metallic sheen of Moroni's *Portrait of a Lady* (fig. 2).

Several Genoese patrons helped Rubens gain significant commissions. For Maria Grimaldi's husband he painted important mythological works,

2
GIOVANNI BATTISTA MORONI (1520/24–1579)
Portrait of a Lady
c. 1555–60
Oil on canvas
155 × 106.8 cm
The National Gallery, London
NG 1023

3
Attributed to PAOLO (1528–1588) or BENEDETTO (1538–1598) VERONESE
Portrait of a Lady
c. 1570
Oil on canvas
112 × 90 cm
National Gallery of Ireland, Dublin, NGI 657

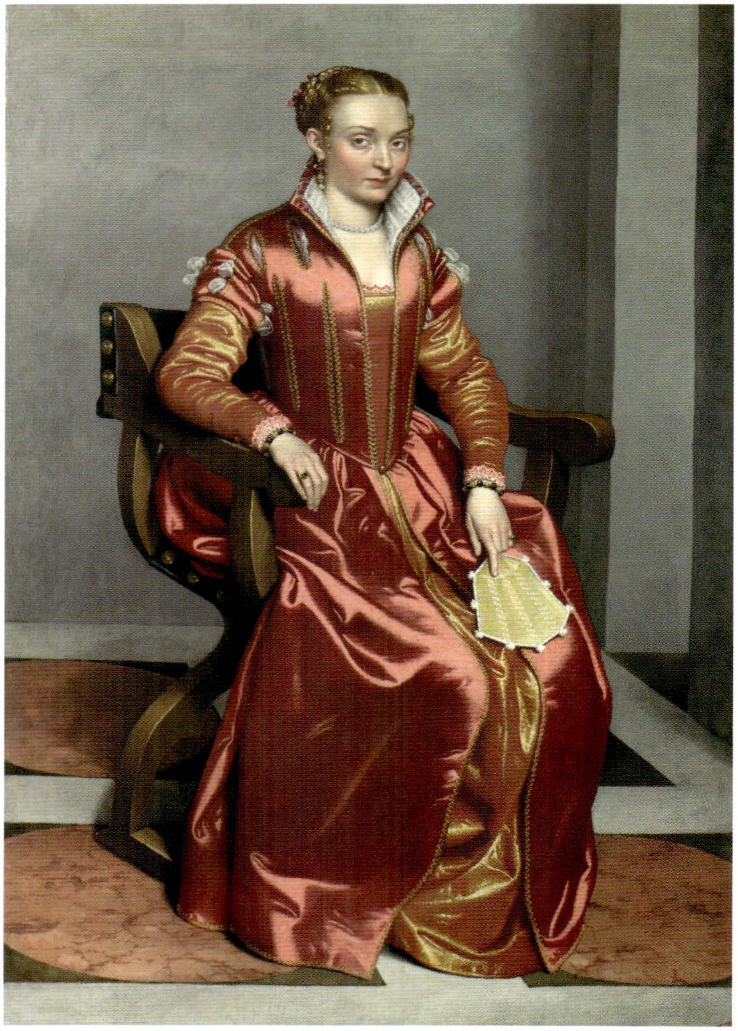

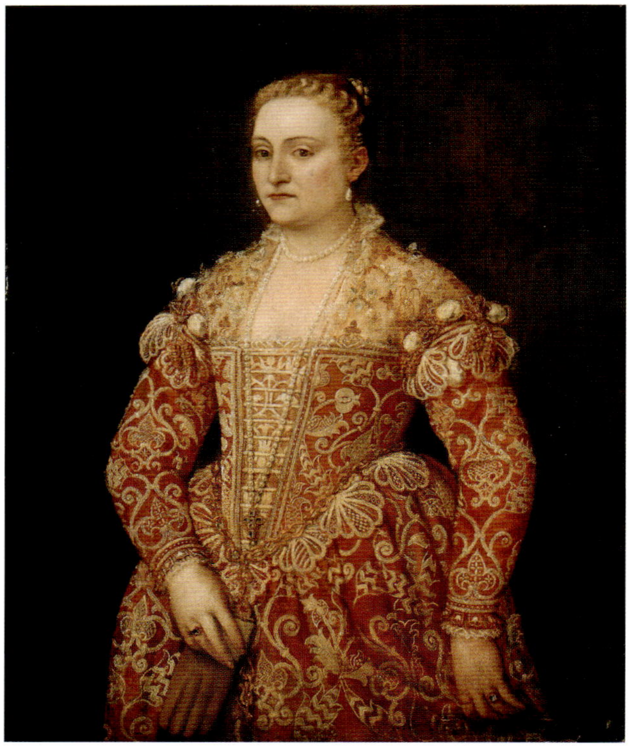

4
PETER PAUL RUBENS
(1577–1640)
Marchesa Brigida Spinola Doria
1606
Oil on canvas
152.5 × 99 cm
National Gallery of Art, Washington
Samuel H. Kress Collection
1961.9.60

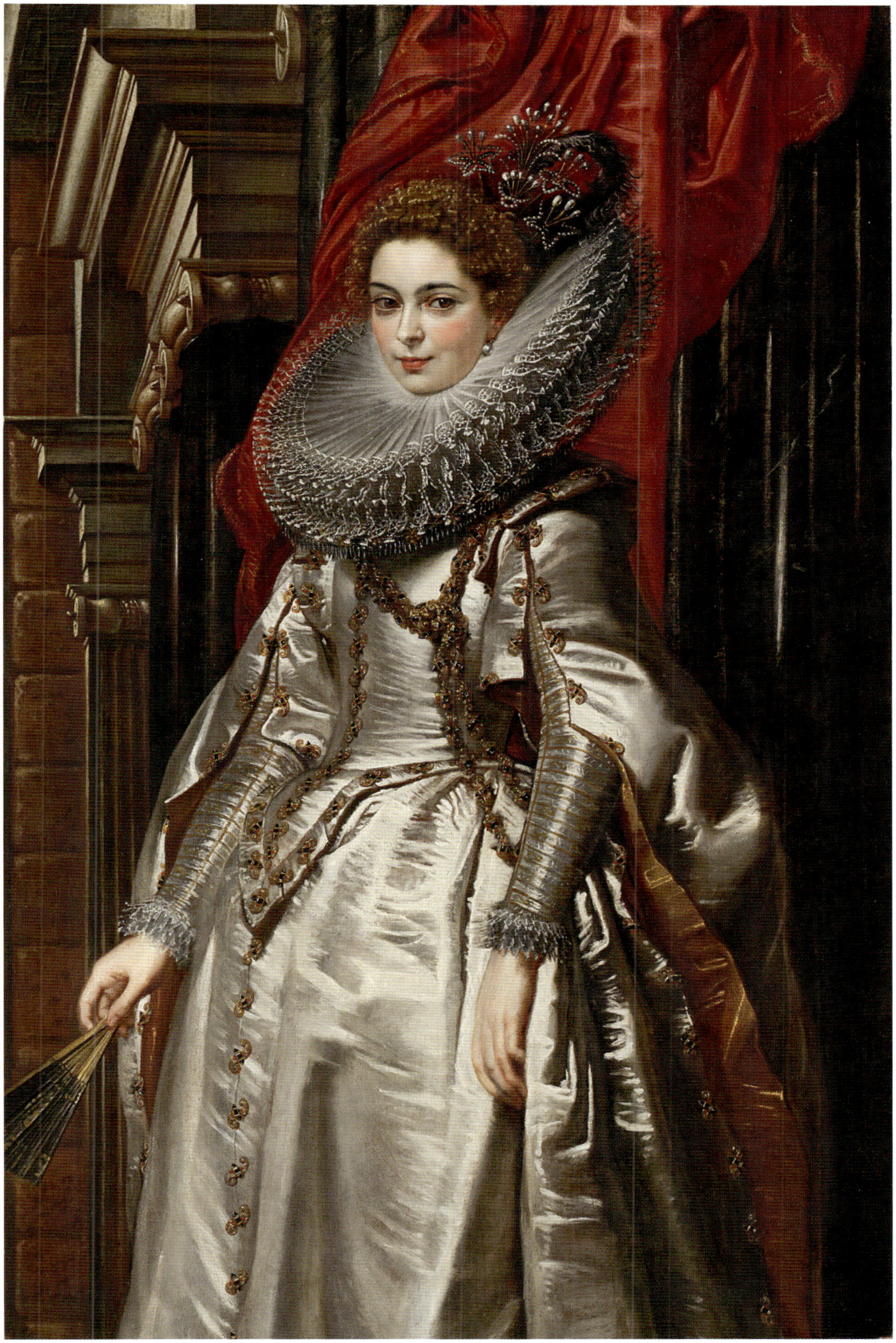

5
PETER PAUL RUBENS
(1577–1640)
The Death of Decius Mus
1616/17
Oil on canvas
289 × 518 cm
Liechtenstein Museum, Vienna, inv. no. GE51

including a *Lament over Adonis* (private collection) and a *Hercules and Omphale* (fig. 6). One of his sitters, Maria Serra, was the sister of Cardinal Giacomo Serra, who procured him a commission for the high altar of the Oratorian church of Santa Maria in Vallicella (then known as the Chiesa Nuova) in Rome; and Marcello Pallavicino, her brother-in-law, was the founder of the Jesuit church in Genoa, Santi Ambrogio e Andrea, for which Rubens painted *The Circumcision* (installed in 1606). Thus Rubens was quick to secure the prime sites – the high altars – in the churches of the vigorous new Jesuit and Oratorian orders. At a later date (*c.* 1616–17), a Genoese merchant living in Antwerp, Franco Cattaneo, financed Rubens's designs (for example, fig. 5) for a series of tapestries on the history of the Roman Consul Decius Mus.[6]

Venice was not the only city to shape the tastes of the young painter. Rubens had travelled to Florence in October 1600, early on in his employment under Vincenzo, for the marriage by proxy of Henri IV of France to the Duchess of Mantua's sister, Maria de' Medici (a future patron). There he would have experienced the dynamism of Michelangelo's figures for the first time. No drawings can be dated securely to the time of this trip, but it is possible that Rubens's drawing after Michelangelo's marble relief of *The Battle of the Lapiths and Centaurs* in the Casa Buonarroti (Institut Néerlandais, Paris) was executed at this moment.

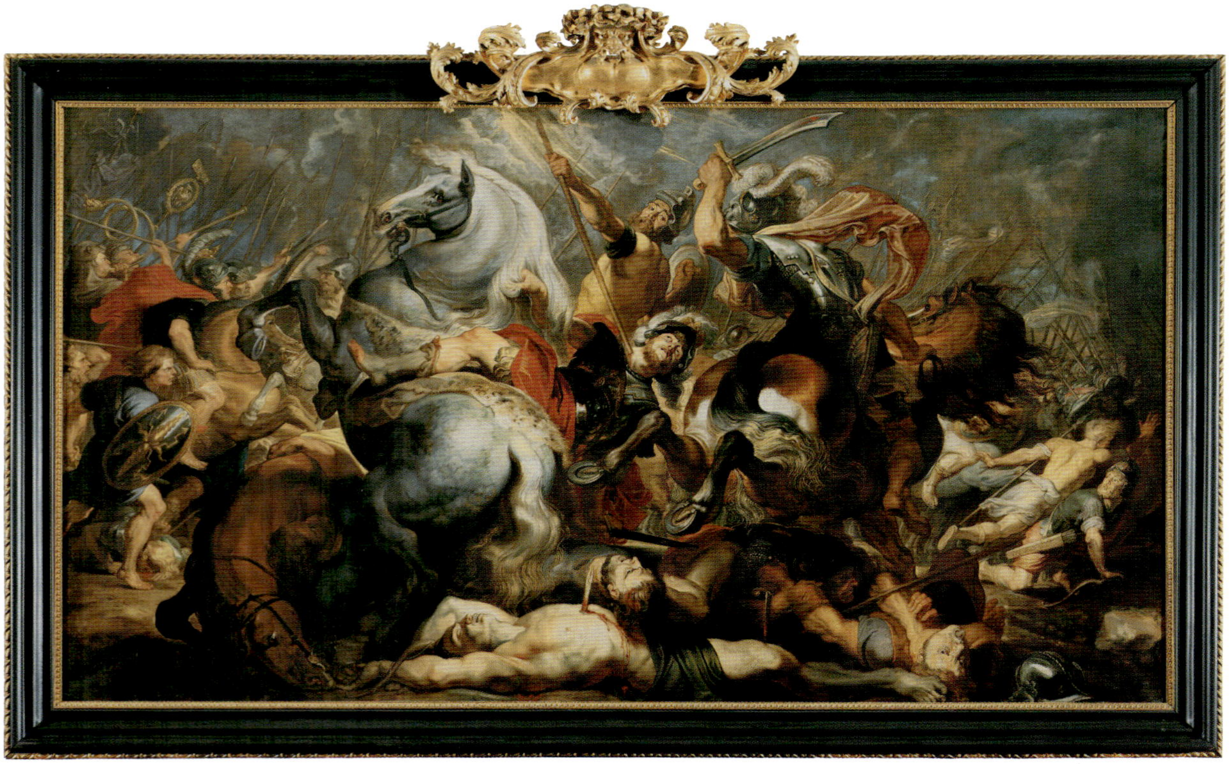

6
PETER PAUL RUBENS
(1577–1640)
Hercules and Omphale
c. 1604–05
Oil on canvas
278 × 215 cm
Musée du Louvre, Paris,
inv. no. 854

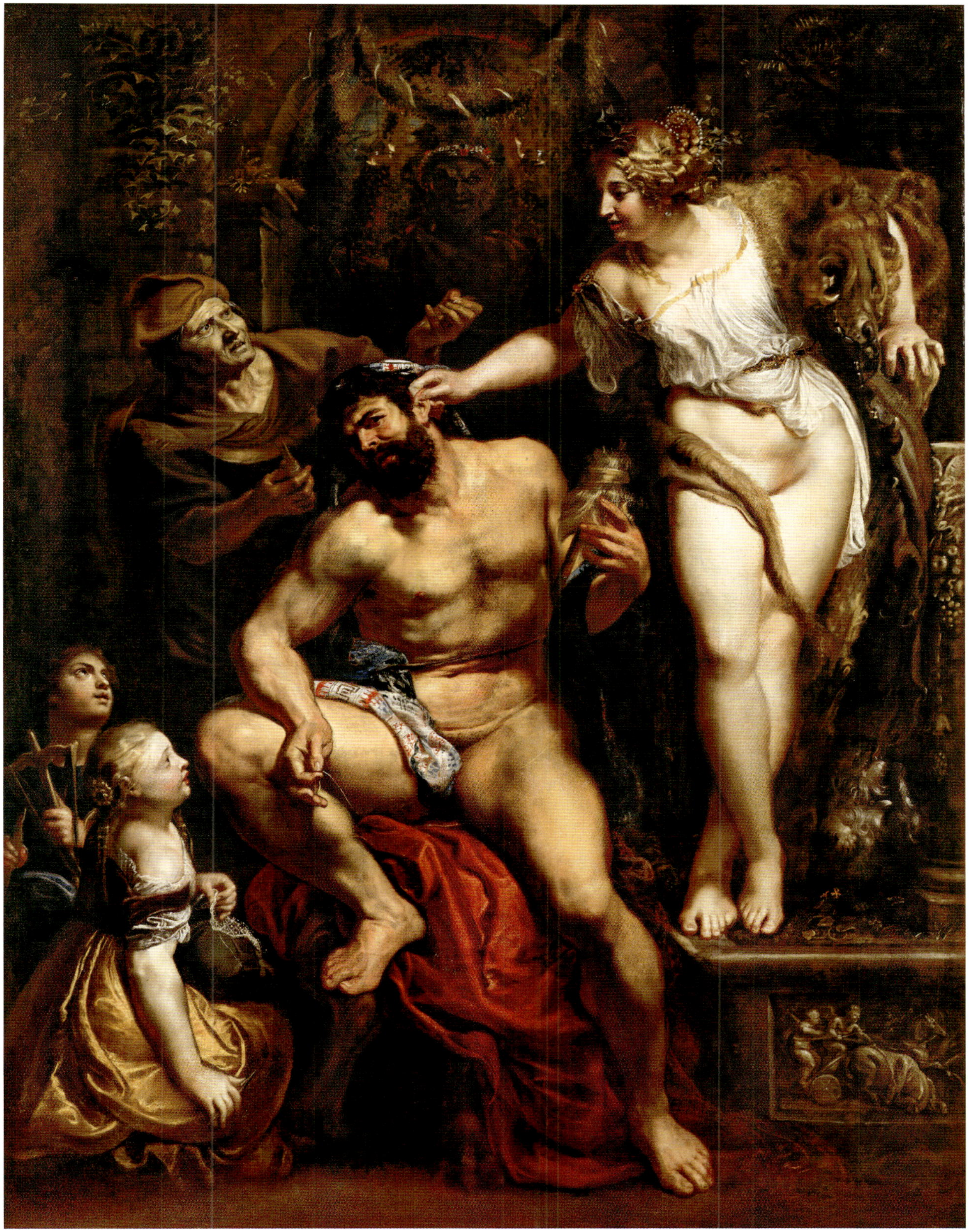

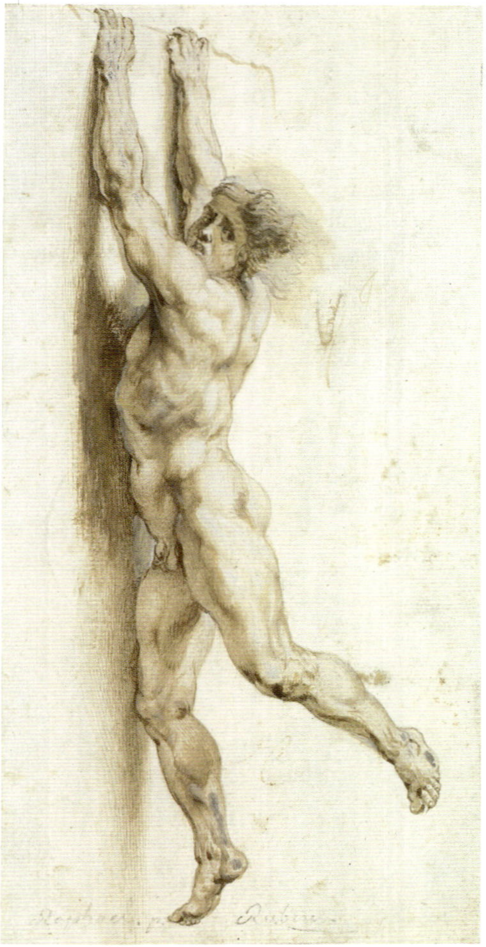

7
PETER PAUL RUBENS
(1577–1640) correcting another artist after RAPHAEL (1483–1520)
A Naked Man clinging to a Wall
c. 1604
Pen and brown ink, with brown wash, heightened with white (partly oxidized)
22.4 × 11.1 cm
The British Museum, London
AN82339001 (OO. 9.23)

In July 1601 Rubens arrived in Rome, with a letter of introduction from the Duke of Mantua to Cardinal Montalto, a nephew of Pope Sixtus IV, whose Roman residence was the Villa Medici. This gave him access to the exceptional collection of antiquities in the villa, and to other important private art collections in Rome. The Vatican contained masterpieces from both antiquity and the Renaissance, and Rubens made various drawn copies of aspects of the Sistine Chapel ceiling, of figures from Raphael's Stanze, and of the *Laocoön* (fig. 123) and other classical sculpture in the Belvedere courtyard. For Rubens copying two- and three-dimensional works was an essential means of learning to draw and paint the human body, and he came to compose his paintings almost as if they were assemblages of sculpture. Rubens gathered a large collection of prints, notebooks and loose sheets of drawings during his Italian trip, of his own and by other artists (some of which he 'corrected'), together with a number of antiquities. Typical of his retouchings is a drawing by an anonymous sixteenth-century artist of a *Naked Man clinging to a Wall* (fig. 7), a figure from Raphael's *Fire in the Borgo* in the Stanza dell'Incendio in the Vatican. Rubens retouched it with brown wash and cream bodycolour in order to heighten the relief, and adjusted the facial features to make them more anguished.[7] Rubens made his own sketches from Raphael's fresco (or a print after it) on one of the few surviving sheets from his lost sketchbook (Kupferstichkabinett, Staatliche Museen, Berlin).[8]

Rubens also owned and retouched nine drawings copying scenes from Polidoro da Caravaggio's painted façade of the Palazzo Milesi in Rome, which had been so admired by the likes of Vasari for its classicizing treatment and invention. Many figures of *The Castration of Uranus* (private collection) and *The Rape of the Sabine Women* (fig. 8) were thoroughly remodelled by Rubens both in outline and internally.[9]

Rome was the focus of Rubens's artistic ambition while he was in Italy. He received his first major public commission in the city from Archduke Albert, Regent of the Spanish Netherlands, for the church of Santa Croce in Gerusalemme. Before Easter 1602, when he was recalled to Mantua, he had completed three impressive panels, *Saint Helena with the True Cross* and, on either side, *The Mocking of Christ* and *The Raising of the Cross* (the former two now in Grasse Cathedral, the last destroyed). Rubens did not revisit Rome until late 1605. In the intervening period he produced an impressive body of paintings, including an equestrian portrait of *The Duke of Lerma* (1603; Prado, Madrid) and a large mythological scene showing *The Council of the Gods* (*c.* 1601–02; Prague Castle). When eventually he did return to the city he was no doubt inspired by the presence of his brother Philip, with whom he took up residence near the Piazza di Spagna. Philip had been made librarian to Cardinal Ascanio Colonna, and would have proved an important intellectual stimulus to Rubens's exploration of Roman antiquities.

8
PETER PAUL RUBENS
(1577–1640) after POLIDORO
DA CARAVAGGIO (*c.* 1499–1543)
The Rape of the Sabine Women
c. 1602–10
Pen and brown ink and wash
over black chalk, heightened
with white and oil paint,
on brown paper
27.7 × 39.7 cm
Art Gallery of Ontario, Toronto

In addition to his brother, Rubens encountered various friends from northern Europe during his stay in Italy. One of them was Jan van den Wouwer (Woverius), in Verona in July 1602; he features, along with the artist's brother Philip and his Antwerp mentor the philologist and humanist Justus Lipsius, in Rubens's group portrait known as *The Four Philosophers* (fig. 9). The German artist Adam Elsheimer, who was living in Rome, was also an important friend to and influence on Rubens. Elsheimer had been converted to Catholicism by the humanist Gaspar Schoppius, to whose circle Philip Rubens belonged. Elsheimer's art, though always on a very small scale, was remarkable for its dramatic lighting and intricate composition. The drooping tendrils of ivy in the *Massacre* might have been inspired by Elsheimer's treatment of foliage (for example in his *Saint Lawrence prepared for Martyrdom*; fig. 10). We know that Rubens owned paintings by Elsheimer, and that he copied his paintings; he even helped Elsheimer's widow sell his work on his death.[10]

However, the most important artist active in Rome at the time was Caravaggio, and Rubens was inspired by his bold figures, dramatic light

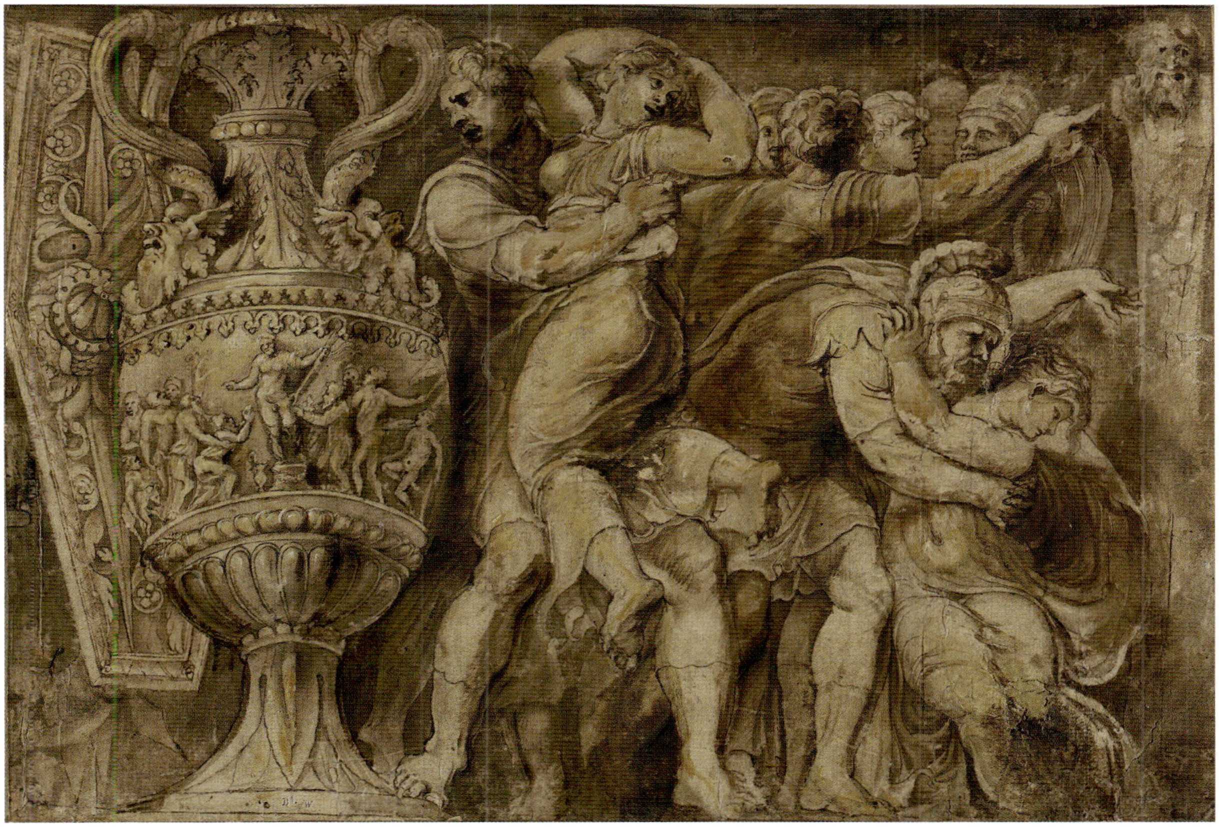

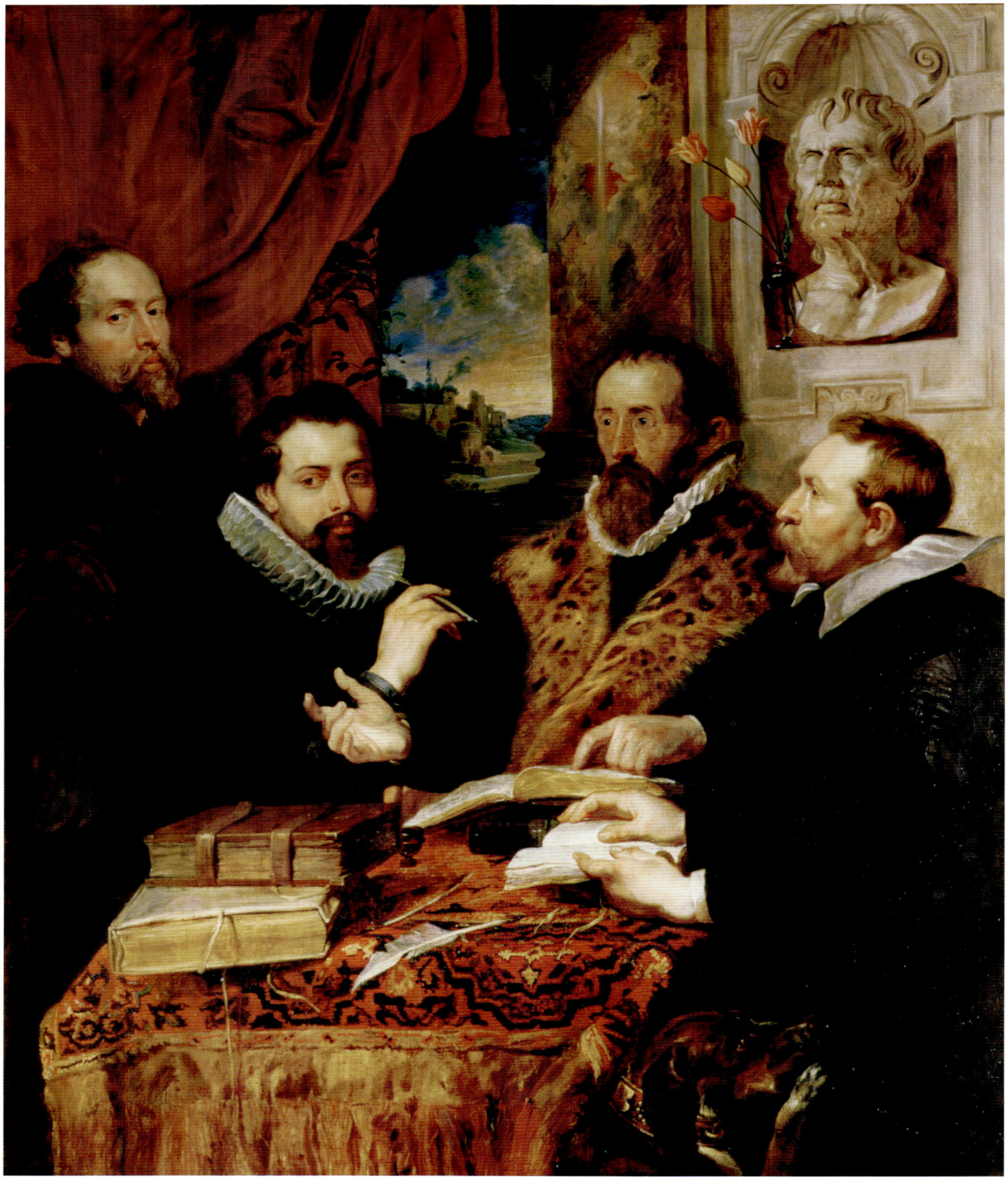

9
PETER PAUL RUBENS
(1577–1640)
The Four Philosophers
after 1611–12
Oil on panel
164 × 139 cm
Palatine Gallery, Pitti Palace, Florence

10
ADAM ELSHEIMER
(1578–1610)
Saint Lawrence prepared for Martyrdom
c. 1600–01
Oil on copper
26.8 × 20.8 cm
The National Gallery, London, NG 1014

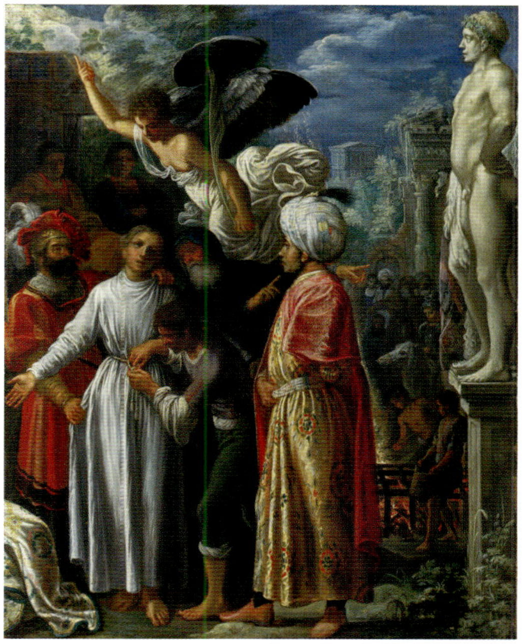

effects and grandiose scale. In the *Massacre*, for instance, he employs a typically Caravaggesque spotlight effect to heighten the theatricality of the scene. After his return to Antwerp Rubens took up a more Caravaggesque style, emphasizing greater contrasts between light and shade. He made a free copy in oils (fig. 12) of Caravaggio's Santa Maria in Vallicella *Entombment* (fig. 11), probably based on a drawing he had made while working in that church (see below). He edited the hand gestures and glances to strengthen the focus on Christ's body. The sense of the body hanging down over the altar and Christ's arm being offered out to the viewer must have influenced Rubens's own attempts to achieve a similar kind of illusionism in the *Massacre* and other works. Such was his admiration of Caravaggio that in February 1607 Rubens recommended the purchase of *The Death of the Virgin* (fig. 13) to Vincenzo Gonzaga, and at a later date led the campaign to obtain *The Madonna of the Rosary* (now Kunsthistorisches Museum, Vienna) for the Dominican church of Saint Paul in Antwerp.

In the autumn of 1606, at the age of twenty-nine, against competition from a depleted field of Italian artists, Rubens won the commission for the high altarpiece of Santa Maria in Vallicella in Rome. This newly rebuilt Oratorian church was important and much visited, for it housed a miraculous thirteenth-century fresco of *The Virgin and Child*. Rubens designed a composition showing various saints in adoration of the fresco above, but felt that it was not properly visible in the church (the rejected painting is now in the Musée de Grenoble). He submitted another design on May 13, 1608, and this time painted three separate paintings on slate, which he hoped would absorb light and minimize reflection. The miraculous image, adored by angels, was placed behind a removable painted copper cover replicating the *Virgin and Child*, flanked by *Saints Gregory, Maurus and Papius* on the left wall and *Saints Domitilla, Nereus and Achilleus* on the right (fig. 14).

Rubens had no time to benefit from the success of this major commission. Before the ensemble could be installed he heard that his mother was dying. He returned to Antwerp in October 1608 only to find he was too late; his mother had died before he had even left Rome. Over her tomb (in the Sint-Michielskerk) he placed the rejected altarpiece. Rubens never returned to Italy, no doubt because he became too busy with artistic commissions, diplomatic duties and his family.

Despite the unhappy circumstances Rubens's return to Antwerp was well timed. He found there a group of wealthy patrician merchants – Nicolaas Rockox among them – who would prove to be important patrons. In July 1609 he was appointed court painter to Archduke Albert and his wife the Infanta Isabella, who, though based in Brussels, gave him the freedom to live in Antwerp and accept commissions from whomsoever he should choose. A twelve-year truce between Spain and the insurgent provinces had been signed on April 9, 1609, in Antwerp Town Hall. Through Rockox Rubens was commissioned to paint for the States reception room there a

11
MICHELANGELO DA CARAVAGGIO (1571–1610)
The Entombment, 1602–04
Oil on canvas
300 × 203 cm
Vatican Museums and Galleries, Vatican City

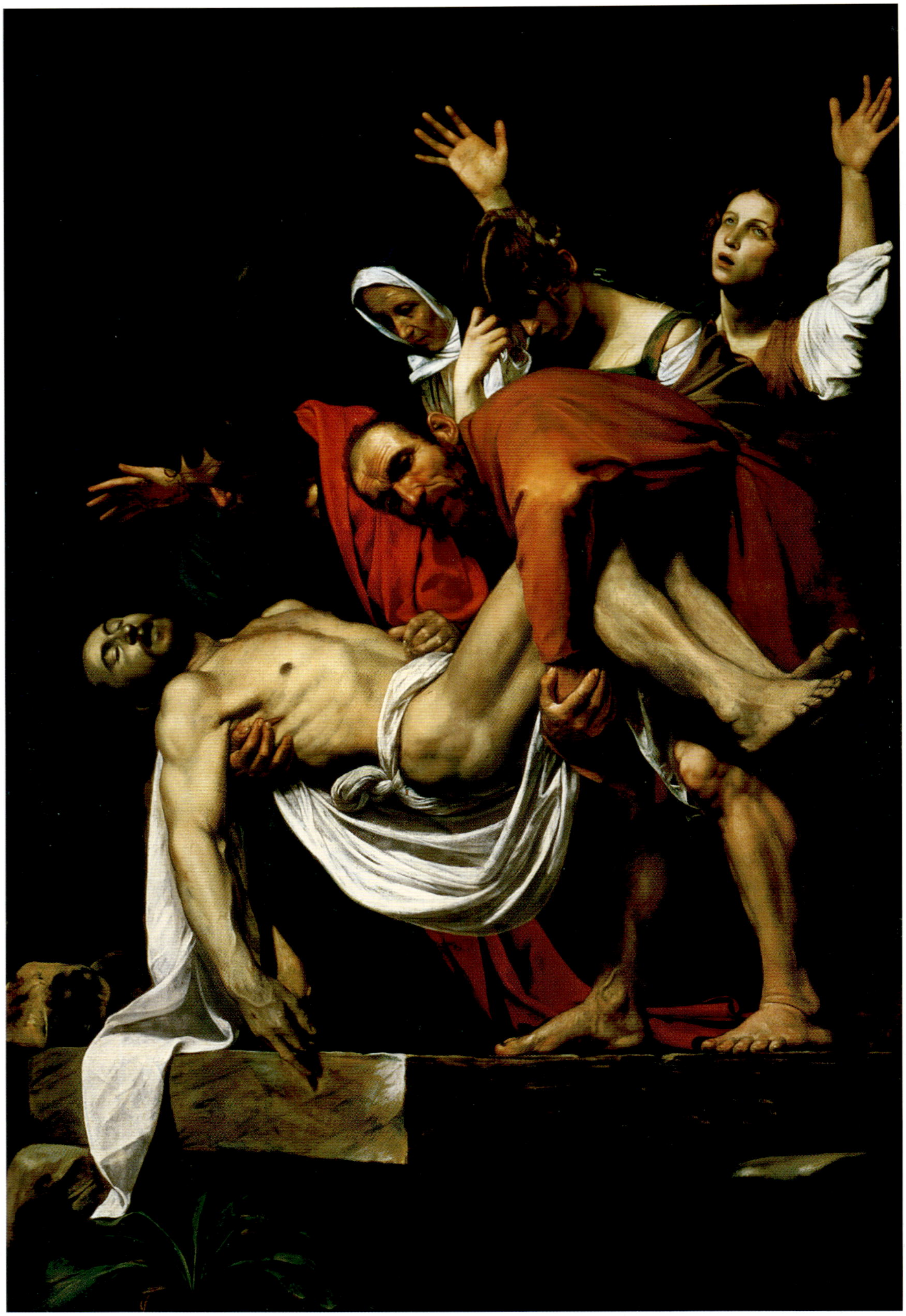

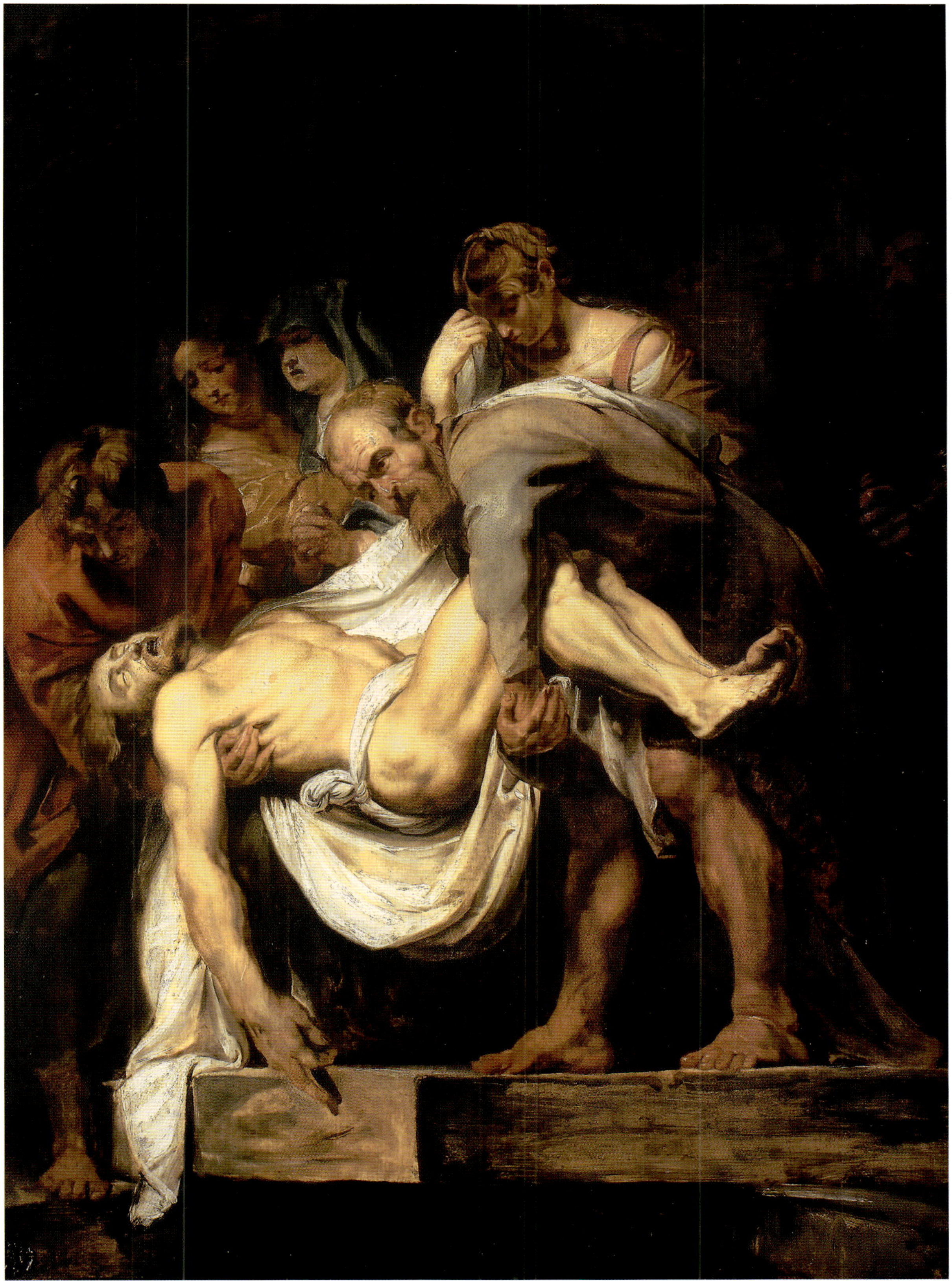

12
PETER PAUL RUBENS
(1577–1640) after
MICHELANGELO DA
CARAVAGGIO (1571–1610)
The Entombment, *c.* 1614
Oil on panel
88.3 × 66.5 cm
National Gallery of Canada,
Ottawa

13
MICHELANGELO DA CARAVAGGIO
(1571–1610)
The Death of the Virgin
1601–05/06
Oil on canvas
369 × 245 cm
Musée du Louvre, Paris, inv. no. 54

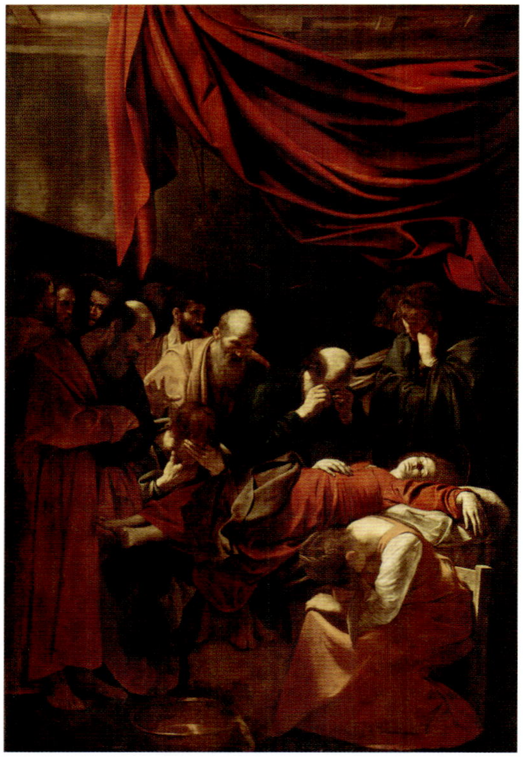

large *Adoration of the Magi* (now in the Prado, Madrid), which served not just as a devotional image but also as a symbol of the peace, with the Christ Child as Prince of Peace receiving gifts from the Magi (representative of the statesmen who had converged on Antwerp).[11] At this time Catholic churches all over the Southern Netherlands were being decorated in a spirit of triumph, and Rubens, fresh from papal Rome, was ideally prepared to respond. He soon painted a major altarpiece, *The Raising of the Cross* for the church of Sint-Walburga (*c.* 1610–11, now in Antwerp Cathedral; fig. 17). Rubens signed the contract for the *Raising* in June 1610; it was partly funded by Cornelis van der Geest, a wealthy spice merchant, church warden and art lover. The enormous triptych was painted on site, but Rubens was provided with a ship's sail with which to partition off his workspace within the church and attain a degree of privacy. The execution of this high altarpiece heralded Rubens as *the* modern painter: Herculean nudes strain at the ropes, figures project from the picture plane; red, straining faces, some contorted with effort, all contribute to a dynamic, emotionally charged whole. This, too, was the period, around 1610–11, in which Rubens probably painted the *Massacre*, another equally 'modern' painting.

There are not enough datable early Antwerp paintings to place the *Massacre* with certainty. It has been suggested that Rubens painted it as soon as he arrived back in Antwerp from Italy, in October 1608,[12] but works like *Cain slaying Abel* (Courtauld Gallery, London) and *The Beheading of Saint John the Baptist* (fig. 15) with their bubblewrap musculature would seem to have a better claim to be made around that time. At least from the beginning of 1609 Rubens was immersed in painting *The Adoration of the Magi* for the Town Hall, and since that painting (in its original form) seems less sophisticated than the *Massacre*, a date for the *Massacre* of shortly after 1609 or 1610 seems most likely.[13] Rubens's stylistic development was rapid at this point, but the composition, observation of anatomical detail and drapery swirls in *The Raising of the Cross*, *c.* 1610–11, match those of the *Massacre*. The occasional lapse in coherence of the composition of the *Massacre* is due perhaps to the speed of its execution rather than to an earlier date. The mother in red from Rubens's *Raising of the Cross* has a highly improbable articulation of her right arm, and so does the crouching woman in white in the *Massacre*. Both paintings show a dramatic use of shadow to etch into torsos, limbs, hyperflexed musculature and extreme poses. On the other hand, *The Descent from the Cross* (1611–14; fig. 16), painted for the Guild of the Arquebusiers (musketeers) for the guild's altarpiece in Antwerp Cathedral (and again secured for Rubens by Rockox, who was *hoofdman*, or captain of the guild) is surely later than the *Massacre*. It represents a more classical strain in Rubens's work, characterized by restraint of attitude and gesture, which was better suited for the cathedral site.

The very specific choice of models, costume and patterning of colour is typical of other paintings by Rubens executed around the same time

14
PETER PAUL RUBENS
(1577–1640)
Saints Domitilla, Nereus and Achilleus, 1608
Oil on slate
425 × 200 cm
Santa Maria in Vallicella, Rome

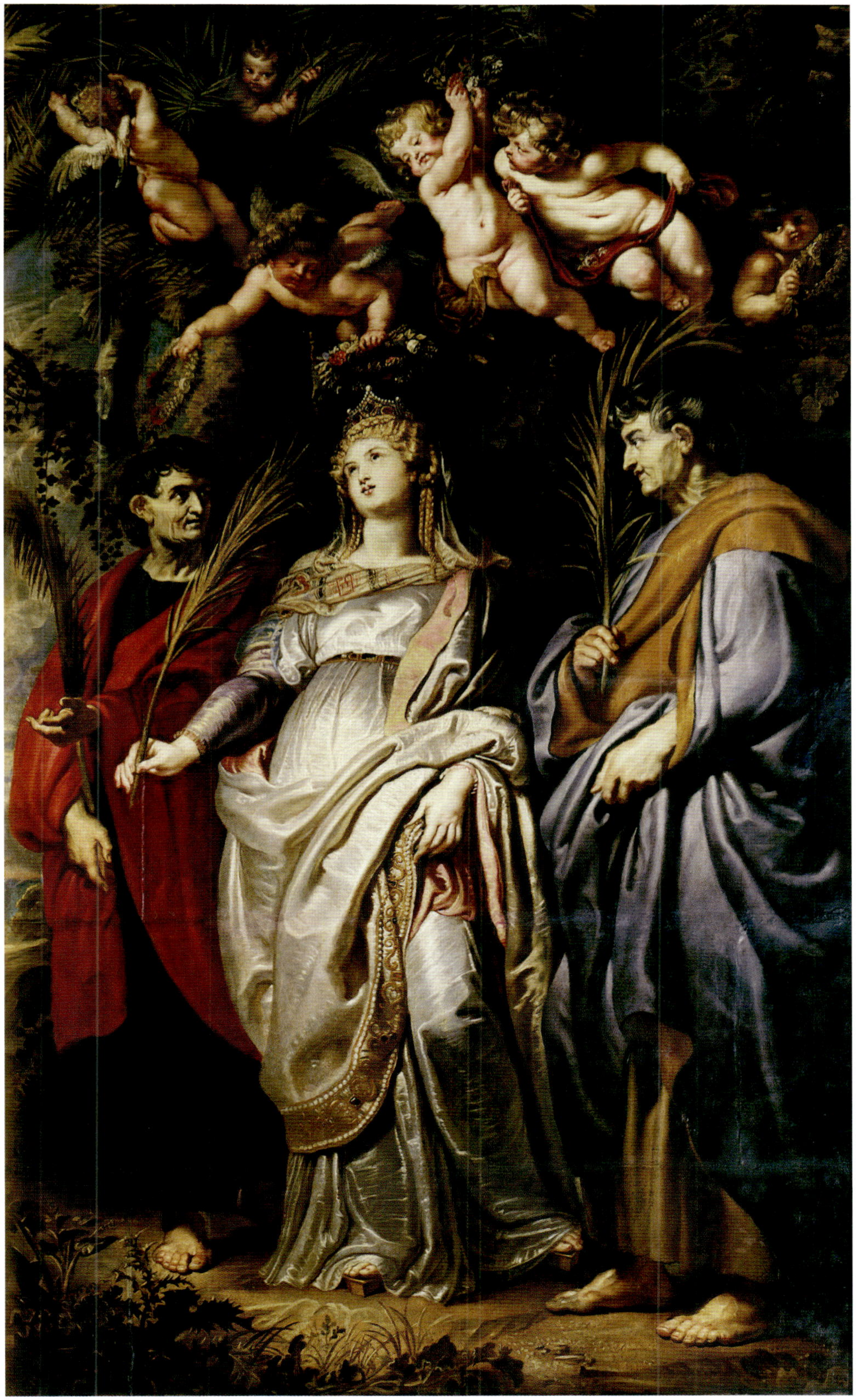

15
PETER PAUL RUBENS
(1577–1640)
The Beheading of Saint John the Baptist, 1609
Oil on oak panel
94 × 101.8 cm
Private collection

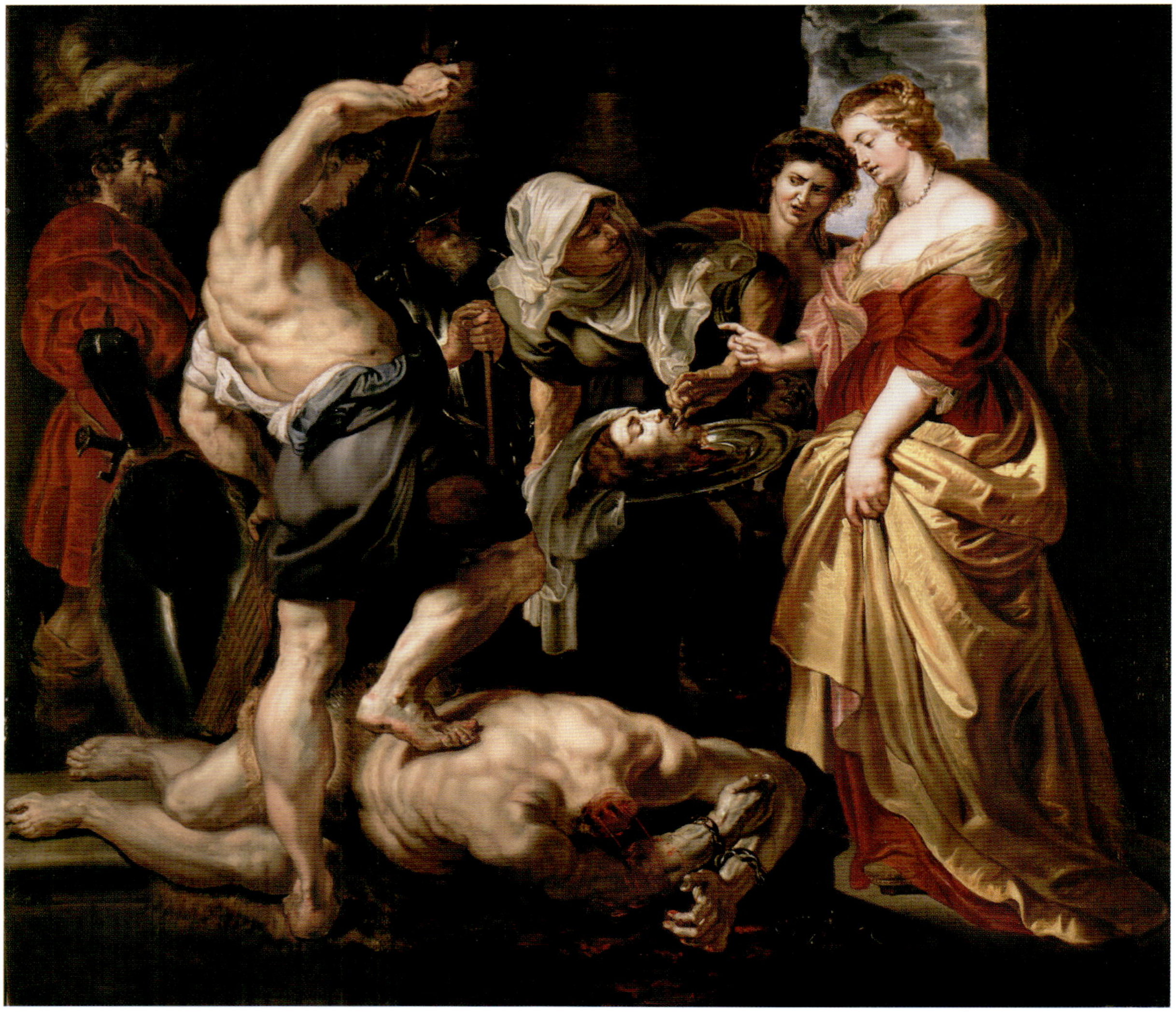

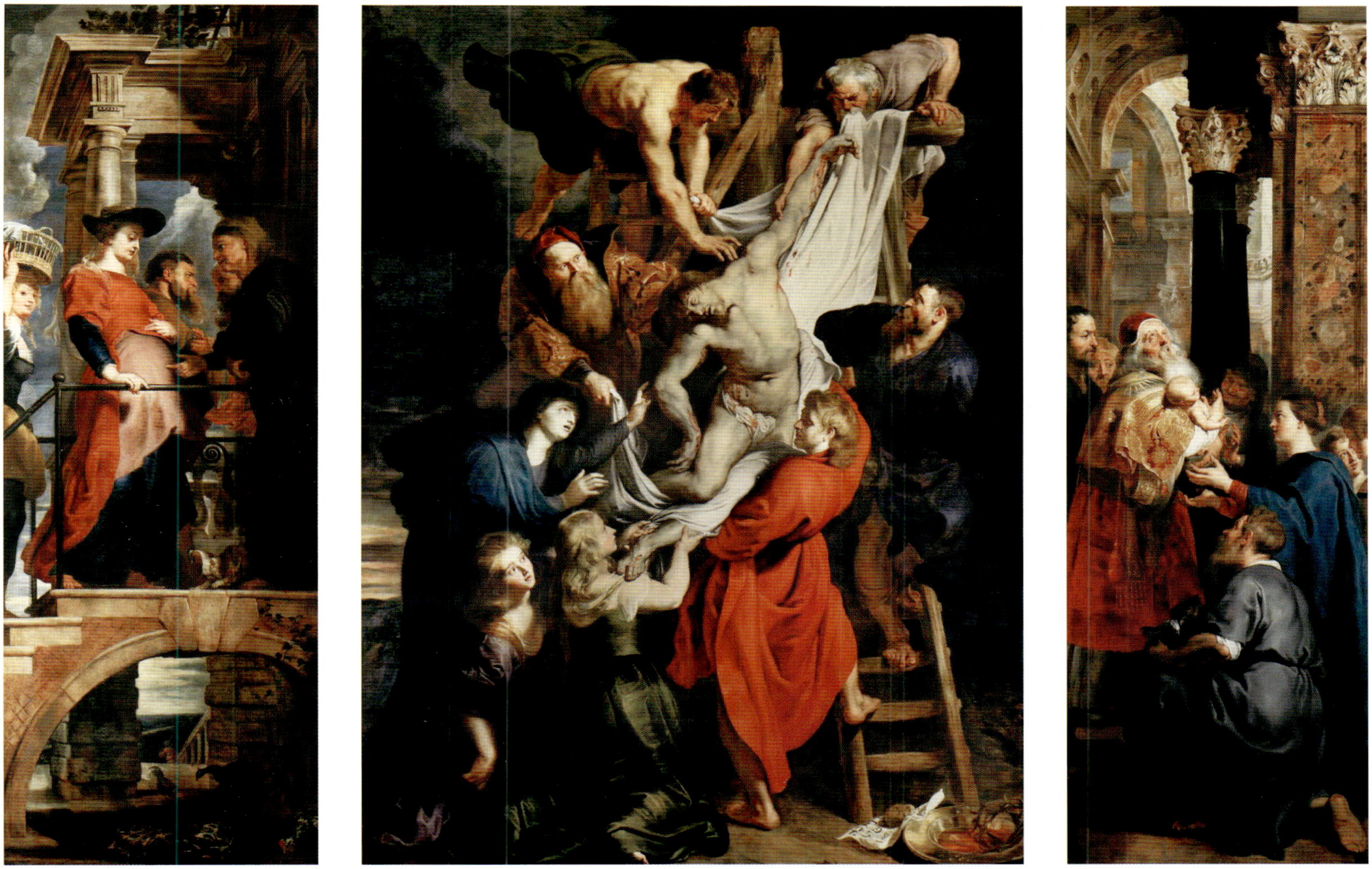

16
PETER PAUL RUBENS
(1577–1640)
The Descent from the Cross
c. 1611–14
Oil on panel
425 × 320 cm
Onze-Lieve-Vrouwekathedraal,
Antwerp

17
PETER PAUL RUBENS
(1577–1640)
The Raising of the Cross
c. 1610–11
Oil on panel
460 × 150 cm; 460 × 340 cm;
460 × 150 cm
Onze-Lieve-Vrouwekathedraal,
Antwerp

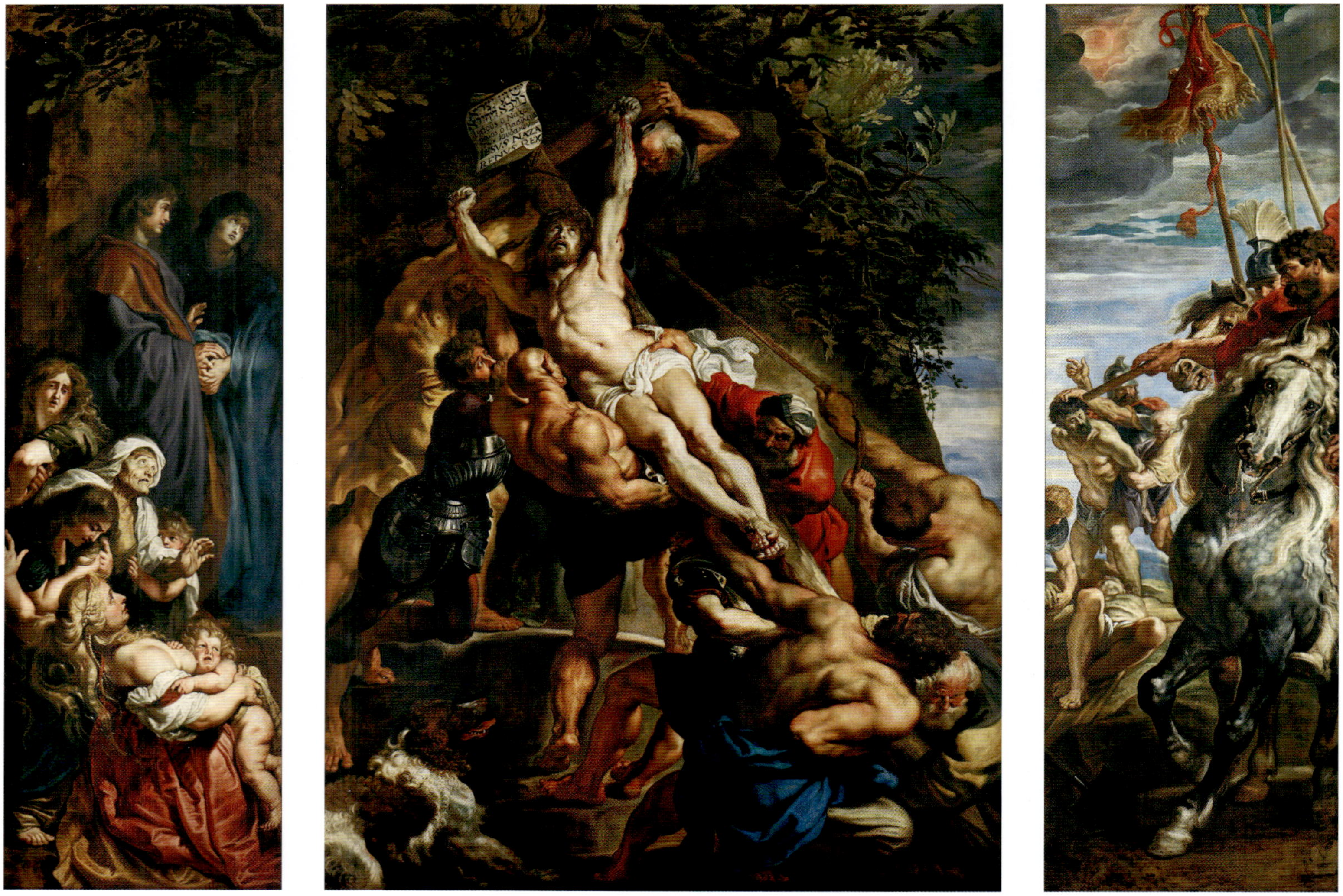

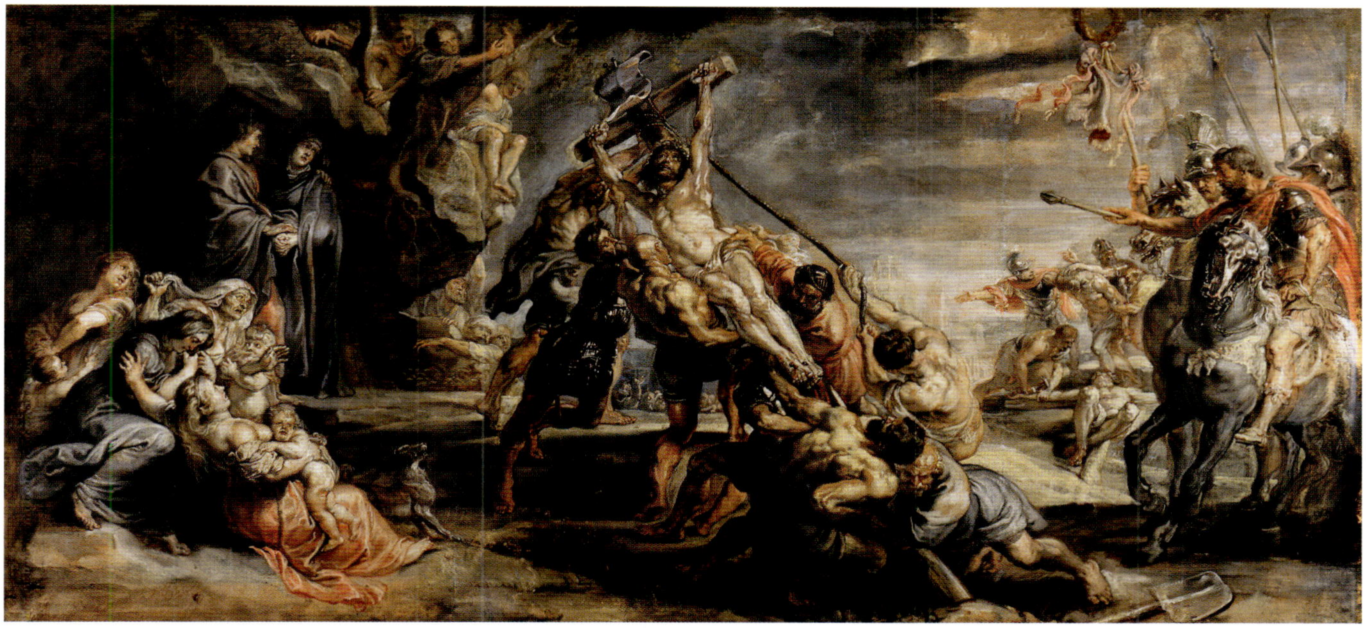

18
PETER PAUL RUBENS (1577–1640)
AND WORKSHOP
Ricordo for The Raising of the Cross, 1637–38
Oil on paper, later mounted on canvas
72.1 × 132.7 cm
Art Gallery of Ontario, Toronto

as the *Massacre*, such as the *Samson and Delilah* (see fig. 45). Narrative details like the exaggerated facial pallor, and anachronistic costume features such as leggings, also link the *Samson* with the *Raising of the Cross*.

As Rubens's success grew, and specifically in order to fulfil the Arquebusiers' commission for *The Descent from the Cross*, he had to extend his workshop. He organized a production line, with young trainee painters, following the example of Raphael and of Frans Floris. At the same time he worked collaboratively with other independent masters, including the specialist flower and still-life painter Jan I Brueghel, the animal painter Frans Snyders and the landscapist Jan Wildens. What makes the *Massacre* so interesting is that it predates this workshop expansion. Though a large-scale work, it is all Rubens's own.

The fever pitch of contorted figures that Rubens achieved in his painting around 1610 was not sustainable. His own reappraisal of a literal transcription of the *Raising of the Cross* composition made by his workshop (fig. 18) for an engraving in the 1630s is revealing. He shifted the scene back in space, so muffled the vertiginous diagonal, and created a lateral sweep across the composition. He added a terrace of spectators and braced the Crucifixion group by moving the dog and extending the anchor figure on the right.

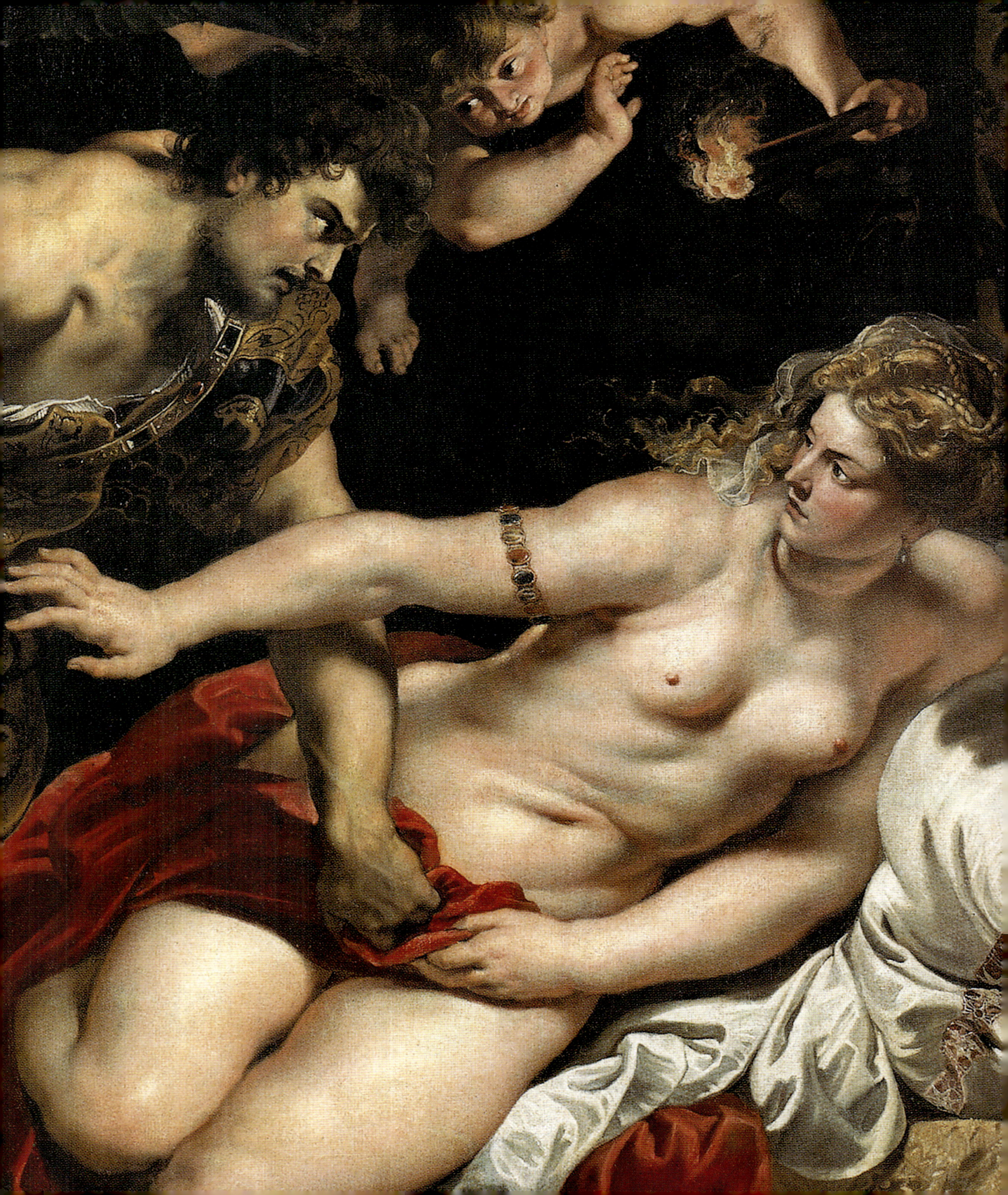

The *Massacre* in context, 2: The painting's history and provenance

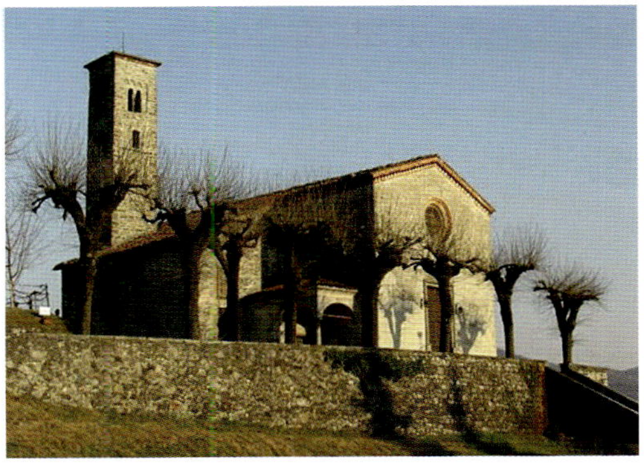

19
Church of San Giorgio, Annone

As they pass from patrons to collectors, as attributions are lost and acquired, great works of art can develop unexpected histories. The *Massacre* is a case in point. In 2002, the picture was consigned for sale from an Austrian monastery, Stift Reichersberg, where it had been placed on deposit by its owners in 1973. It had last been recorded as a work by Rubens at the end of the seventeenth century; since then it had been 'lost' and was effectively unknown to the market, collectors and scholars. Its emergence on the London market in 2002 was a sensational event, and even so its sale exceeded all expectations when it was bought by the second Lord Thomson of Fleet for a world record price at auction for an Old Master painting.[1]

The earliest recorded owner of the *Massacre* was Giacomo Antonio Carenna (1591–1672), a prominent Milanese financier living in Antwerp (fig. 20). The first known mention of the *Massacre* is found in his will of 1669,[2] in which it is described as hanging above a chimney-piece in the major reception room (described with modesty as "*saletta maggiore*") of "his big house" (*sua casa grande*): "*item una pittura sopra la cheminea, del infanticidio di Herodes, sendo originale et fatta dal quondam Cavagliere Pietro Paolo Rubbens*" (a picture above the chimney-piece, of Herod's infanticide, which is original, and made by the late Sir Peter Paul Rubens).

Since Carenna does not seem to feature in surviving contemporary correspondence or other historical sources, the little we know about him comes from legal documentation and parish records.[3] The Carenna family came originally from the small town of Annone in Brianza, north of Milan. There, in the church of San Giorgio (fig. 19), his ancestors were buried and Giacomo Antonio himself was christened.[4] The Carenna had close links with another, very well established merchant family, the Annoni, who were also based between Annone and Milan; Giacomo Antonio's mother, Giovanna, was an Annoni, he himself married another, Maria, and he and three of his brothers were all at some time employees or business partners of the Annoni. In 1604, aged fourteen, Giacomo Antonio had been sent to start work as an apprentice in the Annoni office in Antwerp. In 1620 he became the chief representative of the firm in the city; by 1629 he was the only non-family partner of the business.[5] Carenna may well have known Rubens personally, for Rubens was not only the most celebrated painter in the city but also his near neighbour. Furthermore, through his in-laws the Picquery and Fourment families, the artist was likewise connected to the leading merchants in the city.[6]

Carenna's in-laws, the Annoni – or Dannoni as they were better known in Antwerp – operated a wide network specializing in the trading of goods between the two Spanish-ruled territories of Milan and the Southern Netherlands. Paintings by Rubens and Brueghel destined for Cardinal Federico Borromeo were among the wide range of luxury goods which the Annoni transported to Milan in the second and third decades of the

Tarquin and Lucretia
(detail of fig. 38)

20
After JORIS HOEFNAGEL
(1542–1600)
Map of Antwerp, *c.* 1572
Coloured engraving from
Civitates Orbis Terrarum by
Georg Braun (1541–1622) and
Frans Hogenberg (1535–1590)

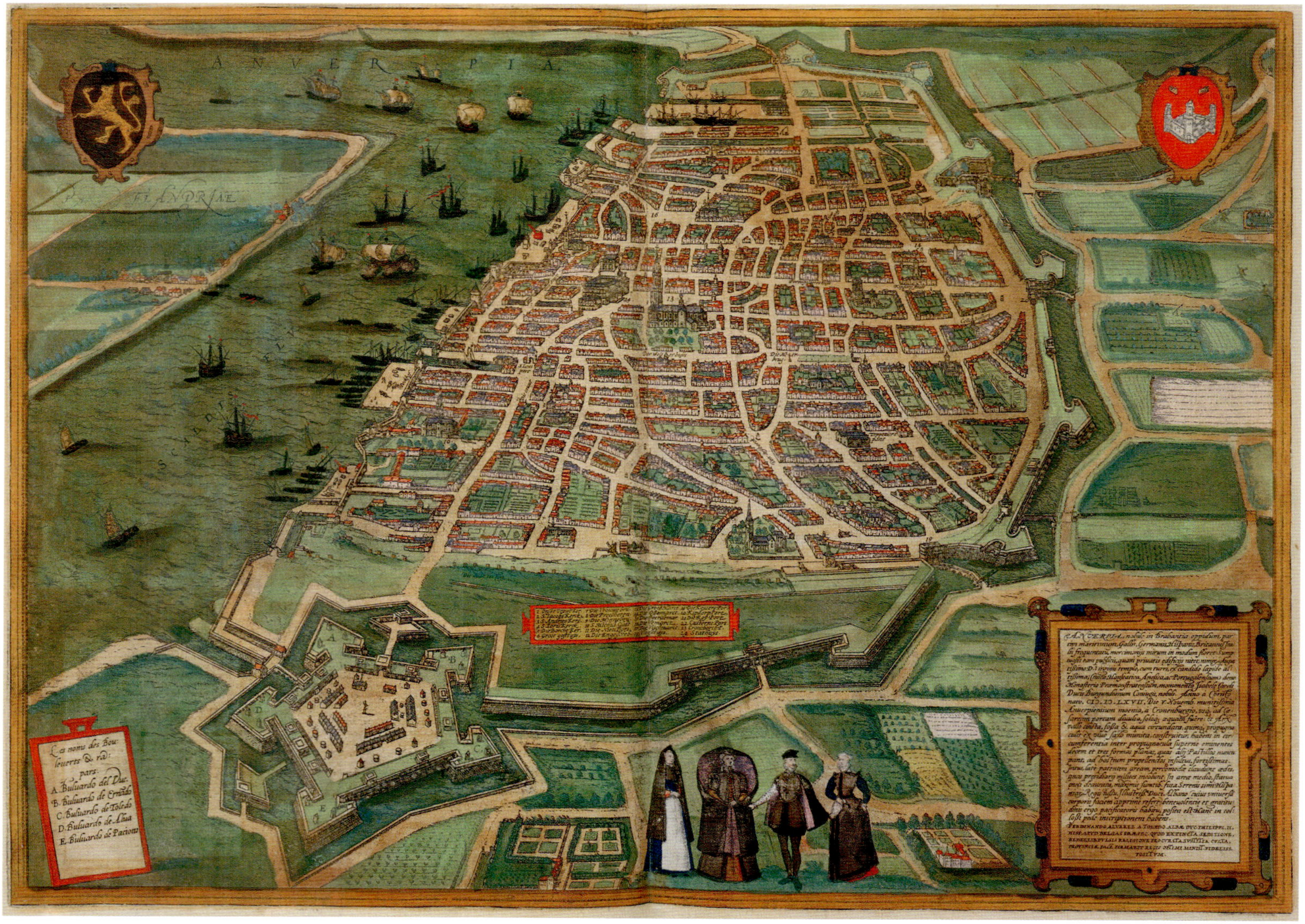

21
Map of Antwerp
after JORIS HOEFNAGEL,
detail of fig. 17 showing the area around the Sint-Jacobskerk

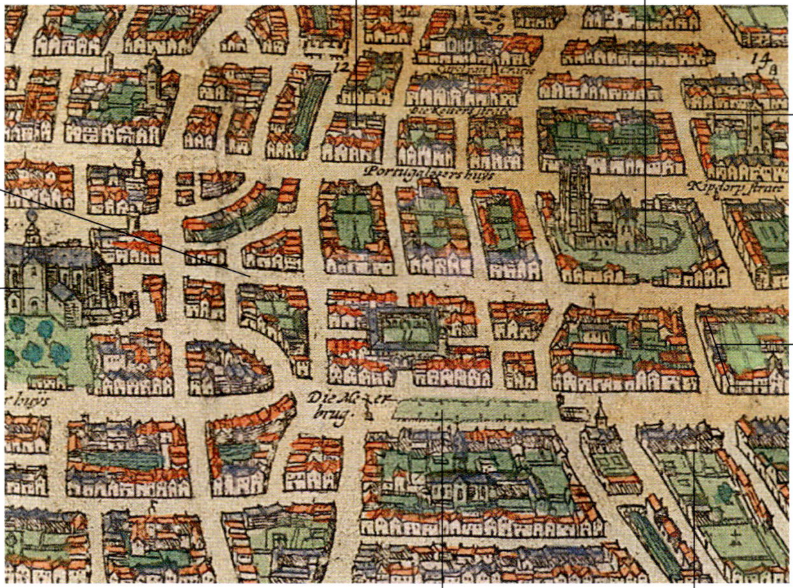

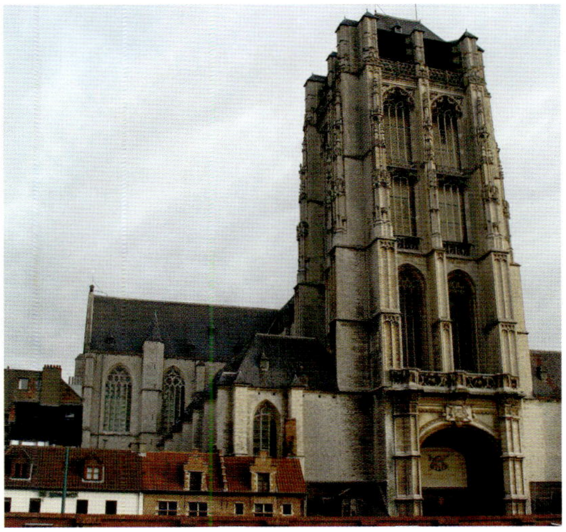

22
Sint-Jacobskerk (Saint James's church), Antwerp

seventeenth century.[7] In 1638 Rubens records having spoken to (Stefano) Annoni concerning the progress of his painting *The Horrors of War*, destined for the Grand Duke of Tuscany.[8] Moreover, in 1649 the Carenna family moved to within a hundred yards of Rubens's residence in the Wapper, a street that ran off the Meir, nearly opposite Eyckestraat,[9] and both the Carenna and Rubens families attended Sint-Jacobskerk (Saint James's church; fig. 22), where their funerary chapels were adjacent in the choir.[10] As we know from Giacomo Antonio's 1655 document of ennoblement, he started his chapel (fig. 23) in the church in that year. Rubens's mother had lived in nearby Keizerstraat and the Carenna family had a house (occupied successively by Giacomo Antonio's sons Francesco and Ignazio), possibly the original family home, on Lange Nieuwstraat – all in close vicinity to Sint-Jacobskerk (fig. 21). There were further similarities in the biographies of owner and painter. Both Carenna and Rubens acquired titles and were knighted by Philip IV of Spain – Carenna on May 14, 1665, Rubens some thirty-five years earlier on August 21, 1630.[11] Carenna's descendants appear to have shown an interest in humanism and history, so it is probable that he also aspired to be part of Rubens's antiquarian circle.[12]

23
The Carenna Chapel in Sint-Jacobskerk, Antwerp, with altarpiece by Jacob Jordaens; Giacomo Antonio Carenna's vault lies in front of the balustrade

24
JACOB JORDAENS
(1593–1678)
Saint Carlo Borromeo interceding with the Virgin for Victims of the Plague
1655
Oil on canvas
285 × 185 cm
Carenna Chapel, Sint-Jacobskerk, Antwerp

A patent of nobility, granted for services rendered to the King of Spain,[13] is effectively our only biography of him. It records that Carenna, born in Milan but living in Antwerp from his youth, held the important voluntary post of city almoner and that he practised as a financier. His services to Spain must have been loans, including the 10,746 ducats that he advanced to the count of Yebes, Juan Esteban Imbrea, towards the refinancing of the Spanish treasury.[14] The Spanish crown accepted that his family had already been ennobled, although the documentation had been lost in the fires associated with the plague in Milan. Carenna thus obtained the right to display his coat of arms in his chapel, and they are indeed to be found on the stone cover to his vault. Jacob Jordaens, who had completed the overdoors in Carenna's house in 1653, supplied an altarpiece for the chapel, representing the Milanese Saint Carlo Borromeo interceding with the Virgin (fig. 24). Carenna's coat of arms consisted of an olive branch between two stars, recalling – and perhaps explaining – the olive branch that the Virgin offers to Christ in Jordaens's altarpiece.[15] His coat of arms is also to be seen in the lower borders of the tapestries that once hung in his larger reception room (fig. 26).

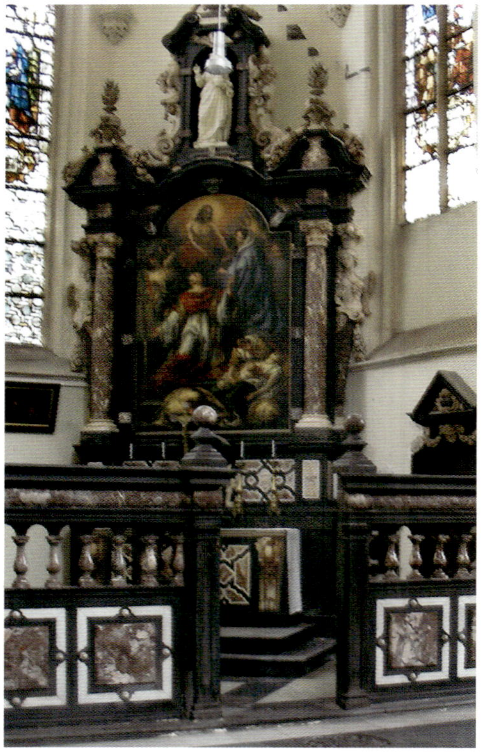

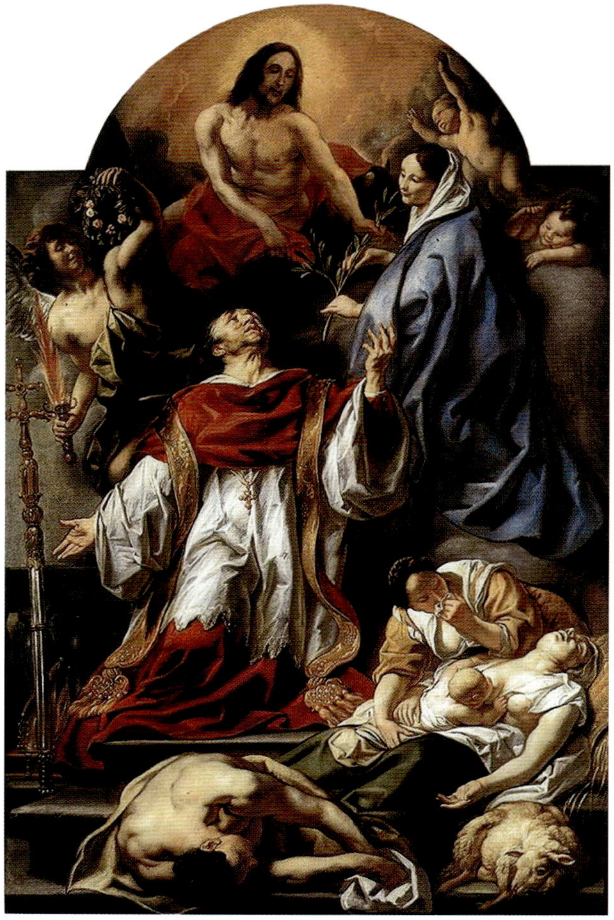

25
Osterriethhuis on the Meir, Antwerp (the site of Giacomo Antonio Carenna's house)

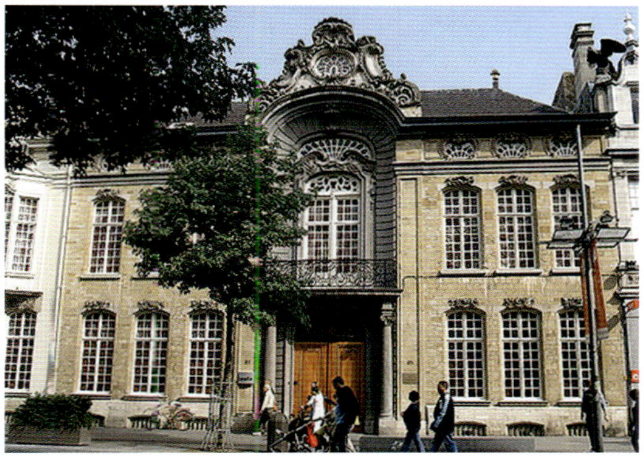

Appropriately to their social aspirations, the Carenna lived from 1649 in a grand house on the corner of the Meir and Eyckestraat (fig. 25),[16] which Carenna had bought from Pieter Hellemans, lord of Aartselaar, in 1649. The building is now known as the Osterriethhuis and is now owned by the Dexia Bank (it was formerly known as Hôtel Jeronimo and Hôtel d'Espinosa). The Carenna family also owned six other small houses on Eyckestraat annexed to their main house (which may have extended to the street behind, the Lange Nieuwstraat). Outside town, in Mortsel, they owned Ter Varent castle, a pleasure house surrounded by water, as it is described in Giacomo Antonio's will. In February 1665 Giacomo Antonio purchased the lordship of Burcht and Zwijndrecht, two villages and a fine castle just across the river from Antwerp, which in 1667 he divided up for his sons Francesco and Ignazio.[17]

Many of Rubens's friends and patrons were city almoners, an office also held by Carenna. The primary function of almoners was to provide for the poor, but as part of their duties they also held a feast on 4 December every year (the day elections were made to their number), and occasionally commissioned altarpieces. In 1518 the Antwerp almoners had asked the Brussels painter Bernard van Orley to paint them a *Last Judgement and the Seven Acts of Mercy* for the Cathedral:[18] completed in 1526, it shows almoners, wearing fur tabards and black flat caps, attending a burial (in the central panel) and aiding the needy (in the wings). Frans II Francken popularized this imagery in a composition, *The Seven Acts of Mercy*,[19] known in nine versions which quite possibly were produced for almoners. We know that the owner of a composition by Jan 'Velvet' Brueghel, of an almoner visiting the poor, was himself an almoner;[20] Giacomo Antonio's cousin Stefano Annoni owned another *Seven Acts of Mercy*.[21] Almoners are identified in portraits by Jordaens and Van Dyck not only by inscriptions but also by the collecting bowls they hold:[22] it was a prestigious office. We may picture Carenna, too, attired in the by then old-fashioned fur coat and black cap. He became an almoner in 1648, and his son Francesco was elected in 1657. Election seems to have involved a year's full-time commitment, and socially it was virtually the equivalent of ennoblement.[23] Earlier in 1655, in support

26
Giacomo Antonio Carenna's coat of arms
from the border of a tapestry woven by JAN II RAES after PETER PAUL RUBENS (see figs. 39–43)

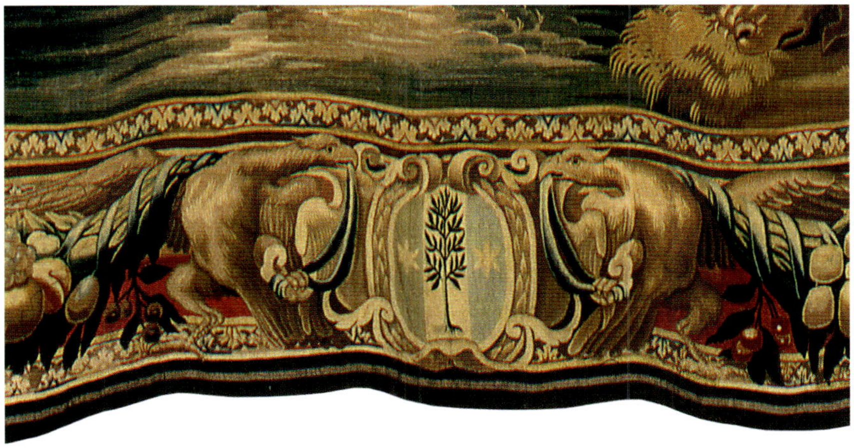

27
Francesco Carenna and his wife Isabella Roelants's coats of arms in the Carenna Chapel in Sint-Jacobskerk

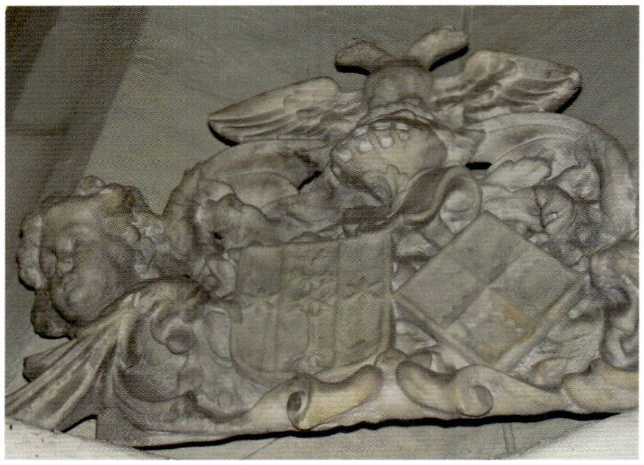

of Carenna's request to display arms, Philip Rubens (secretary to the city and the painter's nephew), had certified that the applicant had held this office.[24] In December 1672 the Antwerp almoners provided a grand feast in honour of 'Almoner Carenna'.[25] This – along with the illustrious names of godparents at the christenings of his children (including Gertrude van Veen, a noblewoman who appears to have been the daughter of Rubens's teacher Otto van Veen, and her husband the prominent Venetian banker Louis Malo)[26] – makes it clear that he was a leading member of Antwerp society. He died on November 25, 1672, and on December 16 mourners were paid to accompany his bier.[27] It seems ironic, given the scarcity of information about his life, that we know, down to the last chicken and almond tart, details of the feast that was ordered and celebrated for 'Almoner Carenna' that autumn across the street from Carenna's house, along the back wall of what had been Rubens's garden.[28]

It is not known when Giacomo Antonio married Maria Annoni, but the short-lived Pietro, the first of the many children she bore him, was baptized in 1623 and the baptism of their last child took place in 1641.[29] Two sons reached adulthood, (Giovanni) Francesco (1626–1691; see fig. 27) and Ignazio (1641–after 1689). Giacomo Antonio seems also to have taken particular care of his younger cousin Stefano Annoni (*c.* 1600–1664), who later worked closely with him in the Annoni business.[30] Stefano, living nearby in Lange Nieuwstraat, became a serious collector in his turn.[31] He owned a *Feast at Cana* by "Giovanni of Bruges" or Jan van Eyck (possibly the same painting as that again attributed to Van Eyck in the collection of Louis XIV and now in the Louvre, thought since the nineteenth century to be by Gerard David), and two Holbein portraits.[32] He also owned five oil-sketches and a *Judgement of Paris* by Rubens (but, since Rubens painted at least three versions, none of which have an unbroken seventeenth-century provenance, we cannot be sure which one). He had owned a painting by Abraham Janssens of "*Diana with Satyrs*" (see fig. 29), which he gave to his mentor Giacomo Antonio in 1657,[33] and he bequeathed a landscape by Paul Bril to Giacomo Antonio's son Francesco when appointing him his executor in 1664.[34] A further 84 paintings are listed in his inventory, including a view of his own garden, one of the many versions of *Andromeda* by Cavaliere d'Arpino, and a portrait by Tintoretto.[35]

Stefano's inventory shows he had a room for a female servant (called Petronella), seven orange trees, a horse in the stable and some tobacco. A set of scales and iron-clad boxes are the only signs of his financier trade. In his will he provided for his illegitimate children Giovanni Stefano (born 1630) and Giuliana Annoni, and left money for the poor and for masses to be held in various Antwerp churches as well as in his family church in Annone in Italy. He expressed the wish to be buried in Sint-Jacobskerk. He left possessions to his nephew Giovanni Antonio Annoni or, in the event of his death, to his cousin Paolo Annoni. Stefano also called

28
Interior of the great reception room of the Osterriethhuis, Antwerp, today, showing the original fireplace

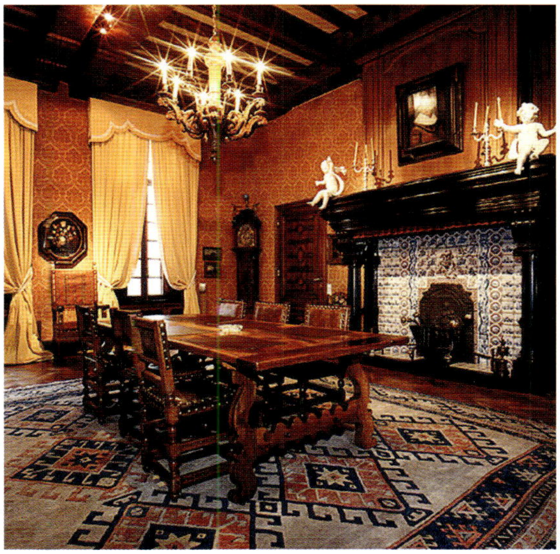

Giovanni Antonio Carenna "cousin"; Carenna's mother must have been related to these Annoni, and was perhaps Stefano's aunt.

The exchange of paintings as tokens of affection between relatives that these wills reveal is perhaps a sign of the increasing affluence and the upward social mobility of these merchant financier families. In Giacomo Antonio Carenna's case, surely the acquisition both of titles and of works of art was as an active strategy to elevate his family from their provincial roots in the Milanese countryside.

Giacomo Antonio's brother Stefano was also a collector, but unfortunately an inventory of November 1680 does not attribute the paintings he owned.[36] Nevertheless it describes still lifes of flowers, a number of landscape paintings that showed *Hermits Praying*, a pair of octagonal panels (perhaps by Brueghel or Bril), a *Rape of Proserpine* and a *Rape of Europa*. Also listed is a picture of a *Boy holding a Rooster*. Stefano owned numerous paintings of religious subjects, including a *Belshazzar's Feast*, and various Madonnas too generic to identify. Pictures of the newly promoted saints Filippo Neri and the Milanese Carlo Borromeo, and of Carlo's beatified brother Federico, suggest an orthodox Counter-Reformation sentiment, with a regional preference that was appropriate for Spanish Lombardy.[37] Stefano Carenna also had likenesses of his brothers Giacomo Antonio and Bartolomeo and a full-length portrait of his third brother Giovanni Angelo. The next generation continued this strategy of upward mobility when, in 1711, Stefano's son, Carlo Francesco, became Count of Merone.[38]

The *Massacre* in the Carenna collection

There is no obvious reason why a painting with the subject-matter of *The Massacre of the Innocents* should have appealed to Giacomo Antonio Carenna. The subject was not a typical choice for a domestic interior. Still, the Holy Innocents (as the slaughtered infants were known) were much venerated in Milan. Particular attention was paid to their feast day on December 28, with a special celebration held in the Cathedral, and it is possible that this date was of some special significance to Carenna. In 1606 another Milanese merchant, Giovanni Giacomo Castoldi, secured two skulls of the Holy Innocents, which were officially recognized by Cardinal Federico Borromeo and distributed amongst Milanese churches.[39] Various other relics of the Innocents had arrived in Milan before that date: in 1399 Luchino Visconti consecrated a chapel built for them in the church of San Francesco Grande, and in around 1448 they were housed in a purpose-built reliquary in the same church.[40]

As we have seen, the *Massacre* features in Giacomo Antonio's will of 1669. Carenna died in November 1672 and presumably the *Massacre* still hung in the larger reception room (fig. 28) at the time of his death. It was not, however, included in a later inventory, dated April 2–4, 1691 and made just before the death of his son Francesco in June 1691 (at which point the house was sold and the contents auctioned off).[41] This distinguishes it from the other works of art mentioned in Giacomo Antonio's will, which were still listed as contents of the greater reception room at the time of Francesco's death in 1691. In place of the *Massacre* over the fireplace the inventory makes reference to "a large chimney-piece (drawn) in front of the mantel shelf showing Diana and other figures." We know that in 1657 Stefano Annoni had given Giacomo Antonio a "*Diana with Satyrs* by Abraham Janssens,"[42] and it is tempting to speculate that this was a picture by Janssens now at Kassel, known as *Diana surprised by Satyrs* (fig. 29),[43] which includes two satyrs admiring Diana and her group of sleeping nymphs.

The circumstances surrounding the disappearance of the *Massacre* from Carenna's collection are unknown. However, we know that in the 1670s the Parisian dealer Jean-Michel Picart and his agent in Antwerp, Matthijs

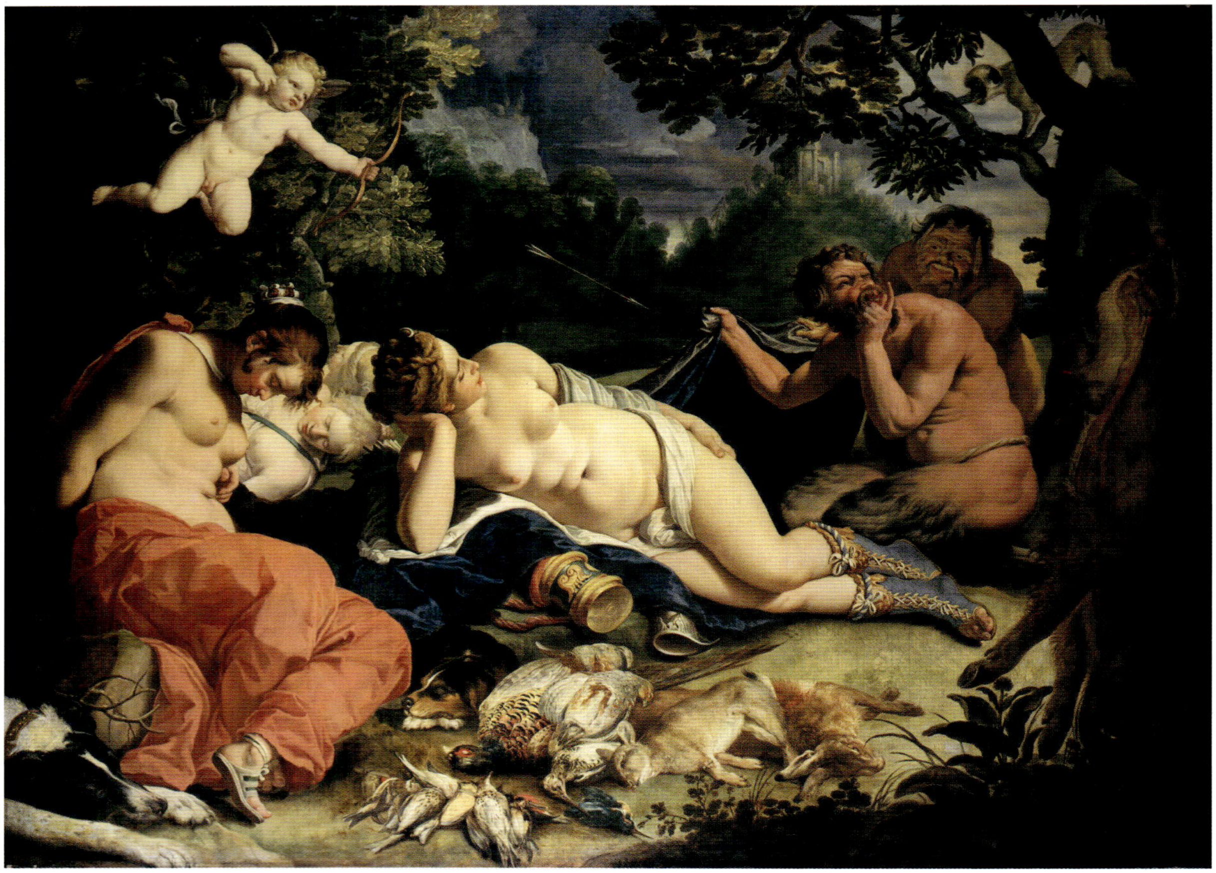

29
ABRAHAM JANSSENS
(1575–1632)
Diana surprised by Satyrs, *c.* 1620
Oil on canvas
169 × 235 cm
Museum Schloss Wilhelmshöhe, Gemäldegalerie Alte Meister, Kassel

30
GONZALES COQUES
(1614/18–1684)
The Family of Jan-Baptista Anthoine, 1664
Oil on copper
56.5 × 73.8 cm
The British Royal Collection
RCIN 405339

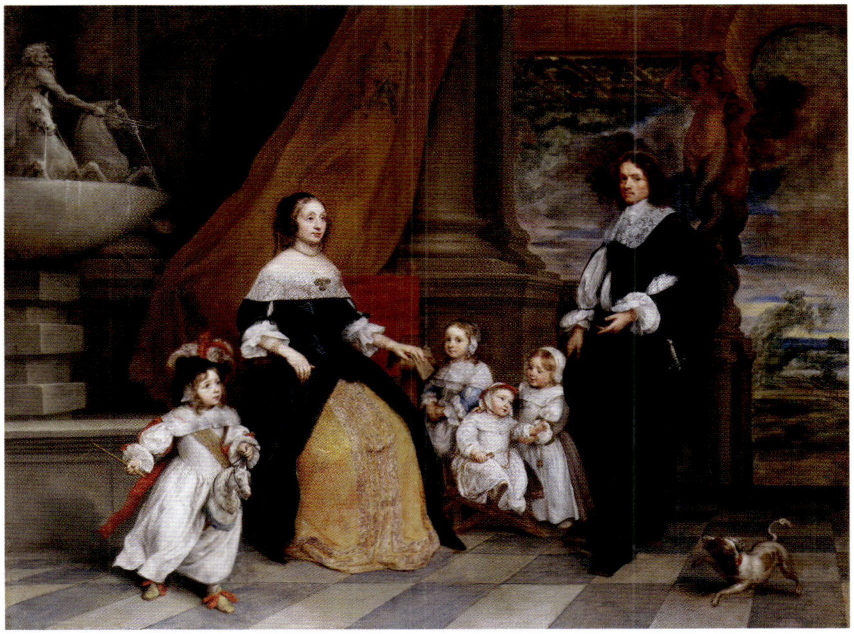

Musson, a pupil of Rubens and an executor of his estate, were searching for pictures by Rubens to sell to the duc de Richelieu. Their correspondence suggests that the Carenna *Massacre* was probably on the market and attracting serious interest from several quarters.[44] Musson was already targeting the *Massacre* on July 26, 1675. Picart told Musson that the *Massacre* was owned by "Carenno" or "Karena," a merchant from Genoa living in Ghent.[45] He warned him, in a vitriolic aside, that the Genoese were "a nation even worse than the Jews," and so he should not expect a bargain. Indeed Musson wrote to Picart in January 1676 that the *Massacre* was too expensive at 2,000 guilders, suggesting that a price of 300 guilders was more reasonable. However, in a document dated June of the same year, Philips Sweerts, a Flemish art dealer, obtained an option to buy an *Adoration of the Magi* by Veronese and with it an "Italian painter's" *Massacre of the Holy Innocents* for 1,100 guilders from its owners Jan-Baptista Anthoine and Antonio van Leijen.[46] The contract specified that the works were for purchase or return within three months. Apparently no buyer was found, as *The Massacre of the Innocents* re-appears, still unattributed but with a very high valuation of 1,200 guilders, in 1691 in the will of one of the owners, Jan-Baptista Anthoine (fig. 30).[47]

A number of links between Anthoine and the Carenna family make it likely that this unattributed *Massacre* was Rubens's early work. Anthoine held the lucrative office of Imperial Postmaster for the Netherlands and was a fellow parishioner and neighbour of Francesco Carenna.

(Coincidentally, Francesco Carenna's wife Isabella was the daughter of an earlier Postmaster, Jan Roelants.) Paulus Pontius's engraving of Jan Roelants, Francesco's father-in-law, was dedicated to Anthoine.[48] The valuation at 1,200 guilders of the unattributed *Massacre* made it the most expensive work in Anthoine's inventory; it is significant that its valuation was higher than the identified masterpieces by Van Dyck, Murillo and Rubens in the same impressive collection. The art experts who compiled the inventory, Jan Erasmus Quellinus and Pieter van der Willige, seem to have appreciated the work's merits but do not seem to have recognized Rubens's early style. That the June 1676 contract had misattributed this *Massacre* to an Italian painter would show how far Rubens had assimilated the innovations of Italian masters such as Caravaggio and the Carracci. The "big" *Massacre* was inherited by Anthoine's daughter, Joanna Maria, a member of a lay order.

The next record of the *Massacre* occurs in December 1698, when, together with Rubens's *Samson and Delilah* (see fig. 45), it was offered by the Fourchardt brothers to Prince Johann Adam Andreas I of Liechtenstein.[49] There is little doubt that the painting on offer was Rubens's early *Massacre* since Anthoine's *Venus with a Mirror* by Rubens, which is valued in his inventory at only 240 guilders, also reached the prince's collection before his death in 1712, and both paintings are listed in the inventory of his estate. Evidently the Fourchardt brothers had obtained Rubens's early works and become effective promoters of them. Once they had overcome his initial resistance, they sold three of his finest paintings to the prince.

The *Massacre* and the *Samson and Delilah*, together with many other masterpieces by Rubens, remained in the Liechtenstein collection for the next two hundred years. In the mid eighteenth century both the *Samson* and the *Massacre* again lost their attributions to Rubens, a turn of events that makes this brief re-establishment of the early phase of Rubens's career by the Fourchardt brothers and their Viennese client all the more remarkable. In the case of the *Massacre*, there was no engraving to support its authenticity, but the *Samson* was engraved and still suffered demotion. It is worth remembering that around the turn of the seventeenth century many works by Rubens had been re-attributed to Van Dyck – whose works were then worth three or four times as much – but it would have been hard to pass off these early works as the product of his pupil; the solid modelling in both works contrasts with the more fluid, decorative curves of the younger artist.

The *Massacre* hung in the Liechtensteins' Stadtpalais in the Bankgasse, Vienna, until it was moved to the Gartenpalais shortly after 1807. Between 1807 and 1815 Josef Braun made a series of detailed drawings of the wall elevations there, which remain in the Liechtenstein collection. They seem to have assisted with planning the hang. Subsequent alterations were recorded by sticking pieces of paper over the original plan. From these drawings, we know that the *Massacre* hung on the second wall of Room 6, in the centre of the wall at the lower level.

The *Samson and Delilah* (see fig. 45) hung on the same wall in the Gartenpalais, and the inscriptions on the drawing plan show that the two pictures were valued for an identical sum. As artistic taste changed to favour the Rococo, both paintings lost their attribution as works by Rubens. As early as 1767 the *Samson* had been demoted to a work by Frans de Neve, and from 1780 it was re-attributed to Jan van den Hoecke, a pupil of Rubens who had become the court painter of Archduke Leopold Wilhelm of Austria.[50] The *Massacre*, too, was re-attributed to Van den Hoecke (who thus became a depository for atypical Rubens paintings) but stayed in the collection for a further forty years after the *Samson* was sold at auction in 1880. It was not until June 11, 1920, that the painting left the collection, when it was sold by Prince Johann II, who had decided to re-hang the gallery in keeping with his conservative tastes. Although he was a scholarly art historian, Johann II was known for his austere disposition and, unlike his namesake, particularly disliked nudity. The *Massacre* was bought by a Viennese dealer, Glückselig, who then sold it to the father of its last European owner. By a remarkable twist of fate, the picture narrowly avoided destruction during the Second World War, having been placed in storage in Salzburg shortly before the office in which it had hung was bombed.[51] It survived to be sold over half a century later, in 2002, in the auction mentioned at the start of the chapter.

While the later provenance of the *Massacre* is now quite well established, in contrast nothing definite is known about the painting before it is recorded in the 1669 Carenna inventory. Conceivably it was commissioned or acquired as a bad debt by the twenty-year-old Carenna around 1610–11; but he may not have consolidated his position in the Annoni firm before his marriage to Maria Annoni (and receipt of the accompanying dowry) shortly before 1623. Rubens may have painted it for another patron who subsequently sold it to Carenna, or, as was also his practice – as with the 1611 *Juno and Argus* now in Cologne (fig. 31) – he may have painted it without any commission, hoping to win new patrons. It may even have hung over Rubens's own fireplace. We know from the artist's 1618 letter to the English ambassador Sir Dudley Carleton that not all of his paintings found a home immediately.[52] In that letter the artist offered Sir Dudley a selection of works including a *Leda*, a *Daniel in the Lions' Den* and a *Prometheus*, all paintings that can be dated before 1613. The *Massacre* is not offered, however, which suggests that, by this date at least, it was no longer in Rubens's possession. Certainly, there were plenty of art lovers in early seventeenth-century Antwerp and elsewhere who would have been eager to obtain pictures by Rubens. One such person might have been the duke of Aarschot-Croÿ. We know that the aforementioned *Juno and Argus* was offered to him, and the *Massacre* would have been a suitable addition to

31
PETER PAUL RUBENS
(1577–1640)
Juno and Argus, 1611
Oil on canvas
250 × 350 cm
Wallraf-Richartz-Museum,
Cologne

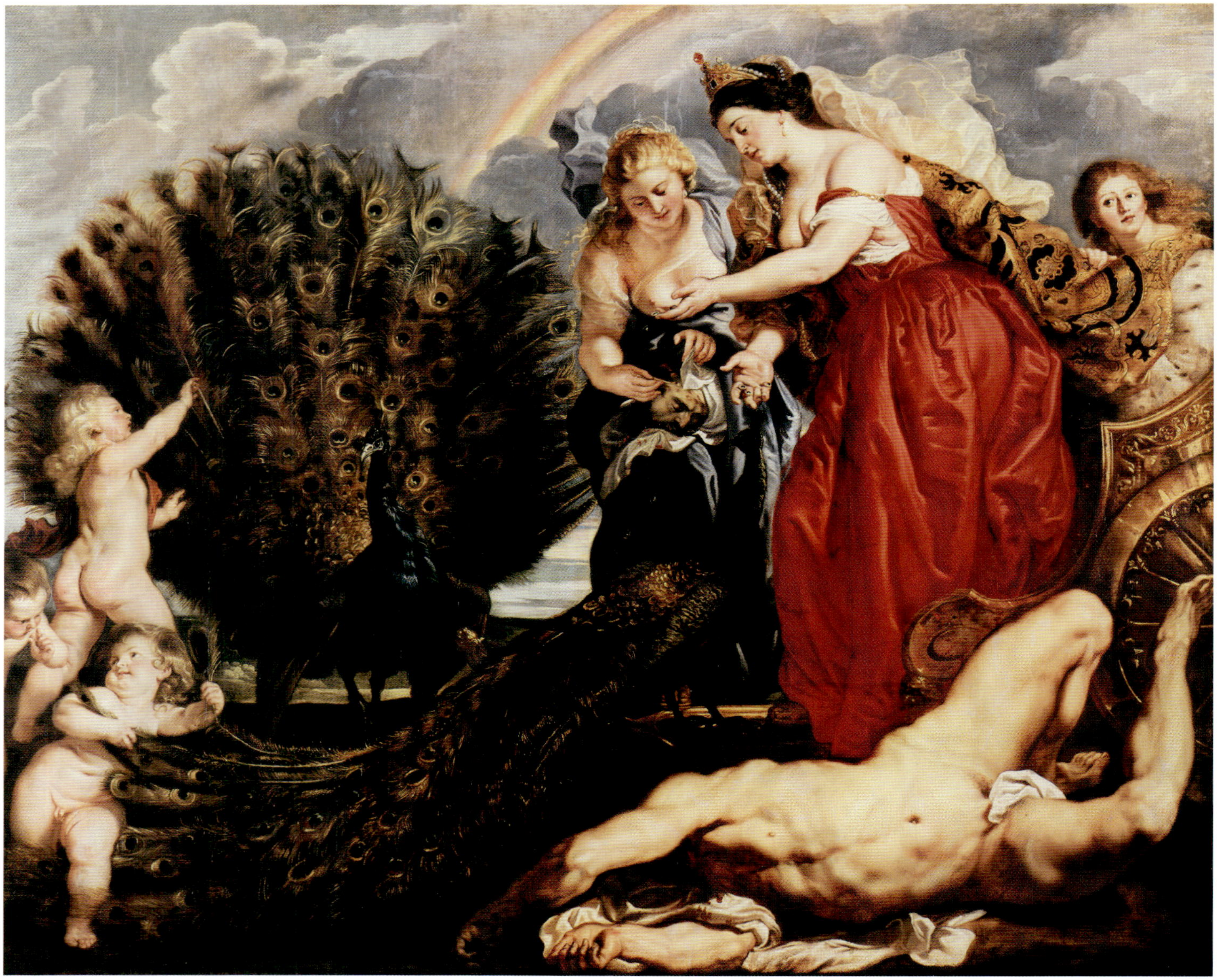

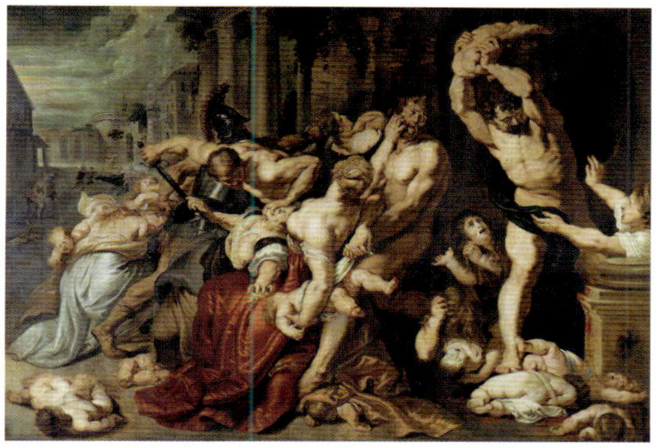

32
After PETER PAUL RUBENS
(1577–1640)
The Massacre of the Innocents
c. 1670–75(?)
Oil on canvas
162.5 × 232 cm
Musées royaux des Beaux-Arts de Belgique, Brussels, inv. no. 3639

33
PETER PAUL RUBENS
(1577–1640)
Roman Charity or **Cimon and Pero**
c. 1612
Oil on canvas
140.5 × 180.3 cm
The State Hermitage Museum, St Petersburg
GE-470

his grand gallery.[53] In general, paintings on canvas, being more easily transportable, tended to be for export. Those on panel were for local consumption, which makes it more likely that Rubens made the *Massacre* for the Antwerp market.

There is an enlarged seventeenth-century copy of Rubens's *Massacre* (fig. 32) on canvas, which, curiously, has the same dimensions as the Janssens which probably replaced the *Massacre* in Francesco Carenna's larger reception room. It is possible, therefore, that Francesco Carenna had this copy made to replace the original work which he sold in the 1670s.[54] (The dimensions of the oak panel on which the *Massacre* was painted are smaller than the standard dimensions of a canvas at the time, which might suggest it was site specific.) Another of Rubens's panels, *Cimon and Pero* (fig. 33), is the same size and we know that that work came to hang in the house of Carel van den Bosch, the Bishop of Bruges, probably above the fireplace.[55] Two other panels, *Leda and the Swan* (Dresden) and *Jupiter and Callisto* (Kassel), are also the same length. This may indicate a standard timber size that suited chimney-pieces, which, in turn, would make it more likely that the *Massacre* was indeed painted speculatively and not on commission. The Thomson Collection picture, which measures 182 cm across without a frame, would have fitted neatly over the only remaining *c.* 1600 fireplace in the larger reception room in Carenna's house, the chimney-breast of which measures 205 cm (fig. 37).

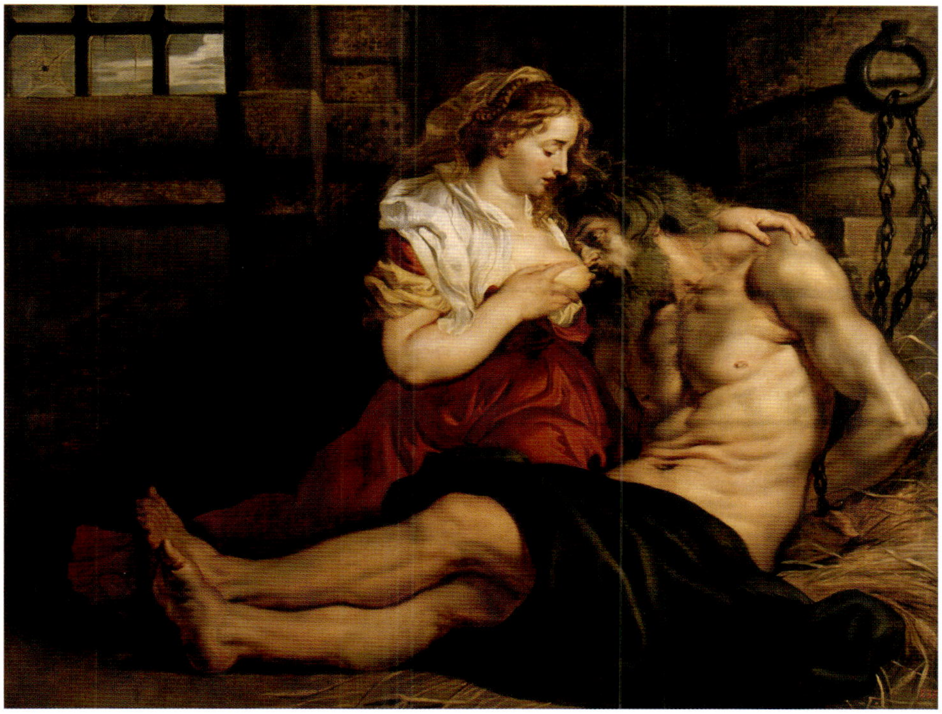

34
PETER PAUL RUBENS
(1577–1640)
The Birth of Venus, *c.* 1616
Oil on canvas
227 × 249 cm
Formerly Schloss Sanssouci, Potsdam (missing since 1942)

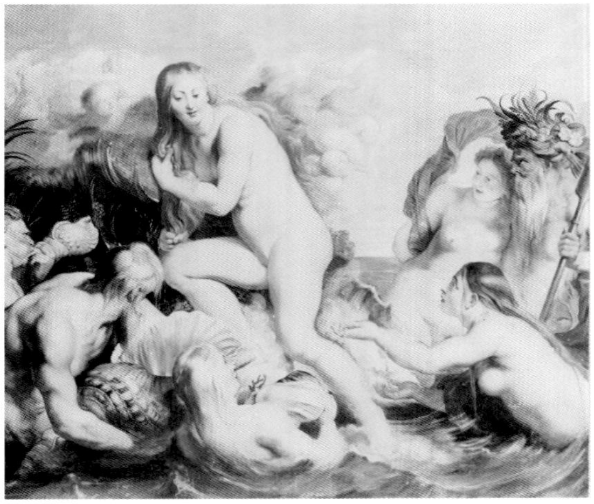

The display of *The Massacre of the Innocents*

Carenna's house on the Meir in Antwerp was remodelled in the eighteenth century, but its imposing scale remains. Early inventories also allow us to gain some idea of the way it looked in the seventeenth century and so give us a sense of the physical context for the *Massacre*. Carenna bought the house from Pieter Hellemans in 1649. Hellemans's inventory has not yet been found but we do possess a room-by-room inventory from an earlier owner. The 1617 inventory of Isabella da Vega, widow of Emmanuel Ximenez,[56] records that the reception room was dominated by a large canvas, Rubens's *Birth of Venus*, which was covered by a blue curtain.[57] This was probably the painting (fig. 34) last recorded in Potsdam in 1942.[58] Both the Portuguese merchant Emmanuel Ximenez and his brother Gonzalo were made knights of the Florentine order of Santo Stefano in 1591.[59] It seems that the house had a tradition of being decorated with Rubens's paintings by foreign ennobled merchants.[60] Most of the other paintings in the Ximenez inventory are not attributed but some were clearly of subjects explored by Rubens (whether by him or not) such as *Saint Ursula*, *The Rape of the Sabine Women* and *Judith and Holofernes*.

The Ximenez inventory also gives an idea of the other furnishings in the rooms. We learn that there were many sets of chairs for both men and women, banqueting tables covered with Persian carpets, colourful objects such as celestial globes, stuffed crocodiles and salamanders as well as a harpsichord decorated by Hendrick van Balen and Jan Brueghel. Storerooms of linen, dresses and wine are described, as are saddles and bedding and fittings.[61]

Giacomo Antonio Carenna's 1669 inventory is unusually short and only describes the works of art in the larger reception room of his house. Its brevity can be explained by the fact that the house and contents would pass to Francesco, his eldest son.[62] As mentioned previously, it describes the *Massacre* as hanging above a chimney-piece in the room. It also notes a series of tapestries of *The History of Achilles* (figs. 39–43) and the overdoors by Jordaens which he had commissioned in 1653 (figs. 35–36). Each tapestry had a lower border with Carenna's coat of arms (see fig. 26). The inventory mentions the chairs and the adjacent chapel before stopping abruptly. There is a sense of proprietorial pride in the description of the room, which stresses that both the tapestries and the Jordaens were made to measure. Apparent confirmation that Giacomo Antonio was behind this description comes with the use of the word *cadregha*, 'chair' in Milanese dialect.

The Carenna collection is listed more fully in his son Francesco's detailed 1691 inventory, which makes for an impressive journey through the family residence on the Meir. After passing through a study with a desk and a picture of *The Virgin and Saint Carlo Borromeo* by Jan Boeckhorst, one enters the smaller reception room with a chimney-piece by Frans Snyders and Rubens showing *Figures, Fruit and Game*. (The Dresden *Diana returning from the Hunt*

35
JACOB JORDAENS
(1593–1678)
The Feast of Cleopatra
1653
Oil on canvas
156.4 × 149.3 cm
The State Hermitage Museum, St Petersburg
GE-3536

36
JACOB JORDAENS
(1593–1678)
The Death of Cleopatra
1653
Oil on canvas
171 × 172 cm, including a strip of about 17 cm added to the lower edge; estimated original format 156 × 172 cm
Staatliche Museen, Gemäldegalerie Alte Meister, Kassel

contains the required ingredients and is a suitable size.)[63] This not so small room (there seems to be a residual Milanese modesty regarding room sizes) had six tapestry scenes from the story of Meleager (and Atalanta). It may be the same set that the Fourchardt brothers were offering to Liechtenstein in the 1690s.[64]

It seems that a courtyard separated the larger (Achilles) room and the adjacent smaller (Meleager) hall from another large room with its own adjoining rooms. Spread over two floors, this large house had at least twelve other significant rooms. Francesco Carenna's inventory again records the Achilles tapestries and Jordaens paintings in the larger reception room, as in his father's 1669 inventory, except there is no mention of Rubens's *Massacre*. This room, an enormous space, must have been sumptuous, featuring as it did Rubens's cycle of Achilles tapestries. The two Jordaens paintings, more fully described in Francesco's inventory as depicting *The Feast of Cleopatra* (fig. 35) and *The Death of Cleopatra* (fig. 36), either occupied the end wall beside the chimney-piece or the long wall opposite the courtyard windows, as they are lit from the right.[65] Both were originally the same height, but the *Death* was some 20 cm wider, suggesting that it was made to fit over a greater door. Crowning the fireplace was "Diana & other figures" (Abraham Janssens's *Diana surprised by Satyrs*; see fig. 29) and, in Giacomo Antonio's day at least, the *Massacre*. The 1669 inventory records that the hearth was covered (when not in use) by a perspectival painting, probably identical to the canvas cover in the 1691 inventory. Giacomo Antonio's white cotton curtains had been replaced by red silk ones and his twenty chairs had been reduced to twelve of red velvet, with two tables covered in red velvet.

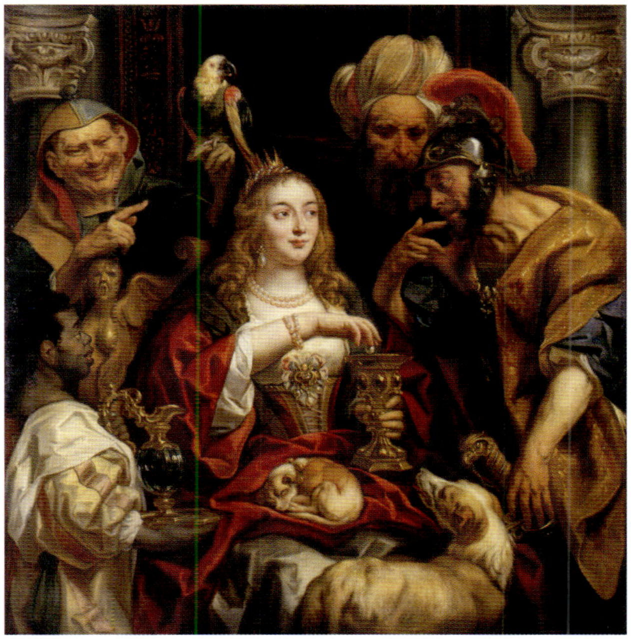

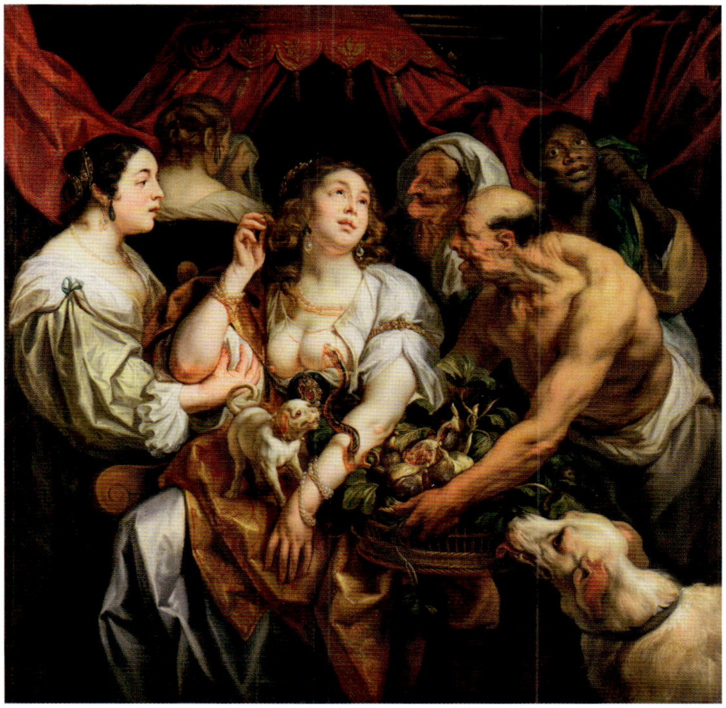

37
Chimney-piece in the great reception room in the Osterriethhuis, Antwerp. Jan Huyghebaert, who stands by the fireplace, is 5′ 10″ (1.77 m) tall.

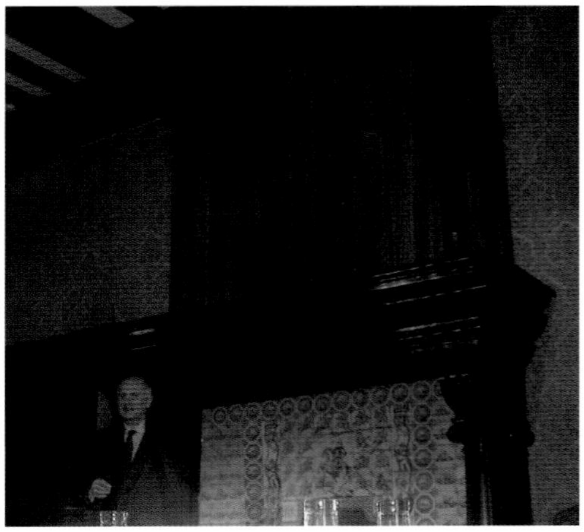

Rubens had emphasized the love element in the Achilles tapestries, and Jordaens's Cleopatra paintings illustrated one of the great love affairs of the ancient world, so Francesco's display of Janssens's painting of a cupid-struck satyr falling for the chaste huntress Diana provided another variation on the theme of love in a predominantly red hall. Since the room would have served as a banqueting hall, the Jordaens painting of Cleopatra dissolving a pearl in wine to create a more expensive feast than Mark Antony had provided had a nice relevance. Giacomo Antonio may have been amused by the happy coincidence of sharing his middle name with the Roman general.

The only remaining *c.* 1600 fireplace stands in the reception room on the west end-wall backing on to Eyckestraat. It has a flat mantel and two free-standing black stone columns each about 2.5 metres high, while painted tiles decorate the hearth (see fig. 28) – a properly grand setting for a picture by such an eminent artist as Rubens. Chimney-piece pictures were given a particular name in contemporary inventories, *schouwstuk*, indicating their importance in domestic interiors.[66] These pictures sometimes had a curtain which could be drawn across them: prized or licentious paintings were often so covered in seventeenth-century collections (already a practice in ancient Greece). The Meleager room also had a Rubens chimney-piece. The *schouwstuk* in other rooms included a *Hart and other Game* by Frans Snyders, a *Still Life* by Jan Davidsz de Heem, a *Democritus and Heraclitus* (perhaps by Bloemaert or Jordaens), and two landscapes by Joos de Momper. Francesco's inventory describes a room with a chequerboard and a painting of an "Italian pleasure house" (*speelhoff*) – perhaps a villa at Annone like his father's "pleasure house" at Mortsel. Portraits of Francesco's parents are also mentioned, but have not been identified. The books and shells listed may have belonged to his father.

The placing of the *Massacre* high on the chimney-breast is important, as it suggests that the painting in the Thomson Collection may have been intended to be viewed from below (fig. 37). This would account for the sharply receding perspective, and in particular for the foreshortening of the mother in the foreground who scratches the face of one of the soldiers: Rubens painted her from above, and when seen from below she seems to fall out into our space. Her child, too, is painted with this perspective in mind, hence his large scale relative to the other infants. There is also a sense that the whole composition is more spatially coherent if read from slightly off to the right, and the painting may have been designed to be seen from this angle. As we know from his handling of another great chimney-piece, the *Samson and Delilah* (fig. 45) for Rockox, Rubens was a master of adapting images to their setting. It is possible that Rubens's *Tarquin and Lucretia* (fig. 38), owned by his brother-in-law Arnold Lunden, also hung above a fireplace as a *schouwstuk*, as it is roughly the same size as the *Samson and Delilah* and again looms over the viewer.[67]

38
PETER PAUL RUBENS
(1577–1640)
Tarquin and Lucretia, *c.* 1612
Oil on canvas
187 × 219 cm
Collection of Vladimir
Logvinenko, Moscow

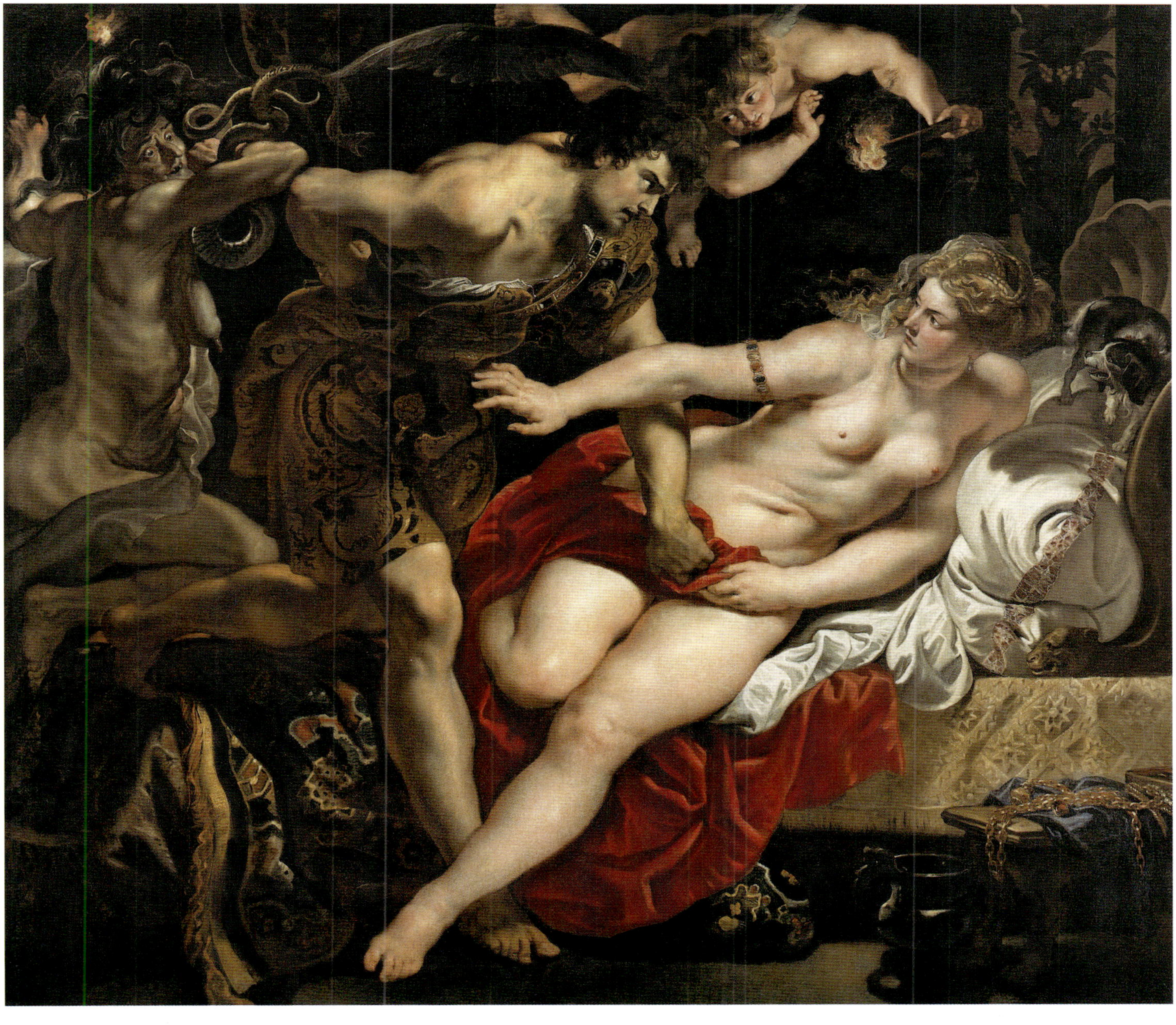

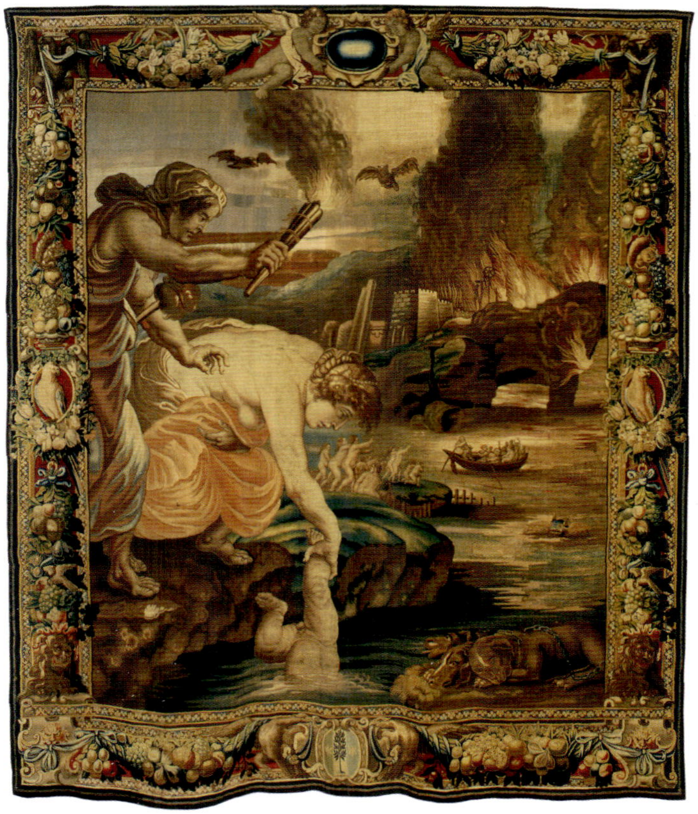

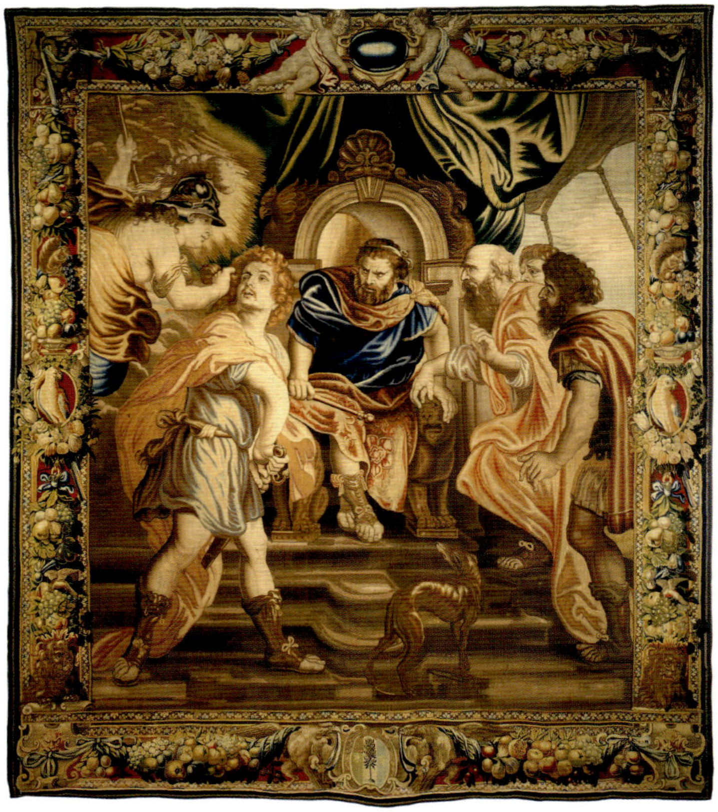

39
JAN II RAES after
PETER PAUL RUBENS
Thetis dipping Achilles in the River Styx, *c.* 1650
Tapestry
423 × 362 cm
Musées royaux d'Art et d'Histoire, Brussels, inv. no. 2107

40
JAN II RAES after
PETER PAUL RUBENS
The Wrath of Achilles
c. 1650
Tapestry
423 × 376 cm
Musées royaux d'Art et d'Histoire, Brussels, inv. no. 2109

Besides the chimney-pieces, there were about a hundred other paintings in the house, including hunting scenes and cycles of the seasons but also, of course, works with a religious subject-matter. The chapel adjacent to the larger reception room contained an altarpiece of *Christ, Saint Joseph and Saint Carlo Borromeo* according to Giacomo Antonio Carenna's inventory, along with three small devotional paintings. The Carennas were evidently devoted to the newly canonized Milanese saint Carlo Borromeo: we noted that Francesco had *The Virgin and Saint Carlo Borromeo* in his study and the altarpiece by Jordaens in the family chapel in the Sint-Jacobskerk (see fig. 24) shows the saint interceding to the Virgin to stop the plague.

In contrast to today's emphasis on paintings, in Carenna's time the most expensive decoration of the reception room was the set of fine made-to-measure Brussels tapestries depicting the story of Achilles. Designed by Rubens much later than the *Massacre* – around 1630–35 – this set was produced by the Antwerp tapestry dealer Jan II Raes before December 1653, after which date the template cartoons were sold to another producer, Jan van Leefdael. The lower borders with the Carenna

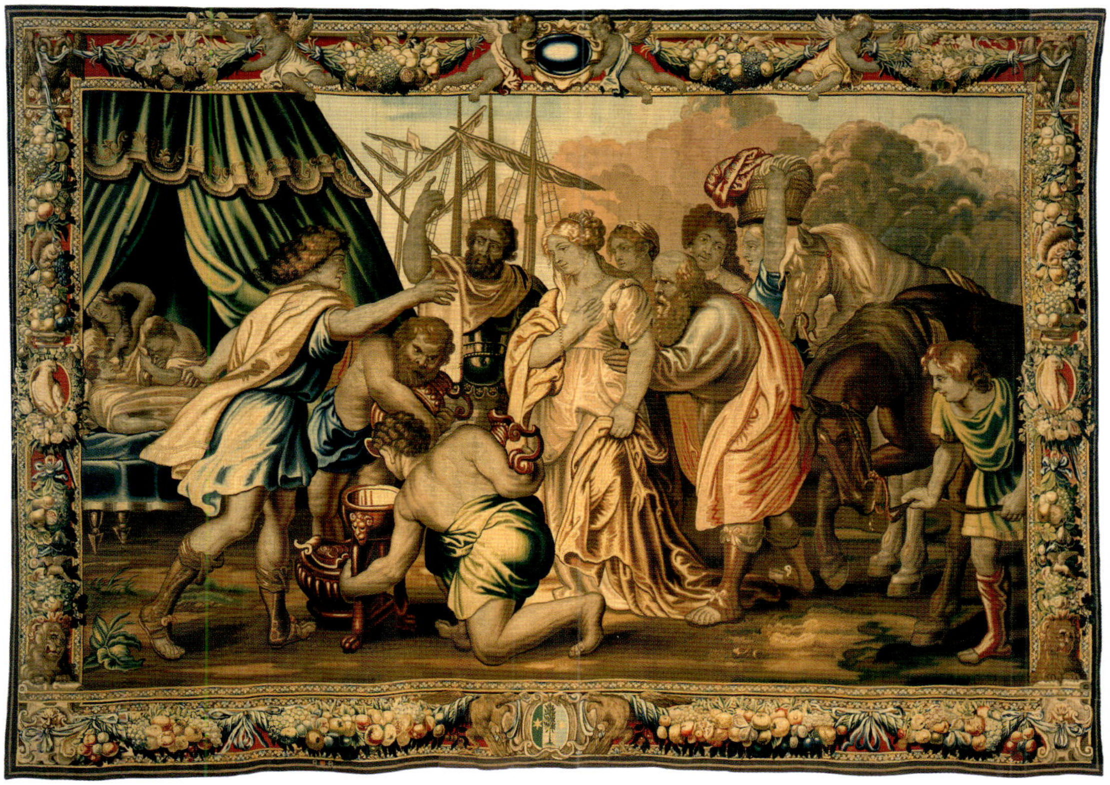

41
JAN II RAES after
PETER PAUL RUBENS
The Return of Briseis to Achilles, *c.* 1650
Tapestry
416 × 593 cm
Musées royaux d'Art et d'Histoire, Brussels, inv. no. 2110

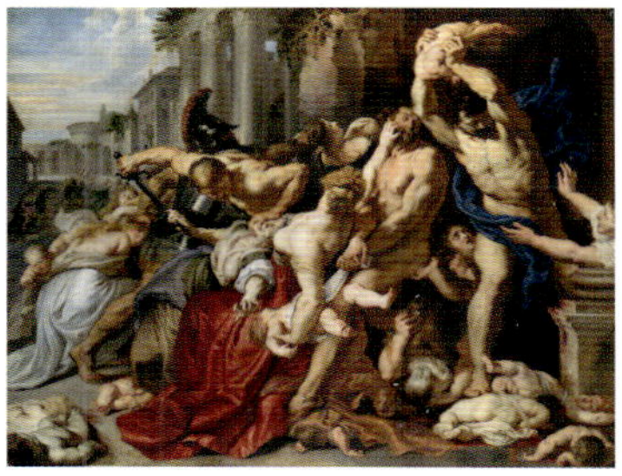

The *Massacre* shown in scale to three of the tapestries which hung beside it in Carenna's larger reception room

coats of arms were presumably added after Giacomo Antonio was ennobled in 1655.[68]

Some seven Achilles tapestries are recorded in the inventory following Francesco's death, five of which are now in in the Musées royaux d'Art et d'Histoire in Brussels – *Thetis dipping Achilles in the River Styx* (fig. 39); *The Education of Achilles* (fig. 42); *The Wrath of Achilles* (fig. 40); *The Return of Briseis to Achilles* (fig. 41); and *The Death of Achilles* (fig. 43).[69] One of the set was burnt in a fire in the eighteenth century: it must have depicted *Achilles and the Daughters of Lycomedes*, *Thetis receiving Arms from Vulcan* or *The Death of Hector*. The enormous dimensions of the reception room would have been ideal for the tapestries, which would have taken up nearly 30 metres of wall space, and the paintings occupied a further six metres. A painting showing the Duke of Savoy's set of Story of Achilles tapestries (fig. 44) gives some idea of the grandiose setting and the size of room that was needed.[70] Playing off these action scenes in these enormous woven images, which were more than twice its height, the athletic exuberance of the *Massacre* would have seemed rather less strident.

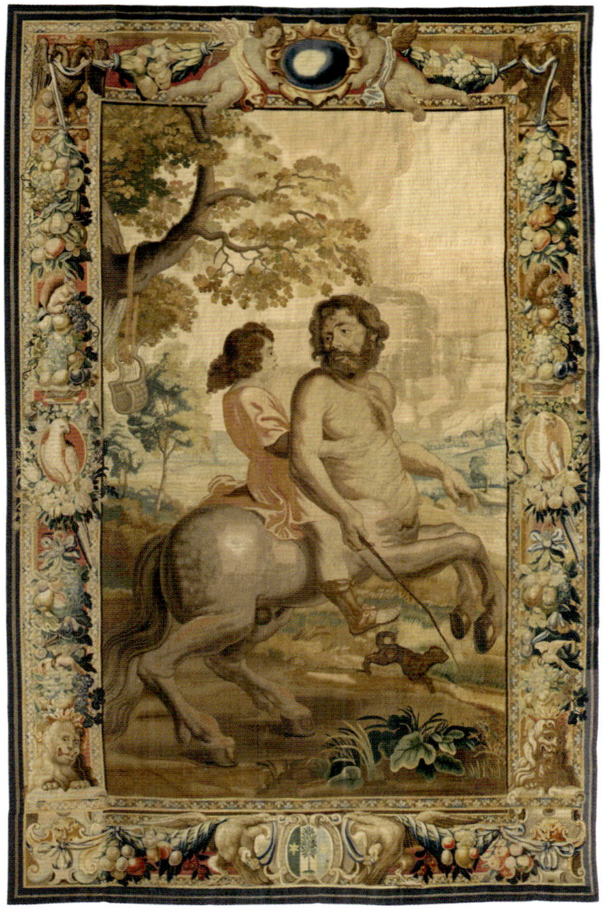

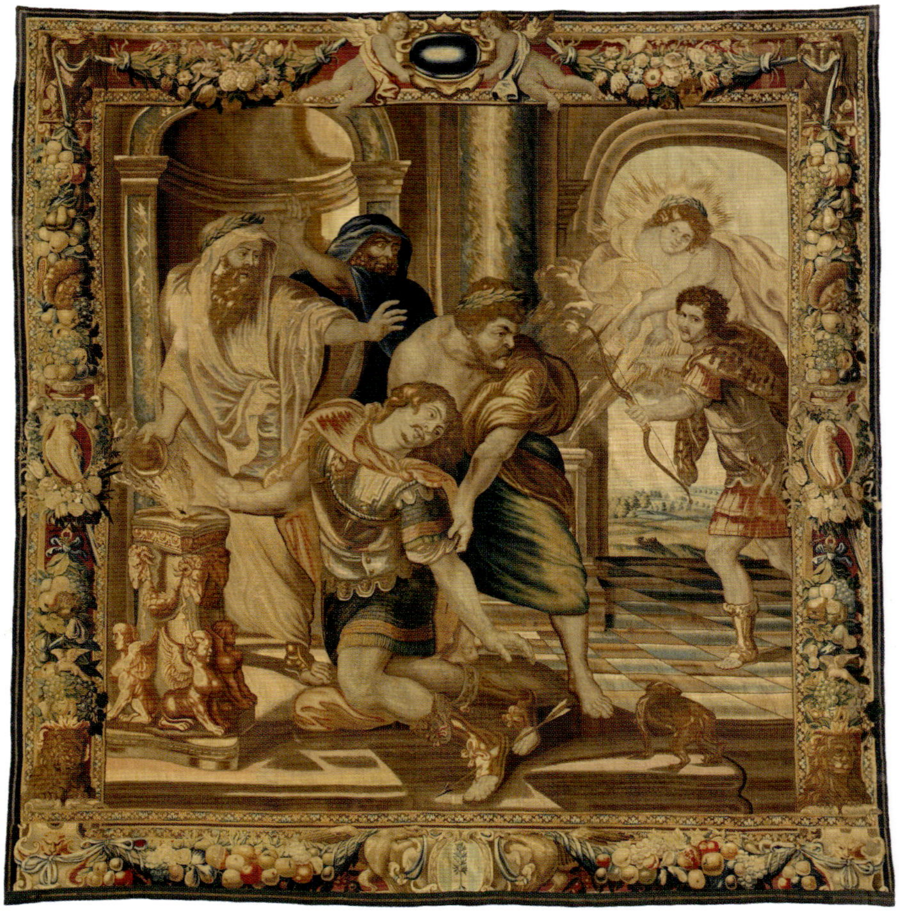

42
JAN II RAES after
PETER PAUL RUBENS
The Education of Achilles
c. 1650
Tapestry
423 × 255 cm
Musées royaux d'Art et
d'Histoire, Brussels,
inv. no. 2108

43
JAN II RAES after
PETER PAUL RUBENS
The Death of Achilles
c. 1650
Tapestry
418 × 390 cm
Musées royaux d'Art et
d'Histoire, Brussels,
inv. no. 2111

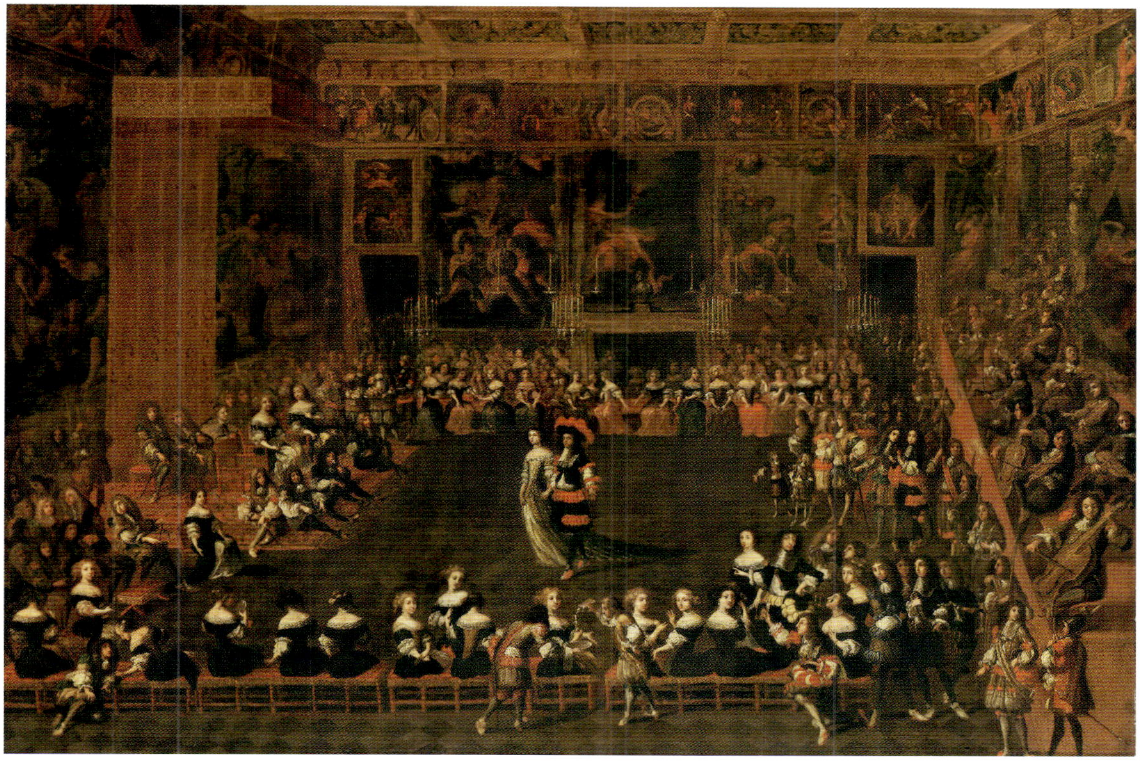

44
LAURENT DUFOUR
(1593–1678)
A Ball in a Royal Palace in Turin in 1663
(showing a set of Rubens's Achilles tapestries on the walls; *Thetis dipping Achilles*, fig. 39, can be identified above the large fireplace)
c. 1663–65
Oil on canvas
89.5 × 128.3 cm
Private collection

Since tapestries were the most prestigious and expensive form of wall decoration in the Renaissance and Baroque eras, European princes and dukes strove to establish tapestry workshops to rival those of Flanders. Carenna's choice of tapestry was also appropriate given his family's involvement in the assembling of thread, both fibre and metal, and dyes from across Europe and the New World, and it promoted the extraordinary craftsmanship that created these luxury images. Francesco Carenna's 1691 inventory shows that the Carenna house had two additional sets, a Story of Meleager and a series of landscapes – making a spectacular display of wealthy furnishings.

Nicolaas Rockox (1560–1640) and the *Samson and Delilah*: a comparative study

Rubens painted *Samson and Delilah* (fig. 45) within a year or so of the *Massacre* for his friend and patron Burgomaster Nicolaas Rockox, whose double-fronted house, known as the 'Golden Ring', stood on Keizerstraat in Antwerp. These contemporaneous works were both painted as chimney-pieces and were both owned (and, in the case of Rockox at least, commissioned) by important civic figures and collectors in Antwerp;

moreover, almost a hundred years later, they were united in the Liechtenstein collection. What makes the Rockox panel unique, and important in understanding the *Massacre*, is the fact that we have so much information about the work and its original location in Rockox's house (fig. 47). This includes a view of the *Samson* set above the fireplace in a painting by Frans II Francken (fig. 46).

Rockox did not own princely tapestries like the Carenna family, but he had amassed a renowned collection of antiquities and curiosities. His 'gallery' was actually spread over several rooms, including a great room housing the main collection and a smaller room behind it which probably served as a place for study and contemplation and held objects such as coins, gems and medals together with his paintings.[71] Frans II Francken's panel, *A Feast in the House of Nicolaas Rockox* (*c*. 1630–35; fig. 46), shows a selection of highlights from the collection arranged in the great room. This was not the only work celebrating his taste, for at least two of Rockox's *all'antica* Renaissance objects, a Paduan oil-lamp and a small bust of Hercules, were chosen to represent the culture of Antwerp in Rubens and Brueghel's *Sense of Sight* (see figs. 117–19). The room is furnished with embossed gilt leather wall-hangings, ancient busts and bronze statuettes as well as images both sacred and secular. From the inventory of Rockox's estate we know that he owned some 82 paintings at the time of his death. Rubens's *Samson and Delilah* was the most important of these pictures and can be seen in Francken's picture hanging in its place above the fireplace.[72]

The *Samson and Delilah* (and perhaps the *Massacre*, too) was designed with its location in mind. The courtyard light from the windows on the left catches the strong forms of Delilah's and Samson's backs, the soldiers in the doorway on the right-hand side recede further in the less intense illumination of a natural light source, while they appear to jump forward in artificial lighting. The cloudy sky sinks into the gloom behind the soldiers. We first view the painting from left of centre – here again there was an angled principal viewpoint. This may seem strange to viewers accustomed to frontal museum displays, but Rubens had just designed two contiguous side-wall scenes in the Jesuit church in Mantua and the Oratorian church in Rome to flank his high altarpieces and so was practised in adjusting compositions for side viewing. As the painting was hung above eye level, Samson's hulking nudity would have borne down from above into the viewer's space in much the same way as the central woman in red does in the *Massacre*. The *Samson* and the *Massacre* were certainly not conceived as a pair but they may have been worked on in the studio together, for they share similar models, costume and sources. The figure of Delilah and the central mother in red in the *Massacre* may well be based upon the same woman, wearing the same dress, and the old woman in each must draw on a common source.[73] Samson's limp yet impressive musculature has correspondence in the more taut modelling of the

45
PETER PAUL RUBENS (1577–1640)
Samson and Delilah, *c.* 1609–10
Oil on wood
185 × 205 cm
The National Gallery, London
NG 6461

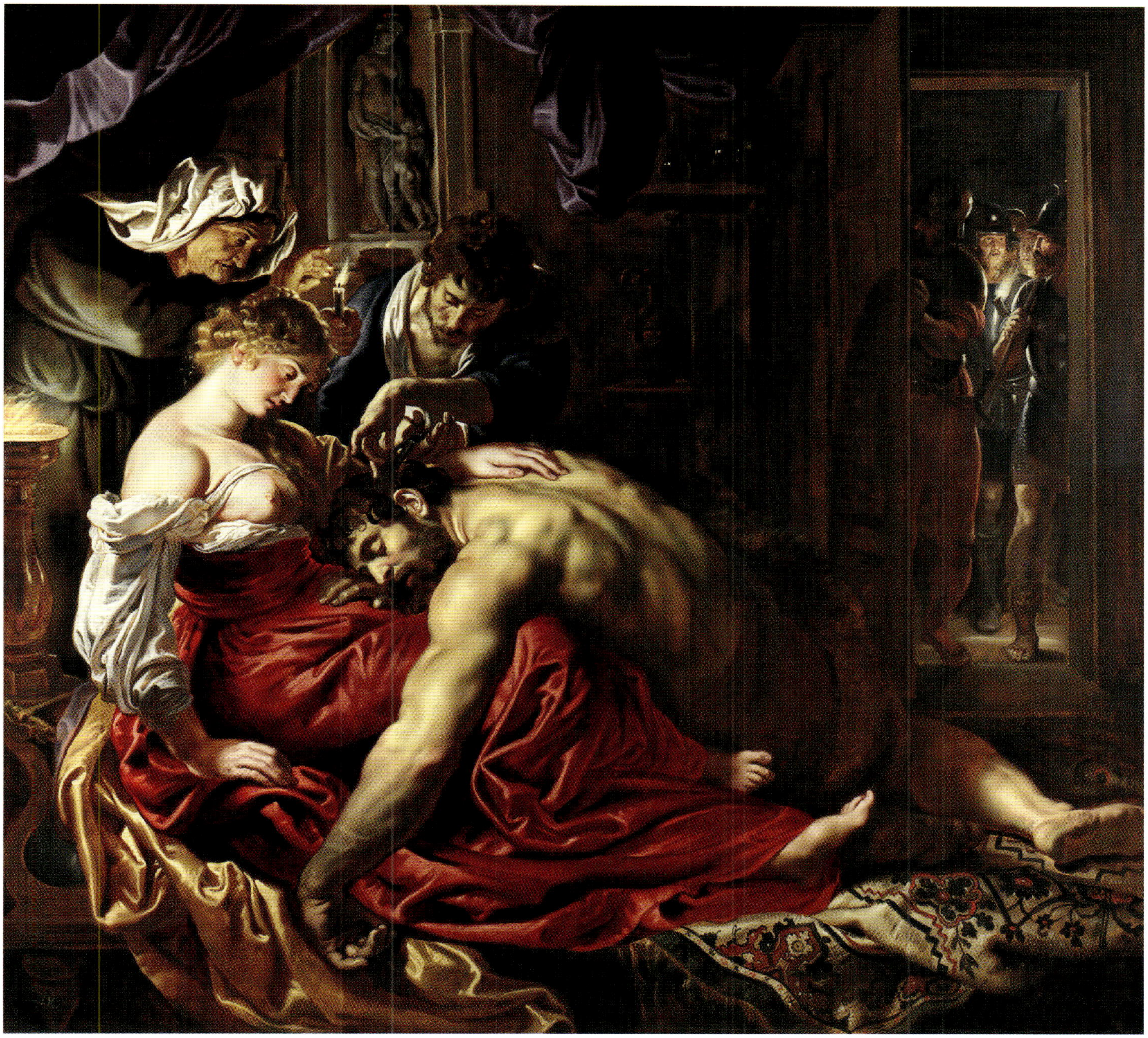

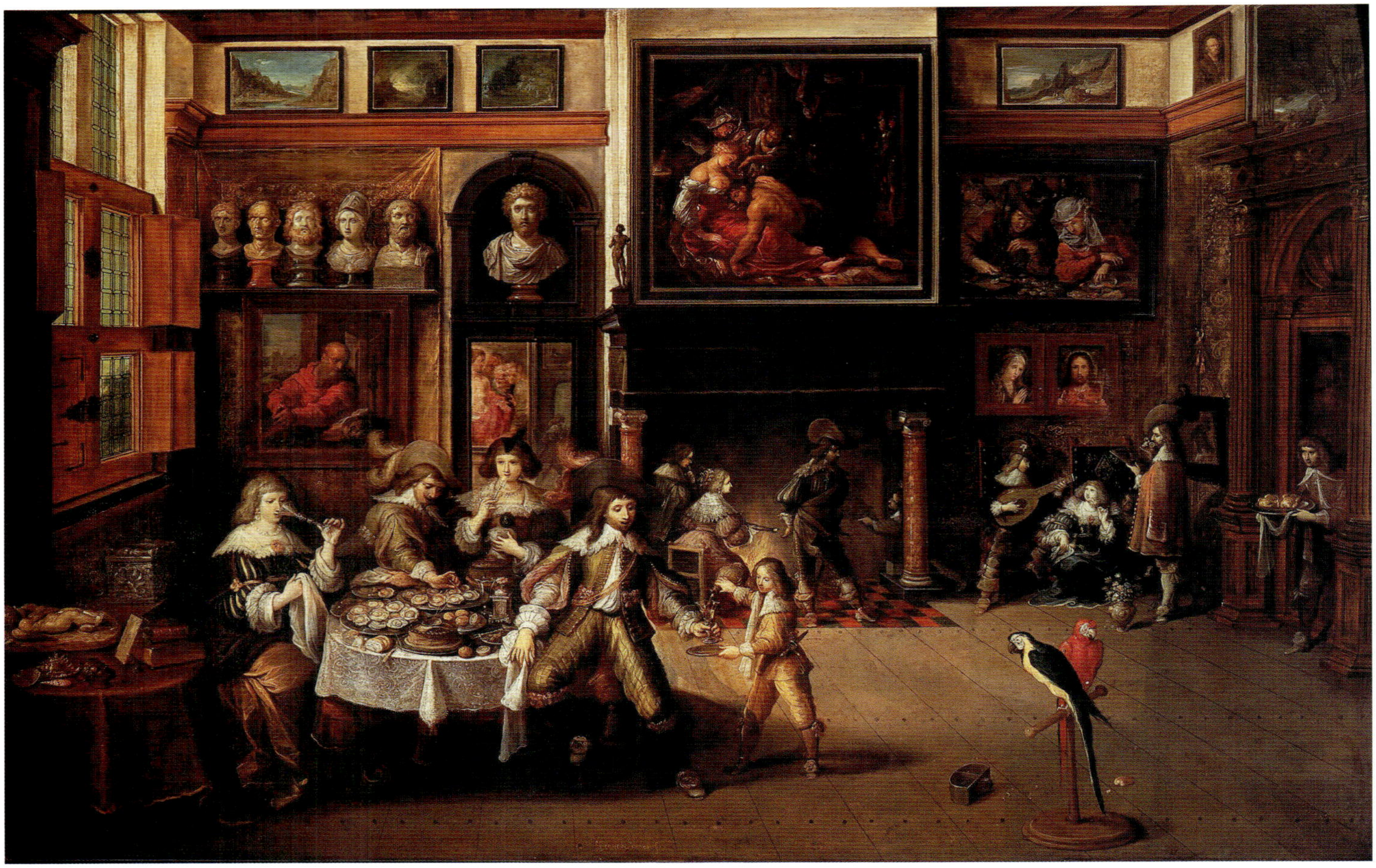

46
FRANS II FRANCKEN
(1577–1640)
A Feast in the House of Nicolaas Rockox
c. 1630–35
Oil on wood
62.3 × 96.5 cm
Staatsgemäldesammlungen, Alte Pinakothek, Munich, 858

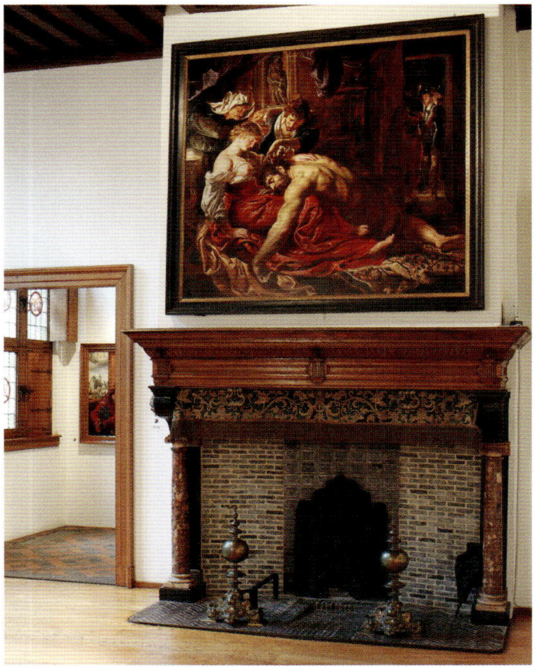

47
Samson and Delilah hung above the chimney-piece in the Rockoxhuis, Antwerp, in 2007

48
PIETER COECKE VAN AELST
(1502–1550) after school of
RAPHAEL (1483–1520)
The Massacre of the Innocents
c. 1524–31
Tapestry, wool, silk and silver thread
574 × 365 cm
Gallery of the Tapestries, Vatican

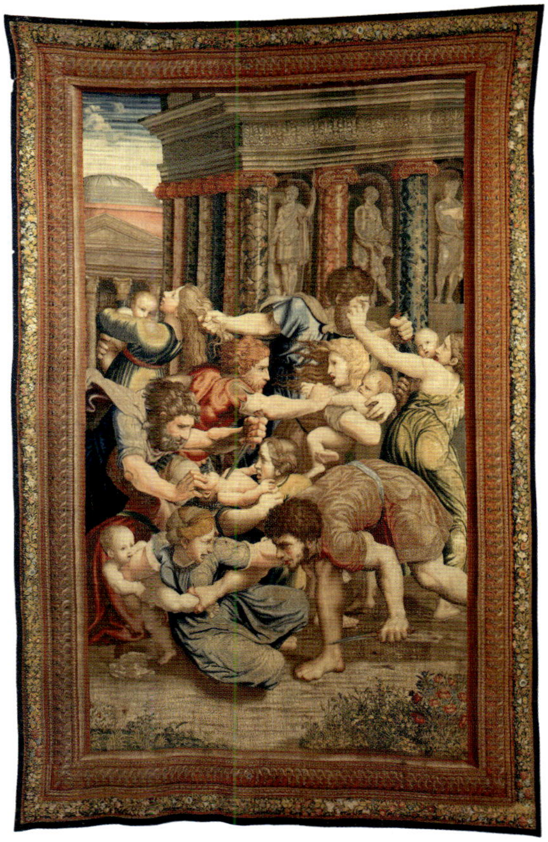

Massacre's executioner as he pulls the swaddling clothes. Moreover, the statue of Venus and Cupid in the background of the *Samson* (see fig. 45) probably derives from a source which informs the *Massacre*, a tapestry after a design by Raphael's workshop of the *Massacre of the Innocents* (fig. 48): this depicts a Venus and Cupid group in a niche set within an *all'antica* building in the background, and the same tapestry shows a woman scratching the face of a soldier, as we find in the *Massacre*. Curiously, Rubens's version of the Venus has been adorned with a diadem of red flowers and a necklace. In mythographic handbooks Venus is described as bearing red and white roses, so Rubens may simply be visualizing this tradition. However, Rubens mentioned bridal roses in his notes on antique customs, so perhaps these roses of Venus are intended to imply that Samson had more serious intentions.[74]

Samson's Herculean back again evokes ancient statues. The Belvedere *Torso*, which has a similar curved back, is a plausible source (see further below, pp. 119ff., for antique sources employed in the *Massacre*). A comparison of a drawing by Rubens of Hercules wrestling the Nemean lion and the original (on the façade of Villa Medici) reminds us that this emphasis of the curve of the back is a very typical Rubens enhancement.[75] This heroic display of 'speed hump' musculature shining in the wind-blown torchlight is a silent night-scene equivalent to the noisy day-lit *Massacre*. Broad, splashy brushwork along the bottom of this painting, as in the *Massacre*, creates the illusion of living flesh while displaying virtuosity.

In about 1611, probably following the preparatory oil-sketch now in Cincinnati rather than the finished product, Jacob Matham produced an engraving after the *Samson* (fig. 49). There, in a detail of the furniture on which Delilah sits, is a reminder of just how absorbed Rubens was with issues of antique culture. Here, far more than in the painting, the elaborate zoomorphic bronze finial on the corner of the couch – crowned with a donkey's head and capped at the foot by a panther's head – becomes clear. Etrusco-Roman tombs have bronze finials with panther and donkey terminals (see fig. 51), and the notes of Nicolas-Claude Fabri de Peiresc, an antiquarian correspondent of Rubens's, suggest that Rubens had discussed these bronze *sponda* (couch) fittings with another expert, perhaps Lelio Pasqualini in Rome. His friend had wondered if they did not function as pins to hold down the bed cover. Rubens perhaps toyed with this idea, as he included a further horse's head below the soldier's feet and above Samson's heel before painting it out. It is just readable in the painting, though it is more visible in an infrared image.[76] Rubens includes a panther-head terminal in his *Tarquin and Lucretia* (fig. 50). Such ancient furnishings were known to Raphael, as we see in his *Joseph with Potiphar's Wife* in the Vatican Loggia, and Giulio Romano seems enamoured with them in his *Two Lovers* (Hermitage).[77] The adjustment from the oil-sketch to the engraving is a typical antiquarian intervention by Rubens, who frequently revised his designs to incorporate more scholarly references.

49
JACOB MATHAM (1571–1631)
after PETER PAUL RUBENS
(1577–1640)
Samson and Delilah, *c.* 1611
Engraving
37.5 × 44.1 cm
Rockoxhuis, Antwerp, inv. no. 81.2.2

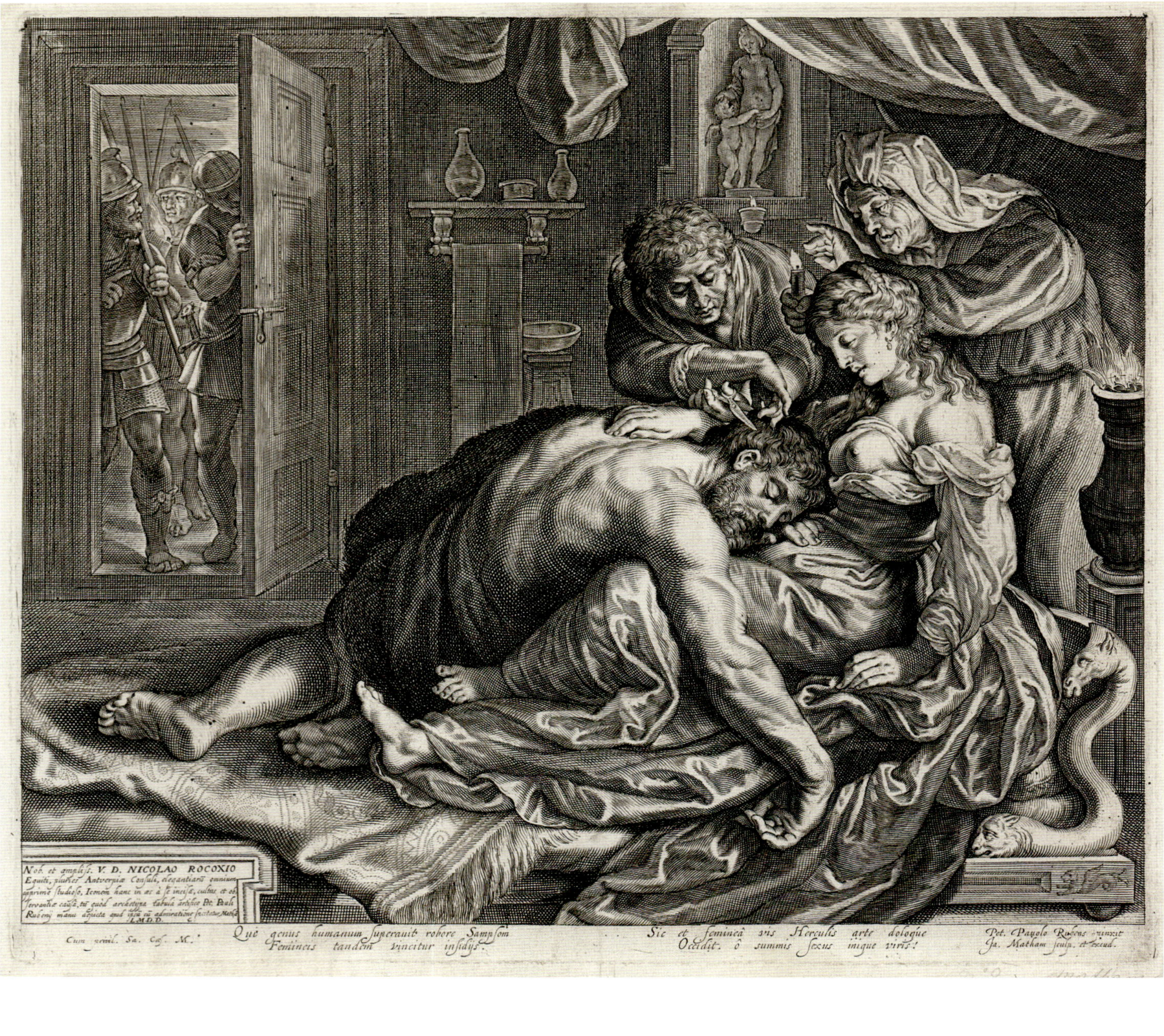

50
PETER PAUL RUBENS
Tarquin and Lucretia
detail of fig. 38

51
Artist active in Rome
c. 1620–30
Sarcophagus
Ink on paper
Cassiano dal Pozzo collection, The British Royal Collection
RN 8544

An inscription in Latin beneath the print bears a dedication to Rockox and states that the original is a true work by Rubens and can be admired in Rockox's house. The subscript goes on to compare Samson with Hercules: "Samson who surpassed the world in strength is finally conquered in a feminine trap. So too the force of Hercules succumbed to a woman's craft and guile. Oh you female sex baneful to the greatest of men!"[78] The comparison of a biblical figure with one from classical literature indicates that the subject-matter of the *Samson*, like that of the *Massacre*, did not operate purely on a religious level. It also served as an exemplary scene in which women are shown to strip men of reason and, in the case of the *Samson*, power. Delilah is represented in the role of seductress, breasts bared and hair loosened, appropriate to her casting as a whore in Josephus's *Antiquities of the Jewish People*.[79] The stories of Aristotle and Phyllis and Hercules and Omphale (see fig. 6), which involved comparable subjugations of men, were frequently the subjects for series of engravings and paintings.

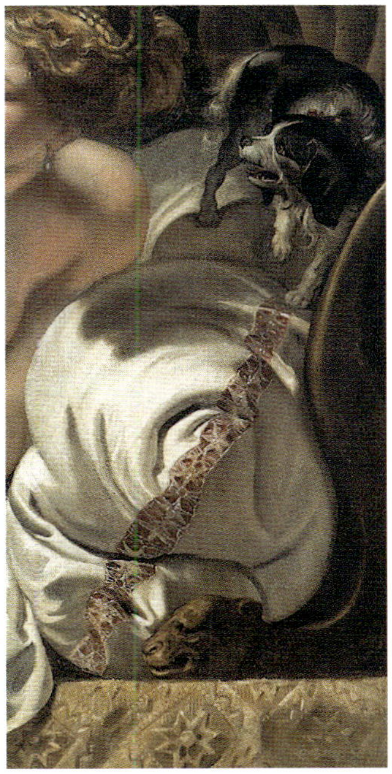

In the *Samson* Rubens uses the streaky yellow priming as part of the painted surface more aggressively than in the *Massacre*: in areas like the white sleeve on Delilah's arm and the edges of Samson's forehead the streaky layer can be seen in reserved gaps. Again, the bold patterning of the Persian carpet appears almost to be splashed on. Flesh highlights are again textured to catch the light and locks of hair and contours of limbs are dug out of the surface with thick blacks. The illusion of purple, achieved using red-lake pigment from Mexico and charcoal black, is applied stridently in the *Samson* (while such coloration is only echoed in the old woman's dress in the *Massacre*). All these techniques help create the illusion that the painting itself is luminous. The focus is on the choreographed hands around the barber, recalling a similar focus in the carefully arranged limbs in some of Rubens's multiple-view anatomical drawings. The old woman can be interpreted as a procuress, although it is worth recalling Rubens's writing to the Duke of Mantua, when offering him his first Santa Maria in Vallicella altarpiece, now in Grenoble, that it showed a great variety of heads, young and old.[80]

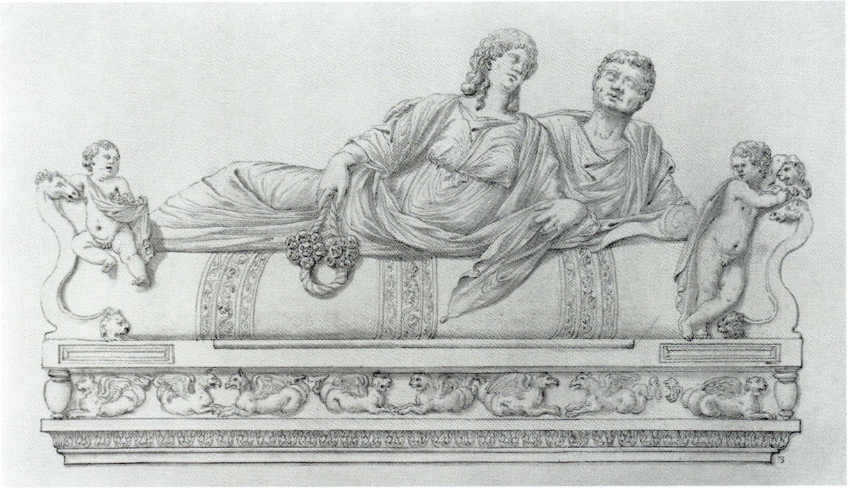

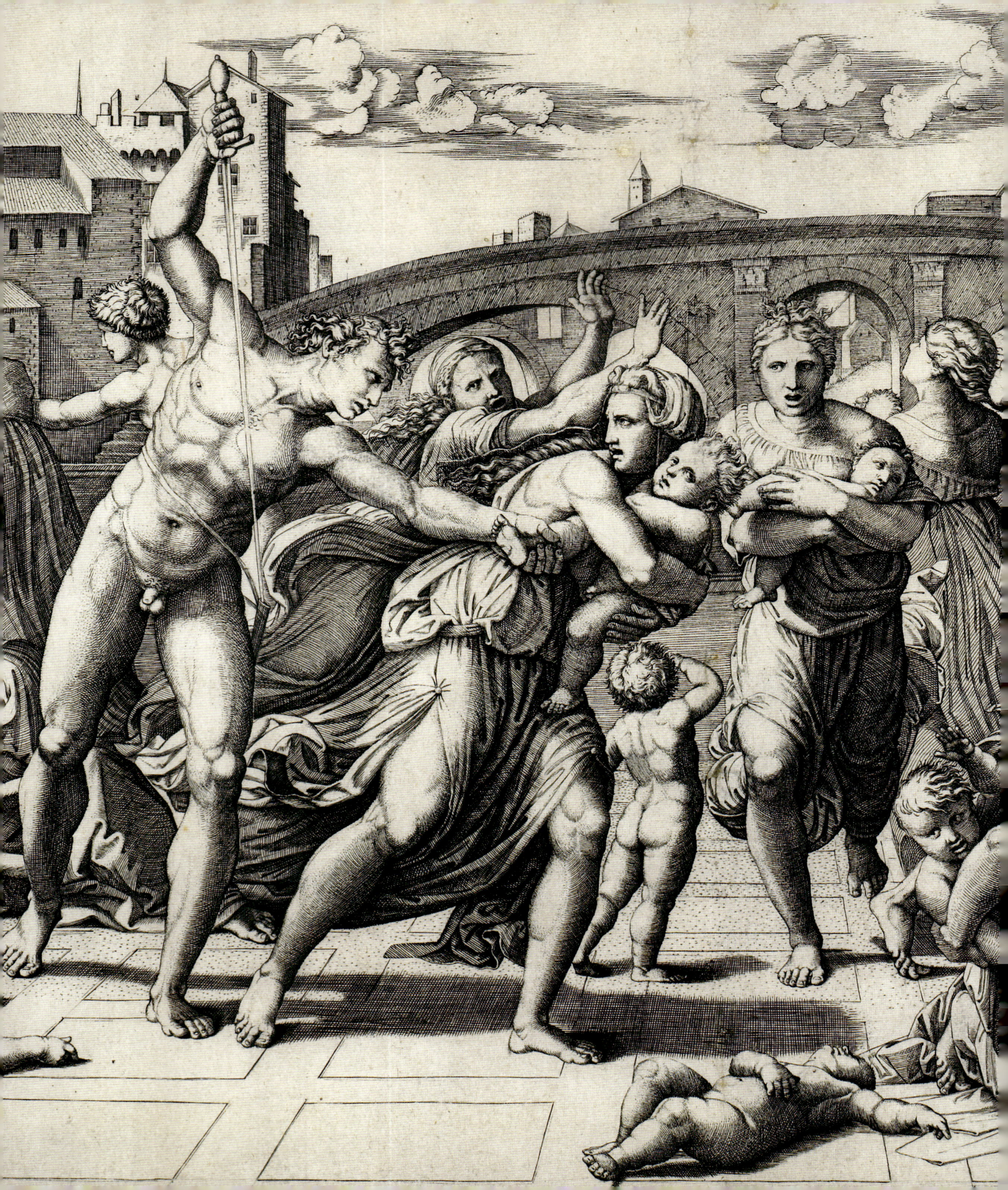

Unravelling the sources: Word and image

The story of the Massacre of the Innocents has a vigorous artistic tradition, due in large part to the various, often highly descriptive, liturgical and other texts that informed its iconography. Identifying particular texts as the source of inspiration for artists or patrons is difficult, however, as the ideas and descriptions given in texts often filtered through unconsciously.

The account told in the Gospel according to Saint Matthew (2: 16) records that Herod ordered the killing of infant boys because he had understood that the Three Magi had predicted that he would lose his throne to a newborn "King of the Jews:" "Herod perceiving that he was deluded by the wise men, was exceedingly angry; and sending forth killed all the male children that were in Bethlehem, and in all the borders thereof, from two years old and under, according to the time which he had diligently inquired of the wise men." Christ was carried to Egypt by his parents and so escaped the slaughter. The episode of the Rest on the Flight into Egypt was also a popular subject for artists and was painted by Rubens shortly after the *Massacre* in 1614 (Gemäldegalerie, Kassel). The Massacre was seen to prefigure the Passion of Christ and Saint Matthew himself (2: 17–18) recalled Jeremiah speaking of the lamentation of Rachel, who once wept for the sons of Ephraim, but now wept again for the children of Bethlehem: "Then was fulfilled that which was spoken by Jeremiah the Prophet, saying: A voice in Rama [where the tomb of Rachel is located] was heard, lamentation and great mourning, Rachel weeping for her children, and would not be comforted, because they are not."

Later texts focused on different aspects of the Massacre: the *Biblia Pauperum* (a form of pictorial Bible with little text) embellished the need to escape, comparing the Massacre with Moses being put in the basket of bulrushes, while the fuller *Bible Moralisée* compared the episode to Queen Athaliah's killing of the sons of King David.[1]

The veracity of Saint Matthew's account has been doubted, and it is surprising that the Massacre is not mentioned either in any of the other Gospels or in the early Apocrypha, with the exception of the Protoevangelium of James, 22. The historian Flavius Josephus similarly omitted the event, but it is conceivable that he regarded it as an episode of comparative insignificance compared to the numerous other atrocities Herod committed.[2] While the Greek liturgy asserts that Herod killed as many as 14,000 boys, modern writers have reduced that number considerably, since Bethlehem was a small town.[3] Some scholars doubt that the massacre really happened, as there is little other evidence of it, and suggest that it was invented to lend credence to Christ's status as Messiah.[4]

It is intriguing that the fourth-century Roman philosopher Macrobius should refer to the massacre in his *Saturnalia*.[5] He places the event in the Roman province of Syria, which at the time included Judaea, and relates that when Augustus heard that Herod's own son had also been massacred, he remarked, "It [was] better to be Herod's hog [*hus*] than his sprog [*huios*],"

The Massacre of the Innocents
(detail of fig. 56)

alluding to the Jewish law against eating, and consequently their not killing, pigs. Although Abelard inserted this vignette into his hymn for the feast of the Holy Innocents, it appears that the son mentioned by Macrobius was actually an adult, who was decapitated for having conspired against his father.[6]

The Latin Church instituted the feast of the Holy Innocents some time before the end of the fifth century. It is still celebrated by the Catholic Church and the Church of England on December 28, a date which has nothing to do with chronological order but was set close to Christmas because the Holy Innocents gave their lives for the newborn Christ.

The biblical account is quite short, as we have seen, but from around the time the feast day was established we find Greek and Latin sermons about the massacre that embellish the story with graphic detail. Their authors would have been able to draw upon a passage in the *Ad Herennium* (a widely used first-century BC textbook on oratory) which describes children being "torn from their parents' laps, slaughtered on their parents' bosom and violated at their parent's feet."[7]

These sermons were not simply descriptive but served a religious purpose. Saint Peter Chrysologus (406–450) talked of children being torn from their mother's arms "[so that] mothers suffered in the martyrdoms of their sons . . . thus it is inevitable that they will be consorts in their reward, as they were companions in their passion."[8] This was, in turn, compared with the suffering of the Virgin and her assumption into heaven.

A sermon by the fifth-century Basil of Seleucia arguably set the pattern which became standard in descriptions of the Massacre, and which was still established in texts for feast days in the Byzantine Church in the thirteenth century.[9] His text is constructed of three parts, as advised by a treatise on rhetorical exercises by Hermogenes of Tarsus (second century AD), though following the basic story as related by Matthew: the prelude (Herod ordering the massacre); the action; and the aftermath (the grieving mothers / Rachel weeping for her children). During 'the action' Basil relates a long catalogue of cruelties, involving mothers warding off the swords' edges with their hands and innocents being murdered in their mothers' arms. In the aftermath the mothers collect together their babies' sundered limbs and search for any body part that might be missing, which they kiss once found. The only character to be given direct speech is a mother holding a dismembered child.

These images are found again in a text by the sixth-century poet Romanus, who added another motif – children being decapitated while they suckled at their mothers' breast. These features appear consistently in subsequent sermons, but it is not until the twelfth century that we find a written description by the Italian preacher Philagathus of a painted massacre which could almost be a description of Rubens's later work.[10] The savage details echo Basil's sermon: "[soldiers], springing like wild beasts,

52
Northern France
The Flight into Egypt, from a diptych with scenes from the Life of the Virgin, 14th century
Ivory
Diptych panels each 7.3 × 11.5 cm
The Thomson Collection,
Art Gallery of Ontario, Toronto

pitilessly dismembered wretched infants. The painter depicted the unhappy mothers given to a piteous lament and mixing tears with blood. And one tore her hair, another scraped her cheeks with her nails, another tore apart her robe, and, bearing her chest, showed her breast, deprived of the feeding baby. Another collected together the scattered limbs of her dismembered child; and another held her newly slain infant on her knee and bitterly wept."

The iconography of these early sermons filtered down to choir books and liturgical texts as well as to medieval mystery plays. *The Pageant of the Shearman and Tailors* included 'The Coventry Carol,' a lament over the massacre which is still sung today. In parallel many of these descriptive clichés were incorporated into visual tradition. There was interchange between visual and textual interpretation of the Massacre, although in general it has been written description which has informed the artistic tradition.

A comparatively sedate example can be found in a mosaic (dating *c.* 432–40) at Santa Maria Maggiore in Rome, where the emphasis is given to Herod instructing his soldiers and the only hint of impending tragedy is one mother, to the right, turning to flee. Early depictions of the Massacre often show soldiers holding babies aloft to dash them to the ground (witness an ivory panel of the early fifth century in the Staatliche Museen, Berlin).[11] A miniature in the Rabbula Gospel Book in Florence, dated 586 and written at the monastery of John of Zagba in Syria, shows a soldier holding a child upside down by its ankle and lifting his sword to dismember the body (details which can be found in Basil's sermon). A fourteenth-century ivory in the Thomson Collection (fig. 52) also shows a soldier holding a child by the ankle, butchering it with a sword.

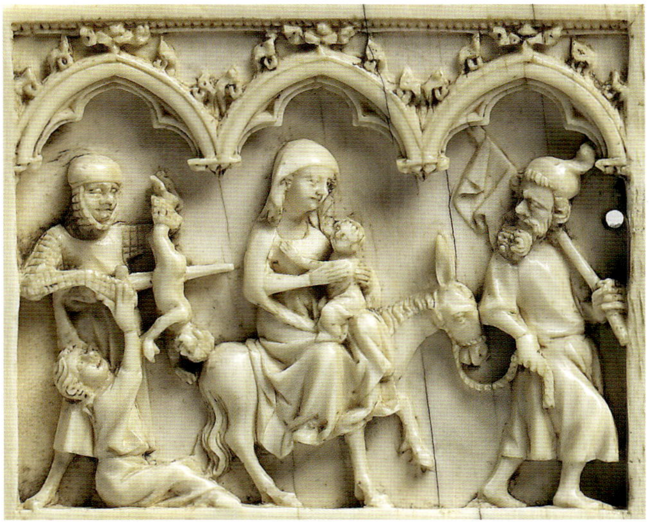

While these standard elements have much in common with Basil's sermon, they were also informed by other biblical or mythological scenes of slaughter. In representations of the Judgement of Solomon, for instance, the disputed child is often held aloft by the soldier ordered to kill it. A painting of this subject by Rubens's workshop exists in the Prado, Madrid. Similar imagery even appears on a vase depicting the Sack of Troy, datable to the seventh century BC, now in the Museum at Mykonos.[12] Among early representations, it is typically sculptures and mosaics that survive. Some of the earliest painted depictions of the massacre are found among the historiated initials accompanying liturgical texts. For example, an *Ordo officiorum* of 1215 (Duomo, Siena, ms. G.V.8, f. 32v) contains an initial I decorated with the decapitated heads of the Innocents, along with rivulets of blood.[13]

Basil's sermon, itself doubtless based on pagan descriptions of massacres, may not have been known directly by later authors and artists, but the imagery he used re-appears in Pietro Aretino's account of the massacre in his *L'Umanità di Cristo*, first published in Venice in 1535. He describes how a "bandit" grabs a woman by the hair, while another "makes a shield with her breast" in an effort to save her child. Infants are described as being trampled underfoot and smashed against a wall. He describes the arms of the executioners as "*scrupulose di muscoli et di vene*" (knobbly with muscles and veins) and how the mothers, on realizing Herod's intentions, are struck dumb like the severed limbs, which at first do not bleed.[14]

Aretino's rhetoric was given further colour by a group of poets, among them Giovanni Soranzo and Giambattista Marino, who celebrated an enormous (more than four metres wide) painting of the Massacre commissioned from the painter Giovanni Battista Paggi by the merchant prince Marcantonio Doria in Genoa in or just before 1604 (see further below and fig. 58).[15] Marino's poem on Paggi's masterpiece, entitled *La strage de' fanciulli innocenti* (The massacre of the innocent little boys), was subsequently published in print in 1619 in *La Galeria*, an anthology of poems about art, on this occasion celebrating Guido Reni's painting of the Massacre (San Domenico, Bologna), and was published again as an extensive poem in its own right, *La strage degli innocenti*, in 1632. It has been argued that Marino had studied Aretino's work as a very young man in Naples, where it was more accessible than in northern Italy, since, having been censored by the Church, after 1558 his writings went almost completely out of circulation.[16] In his text Aretino had compared a mother to a sculpture of Charity, which, after the slaughter, resembled a marble stained with vermilion.[17] Marino adopted the same simile: a mother in his poem has five infants and is compared with a painting by Cavaliere d'Arpino and also to the Niobid sculptures at the Villa Medici (for which see below, figs. 131, 133).[18] The mother's white marble form is stained by her children's blood and the executioner's heart is described as "*macigno*" (sandstone).[19]

Marino echoed Aretino in other passages: "a threatening and cruel man . . . had wrapped her golden hair around his arm, and jerk by jerk he uprooted and broke the curling and fine gold of her blonde splendour. She, just as the ivy clings to a trunk, stayed rooted to her sweet charge, but the beast on foot squeezed her hair so hard that in the end she had to let go. Then with a robust hand he hurled the child, and threw him against the nearby wall among the hard rocks. Before he hurled him, however, and before he struck him, he swung him around three or four times."[20] The parallels with Rubens's picture are obvious, including the pulling of blonde hair, the reference to ivy and the hurling of the child, which are all found in his picture. Certainly artists were inspired by poetry and, although Marino's poem was published after Rubens's *Massacre*, it is likely that Rubens knew it in manuscript form.

These contemporary poems are important as they illustrate the precarious balance and contrast, in all artistic forms, between beauty and horror.[21] Marino, in particular, succeeds in balancing the horrific content with the eloquence of his verse, and uses consciously antiquated Petrarchan vocabulary to subvert the realism. He also 'suspends' time, taking the mothers and sons out of the action as if they themselves were works of art.[22] These literary descriptions also served to popularize the subject of the Massacre as, like engravings, they were easily reproduced and disseminated.

Tintoretto would certainly have known and read Aretino's prose. Venice was one of Rubens's first stops when he arrived in Italy in 1600, and in the Scuola Grande di San Rocco he would have seen Tintoretto's *Massacre* (*c*. 1582–87; fig. 53). Rubens certainly responded to Tintoretto's dramatic style and theatrical lighting effects, and there is some evidence to suggest that he made a copy of the work. The composition of Tintoretto's picture is, typically, more disparate, but it shares the intensity of violence that is seen in the Rubens panel. The small running figures in the background of Rubens's picture echo those by Tintoretto: they share the same billowing draperies and the architectural vista which recedes into the background. Parallels can be drawn between the figure at the bottom left of Tintoretto's picture and Rubens's swordsman, too (figs. 55 and 54), although Rubens would have been aware that this figure was drawn from Michelangelo's *Battle of Cascina*, a tightly woven composition which in itself must have inspired him. The telescopic perspective was a Mannerist device much used by Tintoretto.

Clearly, in creating an original depiction of the subject, Rubens drew on an iconography common to many representations of the Massacre – the brandishing of swords, the exposure of breasts torn from the mouths of babes and the pulling of hair. These had already appeared in Raphael's composition of the subject engraved by Marcantonio Raimondi (*c*. 1511; fig. 56), which was perhaps the most widely known depiction of the

53
TINTORETTO
(1518–1594)
The Massacre of the Innocents, *c.* 1582–87
Oil on canvas
422 × 546 cm
Scuola di San Rocco, Venice

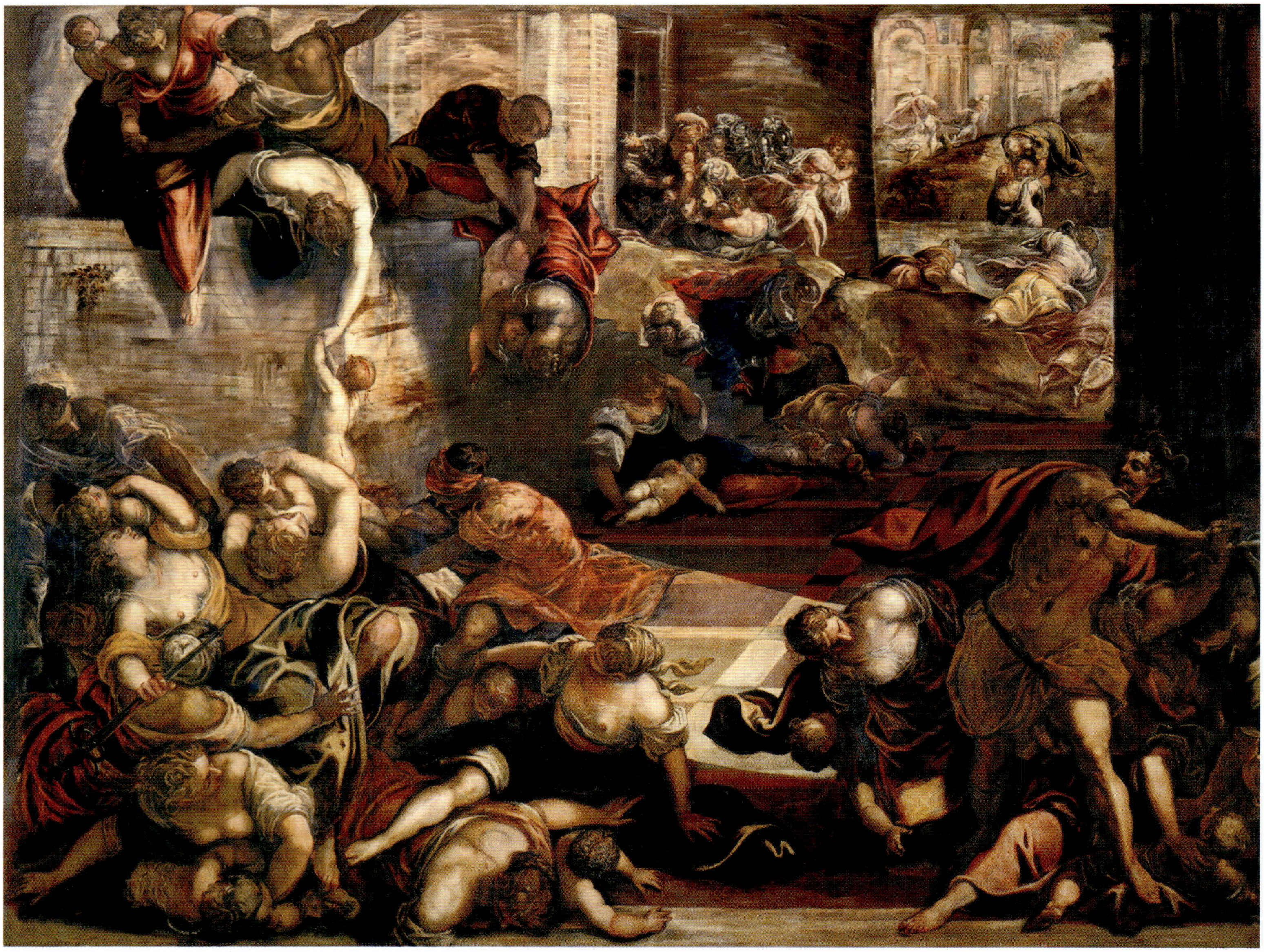

54
PETER PAUL RUBENS
The Massacre of the Innocents, detail

55
TINTORETTO
The Massacre of the Innocents, detail

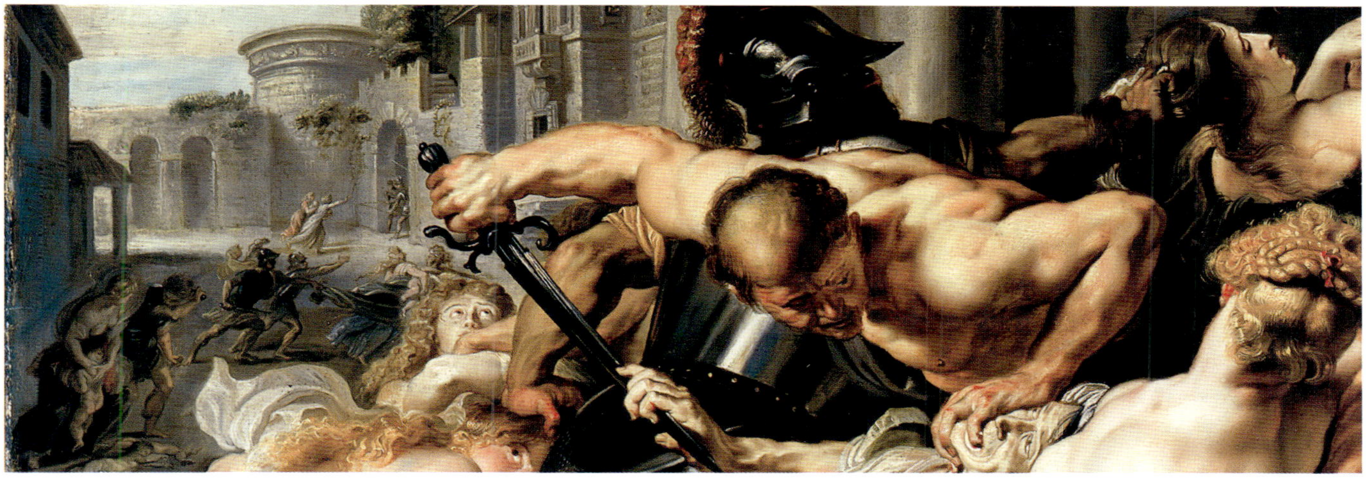

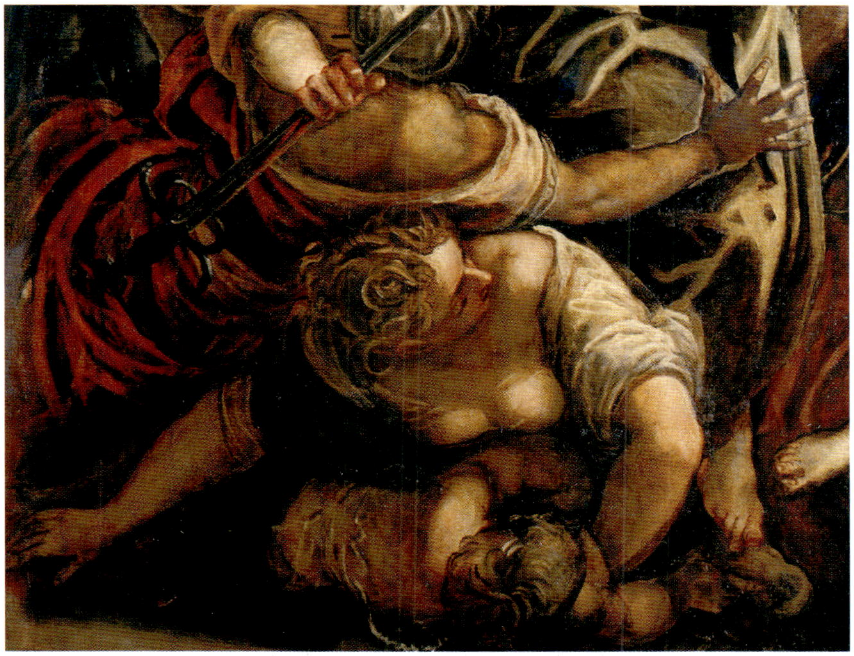

56
MARCANTONIO RAIMONDI
(1518–1594) after
RAPHAEL (1483–1520)
The Massacre of the Innocents
c. 1511
Engraving
28.3 × 43.4 cm

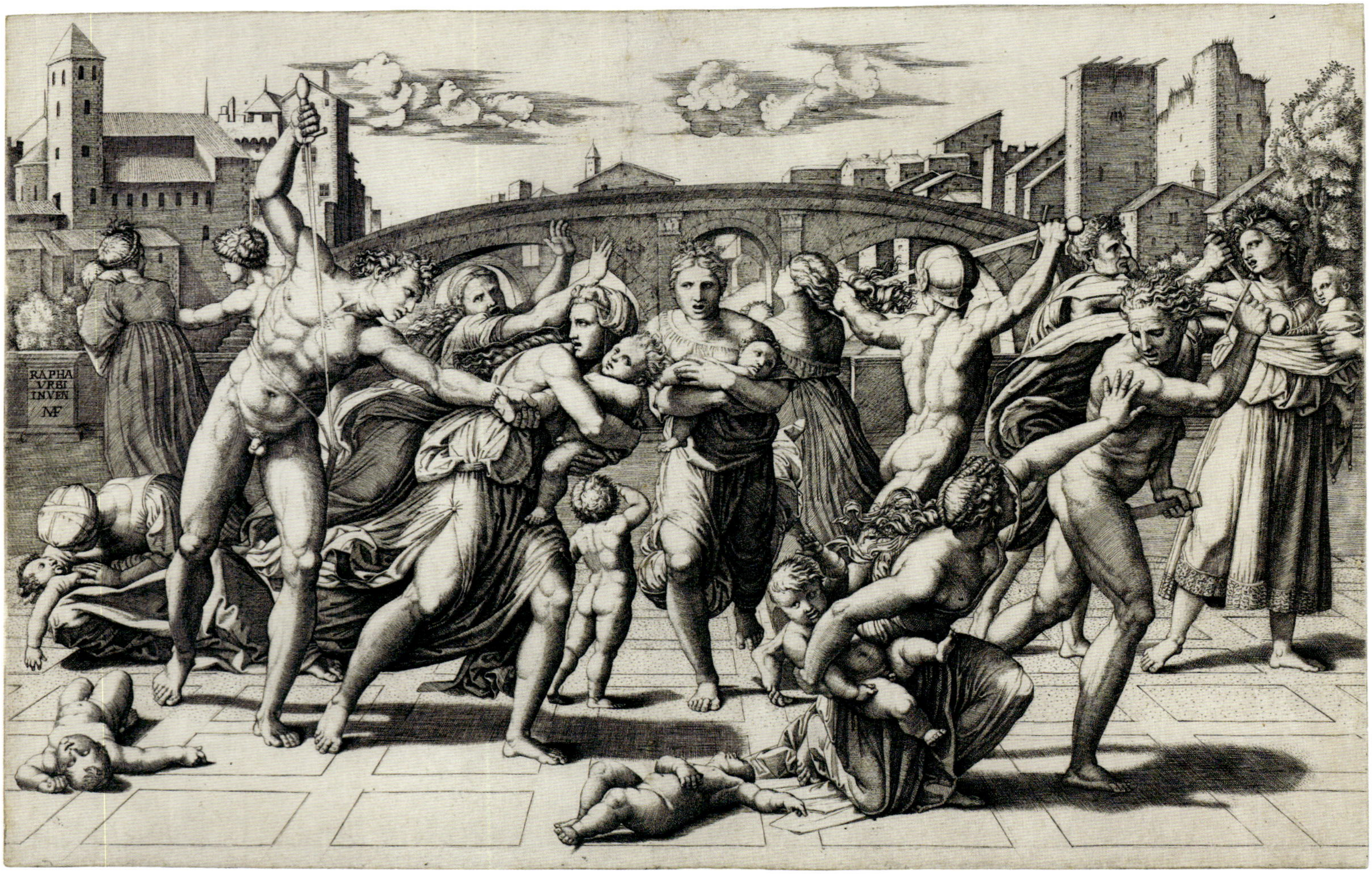

57
PETER PAUL RUBENS
The Massacre of the Innocents, detail

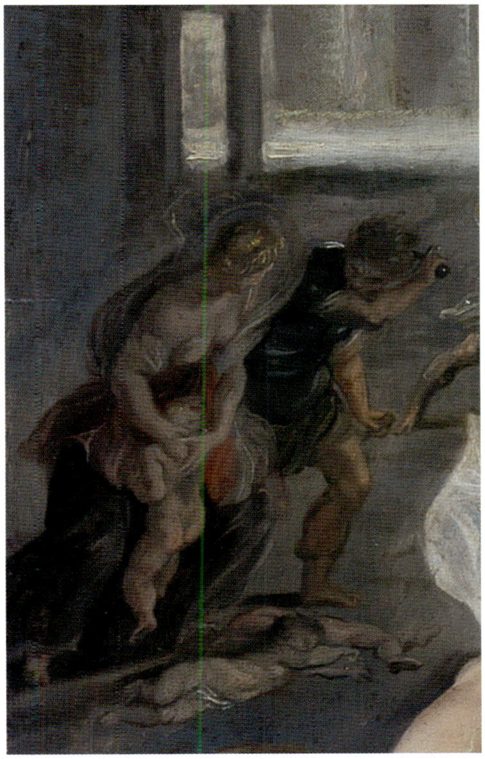

Massacre. For Raphael the print was an exercise in self-promotion: the subject of the Massacre presented a complex design problem suitable for the assertion of invention and skill. Depicting violence, love and loss in a credible, affecting and beautiful way was a test of any artist's ability. In a later print, the *Morbetto* (*c.* 1512–13), Raphael illustrated an episode in Virgil's *Aeneid* (Book III) in which Aeneas and his Trojan followers are struck by plague in their new settlement in Crete. Raphael showed a child trying to suckle its dead mother even as a bystander, holding his nose, pushes the infant away. There was in this perhaps a resonance of a painting by the Greek artist Aristides which is described by Pliny in his *Natural History* (35, 98–99): Aristides had painted the capture of a town, including an infant creeping to the breast of its mother who is dying of a wound but is afraid that, as her milk is exhausted by death, the child may suck her blood. Pliny's description had captured the imagination of Renaissance artists and theorists alike, and in Vasari's *Lives of the Artists* (1550) this passage is evoked in a discussion of Ghirlandaio's *Massacre of the Innocents* in Santa Maria Novella in Florence.[23] Ghirlandaio had not illustrated the motif but Raphael's image is revived in the lower right of Jordaens's altarpiece for the Carenna Chapel (see fig. 24).

Compared with the *Morbetto*, Raphael's print of the *Massacre* is consciously balletic and graceful. One has a sense that the Massacre, much like Christ's Entombment or Deposition, had become a suitable vehicle for artists to show emotion and movement. It is testament to Raphael's skill that the predominant effect of the image is of harmony, given that the central mother is clutching her dismembered child to her breast much like the central character in Basil's sermon.[24] Rubens acknowledged Raphael's design by paraphrasing the executioner on the extreme right in the left-hand background of his panel (fig. 57), and the portrayal of the soldiers as nude, athletic heroes is itself a legacy from Raphael (and some earlier Italian artists such as Ercole de' Roberti).

Sources after Raphael, too, may have had an impact. The mid-sixteenth-century Dutch artist Maarten van Heemskerck had taken the anatomical display a stage further by undressing the mothers as well.[25] The subject was also revisited by Raphael's students in a trilogy of tapestries (*c.* 1524–31) now in the Vatican Museums, where the violence is more exaggerated by scenes of eye-scratching and hair-pulling (see fig. 48). As we have noted (p. 69), the niche sculpture of Venus and Cupid in one of these tapestries found its way into the background of Rubens's *Samson and Delilah* (fig. 45), evidence again of the migration of ideas and images between his works.[26]

We know that Rubens also studied Marco Dente's print after Baccio Bandinelli of the Massacre, of *c.* 1520. In that work the grace of Raphael's design was reconceived in more emotive terms, and grieving mothers dominate the foreground. A copy of Rubens's sketchbook includes copies of

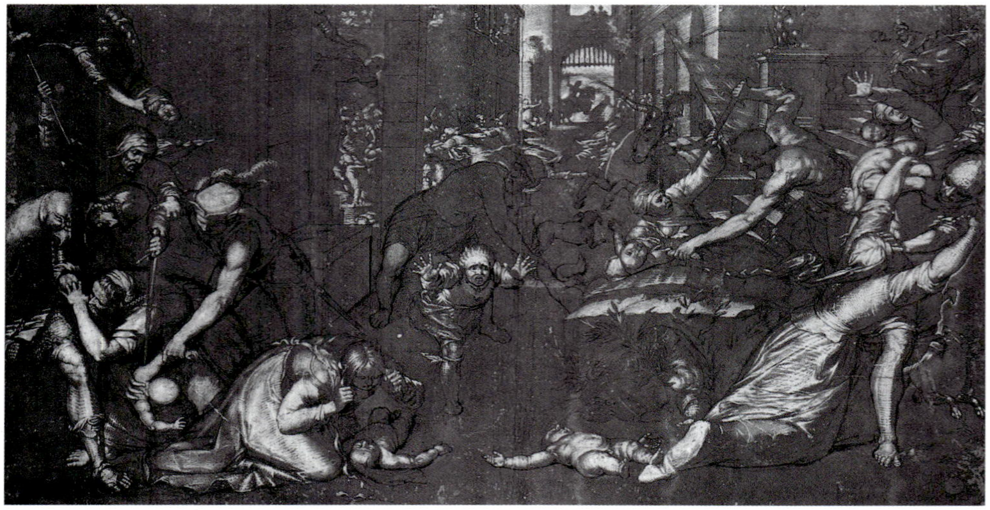

58
GIOVANNI BATTISTA PAGGI
(1554–1627)
The Massacre of the Innocents
1604
Oil on canvas
Stolen and since lost; only a fragment (below, of the left-hand part of the painting) survives; this
255 × 178 cm
Museo Civico e Diocesiano d'Arte Sacra, Colle di Val d'Elsa, Siena

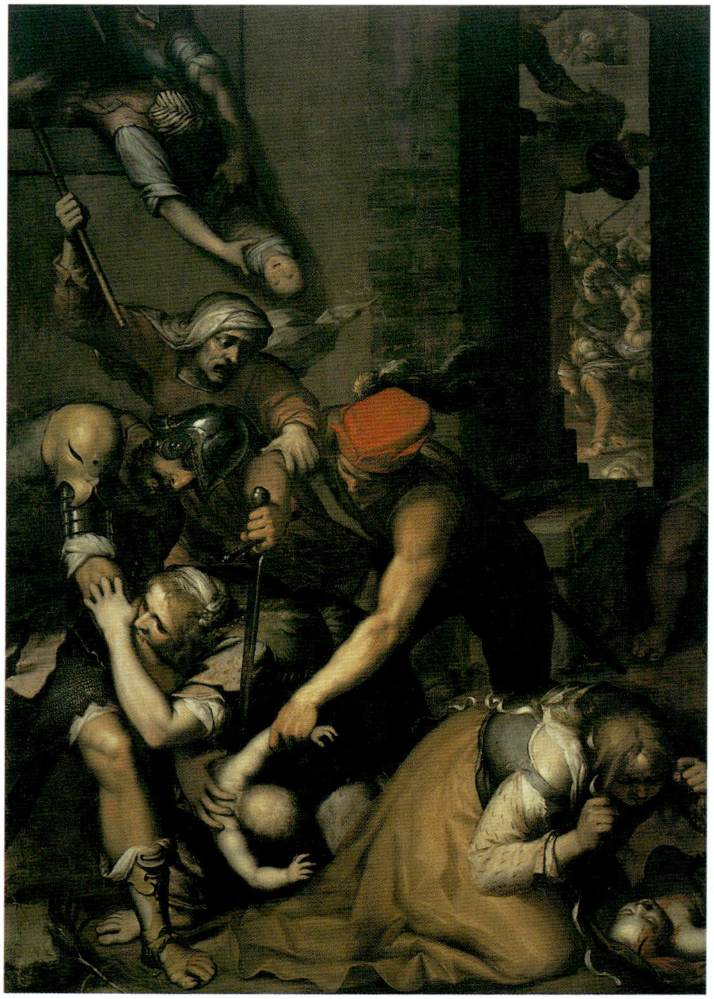

59
PETER PAUL RUBENS
The Massacre of the Innocents, detail

60
MICHELANGELO BUONARROTI
(1475–1564)
The Resurrection, *c.* 1532
Black chalk
28.3 × 43.4 cm
The British Royal Collection
RL 12767r

some of Bandinelli's babies, and they are recommended in the text as a prototypes for putti. The same sketchbook (ff. 14v–15r; see fig. 84) suggests that Rubens also copied Paggi's *Massacre* (fig. 58).[27] The sketchbook drawings are literal copyings, and Rubens took the opportunity to explore in detail the motif of the mother cowed over her dead child while pulling her hair back from her face. The Bandinelli print seems to show the three phases of action stipulated by rhetoric and followed by Basil of Seleucia. Herod is shown at the centre, on a dais giving orders, the action takes place to the left and right, and the aftermath is shown in the foreground, where a mother close to the centre holds a decapitated head while weeping inconsolably, recalling Basil's words: "How will I put your limbs back together again that he so mercilessly has cut up with his sword?"[28]

Bandinelli and Daniele da Volterra are two of the few contemporary artists that Rubens mentions by name in his sketchbook. The latter had painted a *Massacre* now in the Uffizi and had frescoed the same subject in the church of Santa Trinità in Rome. Both of these sculptor/painters were hugely influenced by Michelangelo and so addressed the subject of the massacre in a sculptural, three-dimensional way which would have appealed to Rubens's visual sensibilities and complemented his study of classical sculpture.[29] The work of Michelangelo is recalled in Rubens's *Massacre* by the soldier holding the baby aloft (fig. 59). This figure bears uncanny similarities to Michelangelo's drawing of *The Resurrection* (fig. 60),

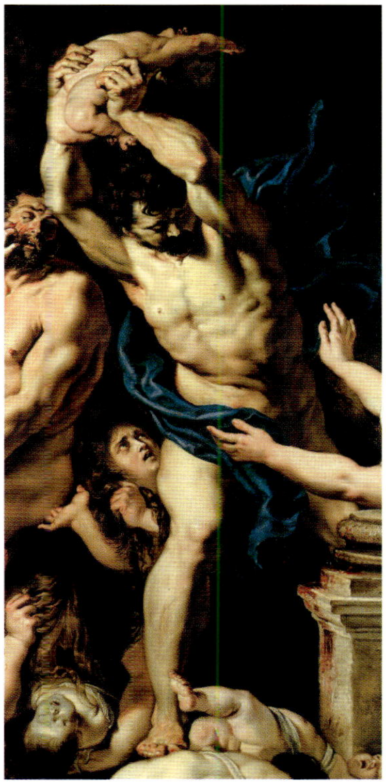

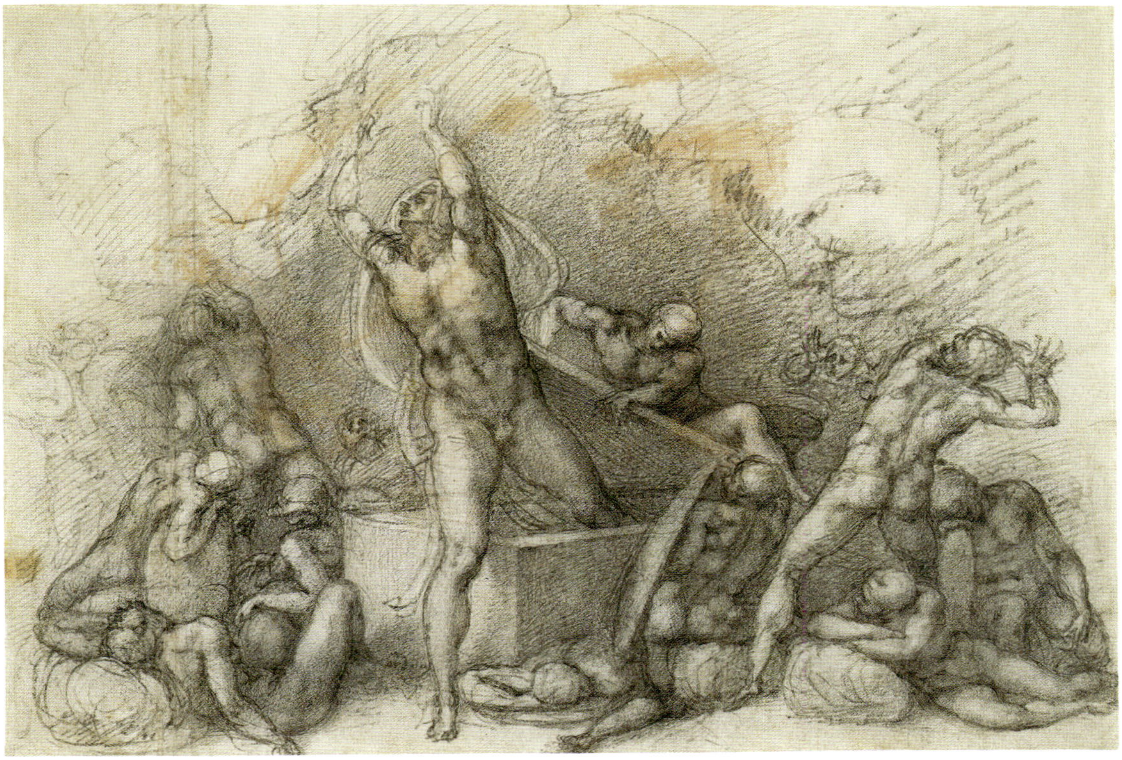

61
PHILIP GALLE (1537–1612)
after FRANS FLORIS
(1519/20–1570)
The Massacre of the Innocents
(painted possibly *c.* 1550–55), *c.* 1600
Engraving
33.1 × 41.6 cm

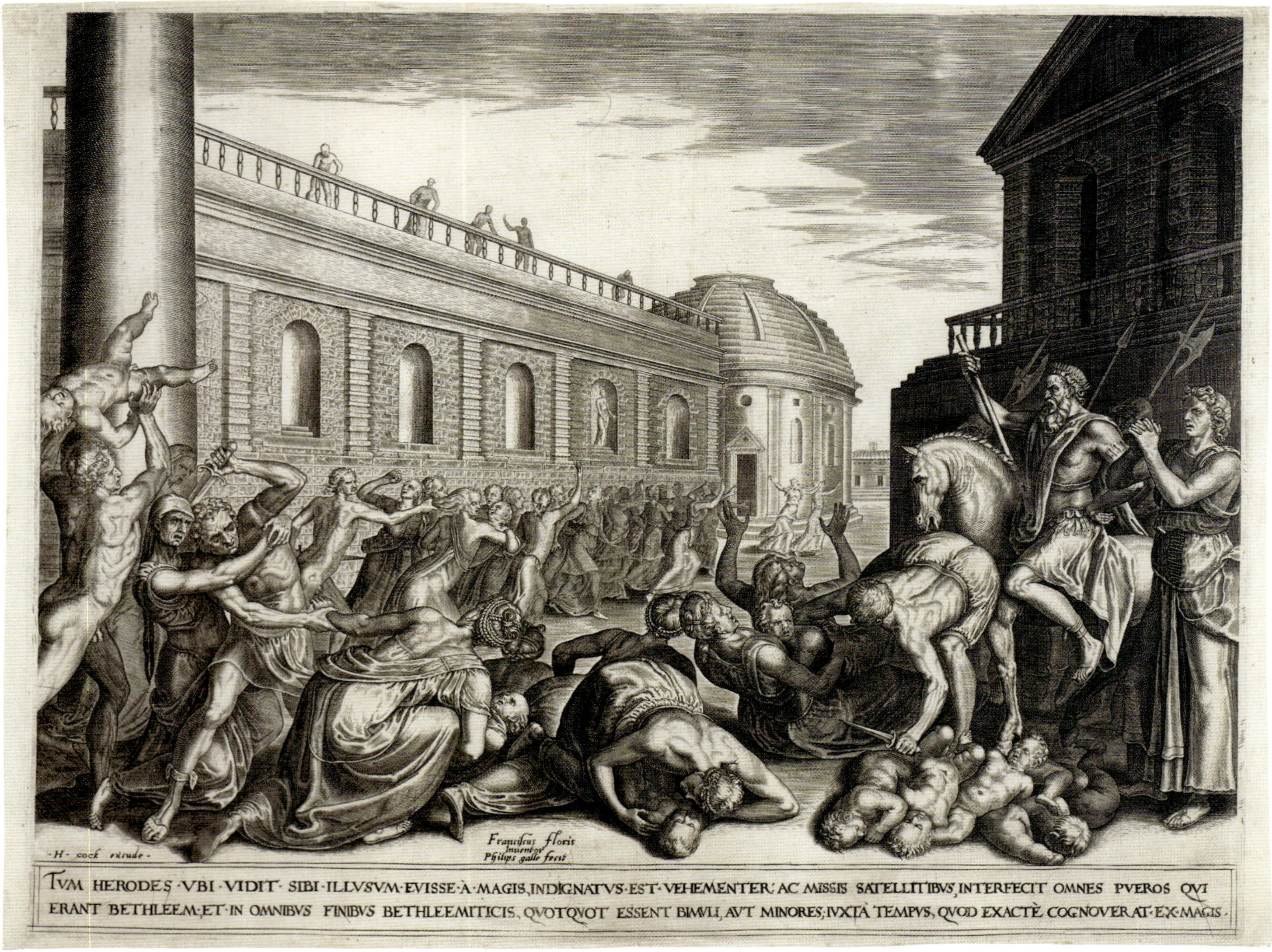

though Rubens has twisted the torso to more of an angle, and the head is turned downwards. It is worth noting that he may have reached this solution via an intermediary model by the sculptor Willem van Tetrode (see below, pp. 103ff., and figs. 90, 93, 94) rather than through direct knowledge of Michelangelo's drawing.

Frans Floris, the leading humanist Flemish painter in the generation before Rubens, painted a *Massacre* in about 1550–55 which in Rubens's day hung in the Town Hall in Antwerp. The work, which is now lost and known only in an engraving by Philip Galle (fig. 61), would have been familiar to Rubens and the patrician elite of Antwerp, given its very public location. The work contains all the iconographic references associated with the narrative of the Massacre used by Rubens. The main soldier with child raised, the central woman in red and the hair-pulling group are all to be found in Floris's work, but in Rubens's hands these images are combined more fluidly and infused with the vigour of his Italian experience. The mother weeping over her dead child is also found in both works but, whereas in the Floris she leans towards the viewer over her child, in Rubens's picture she hangs over her baby, her body heavy with grief, her anguish obscured by the hair she clutches in despair.

Adjusting for the fact that this is a copy print of the Floris rather than the original, there are parallels in the rippling muscular backs of the soldiers and the precariously twisting women. The telescopic streetscape, a rarity in Rubens's work, and the diminutive figures peering down are all anticipated by Floris. It seems probable that the commander on horseback painted out by Rubens (visible in an x-ray; see fig. 68) was also inspired by his Flemish predecessor, but it seems that Rubens found it too top-heavy for his own scheme. Fired with the success of his Italian experience, he may have painted the *Massacre* on his return as a direct response to Floris's masterpiece. In making such a move he sought to claim from him the mantle of Antwerp's leading painter.

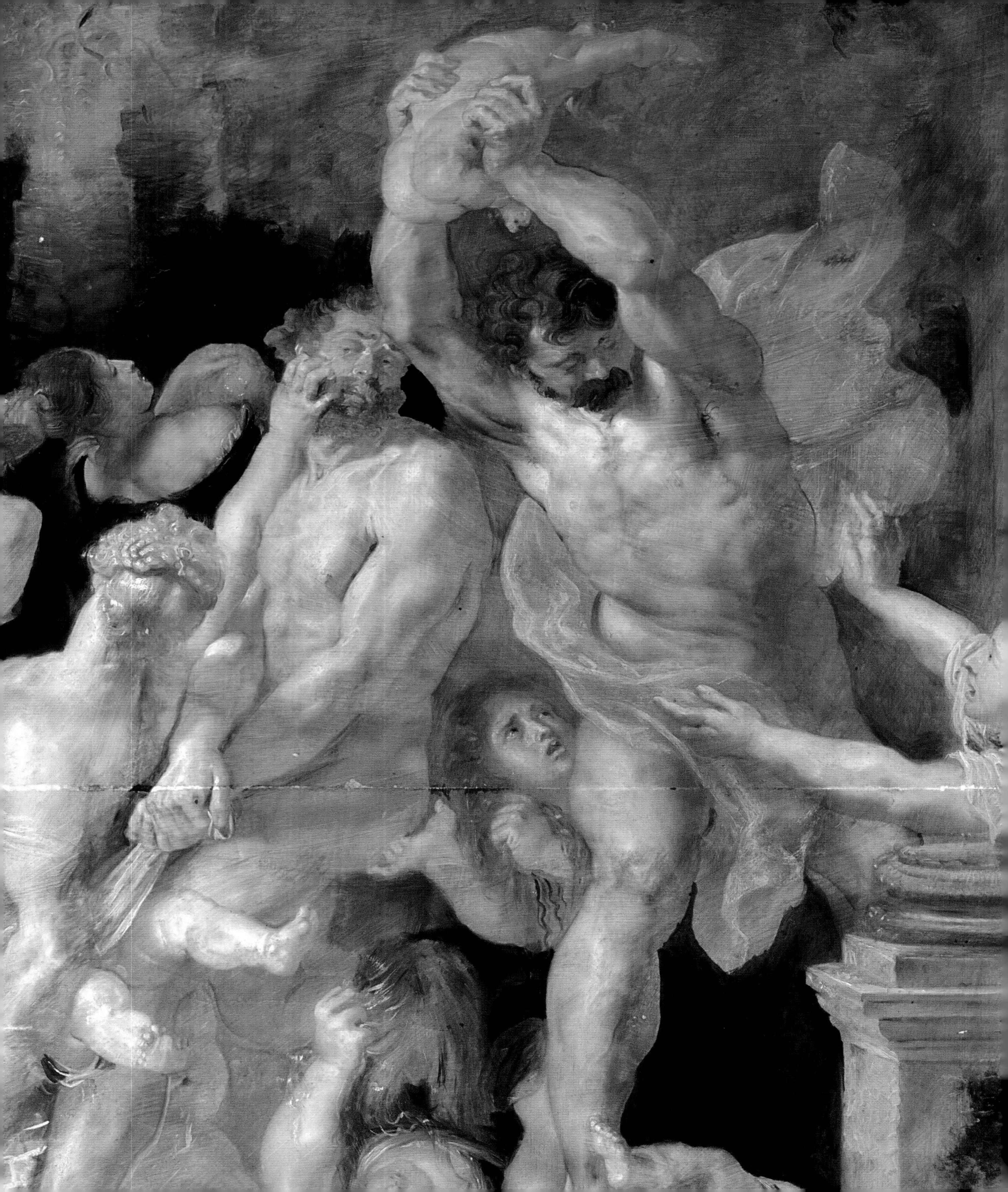

Designing the *Massacre*

There are no surviving preparatory drawings for the *Massacre*, as there are for many other works by Rubens. This means that we have to reconstruct the process of its making from technical examination, extrapolation from other projects and, with particular reference to his sketchbooks, from the way that Rubens generally gathered and developed his visual material. In his sketchbooks he made notes on ancient sculpture; the *Massacre*'s relationship with the works of Antiquity is considered in the next chapter.

Rubens's complex and powerful composition for *The Massacre of the Innocents* appears at first to be dominated by a circular mass of tightly bound figures at the centre of the picture. On a closer reading, the main protagonists are found to be conceived in groups and placed along diagonals which converge to the right; from here the figures surge upwards and are joined together in a series of violent, contrasting gestures. Though the clusters of figures are conceived separately they interlock with each other, unified as if by centrifugal force. The rhythm of these interacting groups leads the eye back and forth and in and out through pose and gesture, creating the overall effect of a writhing knot of destruction which flings dead and dying infants into the furthest corners of the panel.

With the benefit of infrared reflectography (IR) (fig. 63), which responds to the carbon in the underlying drawing or brushwork, and x-radiography (fig. 62), which captures the presence of lead white, we can discover information about the application of paint below the surface of the painting which provides vital clues as to how it was made. We know from technical analysis that Rubens was still resolving the composition of the *Massacre* when he started work. He began the painting with a white ground which he then primed with a tinted browny-grey wash-like layer, streaked diagonally across the panel.[1] This wash shows through in places, such as under the sword arm of the armed soldier, where the thin diagonal strokes are visible (fig. 64). Below the paint surface there are also traces of vertical strokes on the base of the bloodstained column and in the figure of the child below which may be associated with this tinted priming.

Rubens then mapped out the design on the panel using black outlines and grey washes to create the desired forms. Some white highlighting was added to build up the figures and IR also reveals (fig. 65) more of a dark curve still partially visible (see fig. 64), which may be an earlier draft of a sword handle. This exemplifies a process typical of the artist. Normally masked by the paint layers above, similar strong black lines can be seen when Rubens adjusts his design in other paintings, for example in the hand of Saint Gregory in Rubens's first painting for Santa Maria in Vallicella in Rome (now in Grenoble). Later unfinished paintings like *Henri IV in the Battle at Ivry* (fig. 67) enable us to visualize this initial blocked-in design and interpret the images technology makes available. The changes in arms and legs in the *Battle* (for example, the soldier in front of the white horse has three arms) might indicate that it was Rubens's practice to adjust the

The Massacre of the Innocents
Infrared reflectogram (detail of fig. 63)

62
PETER PAUL RUBENS
(1577–1640)
The Massacre of the Innocents
X-radiograph

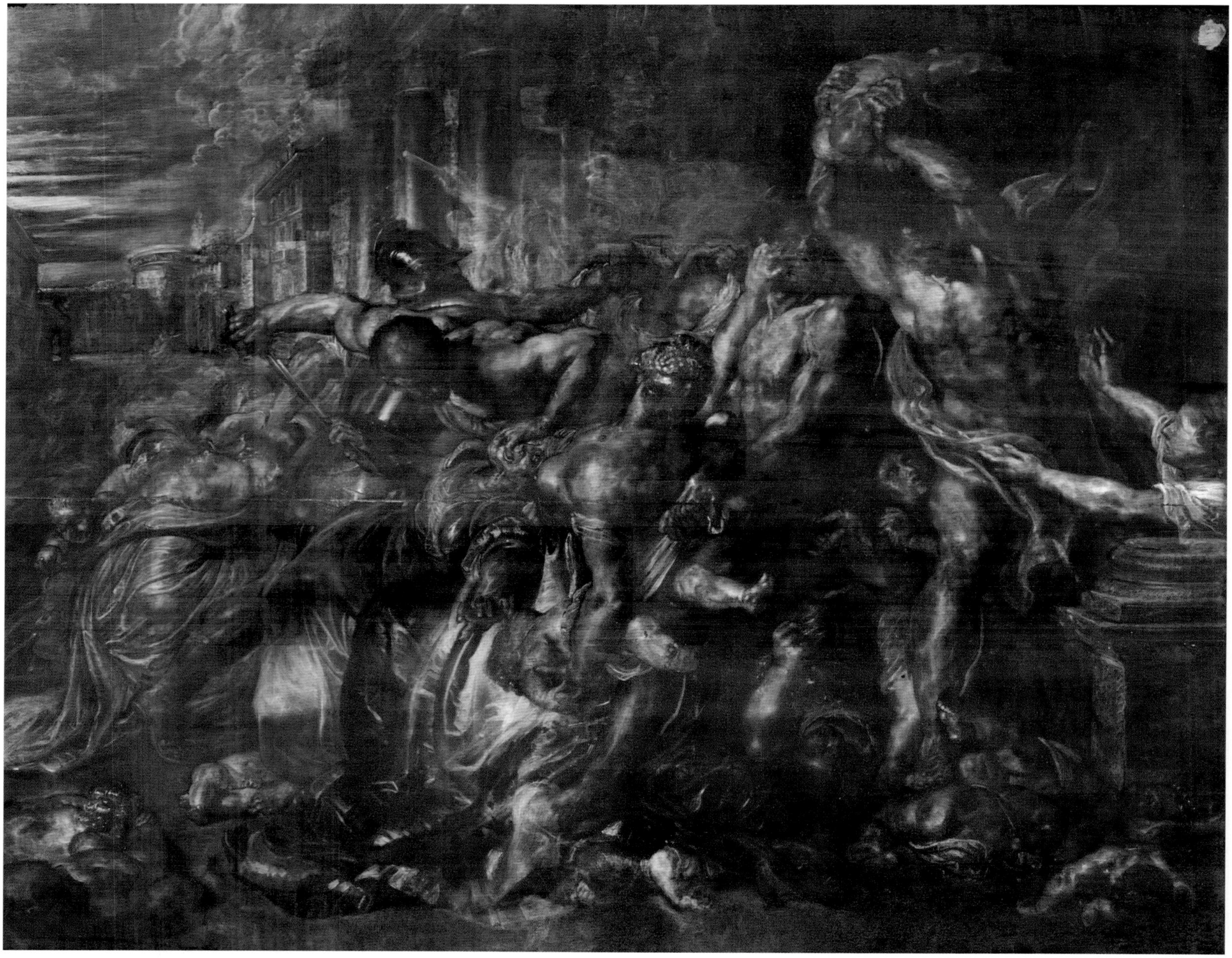

63
PETER PAUL RUBENS
(1577–1640)
The Massacre of the Innocents
Infrared reflectogram

64
PETER PAUL RUBENS
The Massacre of the Innocents, detail

65
PETER PAUL RUBENS
The Massacre of the Innocents
Infrared reflectogram, detail

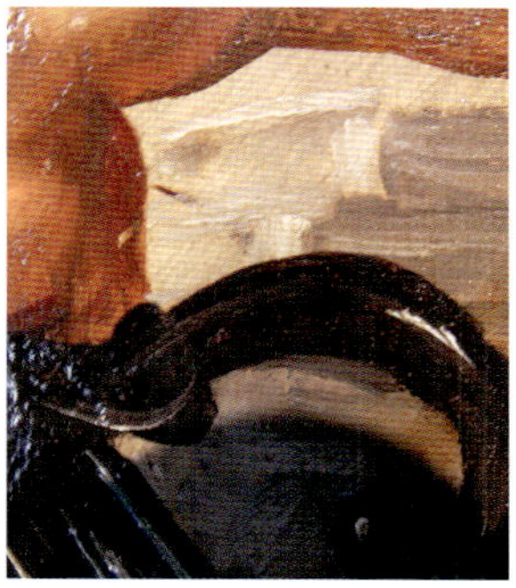

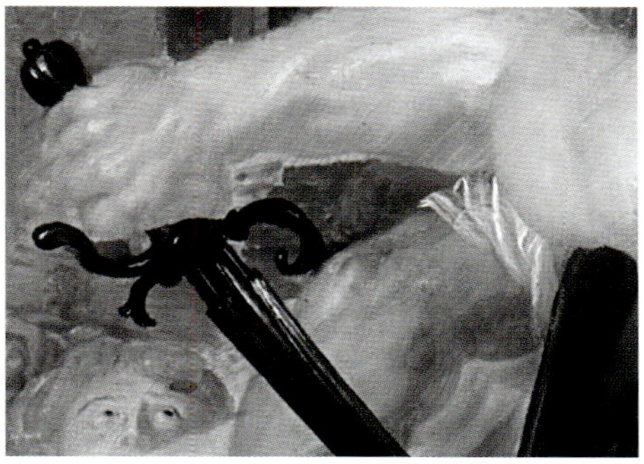

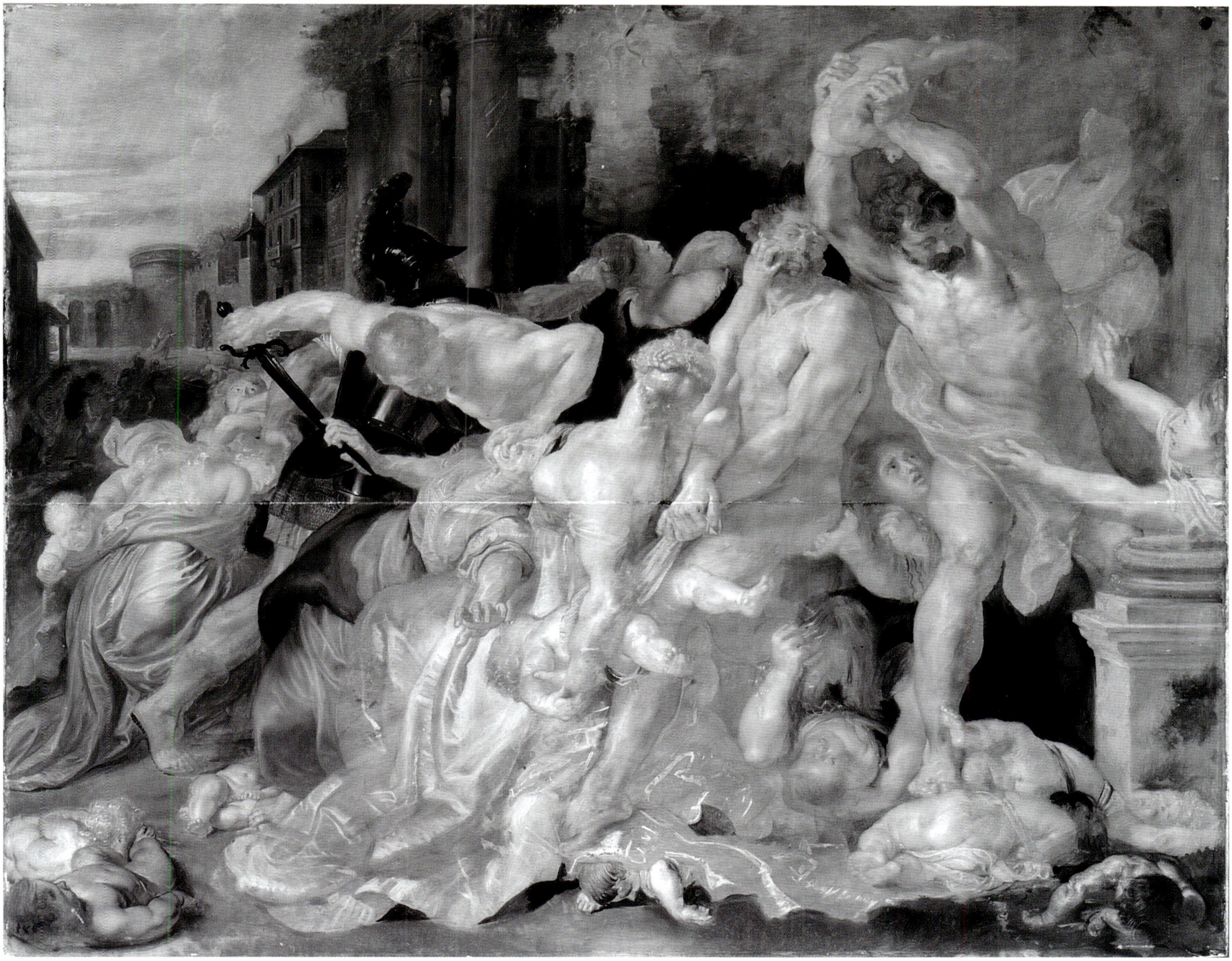

66
PETER PAUL RUBENS
(1577–1640)
A Lion Hunt
c. 1614–15
Oil on oak
74 × 105.7 cm
The National Gallery, London
NG 853.1

67
PETER PAUL RUBENS
(1577–1640)
Henri IV in the Battle at Ivry
c. 1630
Oil on canvas
174 × 260 cm
Rubenshuis, Antwerp

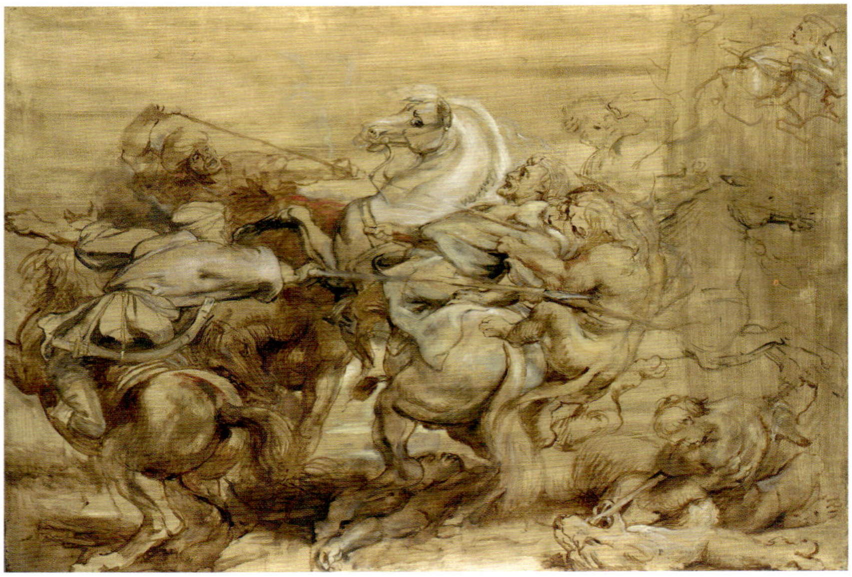

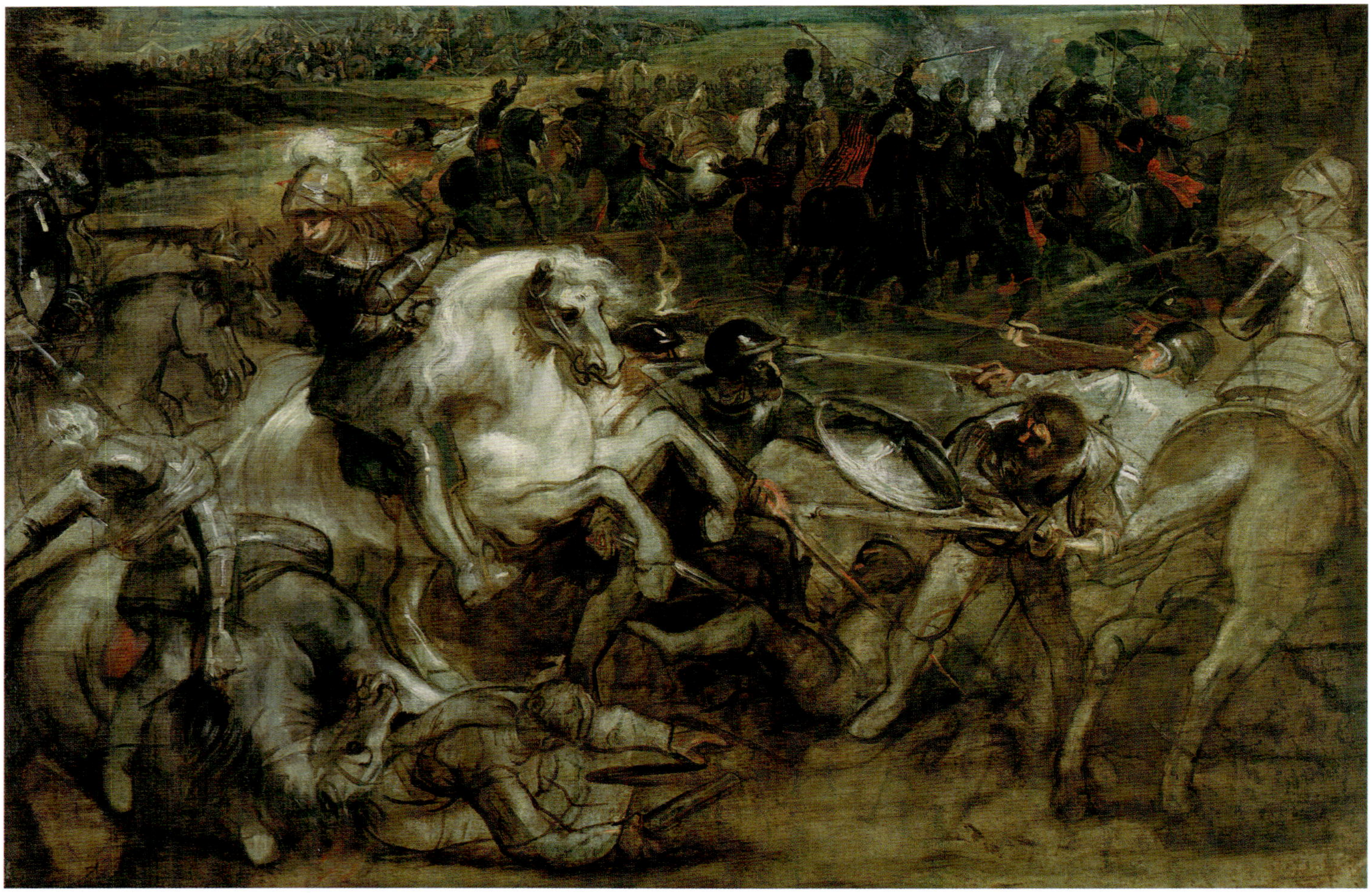

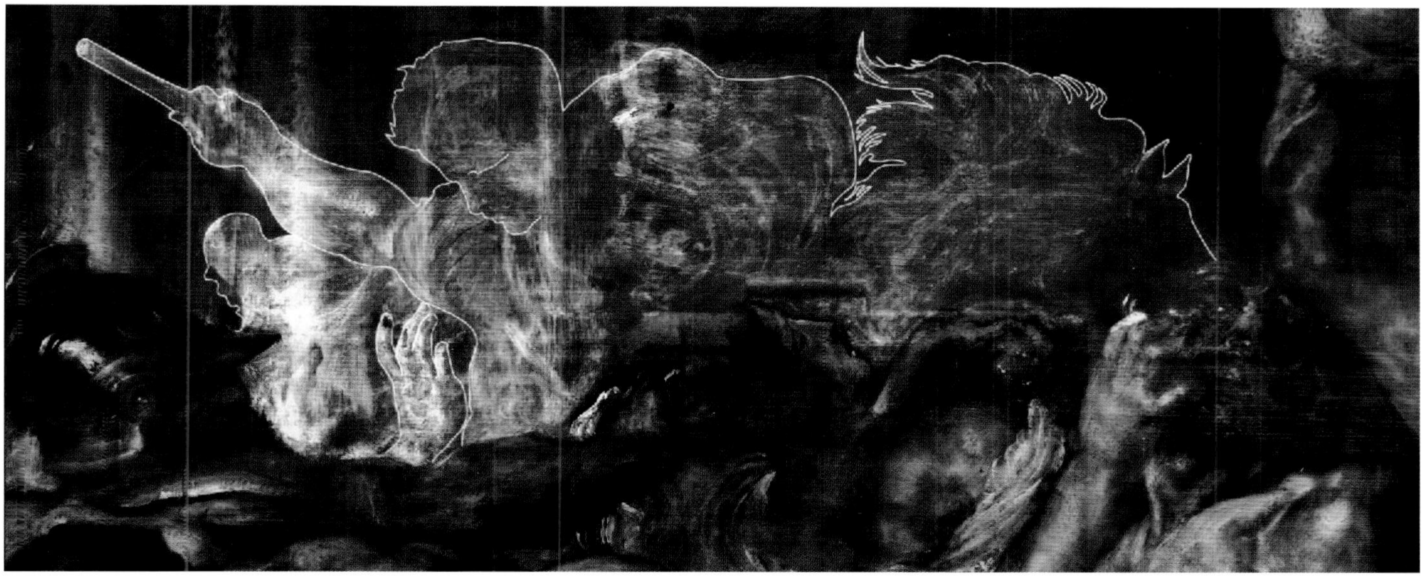

68
PETER PAUL RUBENS
(1577–1640)
The Massacre of the Innocents
X-radiograph (with outlines strengthened), detail

composition at this stage. The beginnings of a large painting like the *Massacre* would in any case have looked very similar to one of Rubens's monochromatic oil-sketches before it was covered over by the addition of coloured paint (fig. 66).

The development of this stage of the composition is well illustrated by the figure of the mounted commander, which Rubens created as part of the original design, but who was eventually removed from the composition (fig. 68). He appears to have blocked in the figure with dark paint alone then built it up with white highlights. There does not seem to be any sign of the pigmentation of this figure's cloak, which presumably was intended to be red.[2] In contrast, the pleading hands of a woman which Rubens also later painted out must have progressed to a more finished state, as they are still just visible, and the hand nearest to the soldier in armour leaves a pink tint beneath the thinly painted column. Some black painted curves which appear to be part of the crest of an earlier helmet decoration are also visible below the finished red crest in front of the armoured soldier's helmet (fig. 69 and detail page 14). It is clear from the x-ray (fig. 70) that the helmet was originally painted without the existing sphinx decoration, and Rubens must have elaborated the helmet design, elevating the height and importance of this armoured figure as if to compensate for the absence of the commander on horseback.[3]

Rubens revised his plans for the painting in other, less dramatic ways. A revision in the position of the armoured soldier's hobnail boot is a good example of a drafting change which may have been made to underline his knowledge of antique costume from Roman literature. The IR image shows

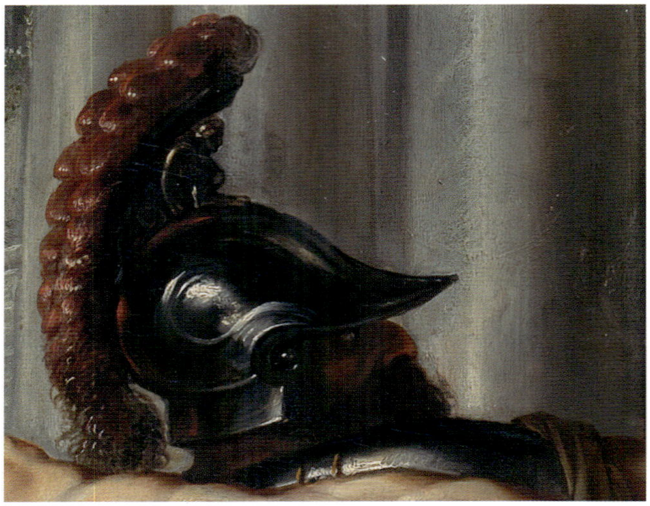

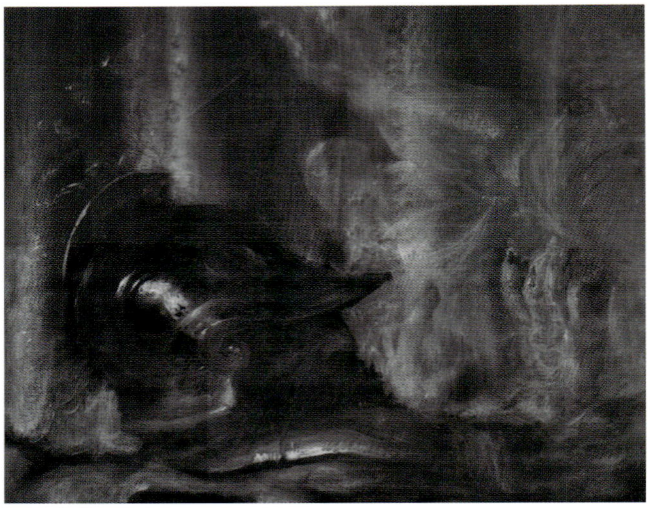

69
PETER PAUL RUBENS
The Massacre of the Innocents, detail

70
PETER PAUL RUBENS
The Massacre of the Innocents
X-radiograph, detail

71
PETER PAUL RUBENS
The Massacre of the Innocents
Infrared reflectogram, detail

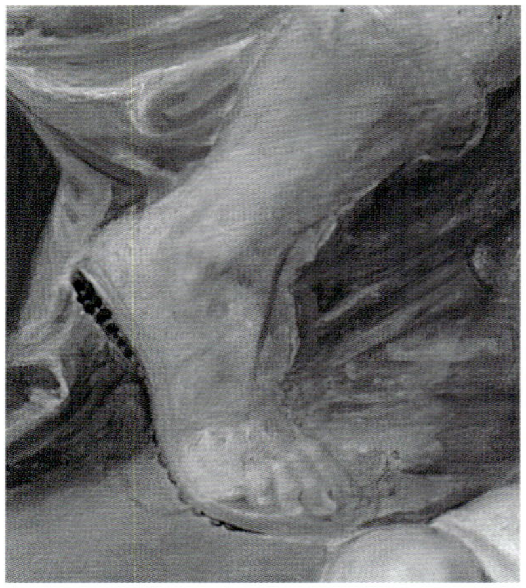

that this soldier's foot was originally further to the left and pointing more sharply down (fig. 71). Rubens was proud of his familiarity with this detail of Roman military costume and had introduced hobnails under the shoe of Saint Papius in his first (1607) scheme for the Vallicella altarpiece (now in Grenoble) and, later, much to the delight of his antiquarian friend Peiresc, he also used the hobnail boot in the 1622 cartoons for his Constantine tapestries.[4]

The IR also shows that there was originally a different pattern of folds on the dress of the woman in red which extended further down below the grey foreground. Some of these draft folds are visible to the naked eye as ridges through the masking surface layers of red paint, but they are more easily read in IR. Otherwise, since the surface colouring-in follows the contours of the underdrawing design exactly in most areas of the carefully painted *Massacre*, there are very few signs of such preliminary laying-out.

The infant on the far right is clearly painted over the grey foreground, rather than in a space reserved for such a figure – so it was obviously a late inclusion – and there seems to have been a different compositional plan behind and to the right of this child which is now illegible. In contrast, the soldier with a sword was painted in a designated area and so was part of Rubens's original design. The underdrawn head of the commander's horse also appears to stop at the point where the scratched man's black hair begins, which indicates that the latter figure was always in the original plan, whereas the grey architecture behind the armed soldier was added afterwards.

The inclusion of the figure of the mounted commander leaning out towards the viewer would have created a very different triangular structure for the work, resulting in a collision of figures rather than the counter-balanced groups of the final work. The missing commander can be visualized

72
PETER PAUL RUBENS
(1577–1640)
Saint George and the Dragon, *c.* 1606
Oil on canvas, 304 × 256 cm
Museo del Prado, Madrid

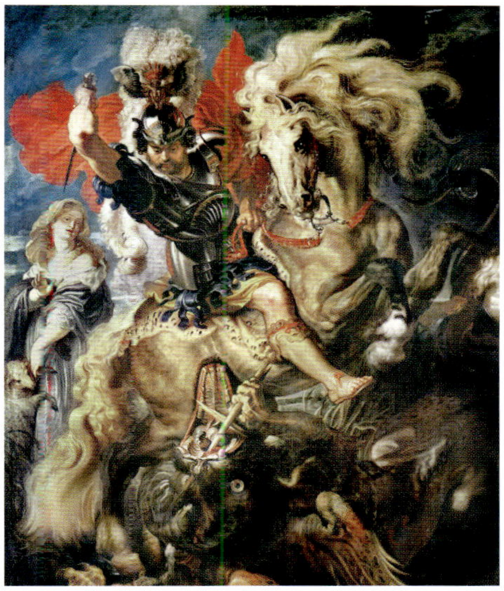

partially from traces of his baton and arm which are still visible under the paint of the column above the plume of the armoured soldier. Figures in an earlier prototype for this composition, *The Martydom of Saint Ursula* of *c.* 1603 (Palazzo Ducale, Mantua), give some clue as to the way the commander figure might have looked. In that work, the Hun leader turns back his horse, raising his baton, in a similar way, and the backward-toppling arched woman of the *Massacre* is prefigured in its bottom left quadrant. Perhaps the clearest precedent is provided by the *c.* 1609 *Saint George and the Dragon* in the Prado (fig. 72). This presents an overhanging rider striking downwards at the dragon, which spirals out into our space in much the same way as the woman in red does in the *Massacre*. The inclusion of the mounted commander in the *Massacre* would have reinforced the circular structure of the composition,[5] and perhaps Rubens removed it because he wanted to make the composition more linear. This would also have served to emphasize the Mars-like armoured soldier, who may personify the *Furor* (fury) of War.

In this sense the *Massacre* has a strong visual and thematic link with a much later work by Rubens. The image of the Cruelty of War (*saevities belli*) – one of a number of scenes in Rubens's *Temple of Janus* arch for the entry to Antwerp of the Cardinal-Infante Ferdinand (figs. 73, 74), of 1634–35 – shows a helmeted soldier in a red cloak who drags a mother by her hair while her child has been thrown to the ground.[6] The image reads as a précis of Rubens's *Massacre*. In that commission Rubens's anti-war message was

73
PETER PAUL RUBENS
(1577–1640)
The Temple of Janus
c. 1634–35
Oil on canvas
70 × 65.5 cm
The State Hermitage Museum, St Petersburg

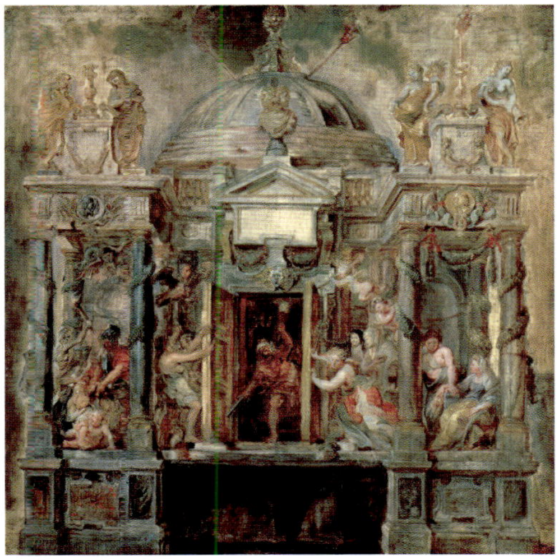

74
PETER PAUL RUBENS
The Temple of Janus
detail of fig. 74, showing Cruelty of War pulling a mother by her hair in front of Death

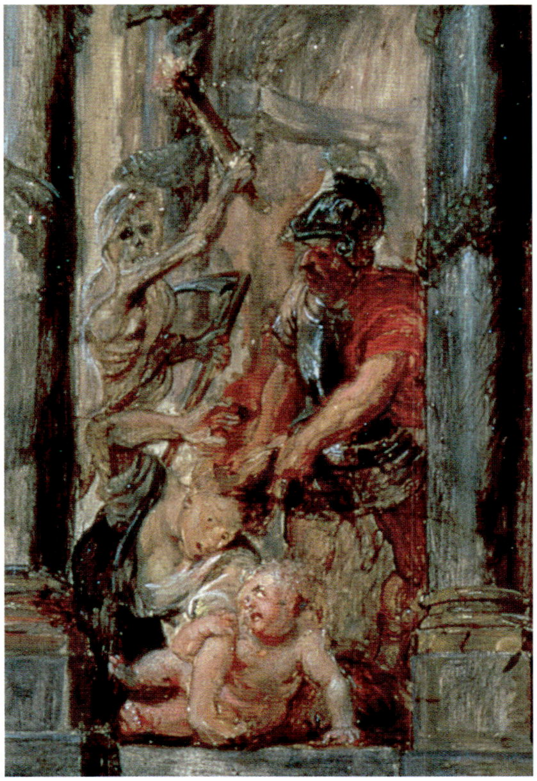

75, 76, 77
PETER PAUL RUBENS
The Massacre of the Innocents, details

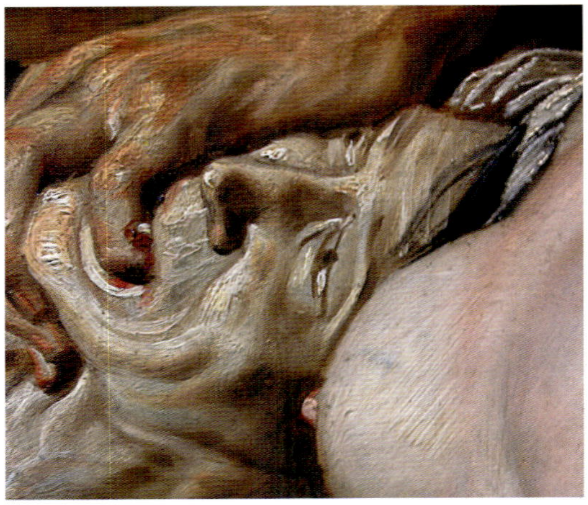

overtly political, addressed to the incoming governor, as we know from Gevaerts's written description of the triumphal arches made to welcome the new Habsburg governor.[7]

The power of the *Massacre* as finally painted lies partly in its remarkable state of preservation. The subtle gradations of tone that create the volumes of the limbs and torsos are an extraordinary survival, since these can so easily be lost by abrasion. It is interesting that the infant on the very far right of the *Massacre* (with his head on his arm) is painted in a looser way than much of the rest of the work, in a style closer to Rubens's small oil-sketches.[8] A simple explanation for this passage may relate to its intended location. The light source in the painting comes from the left and, if the work was designed for a specific site, Rubens may have wanted the infant figure to catch the more distant light in the less illuminated part of the painting. It is even possible that this dead infant was added when the painting was placed *in situ* (a point to which we shall return). Whatever the explanation, the two infants which frame the lower corners of the panel like bookends are painted with virtuoso economy as if to preserve the freshness of an oil-sketch in the section of the painting which is most visible to a viewer standing beneath the work.

The central woman dressed in flaming red is apparently bathed in the light emanating from the dawn sky on the left of the painting, yet she is also strongly illuminated by the light of the room into which she projects illusionistically. On the right-hand side, which is designed for the lowest illumination, other figures gain form and relief as if cut from deep shadows. In contrast to the *Samson and Delilah* (fig. 45), which we know was approached and intended to be viewed from the left, the *Massacre*'s primary viewpoint was from the right. Only from this angle can we fully make sense of the stance of the soldier, raising the child aloft, whose arm overlaps the man being scratched. The latter can be read as standing 'behind' the soldier raising the child: when seen in this way he becomes fully

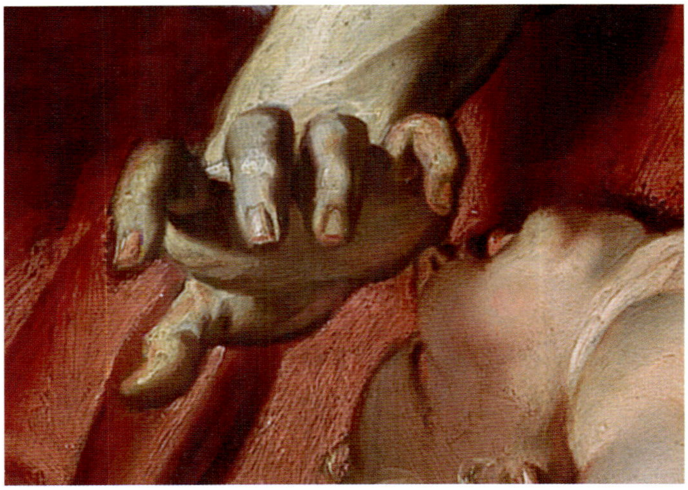

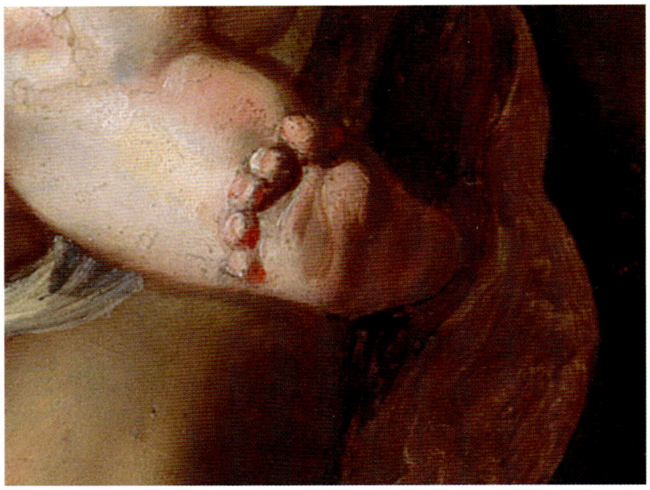

78, 79, 80
PETER PAUL RUBENS
The Massacre of the Innocents, details

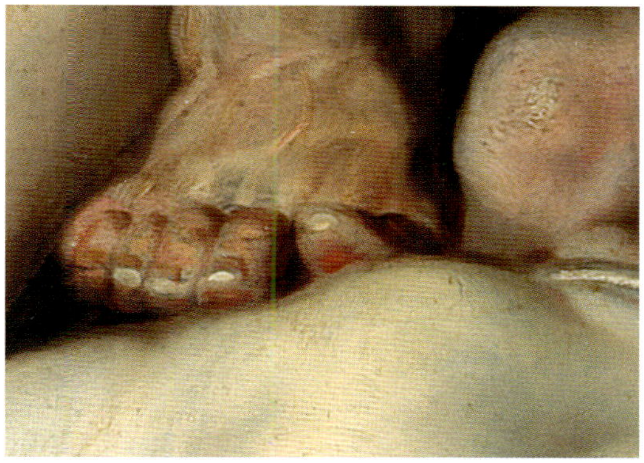

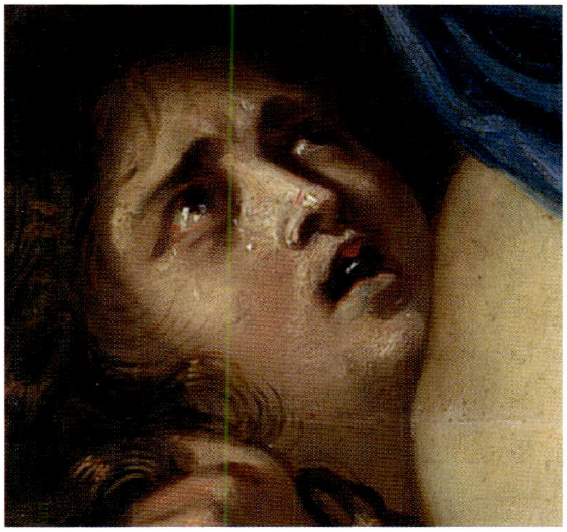

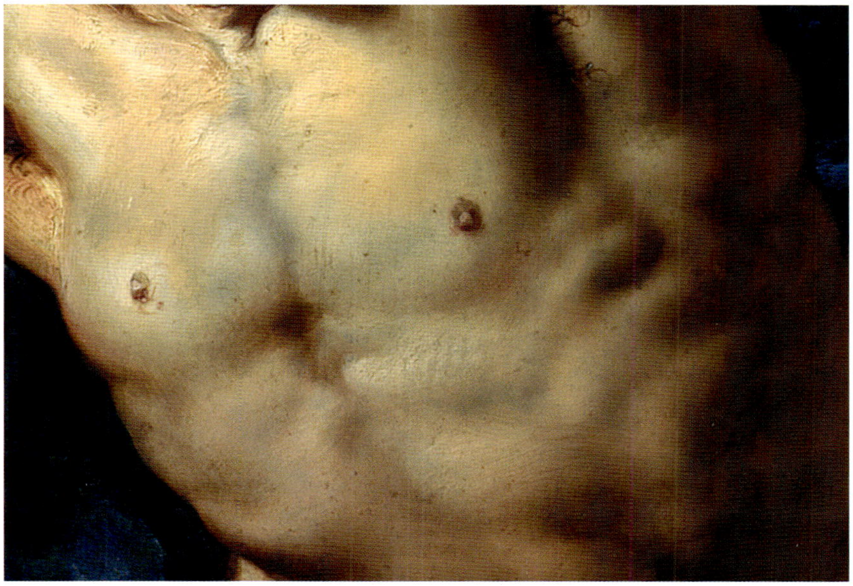

coherent as a figure. The cityscape also works better from this principal viewpoint. Compositions for chimney-piece paintings, like altarpieces, were conceived with their site in mind, and, as we have seen with the *Samson and Delilah* (pp. 65–71), placement was critical. We know Rubens painted large altarpieces *in situ* – for example, *The Raising of the Cross*, the Sint-Walburga and the Santa Maria in Vallicella commissions – so it is certainly possible that he retouched a work upon its installation in a domestic setting.

The creation of striking visual effects by seemingly effortless brushwork was a form of artistry praised since antiquity. Rubens depicted a horse's foaming mouth in his equestrian portrait of Gian Carlo Doria (Galleria Nazionale della Liguria, Genoa) with no more than a single brushstroke, perhaps imitating the bravura of the antique painter Protogenes whom Pliny describes as creating such a virtuoso visual effect with no more than a thrown sponge.[9] The similarly abbreviated application of paint in the *Massacre* amply signals the violence of the scene – a smudge of paint for red blood on fingers, a deft fleck of white to convey the old woman's single tooth (fig. 75) and red ribbons to signify scratches on a face. Rubens uses small patches of colour with extraordinary effect, in the touches of blue in the lips of the distressed mother on the right (fig. 79), for example, and for the dabs of red on the old woman's fingertips (fig. 76), on the foot pads of the child hanging from his mother's arms in the centre of the picture (fig. 77) and the toe of the right-hand executioner (fig. 78). Hatched strokes convey musculature and textured white highlights catch the fall of light on the torso of the soldier wielding the infant (fig. 80). Looking in raking light at the breast of the woman in red reveals just how Rubens models the paint to create a surface of light-catching furrows.

81
PETER PAUL RUBENS
The Massacre of the Innocents, detail

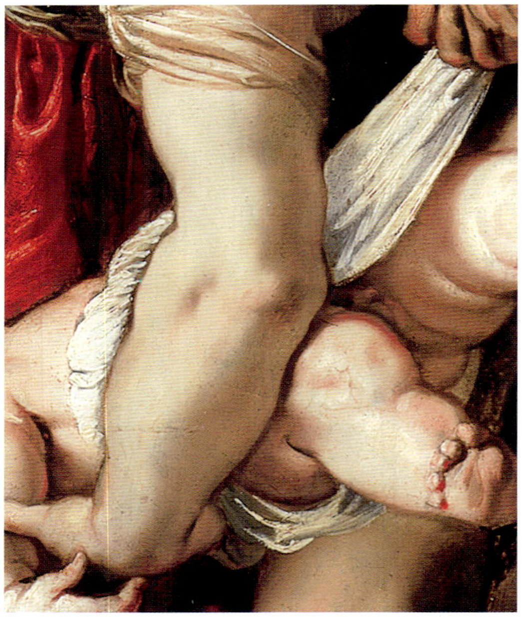

The pasty application of white, especially in the drapery and swaddling clothes (fig. 81), is also evident in the preliminary sketch in the Groeninger Museum, Groeningen, for the Antwerp Town Hall *Adoration* and is generally characteristic of Rubens's oil-sketches. Details like the flashing white hair highlights and the long golden swirling locks show the brushwork of the thirty-something artist at his most daring and inventive, claiming his right to be Antwerp's leading painter. Indeed the energy of the painting makes the work of Rubens's predecessors like Maarten de Vos and contemporaries like Abraham Janssens and Wenzel Coebergher (1560–1632) look stilted and schematic. Rubens shifted the depiction of action to another level, above even Caravaggio's breathtaking achievement.

Rubens's lost sketchbook

The destruction of Rubens's original sketchbook (also known as his notebook or pocketbook) is one of the great losses of art history. It was destroyed in a fire at the Louvre in 1720 while in the possession of André-Charles Boulle, the cabinetmaker to Louis XIV. It is some consolation that various fragmentary records of the book exist, from which we can at least partially reconstruct its content. There remain four copies of the original (the de Ganay, Johnson, Madrid Bordes and 'Van Dyck' sketchbooks or notebooks), one series of engravings after it (published, with a French text, by Charles-Antoine Jombert in 1773), and at least three original sheets from the sketchbook (in the Staatliche Museen, Berlin, and included among the Johnson and Madrid Bordes copies; see figs. 86–88). It seems likely that the four sets of copies, none of which are identical or apparently a complete copy of the original, were made by young artists seeking to learn figurative narrative and compositional structure from Rubens's example.[10]

Rubens's sketchbook must have been assembled between 1595 and 1610, as it records his artistic progress from his earliest training through to his stays in Spain (1603–04) and Italy (1600–08). It seems to have functioned as a compendium of images which Rubens copied from the wide range of sources he viewed, arranging the images by topic and then developing compositional variations from them. Although it was chiefly concerned with invention and the creative process, it also contained Rubens's written annotations and observations about the images he was copying and reworking. The sketchbook would have shown a voracious appetite for prints, a taste for late Raphael and surprisingly little copying of the antique. This suggests that he had separate books for the study of ancient art and for the study of anatomy.

The remains of Rubens's sketchbook are a key source for understanding both Rubens's early development and works of around 1610, including the *Massacre*, and the aesthetics and inventive process which informed his entire oeuvre. Though there are no known preparatory drawings or oil-sketches

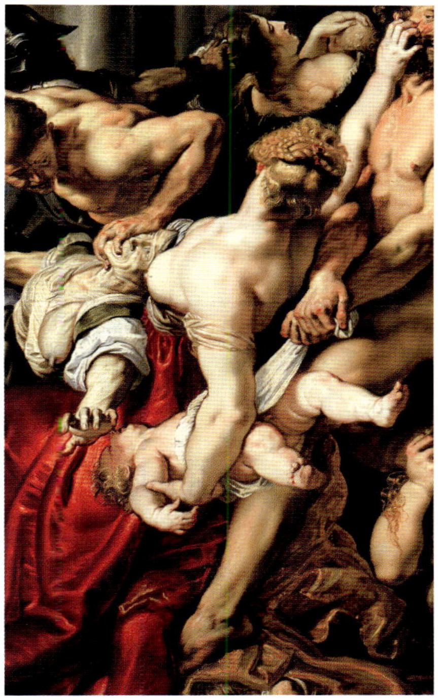

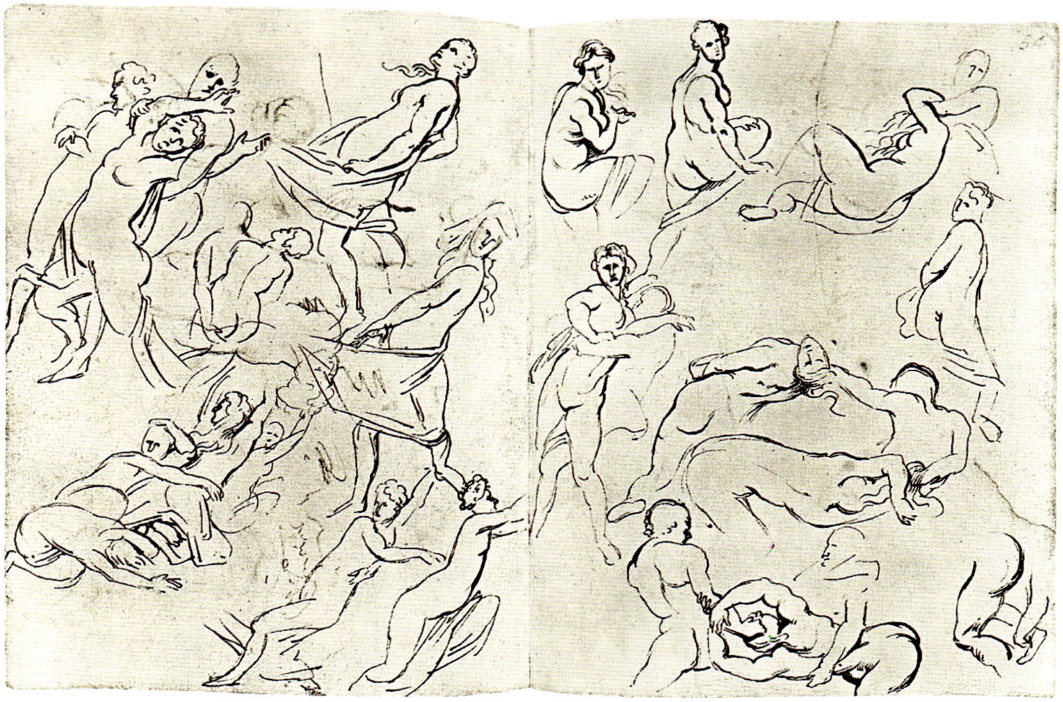

82
PETER PAUL RUBENS
The Massacre of the Innocents, detail

83
Copy after
PETER PAUL RUBENS
(1577–1640)
(sometimes attributed to
ANTHONY VAN DYCK)
'Van Dyck' sketchbook, ff. 55v–56r, *c.* 1598–1609
Devonshire Collection, Chatsworth

made specifically for the *Massacre*, many of Rubens's anatomical drawings and drawings after the antique as well as sketchbook adaptations served as prototypes for some of the figures. He may well have made detailed sketches of individual figures as well as more worked-up compositional drawings for the painting. His method of picture-making was not restricted to the two dimensions pre-ordained by a flat picture plane. Like a choreographer or animator of images, Rubens conceived figures spatially, almost like sculptures he could rotate. The sequences of figures drawn from different viewpoints, some of which are also found in copies of his lost sketchbook, attest to this constant reappraisal of the graphic ideas which captured his imagination. The central female figure in red in the *Massacre* (fig. 82) may also be associated with Rubens's general interest in motifs of women being pulled into backward-arching falls such as we see in the early *Battle of the Amazons* (see fig. 121), the *Martyrdom of Saint Ursula* (Mantua) and in the 'Van Dyck' sketchbook (fig. 83).[11] The triplet of twisting figures in the lower right corner of the sketchbook is inspired by Michelangelo's *Battle of Centaurs* (Casa Buonarroti, Florence), and the imaginative transformation of the group, above, into a man pulling two women by their hair leads to the hair-pulling helmeted soldier in the *Massacre*.

In the same version of Rubens's sketchbook we find a record of another *Massacre of the Innocents*, that of Giovanni Battista Paggi (see fig. 58), dating to 1604. Rubens's copying of two details (the mother lowering her child and the mother biting the soldier's arm, on ff. 14v–15r in the top left corner; fig. 84) of Paggi's *Massacre* (fig. 58) while in Genoa in 1606 would suggest he had been considering the subject for some time before he initiated his painting in Antwerp. Rubens was engaged by the task of showing the varied expressions and gestures of maternal grief and made a series of explorations of that subject on this sheet,[12] developing the idea of a grief-stricken mother bending over her dead child and pulling at her own hair in despair. (The foreshortened view of the mother with her hair cascading down in swirling arabesques across her dead child also recalls Enea Vico's engraving after Raphael's *Pietà*.)[13] A similar figure can be found in the *Massacre*, rotated to give a frontal view (fig. 85). The two views of the mother raising up her dead child were incorporated into Rubens's Courtauld *Brazen Serpent* (see fig. 128).

Rubens's concept of female beauty is stated emphatically in the *Massacre*. The long neck of the central female figure reflects his early interest in comparing the aesthetic qualities of mares' and women's necks, which is graphically recorded and described in several versions of the sketchbook. Rubens notes his preferences for black eyes and silver manes – or their

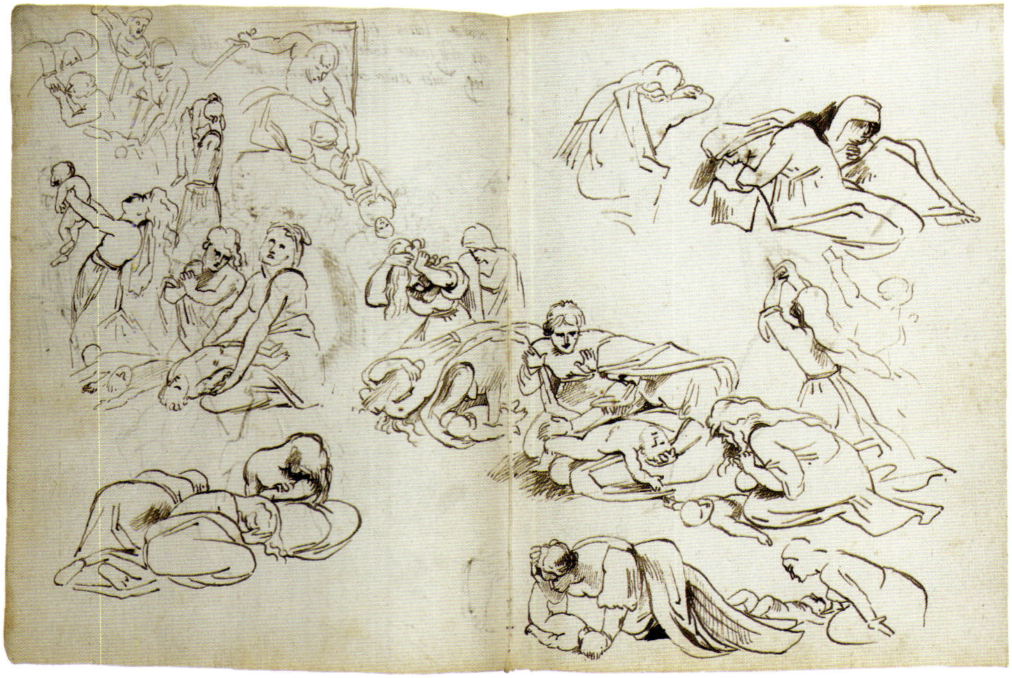

84
Copy after
PETER PAUL RUBENS
(1577–1640)
(sometimes attributed to
ANTHONY VAN DYCK)
'Van Dyck' sketchbook, ff. 14v–15r, *c.* 1598–1609
Devonshire Collection, Chatsworth

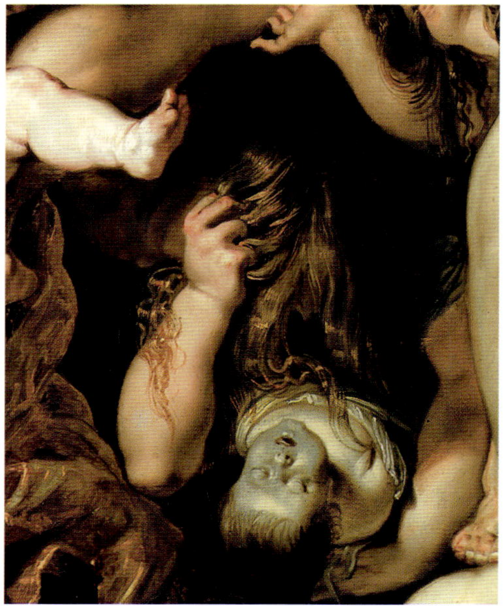

85
PETER PAUL RUBENS
The Massacre of the Innocents, detail

equivalent, long blonde hair – and firm stomachs and rumps.[14] Like Delilah in *Samson and Delilah* (fig. 45), the more anatomically correct central woman in red in the *Massacre* demonstrates Rubens's interest in the equine curved neck and in the ideal human form.

Rubens began analysing the human body early in his career. There are subtle signs of this ambition in paintings he made before he left for Italy in 1600. These somewhat awkward efforts to paint the human anatomy can be found in his earliest paintings, including the 1597–99 *Judgement of Paris* (fig. 1). The description of the upper muscle groups on the back of Paris on the left, the articulation of the lower back and buttocks of Minerva in the centre right and the abdomen of the river god at the far right all show him trying to come to grips with the muscular structure over the skeleton. A similar fascination with knobbly muscles (*serratus anterior*) at the top of the ribs can be seen in the man who tries to assist Paul in the *Conversion of Saul* in the Liechtenstein Collection in Vienna.

We know that Rubens studied anatomy from the evidence of several of his own drawings (in the Rubenshuis, Antwerp, and at Chatsworth) and of copies.[15] Some of these anatomical drawings were derived from Juan de Valverde de Hamusco's *Historia de la Composicion del Cuerpo Humano*, first published in Rome in 1556 and later appearing in 1566 and 1572 Antwerp editions. These drawings were themselves versions of the 1543 illustrated publication of Andreas Vesalius, the celebrated Brussels anatomist. Valverde's *Historia* was illustrated by Nicole Beatrizet and, apart from a few reversals, its plates were recut reasonably accurately in successive editions. Rubens's own records of its illustrations are known from drawings made in his studio by Willem Panneels. Panneels's *c.* 1628 copies of three drawings of torsos have been sourced to Rubens's 'anatomy book.' Further anatomical drawings also appear in the Madrid Bordes copy of his lost sketchbook. All these drawings show Rubens extracting and adapting information, especially about the torso and the head, from these diagrams of muscles, nerves and skeletons. Even in the crudest copies, the drawings show Rubens's ambition to understand the human machine. As a result he sometimes seems to be pulling the skin back on over his subcutaneous investigations; and the lower arm of a victim in his *Saint George and the Dragon* in the British Royal Collection has actually been flayed.[16]

While Rubens sought to understand anatomical structures he also explored ways of codifying this information in geometric form. In famous drawings of the antique Farnese *Hercules* sculpture (fig. 89) he simplified a procession of views of the male form into powerful minimal blocks (figs. 86, 88). Although this technique has precedents in some generic drawing books of the time and is seen in sketches by the sixteenth-century Genoese painter Luca Cambiaso, these cubic analyses were certainly Rubens's own. Naturalistic drawings in his own hand (see fig. 87) exist

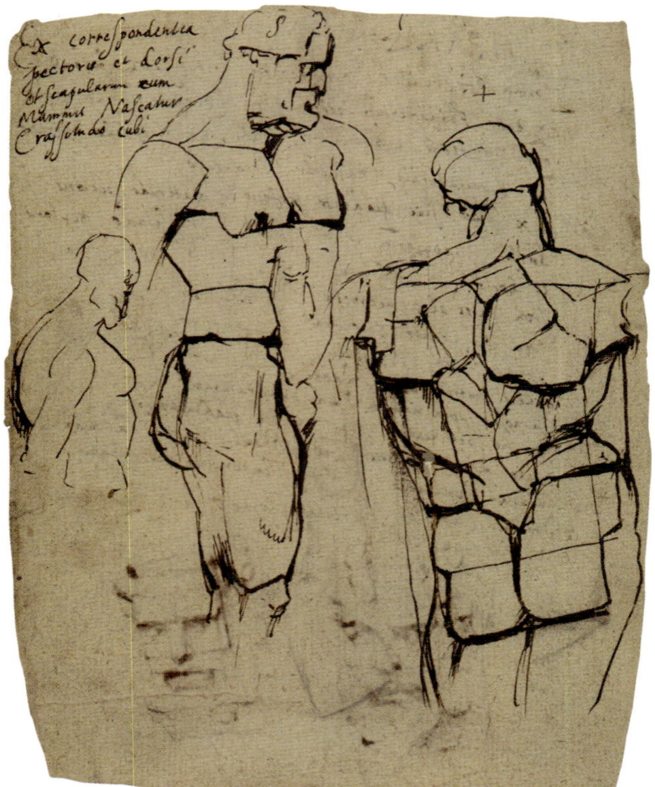

86
PETER PAUL RUBENS
(1577–1640)
Johnson sketchbook page: Studies of the Farnese Hercules, *c.* 1602
(recto of fig. 88)
Pen and ink on paper
19.6 × 15.3 cm
Courtauld Gallery, London
D.1978.PG.427

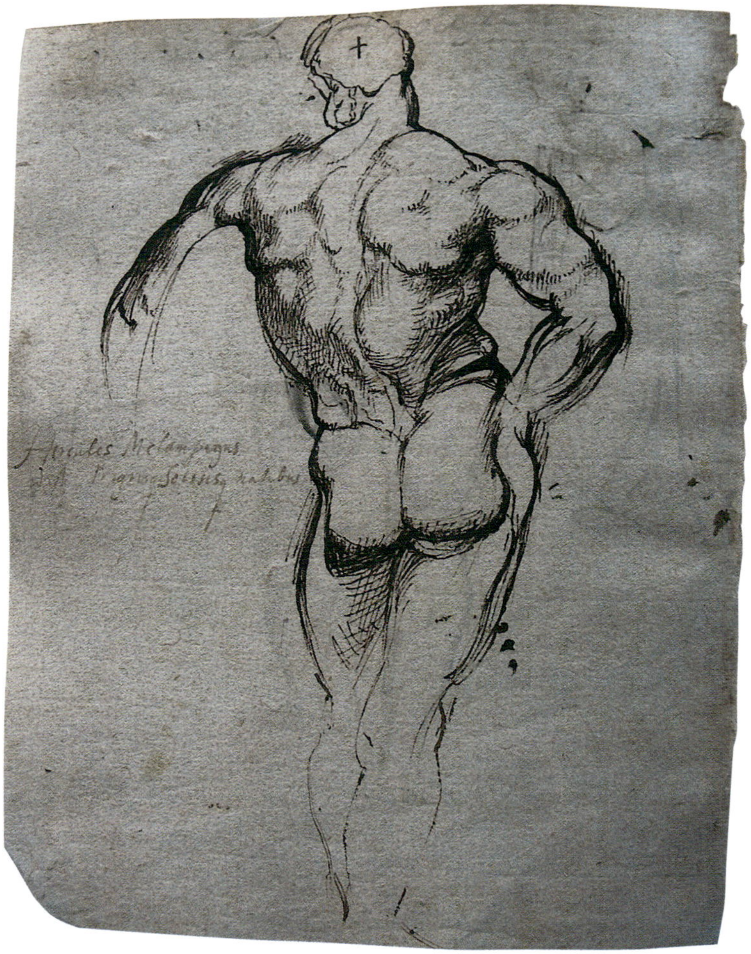

87
Here attributed to
PETER PAUL RUBENS
(1577–1640)
Madrid Bordes sketchbook page: Study of the Farnese Hercules, *c.* 1602
Madrid Bordes sketchbook
22 × 17 cm
Private collection, Madrid

of the same views of the Farnese *Hercules* which serve as a starting point for the abstracted rectangular versions. One of these (fig. 86) explores the stereometric possibilities of the Farnese *Hercules*, while on the verso of the same sheet (fig. 88) in the Johnson copy of the sketchbook Rubens states that the human form is constituted of three elements – the triangle, the square and the circle (in an extension of Aristotelian philosophy).[17] For Rubens the Farnese *Hercules* represented the ultimate robust male form. It is no coincidence that he chose this antique statue as the basis for his studies (see the following chapter).

In the surviving original sketch in the Madrid Bordes sketchbook, which shows the *Hercules* from behind (fig. 87), Rubens added an inscription, "*Hercules melampygus nigris*" (Hercules of the black buttocks). This line associates the view of the statue with an antique story in which two mischievous boys, destined to become tree monkeys, were warned to avoid a man answering to this description. This dialogue between image and text is typical of Rubens, who was always making links between

88
PETER PAUL RUBENS
(1577–1640)
Johnson sketchbook page
c. 1602 (verso of fig. 86)
Pen and ink on paper
19.6 × 15.3 cm
Courtauld Gallery, London
D.1978.PG.427

89
After LYSIPPOS
(fl. 370–310)
The Farnese Hercules
Marble
Height 317 cm
Museo Archeologico
Nazionale, Naples

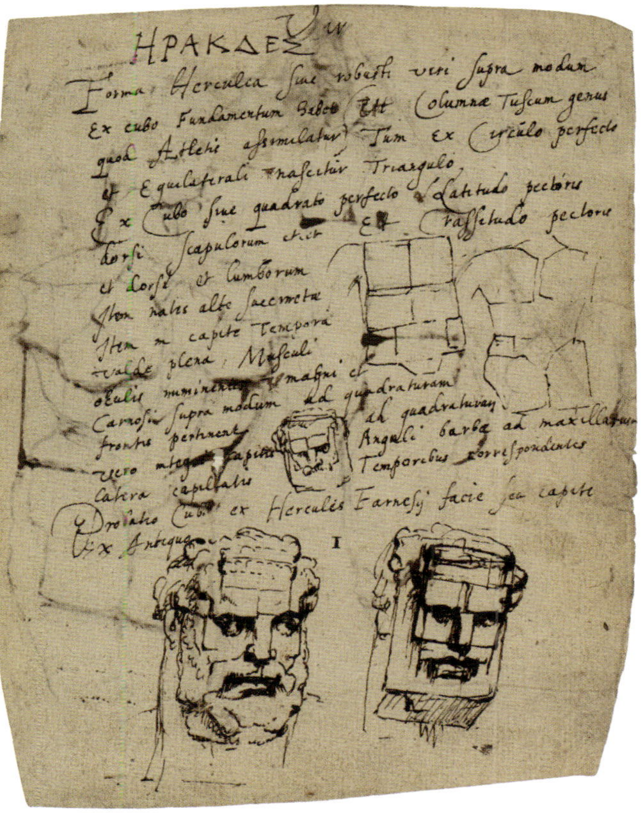

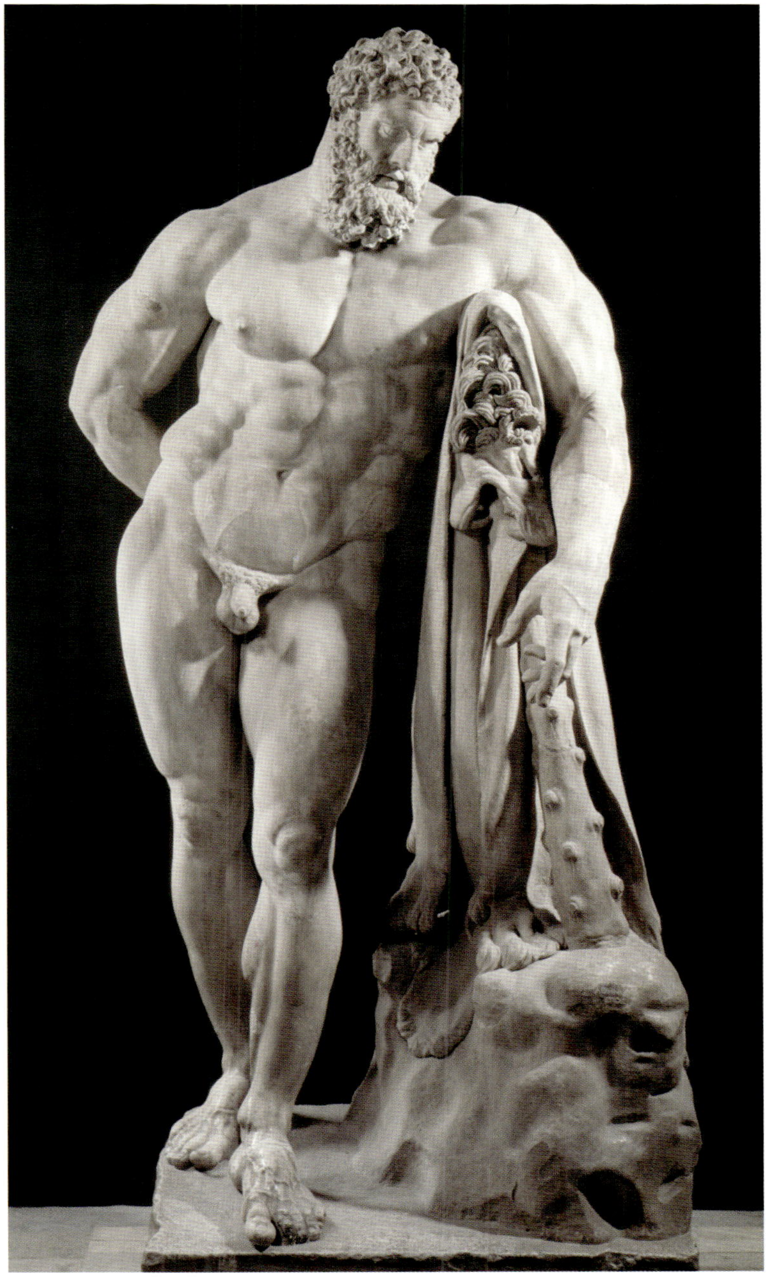

verbal imagery and pictorial ideas.[18] On the recto of the same sheet he drew a figure from Raphael's template for the Sistine tapestry of *Saint Paul preaching at Athens* while stating (recalling Vitruvius) that the cube is the basis of all things and that nothing stands without it.[19]

Many of the sketchbook drawings were annotated in this way.[20] An inscription referring to a passage from a boxing match in Virgil's *Aeneid* is noted on a sheet from the de Ganay copy of the sketchbook which shows a slumped figure. The passage in Virgil, in which the victor spits out gore and blood, does not appear to have been painted by Rubens, but the spirit of it can be found in the injured dragon's mouth in the Prado *Saint George* (fig. 72) and equally in the bloody horse's teeth in the Liechtenstein *Death of Decius Mus* (fig. 5). It can also be felt in the *Massacre*, for while the bloodiness of the scene is not the main focus, blood from acts of indescribable violence stains the marble plinth and trickles to the ground, catching on fingers and toes. Ultimately it is the blue, lifeless limbs of dead infants which are more disturbing than the gore in the *Massacre*.

Rubens and sculpture

Although it is curiously under-represented in the sketchbook copies, we still have many of Rubens's drawings of antique and Renaissance sculpture which record his interest in and use of sculpture for his painting designs. Rubens also designed sculpture in the form of altar frames to set off his paintings as well as works for specialist ivory carvers like Georg Petel. There was a tradition of Italian artists, painters such as Tintoretto as well as sculptors like Alessandro Victoria, seeking models after Michelangelo's sculpture to explore Michelangelo's figural ideas. Michelangelo's *Samson and the Philistine* is quoted by painters as diverse as Daniele da Volterra (1550 *Massacre*), Pellegrino Tibaldi (1549 *Adoration of the Shepherds*) and Willem van Haecht (his collector's cabinet, 1628). Rubens also drew a bronze copy of Michelangelo's *Night* (Lugt collection, Paris) from three different angles, showing details like the plaited hair which occur only in the more elaborated replicas, and he incorporated the pose in his *Battle of the Amazons* (private collection) and in *The Council of the Gods* (Prague Castle). Michelangelo's *David* is found in the Johnson and Madrid copies of the sketchbook and is included among the engravings published by Jombert in 1773. Giambologna's *Rape of the Sabines* provided a range of tempting images for Rubens to copy and adapt. The man anchoring the cross in the Louvre sketch for *The Raising of the Cross* is almost identical to Giambologna's crouching base figure, while the woman being held aloft in that sculpture was easily grafted into various Rubens compositions, often with limb positions adapted to fit the composition.

90
WILLEM VAN TETRODE
(*c.* 1525–1580)
Ecorché (The Horse-tamer)
1562–67
Bronze
Height 43 cm
The Hearn Family Trust, New York

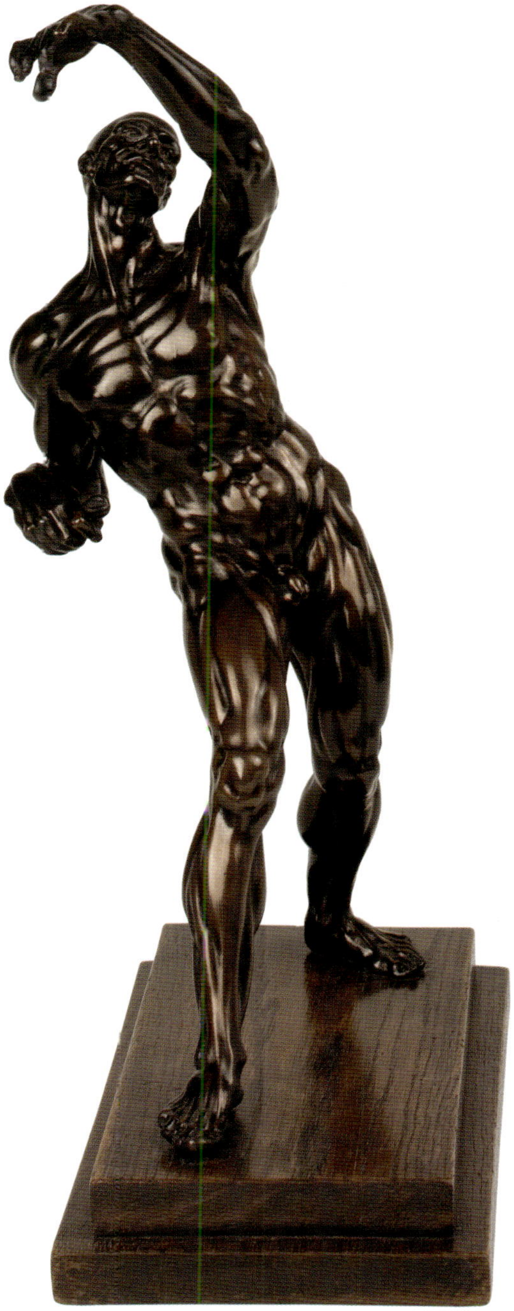

A further source for the pose of the central woman in red in the *Massacre* may have been Rubens's recall of *Samson and the Philistine*, Giambologna's monumental masterpiece which was in the Duke of Lerma's collection when Rubens visited Spain in 1603 (now in the Victoria and Albert Museum). A Rubens drawing in Amsterdam (on deposit at the Rijksmuseum) which shows some knowledge of the forced-back pose of the Philistine supports this hypothesis. Rubens played with this pose in his two oil-sketches for *The Capture of Samson* (see figs. 107–08), exploring the potential of leaning forward or back as alternative solutions for the figure of the struggling Samson. Lunging gestures are again key to in his oil-sketch for *The Deposition* (Louvre), in which the kneeling thieves are oscillated through a similar back and forward succession of poses.[21]

Above all, it was Rubens's study of a flayed (or écorché) bronze by Willem van Tetrode (figs. 90, 94) that enabled him to explore not only the anatomy of the human form but also the spatial relationships between figures. Tetrode, whose design was inspired by the antique *Horse-tamers* on the Quirinal Hill in Rome, probably made his sculptures precisely to aid artists, and the fact that Rubens's drawings were also engraved after Rubens's death by the painter's preferred in-house engraver Paul Pontius suggests that they were indeed used didactically. The pinwheel effect of limbs going in all directions made the model especially useful. Rubens's sketches after Tetrode's bronze detail every muscle and sinew, although, ironically, the Mannerist distortions of Tetrode's figure fell some way short of anatomical exactitude. In true Baroque style, Rubens introduced further exaggerations, artistic folds and muscular swirls into his own copies and seemed especially to admire the dynamic choreography of this bronze (see figs. 91, 96, 99, 100, 102).[22] There is evidence of Rubens's detailed study of the occipital fold (the fleshy crease where the skull joins the neck), just visible in the Tetrode (fig. 92), which Rubens uses and exaggerates in his drawings after it (see notably fig. 91) and again in the central woman in red in the *Massacre* (fig. 93). Her hairline is unnaturally high, allowing Rubens to demonstrate his knowledge of this anatomical detail, which is otherwise usually visible only on the necks of bald men. The detail must have held particular appeal for him. The occipital fold can also be seen on the neck of the bald man in his *Raising of the Cross* (fig. 95), though it is absent in the oil-sketch for that work, which was obviously modified to incorporate it. Rubens's interest in the anatomical foundations for his paintings seems to have been at a peak during the period 1609–11. In Rubens's *c.* 1607 essay on the advantages and limitations of copying ancient sculpture he noted that most sculptors ignored the shadowy depressions caused by the expansion and contraction of the skin, but that this should concern painters. The neck fold illustrates this natural observation.[23]

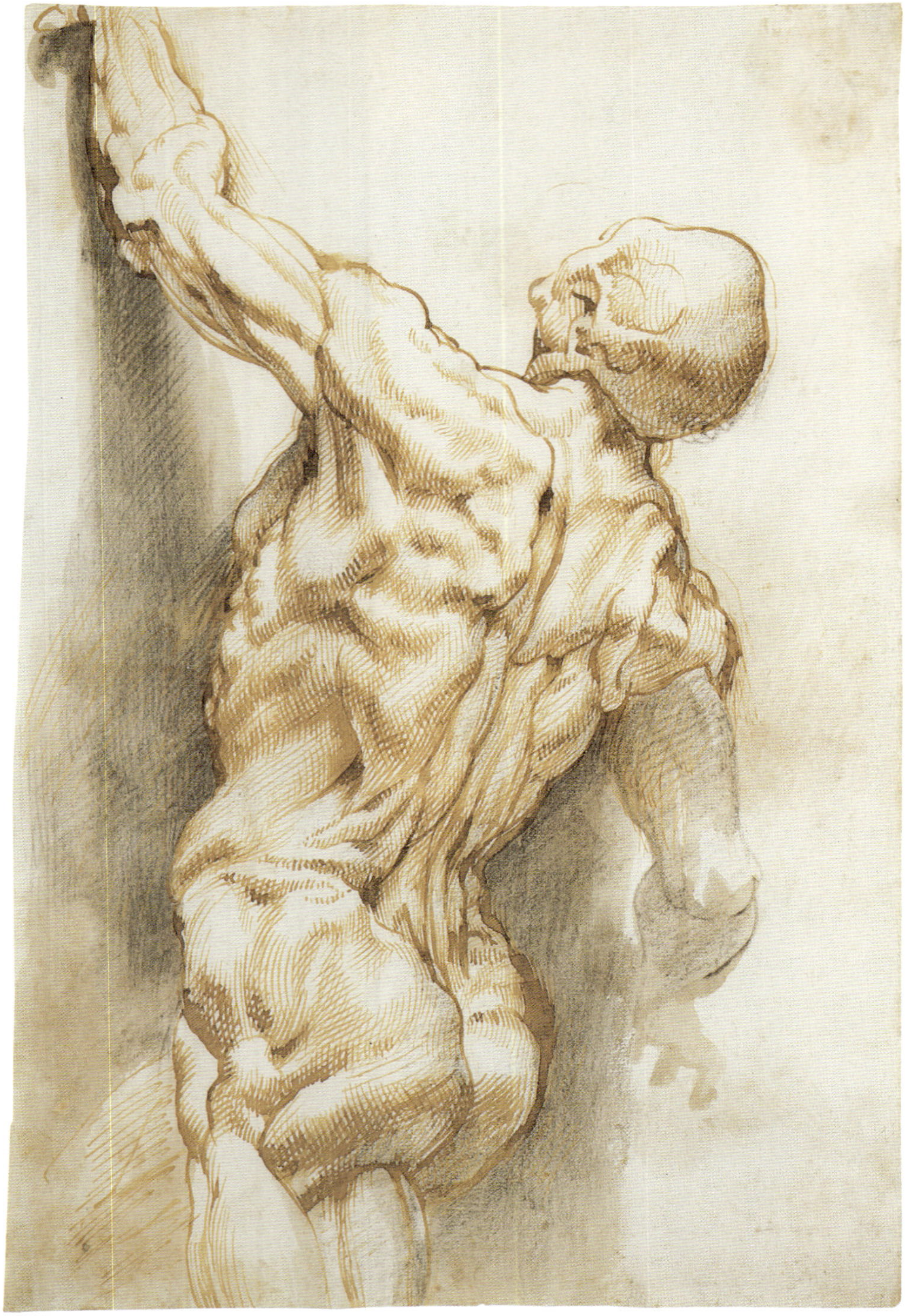

91
PETER PAUL RUBENS
(1577–1640)
Anatomical Study of a Nude, *c.* 1608–10
Black chalk, pen, brown ink, light brown wash
28.8 × 18.5 cm
The Thomson Collection,
Art Gallery of Ontario, Toronto

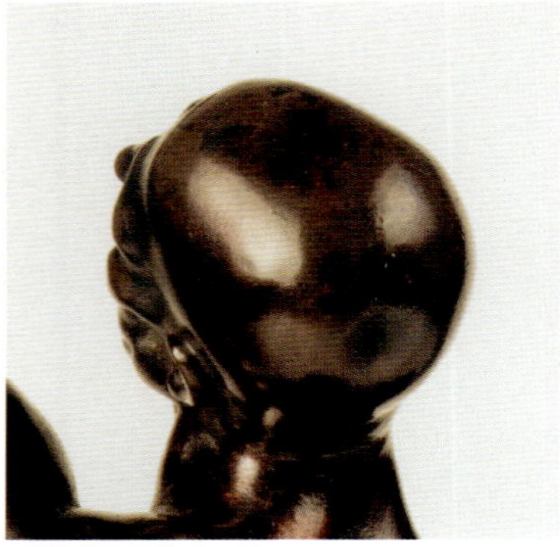

92
WILLEM VAN TETRODE
Ecorché (The Horse-tamer)
detail of fig. 94

93
PETER PAUL RUBENS
The Massacre of the Innocents, detail

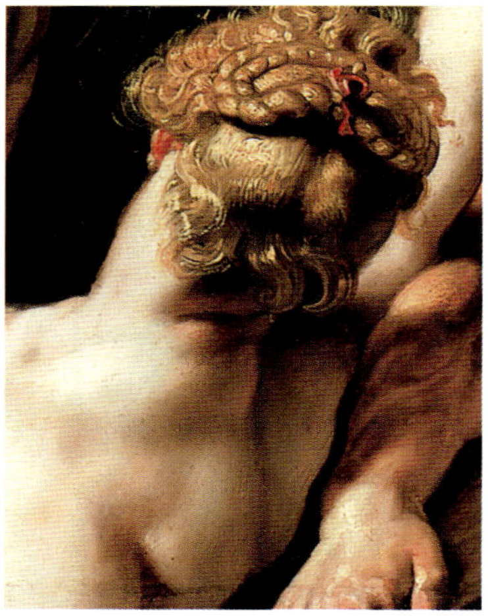

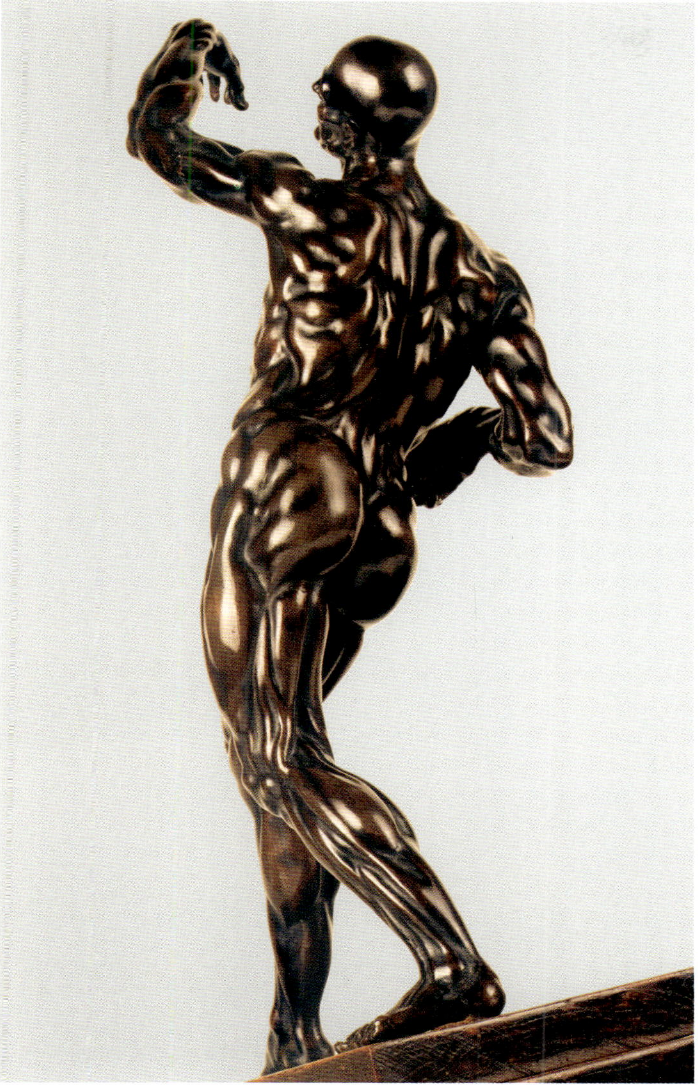

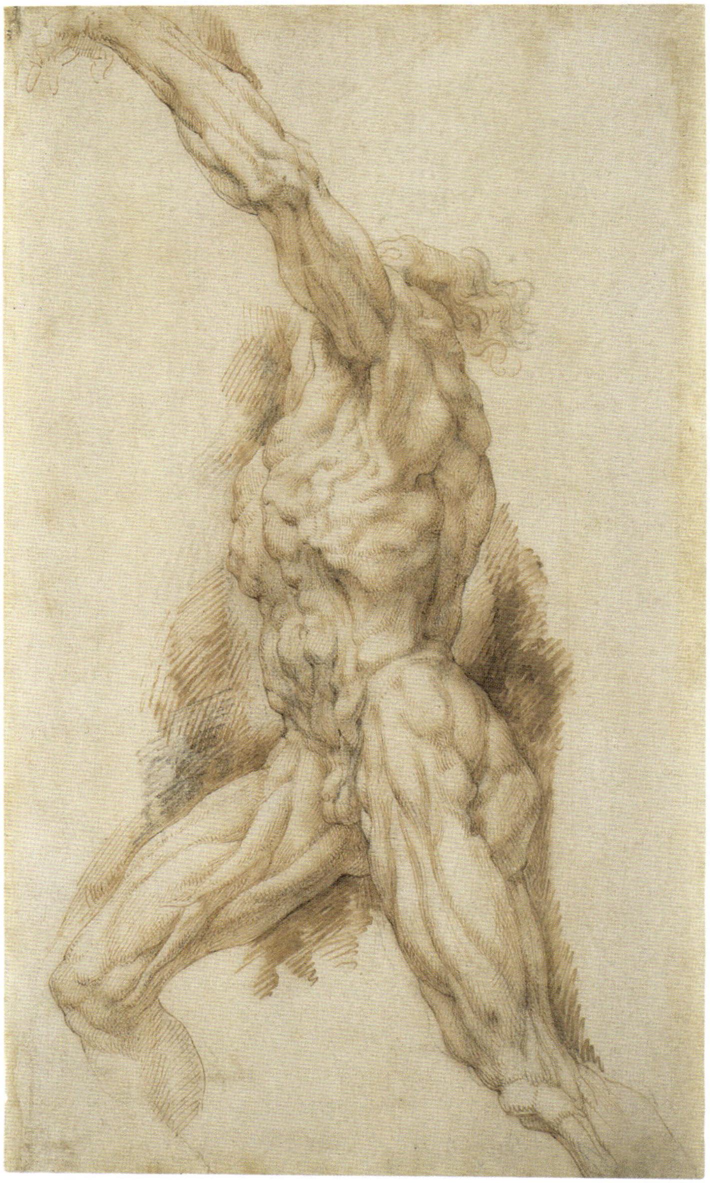

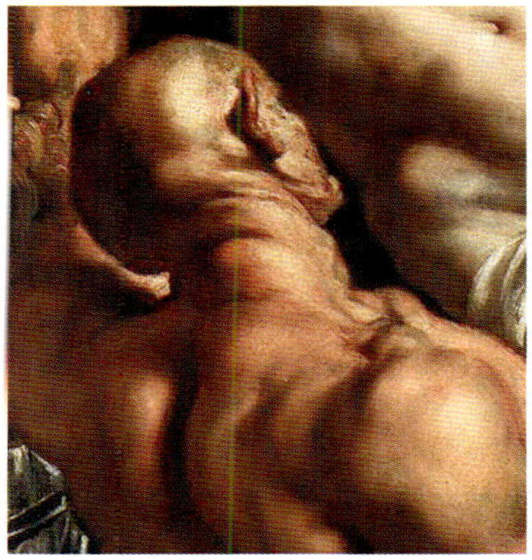

94
WILLEM VAN TETRODE
(*c.* 1525–1580)
Ecorché (The Horse-tamer)
1562–67
Bronze
Height 43 cm
The Hearn Family Trust,
New York

95
PETER PAUL RUBENS
(1577–1640)
The Raising of the Cross
detail of fig. 17

96
PETER PAUL RUBENS
(1577–1640)
Study of an écorché
c. 1608–10
Black chalk, pen and brown ink,
brown wash, watermark
29.8 × 17.2 cm
The Thomson Collection,
Art Gallery of Ontario, Toronto

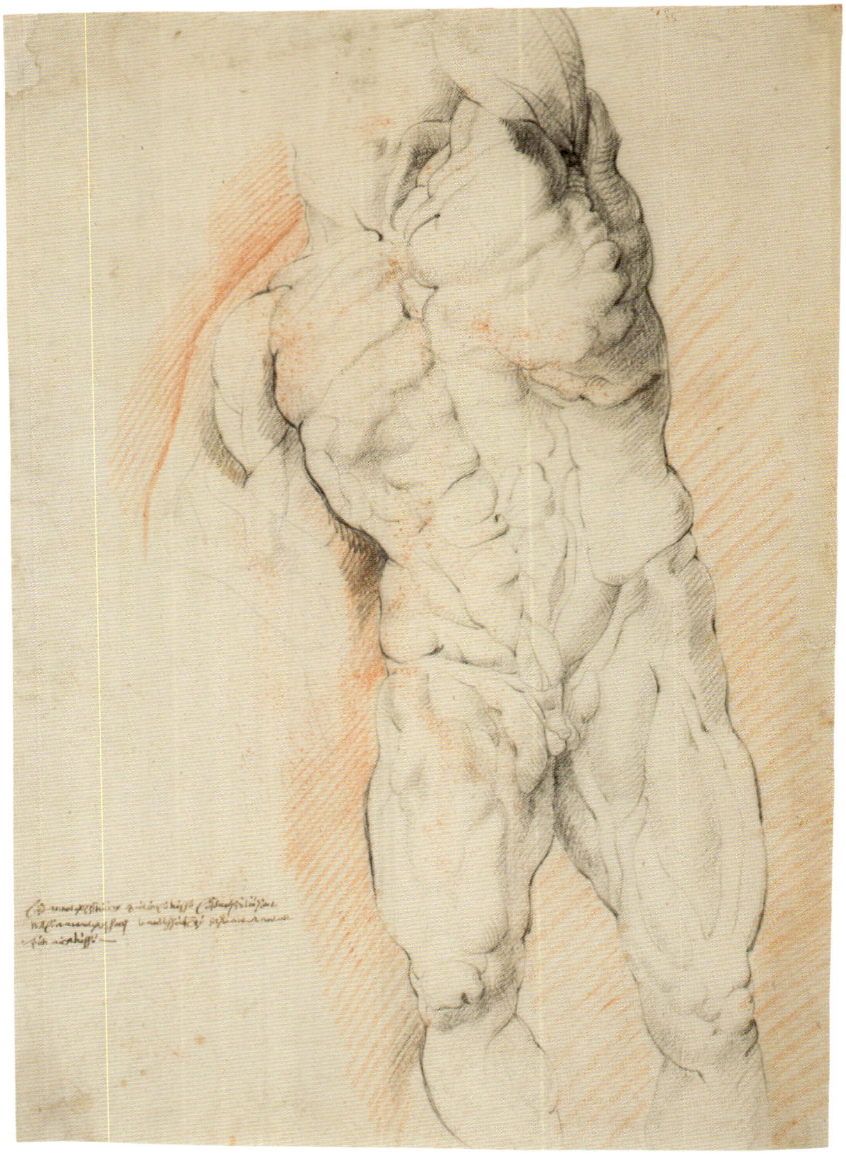

97
WILLEM PANNEELS
(*c.* 1600–*c.* 1640) after
PETER PAUL RUBENS
(1577–1640)
Study of an écorché
(The Horse-tamer)
Graphite, black and red chalk on
yellowish paper, 41 × 28.8 cm
Statens Museum for Kunst,
Copenhagen KKSgb8373

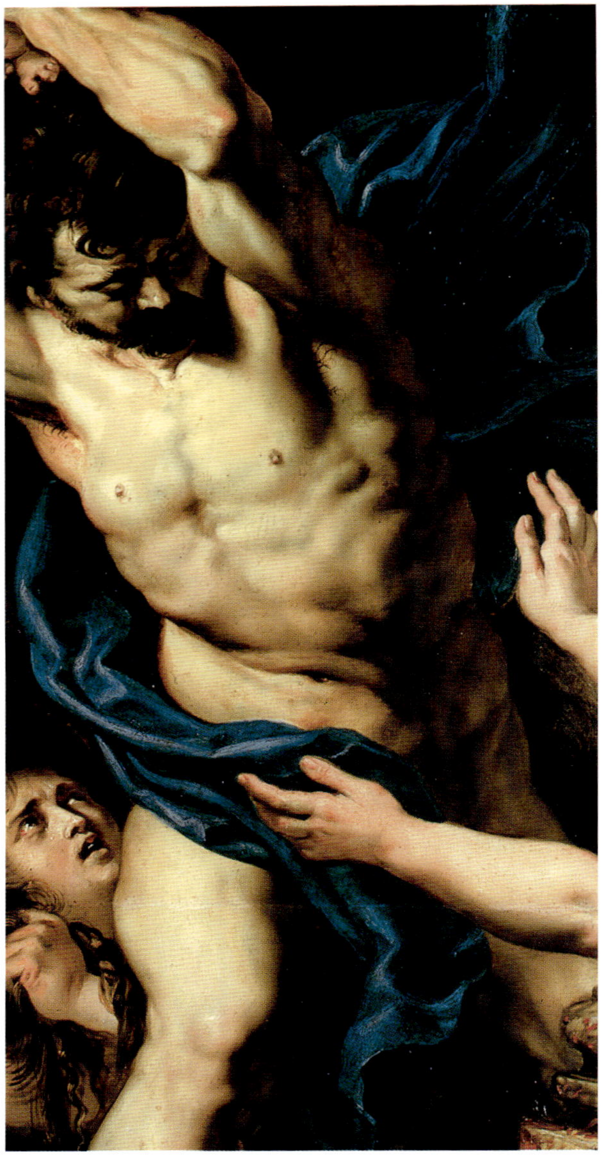

98
PETER PAUL RUBENS
The Massacre of
the Innocents, detail

99
PETER PAUL RUBENS
(1577–1640)
Anatomical Studies of an Arm (verso of fig. 102)
c. 1608–10
Black chalk
26.4 × 19.6 cm
The Thomson Collection, Art Gallery of Ontario, Toronto

Tetrode's influence is felt equally in the executioner on the right of the *Massacre*, not only in the knobbly bones of the elbow but also in the musculature of his torso (fig. 98). A copy of a lost drawing by Rubens (fig. 97) after a tilted frontal view of Tetrode's *Horse-tamer* écorché closely matches the executioner's torso. This missing drawing seems to have had a special place in Rubens's work. He used it again in the bottom right of his 1620 *Last Judgement* in Munich, and his engraver Pontius appears to have based his bound figure on this invention in his book of designs after Rubens.[24] Further evidence of the use of Tetrode's bronze in the *Massacre* can be found on the recto and verso of another sheet of drawings (figs. 99, 102): on the verso (fig. 99) Rubens continued the arm that is truncated in his view of the torso of the écorché (fig. 97) and adapted it for the upper arm of this same executioner (fig. 98). He repeats this upper arm, this time including the neck, in the middle figure of another magnificent study (fig. 100). Here the main figure has gained a shield and hair while his Tetrode-like physique has been 'morphed' onto the pose of the famous

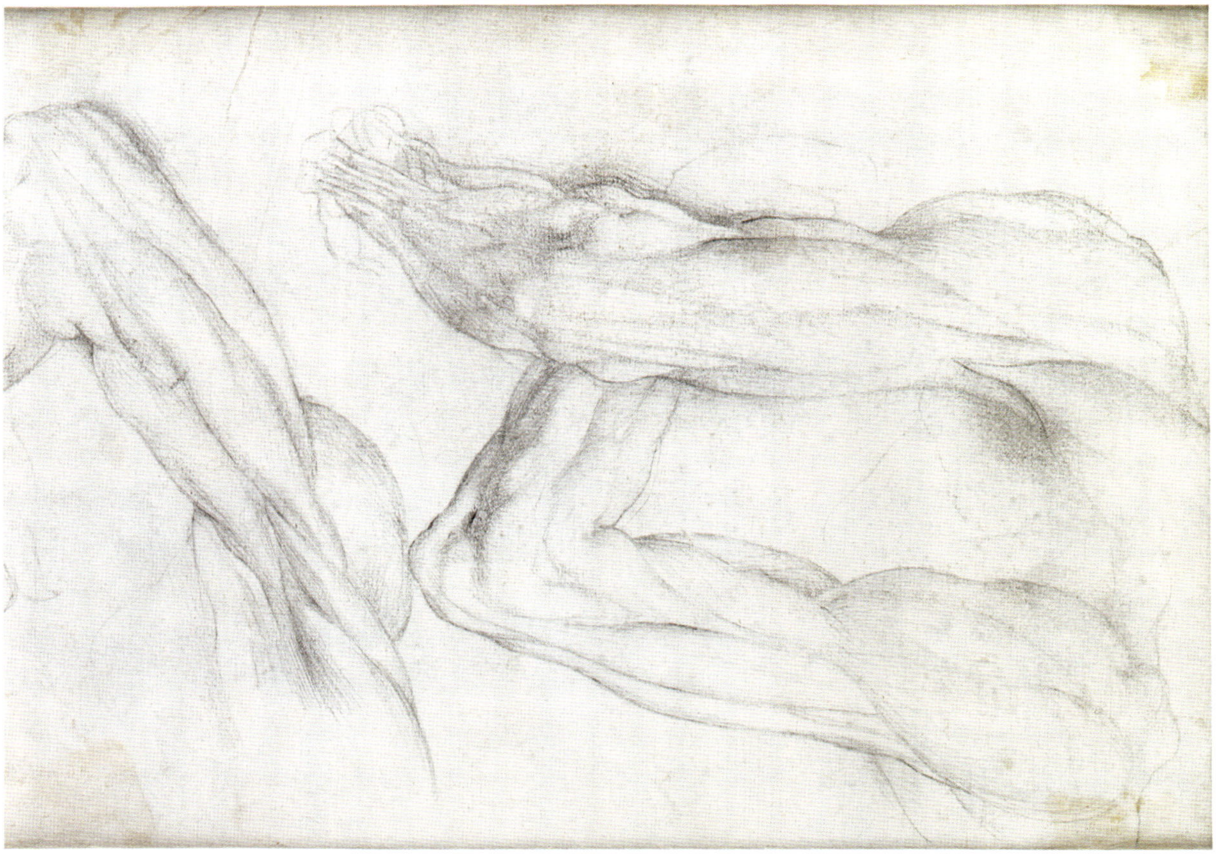

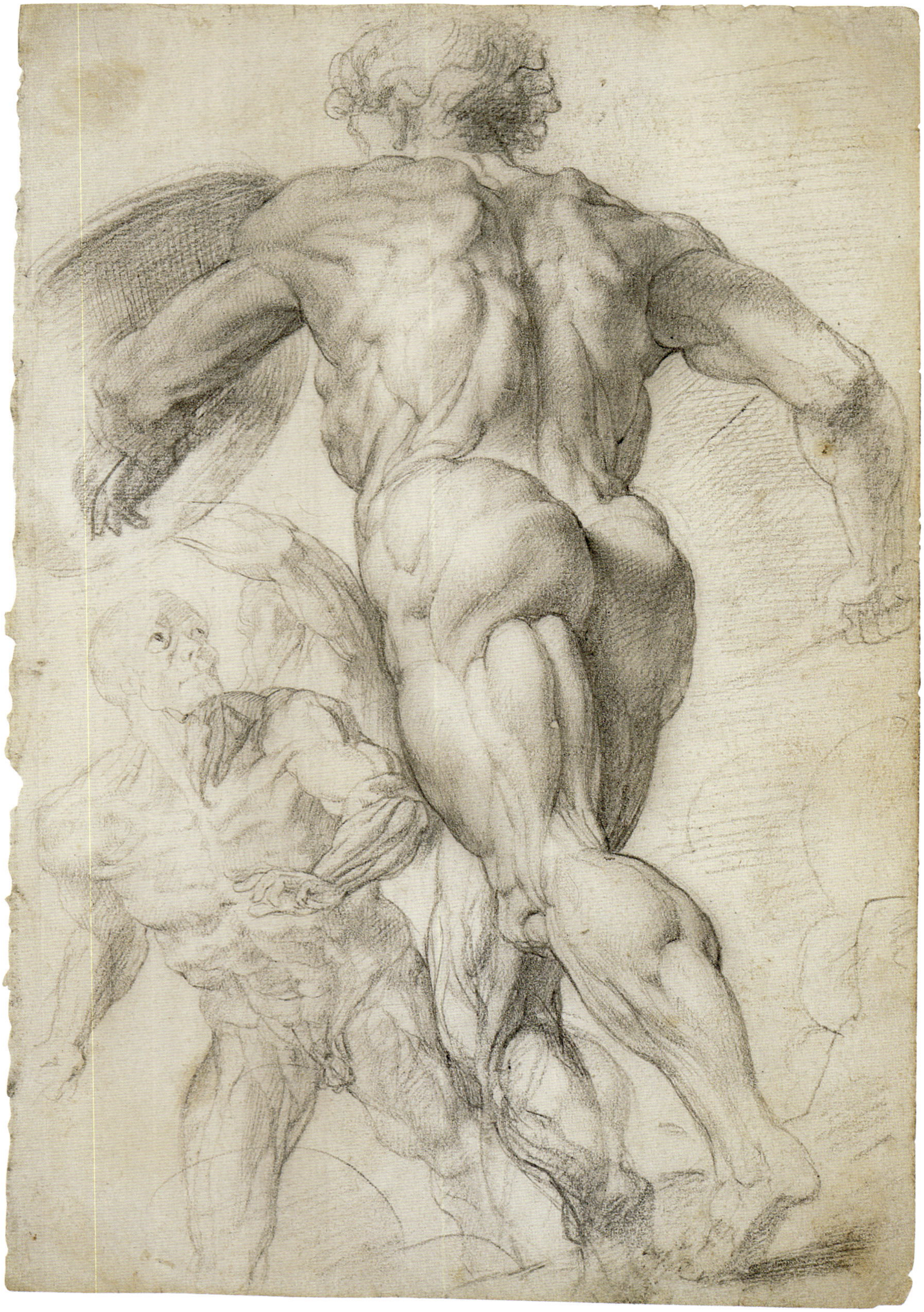

100
PETER PAUL RUBENS
(1577–1640)
Study of three écorché nudes in combat
c. 1608–10
Black chalk, 29.1 × 20 cm
The Thomson Collection, Art Gallery of Ontario, Toronto

ancient sculpture known as the Borghese *Warrior* (see fig. 120). The redrafting of his calf blurs the line between the use of the model and imagination. The design on the recto of the drawing mentioned above (fig. 102) relates to the upper arm and elbow of the soldier holding the sword (fig. 101).[25] Rubens clearly enjoyed painting the musculature of this sword-wielding soldier and introduced a fantasy loop of muscle above his shoulderblade characteristic of his expansive interpretation of Tetrode's flayed figure. This swordsman can be read as a bird's-eye view of the Tetrode. Since Rubens was especially gifted at taking a source pose from another artist and then moving the limbs to any desired position to suit his composition these almost literal quotations must be seen as a homage. Such is his skill, it is hard to distinguish when he is freely manipulating the flayed models and when he is using life models for his human poses.

The figure of the soldier being scratched, which is also inspired by Tetrode's *Horse-tamer*, is possibly the least satisfactory figure in the *Massacre*. The play of energy has become too complicated: he runs on tiptoes tugging at a baby's swaddling clothes, reeling back from the mother's scratch. It seems as if Rubens was intent on showing off his sculptural knowledge and his allegiance to Tetrode's écorché to the

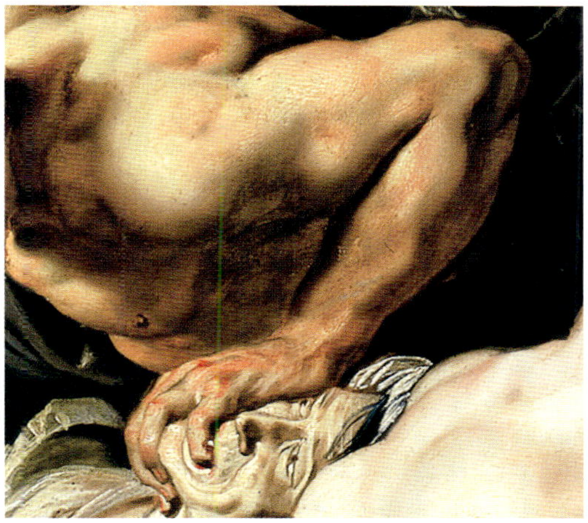

101
PETER PAUL RUBENS
The Massacre of the nnocents, detail

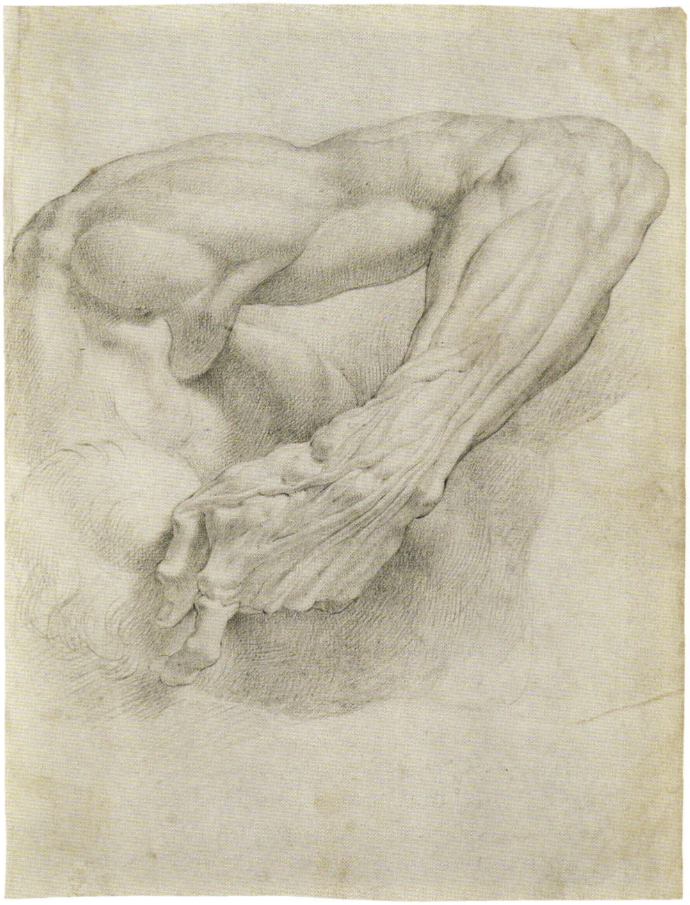

102
PETER PAUL RUBENS
(1577–1640)
Anatomical Study of an Arm (recto of fig. 99)
c. 1608–10
Black chalk
26.4 × 19.6 cm
The Thomson Collection, Art Gallery of Ontario, Toronto

103
PETER PAUL RUBENS
The Massacre of the Innocents, detail

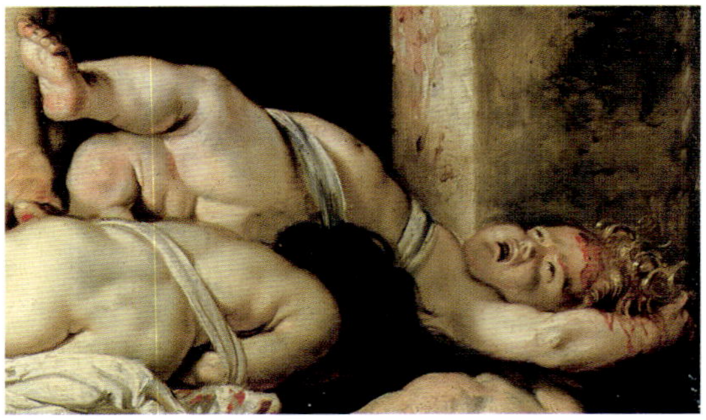

detriment of the composition. The infant at the base of the plinth is, apart from its arm, a rotation of the same pose with one leg up, one pointed forward and the torso twisted (fig. 103). Rubens used the *Horse-tamer* pose not only in the *Massacre* but again in *Tarquin and Lucretia* (see fig. 38), in which the torso leans forward rather than back, and in other dynamic compositions of this time, such as *The Transfiguration* (*c.* 1605; Nancy) and *The Conversion of Saul* (*c.* 1612; Courtauld Gallery, London).[26]

There are various instances of Rubens using drawings like these over a period of years in successive commissions, and this ability to use the same models in new guises and poses repeatedly is one of the most important features of his work. Rubens was a genius at stage-managing both elements from earlier compositions and those drawn from heterogeneous sources: he assimilated these with ease to develop his own unique style.

Many of the sheets in the sketchbook copies show imaginative doodles and explorations of sequential movement similar to those in Rubens's autograph drawings. He continually made alterations in working up an idea towards a solution. Rubens's studies for *The Labours of Hercules* (see fig. 104) constitute progressive sequences, in which Hercules and Antaeus and the Nemean lion are tilted, rotated and bent to explore the energy of a curved back and to find the perfect composition. A similar change of pose occurs between the *Raising of the Cross* oil-sketch (Louvre) and the final version of the work, in the figure of the man lifting the cross under Christ's body (the leg change is rehearsed in the 'Van Dyck' copy of the sketchbook, f. 40v). The sheet of *Dancing Peasants* (British Museum, inv. 1885-5-9-50, recto) is another graphic exploration of the sequences of a dance, one which he used for the rollicking peasants in the Louvre's *Kermesse* of 1630–36.

Rubens quickly became an exponent of the oil-sketch as a means towards resolving a composition. Polidoro da Caravaggio, a pupil of Raphael, was one of the earliest artists to use the oil-sketch as part of the creative process. Frans Floris, Rubens's Flemish predecessor, is known to have painted studies of heads and Rubens's teacher, Otto van Veen, made oil-sketches on paper. It was the Venetians in particular, though, who were most revered for painting in this way and Rubens owned oil-sketches by Tintoretto, Titian and Veronese.[27] Andrea Schiavone, who worked in Venice in the 1550s, produced various oil-sketches which became sought after by other artists, and the Sienese painter Beccafumi and the Emilian Parmigianino also produced them. In Parmigianino's paintings the virtuoso abbreviations found in the sketch migrate across to the broadly finished work itself. This same sketchiness can be found in the *Massacre*, particularly in the dead child at the bottom right, where sheaves of unblended brushwork are left in a spontaneous state.

This discussion of oil-sketches serves to remind us that Rubens may have made a painted sketch for his *Massacre* composition that has since been lost. Oil sketches exist for *The Circumcision*, 1606, the Santa Maria in Vallicella altarpiece, 1608, the *Samson and Delilah*, *The Raising of the Cross* and *The Recognition of Philopoemen*, c. 1609. Under *The Capture of Samson* (fig. 107) there is a second oil-sketch, for his 1609 *Adoration of the Magi*. Even at this early stage Rubens clearly regarded the oil-sketch as an important step in refining the compositional structure for a finished painting, and it is intriguing to imagine the sketches that Rubens might have prepared in this instance. He might have worked up an oil-sketch based on images from his Italian sketchbook, his expanding bank of drawings after the antique, and his detailed anatomical studies. Rubens drew in paint with as much ease as he used black or red chalk to record his ideas, and referred to his oil-sketches as coloured inventions. On March 19, 1614 he wrote to Archduke Albert: "Thanks to his extremely good memory, the Archduke

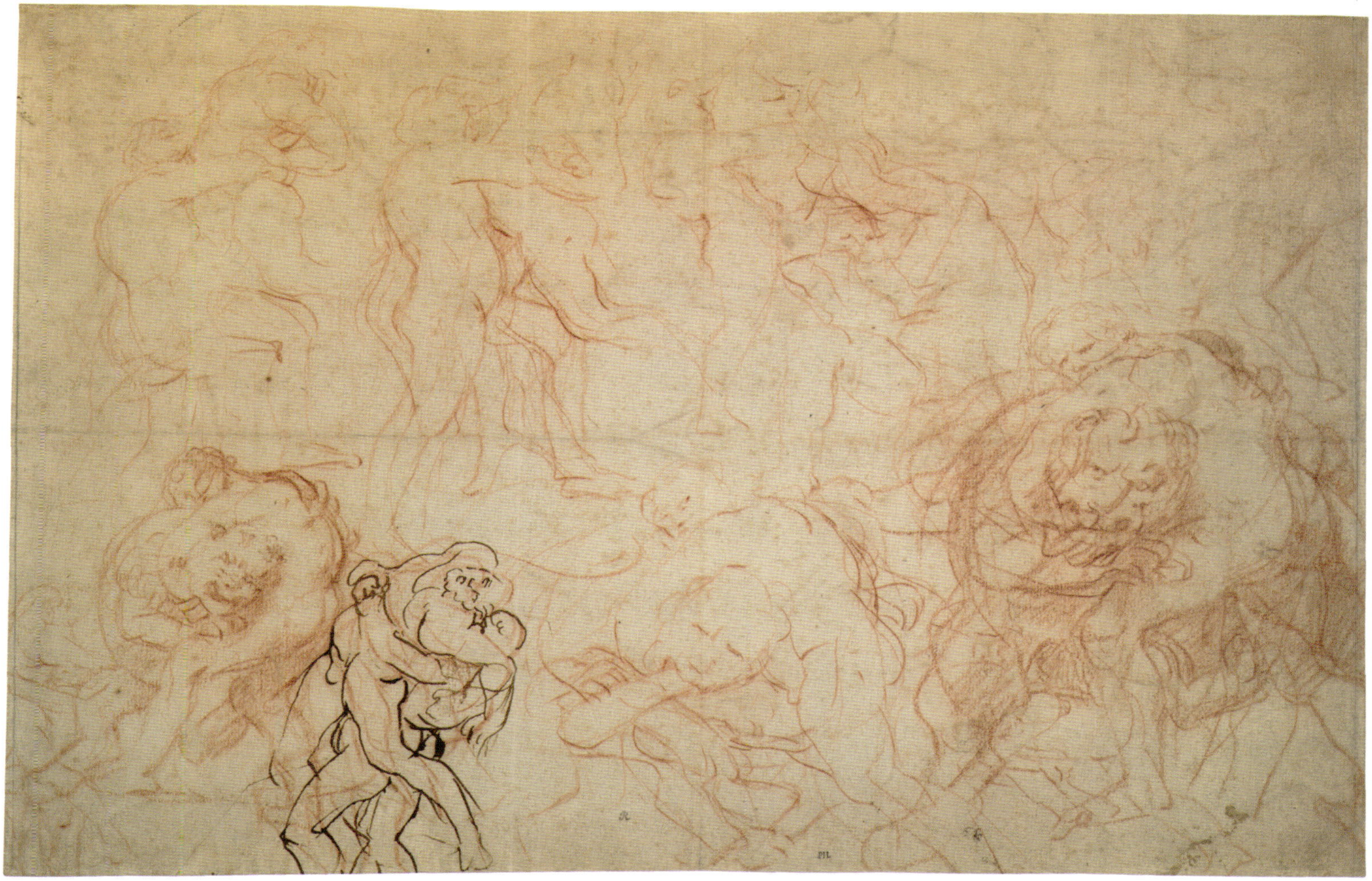

104
PETER PAUL RUBENS
(1577–1640)
Studies for the Labours of Hercules: Hercules struggling with Antaeus and (below, three sketches) Hercules and the Lion
c. 1600–08
Red chalk, with some pen and brown ink
31.1 × 47 cm
The British Museum, London
AN186736001

105
PETER PAUL RUBENS
(1577–1640)
The Descent from the Cross
c. 1602
Pen and brush and brown wash over sketch in black chalk
43.5 × 38 cm
The State Hermitage Museum, St Petersburg
OR-5496

must remember well having seen, two years ago, a coloured design [*dissegno colorito*], done by my hand, to serve for the triptych of the high altar of the Cathedral at Ghent." (*Saint Bavo about to receive the Monastic Habit* in the National Gallery, London, is probably the oil-sketch in question, or there may have been an earlier now lost study.)[28]

Of course Rubens's oil-sketches also served as presentation pieces to impress patrons or as records for projected engravings: a sketch of *The Descent from the Cross* (fig. 106) which is very close to the finished work (see fig. 16) is probably one such example. In 1611 Rubens presented two painted *modelli* to win the commisson of *The Assumption of the Virgin* for the high altar of Antwerp Cathedral. At other times an oil-sketch was in effect a brush drawing in brown which happened to be on panel. In *A Lion Hunt* (see fig. 66) Rubens changed the lion's angle of attack in the centre of the painting and then reworked it in a thumbnail sketch in the upper right-hand corner. Sometimes a drawing such as the *Descent* in St Petersburg (fig. 105) can consolidate many of his earlier ideas while carrying written tags for visual sources he wishes to include (in this case a note in the upper left portion of the drawing of the figure leaning over the crossbar

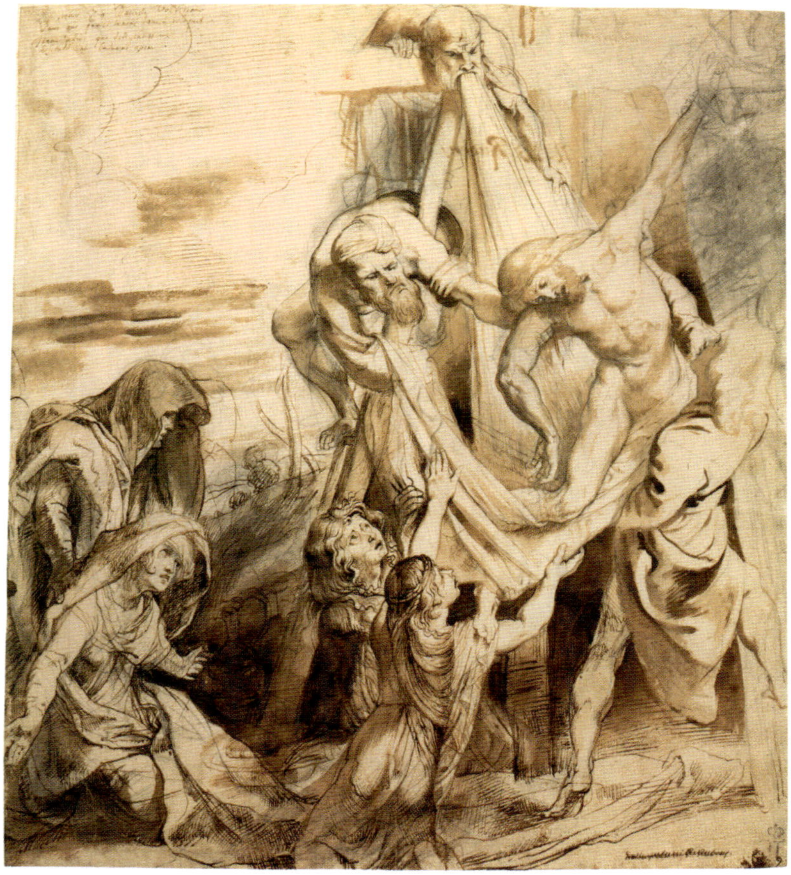

106
PETER PAUL RUBENS
(1577–1640)
The Descent from the Cross
(central panel of triptych), 1611–12
Oil on panel
115.2 × 76.2 cm
Courtauld Gallery, London
P.1947.LF.359

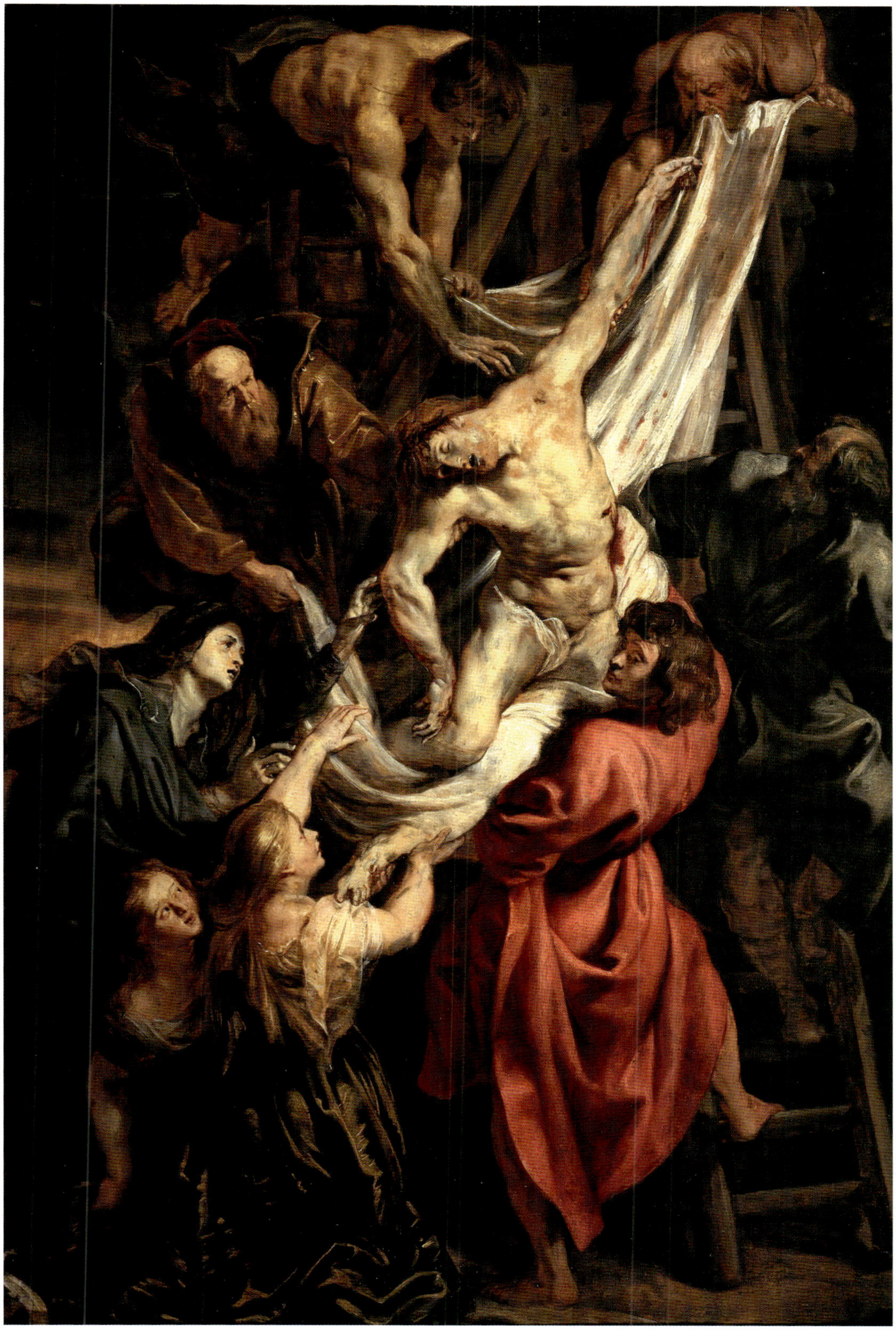

107
PETER PAUL RUBENS
(1577–1640)
The Capture of Samson
1609–10
Oil on panel
50.4 × 66.4 cm
Robert A. Waller Memorial Fund,
The Art Institute of Chicago
inv. no. 1923.551

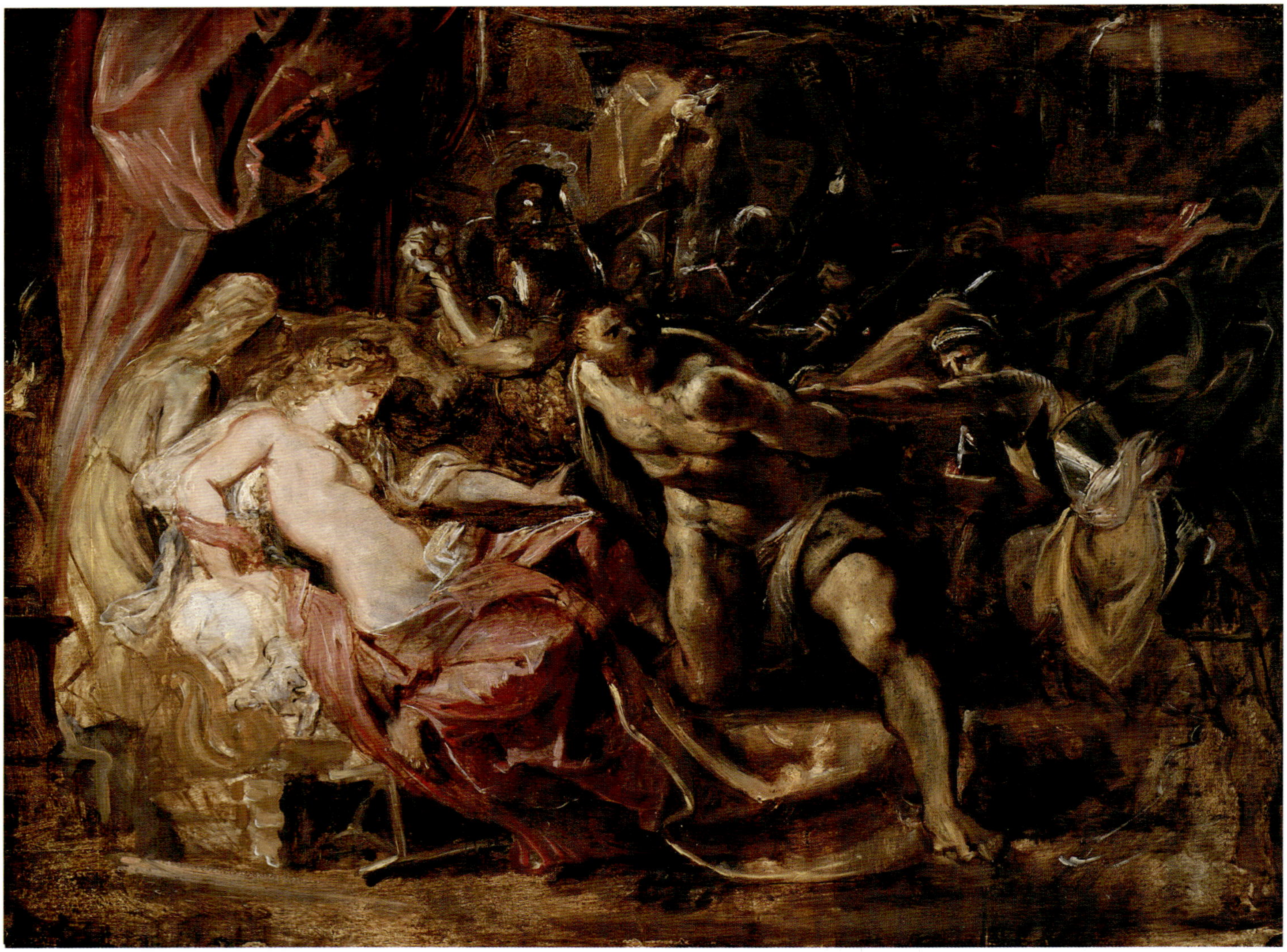

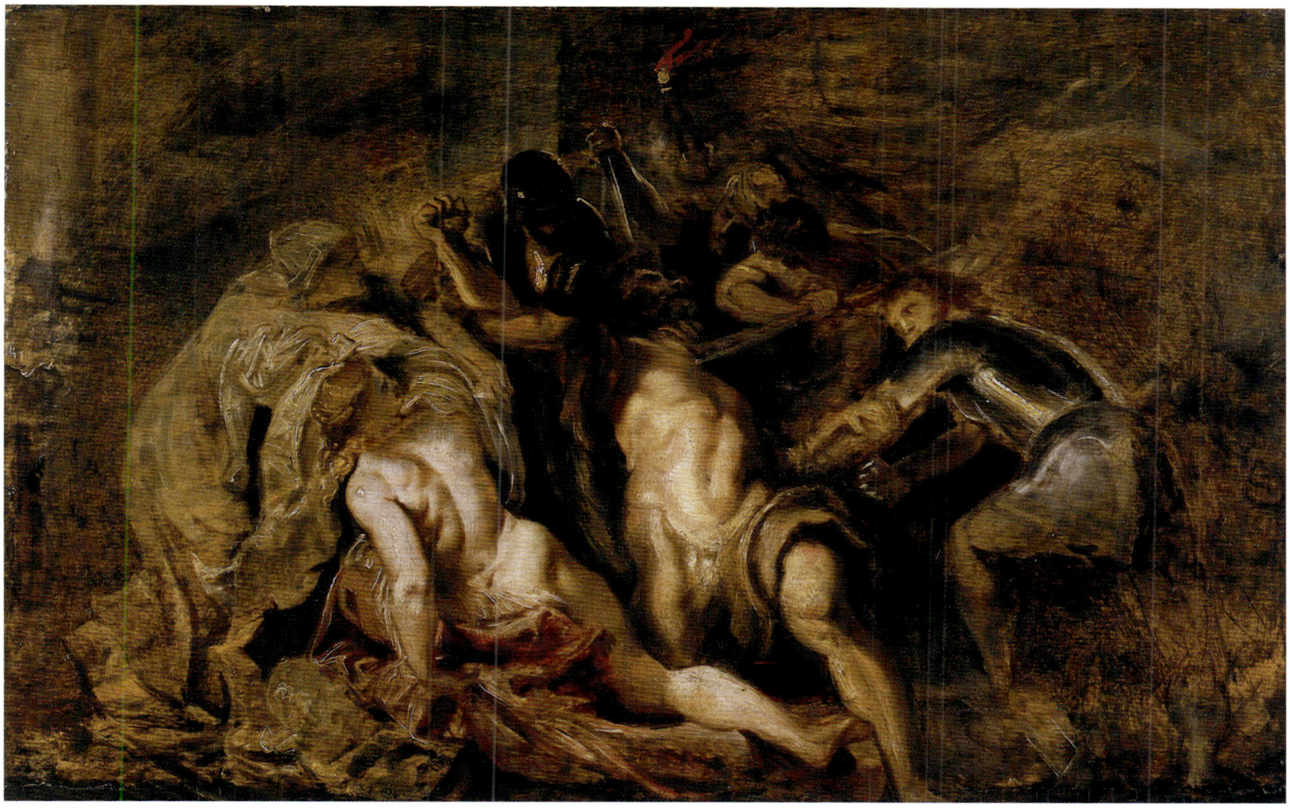

108
PETER PAUL RUBENS
(1577–1640)
The Blinding of Samson
1609–10
Oil on panel
37.5 × 58.5 cm
Museo Thyssen-Bornemisza,
Madrid

from Daniele da Volterra's painting of the subject in Santa Trinità in Rome), and in this way anticipates the oil-sketch (fig. 106).

We have two oil-sketches showing different episodes from the story of Samson and Delilah. *The Blinding of Samson* in Madrid (fig. 108) depicts the violent cleaving apart of the counterposed lovers.[29] The sketch of *The Capture of Samson* in Chicago (fig. 107) – with Delilah in a pose recalling Michelangelo's *Leda* and approaching that seen in the National Gallery *Samson and Delilah* (see fig. 45) – also bears some similarities to the *Massacre*. Samson is shown lunging forward, one leg projected in front and the other bent behind him; he is similar in physique to the soldier wielding the infant in the *Massacre* and to *Prometheus* (Philadelphia Art Museum).

Rubens's need for worked-up oil-sketches grew in later years, owing to the increasing size of the projects he undertook (such as the Banqueting House ceiling in London and the Marie de Médicis cycle in Paris) and the complexity of multi-figure compositions which themselves might form part of a larger cycle of work. In later years, Rubens's oil-sketches also provided a template allowing his compositions to be consistently produced by his studio.[30] This would not have been the case with the *Massacre*, which, as noted already, is entirely autograph. Any preparatory oil-sketch would have been used for resolving the design (or possibly for marketing purposes). The fact that Rubens used the panel itself to alter his design, however, by blocking in and then removing the figure of the mounted commander, is perhaps the strongest evidence that he did not in fact use an oil-sketch to prepare his composition for the *Massacre*.

Rubens returned to the subject of the Massacre of the Innocents in about 1635.[31] The picture, now in the Alte Pinakothek, Munich (fig. 109), is quite different in feel from the Thomson Collection picture. It is much more fluidly painted, as is typical of this later date, with loose, dry brushwork and a shimmering palette. The later version, in contrast to the relentless killing frenzy of the earlier treatment, offers some promise of divine redemption in the angels who scatter the young martyrs with rose petals.[32] The nucleus of figures in the early work disperses into several groups in the later version, although both images climax in the raised arms of a protagonist (which in the later version is a central female figure holding up a bloody veil rather than a dead child). Infants in contemporary smocks have replaced the more authentically *all'antica* swaddling clothes of the earlier version, in keeping with the almost low-life realism which suffuses the later work. The pose of the Laocoön-type besieged executioner to the left appears to be a rewriting of the soldier on the far right of the earlier panel version. In general the ennobling classical forms of the early *Massacre* have been replaced by a more animalistic struggle in the Munich painting, in which Rubens revisits Floris's formulation (fig. 61) and also his own summary of Paggi's arm-biting woman (see figs. 58, 84) for the same motif on the top right of this painting.

In the late seventeenth century some French critics did not approve of the late version of the *Massacre*, then in the duc de Richelieu's collection. They found the Flemish landscape and architecture of the Munich picture an unlikely representation of Bethlehem.[33] One suspects Rubens's grand cityscape in the early *Massacre*, with its mixture of ancient Roman and Renaissance palaces, would have raised the same eyebrows. Such criticism misses the point, however, because, in constructing this landscape, Rubens did not try to recreate an authentic Palestine. Instead he displayed his knowledge of Western culture. Accordingly, the Renaissance antiquarian Sebastiano Serlio's reconstruction of Vitruvius's cityscapes and Flemish reactions to it (such as Maarten de Vos's *Tribute Money* in the Koninklijk Museum voor Schone Kunsten, Antwerp) are more relevant comparisons.

In both versions Rubens was searching for the most dramatic presentation of the striking action. Always an action painter, Rubens has shifted from a Herculean idealization to a much more Flemish earthy brawl, with the mothers decked out in the latest hairstyles and dresses to facilitate the audience's identification with their anger and grief.[34]

109
PETER PAUL RUBENS
(1577–1640)
The Massacre of the Innocents
c. 1635
Oil on oak
199 × 302 cm
Alte Pinakothek, Munich

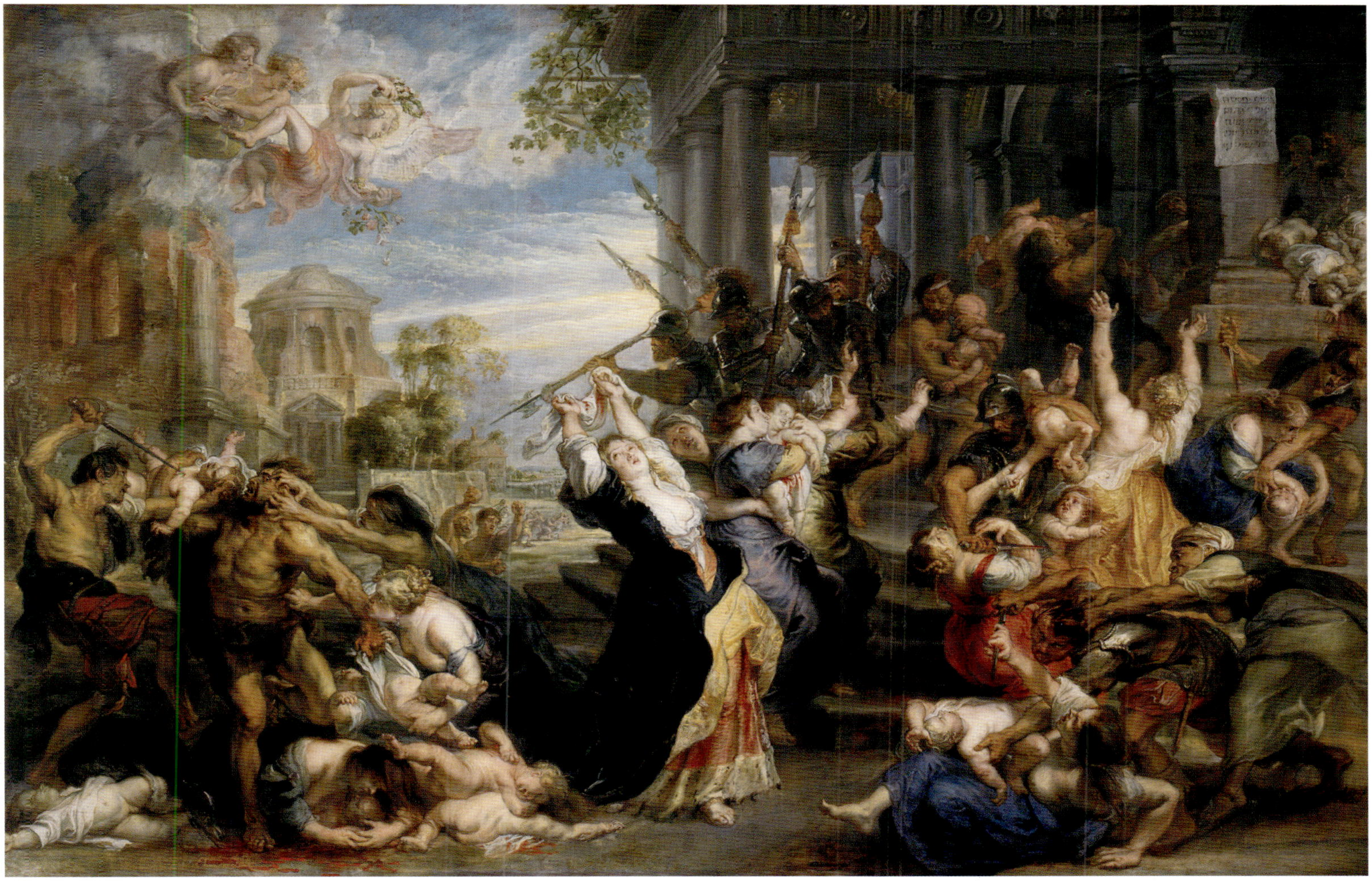

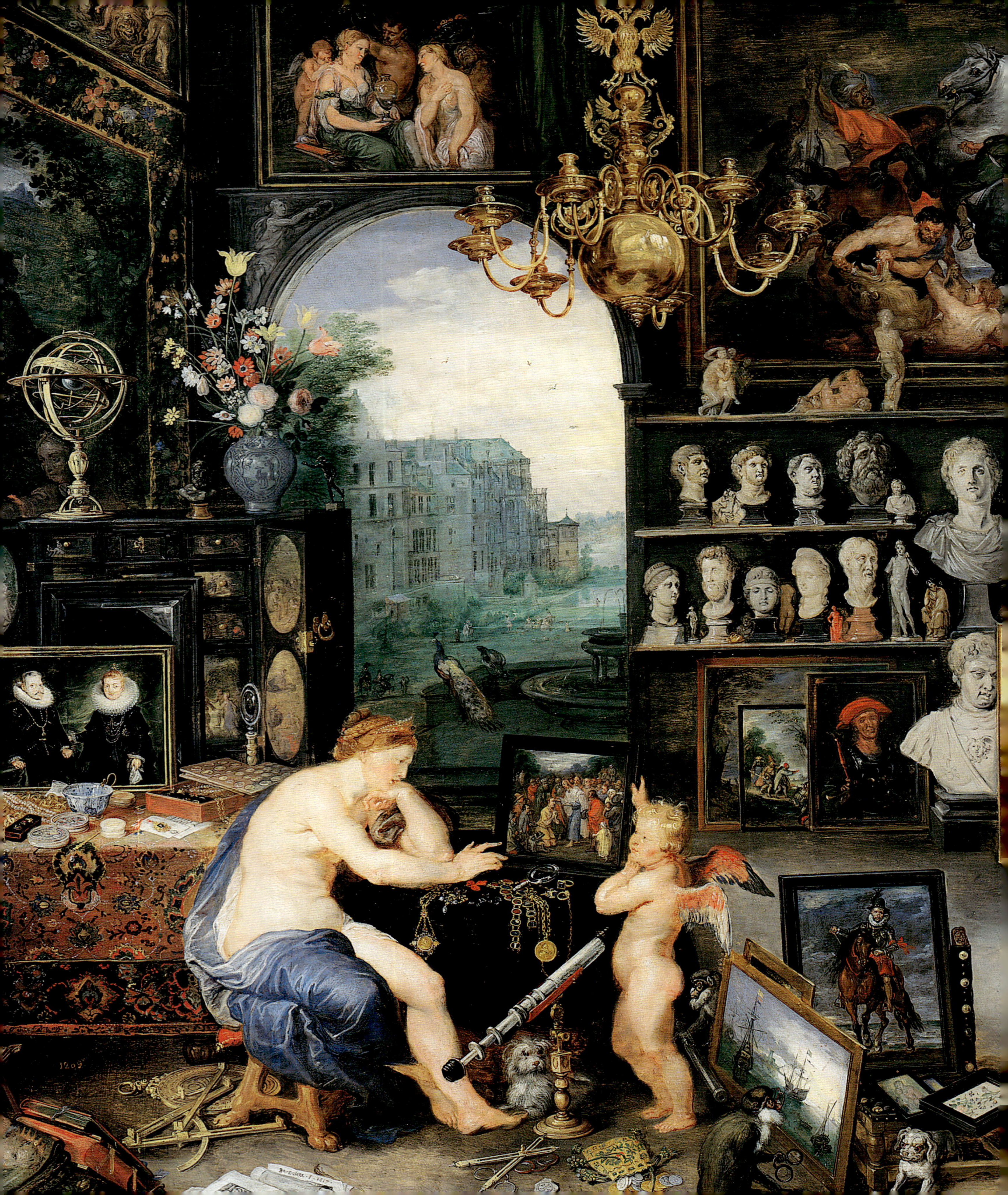

The inspiration of Antiquity

Nicolas-Claude Fabri de Peiresc, the French savant and friend of Rubens, wrote that "in matters of antiquity he [Rubens] possesses the most universal and remarkable knowledge I have ever seen."[1] This was no small compliment coming from one of the most eminent antiquarians of the day. Rubens was fascinated by the study of the antique throughout his life and it influenced the way he spoke and wrote, his circle of friends and, of course, his art. At an early age he was sent to the famous school of Rombout Verdonck in Antwerp, where he attained a proficiency in Greek and became very well versed in Latin. Rubens added appropriate Latin quotations to his sketches and drawings, and often paired iconographical references with Latin text. His sketches of Roman emperors show both erudition and imagination – for example, his drawing of the frenzied Domitian stabbing flies with his pencil is inscribed with the words "*ne musca [quidem]*" (not even a fly . . .), taken from Suetonius's *Life*.[2]

Such a level of humanist learning and culture was expected amongst the educated elite in Antwerp. Jan Caspar Gevaerts (Gevartius), the Secretary of the City of Antwerp, was, in addition to his civic duties, an internationally renowned classical scholar. He had written, though not published, a commentary on the writings of Marcus Aurelius and we know that Rubens had tried to assist him with his research.[3] Rubens painted Gevaerts seated, pen in hand, before a bust of the emperor (fig. 110), reminding the viewer both of the sitter's learning and of the subject that engaged him.[4]

Christopher Plantin, who arrived in Antwerp in 1549, founded the Plantin press, which was responsible for the publication of numerous scholarly texts, classical works and translations. Later inherited by his learned grandson, Balthasar Moretus, the Plantin press became a centre of intellectual thought in Northern Europe as well as a meeting place for scholars. The famous Neo-Stoic philosopher Justus Lipsius became such a frequent visitor that the guest room in the Plantin house was christened the Lipsius room.

Antwerp was a hub of learning and scholarship and an ideal place for the young Rubens to pursue his interests in the antique. His enthusiasm for classical antiquity was shared with his brother Philip, who, before he died at the age of thirty-seven, was perhaps Justus Lipsius's most eminent pupil and one of the greatest scholarly hopes of his day. The brothers collaborated on a book entitled *Electorum Libri II* (published in Antwerp in 1608), which included essays on ancient life and discussions of ancient language and life. Peter Paul provided five illustrations for the book and it is likely that he also contributed to its intellectual content, interpreting passages of classical text using surviving images.

Rubens owned an extensive library. Although none of his own inventories survive, we have a good idea of the books he read from Plantin press invoices, references in his own letters and from an auction catalogue of books owned by his eldest son, Albert, which would have included books inherited

The Sense of Sight
(detail of fig. 119)

110
PETER PAUL RUBENS
(1577–1640)
Jan Caspar Gevaerts
c. 1628
Oil on panel
119 × 98 cm
Koninklijk Museum voor Schone Kunsten, Antwerp

111
PETER PAUL RUBENS
(1577–1640)
The Death of Seneca
c. 1611
Oil on oak
185 × 154.7 cm
Bayerische Staatsgemäldesammlungen, Alte Pinakothek, Munich

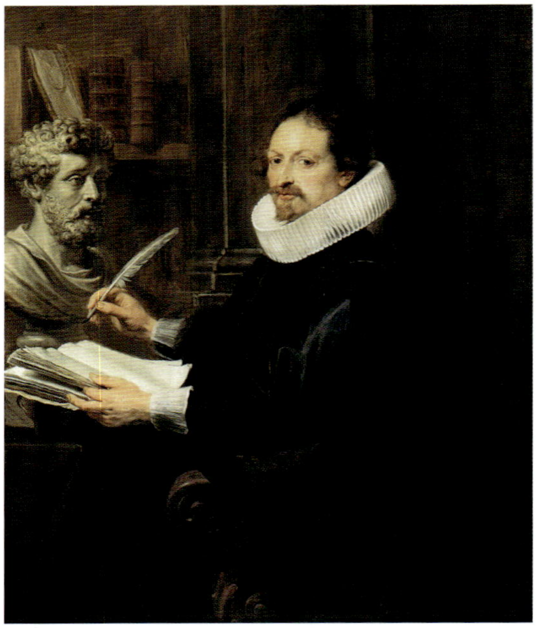

from his father.[5] His library included works by Virgil, Ovid, Pliny, Herodotus, Thucydides and all the Roman historians, alongside volumes on an eclectic range of subjects typical of the interests of a seventeenth-century scholar, such as natural history, geology and hieroglyphs. It has been shown, too, that Rubens acquired books as he needed them to research particular painting projects: so, for example, he collected natural history books when he was working on hunt scenes, and he obviously enjoyed the intellectual exercise of designing erudite frontispieces for new publications.[6]

Rubens's library was integral to his creative process, just as the study of classical literature was intimately connected with the study and understanding of antique sculpture. Rubens built a semi-circular room on to the back of his house in order to accommodate his growing collection of antiquities. The room was lit by an oculus recalling that of the Pantheon in Rome. In 1618 Rubens acquired the collection of Dudley Carleton, the English ambassador in the Hague, which would have greatly supplemented his existing works in both quality and number. Items from Rubens's antiquities collection such as his marble bust of 'Seneca' often feature in his paintings.[7] Rubens brought the bust back with him from Italy and it appears in a number of his works. He used it as a model for engravings, including the title page of Lipsius's *Annaei Senecae ... Opera ... Omnia* (1615, engraved by Cornelis I Galle) and for part of a print series of twelve *Famous Greek and Roman Men* (published 1638, engraved by Lucas I Vorsterman). It was used most memorably in *The Four Philosophers* (see fig. 9) and *The Death of Seneca* (fig. 111).[8] In the latter, Rubens typically takes the sculptural design and animates the surface to enhance the portrait. Using his own 'worm's-eye' drawing of the marble bust he also inserted the image in the final painting of Saint Ignatius of Loyola which he made around 1618 for the high altar of the Jesuit church in Antwerp (now in the Kunsthistorisches Museum, Vienna).[9] As we have seen, such learned embellishments were often added by Rubens between oil-sketch and the finished work or recording engraving. The bust is possibly the same object that is now in the collection of the Rubenshuis. (In fact the bust is no longer believed to be of Seneca; it was identified in 1813 as a Roman copy after a Hellenistic bronze.)

In the depiction of Seneca's suicide at the behest of Nero,[10] Rubens eloquently conveys the philosopher's resolve to endure death without yielding to fear or self-pity. The body of Seneca was modelled on an antique sculpture then in the collection of Cardinal Scipio Borghese (now Louvre) and believed at the time to represent the *Dying Seneca* (now known as *An African Fisherman*).[11] Rubens made detailed studies of this black stone statue showing an emaciated old man with prominent veins.

As well as antique sculpture, Rubens collected cameos and engraved gems. We know this was a lifetime pursuit, as he was already drawing a

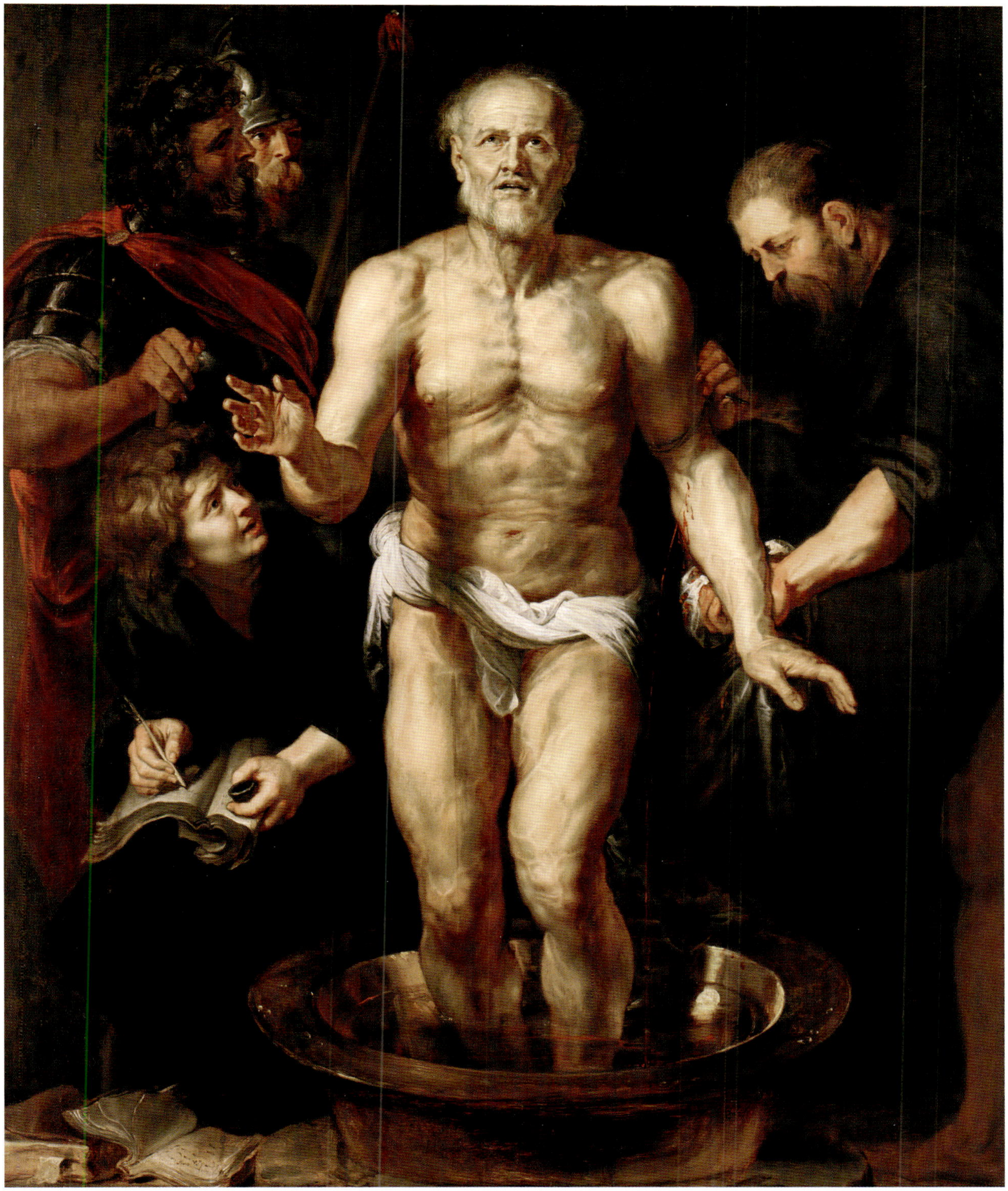

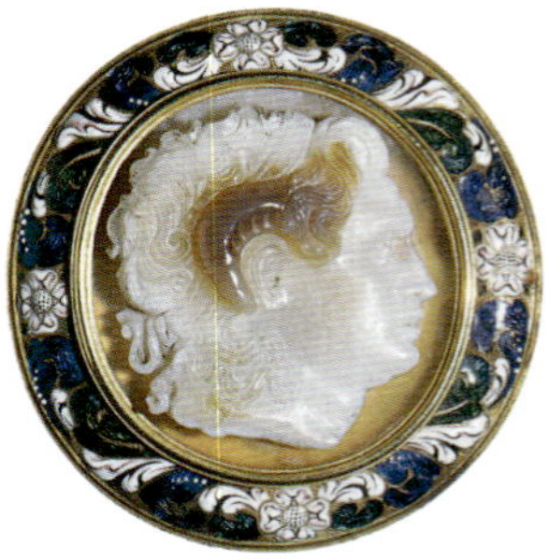

112
Roman, 1st century AD
Jupiter Ammon
Leopard sardonyx
9.3 × 7.9 cm
Bibliothèque nationale de France, Paris

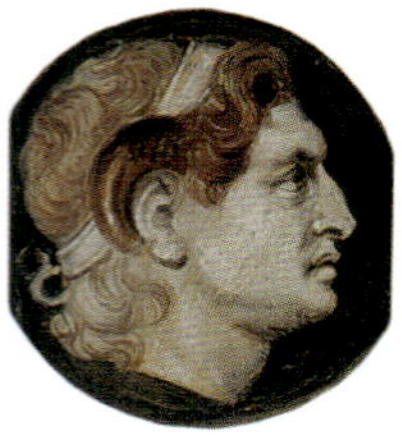

113
PETER PAUL RUBENS
(1577–1640)
Jupiter Ammon, *c.* 1606
Bodycolour on board
6.1 × 4.9 cm
Museum Briner und Kern (Stiftung Jakob Briner), Winterthur

beautiful cameo of Jupiter Ammon (figs. 112, 113) in about 1606 and much later in his life recalled handling the Gemma Augustea (fig. 114), then owned by the Gonzaga, when he was in Mantua between 1600 and 1606. He owned some of the most spectacular gems then known, such as *The Wedding of Psyche* (now Museum of Fine Arts, Boston) and *Messalina*. He also owned cameos of *The Triumph of Constantine*, *The Triumph of Luna*, *Harpocrates* and *The Hunt of Marcus Aurelius* and was an authority on the identification of the subject-matter of such glyptic material. Gems were the most sought-after antiquities in the seventeenth century and casts and drawings of these small, jewel-like carvings were often exchanged by scholars.[12]

Rubens's collection of antiquities was apparently not just for study, for he once confided in Peiresc that he used his cherished silver spoon depicting Mercury to feed his wife during her confinement. Peiresc had discovered the original Roman spoon from which Rubens's example was skilfully replicated (now in the Bibliothèque nationale, Médailles, Paris).[13] The incident shows how deeply immersed in the antique he was and also that the demand for ancient material spawned an industry for forgeries. Rubens brought back from Rome an early Christian sarcophagus which showed an infant wrapped in swaddling clothes and this imagery may well have influenced the design for the infants' swaddling in the *Massacre*.[14]

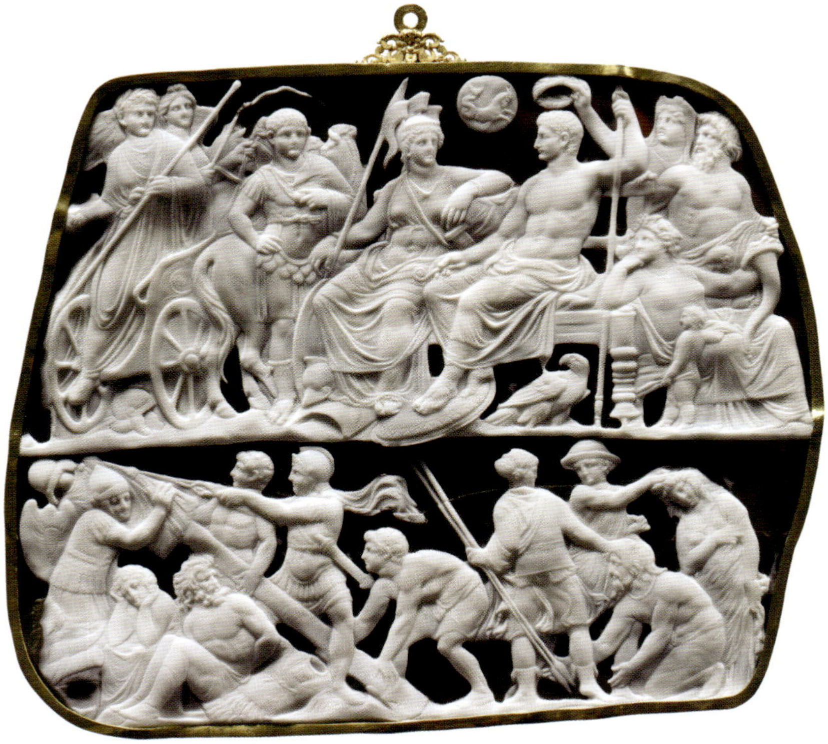

114
Roman, after AD 10
Gemma Augustea
Two-layered onyx; setting, gold frame
19 × 23 cm
Kunsthistorisches Museum, Vienna

The greatest accolade one could bestow upon a painter was to describe him as the 'new Apelles,' a reference to the revered ancient Greek painter who lived in the first half of the fourth century BC and was a favourite of Alexander the Great. Rubens had already been described in such terms in 1611 but nothing by this antique painter had survived and no-one knew what the works looked like. Classical texts, which were often brief references rather than extended descriptions, were the only source of information.[15] Pliny the Elder's *Natural History* (35, 86–87) and, to a lesser extent, the works of Lucian were the prime sources for descriptions of Apelles's paintings.

On August 1, 1637 Rubens wrote to Franciscus Junius, who had just published a compendium of ancient written sources on art: "Who amongst us, if he were to attempt in reality to represent a celebrated work of Apelles or Timanthus, such as Pliny describes them, but would produce something absurd, or perfectly foreign to the exalted greatness of the ancients? Each one, relying on his own powers, would produce some wretched, crude, unfermented stuff, instead of an exquisite old wine, uniting strength and mellowness, outraging those great spirits whom I endeavour reverently to follow, satisfied, however, to honour the marks of their footsteps, instead of supposing – I acknowledge it candidly – that I can ever attain to their eminence even in mere conception." Rubens's mention of the fourth-century BC artist Timanthes (or Timanthus) is worthy of comment. Pliny's account (35, 74) of that ancient artist's painting of *The Sacrifice of Iphigenia* proved particularly evocative for artists of the Renaissance and onwards and Rubens probably supplemented his knowledge of the lost work by also reading the response of the orators Cicero and Quintilian to it.[16] Timanthes was famed for his depiction of emotion and with *The Sacrifice of Iphigenia* defeated Kolotes of Teos in a competition. Iphigenia's father, Agamemnon, was compelled to sacrifice his daughter in order to appease the goddess Artemis, who was keeping the Greek fleet from leaving Aulis for Troy. Pliny describes the different expressions of distress on the participants' faces and records that Agamemnon's own face was shrouded, thus leaving the spectator to imagine his grief. This artistic device of suggesting by concealing inspired artists of the Renaissance and Baroque periods and is used by Rubens in the *Massacre*.[17]

The famous Renaissance theoretician Leon Battista Alberti suggested that this same subject, along with *The Calumny of Apelles* and *The Three Graces*, might be the highest challenge an artist could aspire to.[18] He describes how Timanthes would have "exhausted his art in showing him [Agamemnon] greatly grief stricken. Not having any way in which to show the grief of the father, he threw a drape over his head and let his most bitter grief be imagined, even though it was not seen." Rubens himself attempted to recreate Timanthes's picture, in one of a series of *grisaille* paintings depicting the lives of the Greek artists and their works

115
PETER PAUL RUBENS
The Massacre of the Innocents, detail

116
MICHELANGELO DA CARAVAGGIO (1571–1610)
The Death of the Virgin
detail of fig. 13

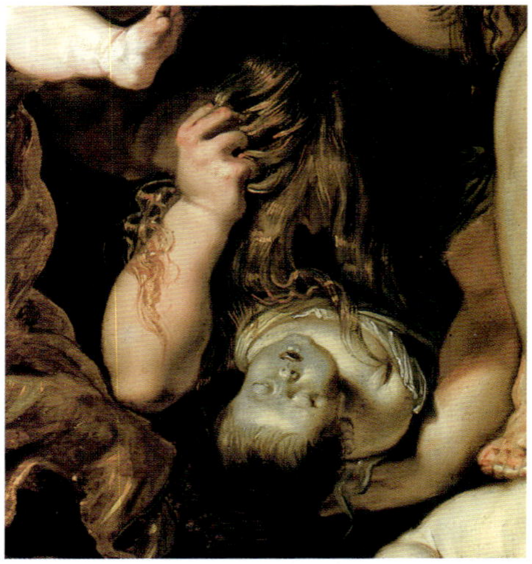

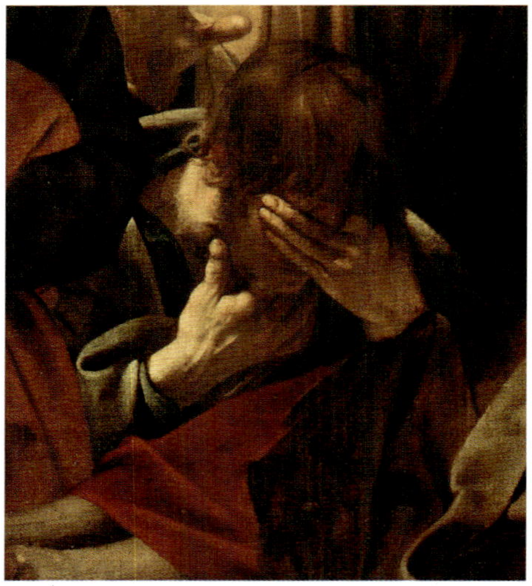

on the façade of his own house around 1618–21. Sadly, these have been lost and we only have desiccated prints and drawings after them with which to reconstruct Rubens's interpretation of this most famous antique subject.

Timanthes's device of subtle insinuation rather than overt illustration can be traced in the *Massacre*. In the lower right quadrant, beneath the surging mass of figures, a mother crouches cradling her dead child, her face not obscured by a cloak but by her hair, which she wrenches in grief (fig. 115). We have seen Rubens developing visual ideas for this figure in his sketchbook (see p. 98 and fig. 84), which he now merges with his textual knowledge. Her hair obscures her face in just the same way that Agamemnon's cloak obscured his. Caravaggio's *Death of the Virgin* (fig. 116) also uses this device of hiding the mourner's face to accentuate the emotion. The female figure in red in the centre of the *Massacre* is also turned away, so that we can only imagine the anger and desperation across her face, a technique which powerfully engages the mind and emotions of the viewer.

While the soldiers are portrayed as emotionless machines who make no eye contact with the terrified gaze of their victims and are deaf to their cries, the viewer's eye is directly engaged by the sightless eyes of the dead child cradled by his mother and by the backward glance of the crouching woman in white on the left. Her enticing glance invites us into the painting, as does the Sabine dressed in pink in Rubens's later *Rape of the Sabines* (National Gallery, London).

There were a few classical murals known in Rubens's time, but these did not manifest the claimed qualities of illusionism and expressiveness described in the ancient texts. Rubens's comments on a newly discovered Roman wall painting, the Barberini *Landscape*, suggest that he was sceptical of the intellectual rigour and perspectival achievements of such work.[19] Antique sculpture more reliably lived up to the expectations raised by ancient literature, and Rome was rich in ancient large figurative marbles and elaborate bas-reliefs, though for the most part ancient copies of the originals. Small-scale copies of famous sculpted works were popular with collectors, and were often displayed on tables and shelves in painted views of these interiors (fig. 119 and detail p. 118). Earlier artists, such as Amico Aspertini, had already assembled drawings after sarcophagi and other antique sculpture into sketchbooks and sought to integrate relief designs into their images. Rubens embarked upon more scholarly research and, as his collaboration with his brother on the *Electorum Libri* proves, was supremely capable of recognizing and distinguishing ancient pieces from Renaissance statuary, a skill prized by artists and admired by patrons.

Rubens's earliest paintings, made before he left for Italy in 1600, show him already responding to prints, casts and models after celebrated antique sculptures. The Potsdam *Battle of the Amazons* (fig. 121) of *c.* 1598

117, 118
Details of fig. 119, showing an oil-lamp and a bust of Hercules owned by Rockox

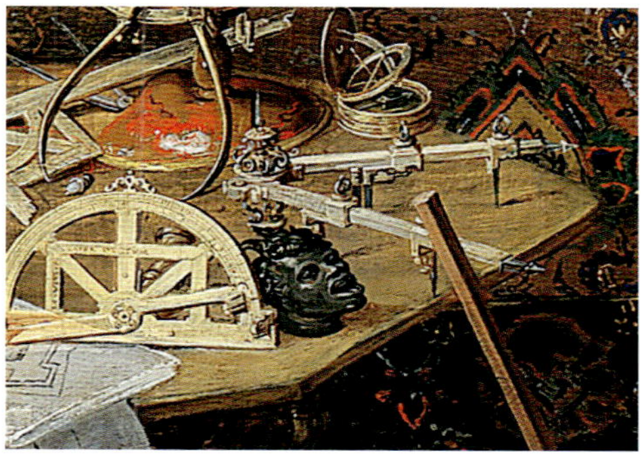

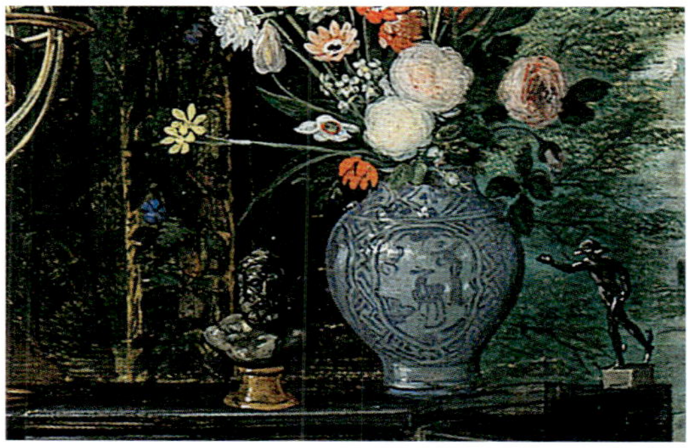

119
JAN I BRUEGHEL (1568–1625) and PETER PAUL RUBENS (1577–1640)
The Sense of Sight, 1617
Oil on panel
65 × 100 cm
Museo del Prado, Madrid

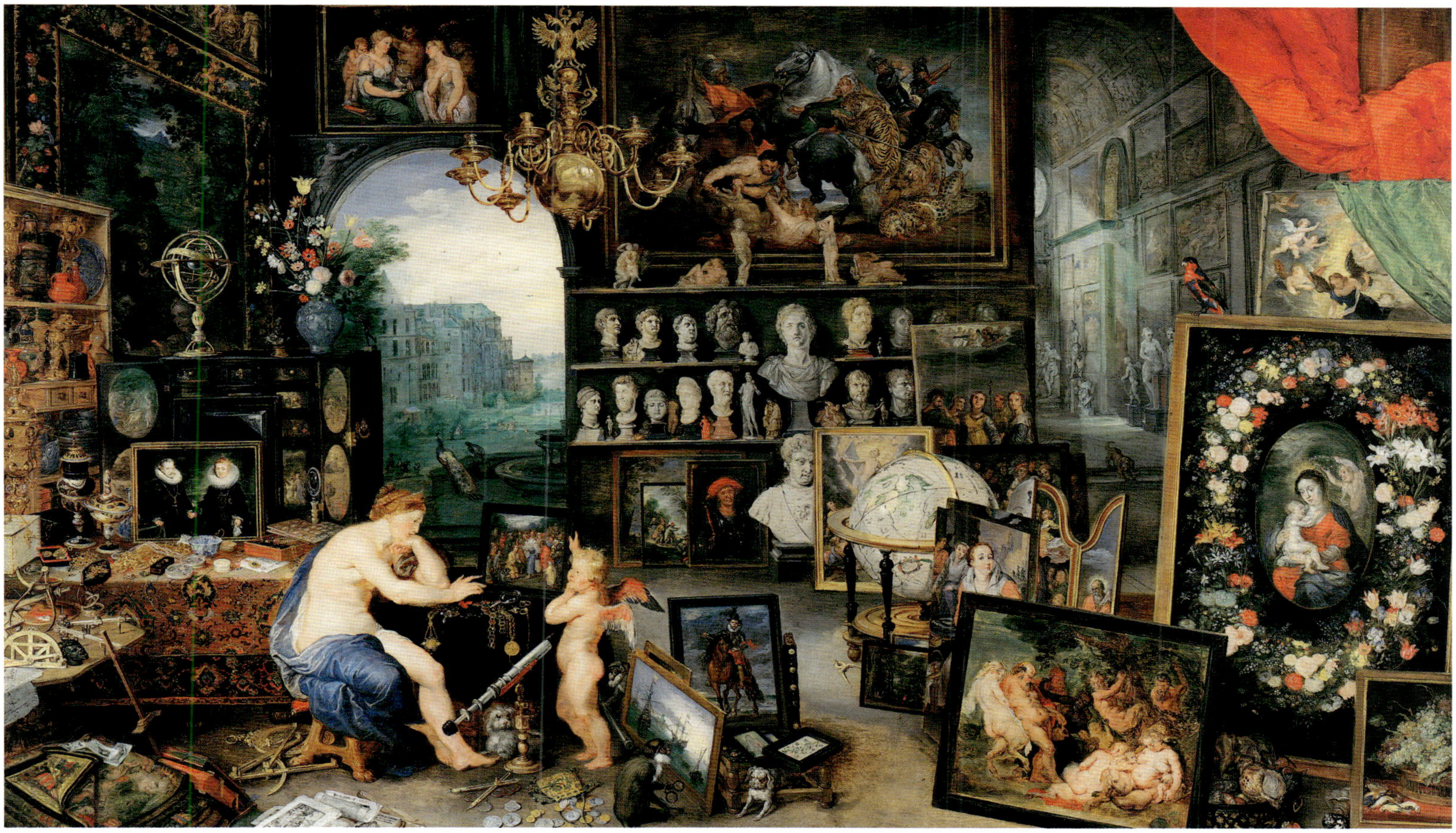

120
After AGASIAS OF EPHESUS
The Borghese Warrior
c. 50 BC
Marble
Height 199 cm
Musée du Louvre, Paris

shows both the Borghese *Warrior* (fig. 120), viewed from above (on the right, below the white horse with a pink tail) and the *Laocoön*, now recast as Hercules grasping two Amazons further to the right. Such exemplary sculptures remained an inspiration for Rubens's compositions throughout his life. It is telling that the *Laocoön* was drawn twice in Rubens's sketch-book, once copied in reverse from a print and again, in a back view, from one of the finished survey drawings Rubens made in Rome (see further below). The apparent absence of any drawing of the Borghese *Warrior* from the sketchbook suggests that Rubens acquired a model of the sculpture, a hypothesis which is confirmed by the fact that aerial views of the sculpture appear in Rubens's paintings throughout his career.[20] A drawing such as fig. 100 shows a clear reminiscence of it.

Rubens also used the famous *Horse-tamers*, then thought to be by the two greatest ancient sculptors, Phidias and Praxiteles, in the 1603 *Battle of the Amazons* (private collection) in which the rearing horse is repeated and rotated in the bottom right corner, a telling indication that a model was being used.[21] Rubens later fully exploited a worm's-eye view of this marble horse in his 1620s *Constantine defeating Maxentius at the Milvian Bridge* (oil-sketch for tapestry in the Wallace Collection, London).[22]

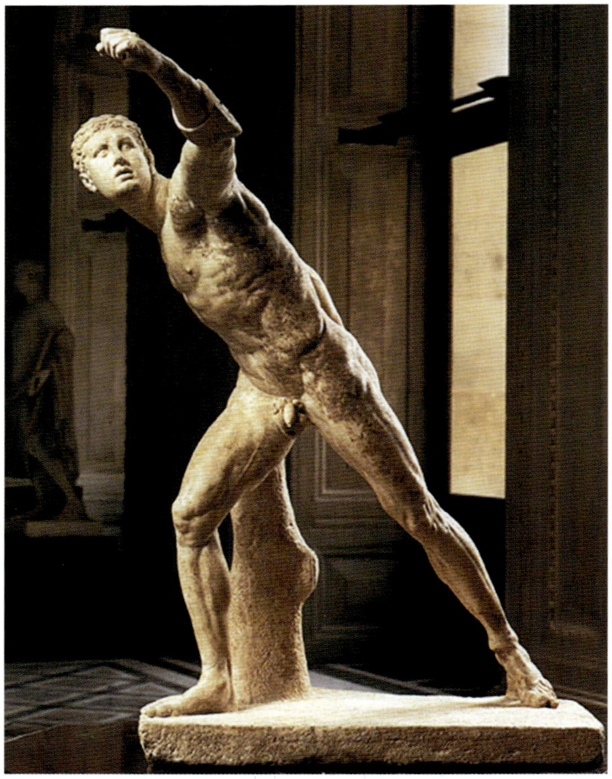

121
PETER PAUL RUBENS (1577–1640) and
JAN I BRUEGHEL (1568–1625)
The Battle of the Amazons
c. 1598
Oil on panel
97 × 124 cm
Sanssouci Bildergalerie, Potsdam
GK 10021

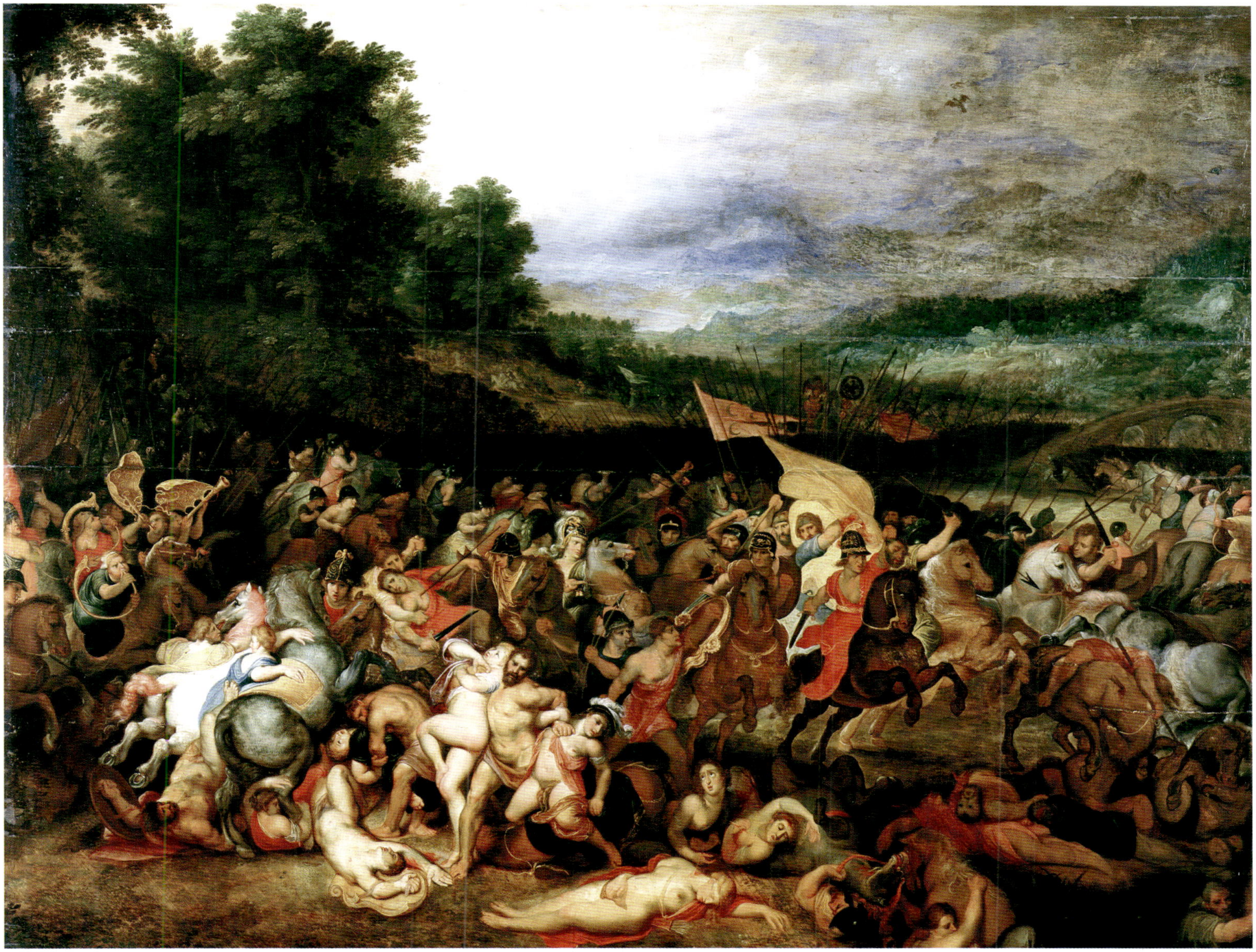

Rubens would have seen the *Laocoön* (fig. 123) in the Belvedere courtyard of the Vatican when he visited Rome in 1602. Unearthed in Rome in 1506, it depicts the story recounted in Virgil's *Aeneid* (II, 199–228) of the priest Laocoön and his sons dying a gruesome death, strangled by serpents that had been sent by Neptune to stop him warning of the dangers of accepting the Trojan Horse. We know from Pliny that the original sculpture (the one in the Vatican Museum is probably a copy from around the first century AD after a Hellenistic original), which adorned the palace of the Emperor Titus, was a work of Hagesander, Polydorus and Athenodorus of Rhodes; Pliny described it as being, "of all paintings and sculptures, the most worthy of admiration" (36, 37).[23]

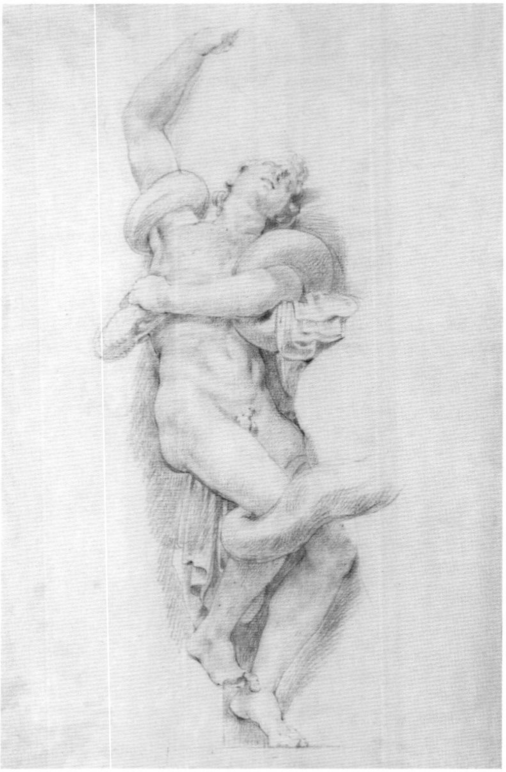

122
PETER PAUL RUBENS
(1577–1640)
The Younger Son of Laocoön seen from the Front
c. 1601–02
Black chalk
41.1 × 26 cm
Biblioteca Ambrosiana, Milan, F 249 inf. no. 6, p. 13

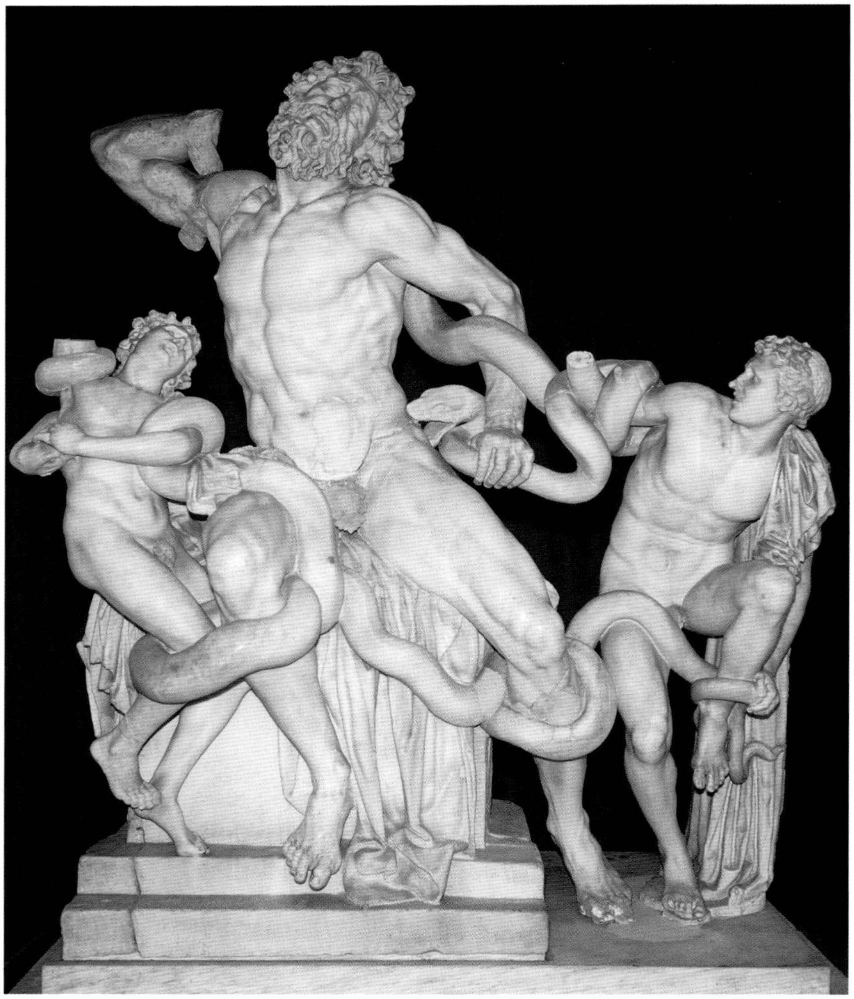

123
After HAGESANDER, POLYDORUS and ATHENODORUS OF RHODES
Laocoön and his Sons
1st century AD
Marble, height 210 cm
Museo Pio-Clementino, Vatican Museums and Galleries, Vatican City

124
PETER PAUL RUBENS
(1577–1640)
Laocoön and his Sons, *c.* 1601–02
Black chalk
48.2 × 37.5 cm
Wallraf-Richartz-Museum, Cologne
CNF 1025/WRM/Z 5889

While Timanthes obscured the physical signs of Agamemnon's grief, the sculptors of the *Laocoön* carved detailed and vivid expressions in the faces of the three figures – one son dying, the other still struggling to escape the serpent and the father straining every sinew in a heroic but doomed attempt to save his sons. The popular sixteenth-century writer Pietro Aretino commented on the use of the diverse facial expressions in the *Laocoön*, raising the question of the proper limits of the visual arts in maintaining a balance between beauty and horror. As soon as the work had been discovered its fame had spread, inspiring artists and captivating scholars across Europe. Small versions of the group in bronze or terracotta were produced and widely disseminated, as were prints. Michelangelo's

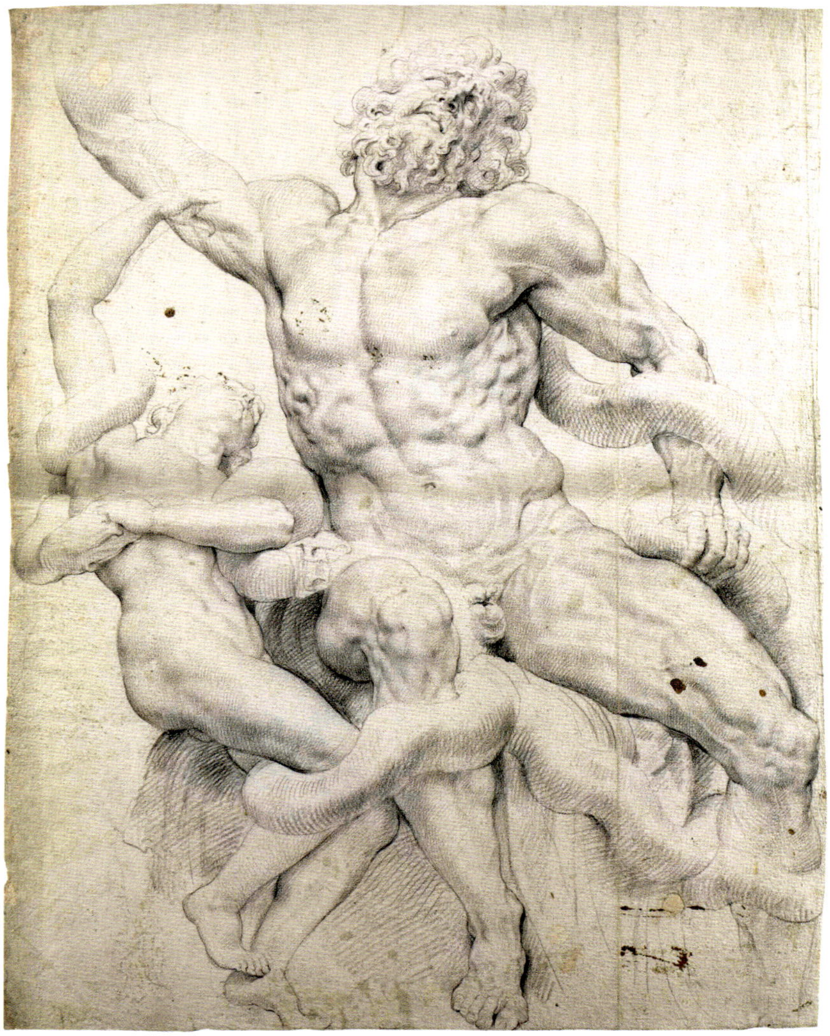

125
After HAGESANDER, POLYDORUS and ATHENODORUS OF RHODES
Laocoön and his Sons
detail of fig. 123

126
PETER PAUL RUBENS
The Massacre of the Innocents, detail

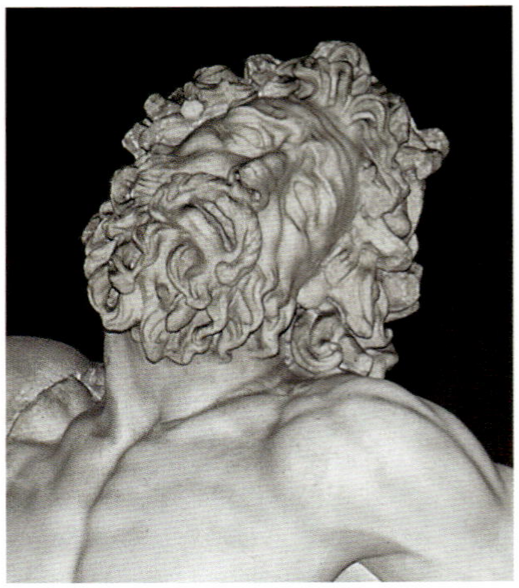

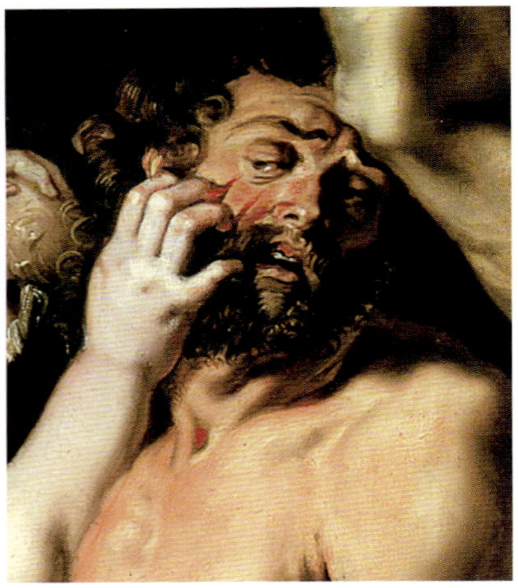

so-called *Slaves* represent a powerful response to the *Laocoön*, and models after the *Slaves* were known in Antwerp (see the top of the central shelf in Brueghel and Rubens's *Sense of Sight*, fig. 119 and detail p. 118). The priest's anguished features appear frequently in Renaissance art. Giulio Romano dedicated the room of *The Fall of the Giants* (Palazzo del Tè, Mantua) to variations of desperation and suffering inspired by the statue, and even Titian, who was not a renowned antiquarian, responded to its imagery in his *Bacchus and Ariadne* (National Gallery, London). Later in his life, having seen the statue in Rome, Titian reinterpreted the figure of Laocoön for his Moses in *The Trinity* (1552; Museo del Prado, Madrid), tightening up the muscles and distended blood vessels to capture the almost feral energy.

Rubens became fascinated with this three-figure group and drew it from many angles, the drawings resembling graphic maps detailing blood vessels and bulging muscle from different viewpoints (figs. 122, 124, 146).[24] The *Laocoön*'s anguished features surely provided inspiration for the *Massacre* (figs. 125, 126). The sinusoidal curve of the furrowed brow is paraphrased in the face of the woman behind the crouching girl in white, and more emphatically in the face and brow of the soldier being scratched. But it is above all the emotional energy and the tension between life and death that Rubens absorbed in his study of the *Laocoön* and used to such effect in the *Massacre*. The central woman in red echoes the predicament of the priest, overcome by superior force but nevertheless struggling tragically against all odds. Details such as the pulsating blood vessels in the soldiers' arms must also be derived from that paradigm of torsos under stress. A *Laocoön*-like triplet of tension can be found in the helmeted soldier grasping the crouching woman's hair with one hand whilst pulling at the fleeing mother with the other. Rubens had no call to entwine his group of figures in serpents but there is a sense of cohesion and sculptural bonding in the

Massacre that mirrors the ancient group and which is found again in works such as *The Battle of the Amazons* (see fig. 121) and *Moses and the Brazen Serpent* (fig. 128). Abraham's imploring face in *The Sacrifice of Isaac* (fig. 127) is a calmer response. Rubens looked to the agonized pose of the *Laocoön* again when exploring imagery to represent Hercules's excruciating death caused by a poisoned cloak.[25] This association of images was clearly a dominant factor in Rubens's art, and may have been understood by the more visually informed of his audience. Certainly the way the cloth snakes around Hercules gives a sense of malicious animation and one also sees serpentine echoes in the snaking ribbons and enveloping blue flame of cloth in the *Massacre*.

In studying these antique sources, Rubens was searching for more than just visual quotations. He wanted to absorb, animate and unravel the compositional possibilities inherent in these great marble groups.

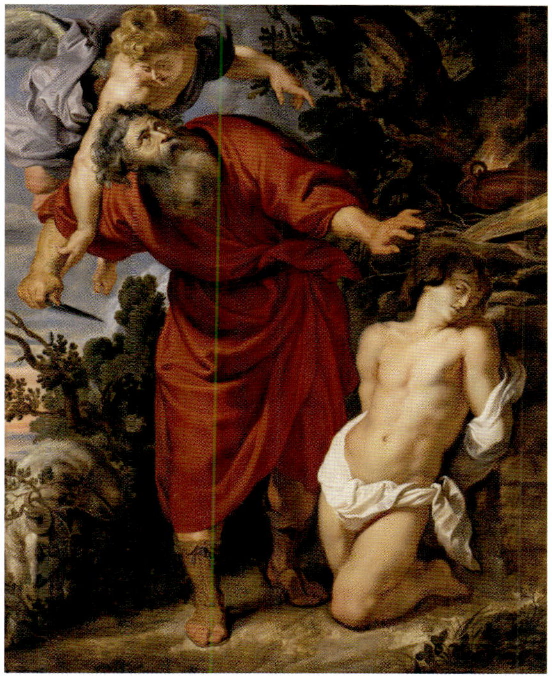

127
PETER PAUL RUBENS
(1577–1640)
The Sacrifice of Isaac
c. 1611–12
Oil on panel
141.0 × 110.5 cm
The Nelson-Atkins Museum of Art, Kansas City, Missouri

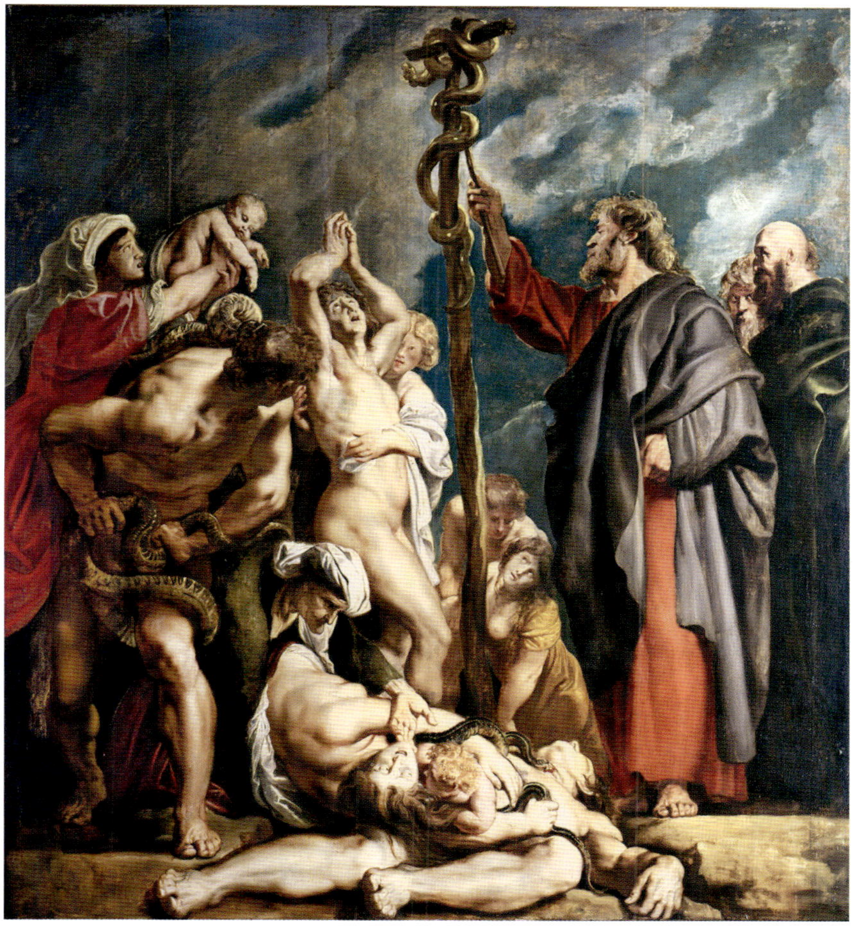

128
PETER PAUL RUBENS
(1577–1640)
Moses and the Brazen Serpent
1609–10
Oil on panel
161.2 × 146 cm
Courtauld Gallery, London

The Farnese *Bull* (fig. 129) is another example of an ancient group straining with energy and latent power. Again the work is described by Pliny (36, 33–34), who says that the sculptors were Apollonius and Tauriscus of Rhodes, and that the scene represented the fable of Dirce who, as punishment for her ill treatment of Antiope (whom she succeeded as wife of the King of Thebes), was tied to a wild bull by Antiope's sons. As in the case of the *Laocoön*, it is now generally agreed that the surviving marble sculpture is a Roman copy of the Greek original. The Dirce may have provided the model for Venus in Rubens's *Venus and Adonis* (*c*. 1610–11; Düsseldorf), right down to the same splayed leg (although the knees are decorously drawn closer).[26] Rubens has also been credited with drawing the head from the *Bull*,[27] but it is the group's diagonal sweep that inspired him, so that the men attempting to restrain the bull, heaving against its bulk with ropes, became the template for the

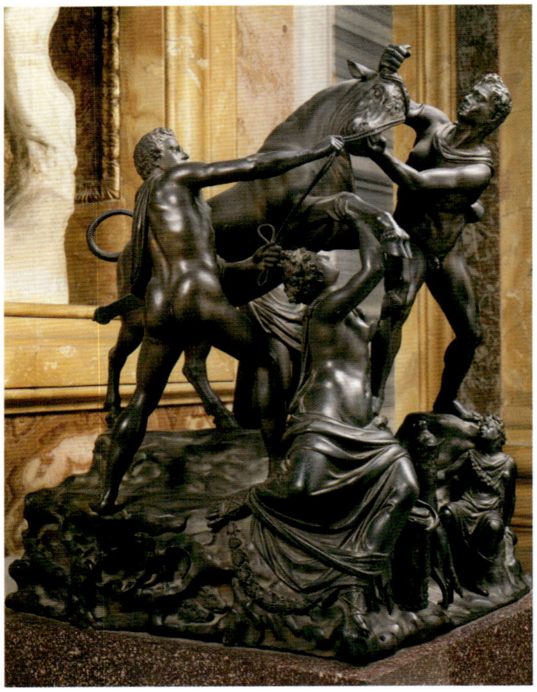

129
ANTONIO SUSINI
(1577–1640) after
a Roman marble copy
(Museo Archeologico
Nazionale, Naples) of a
Hellenistic original
The Farnese Bull
Bronze
Galleria Borghese, Rome

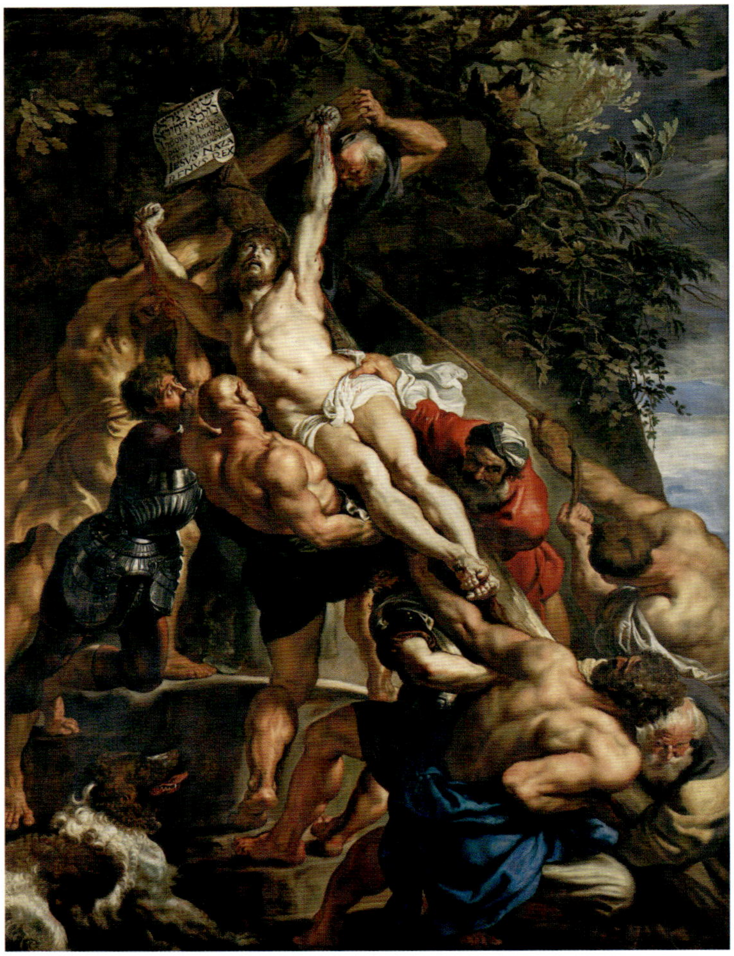

130
PETER PAUL RUBENS
(1577–1640)
The Raising of the Cross
(central panel of triptych)
c. 1610–11
Oil on panel
460 × 340 cm
Onze-Lieve-Vrouwekathedraal,
Antwerp

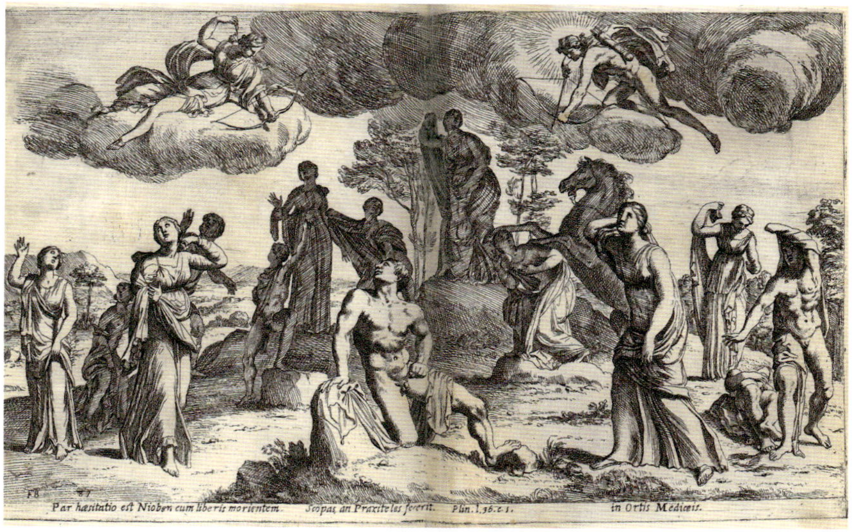

133
FRANÇOIS PERRIER
(1590–1649)
Niobe and her Children
1638
Engraving from François Perrier, *Les statues antiques de Rome*

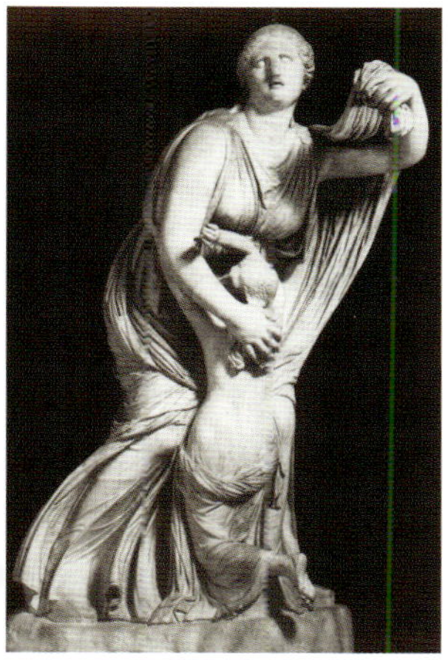

131
ROMAN copy of a HELLENISTIC figure from a group
Niobe
Marble
Galleria degli Uffizi, Florence

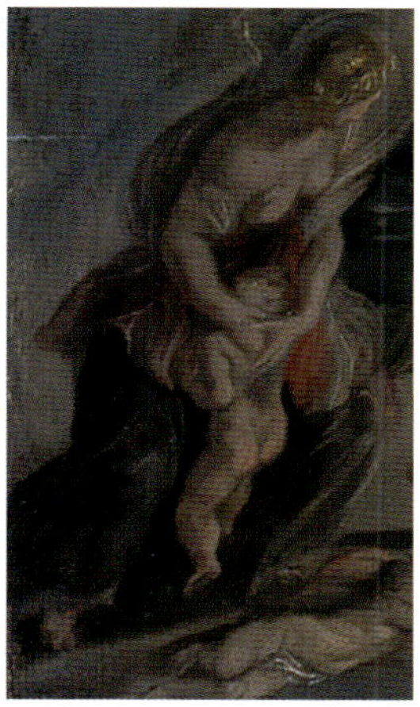

132
PETER PAUL RUBENS
The Massacre of the Innocents, detail

straining figures pulling on ropes in his *Raising of the Cross* (fig. 130).[28] It is hard to believe that Rubens would have created the complex interaction of figures in the *Massacre* without inspiration from these ancient multi-figure groups.[29]

Most surviving free-standing Roman sculpture was of single figures, or occasionally figure pairs. More complex groups such as the *Laocoön* and the Farnese *Bull* were comparatively rare and elements of a group work would often have been dispersed or lost. A prime example of such dispersal is the *Niobe* group (figs. 131, 133), of which the scattered components were discovered in 1583.[30] Niobe had boasted of her many progeny, declaring that she was worthy of the worship normally accorded to Leto, who only had two children, Apollo and Diana. Apollo and Diana avenged their mother by killing the Niobids with arrows. These statues, after their discovery and restoration, were displayed in the garden of the Villa Medici in Rome, where Rubens would have seen them. A 1638 engraving shows that six Niobids and a horse were on show there (fig. 133). Again it is the emotion in the faces of the protagonists that appealed to critics: grief, dread and supplication are all evident here.

These figures must have intrigued Rubens, not least in making him consider how to arrange the individual pieces to make a convincing group. In the background of the *Massacre*, on the far left, Rubens quotes Niobe shielding one of her daughters, although here the daughter has become a son (fig. 132). The antique Niobe's cloak, which serves to shield her daughter, drapes limply from her left hand, but Rubens has inflated the cloak so that it billows above and behind the mother – an adaptation which is typical of his confidence in enhancing a design and endowing it with Baroque emotion. Rubens would have been familiar with the reference to a *Niobe* group in Pliny and it seems too much of a coincidence that a few lines below (36, 29) Pliny describes two *Breezes* "who are spreading their cloaks like sails" (*Aurae velificantes sua veste*). The parted lips, eyes appealing to heaven and expressive hand gestures found in the *Niobe* group are also used in the *Massacre* by Rubens, in particular in the two crouching women flanking the soldier holding the infant aloft. As noted above (p. 76), the Italian poet Giambattista Marino, in a poem of 1632, compared the mothers of the Massacre to these same Niobid sculptures, which confirms the supposition that some of Rubens's audience would have recognized such allusions. The poem, inspired by Paggi's painting of the Massacre, was begun in 1604 and probably circulated well before its publication in 1632, so Rubens may well have seen a manuscript version.

The crouching mother dressed in white and gazing into our space also serves to connect scene and viewer (fig. 135). She was inspired by the renowned antique statue of the *Crouching Venus*, which Rubens would certainly have known in the version owned by the Gonzaga in Mantua (fig. 134). Rubens used a mirror image of the same model, in a more literal quotation, in his near contemporary (1614) painting of *Venus Frigida* (fig. 136). In the *Massacre* Rubens was so satisfied with the impact of the

134
After DOIDALSES
(3rd century BC?)
Venus crouching at her Bath
Marble
Height 112 cm
The British Museum, London
on loan from Her Majesty Queen Elizabeth II
GR 1963.10-29.1
(formerly Gonzaga collection, Mantua)

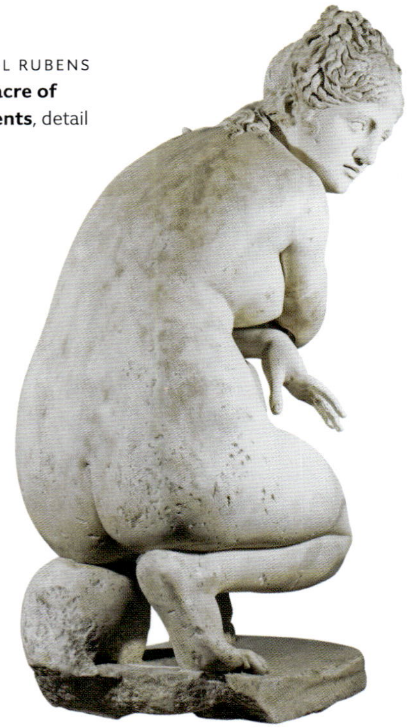

135
PETER PAUL RUBENS
The Massacre of the Innocents, detail

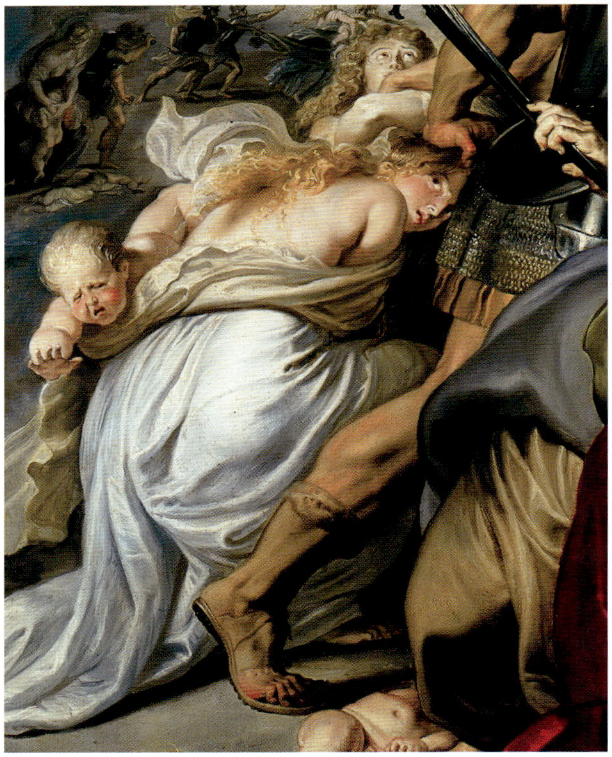

136
PETER PAUL RUBENS
(1577–1640)
Venus Frigida, 1614
Oil on panel
142 × 184 cm
Koninklijk Museum voor Schone
Kunsten, Antwerp, inv. no. 709

Roman torso – now with riverlets of golden locks tumbling down her back – that he took liberties with the attachment of her arm.

The inspiration of the antique can also be found in the soldiers, whose sheer muscularity owes much to the colossal physiques of statues such as the Farnese *Hercules* (see fig. 89) and the *Laocoön*. The great arm and torso of the soldier being scratched, which are etched in shadows to dramatize their bulk, recall the physique of the Farnese *Hercules*.[31] Rubens lamented the loss in his own day of the superior physical stature of the ancients and claimed that their physiques were to be only matched in the backs of porters, the arms of fighters, the legs of dancers and most closely in rowers.[32] Indeed his older contemporary Hendrick Goltzius had taken the

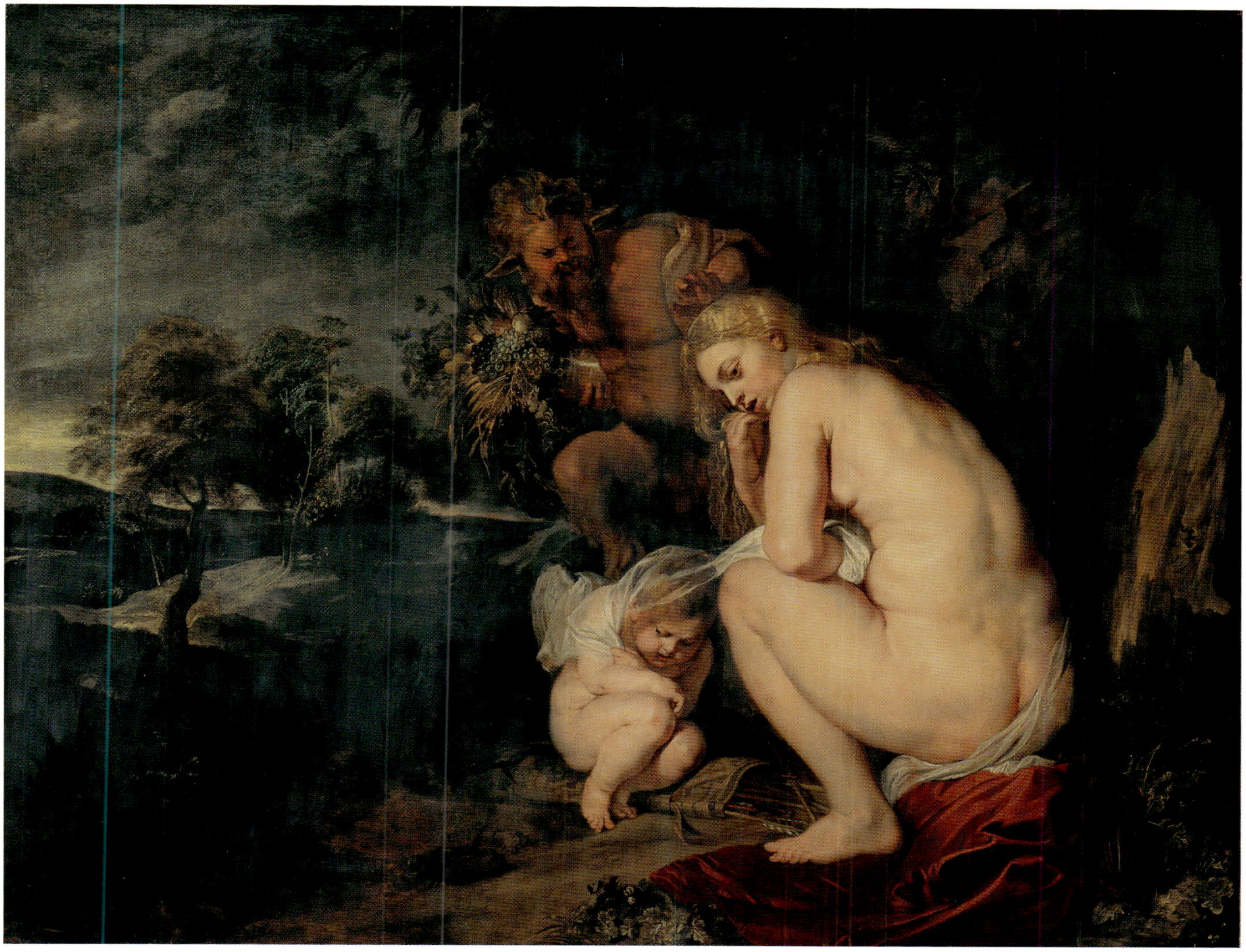

137
WILLEM PANNEELS
(1600–1632), *c.* 1628, after
PETER PAUL RUBENS
Detail of the Wrestlers
c. 1602–08
Red chalk
180 × 195 cm
Statens Museum for Kunst,
Copenhagen

138
PHILIPPE MAGNIER
(1647–1715)
after SCHOOL OF
LYSIPPUS (?)
The Wrestlers, 1684?
Marble
Height 100 cm
Musée du Louvre, Paris

papal galley from Naples to Rome especially to study the slaves' muscular forms, and Rubens, too, drew such oarsmen, perhaps while waiting for a boat to Spain from Pisa in 1603 ('Van Dyck' sketchbook, f. 16r).[33] The link with Hercules may be more than visual, as Rubens may also have been playing on the fact that Hercules, in a fit of madness, had slaughtered his own children. Rubens may also have had in mind the biblical reference (Psalm 136: 9) to dashing children like evil thoughts.[34]

The soldier with the sword in the centre of the composition recalls the antique two-figure group known as *The Wrestlers* (figs. 138, 139). Rubens would have seen the sculpture, which at that time was thought to belong to the *Niobe* group, in the Villa Medici. The bent left arm and clutching hand of the lower figure is mirrored almost exactly in the *Massacre*. Michelangelo had also used a similar pose in his *Battle of Cascina*. Rubens must have drawn both figures, as there are Panneels drawings after Rubens of these figures seen from the front and above in Copenhagen (fig. 137). Rubens used the composition in other works, including a back view of it for the devil in his drawing for *The Martyrdom of Saint Gregory* (Fogg Art Museum, Boston) and again for the devils in *Saint Ignatius Loyola* (Kunsthistorisches Museum, Vienna). Again, reductions of this antique

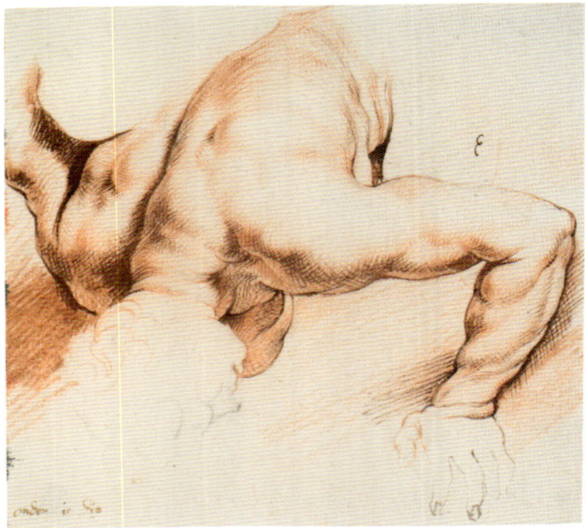

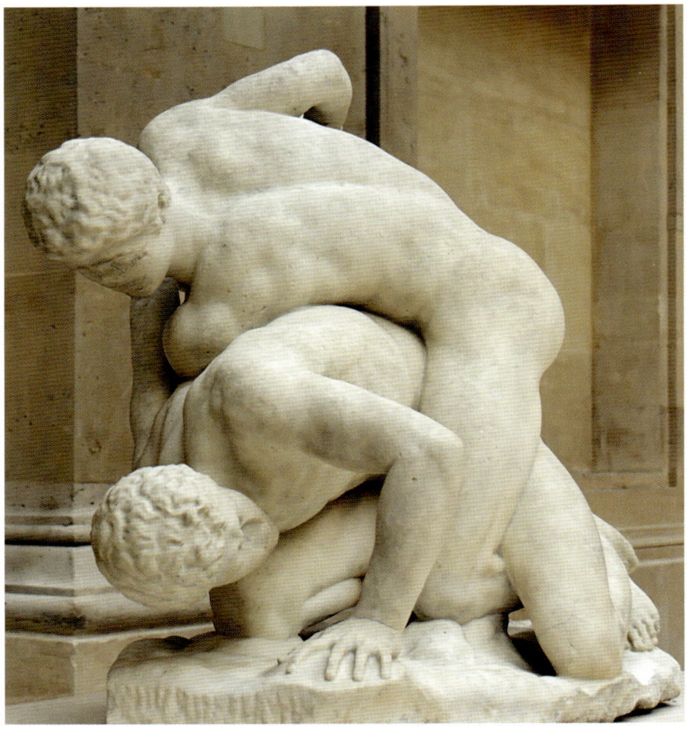

139
PETER PAUL RUBENS
The Massacre of the Innocents
detail

group were popular and are depicted in collector's cabinet paintings in Antwerp, such as Brueghel's *Sense of Sight* (in the centre of the bottom shelf beside the socle of the large bust; see fig. 119 and detail p. 118).

References to the great works of antiquity can even be found in the forms of the slain children. Here we can be guided by Rubens's own views on the use of antique statues for models of child development: "When taking statues [of antiquity] as models the best ones should always be selected and imitated as models of the different ages concerned – infancy, say, of which the nicest example is provided by the putti on the statue of the Nile [fig. 140] and of the Tiber in the Vatican Gardens. 'Self-contained in their smooth rotundity,' they are playful in their gestures, crawling on the ground and clambering over the massive limbs of their father as if they were mountains. Similar to these are the ones next to the Tiber statue in the same place, being suckled by the she-wolf. Next a slightly more advanced age, but still that of a baby, was illustrated by the ancients in the Cupid asleep on an outspread lion skin, with a torch in his left hand. A later stage than this is shown in the boy next to Leda where he is struggling with the swan, and in the Hercules crushing the serpents in his cradle. Finally a somewhat more substantial age is represented in the little Greek

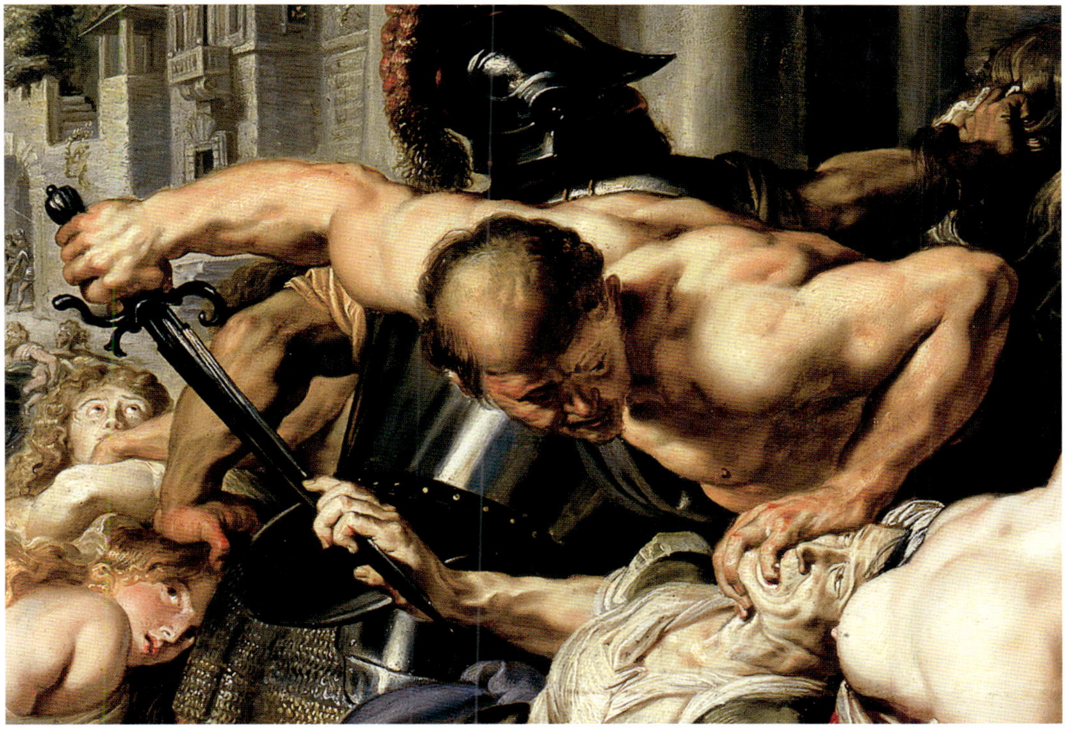

140
Roman copy of
a Hellenistic group
The River Nile
Marble
Height 133 cm
Vatican Museums and Galleries,
Vatican City

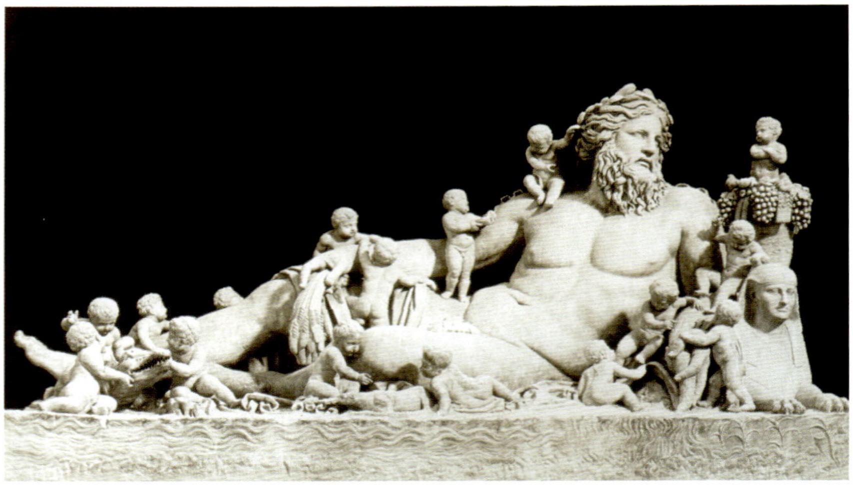

boy fighting with boxing gloves. All these children of different kinds, yet still possessing the chubbiness of infancy, can be seen in ancient marbles in Rome."[35]

Apart from the *Sleeping Cupid,* Rubens is of course thinking of active children, not corpses, with this recipe list of models. The richest source of ancient images of children for him was the statue of *The River Nile* (fig. 140) and we can see scrambling infants from that work in a number of Rubens's paintings, even up to the 1622 *Education of Maria* from the Marie de Médicis cycle.

In the above passage Rubens's reference to "smooth rotundity" was a quotation from Horace's *Satires* and is typical of his fluency in adopting verbal images from textual sources to describe the ideal he was seeking from his models. The desired effect is well illustrated in his drawing of the back view of Laocoön's son and equally in the corpulent stomach of his Dresden *Silenus*. We can approach the *Massacre* armed with this insight. Rubens admired the authority of ancient sculpture and also the curving surfaces of ancient carving. It was his ambition to match the plastic forms of their limbs and their smooth rotundity in his own painting. The sensation that one can grasp hold of the arm of the woman in red in the *Massacre* (or Samson's arm in the *Samson and Delilah*) as if it were a handle of flesh was deliberate, as was the sense of traversing the contours and dimples of the dead infant's back at the bottom right, a tactile involvement that is violently stopped when one realizes his head is baptized in a pool of his own blood.

Rubens also used as a source for the dead children a sculpture of great interest even though its authenticity as antique is dubious. This is a marble *Three Sleeping Cupids* that mysteriously entered the Borghese collection in 1608 and which Rubens would have seen there (fig. 141).[36] The infant

141
ANGELO BEZZI (19th century) after an unidentified sculptor (*c.* 1600)
The Borghese Sleeping Cupids
Marble
Width 94 cm
Devonshire Collection, Chatsworth

142, 143, 144
PETER PAUL RUBENS
The Massacre of the Innocents
details

lying in the foetal position to the left in the *Massacre* (fig. 142) is a quotation, although mirrored, from this group, as is the boy in the bottom right with his hand held in an awkward cupped position (fig. 144). The cupped hand is found again in the corresponding figure of the dead child being squashed under the gold shawl (fig. 143), and was used by Rubens in his *Deposition* and for the doomed, slumbering Samson. It seems to prefigure or represent death in his art. The rotation of the infant's arm outwards gives the pose a distorted, dead feeling. It is worth noting that Rubens's infants have short, plump toes matching the proportions of their bodies, whereas those of the *Sleeping Cupids* have prominent tendons. The child to the right with his back to the viewer (fig. 148) has an androgynous quality similar to that found in Rubens's drawing from behind of the younger son of the *Laocoön* (fig. 146). The ribbons against the flesh in the same dead infant

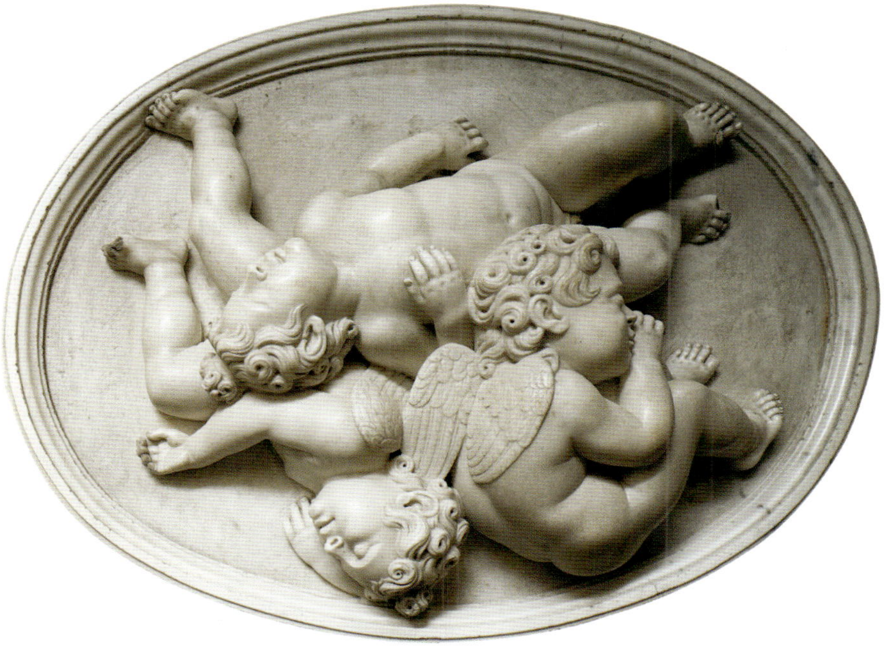

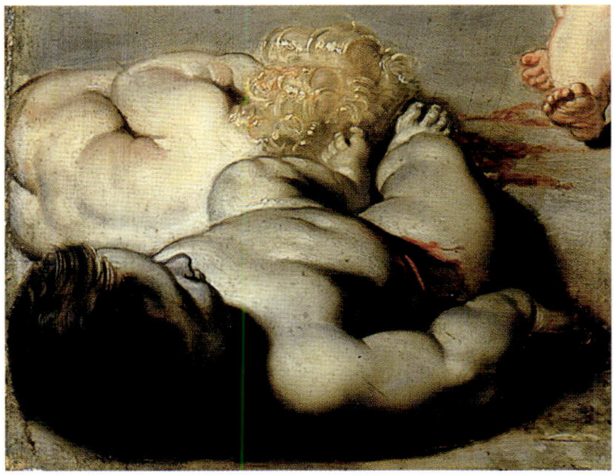

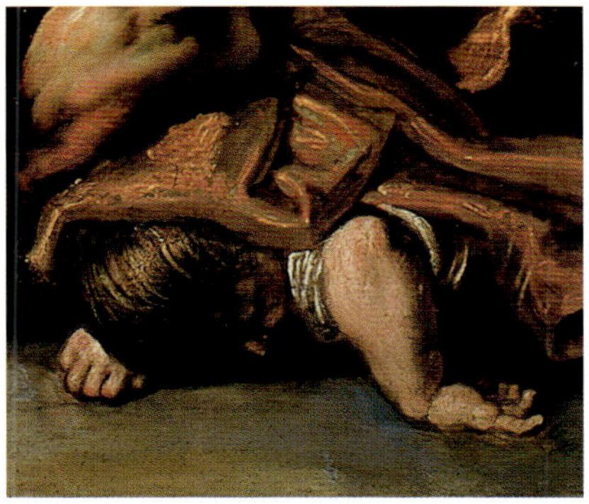

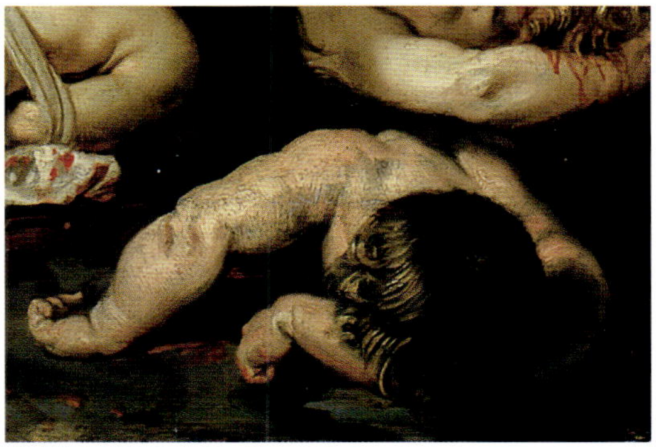

145
Artist working for NICOLAS-CLAUDE FABRI DE PEIRESC (1580–1637)
Sleeping Cupid, 1620
Red chalk
18 × 23 cm
Réserve des Estampes, Bibliothèque nationale de France, Paris, MS Aa 54, f. 53

146
PETER PAUL RUBENS (1577–1640)
The Younger Son of Laocoön seen from the Back, *c.* 1601–02
Black and white chalk
44.4 × 26.5 cm
Biblioteca Ambrosiana, Milan, F 249 inf. no. 6, p. 11

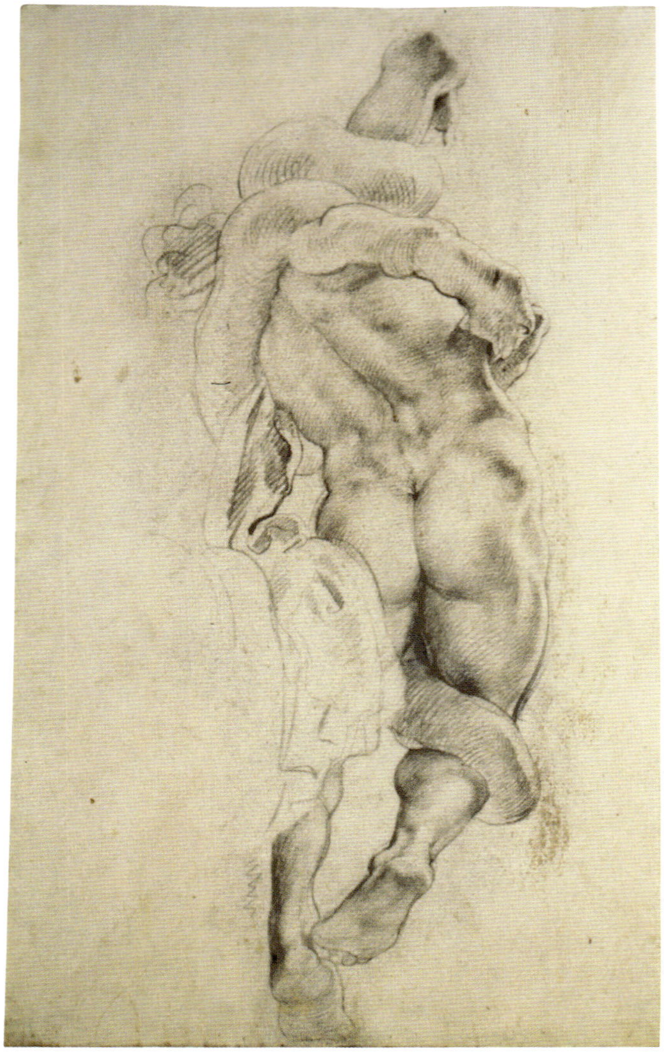

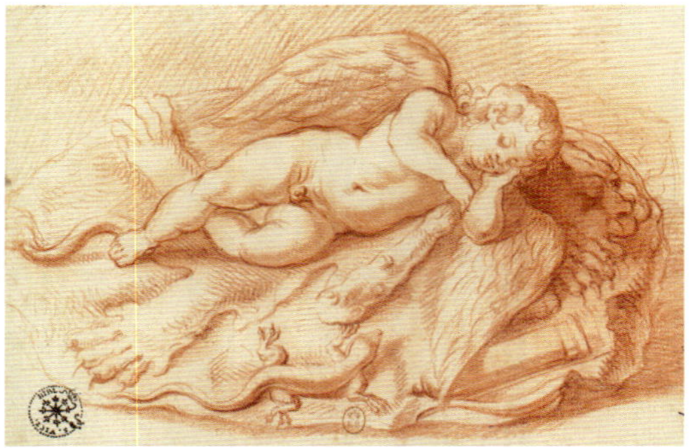

are a device Rubens had fastidiously copied from the putto's waist in the antique Roman marble of the Borghese *Centaur*.[37] The motif here has nothing of the provocative charge of the ribbon across Delilah's breast, which has connotations of Venus's girdle, but Rubens seems fully aware of its tactile qualities. Rubens had painted Venus herself wearing her irresistible girdle in his *Council of the Gods* of 1602 (Prague Castle), so he understood the potential of a contour-hugging ribbon. The slipped-down chemise binding the arm of the woman in red makes equally ambiguous tactile and maternal references. Rubens's friend and patron Nicolaas Rockox also owned a *Sleeping Cupid* – a single figure – seen from the side on the very left of the Francken *Interior*

147
FRANÇOIS DUQUESNOY
(1597–1643)
The Van den Eynde monument
1633, detail
Marble
Santa Maria dell'Anima, Rome

148
PETER PAUL RUBENS
The Massacre of the Innocents, detail

(see fig. 46) and better understood from the frontal view of the Cupid in Peiresc's drawing after it (fig. 145),[38] whose crossed legs are echoed in the infant lying beneath the old woman's knee.

Around 1602, at the time of Philip Rubens's residence there, experiments on the circulatory system had been conducted at the University of Padua, and Peter Paul, given his naturally inquisitive mind, might have been aware of them. He would also have known the work of earlier artists in which blue paint was used to convey death: the blue-tinged lips of Rosso Fiorentino's *Dead Christ* (Museum of Fine Arts, Boston) is a notable example. Another example admired and copied by Rubens is the pallid flesh in Caravaggio's *The Entombment* (see figs. 11, 12). Rubens must have been especially intrigued by the veins in the dead Christ's projecting arm. In the *Massacre* Rubens places the infants firmly in the realm of the dead through his use of greyish skin-tones and judiciously applied red highlights, which have a macabre beauty of their own.

In his treatise *De imitatione statuarum* (written probably about 1607), Rubens warned: "in order to attain the highest perfection in painting, it is necessary to understand the antique, nay, to be so thoroughly possessed of this knowledge, that it may diffuse itself everywhere . . . though it must be judiciously applied . . . so that it may not in the least smell of stone."[39]

The dying Rubens returned to the theme of achieving aesthetic perfection when praising some casts after sculpture in his last extant letter, to the sculptor Francois Duquesnoy, who was then working in Rome. He wrote on April 7, 1640 thanking him for models "and for the plaster casts of the two putti from the epitaph of Van den Eynde in the Chiesa dell'Anima [fig. 147]. Still less can I praise their beauty: properly it is nature, rather than art, that has formed them; the marble is softened into living flesh."[40] The statues might provide the best models but the ultimate goal was to convey a sense of living flesh and Rubens, as a painter who also designed sculpture, was trying, like Pygmalion, to breathe life into form.[41]

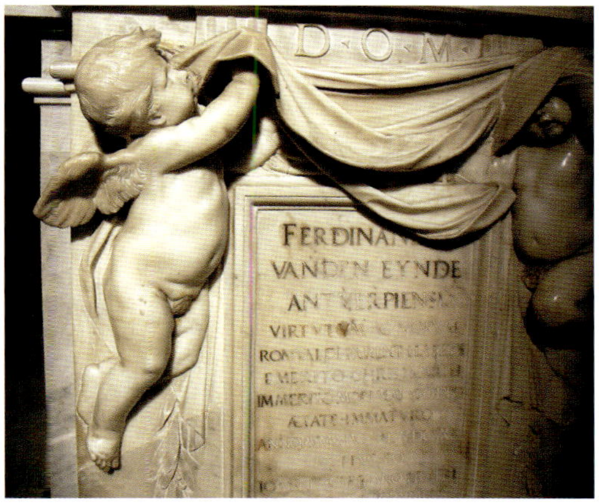

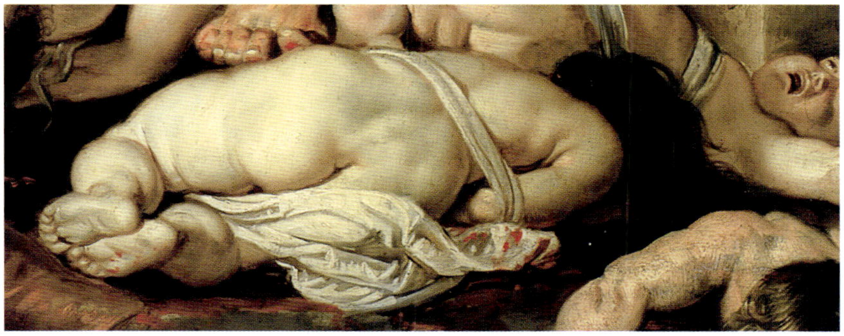

Bibliography and notes

Bibliography of frequently cited works

ANTWERP 2004
K.L. Belkin and F. Healy, *A House of Art: Rubens as Collector* (exhibition catalogue, Rubenshuis, Antwerp, March 6 – June 13, 2004)

ANTWERP 2007
H. Van de Velde, J. Kräftner and A.-M. Leander Touati, *Samson and Delilah: A Rubens Painting Returns* (exhibition catalogue, Rockoxhuis, Antwerp, November 6, 2007 – February 10, 2008)

BARNES ET AL. 2004
J. Barnes, N. De Poorter, O. Millar, *Van Dyck: A Complete Catalogue* (London, 2004)

BAUDOUIN 2005
F. Baudouin, *Rubens in Context. Selected Studies. Liber Memorialis* (Antwerp, 2005)

BELKIN 2004
K.L. Belkin, *Rubens* (London, 1998)

BRUNSWICK 2004
N. Büttner, U. Heinen *et al.*, *Peter Paul Rubens, Barocke Leidenschaften* (exhibition catalogue, Herzog Anton Ulrich-Museum, Brunswick, August 8– October 31, 2004)

BRUSSELS 2007
J. Vander Auwera and S. Van Sprang, *Rubens: A Genius at Work* (exhibition catalogue, Musées Royaux des Beaux-Arts de Belgique, Brussels, September 14–January 27, 2007)

CROPPER AND DEMPSEY 1996
E. Cropper and C. Dempsey, *Nicolas Poussin: Friendship and the Love of Painting* (Princeton, 1996)

DENUCÉ 1931
J. Denucé, *Export of Works of Art in the 17th century from Antwerp: The Firm Forchoudt* (Antwerp, 1931)

DENUCÉ 1932
J. Denucé, *De Antwerpsche konstkamers. Inventarissen van kunstverzamelingen te Antwerpen in de 16e en 17e eeuwen* (Amsterdam, 1932)

DENUCÉ 1949
J. Denucé, *Na Peter Pauwel Rubens, documenten uit den kunsthandel te Antwerpen in de XVIIe eeuw* (Antwerp, 1949)

DUVERGER
E. Duverger, *Antwerpse Kunstinventarissen uit de Zeventiende Eeuw*, vol. 1 (Brussels, 1984); vol. 7 (1993); vol. 8 (1995); vol. 9 (1997); vol. 10 (1999); vol. 12 (2002)

GENOA 2004
P. Boccardo *et al.*, *L'Età di Rubens, Dimore, committenti e collezionisti genovesi* (exhibition catalogue, Palazzo Ducale, Genoa, March 20 – July 11, 2004)

HELD 1980
J.S. Held, *The Oil Sketches of Peter Paul Rubens: A Critical Catalogue*, 2 vols. (Princeton, 1980)

JAFFÉ 1966
M. Jaffé, *Van Dyck's Antwerp Sketchbook*, 2 vols. (London, 1966)

JAFFÉ 1977
M. Jaffé, *Rubens and Italy* (Oxford, 1977)

JAFFÉ AND BRADLEY 2003
D. Jaffé and A. Bradley, 'Rubens's Massacre of the Innocents', *Apollo*, CLVII (2003), pp. 11–20

LONDON 2005
Rubens, A Master in the Making, essays by David Jaffé and Elizabeth McGrath, catalogue by D. Jaffé and M. Moore Ede (exhibition catalogue, National Gallery, London, October 26, 2005 – January 15, 2006)

MCGRATH 1978
E. McGrath, 'The Painted Decoration of Rubens's House', *Journal of the Warburg and Courtauld Institutes*, XLI (1978), pp. 245–79

MCGRATH 1997
E. McGrath, *Rubens. Subjects from History* (Corpus Rubenianum Ludwig Burchard XIII, I, London, 1997)

MAGURN 1955
R.S. Magurn, *The Letters of Peter Paul Rubens* (Cambridge, Mass., 1955)

VAN DER MEULEN 1994
M. Van der Meulen, *Copies after the Antique*, 2 vols. (London, 1994)

MULLER 1993
J. Muller, 'Private Collections in the Spanish Netherlands: Ownership and Display of Paintings in Domestic Interiors', in *The Age of Rubens*, ed. P.C. Sutton (exhibition catalogue, Museum of Fine Arts, Boston, September 21, 1993– January 2, 1994)

ROTTERDAM 2003
F. Lammertse and A. Vergara, *Peter Paul Rubens: The Life of Achilles* (exhibition catalogue, Museum Boijmans Van Beuningen, Rotterdam, October 6– December 10, 2003)

WHITE 1987
C. White, *Peter Paul Rubens: Man and Artist* (New Haven and London, 1987)

WOOD 2002
J. Wood, *Rubens. Drawing on Italy* (exhibition catalogue, National Gallery of Scotland, Edinburgh; Djanogly Art Gallery, Nottingham, 2002)

The *Massacre* in context, 1 (pp. 24–43)

1 This summation, organized by Amanda Bradley, is based on information in the following publications: D. Jaffé in London 2005, pp. 11–20; F. Baudouin, 'Rubens kinderjaren in Keulen en in Antwerpen', in Baudouin 2005, pp. 44–65; Brunswick 2004, pp. 13ff.; F. Huemer, *Rubens and the Roman Circle: Studies of the First Decade* (New York and London, 1996); White 1987; and for the school framework Jaffé 1977 .

2 A detailed discussion of the date when Rubens may have met Rockox can be found in F. Baudouin, 'Nicolaas Rockox, friend and patron of Peter Paul Rubens', in Baudouin 2005, pp. 71ff.

3 September 13, 1621, Rubens to William Trumbull. See Magurn 1955, p. 77, no. 46.

4 See H. Goldfarb *et al.*, *Titian and Rubens. Power, Politics and Style* (exhibition catalogue, Isabella Stewart Gardner Museum, Boston, 1998), p. 31.

5 See Antwerp 1997, p. 97, and entry by K.L. Belkin in Antwerp 2004, pp. 95–97, no. 3; and further below, 'Designing the *Massacre*', note 27.

6 For details of the commission see G. Demarcel, 'The History of Decius Mus', in *Rubens's Textiles* (exhibition catalogue, Hessenhuis, Antwerp, 1997), pp. 45–47. See also A. Wheelock Jr., *Flemish Paintings of the Seventeenth Century* (National Gallery of Art, Washington, 2005), no. 1957.14.2.

7 A full discussion of this drawing can be found in Wood 2002, p. 51, no. 22. The model may be the drawing in the Albertina: see P. Joannides, *The Drawings of Raphael* (Oxford, 1983), p. 226, no. 368.

8 Another sheet survives in the Courtauld Collection, and another in a private collection – recently discovered – showing the Farnese *Hercules* (here fig. 89).

9 The two sheets of the *Castration* and the *Rape* may once have been joined together: see Wood 2002, p. 58, no. 32. Cf. Bartsch XVII (109), 154 (2), for engravings after Polidoro's fresco.

10 Elsheimer's *The Mocking of Ceres* (Prado, Madrid) was acquired by Rubens on his return to Antwerp, some time in the late 1610s. He proceeded to acquire others later in life, but the impact of Elsheimer's work predates these acquisitions. See K.L. Belkin in Antwerp 2004, pp. 98–101, no. 4.

11 F. Baudouin, 'Nicolaas Rockox, friend and patron of Peter Paul Rubens', in Baudouin 2005, p. 76. The sketch in the Groeninger Museum is the template for the first formulation of the Prado picture. Only three years after its conception, the painting was given to the Spanish Ambassador, Rodrigo Calderón, by the city of Antwerp. When he was executed in 1621, Philip IV obtained it from his estate, and thus, when Rubens visited Madrid in 1628 and 1629, he was reunited with the picture, and added a strip on the right, which included a self-portrait on horseback. As Joost vander Auwera has discovered, the office bearers of the Town Hall had a special devotion to the Adoration: see also *Rubens: The Adoration of the Magi* (exhibition catalogue, ed. Alejandro Vergara, Museo del Prado, Madrid, 2004–05), pp. 27ff.

12 Elizabeth McGrath and Walter Liedtke have (in conversation) suggested that Rubens painted it in early 1609. Rubens was exploring larger-than-life figures at this time, which almost burst out of the frame, but the *Massacre*, like his later *Rape of the Sabines* (National Gallery, London), seems to belong to a different 'Renaissance' model. See also J. Müller Hofstede, 'Rubens' "Bethlehemitische Kindersmord"', in *Munuscula Amicorum: Contributions on Rubens in honour of Hans Vlieghe* (Turnhout, 2006), pp. 283–91.

13 It should be pointed out that the truce was much anticipated in diplomatic letters written during 1608, therefore it is possible that the Adoration was initiated before it came into effect.

The *Massacre* in context, 2 (pp. 44–71)

1 The picture was auctioned at Sotheby's, London, on July 10, 2002, lot 6. I am much indebted to the information in George Gordon and Judith Niessen's catalogue entry for that sale, and in particular their research with regard to provenance.

2 The earliest published reference to Carenna dates to 1678 (see Appendix, Documents A, no. 7). Carenna's 1669 will was published for the first time in an often overlooked sale catalogue which summarized some of his gifts to religious orders: P. Génard, 'Notices sur les riches tapisseries flamandes de Van Dyck dans la galerie de l'art de ce dernier', in sale catalogue, Rue Baeckelmans, Brussels (January 18, 1875). It is also excerpted in Denucé 1932, pp. 189–90, and in Duverger, vol. 9 (1997), pp. 259–60. It is more fully published here in the Appendix, Documents A, no. 3.

3 The only candidate for Carenna's portrait I can suggest is Pieter I Thys, *Man with a Letter in his Hand* (112 × 89.5 cm), in the State Hermitage Museum, St Petersburg. The letter the sitter holds is inscribed *Per A Antonio* . . . . See N. Gritsay and N. Babina, *Seventeenth and Eighteenth-Century Flemish Painting: State Hermitage Museum Catalogue* (London, 2008), p. 389, no. 471. Giovanna Tonelli has discussed the Carenna and the Annoni in her work, 'Il Notarile come fonte per la storia del commercio e della finanza a Milano (1600–1650)', *Mélanges de l'Ecole française de Rome*, 2002, pp. 79–104; she has since carried out important further research on the Carenna and Annoni families: see her essay here, pp. 154ff.

4 For the baptismal document see Giovanna Tonelli's essay, note 86.

5 On Carenna's business activities and his relationship with the Annoni family see further Giovanna Tonelli's essay, pp. 159–60.

6 The merchant and almoner (1642) Nicolas Picquery (buried Sint-Jacobskerk, 1661) married Elizabeth Fourment, sister of Rubens's second wife Helena. Their father Daniel was a tapestry and silk dealer. The heirs of Rubens's youngest son Franciscus (1633–1678) were in dispute with Lord (Paolo?) Carenna in 1703–06: see K. van Honacker, *Het archief van de families Rubens en van Parys* (Brussels, 2002), p. 22.

7 For the Annoni despatch of the *Madonna in a Garland* by Rubens and Brueghel (now in the Musée du Louvre) see the letter of September 5 [1621?] cited in S. Bedoni, *Jan Brueghel in Italia e il collezionismo del Seicento* (Florence and Milan, 1983), p. 136. Andrea Annoni had himself portrayed in the Flemish altarpiece of *c.* 1550 formerly in San Giorgio, Annone, now in the Museo Diocesano, Milan (see P. Biscotti, *Il Museo Diocesano di Milano* (Milan, 2005), pp. 234–37).

8 Magurn 1955, p. 408, letter 242, March 12, 1638, Rubens to Sustermans in Florence: "M. Annoni . . . tells me that he sent the case with the picture three weeks ago via Lille, whence it will go to Italy."

9 For the house, the present Osterriethhuis, see Ministerie van Nationale Opvoeding en Nederlandse Cultuur. Rijksdienst voor Monumenten- en Landschapszorg, *Bouwen door de eeuwen heen: Inventaris van het cultuurbezit in Belgie. Architectuur. Deel 3nb Stad Antwerpen* (Ghent, 1979), pp. 316–19.

10 T. van Lerius, *Notice des Œuvres d'Art de l'Eglise Paroissiale et Ci-devant Insigne Collégiale de Saint Jacques à Anvers* (Borgerhout, 1855), p. 125. We know from his ennoblement letter and his will that Carenna built a sacristy and chapel in 1655. Rubens's chapel, built in 1641, is directly behind the main altar, and Carenna's chapel abuts the left side of Rubens's chapel. See also *Bouwen door de eeuwen* . . . (cited note 9), pp. 474–78, and the ground-plan pl. XXXI. The terms flanking the altar recall those Rubens designed for his Achilles tapestries (of which Carenna owned a set; figs. 39–43), on which see Guy Delmarcel in *Tapisseries bruxelloises au siècle de Rubens* . . . (exhibition catalogue, Musées royaux d'Art et d'Histoire, Brussels, 1977), pp. 103–08, nos. 33–37. For the series see F. Lammertse and A. Vergara, *Peter Paul Rubens's The Life of Achilles* (Rotterdam, 2004), pp. 40, 65, 70–71.

11 Neither Carenna's nor Rubens's knighthoods are mentioned, since they were less prestigious than military orders, in Francisco Fernandez Izquierdo, 'Los flamencos en las órdenes militares españolas', in *España y las 17 provincias de los Paises Bajos*, ed. Ana Crespo Solana and Manuel Herrero Sánchez, vol. 1 (Universidad de Cordoba, 2002), pp. 101–36 (John Elliott kindly signalled this reference). However, in the Brussels state archives there are documents of ennoblement dated Madrid, December 30, 1655 (Appendix, Documents A, no. 2), and of his knighthood, bestowed by Philip IV on January 14, 1665 (Ms divers/ Handsschriftenverz. 270, f. 221, seemingly copies made by the notary Ambrosio Sebille, on August 20, 1666, and again on June 18, 1667); the same notifications are to be found in the Archivo General de Simancas (Valladolid), Secretarías Provinciales, *libro* 1435 (*legajo* 2498), together with certification by the notary Philip Rubens (nephew of the painter) that Giacomo Antonio Carenna was an almoner in 1648 (see Documents A, no. 1). I owe these Spanish archival references to Angel Alloza and Francisco Fernández Izquierdo. I also thank José Luis Colomer and Monica McConnell for investigating the knighthood. See also P. Janssens and L. Duerloo, *Armorial de la Noblesse Belge*, 4 vols. (Brussels, 1992), *s.v.*

12 Ignazio was a member of the humanist group known as 'the Romanists' which Rubens and many other painters had joined after travelling to Italy: see E. Dilis, *La confrérie des Romanistes* (Antwerp, 1923), p. 54. Alessandro's 1699 inventory (Duverger, vol. 12 (2002), pp. 517–19), shows he owned books on Elizabeth I and Cromwell, and Francesco's 1691 inventory mentions books.

13 Appendix, Documents A, no. 2.

14 For Juan Esteban Imbrea, who was made count of Yebes on 21 October 1649, see C. Álvarez Nogal, *Los banqueros de Felipe IV y los metales preciosos americanos* (Madrid, 1997), pp. 70–72. For the loan, involving also Etienne Spinola, see Stadsarchief, Antwerp, notary archive Ambrosio Sebille, Ms 3009, for January 22, 1649. The Sebille files contain documents showing

Carenna appointing his brother as his proxy in Milan and fixing the postal charge to Venice (Ms 3013, February 1, 1663) but few other financial transactions. In her essay (see below, p. 164 and note 156) Giovanna Tonelli indicates the involvement of Carenna and the Annoni 'group' in numerous transactions involving war financing, and, in 1650, a loan by Carenna to King Philip IV that seems never to have been repaid.

15 The branch is identified as laurel in *Jordaens in Belgisch bezit* (exhibition catalogue, Koninklijk Museum voor Schone Kunsten, Antwerp, 1978), p. 89, no. 32. In a study drawing Christ holds the 'olive branch.'

16 See note 9. The house was built in 1570, and was initially owned by the de Wals family, but was sold between 1609 and 1610 to Portuguese merchants, the Duarte Ximenez, who, in turn, sold it on July 4, 1622. The house was sold to Carenna by Pieter Hellemans. It is worth noting that in 1608 Pieter's father Ferdinand Hellemans acquired from Francisco Godimez a house on the Meir which stretched through to the Nieuwstraat: this must have been comparable, if not identical, to Carenna's (see R. Baetens, *De Nazomer van Antwerpens Welvaart. De diaspora en het handelshuis De Grootte tijdens de eerste helft van de 17de eeuw*, 2 vols. (Brussels, 1976), I, p. 178). This information was kindly provided by Dorrit Van Camp.

17 D. Verelst, *Geschiedenis van Zwijndrecht en Burcht* (Zwijndrecht, 1990), p. 129. In January 1619 Nicolaas Rockox inherited from his brother Jan a farm between the two towns (Zwijndrecht and Burcht) which he sold to Rubens on 15 June 1619: see Baudouin 2005, p. 84.

18 M. Friedländer, *Jan Gossaert and Bernard van Orley* (Brussels, 1972), p. 69, pls. 84, 85.

19 See U. Härting, *Frans Francken der Jüngere* (Freren, 1989), pp. 306–10, nos. 269–79a. Other painters, including David Teniers the Younger, were also engaged by the subject: see *Antwerp, Story of a Metropolis: 16th–17th Century*, ed. J. Van der Stock (exhibition catalogue, Hessenhuis, Antwerp, 1993), p. 313, no. 175 (*An Almoner and his Wife* by Gonzales Coques), with reference to another by Pieter I Thys.

20 See the inventory of Peeter Stevens (1662): Duverger, vol. 9 (1997), p. 145, no. 27, Jan 'Velvet' Brueghel, "*Un aumônier visitant les pauvres*" (probably the work now in the Koninklijk Museum, Antwerp or a version of it; see *Pieter Breughel der Jüngere – Jan Brueghel der Ältere. Flämische Malerei um 1600. Tradition und Fortschritt* (exhibition catalogue, Villa Hügel, Essen, 1997), pp. 116–20, nos. 15–18).

21 Duverger, vol. 8 (1995), p. 382, "*Una pittura delle Sette Opere di Misericordia.*" For Stefano Annoni's inventory see below and Appendices, Documents A, no. 4.

22 See Van Dyck's portrait of the almoner Adriaen Stevens (1561–1640) showing a bowl behind him: Pushkin Museum, Moscow; Barnes *et al.* 2004, p. 352; and Jordaens's of Rogier Le Witer of 1635 also shows a collecting figure and the date of his election as an almoner, 1623: Rijksmuseum, Amsterdam; R.-A. d'Hulst, *Jacob Jordaens* (London, 1982), pp. 273, 340 note 10.

23 L. Robyn de Schneidauer, 'Les grands-aumôniers d'Anvers', *L'intermédiaire des généalogistes*, no. 57 (May 1955), pp. 113–25, at p. 119, lists Giacomo Antonio Carenna as an almoner in 1648 and his son Francesco as an almoner in 1657. According to Schneidauer the office ran for five years.

24 Appendix, Documents A, no. 1.

25 Schneidauer 1955 (cited note 23), p. 119. It may be that Carenna was commemorated at the feast the almoners regularly held on Saint Barbara's day (December 4).

26 P. Génard, *Anvers à travers les âges* (Brussels, 1888), II, p. 349. Susan Ryckaert was another noble godmother. Her coats of arms are on a bronze balustrade of the Chapel of Saint Anthony in the Sint-Jacobskerk, where Gertrude van Veen was also buried. Louis Malo was still alive in 1659 and had an engraving after Van Dyck's *Margaret Lemon as Erminia* (Blenheim Palace) dedicated to him (Barnes *et al.* 2004, p. 552, no. 158).

27 Verelst 1990, p. 130 (cited note 17); for the date of Carenna's death see Jacques le Roy, *Notitia Marchionatus Sacri Romani Imperii, hoc est urbis et Antverpiensis* (Amsterdam, 1678), p. 386 (see Appendix, Documents A, no. 7). For the Le Roy family and their comparable advancement in Antwerp see J. Hedley, *Van Dyck at the Wallace Collection* (exhibition catalogue, The Wallace Collection, London, September 23– December 15, 1999), pp. 50–77. Le Roy accurately records Carenna's funeral chapel and the inscription on his vault lid, and on p. 158 illustrates Carenna's castle at Burcht, which is described as having good views of the city of Antwerp. A view of the city apparently taken from a point close to the castle by Abel Grimmer and Hendrik van Balen is now in the Koninklijk Museum voor Schone Kunsten, Antwerp: see B. Werche, *Hendrik van Balen (1575–1632)* (Turnhout, 2004), p. 154, no. A55; also *The Age of Rubens*, ed. P.C. Sutton (exhibition catalogue, Museum of Fine Arts, Boston, 1993), p. 116, fig. 13, and Antwerp 1993 (see note 19), pp. 163–63 (for Bonnecroy) and 285 (for Grimmer and Van Balen's view of the port of Antwerp).

28 Schindler archive, Plantin Museum, Antwerp, which is being catalogued by Dorrit Van Camp, who kindly shared the receipts for the December feast for 'Almoner Carenna' with me. Carenna left money for masses to be held in two religious institutions in the same block as his house, of Poor Clares and Minims.

29 Maria Annoni appears as the mother on the birth certificates of Giacomo Antonio's children, recorded in the registry of baptisms (*dopen*) at Sint-Jacobskerk; photocopy in the library of the Stadsarchief (or 'Felix' Archief, or city archive), Antwerp.

30 Giovanna Tonelli notes that in 1627 Giacomo Antonio engaged Paolo Annoni, the son of his former employer, Giovanni Pietro Annoni, and his eleven-year-old brother as trainees.

31 The paintings in Stefano Annoni's inventory were published in Duverger, vol. 8 (1995), pp. 380–83, doc. 1664; this is here (Appendix, Documents A, no. 5) more fully published, including the furniture; and his will is published for the first time (Documents A, no. 4).

32 For the Louvre painting see H. Adhémar, *Les primitifs flamands* (Brussels, 1962), pp. 114–34. This identification was suggested by Lorne Campbell.

33 28 January 1657, Duverger, vol. 7 (1993), p. 308, doc. 2130 (G. Le Rousseau, 2446 (1657), ff. 60–61v). "*Per una recognitione o memoria la suo al suditto Senor Giacomo Antonio Carenna, mio cogino, una mia pittura el Diana con Satyri fatta dal Abraham Janssen.*"

34 See Appendix, Documents A, no. 4.

35 We know also that Stefano Annoni was buying ten 'history' paintings from Fourchardt on June 20, 1655 (Denucé 1931, p. 57), and that on another occasion Jan II Brueghel received two "*trophkines*" on Annoni's behalf (*ibid.*, p. 153). Stefano's Bril is no. 26 in Francesco's 1691 inventory (Duverger, vol. 12 (2002), doc. 3989, pp. 99–105). From about 1700 there is notice of a Rubens painting in the Palazzo Annoni: this appears to be a copy of the Louvre *Tomyris and Cyrus*, measuring 205 × 155 cm; see McGrath 1997, II, pp. 33, 37. The Getty Provenance Index database of archival documents has the wills of Giovanni Francesco Annoni (1706), Carlo Francesco Annoni (1713) and Giovanni Battista Annoni, son of Antonio (1737), who owned a "*stragge degli innocenti*" (signalled by Burton Fredericksen).

36 See Giovanna Tonelli's essay, note 173, and Documents B.

37 The shape of the collection seems very similar to that of Cardinal Federico Borromeo, who had died in 1631.

38 See further Giovanna Tonelli's essay, pp. 167ff.

39 See *Arte lombarda dai Visconti agli Sforza*, ed. G. Gronchi (1958), p. 110, for which reference, and her help on the Holy Innocents and Milan in general, I am grateful to Anthea Stevens. See further M.P. Carroll, *Veiled Threats: The Logic of Popular Catholicism in Italy* (Baltimore and London, 1996), pp. 181–83: this reference Amanda Bradley brought to my attention.

40 The reliquary was transferred from the deconsecrated San Francesco (now destroyed) in 1803 and is currently in the Museo della Basilica di Sant'Ambrogio, Milan. The "*reliquiario degli Innocenti*" (60 × 35 × 23 cm) is enamelled and embossed in silver with six related scenes on the front.

41 Duverger, vol. 12 (2002), doc. 3989, pp. 99–105.

42 See note 33.

43 B. Schnackenburg, *Gemaldegalerie Alte Meister. Gesamtkatalog* (Kassel: Staatliche Museen, 1996), pp. 150–51, pl. 54, fig. 83.

44 See Musson to Picart, January 6, 1676: Denucé 1949, p. 428. See also D. Widmaer Picasso, *Jean-Michel Picart (1600–1682)* (PhD thesis, Sorbonne, Paris, 2000), and J. Blažkova and E. Duverger, *Les Tapisseries d'Octavio Piccolomini* (Ghent and Sint-Amandsberg, 1970), p. 72.

45 Picard wrote from Paris to Musson on July 26, 1675: "*een stuk van Rubens de Kinderdooling die eenen persoon toukompt ghenamt Mr Careno … Gent … Karena*": Denucé 1949, pp. 411, 412; and on August 16, 1675: "*maer ghelyc ic verstaen soo is dien Carena, die komt van Genevoyse afkomsten, dat is een uasie erger als Joden … 2 ofte 3 dusent guldens*": *ibid.* Already, on January 10, 1675, Cornelis de Baillieur had mentioned "*dese soude aengekocht door Jonker Jacomo Antionio Carenna:*" *ibid.*, p. 168. On the likelihood of Giacomo Antonio Carenna having also operated in Genoa see Tonelli's essay below, p. 163.

46 Denucé 1932, p. 364; Duverger, vol. 10 (1999), June 3, 1676, pp. 114–15. See N. Penny, *National Gallery Catalogues: The 16th-Century Italian Paintings, Volume II: Venice 1540–1600* (New Haven and London, 2008), p. 408, for a 1607 Flemish copy of the London National Gallery *Adoration*. The painter Erasmus II Quellinus's inventory of 22 March 1679 records a copy of Veronese's *Adoration* (Duverger, vol. 10 (1999), pp. 347–74, at p. 356, "*Een Drij Coninch naer Paulo Veronese*") and this may be Quellinus's copy after Veronese in Anthoine's 1691 inventory, but there is no clear link to the 1676 conditional sale or return document.

Provisional family tree of Giacomo Antonio Carenna and his son Francesco in Antwerp

GIACOMO ANTONIO (1591–1672)[a]
Lord of Zwijndrecht and Burcht
Married
Maria Annoni[b]

Children:

- Pietro (March 11, 1623–) Godfather: Giovanni Carenna
- Pietro (March 13, 1624– ...) Godparents: Jan Pieter Hannon, Suzanna Ryckaerts
- Giovanni (??– ...)
- Giovanni Francesco (November 12, 1626–1691) Godmother: Grazia Belle *Married* Isabella Roelants *Lord of Zwijndrecht*
- Paolo (January 6, 1628– ...) Godparents: Paolo Carenna, Suzanna Ryckaerts
- Theresa (July 29, 1631– ...) Godparents: Battista Culgaro, Clara Annoni
- Ludovica (November 27, 1633– ...) Godparents: Stefano Annoni, Gertrude van Veen (?)
- Ludovico (May 21, 1635– ...) Godparents: Louis Malo, Suzanna Ryckaerts
- Giovanni (October 8, 1636– ...) Godparents: Stefano Carenna, Anna Bierens
- Anna Maria (August 27, 1639– ...) Godparents: Pietro Annoni, Gertrude van Veen
- Ignazio (September 17, 1641–1689) Godparents: Stefano Annoni, Gertrude van Verschueren[c] *Married* Suzanna de Thosse[d] *Lord of Burcht*

Children of Giovanni Francesco:

- Alessandro (– 1697)[e] *Lord of Zwijndrecht, Mol, Balen, Dessel*
- Paolo (– after 1691)
- Francesco (alive 1691) *Canon at Sint-Jacobskerk*
- Giacomo Antonio (May 31, 1657–1727) Godparents: Giacomo Antonio Carenna, Maria Anna Vandergoet *Priest*[f]
- Giovanni Maria (July 9, 1666–...) Godparents: J-Maria Charlet, Antonio Carenna, Maria Alessandra Roelants
- Ignazio Giuseppe (July 22, 1667– after 1691) Godparents: Giacomo Antonio Carenna, Maria Alessandra Roelants
- Maria (August 28, 1668– probably before 1691) Godparents: Giacomo Antonio Carenna, Maria (Agut Combe?) *Married* Meuleniere of Bruges[g]
  - Nicolas (–1744)
- Caterina (December 13, 1668[?]– after 1691) *Married* Etienne Caro of Brussels[h]
  - Philip Joseph (–1726) *Canon at Sint-Jacobskerk*[i]
- Jacopo Antonio (July 12, 1669–)
- Jacopo (July 23, 1670– ...) Godparents: Jacques Roelants, Maria Alessandra Roelants
- Domenico (1671– after 1691)

Initial dates given are baptismal, not birth. Information on baptismal dates and godparents is taken from 'Historische documentatie verzameld door F. Donnet', Stadsarchief, Antwerp, PK 3284. The 1691 will of Francesco Carenna (see notes 41 and 62) and the 1699 will of Alessandro Carenna (Duverger, vol. 12 (2002), pp. 517–19) list Francesco Carenna's children then alive.

a) Baptismal certificate of March 8, 1591 (*Parrocchia di Ss. Maria e Giorgio, Annone di Brianza, Anagrafe-registri antichi. Registro dei battesimi dal 1575 al 1605 (1)*).
b) Maria Annone appears as mother on Giacomo Antonio Carenna's children's baptismal certificates (Stadsarchief, *Sint-Jacob, Dopen*).
c) She appears to have been a relative of the mother of this illegitimate Ignazio.
d) Will of Suzanna de Thosse, May 7, 1698: Duvergier, vol. 11 (2001), p. 540.
e) For Alessandro's will see Duverger, vol. 12 (2002), pp. 517–19, as above; his inventory of April 9–14, 1699 is Stadsarchief, Staaten/Rekeningen Ms 1151.
f) For his career see *Nieuw Nederlandisch Biografisch Woordenboek*, vol. 3 (Leiden, 1914), pp. 204–05.
g) J. De Herckenrode, *Nobiliaire des Pays-Bas* (Ghent, 1865), I, p. 388.
h) Albert Royal Library, Brussels, Ms II 1208, f. 60v (reference given by Michiel Verweij). Etienne Michel Cano was the son of Jean-Baptiste Cano of Brussels. Caterina signed Alessandro Carenna's will as "C. Cano;" this will was also signed by A.J. and P.C. Halmale (Francesco's wife's sister Claire Roelants married Nicolas van Halmele, mayor of Antwerp, so they may have been guardians).
i) See note 48 on the following page.

47 See Denucé 1932, pp. 353ff.; Duverger, vol. 12 (2002), pp. 85–98: Anthoine's will of March 28, 1691 (notary J.M. Lodewijcx) left to Joanna Maria Anthoine "*Een groot stuck Kinderdoodinge fl 1,200*." This large unattributed *Massacre* was the most expensive painting of the 306 in his collection, which included works given to Rubens and Van Dyck. Rubens (or possibly Frans Floris) is the most likely author of an expensive *Massacre*; Rubens's later *Massacre* now in Munich would appear from de Piles's accounts of the 1670s to have already reached the duc de Richelieu, having being owned by Canon Antoine de Tassis and engraved by Pontius in 1643: see K. Renger and C. Denk, *Flämische Malerei des Barock in der Alten Pinakothek* (Munich, 2002), p. 300. Most paintings were valued at 800 guilders or less, for example no. 24, Jan 'Velvet' Brueghel, *Saint John Preaching*, fl. 600; no. 63, Van Dyck, *Portrait of Cornelius and Lucas de Wael*, fl. 600 (now Capitoline Museum, Rome; Barnes *et al.* 2004, p. 210, no. II.71); no. 116, Veronese, *The Finding of Moses*, fl. 800. No. 95, "*Een groot stuck Twee Miloeneters van Morillo*," fl. 1000, is to be identified with Murillo's *Melon Eaters* (146 × 104 cm, Munich; see X. Brooke, *Murillo, Scenes of Childhood* (exhibition catalogue, Dulwich Picture Gallery, London, 2001), p. 90, no. 6, as in Antwerp by "1678;" in the Spanish edition of the same catalogue (2001) it is claimed that it was bought by Max Emanuel in 1691; see further U. Krempel, 'Max Emanuel als Gemäldesammler', in *Kurfürst Max Emanuel: Bayern und Europa um 1700*, ed. Hubert Glaser (exhibition catalogue, 2 vols., Munich, 1976), I, pp. 221–38: she gives Gisbert van Ceulen's inventory, the contents of which were acquired by Max Emanuel in 1698). No. 108, "*Een Vrouken met Pekelharinck in de handt van Geeraert Dauw 1,000*," is Gerrit Dou's *Woman with Fish* (one of the paintings in the Hermitage or at Karlsruhe). No. 168, fl. 150, is Poussin's *Satyr carrying off a Nymph*, now in Kassel. Nos. 134–36 are given to Rubens: no. 134, "*Een Venus die haerselven spiegelt van Rubens fl 240*", is probably *Venus with a Mirror* (in Vienna, recorded in the 1612 Liechtenstein inventory); no. 135, *The Visitation* (fl. 800); no. 136, *Mary Magdalene*. No. 137, *Woman in a Fur Wrap* (after Titian) is valued at fl. 240 (now Queensland Art Gallery, Brisbane; see Antwerp 2004, p. 111, note 8). Nos. 139–46 are eight 'Histories of Achilles', valued at 1,200 guilders, the same as the unattributed *Massacre* ("*De Historie van Achilles bestaende in acht stucxkens van Rubens welcke stucxkens tesamen sijn gewerdeert Fl 1,200*"; see Rotterdam 2003, p. 59, suggesting they can be identified in Fourment's 1643 inventory; see also M.E. Wieseman, 'Pursuing and Possessing Passion: Two Hundred Years of Collecting Rubens's Oil Sketches', in *Drawn by the Brush: Oil Sketches of Peter Paul Rubens* (exhibition catalogue, Bruce Museum, Greenwich, Conn.; Berkeley Art Museum; Cincinnati Art Museum, 2004–05), p. 49. One of the surviving oil-sketches for the Achilles tapestries, at Winterthur, has an inventory number written *199*, resembling the *18* on the National Gallery *Samson and Delilah* – suggesting a common mystery owner). No. 59, valued at fl. 300, is (as Neil MacLaren first observed) Van Dyck's *Rinaldo and Armida* (National Gallery, London), and no. 148, at fl. 150, is Rubens's *Saint Ursula* (now in the Musées royaux des Beaux-Arts, Brussels, as is proved by the presence of Anthoine's seal on their backs – as first suggested by M. Jaffé, 'Rediscovered

Oil Sketches by Rubens', *Burlington Magazine* (1970), pp. 432–36, at p. 435 note 7; see now Brussels 2007, pp. 96–97, note 46). There is also a Rubens *Saint George* (see fig. 73), which remains a mystery. For nos. 76–77, portraits of Charles I and his Queen, see Barnes *et al.* 2004, p. 519, no. IV.113: it is proposed that these were the portraits, now lost, engraved by Pieter de Jode for Karel van den Bosch. Barnes *et al.* (2004, p. 248, no. III.2) note that a "Van Dyck" *Adoration* oil-sketch also has Anthoine's seal.

48 For the Pontius print of Jan Roelants (1568–1651) see Génard 1888 (cited note 26), II, pp. 397, 474: it is inscribed *Jacobus Roelans comitis de Tassis* and dedicated to *Io. Bapt. Antonius*. The Imperial Postmaster General count Lamoral II of Thurn and Taxis had the international monopoly and his visit to Alexander Balthazar Roelants, Postmaster of the Netherlands, was celebrated in prints by Wenceslaus Hollar of 1651. Jan-Baptista Anthoine succeeded Jan Roelants as Imperial Postmaster for Antwerp in 1675 and was knighted on May 9, 1678. Following Giacomo Carenna's acquisition and building of the Borromeo Chapel in 1655 Alexander Roelants had obtained from the cash-strapped church (the plagues of 1552–53 and 1555–56 and the building of the choir and ambulatory chapels having exhausted its funds) control of the Saint Roch Chapel in 1657 for his use as a family funerary chapel, and set up a very select Brotherhood of Saint Roch. In 1726 the director was Canon Philip Joseph Cano, the son of Etienne Cano and Caterina Carenna, daughter of Giacomo's son Francesco. See J. Muller, 'Confraternity and Art in the St Jacobs's Church', in H. Vlieghe, *Concept, Design and Execution in Flemish Painting* (Turnhout, 2000), pp. 110ff. For the Cano arms quartered with the Carenna, see *ibid.*, p. 103, fig. 8 (but not there identified).

49 For the the firm Fourchardt see Denucé 1931, p. 259. (George Gordon, in Sotheby's sale catalogue of 2002, has established that Denucé's spelling 'Forchoudt' was not the form used in his correspondence, although names were not spelled systematically during this period.) See also J. Kräftner, 'The Rubens Collection of the Princes of Liechtenstein', in Antwerp 2007, pp. 57–65. The *Massacre* is mentioned in a letter dated December 13, 1698 from Marcus Fourchardt in Vienna to his brother Guilliamo in Antwerp. Marcus tells his brother that he had told Prince Johann Adam Andreas I of Liechtenstein about the Rubens *Massacre of the Innocents*, but that the prince wanted to know more about the artist before embarking on a purchase. It is possible that the *Massacre* was also the subject of an earlier letter of December 3, 1698, which points out that the prince did not want to buy a Rubens which had been painted before his Italian trip. This would explain why the prince did not initially proceed with the purchase – because, not having been in a position to view it (presumably in Antwerp), he (an esteemed connoisseur) could not have appreciated that it was clearly a post-Italian work. The prince eventually saw it on September 5, 1699, and nearly four years later, on August 2, 1702, it arrived in Vienna, in a crate along with various other pictures: "*No. 3 en 4: 1 Kinderdoodinge van Rubbens, met 1 Korfken van Bandora van Rubbens, met 1 Visserijken van Tenniers; dese 3 stuck syn samen vercocht egen Ryxd 2733–30*" (one *Massacre of the Innocents* by Rubens, one *Pandora's Box* by Rubens, one fishing piece by Teniers; these three pieces sold together for 2733.30 *Reichstaler*). It seems that the "Pandora" must have been *The Discovery of Erichthonius*, acquired by Johann Adam from Fourchardt in 1704, as both stories involve the opening of a box: painted around 1615, it measures 218 × 317 cm. It is likely that the *Massacre* went straight to the princely collection, from which it bears a black seal of 1733 on the front of the picture (upper right-hand corner) and a red seal of the same year on the reverse. (The seals were to identify the works left by the prince in 1612 in perpetuity in fidei-commissum.) The prince had already acquired Rubens's Decius Mus tapestry cartoons in 1694. He was the grandson of one of the greatest Catholic winners of the Thirty Years' War. Immensely rich, he acquired the principality so he would rank just below the emperor. He established a bank in Vienna.

50 The first printed catalogue of the collection was produced by Vicenzo Fanti in 1767. Subsequent catalogues were published in 1780 and 1873. See Kräftner in Antwerp 2007, p. 57.

51 Coincidentally, another of Rubens's early masterpieces, *Tarquin and Lucretia* (see fig. 38), had just emerged at this time (shortly before the Second World War), only to disappear for another sixty years in 1945.

52 April 28, 1618; Magurn 1955, pp. 60–61.

53 Rubens to de Bie, May 11, 1611; Magurn 1955, p. 55.

54 See entry by Joost van der Auwera in Brussels 2007, pp. 150–52, no. 41. In the past, some scholars had attributed the Brussels canvas version of the *Massacre* to Rubens, but the discovery of the Thomson Collection picture confirms the derivative status of the Brussels painting. The attribution of the Thomson Collection picture was nevertheless doubted by B. Fassbinder, 'Rubens oder nicht Rubens? das ist hier die Frage', *Zeitschrift für Kunst- und Denkmalpflege*, LVII, no. 2 (2003), pp. 233–48.

55 McGrath 1997, II, p. 101; see also Brunswick 2004, p. 129, for Cornelis de Vos's *Interior* in Stockholm depicting *Lot and his Daughters* hung above a fireplace.

56 Duverger, vol. 1 (1984), pp. 400–61, esp. p. 404. There were also paintings showing Susannah, Venus and Cupid, Hercules and the Centaur (by Floris), Saint Ursula (possibly the panel in Brussels; see Jaffé 1977, p. 233, no. 459), a banquet, Judith and Holofernes, Marcus Curtius, Salome, the Good Samaritan, and the Horatii. Emmanuel's will seems to have been drawn up by the notary Jan Walewyms on September 15, 1604, and he had two children. It seems the Ximenez family won the patronage of Pope Sixtus V before it was discovered they were converted Jews. They were then adopted by the Medici Grand Dukes of Tuscany, which explains the series of Medici papal portraits in their inventory.

57 F. Baudouin, 'Schilderijen van Rubens en van Dyck in het bezit van Filips Godines en Sebilla van den Berghe', *Academiae Analecta*, LI (1991), pp. 63–66, supposes (p. 66) that the painting was covered because it showed female nudity. Philip Godines (1603–1633; widow alive until 1661) subsequently owned Rubens's *Birth of Venus*, which was bought by William III of Orange in 1667 before going to Berlin in 1741.

58 See Jaffé 1977, p. 209, no. 323; G. Bartoschek and C.M. Vogtherr, *Zerstört Entführt Verschollen: Die Verlüste der preussischen Schlösser im Zweiten Weltkrieg* (Potsdam, 2004), p. 428, photo GK 17599; Krempel 1976 (as cited in note 47 with reference to Murillo). Anthoine's Murillo and his Rubens *Birth of Venus* were both bought by Max Emanuel in 1698, with other paintings, from Colen for 100,000 guilders; see note 47.

59 See the will of Marie Ximenez d'Aragón, daughter of Gonzalo and Catherine Eecheren, July 14, 1654 (notary Le Rousseau): Duverger, vol. 7 (1993), p. 259.

60 H. Pohl, *Die Portugiesen in Antwerpen (1567–1648)* (Wiesbaden, 1977), pp. 80–81. Lorne Campbell kindly drew this publication to my attention.

61 One imagines such furnishings were also in Carenna's house. The inventory describes a 'fore-house' or front room, which may have run down the Meir or the side street, leading to two kitchens. It is tempting to suppose that many of the eleven paintings listed in the inventory, which were spread over a similar number of rooms, were also chimney-pieces, and many of the same rooms also had beds and some had bellows listed among their contents.

62 There follows an English translation of the relevant parts of the inventory (published by Duverger, see note 41).
"Extract of the inventory of goods left by MICHEL JOAN FRANCISCUS CARENNA, Knight, Lord of Zwijndrecht etc., widower to ISABELLA ROELANTS. On April 2, 1691 he died in his apartment on the Meir and leaves behind six children: ALEXANDER and PAULO Carenna, FRANCISCUS Carenna, priest and canon of Sint-Jacobskerk, and three minors, Ignatius Josephus, Catharina and Dominicus Carenna. On March 30, 1691 the deceased read his will to the notary J. de Vos. The inventory was put together by this same notary on the request of and in the presence of the children . . .:
Everyday silverware in the kitchen . . . Silverware in the room of Ms Catharina Carenna . . . this is the room of C. Carenna: A tortoiseshell crucifix with a silver figure of Christ under a silver Our Lady In the kitchen . . .
In the antechamber: 17 orange and lemon trees in wooden pots in iron hoops / 3 Maps of the oceans, in black frames / 2 still lifes with fruit Nos. 1 and 2 / A large painting with a boar hunt No. 3 / A painting with a heron hunt No. 4 / A painting with parrots No. 5
In the first room after the antechamber: The room [is] decorated with gold leather on a white ground / A fireplace valance with a flowerpot in the chimney / Two portraits of the mother and father of the deceased / A chimney-piece of Langen Jan [Jan Boeckhorst] representing a statue of Mary and Charles Borromeo No. 6 / Six landscapes of the seasons Nos. 7–12
In the next chamber or salon: This room is decorated with tapestries representing the history of Meliaser [Meleager] in 6 pieces / A painting by Rubens for the chimney with figures, fruit and game No. 13 / A painting above the door with a swan, a heron, a hart etc. No. 14 / A fireplace valance or 'cover' with flowers and three angels in the chimney
In the big *salette* next to the courtyard: A series of tapestries depicting the story of Achilles in 7 pieces / Three red silken curtains for the windows / A large chimney-piece depicting Diana and other figures No. 15 / A painting by Jordaens depicting Cleopatra bitten by the serpent No. 16 / Another painting by

Jordaens also depicting Cleopatra and Mark Antony No. 17 / A fireplace valance in the chimney / A red silken curtain hanging in front of the door
In the entrance to the courtyard: 4 Maps depicting the four parts of the world
In the dining room next to the courtyard: The room [is] decorated with gold leather on a blue ground / A painted screen of 6 components, decorated with flowerpots / A big chimney-piece by Snij[d]ers with a hanging hart and other beasts [game] No. 18 / Another big painting depicting a farm with a variety of animals No. 19 / 4 Paintings depicting the 12 months of the year Nos. 20–23 / 2 Round, small paintings by Bruegel Nos. 24, 25 / A landscape by Bril No. 26 / Two other small landscapes Nos. 27, 28 / A painting of a vase with flowers by Verendael No. 29 / A small painting of a swan No. 30
In the *Roeffken* [?]: The little room [is] decorated with gold leather on a blue ground / A chequerboard / 4 Small paintings of the 4 seasons Nos. 31–34 / A large painting of a Fair No. 35 / A painting of an Italian pleasure garden No. 36 / A painting on wood for the chimney by Mompart [de Momper] No. 37 / A small still life No. 38
In the kitchen: . . .
In the wash house: A [painting of] landscape for the chimney No. 39
In the passage to the cloakroom: a landscape painting of the Court of Brussels No. 40 / A small sculpure of Mary No. 41 / A painting of ships and a fish market No. 42
In the cloakroom: A big painting for the chimney No. 43 / 4 paintings of the seasons Nos. 44–47 / Another fireplace valance / A small painting of a woodpecker [?] No. 48 / A large map
On the square [?]: A portrait of an emperor No. 49 / A large lion, carved from white stone, on a blue socle
In the antechamber to the street: The room [is] decorated with gold leather on a black ground / A chimney-piece with a depiction of fruit and other things [?] by De Heem No. 50 / A fireplace valance with a dog and a cat by the roast
In the summer-house (*gloriette*) near the courtyard [?]: An octagonal table of black stone on a pedestal / A painting of Achilles No. 51 / A painting of ships No. 52
In the garden or summer-house (*gloriette*) behind the courtyard: Two stone figures of Venus and Adonis on pedestals / 8 children on blue pedestals showing the quarters of the coats of arms
Upstairs in the stone children's room: A landscape for the chimney No. 53 / 2 Other small paintings and some prints in frames / 12 Tapestry cushion covers, a tablecloth / 2 large horns
In the room of Master Dominicus: The room is decorated with tapestries of landscapes [probably from his mother: see note 64 below] / A black crucifix with a boxwood [figure of] Christ / A landscape for the chimney No. 54 / A Vanitas still life No. 55 / A painting of the Annunciation No. 56 / A painting of a caravan [Castiglione, gypsies] No. 57 / A small painting of the Offering No. 58 / A small sculpture of Mary No. 59 / Another even smaller sculpture of Mary No. 60
In the room of Master Alexander: The room [is] decorated with gold leather on a red ground / A painting of a landscape for the chimney No. 61
The room of Mr. Van Borcht [the Lord of Burcht?]: The room [is] decorated with gold leather on a green ground / A rug / A carpet on the floor / A table with walnut inlay, a drawer and a tapestry tablecloth / Two paintings of Ships Nos. 62, 63 / A painting of the Annunciation No. 64 / A painting of Abraham and Agar No. 65
In the room called the Ladies' room: A rug / The room is decorated with gold leather on a blue ground / Two portraits Nos. 66, 67 / A painting of the Pietà No. 68 / A landscape No. 69 / A small painting of the Nativity No. 70
In the alcove room of the deceased: The alcove is decorated with a silken and cotton drapery / A small painting of the Nativity No. 71 / a small portrait of the deceased mistress of the house *Memorie* / A portrait of the deceased *Memorie* / a small sculpture of the Immaculate Conception of the Virgin Mary [?] No. 72
In the large chamber before the alcove: The room [is] decorated [with] gold leather on a red ground / 3 White curtains for the windows / 2 Paintings of flower garlands Nos. 73, 74 / A small painting of birds and a game-bag No. 75 / A portrait of the deceased *Memorie* / A painting of the Nativity No. 76 / A large painting of a Landscape No. 77 / A small sculpture of Mary No. 78
In the passage above the first gallery: 4 Paintings of the Seasons Nos. 79–82 / A gold leather screen / A small lavatory covered in gold leather
In the room of Miss Carenna: An oak [?] writing desk with a drawer and leather writing pad / The room [is] decorated with gold leather on a blue ground / A landscape for the chimney Mompart [de Momper] No. 83 / A painting of The Adoration of the Magi No. 84 / A miniature of the Christ Child No. 85 / A painting of a sculpture of Mary inside a flower garland No. 86 / Another miniature of Saint Rosa No. 87
In the glass comptoir: 4 Small paintings and 2 Portraits drawn with the pen / A rug which was formerly in the room of Master Dominicus / An oak dolls cabinet
In the *Maertencamer* [?]: A painting of a game house in water colour No. 88 / A painting of the Battle of Nordlingen in water colour No. 89 / . . .
In the chamber of a servant: A water colour No. 90 / 3 Drawn portraits Nos. 91–93
In the writing room: A painting for the chimney with Democ[r]itus and Heraclitus No. 94 / A painting of Mary No. 95 / A small landscape No. 96 / A small altarpiece with two doors, in the middle the crucified Christ No. 97 / 2 Depictions of flowerpots on paper Nos. 98, 99 / 12 Small paintings depicting the 12 months Nos. 100–111 / 2 Spanish chairs covered with gold leather / 4 prints on paper in black frames / A collection of books, in folio, quarto, as well as in octavo . . . / A book of prints and an atlas / A fine books of prints / A large number of prints of the Triumph of the Seizure of Breda [?] (*Buda*) / A number of small prints on satin with the same subject / A set of drawings and prints of little value."
(This translation was kindly made by Veronica Kopecky with assistance from Ben van Beneden and Bart Cornelius.)

63 See Jaffé 1977, no. 450. Another candidate would be the Oakley Park (Lord Plymouth) *Shepherd and Shepherdess* (*ibid.*, no. 202) but it is much larger; this might be a candidate to be matched with the big Snyders noted in Francesco Carenna's inventory in another room.

64 It is possible that they were the famous Le Brun sequence designed in the 1650s but there were also Flemish designs of this Meleager story. Peter Crijnse Volmarijn (*c.* 1612–1657) painted a *modello* of Meleager presenting Atalanta with the head of the Calydonian boar – see *Old Master Pictures* (sale catalogue, Christie's, New York, January 27, 2009), lot 31 – which may have been for the tapestry series. In Alessandro Carenna's inventory of 1699 (Duverger, vol. 12 (2002), p. 517) there is listed a series of nine tapestries woven with gold thread, showing "figures in a landscape" and bearing the Roelants coat of arms. They must have come from his mother's family, so may have been the Meleager series – though this consisted of seven, as opposed to nine, pieces. The most distinctive paintings in Alessandro's inventory are a *Vanitas* (also found in Francesco's inventory), a *Vase of Flowers with a Monkey*, and a *Hercules* (in fact a statue?) with family portraits.

65 See R.-A. d'Hulst, N. de Poorter and M. Vandenven, *Jacob Jordaens (1593–1678). Paintings and Tapestries* (exhibition catalogue, Koninklijk Museum voor Schone Kunsten, Antwerp, 1993), I, p. 268, no. A87. For Jordaens's *Death of Cleopatra*, see M. Jaffé, *Jacob Jordaens* (Ottawa, 1968), p. 135, where the link to Carenna is first made, and for *Cleopatra's Feast* see Gritsay and Babina 2008 (cited note 3), p. 160, no. 215.

66 See Muller 1993, p. 202.

67 H. Vlieghe, 'Une grande collection Anversoise du dix-septième siècle: le cabinet d'Arnold Lunden, beau-frère de Rubens', *Jahrbuch der Berliner Museen*, XIX (1977), p. 200.

68 M. Krick-Kunstziger, *Bulletin Musée royal des Beaux-Arts*, vol. 4 (1934), pp. 2–12. See also E. Haverkamp-Begemann, *The Achilles Series* (Corpus Rubenianum Ludwig Burchard, X, Brussels, 1975), p. 88; and Rotterdam 2003, pp. 40, 65, 70–71. It has been supposed that Pieter Hellemans, the former owner of the house, owned the set initially, which would then have been bought by Carenna with the house, but against this is the proud claim in Carenna's inventory that they were made to measure. Pieter Hellemans's heir was his daughter Anna Catherina, who married Franciscus Paschalis van den Cruyce; the son-in-law assumed the title of Lord of Aartselaar and Cleydael. Hellemans acquired these titles in 1644 from Philip IV for 19,200 florins, and seems to have been knighted in 1659 and died soon after (see Le Roy 1678 (cited note 27), p. 241). There is a document of May 13, 1664 concerning his legacy for Santa Maria Formosa in Venice (see Stadsarchief, Antwerp, notary Ambrosio Sebille, Ms 2024).

69 G. Delmarcel, *La tapisserie bruxelloise au siècle de Rubens* (exhibition catalogue, Musées Royaux des Beaux-Arts, Brussels, 1977), pp. 103–18.

70 *Old Master Pictures* (sale catalogue, Christie's, London, July 7, 2004), p. 53, lot 27: 89.5 × 128.3 cm, a version of one illustrated in Mercedes Viale Ferrero, *Feste delle Madame Reali di Savoia* (Turin, 1965), p. 58, and discussed by C.E. Bertana, 'Un dipinto del 1663 per il ballo di Corte al Palazzo Reale di Torino', *Studi Piemontesi*, V, no. 16 (1987), pp. 371–76; now in the Geneva foundation of Umberto II and Marie José di Savoia.

71 See H. van de Velde, 'The Painting Collection of Burgomaster Nicolaas Rockox (1560–1640). A Discussion of the Inventory drawn up after his Death', in Antwerp 2007, pp. 33–55, esp. p. 36.
72 D. Jaffé, 'Rubens back and front: the case of the National Gallery Samson and Delilah', *Apollo*, CII, no. 462 (2000), pp. 21–25; and 'Rubens's Samson and Delilah, an Antwerp Chimney Piece in Context', in Antwerp 2007, pp. 11–17. See *Old Master Paintings* (sale catalogue, Sotheby's, London, July 8, 2008), lots 101–02, for other Nuremberg block boards.
73 Giulio Romano's *Two Lovers* in the Hermitage is a good candidate but Caravaggio's *Judith and Holofernes* in the Borghese collection may have been the intermediary.
74 Van der Meulen 1994, I, pp. 115, 156.
75 See Jaffé 1977, figs. 286, 287.
76 Michael Daley alerted me to the still legible overpainted horse's head.
77 For the Savelli sarcophagus, known from 1510, see G. Denhaene, *Lambert Lombard: Renaissance en humanisme te Luik* (Brussels, 2006), p. 354, no. 16, dated to the 2nd century AD; the drawings are illustrated in Pierre Rosenberg and Louis-Anthoine Prat, *Nicolas Poussin (1594–1665)* (Milan, 1994), vol. 1, p. 368, no. 193, fig. 193e; Van der Meulen 1994, I, pp. 116, 156, 206.
78 McGrath 1997, p. 50, note 111.
79 The ribbon across her breast may be a reference to Venus's potent girdle, but Rubens, like Michelangelo, loved binding flesh in ribbons. Michelangelo's *Leda* is the obvious source for Delilah's pose, as was aptly observed by White 1987, p. 100.
80 His claim that the saints could be easily substituted is also interesting given the way the soldiers's attributes were altered in the painting when it became the marker of his mother's tomb. Saint Papius (rather than 'Papianus', as favoured in the art historical literature; I follow Baronius, *Annales Ecclesiastici* (1597, vol. II, pp. 622, 775) and Rubens's own contract) had his palm of martyrdom (he was beaten to death) changed for arrows, suggesting Rubens was rechristening him Sebastian for his mother's tomb in Sint-Michiels, Antwerp.

Unravelling the sources (pp. 72–85)

1 Amanda Bradley kindly surveyed the early Church literature on the subject. I am indebted to Elizabeth McGrath for these references.
2 "[Herod] never stopped avenging and punishing every day those who had chosen to be of the party of his enemies:" Josephus, *Jewish Antiquities*, 15, 2. Also recorded is the murder of Herod's two sons and wife, because they were believed to pose a threat: see Josephus, *The Jewish War*, I, 535–37, and *Jewish Antiquities*, 16, 121–27, 356.
3 *The Catholic Encyclopaedia*, vol. VII (New York, 1910), pp. 290, 419, refers to Herod's hog and suggests that between six and twenty children would have been killed, with a dozen or so more in the surrounding areas.
4 See, for example, E.P. Sanders, *The Historical Figure of Jesus* (London, 1993), pp. 87–88, and P. Maier, 'Herod and the Infants of Bethlehem', in *Chronos, Kairos, Christos II* (Mercer University Press, 1988), p. 170.
5 Macrobius, *Saturnalia*, trans. P. Davies (New York, 1969), p. 171 (IV, XIV).
6 P. Abaelardus, *Petri Abaelardi Hymnarius Paraclensis*, ed. G. Dreves (Paris, 1891), pp. 224, 274: "*... malum, inquit, est Herodis esse natum. / prodest magis talis Regis esse porcum*."
7 *Ad Herennium*, ed. H. Caplan (London, 1968), IV, 51.
8 Cited in P. Hayward, 'Suffering and Innocence in Latin Sermons for the Feast of the Holy Innocents, c. 400–800 A.D.', in *Church and Childhood*, ed. D. Wood (Studies in Church History, 31; Oxford, 1994), pp. 70–71.
9 The following discussion of Byzantine sermons owes much to H. Maguire, *Art and Eloquence in Byzantium* (Princeton, 1981), pp. 22–34 (as cited in Cropper and Dempsey 1996, p. 258).
10 *Ibid.*, p. 27.
11 *Ibid.*, p. 29.
12 L. Kotzsche-Breitenbruch, 'Zur Ikonographie des bethlehemitischen Kindermordes', *Jahrbuch für Antike und Christentum*, nos. 11/12 (1968–69). The British Museum has a vase (B205; GR 1842-3-14.3) showing Priam of Troy being struck by an assailant wielding the king's grandchild.
13 This was illustrated in a lecture given by Anthea Stevens on 'The Good, the Bad and the Defaced – the Representation of the Holy Innocents in Italian Liturgical Manuscripts between 1300 and 1500', at the Courtauld Institute of Art, February 23, 2008.
14 P. Aretino, *L'Umanità di Cristo* (edn. Rome, 1945), pp. 48ff. See Cropper and Dempsey 1996, p. 258.
15 For Soranzo, Marino and Paggi see Genoa 2004, p. 22, entry by Salassi.
16 Cropper and Dempsey 1996, p. 263.
17 Aretino (see note 14), pp. 55–56: "*E chi ha mai visto la Carità scolpita con le chiome raccolte sopra la fronte, scoprendo il bel collo, e la bella gola ... vede la dolorosa assalita dall'uomo fiero ... sembrava un marmo macchiato di vermiglio*."
18 Cropper and Dempsey 1996, p. 264.
19 G.B. Marino, ed. G. Pozzi, *Dicerie sacre e la strage degli innocenti* (Turin, 1960), p. 557, III, 65, line 5: "*che il petto ha di macigno*;" p. 558, III, 70, lines 7–8: "*Di bianco marmo, se non quanto i figli / Fatto i candidi membri avian vermigli*;" cited in Cropper and Dempsey 1996, p. 271, note 54.
20 *Ibid.*, p. 547, III, 34–38, cited in Cropper and Dempsey 1996, p. 264, note 35.
21 Cropper and Dempsey 1996, p. 273, quoting Marino in praise of Guido Reni's *Massacre* in San Domenico, Bologna (painted after Rubens had left Italy): "*spesso l'orrore va col diletto*."
22 This idea is propounded in Cropper and Dempsey 1996, pp. 265ff.
23 See *ibid.*, pp. 267 (Ghirlandaio), 269 (*Morbetto*).
24 Cited *ibid.*, p. 259.
25 See Dirck Volkertsz Coornhert after Heemskerk, *The Massacre of the Innocents*, 1551, engraving (42.7 × 59.2 cm); see further D. Kunzle, 'Spanish Herod, Dutch Innocence', *Art History* (XXIV, 2000), pp. 51–82.
26 See Jaffé in Antwerp 2007, pp. 12–13.
27 Genoa 2004, pp. 224–26, no. 37.
28 As cited in Cropper and Dempsey 1996, p. 259.
29 Daniele self-consciously included views of Michelangelo's own *Samson and the Philistine* bronze to authorize his invention.

Designing the *Massacre* (pp. 86–117)

1 See J. Kirby, 'The Painter's Trade in the Seventeenth Century', *National Gallery Technical Bulletin* (20), 1999, pp. 5–49, esp. pp. 27–28.
2 Saint George's red cloak in the *Saint George and the Dragon* (fig. 72) in the Museo del Prado, Madrid, was originally larger, and the red can be seen coming through the sky below his shoulder.
3 See also the mounted commander in the workshop copy of an early lost *Rape of the Sabines* composition (J. Garff, *Rubens Cantoor*, vol. I (Copenhagen, 1988), p. 178, nos. 240–41), which is revived in the late Dexia Bank *Intervention of the Sabine Women*. Maarten de Vos (*The Martydom of Saint James*, Sint-Jacobskerk, Antwerp), like Floris in his lost *Massacre*, liked to include mounted commanders.
4 Rubens shows the sole of an antique boot which appears to be studded in *The Victory of the Eucharist over Pagan Sacrifices*, c. 1625 (Held 1980, p. 150, no. 98) and in the *Triumph of Constantine* tapestry (Philadelphia). See Belkin 1998, pp. 190–91, fig. 130.
5 The x-ray also shows two pleading hands, probably belonging to a female figure, reaching towards the commander on horseback; these bear some similarity to the hands reaching up towards the Virgin in the *Assumption* painted for Antwerp Cathedral (c. 1613–14). Michelangelo had introduced two disembodied hands in the *Battle of Cascina*.
6 R. Martin, *The Decorations of the Pompa Introitus Ferdinandi* (London, 1972), p. 171.
7 See Held 1980, pp. 238–40, esp. p. 239, citing Gevaerts, who notes *Iliad* XXII, "War deprives children of their mothers' breasts," and Hesiod's claim that peace is the nurse of children.
8 The nearest parallel in a large painting to this loose style is *Moses and the Brazen Serpent* of c. 1610 in the Courtauld Gallery, London (fig. 128); in that work the diffusion of sketch technique to large work is at its most ambiguous.
9 Rubens repeats the effect of mouth foam in the horse on the right of *The Raising of the Cross*. An ancient painter had captured the spittle of a dog, according to Pliny, XXV, 101 (see S. Koslow, 'Law and Order in Rubens's *Wolf and Fox Hunt*', *Art Bulletin* (LXXVIII, 1996), pp. 681–706, at p. 695).
10 For further background on the pocketbook see Jaffé 1966; Van der Meulen 1994, pp. 72–77; J. Bolten, *Method and Practice: Dutch and Flemish Drawing Books 1600–1750* (Landau, 1985), pp. 101–16; D. Jaffé and A. Bradley, 'Rubens's "Pocketbook". An Introduction to the Creative Process', in London 2005, pp. 21–27; T. Meganck, 'Rubens on the Human Figure: Theory, Practice and Metaphysics', in Brussels 2007, pp. 52–64. For the idea that the Madrid version is by Erasmus Quellinus see the entry by Juan Bordés Caballero in J.M. Luzón Nogué, *Velázquez: Esculturas para el Alcázar* (exhibition catalogue, Real Academia de Bellas Artes de San Fernando, Madrid, 2007), pp. 522–24, no. 96.
11 Jaffé 1966; Van der Meulen 1994, pp. 72–77. Jessica Cerasi first made this link (in conversation).
12 Genoa 2004, pp. 224–25, no. 37.
13 Illustrated Bartsch, XXX (Italian Masters of the Sixteenth Century), no. 8 (284). The hair pulling goes back to Rogier van der Weyden and Lucas van Leyden, and can be found in Roman sarcophagi

and cameos showing Amazons; for the Amazons see Cropper and Dempsey 1996, p. 340, note 36.

14 See N. Laneyrie-Dagen, *Théorie de la figure humaine: planches gravées par Pierre Aveline d'après Rubens* (Paris, 2003), p. 108. The pairing of the princess and the horse in both *Saint George and the Dragon* (fig. 72; perhaps inspired by Maarten de Vos's 1601 painting then in Sint-Walburga of the same subject) and the book-ending of the mother and the horse both with swirling manes of hair on opposite wings of *The Raising of the Cross* (fig. 17) may be viewed as more intentional in the light of Rubens's list of shared features.

15 See J. Muller, 'Rubens's Anatomy Book', in *Rubens Cartoor: een verzameling ontstaan in Rubens' atelier* (exhibition catalogue, Rubenshuis, Antwerp, 1993), pp. 78–94.

16 See C. White, *The Later Flemish Pictures in the Collection of Her Majesty the Queen* (London, 2007), pp. 215–25, no. 63.

17 The inscription on the Johnson sheet states: *Qvare Figurae Humanae Elementa Tria constitantur*. See J.M. Muller, 'Rubens's Collection in History', in Antwerp 2004, p. 18. See Cropper and Dempsey 1996, pp. 271, 340 note 54.

18 Venus trying to inhale the soul of the dying Adonis, inscribed on a drawing of this subject in Washington, and Rubens's description of Pasqualini's sarcophagus are other examples: see Van der Meulen 1994, p. 84, and E. McGrath, 'Words and Thoughts in Rubens's Early Drawings', in London 2005, p. 35.

19 Rubens owned copies of Raphael's Sistine cartoons; he extracted the columnar figure to illustrate its 'cubic' solidity.

20 See E. McGrath 'Words and Thoughts in Rubens's Early Drawings', in London 2005, pp. 28–37. The bloody head of Christ in Rubens's *Pietà* (J. Paul Getty Museum) may reflect Virgil's text about the boxing match, but Ann Woollett has suggested that the unusual gore may have been catering for a Spanish patron. Cf. the Johnson copy of Rubens's sketchbook, f. 12v.

21 The prisoners in the *Battle of Ostia*, as found in Rubens's lost sketchbook, are another possible seed for this idea. In London 2005 I have suggested that the baby in the *Circumcision* may be a sculptor's model, used again for the baby with the woman in red. The fact that Rubens seems to draw such a model in the 'Van Dyck' sketchbook (f. 54v), again lying on his back, and uses it for one of the flying putti hovering over the *Exchange of Princesses* from the Marie de Médicis cycle (Held 1980, p. 115, no. 74) only increases the probability that such a model existed. See London 2005, p. 136, and *ibid.* p. 24, fig. 12, for the sketchbook illustration (f. 54v) of the boy on his back.

22 See U. Heinen in London 2005, p. 106. Rubens's anatomical knowledge is said to have been enriched by his study of Leonardo da Vinci's drawings; however, the only possible link is the Windsor drawing of a horse baring its teeth, which is picked up either directly or indirectly by Rubens in his sketchbook: see P. Motture, entry in *Andrea Riccio* (exhibition catalogue, The Frick Collection, New York, October 13, 2008– January 18, 2009), pp. 216–21, no. 19: Andrea Riccio seems to have observed this, too.

23 See Roger de Piles's transcription, as discussed below on p. 141 and note 39 to it. The use of Italian words in this 'Latin' text suggests it was written some time between 1602 and 1607.

24 Victoria Sancho Lobis, who is researching the prints, has followed the view held in the exhibition catalogue *Rubens in Oxford* (Picture Gallery, Christ Church, Oxford, 1988), p. 50, in suggesting that Prometheus is behind this invention, and referring to a workshop drawing in the Altman collection reproduced in M. Giltay, *Le Cabinet d'un amateur: Dessins flamands et hollandais des XVIe et XVIIe siècles d'une collection privée d'Amsterdam* (Museum Boijmans Van Beuningen, Rotterdam, and Institut Néerlandais, Paris, 1976–77), p. 61, no. 104. In the Oxford catalogue, p. 30, there is a drawing after a female (model or sculpture) showing a similar long neck and hair arrangement.

25 Veronika Kopecky drew this connection.

26 There was an antique convention for the running figure, leaning back on tiptoe, which Rubens must have known and enjoyed adapting and which may also have been the source for Tetrode's own design. A similar type can be seen in the parrying soldier on a Greek vase showing *The Death of Hector and Achilles* (attributed to the Berlin Painter, British Museum). Rubens's early *Conversions of Saint Paul* (Liechtenstein and Courtauld Gallery, London) are dependant on Coeck's tapestry designs of the same subject of *c.* 1530–40. See G. Marlier, *Pierre Coeck d'Alost* (Brussels, 1966), p. 316, figs. 253–54.

27 For the oil-sketches of Titian, Tintoretto and Veronese see 'The *Massacre* in context, 1', p. 27 and note 5 to it. His Tintoretto may have been a copy of *Saint Roch in the Plague House*, as Quellinus owned a copy of this painting; his inventory records many Rubens paintings, drawings and sketchbooks, including Titian compositions that Rubens reacted to (Venuses, *The Battle of Cadore*: compare with Rubens's (?) oil-sketch for *The Martyrdom of Livinus*: see Jaffé 1977, fig. 51, and Brussels 2007, p. 198, no. 668: this has Titian's slain horseman and his mount charging out on the left), anatomies, and the *Laocöon* and other small sculptures of the sort that Rubens must have owned. As noted in 'The *Massacre* in context, 2', note 46, Quellinus's studio even contained Veronese's *Adoration*, and may have preserved much of Rubens's own material. See Duverger, vol. 10 (1999),pp. 347–74.

28 Magurn 1955, p. 56; G. Martin, 'Rubens's "Disegno Colorito" for Bishop Maes reconsidered', *Burlington Magazine*, CX (1968), pp. 434–47; G. Martin, *National Gallery Catalogues: The Flemish School, c. 1600–c. 1900* (London, 1970), pp. 182–87; H. Vlieghe, *Saints* (Corpus Rubenianum, VIII; London, 1972), pp. 102–07, no. 71.

29 One can only speculate that Rubens drew the *Samson and Delilah* study for the Cincinnati/London National Gallery solution, perhaps made the oil-sketch, then explored the two captures; it is more likely that he progressed from the Chicago/ Thyssen solution to a calmer Cincinnati/National Gallery arrangement.

30 A. Balis, 'Working it out: Design Tools and Procedures in Sixteenth and Seventeenth-Century Flemish Art', in H. Vlieghe *et al.*, *Concept, Design and Execution in Flemish Painting 1500–1700* (Turnhout, 2000), pp. 129–30.

31 We cannot be sure exactly when the painting was executed, although it must have been at some time after 1635. The identity of the patron is equally uncertain, but it is known that by 1642 it was in the possession of the collector Canon Antoine de Tassis. See K. Renger and C. Denk, *Flämische Malerei des Barock in der Alten Pinakothek* (Munich 2002); Cropper and Dempsey 1996, p. 267.

32 The motif of the mother biting the soldier in the top right of the Munich painting probably derives from Rubens's copy (see fig. 84) of that episode from Paggi in the left corner of his *Massacre* (fig. 58).

33 F. Healy, *Rubens and the Judgement of Paris: A Question of Choice* (Turnhout, 1997), p. 120.

34 See McGrath 1997, I, pp. 68–73, esp. p. 70. Rubens wrote on June 10, 1628, to advise Dupuy on picking a theme, suggesting "*attione di maggior rilievo*." Held (1980, pp. 379–82) draws attention to the flow and revision of ideas between the *Sabines* and the *Massacre*.

The inspiration of Antiquity (pp. 118–41)

1 Letter February 26, 1622, Peiresc to Gevaerts, in C. Ruelens and M. Rooses, *Correspondance de Rubens et documents épistolaires concernant sa vie et ses œuvres*, 5 vols. (1886–92), II (1898), p. 337; translation from White 1987, p. 174, note 24.

2 E. McGrath, 'Not even a fly: Rubens and the mad emperors', *Burlington Magazine*, CXXXIII (1991), pp. 699–703.

3 In a letter dated December 29, 1628 Rubens wrote to Gervaerts that he had unsuccessfully tried to trace writings by Marcus Aurelius in Spain. See Magurn 1955, pp. 293–95.

4 H. Vlieghe, *Portraits of Identified Sitters Painted in Antwerp* (Corpus Rubenianum, XIX, II; London, 1987), pp. 113–16, no. 106.

5 See F. Baudouin, 'Rubens and his Books', in Baudouin 2005, pp. 125–35.

6 See McGrath 1997, pp. 55–67, esp. p. 61; P. Arents, *De Bibliotheek van Pieter Pauwel Rubens* (Brussels, 2001).

7 Van der Meulen 1994, II, pp. 34–40, 135–39, 142–43.

8 For additional information on the bust see *ibid.*, II, no. 117; F. Healy in Antwerp 2004, pp. 268–69, no. 65. The bust had been identified as a portrait of Seneca by the antiquarian Fulvio Orsini in the 1590s. The bust is not literally translated in the picture: Rubens – as usual – enlivened it. See Van der Meulen 1994, II, p. 137.

9 See Van der Meulen 1994, II, fig. 225, for the Hermitage drawing.

10 The account of Seneca's death can be found in Tacitus's *Annals*. See also V. Sørensen, *Seneca: The Humanist at the Court of Nero* (Edinburgh, 1984). Rubens also painted a portrait of *Seneca and Nero* on the same panel (*c.* 1608, private collection, London): see M. Jaffé, *Rubens: Catalogo completo* (Milan, 1989), p. 161, no. 73. See Van der Meulen 1994, II, pp. 34–40.

11 The statue (F. Haskell and N. Penny, *Taste and the Antique: The Lure of Classical Sculpture. 1500–1900* (New Haven and London, 1982), pp. 303ff., no. 76, figs. 160, 161) was identified as Seneca from the similarity of its head to the bust taken to be of Seneca.

12 For a full discussion of Rubens's collections, including his antique works and cameos, see Antwerp 2004 and Van der Meulen 1994 (in which last, for the Jupiter Ammon from Rubens's own collection, see pp. 193–96, Babelon 222, and also Peter Wegmann, *Die Kunst des Betrachtens: Museum Briner und Kern,*

Winterthur (Berne 2006), p. 46f. Rubens records that the gem was owned by the Lipsius pupil Hemelaer, so the drawing (made in Rome) must date from between 1600 and 1606, when its owner was in Rome (see Baudouin 2005, p. 75).

13 See Rubens's letter to Peiresc of December 18, 1634 (Magurn 1955, pp. 393–94). For the identification of the spoon, see D. Jaffé, 'Peiresc and New Attitudes to Authenticity in the Seventeenth Century', in *Why Fakes Matter, Essays on Problems of Authenticity* (London 1993), pp. 157–73; and Van der Meulen 1994, pp. 227–29.

14 McGrath 1997, p. 59, and Van der Meulen 1994, II, pp. 162–63, for the sarcophagus showing a shrouded and swaddled dead child.

15 Translation from White 1987, p. 174; he gives a summary of the praise Rubens received, starting with comparison to Apelles in 1611.

16 Quintilian, II, XIII, 13; Cicero, *Orator*, XXII, 74.

17 Timanthes's painting appears to have been influential throughout Roman times, as various copies not known in Rubens's day attest, including a painting from the House of the Tragic Poet at Pompeii (now in the Museo Nazionale, Naples) and a mosaic from Ampurias in Spain (both first century AD). See J. Montagu, 'The Interpretation of Timanthes's Sacrifice of Iphigenia', in *Sight and Insight*, ed. J. Onians (London, 1994), pp. 305–25, and McGrath 1978, pp. 258–59.

18 Leon Battista Alberti, *On Painting*, trans. John Spencer (revised edn, New Haven and London, 1966), Book II, p. 78.

19 For the landscape see D. Jaffé, 'The Barberini Circle – Some Exchanges between Peiresc and Rubens', *Journal of the History of Collecting*, vol. 1, no. 2 (1989), pp. 120–47, esp. pp. 131–33.

20 The Borghese *Warrior* is also found in the 1620 Munich *Last Judgement* and the National Gallery, London, 1636 *Rape of the Sabines*. The *Laocoön* was also to reappear in his painting – the Courtauld *Atlas*, the Louvre *Hercules and Omphale* (fig. 6), to name just two works.

21 In the 1603 *Battle of the Amazons* (London 2005, pp. 48–49, no. 4) the central foreground figure is modelled on Michelangelo's *Night*, seen from the back, and there are also variations on Michelangelo's *Battle of the Centaurs* (which we have seen copied in fig. 83) and on the *Laocoön*.

22 A reduction (perhaps by Tetrode) of the rearing horse from the *Horse-tamers* model may be shown in Brueghel and Rubens's *Sense of Hearing* (Museo del Prado, Madrid) above the wall clock. This may have been the model Rubens owned. For the *Horse-tamers* see Van der Meulen 1994, II, p. 92.

23 Antwerp 2004, p. 23, note 102.

24 From these drawings we can also tell that he – like others among his contemporaries – experimented with the positioning of the priest's missing arm. See S. Settis in F. Buranelli, P. Liverani, A. Nesselrath, *Laocoonte alle origini dei Musei Vaticani* (Vatican, 2006), p. 27, for a suggested change of dating to 40–20 BC.

25 See the Johnson sketchbook, f. 65r (Courtauld Gallery, D.1978), summarizing *Hercules tearing off the Shirt of Nessus* (Musée du Louvre); L. Burchard and R.A. d'Hulst, *Rubens Drawings* (1963), no. 189, pp. 293–94. *The Death of Prometheus* (Museum of Fine Arts, Philadelphia) is another bird's-eye response; see also London 2005, pp. 89–90, esp. figs. 42, 43.

26 Even before the discovery of the Farnese *Bull* in 1545 – suggesting that this antique pose had survived in other versions – Giulio Romano (*The Death of Procris*) and Michelangelo (*The Last Judgement*) seem to have known and explored a similar twisting pose. Giulio's frescoes in the Palazzo del Tè, especially the giants falling into the viewer's space, must have impressed Rubens during his stay (1600–07) in Mantua.

27 For the oil-sketches see Antwerp 2004, p. 97.

28 Van der Meulen 1994, II, pp. 88–89.

29 U. Heinen, *Rubens zwischen Predigt und Kunst* (Weimar, 1996), pls. 11 and 12, pairs the *Raising* and the Farnese *Bull*. An honorary ancient sculptor, Giambologna might have inspired the bottom-right-corner figure in the sketch (as noted on p. 102), it recalls his *Rape of the Sabines* – but it is the rope-pulling in the finished painting that shows the commitment to the Farnese *Bull* sculpture, as well as the shared sacrificial nature of the two stories. Michelangelo was the other ancient hero reborn and it is not a surprise that his *Night* and *Moses* came under Rubens's scrutiny, as we have also already seen.

30 For *Niobe*, see see McGrath 1997, p. 212. Around 1632 Rubens introduced a pleading Niobid at the bottom right of his sketch for *The Rape of the Sabines* (Held 1980, pp. 379–82, no. 283).

31 For the *Hercules* see Van der Meulen 1994, pp. 40–48.

32 See below, note 39, for the quotation.

33 See London 2005, p. 26, note 45.

34 See Elizabeth McGrath's suggestion, noting this verse and the 1613 edition of Ripa's *Iconologia*, where smashing infants against stones is made emblematic of 'evil thoughts,' in Jaffé and Bradley 2003, p. 11, note 5.

35 Van der Meulen 1994, I, pp. 250–53; pp. 65 (for infant Hercules with snakes; fig. 25), 71–75, 251–52. The quotation "self-contained in their smooth rotundity" has been identified as from Horace's *Satires* II, VII, 86 by Elizabeth McGrath.

36 Rubens's views on the origin of the sculptural group are not known, but we can surmise that his pupil Van Dyck copied the figures in his Italian sketchbook (British Museum) on his master's recommendation, transforming them into seasons. It was still considered ancient at the end of the nineteenth century.

37 Van der Meulen 1994, II, pp. 83–86.

38 See D. Jaffé, 'An Antwerp Chimney Piece in Context', in Antwerp 2007, p. 15, fig. 9, and *Rubens' Self-portrait in Focus* (exhibition catalogue, National Gallery of Australia, Canberra, 1988), p. 54, note 2.

39 "To some painters the imitation of the antique statues has been extremely useful, and to others pernicious even to the ruin of their art. I conclude, however, that in order to attain the highest perfection in painting it is necessary to understand the antiques, nay, to be so thoroughly possessed of this knowledge that it may diffuse itself everywhere. Yet it must be judiciously applied so that it may not in the least smell of stone. For several important painters make no distinction between the matter and the form, the stone and the figure do but disgrace nature; since instead of imitating flesh they only represent marble tinged with various colours. There are, besides, certain places in the natural which change their figure according to the various motions of the body and by reason of the flexibility of the skin, and sometimes dilated, sometimes contracted. These are avoided by the generality of sculptors, certainly necessary to painting, used in moderation [p. 89] . . . . We of this erroneous age are far to[o] degenerate that we can produce nothing like them. [Antique statues] heroic sense, and superior parts, or that we are wrapped up in darkness that clouded our fathers . . . . Nature herself furnished the human body in those early ages, when it was nearer its origin and perfection, with everything that could make it a perfect model. But now being decayed and corrupted by a succession of so many years of sloth and want of exercise for most men give no other exercise for their body but eating and drinking. No wonder therefore, if we see so many paunch-bellies, weak and pitiful legs and arms. Whereas the ancients exercised their bodies every day in the academies and thus [through exercise] increased exceedingly both in strength and size as it appears from the backs of porters, the arms of prize fighters, the legs of dancers, and almost the whole body of watermen [p. 92]:" transcribed from Rubens's notes by Roger de Piles and printed in his *Cours de peinture par principes* (Paris, 1708), pp. 139–47; English translation *The Principles of Painting* (London, 1743), reprinted in J.R. Martin, *The Baroque* (London, 1977), pp. 27–73. Note that G. Waagen, *Peter Paul Rubens: His Life and Genius* (originally published as *Ueber den Maler, Petrus Paulus Rubens*, 1833), translated by Robert Noel, ed. Mrs A. Jameson (London, 1840), gives a different translation (pp. 123–26). See also the partial translation of de Piles's 1743 edition in J. Muller, 'Rubens's Theory and Practice of the Imitation of Art', *Art Bulletin*, LXIV, 1982, pp. 229–47. The stretching and bunching of the skin, which seems to match Rubens's interest in the occipital fold (see p. 103), is preceded by an Italian rather than a Latin word, "*ammaccatura*" ('bruising,' but in painting a hollow represented by shading), as George Lemos has pointed out to me: so perhaps the tract was written around 1608, just before the painting.

40 Magurn 1955, p. 41.

41 Pliny admired the ability of ancient artists to create such convincingly realistic images that birds were deceived into eating painted grapes and viewers fooled into trying to pull back painted curtains.

APPENDICES

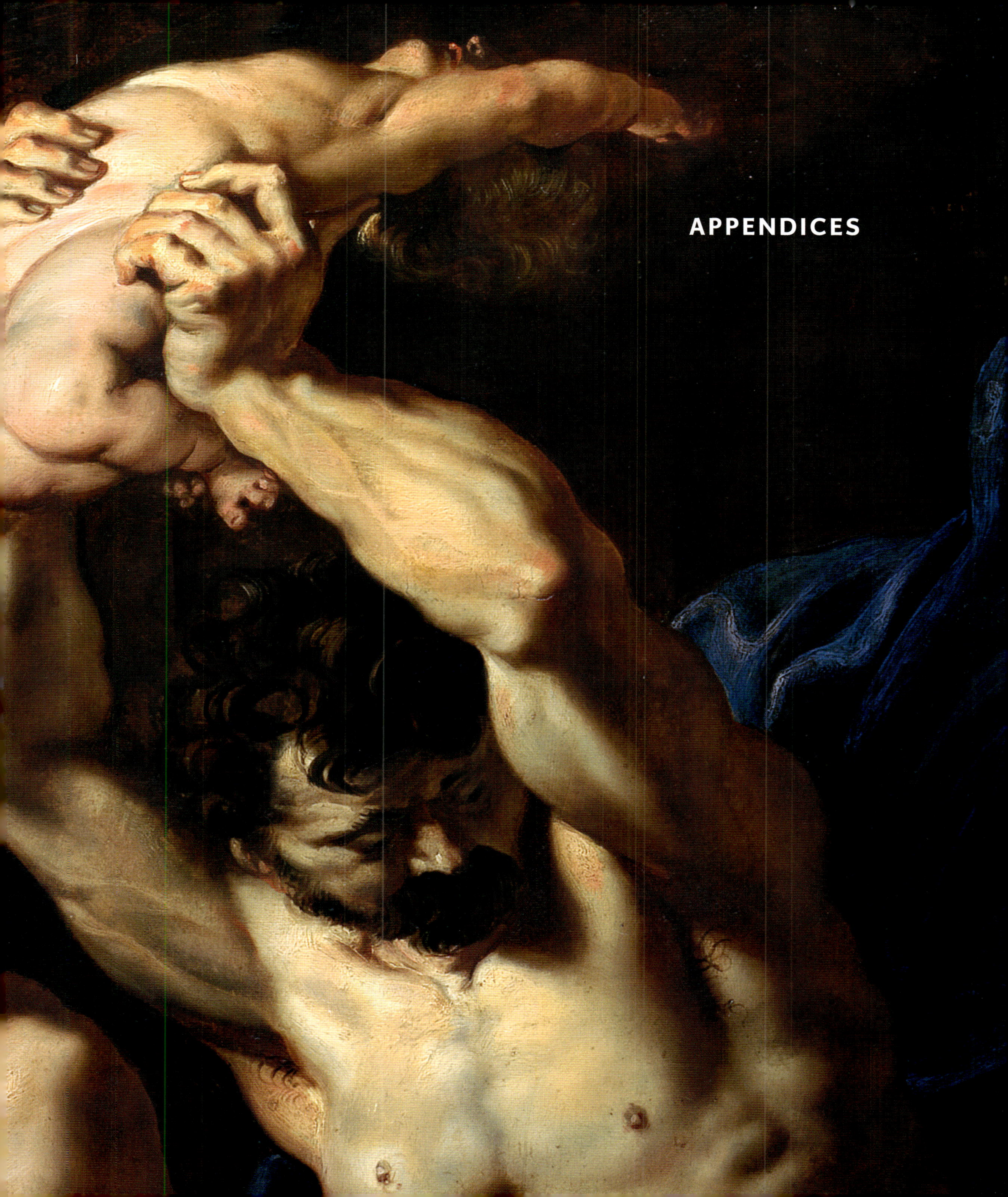

APPENDICES

Introduction

Rubens returned to Antwerp (see p. 38) in late 1608, just before a twelve-year truce was signed between the Catholic Spanish Southern Netherlands and the Non-Conformist United Provinces or Northern Netherlands. This war in what is now Belgium and the Netherlands (Holland) had international dimensions, as the English and French supported the Dutch against the Spanish while the French were also trying to subdue their own Huguenot rebellions. On a larger scale the war was a side show in the Thirty Years' War, commencing in 1618, during which Danish and Swedish forces turned the various Catholic and Lutheran/Protestant city states and territories of Germany into a battleground, while the French invaded Spanish-held northern Italy (Lombardy). The Habsburg Empire, ruled from Spain and Austria, struggled to assert control over its territories. Its aggressive policies pursued on many fronts were disastrous for the prosperity of such cities as Antwerp and Milan, so it is remarkable that the merchant financiers of these cities, such as the Annoni and Carenna families, succeeded in trading across war zones and prospering during such volatile economic and political times, especially when Antwerp's port on the river Scheldt had been reduced to a fraction of its sixteenth-century activity by Dutch blockade.[1]

The city of Antwerp's financial straits affected the public art commissions Rubens won.[2] We know from Rubens's correspondence that he was keenly aware of the precarious state of Spanish finances, which, because they depended on gold from its possessions in South America, were tied to the arrival of the fleets transporting back these riches. He predicted there would be mutinies amongst the soldiers if the treasure ships did not arrive.[3] On March 4, 1627 Rubens picked up rumours from the Genoese bankers that the King of Spain was going to default.[4] Spanish debts and the millions required from Italian bankers to refinance the empire were matters of concern to a painter with Genoese and Antwerp merchant patrons.[5]

In Giovanna Tonelli's essay we are given a fascinating insight into the financial and mercantile life of Antwerp's sister city Milan in Spanish Lombardy, as well as detailed analysis of the trade routes of this time. The owner of the *Massacre*, Giacomo Antonio Carenna, and his in-laws the Annoni, were vital players in financing this trade and Antwerp was a crucial link in the mercantile network. Anyone who has passed the former warehouse known as the Hessenhuis, just south from the Sint-Jacobskerk, grasps the logistical sophistication of the trade. Whole caravans of wagons could be loaded and unloaded under cover and repowered from the adjacent horse and ox markets. The Carenna-Annoni companies secured a virtual monopoly on the transport of these wagons through the Saint Gotthard Pass and seized control of the busy Milan-Antwerp trade in the early 1630s.[6] The impressive row of English trading-houses, now part of the university, is a further reminder of the scale of this industry.[7]

Tonelli's essay explains the context in which these financiers prospered – against the background of the Thirty Years' War – as well as providing a valuable window into the world of these important new patron collectors who, now largely unknown, were so influential in seventeenth-century Antwerp. The related documents have been published in full so as to give a better idea of the style in which these patrons lived and of the kind of possessions beside which their paintings had their place.

Crucial for Carenna, as earlier for Rubens himself, were the deeds of ennoblement from the Spanish Crown. Lordships and ennoblement were important social achievements in the seventeenth century. In the 1610s Rubens had renovated his own house and begun acquiring rural property and finally the country estate of Het Steen (1635). Yet his diplomatic career was dogged by criticism that he was "so mean a person" – not an aristocrat. (A letter from Philip IV of June 6, 1628 raises this issue.)[8] On June 5, 1624 Rubens's ennoblement document stresses his father's legal qualifications and his brother's role as secretary to the city of Antwerp as well as Rubens's own "*virtu*" and "*bonnes lettres et peinture*," his international travel and also the knowledge he had of history and languages.[9] He was knighted by Charles I of England at Westminster on Christmas Day 1630, and by Philip IV in Madrid on August 20, 1631. He might have been amused to see his *Massacre* being owned by two knights (Carenna, 1665, and Jan-Baptista Anthoine, May 9, 1678), a princely family (1702–1928) and finally a Lord. His own career, beginning with apprenticeship to the noble painter Otto van Veen, followed by admiration of another nobleman painter, Giovanni Battista Paggi, in 1606, is a reminder that he aspired to follow the achievement of Titian and make painting a socially respected career. His chapel behind the choir in Sint-Jacobskerk, which was embellished with monuments to his in-laws (the Fourment and Picquery), is evidence of just how well he had succeeded in this endeavour.

1 The population of Antwerp had fallen from 105,000 in 1568 (almost the same as Milan) to 42,000 in 1589, following its recapture by Philip in 1584. It gradually rose again, reaching 67,000 at the time of Rubens's death in 1640 (see P. Bowron in Genoa 2004, p. 114, note 13). Brussels tapestry manufacturers had petitioned for special dispensations so that they and their 600 employees could revive the industry. Financiers became involved with the manufacturers to make these luxury products. In 1650 it has been estimated that there were 800 people working in the tapestry industry, about 6,000 in the linen industry and 9,000 in the Antwerp silk industry. Silk features in the inventories given below.

2 Rubens viewed progress of this conflict not only as a citizen and diplomat but also from the perspective of an artist when he was required in December 1634 to design the welcoming entrance arches and stages for the new ruler of the Spanish Netherlands, the Infante Ferdinand. Despite the fact that Ferdinand, together with his Austrian cousin, had just won a rare Habsburg victory at Nördlingen the commissioning magistrates of Antwerp were preparing a welcome far more modest than usual, and had to extend an unpopular beer tax introduced during the plague to service the loans required to pay for the event. Once many of the 'nations' would sponsor a welcoming arch, but in the bleak economic times only the Portuguese community offered funding. After the event the paintings and sculptures were refreshed and auctioned to try to recoup some of the costs. The Arch of the Mint showing the dream of New World gold must have been tantalizing, and the Stage of Mercury, with the image of the god of commerce flying away from the chained Scheldt especially poignant. In his commentary on the entry, written after the 1635 event, Gervaerts could allude to the sixty ships which had been observed in Antwerp harbour by a mid-sixteenth-century Italian visitor (Lodovico Guicciardini, 1567) as something that happened no longer. Instead trade had to go through Lille or Delft and faced penalizing taxes. See R. Martin, *The Decorations of the Pompa Introitus Ferdinandi* (London, 1972), pp. 27, 179, 189. As has been noted, Rubens also saw his Antwerp Town Hall *Adoration* stripped out and given away as a cheap diplomatic gift a few years after he had painted it.

3 On November 19, 1626 Rubens wrote to Pierre Dupuy, ". . . no news of fleet from Peru . . . [fears of troop] disorders resulting from lack of payments" (Magurn 1955, p. 157).

4 On March 4, 1627 Rubens wrote to Dupuy, "The king of Spain wishes once more to make a decree suspending payment of the notes they hold on the capital credited to him. His Majesty wants to reduce the interest to four per cent." Philip II had repudiated his debts in 1575, so these fears were real. On April 9, 1627 the decree was suppressed and Rubens could report to Dupuy that the bankers were not ruined (Magurn 1955, pp. 172, 173).

5 On April 22 and May 6, 1627 Rubens discussed with Dupuy the national debt of Spain, the new Lucchese and Genoese loans being raised and the Spanish government's decision to devalue its currency by 75% (Magurn 1955, pp. 176–77, 179).

6 For the protests by their competitors see R. Baetens, *De Nazomer van Antwerpens Welvaart. De diaspora en het handelshuis De Grootte tijdens de eerste helft van de 17de eeuw*, 2 vols. (Brussels, 1976), I, pp. 86–87. Dorrit Van Camp kindly drew my attention to this passage. For the monopoly see further Tonelli's essay.

7 More work could be done on other Italian merchants living in Antwerp. The inventory of Jehan Baptiste Cattaneo, the Genoese intermediary for Rubens's Decius Mus tapestries, of April 21, 1671 (Duverger, vol. 9 (1997), pp. 298–300), sadly has no attributions, but he had tapestries, including a set of the story of Cleopatra (by Jordaens?) and paintings of subjects treated by Rubens such as *The Rape of Proserpine*, *Susannah* (Academy, Madrid?) and versions of *Venus Frigida* (by "Titian"? or Rubens?). The last two were chimney-pieces, so it is tempting to link them to Rubens's paintings. A Japanese robe and a "*coc de chocolate avecq des pieds d'argent*" convey the wealth. The inventory of January 21–26, 1669 of the Knight of St James Jean Etienne Spinola, who was involved in Carenna's 1649 note of exchange, included a clock, a Japanese robe, chocolate holders and, again without attribution, a big painting of *The Judgement of Paris*, *Herod with the Head of John the Baptist*, and "*une peinture de trois personnes représentant une teste Décolée*." Again, he was one of the few that owned tapestries and he had Grimaldi silver, perhaps through the wife of his father, Francesco Giovanni Battista Spinola: see Duverger, vol. 9 (1997), pp. 177–79.

8 See Belkin 1998, pp. 206, 232; and N. Büttner, 'Aristocracy and Noble Business: Some Remarks on Rubens's Financial Affairs', in *Munuscula Amicorum: Contributions on Rubens in honour of Hans Vlieghe* (Turnhout, 2006), pp. 67–78, and B. Timmermans, 'The Elite as Collectors', *ibid.*, pp. 343–62.

9 C. Ruelens and M. Rooses, *Correspondance de Rubens et documents épistolaires concernant sa vie et ses œuvres*, 5 vols. (1886–92), III, pp. 295–99.

The Annoni and the Carenna in seventeenth-century Milan

GIOVANNA TONELLI

One can only imagine the amazement felt by young men – such as the brothers of Giacomo Antonio Carenna – on reaching the city of Milan after leaving their small villages in the Alpine foothills in search of fortune. The city of Milan at the turn of the seventeenth century aroused marvel even among experienced travellers and diplomats, accustomed to other European cities.

Milan would have induced wonder above all for its huge size. With 115,000 inhabitants, Milan was then one of Europe's largest cities, rivalling London, Antwerp, Amsterdam, Lisbon, Seville, Venice, Rome and Palermo, all of which were home to between 100,000 and 200,000 people, while only Constantinople, Naples and Paris had more than 200,000 inhabitants.[1] But contemporary observers were also struck by the city's beauty, the outcome of the lavish attention paid to its embellishment during the Middle Ages by one of the most refined courts in Europe.[2] For example, its Cathedral was called "marvellous" by an anonymous writer of the early seventeenth century, who took pride and pleasure in its "immeasurable greatness and height," and could scarcely believe it was built entirely of white marble.[3] Even though in the heyday of the Carenna and Annoni families the city was no longer autonomous, having since 1535 been subject to Habsburg Spain, Milan was still the capital of a State, and had the air of one. Visitors admired its sumptuous palaces built around spacious courtyards; its castle, held to be one of the greatest fortresses of Europe; its wide streets full of carriages of fine manufacture in which rode richly dressed citizens; and its numerous churches, splendidly decorated outside and furnished with refinement inside, for which Milan (perhaps with excessive enthusiasm) was claimed to be Italy's second city, after Rome.[4] Moreover, observers were impressed not only by the luxurious apparel and evident wealth of Milan's affluent classes, but also by their largesse: the anonymous witness already cited claimed that there were an "infinite" number of charitable organizations, who gave "copious alms" to the poor – pious institutions, '*scole*' and other confraternities, and the 'Great Hospital,' or Ospedale Maggiore, dispensing charity as well as medicine.[5] He could only suppose the Milanese "good people," not only by virtue of their care for the poor but also, in his opinion, because they were loyal, courteous, ingenious and "dedicated to virtue and letters."

The early seventeenth century was indeed a good moment for letters. In 1603 works were started on the Biblioteca Ambrosiana, which by 1609 held 15,000 manuscripts and 30,000 printed works (seven times more than those listed in 1608 in the Vatican Library), acquired in Europe and the Middle East on the initiative of Cardinal Federico Borromeo from 1601 onwards. In 1609 the library was opened to the public and a few years later it was given its own printing press. From 1613 the cardinal had set up an academy of the fine arts, though it was not officially founded until the 1620s. In 1618 he inaugurated the Museo Ambrosiano, open, like the Library, to whoever wished to enjoy it. There would be kept the cardinal's collection of drawings, sculpture and paintings, some of which were brought from Flanders to Milan through the offices of Giovanni Pietro Annoni, the head of the branch of the Annoni family with which this essay is concerned.[6]

The economic basis of the magnificence of the capital of Lombardy was the prosperity of its agriculture, its flourishing manufactories and its intense 'tertiary sector' activities. The southern part of the State, where the richest Milanese had their lands, was one of the most fertile in Europe. The soil's yield was increased by a system of irrigation initiated probably in the twelfth century and developed to an impressive efficiency during the fifteenth.[7] Flax, cheese and especially cereals were produced in quantities to satisfy, and more, the needs of the State,[8] one of the most densely populated and urbanized areas of Europe (75 people per square kilometre) at the turn of the seventeenth century; the surplus produce was exported. Apart from the capital, Spanish Lombardy,[9] within a mere 16,000 square kilometres, counted five towns with a population of between 10,000 and 30,000 inhabitants and at least as many with 5,000 to 10,000 residents.[10]

Many of Milan's leading merchants had their origins in the hilly and mountainous regions to the north of the capital.[11] In the course of the seventeenth century they increased their holdings of land in that area; the investments of the Annoni and the Carenna, as we shall see, exemplify this profitable strategy of diversification. This part of the State was not so fertile as the plain, however, and the local population supplemented their meagre harvests with proceeds from the manufacture of less valuable products – cloth of mixed cotton and linen, of wool or of hessian, or leather goods – and from mining and ironworking.[12] In the course of the seventeenth century, however, the area became favoured for the production of silk, which, in raw or semi-worked state, was in increasing demand on the international market, so that eventually it would become the second largest Milanese export after grain.[13]

Milan itself, like other towns of the State, was a centre of production of high-quality goods – velvet, ribbons, braid, lace, hosiery, coifs in silk, often also embellished with gold and silver. By the end of the sixteenth century silk textiles were Milan's most prestigious export, together with woollen and leather goods and armour, especially parade armour.[14]

The quality goods that left Milan and other cities of Lombardy, and indeed those of not such high value produced in areas north of the capital, together with the excess of the cereals grown in the fertile Lombard plain and fibre crops such as flax and silk, all reached their foreign markets by a number of established overland and water routes. Milan lay at the centre of a network linking north and south, east and west.[15] Her luxury products were in demand both in neighbouring states and much further afield – in Savoy as in England,[16] in France, Flanders, Poland and Hungary. Spain was importing Milanese armour at the end of the sixteenth century, while the Grisons and the Swiss cantons as well as the cities of Bergamo and Brescia (under Venetian rule) had long proved a ready market for her cereals; Milan's raw and semi-worked silk departed in the direction of Lyons, Geneva, Genoa or Florence. However, extraterritorial demand was subject to an international economy that took shape towards the end of the sixteenth century and became established in the seventeenth. In this period the State of Milan gradually lost its long-held primacy as a supplier of luxury goods, its main exports becoming predominantly agricultural – cereals, raw or processed silk, cheese and flax.[17]

The signs had been there at the end of the sixteenth century, but this shift was felt particularly during the recession that affected almost all Europe towards the end of the sixteenth century and especially from 1619 to 1622.[18] Several factors particularly affected Spanish Lombardy – the disruption of German markets by the Thirty Years' War; the setting up of local industries by former importers; the trailing in 1618 of the revaluation of the Milanese currency the following year, which led to fears of rising prices and in consequence the hoarding of goods, reducing subsequent demand.

The Annoni in early seventeenth-century Milan

It was in 1621, while the Milanese economy was still mired in the recession that had first been felt in 1619, that Giovanni Pietro and Giacomo Antonio Annoni requested admission among the *Mercatores utentes stratis vel mittentes per stratas* ('traders using the roads or sending by the roads'),[19] the leading mercantile association in the city. It was open only to the leading bankers and merchants operating in and around Milan, who, with the money-changers, constituted the *Universitas mercatorum Mediolanensis*, the most important Milanese commercial and financial institution, which regulated trading practice and so assured the city's credit.[20]

In taking this resonant diplomatic initiative the Annoni made no secret of their intentions. In their request for admission they not merely declared their activity as merchants and bankers, as others had done in comparable submissions,[21] but they added that, as was "particularly" known in Milan, Giacomo Antonio had been in the past a member of the committee that steered the *Universitas mercatorum*.[22] They wished to be admitted, as dealers buying and selling all kinds of goods and bills, "for their satisfaction" above all, but also so as to be able to enjoy the services the association could offer, "with no exceptions being made" (in this time of recession). In other words they sought not merely to be equals ("with no exceptions being made") but to have their status among the leaders in the field recognized "particularly," though not only, in Milan. The Annoni had indeed since the early sixteenth century been prominent in the organization of transport and the buying and selling of goods between the Po Valley and Antwerp, through the Swiss passes and up and down the Rhine.[23] Outside the borders of the Spanish Duchy they were undoubtedly among the best known Lombards operating in a sector in which the Milanese were not in fact very numerous: other than the Annoni, we know to have been operating as early as the sixteenth century on the various routes from North Italy to Brabant the Lorenzi, the Vergani (partners of the Annoni from the early seventeenth century) and the Flemish Doniquart (perhaps only in the seventeenth century). The Volpi had long sent goods from the Lombard capital to Germany, and their caravans also reached Brabant and England; in the seventeenth century the Guidetti also worked these routes. The Figino and the Ponsampieri, originally from Lucca, but resident in Milan, looked after Milan–Lyons.[24] The fact is that transport of goods at an international level required huge capital and no small commercial and financial experience and competence. It required a network of correspondents or agents fully conversant with the local context and capable of procuring business, buying and selling, paying and receiving moneys, and representing the firm before foreign institutions including, in the case of dispute, the courts. Not least, they had to hire and direct suitable handlers of the goods along the route, because it was obviously important these should not be damaged in their travels up and down mountains, or get damp from bad weather, rivers, lakes, canals or seas – or indeed be stolen by any number of ambushing marauders or raiding soldiers.[25]

However, the risks involved in the transport of goods were amply compensated by the profit that might be made, and that we shall see the Annoni and Carenna were able to make. To appreciate fully the paramount importance of the sector let us consider the diversity of the needs even of a small state like Milan.[26] It needed to maintain its supply of food or foodstuffs that were not available within its borders: there were times of famine, when grain would, traditionally, be imported from the Mediterranean, especially Sicily, but also, from the second half of the sixteenth century, from the Baltic, through English and Netherlandish intermediaries. These also procured anchovies, herrings and other dried fish, for which there was great demand in Milan; fresh fish was imported from Mantua, Ferrara and the Romagna, dried fruit, sugar and choice wines such as malmsey from Venice and Genoa – this so-called Lenten fare was consumed instead of meat in the two fasting periods of the liturgical year, Advent and Lent.[27] From the Swiss cantons and from the neighbouring territories of Bergamo, Brescia and Piacenza the State imported animals for slaughter – poultry, pigs, horses, cattle – and perishables such as dairy products and eggs. Cured meats came from Ferrara, wines from Monferrato, olive oil and fresh fruit from Genoa, spices from Genoa and Venice. Spanish Lombardy also imported manufactured goods. These included woollens from England, Catalonia, France, Flanders, Germany and the Veneto. Silks, sometimes interwoven with wool, came from Bergamo, silk veils from Bologna, pictures and tapestries from Flanders, carpets from Germany and from the East through Venice. Canvas was obtained in Flanders, South Germany, Switzerland (St Gall and Zurich), clocks from Augsburg, lenses and soap from Venice, ironwork from Brescia. Furthermore, as we have seen, Milan had its own range of manufactories, and these needed raw materials, those available in the State not necessarily being sufficient. The local production of silk was supplemented by imports from Piedmont, Venice, Calabria and the Levant. Wool of the best quality was imported from England, Flanders, Spain and southern Italy, and coarser wool from Germany (Nuremberg, Ulm, Augburg); spun flax from Brittany, Nuremberg and the Veneto; cotton from the Levant. Besides textiles Milanese traders imported metals, including precious metals for goldsmiths, primarily from the Venetian and German Alpine valleys. Leather and raw materials for tanning were procured in central and northern Europe; sheepskins from the Levant; oxhides from Russia and Nuremberg; tannins from Venice.

Having arrived in Milan laden with these goods from foreign parts, the merchants' convoys left again carrying local goods or imported ones for re-export. The Duchy was an entrepôt for wool cloth from France, England and the Netherlands destined for other parts of the Italian peninsula, as also for textiles produced over an area extending from around Lake Constance to South Germany, going to Genoa and Tuscany, for arms assembled in and around Brescia and directed to France, and for glass, oil and soap from Venice to cross the Alps.[28]

Thus, even during a period of relative stagnation, like that in Milan from 1619 into the early 1620s, the transport firms were always busy. Traders such as the Annoni handled both their own goods and those of others entrusted to them either simply for transport or also for sale at the other end, through the branches of their business at points along the convoys' routes – in Antwerp, Brussels, Lyons, Leipzig, Cracow, Augsburg, Nuremberg, Basle, Turin and Siena.[29] In this way the Annoni stood to gain a commission not only on the sale but also on the financial transfer (these services being quite inseparable in the early modern era). They moved money around numerous European markets, and not only at those where they had branches – for example from Antwerp and Amsterdam to unspecified locations in Poland and Germany, from Lyons to Frankfurt or Constance, from Venice and Verona to Bologna, Pisa, Florence, Rome, from Piacenza to Genoa.[30] According to the procedure of the time, either the Annoni themselves or their correspondents made payments in cash in order to honour letters of credit or to settle a debit and credit account kept with other international traders over a period of time.[31]

The Annoni were also able to serve as intermediaries in the making of payments or receipt of money for rulers (or their families) such as the Grand Duke of Tuscany or the Gonzaga.[32] But they advanced cash or took cash on deposit also for private individuals: we have proof of credits being given by the Annoni to fellow parishioners living in their native Brianza,[33] the area around Como and Lecco north of Milan towards the Lakes. Giacomo Antonio Annoni came in fact from Merone,[34] his relatives the brothers Giovanni Pietro and Cristoforo Annoni from Annone di Brianza. The latter branch of the family had property there, a house *da nobile* and a family vault in the local church, to which, as to the poor of the parish, they habitually left something in their wills, for masses were offered there for the souls of the dead; and in the sixteenth century they had commissioned a Flemish painting to be set above the altar.[35] Their families would commonly spend the summer period there, as the more affluent Milanese would usually move to the countryside during the hottest months of the year.[36] In and around Annone, furthermore, the Annoni would recruit the manpower they needed for their business in Milan and to tend the fields they owned and continued to acquire, often by default on payment of mortgages secured on property.[37]

The Annoni also invested in land in the fertile plain of the Po Valley. At Vittuone and Corbetta, to the east of Milan, Giovanni Pietro Annoni owned parcels of land where he grew grain, vines and mulberry trees.[38] Strategically diversifying their assets, the Annoni also used their money to buy state bonds[39] and stakes in manufacturing and in financial and commercial brokerage firms run by others. In the 1620s they formed a company for the production of silk textiles with the Lumaga, a very powerful family of merchants and bankers operating in all the important European markets – Milan, Genoa and Venice, Lyons, Paris and Nuremberg.[40] They also took a stake in a company with Daniele Delubert, a Frenchman, and two of their long-established trading partners, Roberto Poquilin of Paris, who had been working with them since 1616, and Lodovico Mizzaferro, who already by 1619 was sending silk to Lyons with Cristoforo Annoni.[41]

Such was the economic leverage and consequent clout of these firms that they were able to make deals with political powers. In 1611, for example, the Annoni, in concert with the Volpi and the Lorenzi, agreed with the Swiss authorities a special toll rate which gave them an effective monopoly of the trade routes through Switzerland.[42] At home Giacomo Antonio, Giovanni Pietro and Cristoforo Annoni, through other branches of the Annoni family, enjoyed close relations with the political establishment and high society in Milan.[43] Some time between 1569 and 1571 Giovanni Battista Annoni had married Silvia, daughter of Pietro Francesco Visconti of Brignano and widow of count Alfonso Cicogna,[44] a marriage memorialized in a bronze bowl now in the Ashmolean Museum at Oxford (illustrated). In 1592 Pietro Francesco and Giovanni Paolo Annoni had been enrolled among the LX Decurioni, the council by which Milan was governed.[45] In the mid 1620s the proprietors of the firm of 'Giovanni Pietro and Giacomo Antonio Annoni' made significant moves towards consolidating their status.

In 1623 Giacomo Antonio Annoni bid successfully at auction for the fiefs of Gussola and Martignana, near Cremona, and the title of count that went with them, a sale authorized by King Philip IV of Spain in order to clear the debts on the estate of their former owner, Don Alonso Pimentel, commander of the garrison of light cavalry stationed in Milan. In 1625 Annoni took formal possession of fiefs and title, which he could pass on to his heirs or sell, subject to the approval of the sovereign. It was undoubtedly the need to raise the money to settle with Madrid that led him to sell to his partners in the firm several lots of ground in his native Merone, an estate which, as we shall see, would eventually be taken over by the Carenna family.[46]

In 1626 Giovanni Pietro Annoni set about entering his posterity into the ranks of the Lombard aristocracy. He made a considerable capital outlay to marry his sixteen-year-old daughter Ottavia to Giovanni Visconti, a descendant of a cadet branch of Milan's medieval ducal dynasty, providing her with a dowry of 46,000 *lire*, as much money as he had settled in initial capital in his transport company some twenty years before.[47] With this sum Annoni, one of the leading financiers in the Milan of his time, became the father-in-law of the feudal landlord of a number of villages situated to the north of the city.[48] This marriage was perhaps Giovanni Pietro Annoni's last achievement. He died in October the following year, leaving a widow, Isabella, and several children still in their minority. To safeguard their interests an inventory was drawn up of his goods, a document from which today we may learn much of the life style of this seventeenth-century Milanese financier.

The fifty-eight-year-old Giovanni Pietro Annoni shared eleven rooms, mainly on the *piano nobile* in a palace near the Cathedral (the 'casa delli Annoni Banchieri' in the parish of San Nazaro), with his wife, sixteen years his junior, and their six children, all except one in their minority.[49] Five other children had died in infancy – Antonio, who was born in 1605 and died before 1607; twins born in 1608 and dead by 1610; Carlo Primo and Carlo Francesco, who predeceased their father. Costanza, born in 1604, must either also have died or been married by 1627, for she is not remembered in her father's will (like any daughter who had already received her dowry). Three other children had left home before their father's death – Bianca Isabella, a nun in the convent of San Bernardo in Milan, and Paolo and Pietro, who had already started their careers as traders, even though Paolo was only eighteen and Pietro a mere eleven. They had been sent as apprentices to the branch of the family firm in Antwerp. Clearly Giovanni Pietro and his wife were ready to bring yet further children into the world, since in one room there was a store of cradles with all their accoutrements, ready for use, and linen for childbirth as well as everyday use.[50] In any case, there were no effective means of contraception available at that time, in despite of human ingenuity, largely because there was little understanding of how conception came about;[51] and the very idea was opposed by the Church then as now.

Filled with children, it must have been a lively and active household. Antonio was twenty, the fecklessness natural to his age perhaps moderated or perhaps made more capricious by his imminent responsibilities in succession to his father at the head of the family. Emilia and Alessandro were fifteen and twelve respectively, old enough to look ahead to the life marked out for them by their family with trepidation, eagerness or resignation. The three youngest children, seven-year-old Carlo Francesco, five-year-old Carlo and three-year-old Francesco, no doubt as yet thought little of the future – the first caught up entirely by study and play, the other two with their games and toys (though none appear in the Annoni inventory, which is not unusual for the period, even though in a household as affluent as this toys would have been objects of some value).[52] The joys and fears of the children, their cares and worries, their pleasures and playtime would have been shared and guided not only by their mother but also by their forty-three-year-old aunt Lucrezia, childless wife to Cristoforo, Giovanni Pietro's brother, and sister or cousin to Isabella (both of them née Bonacina).[53] We know that the brothers Annoni were living in the same house some years earlier, and there is no sign that they had moved in the meantime.[54] Undoubtedly the two families shared some rooms, and in Giovanni Pietro's inventory the furnishings of the dining table, for example, are not listed, with the exception of some pewter, the table-cloths and napkins (ranging from the most ordinary to the most precious that

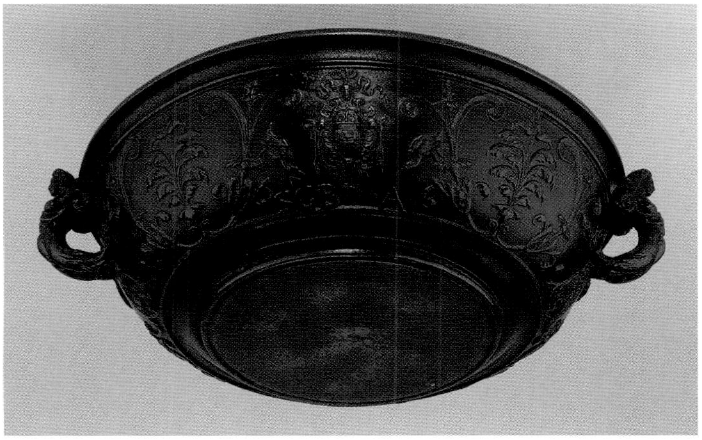

The Visconti-Annoni marriage bowl, Milan, *c.* 1580, The Ashmolean Museum, Oxford

Flanders could provide), one salt cellar, various cups and saucers and silver cutlery (this last reserved for the master of the house and his guests).[55] Giovanni Pietro's rooms do not include any set aside as an office, even though in the inventories of other Milanese merchants of the time such a space is explicitly identified as "*studio de' negotij*" or is immediately recognizable by the presence of things pertaining to trade, such as steelyards and balances, account books, copies of letters, rough paper, unsold goods, spare money, objects in pawn.[56] Probably the office used by Giovanni Pietro and his brother was in Cristoforo's wing of the palace, as perhaps also the 'front room' or '*sala di rappresentanza*' for the reception of visitors, which we know in Stefano Carenna's case, for example, to have been on the ground floor.[57] In Giovanni Pietro's inventory we read of a "room below" which might have served such a purpose, since there were expensive wall-hangings destined for it,[58] some from Flanders, others of gilt green leather. They would have been set off to great effect by the furniture of dark walnut, the favourite material of cabinetmakers in Lombardy of the time and used for beds, chests and tables elsewhere in the palace.[59] At the time of the inventory they had been removed to another room, possibly as a gesture of mourning. There emerge in fact from the inventory several hints of private homage to the memory of the deceased, amidst the patent indications of considerable comfort and luxury.[60]

In the first place the Annoni were able to eat well, witness the battery of utensils in the kitchen. The diet of this rich household was varied and full in comparison to the cereals and pulses on which the vast majority of people in Europe lived:[61] to these, which would have come from their own estates, they added that elite food, meat, not only fresh but preserved, salted in their own cellar in their *salator di carne*.[62] They had their meat cooked in pans of copper – the best kind of metal for the purpose – and game in a special casserole, the *padelotto di anetra*; or they had it roasted on a spit, beneath which there was a dish to collect the dripping fat. They sautéed their vegetables in their *padella da rostire*. They would accompany all this with wine (their pantry contained some fourteen barrels of the finest – aged – wine), served cold during summer in the cooler listed among the copper utensils kept in the kitchen.[63] They ended their meals with tarts baked in various shaped containers made of different materials and undoubtedly with fresh fruits, perhaps even with oranges from their porch at Vittuone, assuming they had ripened, for the sun that shines on the Po valley, though certainly hot, is not hot enough to ripen such fruit properly.[64]

Another element of the comfort that the Annoni enjoyed was space: every member of the family, child and adult, had his or her own bedroom, both in the Milan palace and in their house in the country, except for the babies and the very young.[65] Their sleep was watched over, as is proved by the presence of both a cradle and a bed in one room in the Milan palace and, in the house at Vittuone, a small-sized four-poster bed in the room of their mother.[66] Unlike the greater part of their contemporaries the Annoni children did not sleep in the servant's room, where in fact there was only one bed.[67] (The nursery was a later invention.)[68]

The Annoni could enjoy further comfort and ease in their beds, which in the Milan palace were draped and in Vittuone, more recently made, were gilt,[69] and provided with mattresses, sheets, pillow-cases, quilts and blankets and, for the cold nights of winter, warming pans of copper.[70] This was not unusual for people of their wealth in that area.[71] It was common, moreover, to use bedrooms not only for sleeping but also for socializing with close friends and to eat in,[72] and accordingly we find that the Annoni also kept in their bedrooms tables large and small, a desk, stools, armchairs (as many as six in a room) and a table clock.[73] Specifically for the night they had a night clock (though it cannot have been a silent one, an innovation first known in Rome in the middle of the century) and also chests and cupboards for towels and linen[74] and the family's underwear and clothes.

The essential garment of the time was the shirt or *camicia*, a hundred and fifty of which are listed in the Annoni inventory, for both men and women.[75] Perhaps, however, these were to be worn not only by the parents and their three children between twelve and twenty years of age but also by their servants (how many these were we cannot know, but there was only one room with only one bed in it set apart for the *servitori*).[76] It should be said that the *camicia* was more frequently changed and washed than any other garment – washed in tubs provided both in the Milan and in the Vittuone residences.[77] As for what might be worn over the *camicia*, there is notice only of *catelonie* – warm woollen gowns for winter – and of a few other articles of everyday use, such as kerchiefs for the head, aprons and the occasional man's house jacket;[78] on the other hand some women's garments of particular value are described in considerable detail. In what was presumably Isabella's bedroom there was a fine dress of dark pink taffetta with gold embroidery and silver sleeves which had been made for Bianca Isabella.[79] But as soon as we imagine the joy the young girl might have taken in such fine garments we sadly remember that her family had reserved for her a future within the walls of a convent, in which the pleasures of life were prohibited, or, if enjoyed, needed to be concealed.[80] The wardrobe of the mistress of the house was more sober: Isabella dressed in grey, green, black and brown, which, however, would have set off well the gold and white of embroidered lace and silk, and jewels – pearls and diamonds – with which the fine fabrics, largely of silk, were further enriched; and, in the colder season, she would have worn over these colourful mantles.[81]

A rich diet, furniture, fine clothing, jewellery, horses and carriages – these are the everyday luxuries of one of the most prominent businessmen of the Milan of his time. But missing from Giovanni Pietro's inventory are pictures, books and valuable furnishings. The absence of pictures is most strange. It was common practice among the rich mercantile class of the time to adorn the walls of their houses with pictures of the Madonna, of saints, of scenes from the Old and New Testament, with portraits of the sovereign or of one's own family, and with landscapes.[82] Paintings were not only objects of beauty and of status but were also an investment, being acceptable as collateral in trading deals.[83] Their absence in the Annoni inventory is particularly strange not least because Giovanni Pietro was well acquainted with the art market. Not only had he transported pictures from the Netherlands to Milan for Federico Borromeo, he had also acted as an intermediary between Borromeo and Jan Brueghel, and had shipped works of art to Brussels for Rubens.[84] We might therefore hypothesize that the walls of the Annoni palace were in fact hung with pictures, but that they belonged to others

– to his brother Cristoforo perhaps, or to his wife's family. Since they did not belong to the deceased himself they were not listed in the inventory. Alternatively, in the interval between Giovanni Pietro's death and the drawing up of the documents for the wardship of his minor children the pictures and objects of value had been sold or pawned.

The Carenna in the early seventeenth century

The Carenna grew to prominence in the shadow of the Annoni. Originally, like the Annoni, from Annone di Brianza, the Carenna were already present in Brabant in the sixteenth century.[85] Giacomo Antonio Carenna was sent to Antwerp in 1604 at the age of thirteen to learn the business, and to work there once he had completed his apprenticeship.[86] His mercantile career was marked out for him, as were those of his brothers Giovanni Angelo, Stefano and Bartolomeo. These sons of Giovanni Francesco Carenna were related to the Annoni – though we do not know if it was to the Milan branch of the family – through their mother Giovanna Annoni; and the trader Cristoforo Annoni, not by chance, was godfather to another brother, Giovanni Battista. To date nothing is known of Giovanni Battista, although it may be supposed he was the Giovanni Battista "Careno" who in 1637 transferred money from Brussels to Milan.[87] Of the other sons of Giovanni Francesco we know that all found a position with the Annoni in Milan or abroad with the foreign branches of Giovanni Pietro and Cristoforo Annoni's companies.

Giovanni Angelo Carenna lived in the same parish in Milan as the Annoni brothers and was a witness to several deeds drawn up for Giovanni Pietro Annoni in the 1610s and 1620s.[88] Bartolomeo is recorded in a deed of 1615, in which, on the authority of the priors of the Camera dei Mercanti (chamber of merchants) of Milan, an inventory was made of the goods in the warehouse of the partnership of one Giovanni Ambrogio de Zanis and Bartolomeo Carenna, with a view to their sale in order to render what was due to their creditors. Their company traded in luxury goods for the Milan market – precious textiles from Cambrai, Ulm, Constance and St Gall; lace from Lorraine, Flanders and the Como region; silk ribbons made in Milan or Genoa; French wool cloth; enamels. The value of their goods was considerable, more than 21,000 *lire*, equivalent to between a sixth or an eighth of the working capital of a company like the Annoni's, operating in an international exchange circuit.[89] Responsibility for compiling the inventory was given to Giovanni Pietro Annoni, and we might speculate that it was the poor outcome of this enterprise that led Bartolomeo Carenna to work thereafter for the Annoni, as we find him doing in 1627.[90]

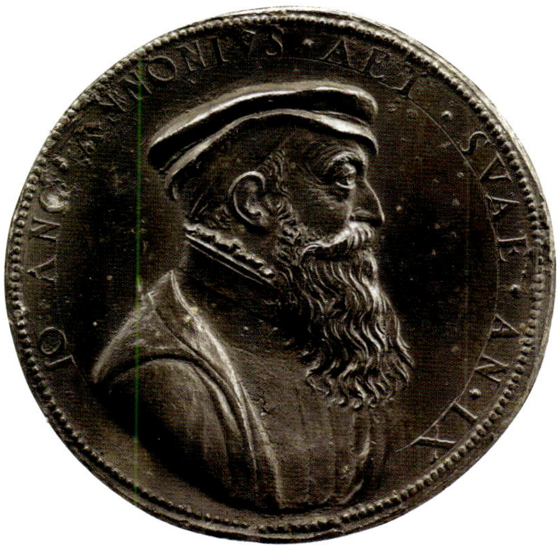

Medal of Giovanni Angelo Annoni, The British Museum, London

Giacomo Antonio Carenna's attachment to the Annoni seems to have been more immediate. In 1615, by this time having become familiar with the market in Antwerp, in which he had now operated for eleven years,[91] he began working for the Brabant branch of the Annoni company of Milan – from the start for the 'Giovanni Pietro and Giacomo Antonio Annoni' company, in fact constituted by a group of members of the various branches of the Annoni family, all resident and active in Milan. Here Giacomo Antonio Carenna worked for more than five years in the business of conveying goods from central northern Europe to Italy and *vice versa*, until the company was liquidated in the 1620s.[92]

In the meantime Giacomo Antonio Carenna became doubly bound to the Annoni in his life of import-export and money transfers. He must have worked in close contact with Giovanni Pietro Annoni, since it was he who, according to the company's articles, was responsible for managing the company both in Milan and in Antwerp and he who in 1620 made Carenna his principal on the river Scheldt.[93] In the early 1620s Giacomo Antonio had married a Maria Annoni.[94] Between 1627 and 1629 he was charged specifically in the 'Giovanni Pietro and Cristoforo Annoni' company's articles to see to the education and training of the young Paolo Annoni, son of Giovanni Pietro, so that he, too, might carry on the family business; he may also have done as much for Paolo's brother Pietro, who had arrived in Antwerp in 1627.[95]

A man, then, whom the Annoni trusted, even for the care of one of their children, Giacomo Antonio Carenna by the end of the third decade of the seventeenth century was an established operator in the Antwerp market, working in an international company with links crisscrossing western Europe – from Antwerp and Brussels to Paris, from Basle and Zurich to Augsburg and Nuremberg, from Turin and Bergamo to Siena, Rome and Naples.[96] But for all his experience and proven competence he remained a subordinate of the Annoni, until the death of Giovanni Pietro in 1627 gave him an opportunity to gain his independence.

On January 1, 1629 a new Annoni company, transporting goods produced in Flanders, Germany, France and "other places" and buying and selling goods both in its own right and on behalf of third parties, was constituted, and Giacomo Antonio Carenna was one of the shareholders.[97] Indeed he was the only shareholder who was not an Annoni and the only newcomer among them: the others were the same Annoni who had been in partnership since the beginning of the century – Giacomo Antonio, son of the late Ambrogio, and Cristoforo Annoni and his nephews, heirs of the deceased Giovanni Pietro.

Carenna had emerged as a pillar of the company. He was named as sole administrator of the Antwerp branch, while the equivalent role in Milan was taken by Cristoforo Annoni, who would rely upon the assistance of his nephew Antonio, eldest son of Giovanni Pietro.[98] Carenna was given power to appoint to deputize for him, in case of emergency, a man of his own choice. He had full authority in the business of the Brabant branch: he could lend and borrow money, buy and insure goods, select clients and suppliers, of all of which he was to give a full account in ledgers that were always to be available for inspection by the other shareholders. And, as mentioned, he was to take Paolo Annoni under his wing and teach him the business.

Giacomo Antonio Carenna staked in the company 'Giovanni Pietro and Cristoforo Annoni' (which continued to be its name even though Giovanni Pietro had been dead for two years at the moment of its constitution) 18,000 *lire*, or about 15% of its starting capital. To appreciate the value of this sum we may compare it to an average take-home salary. The archives reveal how much the collectors of tolls on the border of the State of Milan during the years 1635–37 were paid – 250 *lire* a year.[99] Carenna invested in the Annoni company a great deal more than such an official might earn (not including extras, the so-called *onoranze*) in a lifetime. And it was an excellent investment, even though within a few months the State of Milan would be assailed by a series of disasters.

War and commerce

There were already signs in 1627 of even worse things to come, with the outbreak of a war over the ducal succession of Mantua that would drag on until 1631. In 1635 the French and their Savoy allies once again attacked Spanish Lombardy, which remained a theatre of war almost without interruption until the Peace of the Pyrenees of 1659.

In any particular point where war was raging the difficulties for commerce were obvious. In 1628, for example, Milan went without its supply of grain from Ferrara because there was no route through the Duchy of Mantua. In 1636 the approaches to the capital across the Ticino and the canal which linked that river to the city, the Naviglio Grande, were impassable because of the fighting taking place.[100]

Overall, however, a state of war was not enough to induce the authorities to compromise the guiding principles of openness and tolerance that had hitherto been a mark of Milanese commercial practice. Conscious that Milan lacked the advantages that the possession of a port brought to Venice or Genoa – the very basis of their mercantile prowess – in Milan care had always been taken not to place any obstacle in the way of free traffic and indeed to encourage the presence of foreign merchants in the State.[101] Even in the sixteenth century, while the State was actively concerned to exorcise the peril of heresy, commercial links with Reformed countries were retained and special privileges continued to be granted to German merchants wherever they might come from. In 1611 the German, Spanish, Savoyard and transalpine merchants in general were relieved from paying certain duties from which otherwise only Milanese citizens had been exempt. Foreign traders and financiers had always been freely admitted to the *Universitas mercatorum Mediolanensis*. Again, in 1635 the Milanese authorities negotiated with Rome on behalf of the Schobinger brothers of St Gall, Protestant members of a *fondaco* in Alessandria, when they got into trouble with the Inquisition.

When war began again in the mid 1630s the acts of reprisal taken against each other by hostile states by no means brought commerce to a halt. In the 1630s and 1640s, for example, the closure of the route from Piedmont across the Savoy to Lyons (one of the greatest importance for Lombard trade) was obviated either by using the Sempione pass or by moving goods through Leghorn and Avignon.[102] From 1635 onwards decrees were passed in Milan expelling from Spanish Lombardy French and Savoyard citizens and barring native Lombards from trading with subjects of states hostile to Spain.[103] These decrees, however, were motivated by the need to exercise greater control over citizens' contacts with outside states, and in their texts stated the conditions under which they would be deemed no longer to be applicable. There was no provision for the expulsion of anyone who had been resident or had worked in the State for more than three years. Lombards were able to trade with anyone they wanted, once they had the permission of the relevant authorities. All that entailed, in practice, was identifying yourself, declaring the value of the goods you wished to trade, and paying for a safe conduct; otherwise there was no hindrance to the activity either of foreign or of native merchants. Great numbers of licenses to trade were issued not only to local operators but also to Piedmontese, Savoyard and French ones, and it is clear from the documents associated with the issue of these permissions that the State of Milan remained as open to the rest of Europe as it had ever been. Spanish Lombardy continued during these years of war to be visited by caravans bearing textiles from Lake Constance or South Germany, bound for Genoa and eventually for Spain; linen, wool, silk and lace from Holland, Flanders, Germany and Savoy bound for central Italy; goods from Germany or Flanders for the Monferrato, whence, taking in new supplies in Genoa, they set off again to cross the Alps; books from Lyons for Venice and Rome; arms and ironwork produced in and around Brescia and bound for Piedmont and Lyons.[104]

This policy of open commerce with other states benefited not only Milan's merchants, but in general its public purse, its toll collectors and its aristocracy, since, besides the luxury goods it manufactured, Milan also exported agricultural products cultivated, in large part, on the hereditary lands of the nobility from which came the men who ran the State. Indeed the new footing on which Milanese economy came to be placed after the setbacks of the late 1620s would prove even more favourable not only to its trading community but no less also to its aristocracy, the men responsible for the state's administration.

A new direction for the Milanese economy: the plague

In 1629 Spanish Lombardy was hit by terrible famine and by an outbreak of plague that lasted until 1632.[105] Within three years the city had lost more than a quarter of its population, if not from death then from dispersal into the countryside, where the open spaces reduced the risk of contagion.[106] Those who stayed and lived witnessed the horrors consequent not only on disease but on ignorance of its causes. There were pogroms against those believed responsible for the plague, means of settling grudges, jealousies and differences of all kinds. Confessions were extorted from unfortunates after torture in order to appease a city at the end of its tether.[107] The elite, however, were only minimally affected by the plague, since they could escape to the countryside and there lead their normal lives, fuelling a demand for articles of quality which, augmented by that of the ruling classes of other northern Italian states, made Milan, even then, an emporium of luxury.

Plague, no more than had war, did not cut European trade links. Milan was isolated only on the outbreak of the plague and only for a short time, in late 1629. The city temporarily closed all trading routes within its territory extending out to north-west Italy, to the Alps and beyond and to southern France, wherever the plague had appeared or was suspected of reaching.[108] Conversely, in the spring of 1630 a number of other cities of central and northern Italy suspended trading with Milan.[109]

The plague deprived the capital of manpower and the price of labour rose. What was more, the shape of international demand was changing: raw and spun silk, grain and cheese were required in greater quantity than the manufactured goods of high quality, above all textiles, that, to Milan's great benefit, had seduced Europe's most refined classes up to the end of the sixteenth century. This brought about a profound change in the years following the plague. Milanese merchants found it more profitable to import luxury goods, above all textiles, than to have them produced locally.[110] At the same time the production of semi-processed silk became more profitable, especially if the spinning was done in the countryside, where the raw material was abundant and the cost of labour was cheaper than in the city. Increasingly silk spinning became established in the countryside north of the city rather than in Milan itself, from which it had more or less disappeared by the beginning of the eighteenth century.[111]

Adapting quickly to the demands of the market, Milan remained an important economic centre even during the plague years, and was able to recover its lost population and to achieve once again 100,000 inhabitants by the middle of the century.[112] Enterprises were founded for the production of luxury goods – silks enriched with filaments of gold or silver, for example – and the raw materials needed by its local manufactories continued to flow into the capital.[113] Even while Milan was invaded by northern European products, particularly in wool and fine linen, highly capitalized Milanese merchants continued to form far-ranging trading companies and a number of bankers continued to gather the credit notes of their colleagues to carry out international payments at the 'Bisenzone' exchange fairs, which by that time no longer took place in the town of Besançon but had been established in Piacenza.[114]

The 'Giovanni Pietro and Cristoforo Annoni' company set up in 1629, with Giacomo Antonio Carenna among its shareholders, did not fall behind in the plague years. Its caravans laden with Italian goods were still travelling across the heart of Europe to reach Brabant.[115] It continued successfully to broker: both native and foreign merchants entrusted goods to the Annoni for sale in the various markets of Europe and handed over their money so that the company should settle their debts, invest it, or move it from one market to another – from Brussels to Lille, from Amsterdam to Cambrai, from St Gall to Vicenza, Florence or Rome.[116]

It is very likely that the positive results enjoyed by the 'Giovanni Pietro and Cristoforo Annoni' company encouraged Giacomo Antonio Carenna to embark on an independent project of his own in the following years. In 1631 he returned to Milan, perhaps recalled by the Annoni to present his accounts and to cash the credits that the company had lodged with Giacomo Antonio Annoni.[117] While there, Carenna also settled his accounts with his own family. He required his brothers Bartolomeo, Stefano and Giovanni Angelo to forego formally all claim on his own 'effects', on property that was his alone, that is to say on the money he had earned in nearly thirty years' activity in the Antwerp market. With this document, drawn up by the Annoni's notary, Ottaviano Belingeri,[118] Giacomo Antonio Carenna separated his own possessions from those of his brothers but at the same time protected the interests of each branch of the family, the Milan as well as the Antwerp branch. In fact Bartolomeo, Stefano and Giovanni Angelo could never have had any claim on Giacomo Antonio's property, but the deed precluded any claim that anyone might make on his brothers, at least in Milan, for damages or debts incurred by Giacomo Antonio.

The documents at our disposal do not permit us to do much more than hypothesize what path Giacomo Antonio's continuing financial rise actually took, although by the middle of the century it had clearly achieved a considerable height. The deed of 1631, if we take it together with the description of him as "*mercante*" given in the document of Paolo Annoni's appointment of him as principal of the firm in Antwerp in the same year[119] – a 'merchant' being someone trading independently for himself – would nevertheless appear to indicate that he had an independent business, even if from the point of view of Milan he was seen only as the head of the branch of the Annoni company in Antwerp.[120]

Paolo Annoni at the head of the family and the Annoni company

In the meantime the role of head of the Annoni family had passed, on his death, from Antonio Annoni (heir to Giovanni Pietro) to his brother Paolo. Though hardly more than twenty years old – but no doubt an able young man quick in taking the initiative and in a position to profit from some years' experience in a professional environment and a city, Antwerp, different from that in which he had grown up – Paolo gave a new direction to the affairs of the Annoni company.

When he took over the firm at first he seemingly ran it entirely along traditional lines. He paid his debts to foreign merchants and he took money in his turn from those who owed it to him; he lent money to foreign peers during their stay in Milan[121] and made sure that he could continue to exploit alternative routes by which to send his goods to Brabant.[122] But from 1631 he also undertook a series of operations designed to increase the liquidity at his disposal. He got married – to Francesca Aliprandi, daughter of the deceased Bonifacio and widow of

Ottavio Frisiani, who brought him some 60,000 *lire* as her dowry, about half the sum he would need to make as an initial investment in an international trading company.[123] In the following years he negotiated to recover the capital owing to him from the companies founded during the 1620s by his father and his uncle in partnership with merchants of other families, with the Lumaga and with Daniele Delubert, Roberto Poquilin and Lodovico Mizzaferro.[124] The greater part of this money he re-invested in the family business, which was renamed 'Heirs of Giovanni Pietro and Cristoforo Annoni' and then, in 1637, after four years, was rebranded again in his own name as 'Giovanni Paolo and Stefano Annoni.' This new company, based in Milan with a branch in Antwerp, went into business from January 1638.[125] Paolo ran the business in Milan, assisted by Giovanni Angelo Carenna, who had been working with him from the beginning of the decade and who from 1633 is attested as a "*complimentario*" of the company, in other words a shareholding officer of it; his cousin Stefano Annoni ran it in Antwerp together with Giacomo Antonio Carenna.[126]

The cash he acquired during this time also permitted Paolo and his family to live in grand style. He had built by Milan's leading architect, Francesco Maria Richino, a new palace in the parish of San Nazaro, a residence which would take its place amongst the finest buildings of the capital (illustrated).[127] Quite possibly Giacomo Antonio Carenna, while in Milan in 1631, would have seen the plans for it, and have been inspired to emulate Paolo's initiative at Antwerp – once he had achieved wealth approaching that of his former apprentice. This he managed to do in little more than fifteen years.

Meanwhile Paolo Annoni encouraged his brother Giovanni Pietro to take up a military career, enrolling him in the Spanish Army as a lieutenant colonel.[128] This was not simply because such a career was a noble one,[129] but had the further design of acquiring honours and recognition in Madrid. An involvement in the defence of the State was in itself a recommendation in the eyes of the Spanish court, and had even greater lustre when the officer in question undertook to cover his own expenses.[130] We may suppose that Paolo Annoni did not stint in making available to his brother any support that he needed, alert as he was, like other Milanese of similar position, to the opportunities offered to a financier by the wars in which Spain was engaged to expand his investments and advance the status of his family.

War as a means to the ends of business and social climbing

War, generally speaking, is and always has been miserable for most involved, but it is and always has been for some an opportunity for conspicuous gain. It was no coincidence that in the years following the 1659 Peace of the Pyrenees (which marked the end of nearly three decades of intermittent war, during which commerce had thrived), several Milanese financial companies went bust.[131]

To understand how war might offer opportunities for Milanese traders in the seventeenth century we have only to recall the positive stimulus that military demand had given the local economy in the years 1613–18, when troops were repeatedly called upon to defend the south-western border of the State, under threat from Piedmont. It was soon noted that in those five years trade had increased, and even (perhaps with some exaggeration) that merchants had succeeded in that time in doubling the value of their investments.[132]

Soldiers, of course, had to be paid, fed and equipped with whatever they needed for battle and campaigning; a standing army was a heavy expense, and would be slimmed down whenever and as soon as the situation permitted.[133] To meet the expenses of an army there were the dual instruments of taxation and billeting. Some towns and villages were forced to pay on the basis of the quotas allotted them specifically for military expenditure; others, should they find themselves in the path of the troops, would be forced to take them in. However, the practice had been found preferable in the sixteenth century, and became prevalent in the seventeenth, of lodging troops in empty houses – or barracks – to avoid the inconveniences or indeed outrageous behaviour associated with such visitors (and the locals' violent reactions to it), and of contracting with merchants for their supplies.[134]

Maintaining an army was not the only military burden laid upon the State. There was also enormous expenditure involved in building fortifications and keeping them in good order, and, despite very heavy taxation during war years, the income of the State of Milan did no more than cover the expenses of the administration and the interest on the public debt.[135] Lombardy, however, could count on huge sums of money coming in from abroad, and not only while it was a war zone. After the extinction of its Sforza dukes Milan had benefited from the financial contribution (known as 'aid' or 'remittance') of several other territories controlled by Madrid, because for Spain Milan was strategically vital to the overland lines between the Mediterrranean and the Netherlands. Huge sums of money raised in Spain itself, Naples and Sicily reached Milan,[136] whether destined to remain there or to be passed on across the Alps to serving Spanish troops or any other soldiers recruited to the Habsburg flag.

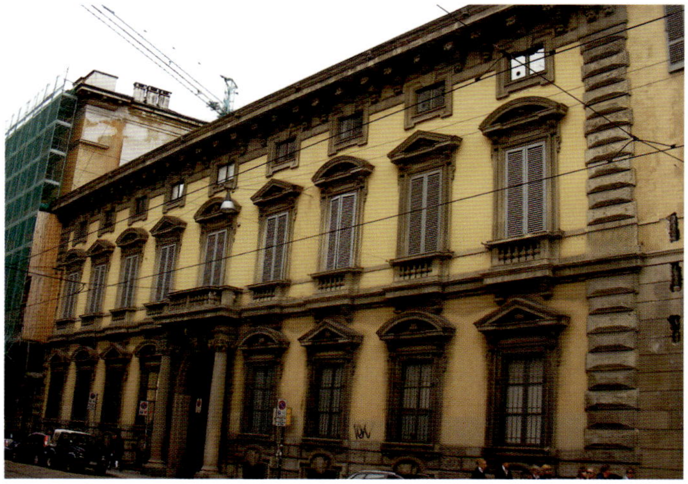

Palazzo Annoni, Milan, built *c.* 1631

The financial mediators whose services were needed to get these 'remittances' to their destination could expect a handsome reward in consideration of the risks involved. The financier needed to guarantee payment of the agreed money by the contracted date; he had to have the necessary sum to hand in advance. In return he took a certain percentage as commission, which varied, for example, with the type of coin in which the loan was made and restituted; he skimmed off some money for interest when the sum concerned was transferred by means of a letter of credit fulfilled at a fair. Different percentages of commission applied in relation to the amount of money involved and the greater or lesser distance between the points of payment.[137] To appreciate just how profitable these arrangements might be, let us take a case in which the financier would charge a comparatively modest commission, for transferring money from Genoa to Milan: suppose a commission of 1% and apply it to a sum of 127,500 *lire milanesi*, which seems to be the lowest sum recorded in this currency among the transactions ordered by the Spanish authorities in Naples between 1637 and 1659.[138] The financier would thus gain 1,275 *lire*, as much as our salaried employee at his customs post would earn in more than five years of duty. And he would gain not only in money but also in favour, since armies were composed of mercenaries, and mercenaries were readily inclined to mutiny or desert if they were not paid on time, and this was a time of constant war – a man who could deliver on this kind of transaction would establish excellent credentials for reward at court.

It was the Genoese who were pre-eminent at moving money around, for all the efforts of the authorities in Milan to free themselves from their costly and not reliably punctual services.[139] They had developed such resources in this market as to give them an unassailable competitive advantage;[140] they were virtually indispensable and as such could insist on their own terms to the Spanish Crown. It is indicative that in the 1630s the Genoese Stefano Balbi opened a public bank in Milan, the Monte di San Carlo, as a means through which he could recover the credit that he had built up with the Regia Camera in Milan.[141]

Compared to the Genoese the Milanese were contractually in a weaker position with the Spanish Crown, and perhaps therefore behaved more cautiously, given the danger that the Crown might not honour its agreements and might suspend payments, as had happened in the sixteenth century and more recently, in 1627, on the outbreak of war in Lombardy. Nonetheless the leading Milanese financiers managed to get their share of the 'remittances', too. We know that the following figures were involved in this business: Francesco Castelli, Geronimo Caimi, Giorgio Clerici, the Durino, Marc'Antonio Lumaga in partnership with Marc'Antonio Stampa, and, in close association with the Carenna, Paolo Annoni and Marcellino Airoldi.[142] Paolo Annoni found a role not in bringing money into Milan, like most of his colleagues mentioned above, but as an intermediary with foreign bankers, no doubt exploiting his north European connections built up over more than a century of trading by his family. He acted, for example, for the Parliament of Burgundy in the transfer of funds from Milan to that region.[143]

It is worth dwelling a moment on Airoldi, because through knowledge of the affairs of this leading Milanese banker we can better appreciate the involvement of Giacomo Antonio Carenna in Antwerp. In 1628 he requested affiliation to the *mercatores utentes stratis* declaring himself to be a businessman particularly active in currency exchange.[144] In the late 1620s or early 1630s he formed a financial and commercial transfer company with Filippo Del Conte, a leading figure in Milanese trade and banking who for several months in 1615 and 1616 had held the highest position of all in the Camera dei Mercanti in Milan. The company traded in wool between the Spanish and Genoese coasts, as Del Conte had been doing in the 1610s.[145] In the 1630s and 1640s Airoldi seems to have played a role as a correspondent in transactions between Naples and Milan, becoming a creditor of the Real Hacienda (royal exchequer).[146] In 1637, while importing silver from Genoa on behalf of the Milanese royal mint, he transferred about 300,000 *lire milanesi* to the Swiss cantons of Uri and Unterwalden, established recruiting grounds for mercenaries. In January 1639, in association with Giovanni Giacomo Durino, he was intermediary between the Real Hacienda and the governor of Burgundy, successfully bringing to Dôle first more than 120,000 *lire milanesi* in order to buy munitions for the defence of the region, then another 240,000 to pay the mercenaries stationed there and finally almost one million *lire milanesi* for the maintenance of the local militias. In 1640, as "*complimentario*," or executive partner of a company formed with Filippo De Latini and Francesco De Baldesis – not coincidentally resident in Naples, whence came the greatest remittances to Milan – Airoldi was the intermediary for loans made to the King of Poland. In 1644 he delivered 4,800 *thalers* to the commander of the Burgundian cavalry so that he could pay his contingent of 840 men.[147] In 1645 he was owed over 120,000 *lire* by the Milanese Camera, and this figure can only have increased in subsequent years, since his family continued to lend money to the Real Hacienda at least until the late 1680s.[148] This was the calibre of man with whom we know that Giacomo Antonio Carenna, as the executive partner of the Antwerp branch of the Annoni company, worked in 1644, making a transfer of money in order to pay soldiers.[149]

This is not likely to have been an isolated occasion. And it may well be that the "Giacomo Corenno" who was a partner of Carlo Rezzonico of Genoa between 1648 and 1654 and collaborated with Airoldi again in the late 1650s was indeed Giacomo Antonio Carenna at work again[150] – 'Corenno' is clearly a variant of 'Carenna', which we also find in the forms 'Carena' and 'Coreno.' However, an element of uncertainty remains because the documentation tells us that the partners Carlo Rezzonico and Giacomo Corenno were "*degentes in civitate Genuae*" (living in the city of Genoa). But it might be that the company in question had a branch in Genoa, run by Carlo Rezzonico, and another in Antwerp, run by Carenna. If this was the case then Giacomo Antonio Carenna was involved once more, in 1648, with Marcellino Airoldi, transferring a huge sum of money for the governor of the State of Milan. In the first half of the 1650s we learn that the company of 'Carlo Rezonico and Giacomo Corenno' was active in the Genoese market, cashing credits for operators of the first order in Milan. In 1650 it was used by Giovanni Pietro Arbona, a very powerful merchant trading with northern Europe,[151] and in 1654 by Alessandro Paravicini, the administrator of the company belonging to his father, Giovanni Antonio, who in 1633 had been director of a financial and commercial transfer company based in Milan and Antwerp and in 1636 of another company based in Rome.[152]

Besides these financial activities on behalf of private individuals, Carenna's upward career received substantial impetus from his willingness to offer his services to the Spanish Crown. Within the span of a decade Carenna and his Milanese colleagues Paolo Annoni and Giovanni Giacomo Durino were able to obtain fiefs and noble titles: the financial transfer business enabled them to gain the confidence of the king and opened up to them positions they could have attained, perhaps, in no other way.

For Paolo Annoni and Durino the opportunity came in 1648–49, very difficult years for Spanish Lombard finances, because revolts against the Spanish Crown in Portugal and Catalonia forced Madrid to direct its financial resources mainly to these areas.[153] In Milan the crisis had to be resolved by selling off tax or toll rights – not temporarily but, in order to make them sufficiently attractive, absolutely and irredeemably – and a huge number of fiefs.[154] Paolo Annoni bought the manor of Merone, in the Como region, where his family had for many years had considerable holdings of land; Giovanni Giacomo Durino acquired that of Monza.[155] Giacomo Antonio Carenna, for his part, in 1649 acquired his fine residence in Antwerp and in 1655 was ennobled. The reason given for the elevation was the generic formula "for services rendered to the Crown," but these services, in those times and circumstances, can only have been financial. Indeed it is more than probable that Carenna was ennobled after releasing the Spanish Crown from a loan for which it had contracted in 1650 and that in 1653 had not yet been repaid.[156]

The rise of the Carenna of Milan

Like their brother in Antwerp, the Carenna in Milan also took it upon themselves to advance their family's standing, and, obviously, the way to do so was by being employed and then becoming stakeholders in the economic colossus that was the Annoni company.

Bartolomeo Carenna we know to have worked for the Annoni abroad. In 1627 he was the representative of the company in Basle and in 1631 he was staying in Bellinzona, undoubtedly to avoid the plague, but it is plausible also that the Annoni had entrusted him with some business outside the State.[157] Giovanni Angelo Carenna we can trace in Milan, where by 1631, after at least ten years working as an agent for the Annoni, he had put down capital in order to become a shareholder, and was working as an administrator beside Paolo Annoni.[158] In the second half of the century Stefano Carenna was also associated with the Annoni company.[159] The Carenna were amply rewarded by gaining a share in the profits of the company, which, as we have seen, grew and grew with the years as Paolo Annoni, like others, took the opportunities offered by the need to make available money to pay for the wars. At the same time the Annoni company continued to organize transport from central North Italy to the Low Countries, and to act as intermediary in making international payments and in buying and selling goods on behalf of their colleagues, both Milanese and foreign.[160] In the mid 1650s, for the Parisian firm of Poquilin alone (with whom they had been trading for about thirty years), the Annoni were handling goods on the Milanese market to a value of almost 100,000 *lire*, a sum far exceeding the capital of a company formed in the same years for the transport of goods between Milan and Lyons.[161]

The Carenna also diversified their investments, depositing sums of money in the Milanese banks of Sant'Ambrogio and San Carlo and acquiring bonds of public debt.[162] The range of their financial activity was varied: they took in bonds offered by private persons or by municipalities in the State of Milan to private persons, taking the interest that mounted up on them until they were discharged.[163] They financed the production of silk thread in the Milanese hills, where there had been silk mills since the second half of the sixteenth century. For this they might make very large loans, as much as 4,000 *lire* in one payment at a rate of 6% a year.[164] In the city they took money on deposit and lent it on the collateral of property, according to an arrangement common at the time known as *retrovendita*. Someone in need of a loan sold a piece of property, which he could reclaim after repaying the sum lent and the interest on it. In the case of the Carenna the official rate of interest was no higher than 6% a year, well below the 10% fixed by the authorities as the maximum permitted before verging on the usurious and criminal.[165] For those who were unable to pay their debts in the time agreed, the Carenna might concede extensions and, sometimes, claim not only the interest owing but also the right to manage the assets or some of the assets of the debtor. For example, in 1656 they succeeded in obtaining directly the rent due to a landowner who was in debt to them, so that the debtor could not deceitfully pay them only part of what he received from his tenants. Should, even after extensions, the loan not be repaid, the *retrovendita* arrangement became void and the property deposited with the financier became his, and it was by this means that the Carenna came by much of their property in Milan and Brianza.[166] The range and rank of the Carenna brothers' debtors and depositors was considerable, from simple peasants in their own native district to Milanese nobles at the head of the State's institutions – in the latter case brokered through the financier Marcellino Airoldi, the associate also of their brother in Antwerp.[167]

The Carenna's financial activities extended beyond the borders of the State: they operated in the international market, transferring money from one market to another, often in collaboration with the Brabant branch of the Annoni firm.[168] They took money on deposit from non-Milanese as well, since we know Jews also to have been their clients, and after their expulsion in 1573 no Jews are recorded on the rolls in Spanish Lombardy.[169] Through their collaboration with the Annoni and their activity in the financial markets in their own right, the Carenna brothers accumulated a fortune that enabled them to live in affluence and move up the social scale, starting, like their brother in Antwerp, with the acquisition of a fine residence.

The Carenna's Milan residence and house in Annone, indicators of their wealth

Before his death in 1670 Bartolomeo had bought a new house in Milan,[170] inherited by his brother Stefano, who enjoyed it for another ten years. When he died in 1680 he left a widow and several minors, in whose interest an inventory of his goods was prepared. We are thus enabled to 'visit' both the town house where he and his family passed the greater part of the year and the country property where they holidayed. It is clear from the documents that both houses served the Carenna brothers' desire to display their wealth to the world. Even a century later the poorer classes in Milan would be living and working in a single room,[171] but the Carenna had at their disposal in the second half of the seventeenth century sixteen rooms in the capital and ten in Annone, not counting the storage areas, corridors, attics and cellars. There was thus abundant space for the family that the financier, at more than forty years of age, had felt it his duty to form, as we may deduce from a study of the genealogical trees of the Carenna and the Annoni (see pp. 176–77): only one of the brothers was to ensure the legitimate continuation of the family, procreated through marriage, in order to avoid splitting the patrimony among too many heirs.[172]

Stefano had married a woman of foreign extraction, Costanza Gallindez, with whom he had fathered many children, not all of whom reached adulthood. Three daughters – two babies named Paola Francesca and their little sister Clara Teresa Maria – certainly died young, for at the time of their father's death they would have been between seven and fourteen years of age, but they are not noted in his will: given their age they could not yet have been married and have been left out of the will for that reason (having already received their inheritance in the form of their dowry). If instead they had been destined for the convent, they would still have been cited, because it was usual for a father to leave some money to daughters who became nuns, and Stefano left some to his surviving daughter Costanza Teresa, who was a religious at Sant'Agostino in Milan.[173] Another daughter, Giovanna, who also does not appear in her father's will, may either have died young or by 1680 have been married.

Stefano lived to the end of his days in a house in the parish of Santa Eufemia – neighbouring San Nazaro, where the Annoni had their residence – with his wife, a serving woman,[174] two daughters, Teresa and Rosa, who had almost reached puberty at the time of his death, and three sons – Carlo Francesco, whose age we do not know, Bartolomeo, eight years old, and Giovanni Angelo, four. The house was 'lived in,' its children much in evidence. A great number of the pieces of furniture were worn, their restoration having perhaps been put off until the children were older and less likely to damage them. The inventory tells us where they kept their clothes and their linen, the toys for the little ones, their books – which perhaps they learnt to read with their father, since their mother, statistically, despite belonging to the affluent classes, is unlikely to have been literate.[175] We learn also where the two adolescent girls kept their little secret things, in a small box that their mother, with tender respect for their feelings, refused to allow the assessor drawing up the inventory to open,[176] although she was meant to have full knowledge of the condition of the estate which she had at her disposal for the bringing up of her children.[177] She will have supposed instead that they kept there some intimate token, some ornament probably of little real value but pleasing to the whims of the two girls coming to terms with the life of society.[178] She must have been her own woman, Costanza Gallindez; at any rate she bought with her own family's money or with an annuity guaranteed her in her marriage contract the clothes and jewellery she wore, given that in her husband's inventory there is no mention of her things, which is unusual for a document of this kind.

The Carenna children were indeed fortunate, living in spacious apartments, kept clean, as the presence of basins, tubs for laundry and cords for hanging out the washing in both houses attests.[179] They were given an education, witness the books mentioned, and they were well fed in an age where hunger was a condition of life for a large part of the population. From the battery of pans in the kitchen and the food stocks in the houses it is evident that they had a varied and full diet. Their staples, as for most European households of the time, were cereals and vegetables. In Milan and Annone the Carenna stored beans, rice and wheat already ground into flour ready for making into dough and baking; in Annone there was a "*panera*" and an oven in the kitchen.[180] There were stores also of more common grains, such as millet, spelt and rye, that might be found in any house,[181] and at Annone also *formentone* or maize, which was being grown in increasing quantities in Lombardy in the seventeenth century.[182] Maize, milled and cooked in water, filled the belly cheaply and for that reason was the most widely eaten food in the countryside and among the poor. However, a diet limited exclusively to maize could lead to pellagra, a disease which may cause mental disturbance, skin rashes and digestive problems and continued to afflict the Italian poor well into the twentieth century.[183] It did not, however, trouble the Carenna, who had access to protein in abundance, above all meat, whether fresh or preserved, for they possessed not only implements with which to cook it – grill, spit, drip-pan – but also cages in which to keep chickens, both in Milan and in Annone.[184] Other protein supplements to their diet came from lard, butter and oils, no doubt also extracted from the walnuts and linseed that the Carenna stored at Annone, where they had a large pot half full of linseed oil.[185] Knowing the predilection in Lombard cooking for the use of butter, one may suppose from the large amount of oil in the house in Milan that the Carenna used their oil primarily for pickling their food, as they did vinegar (of which there was a small barrel in Milan) or salt (over 13 kg at Annone).[186] Like Giovanni Pietro Annoni and family in their house (see above, p. 158), the Carenna, too, washed down their food with wine, red and white,[187] but there is no trace among the kitchenware of any consumption of a comestible that had become popular in Milan from the beginning of the seventeenth century, chocolate. Until the beginning of the nineteenth century chocolate was mostly consumed as a liquid, with the addition of vanilla, cinnamon and sugar,[188] ingredients that were readily available in the city even if the Carenna had not been able to procure them from their colleagues and business partners in the northern ports. Such favours were done not only for clients but also for family. The porcelain bowl treasured in the Carenna household must have come from Antwerp or Amsterdam, given that porcelain was not produced in Europe until the second decade of the eighteenth century.[189] Many of the pictures that adorned the walls of the Carenna's houses were without doubt Flemish, even if they are not declared to be so in the inventory. One may recall Girolamo Borsieri, writing in the late 1610s, noting the pride of the Milanese with regard to their picture collections: anyone with a picture gallery was careful to put on display only original works, "not wishing that strangers should go around saying that in their galleries they gave title of original to copies."[190]

Without being excessive, the Carenna houses typify the *horror vacui* of the Baroque period.[191] Pictures hung in all the rooms in both houses except the attics, cellars and storerooms but including the entrance hall and lumber room in the house in Milan, in which, besides axles, timber, boots and so on, there were deposited, no doubt temporarily, three landscapes on paper and two representations of Christ.[192] Other paintings were more worthily located, above all a portrait of Giacomo Antonio Carenna (who had predeceased his brother Stefano), the pride of his family not only for the fortune he had made but also, by contrast to his brothers in Milan, for having been granted a title. His effigy looked down on the main reception room of the palace.[193] It was the only portrait on display in that room, and it is evident from the description in the inventory that it was so hung that it could not fail to be noticed – beside the fireplace, the centrepiece of the room. Beside his portrait was a painting of Proserpina, rather as if he, too, were returning from the dead for a time to satisfy his family as Proserpina was permitted to return intermittently from the Underworld for her mother's sake. Besides this work, one of the six mythological paintings possessed by the Carenna, all of them kept in the town house, there were hung pictures of saints and of landscapes, and above the mantel a large night scene with numbers of figures.[194] The intervals between the pictures were filled with mirrors, a fixture that had grown in importance during the century,[195] but there is no mention of a chandelier, though this too had become an increasingly significant decorative element. In being lit only by candlesticks the Carenna house was not unusual for its time and place, since chandeliers were costly. (Wax candles were also costly; tallow was cheaper.) A chandelier, furthermore, had to be cleaned every so often, and if it was at all valuable that could not be done by the household servants but required specialist artisans.[196]

Off the main reception room was Stefano's office, where a portrait of the deceased Bartolomeo Carenna had pride of place.[197] It was the only portrait in the room, reminding Stefano of his late brother and keeping alive for his business associates the memory of a capable entrepreneur. Otherwise there were another mythology and a small Madonna and Child among still lifes (mostly of flowers) and landscapes; a picture of a chained tiger closed off the hearth, no longer now to be lit.[198] Still lifes, and perhaps landscapes, could be acquired at a lower cost than other subjects, though we may imagine that the vigorous seventy-year-old Carenna, surrounded by children, some of them very young, would have raised his eyes from his work to lose himself in these representations of nature in all its variety – flowers, fruits, landscapes, pleasure (Bacchus prostrate with drink) – by preference to the sacred themes that otherwise predominated on the walls of his Milan house. These accounted for 39% of the pictures on display, which is a percentage in line with that for religious pictures in houses in Antwerp some years before (40.2% between 1643 and 1652)[199] as well as with noble houses in Milan itself in the eighteenth century (35–40%).[200] In his office Stefano had around him, besides these pictures in which he might take recreation, what he needed for his trade – three small tables, notepaper, ledgers, bonds, documents pertaining to the management of the family assets, balances to weigh gold and silver, objects left in pawn (silver cutlery and candlesticks, pearl necklaces, gold rings set with gems, a clock) and money in more than one currency, a sign not only of the international reach of the Milanese economy but also of the inconsistencies in the issue of coinage that would not be redressed until the end of the eighteenth century.[201] Stefano would probably have been glad to escape to the hills to the north of Milan even if it was only to look after his business there, of which there are signs again in the house in Annone – among the furniture with coverings in silk, silver cutlery and more pictures, again representing mostly still lifes and landscapes, we find silk and silk remnants, balances for weighing precious metals and silk, and documents recording loans.[202] He went to the house frequently and regularly, as he declares in his will, and he would have liked to die there, had he not died in Milan.[203]

He passed away, in October 1680, having set his family a further stage down the road of social advancement by ensuring that his daughter had a dowry large enough to marry her into the nobility. Stefano's wishes were fulfilled nine years after his death, on September 12, 1689, when his daughter Rosa celebrated her marriage to the nobleman Dionigi Aliprandi,[204] to whom she brought a dowry of 18,000 *lire* left to her in her father's will, and perhaps other money.[205] Thus the Carenna guaranteed the future nobility of at least one branch of their family, and the Aliprandi refreshed their coffers, following established practice. Giovanni Pietro Annoni had married his daughter to Giovanni Visconti in a similar pattern, and a colleague of the Annoni, Giulio Volpi, had married his daughter to count Lorenzo Salazario. Traders' money could seduce even the upper ranks of the nobility: the powerful Senate president Bartolomeo Arese had taken the hand of the niece of the wealthy financier Emilio Omodeo.[206]

With her marriage Rosa Carenna had fulfilled her role, but, in the early eighteenth century, following the death without issue of her brother Carlo Francesco (through whom her family had taken the final step out of trade into nobility) she it was who became head of the family.

At the top of the ladder

Carlo Francesco Carenna was able to gain entry into the nobility through the misfortune of the Annoni. From the early sixteenth century to the 1680s, when Antonio Annoni formed a company that extended the range of his transport business to Amsterdam,[207] the house of Annoni had been guided by extremely able businessmen. But the last seventeenth-century head of the family, Carlo, and his son Giovanni Pietro, were not in the same mould. Carlo decided in 1696 no longer to take an executive role in the family business. He leased out the transport side of the business to Antonio Perego, on condition that he continued to use the Annoni name for the company – Carlo would take the credit, Perego would have the credentials attached. In fact the Perego continued the business profitably and did so for a long time, until the late eighteenth century, the company being known by this time as 'Annoni and Perego.'[208]

However, by the early eighteenth century Carlo and Giovanni Pietro Annoni had accumulated debts of 180,000 *lire* and were no longer able to honour commitments towards their own family to which they were legally bound, for instance payment to their cousin Francesco, an illegitimate son of their deceased uncle Alessandro, of the stipend that his father had consigned him in his will.[209] It is difficult to know whether or not to believe the reasons given by trusted associates of the Annoni for their exposure to such a colossal debt – large amounts of money invested in the running of the transport business; enormous sums spent on acquiring bonds of public debt. That does not seem a sufficient explanation, nor does it mention that Carlo had drawn on the company funds in order to buy the manor of Cerro, near Lodi, in 1674.[210] It does not even seem that Carlo had been improvident. Reared as a future head of the family, he had been taught how to handle his affairs properly, and evidently managed his family holdings at Vittuone and Merone cannily, for they were found to be in an excellent state by an engineer who visited them in the early eighteenth century.[211] He found that Vittuone had flourishing cereal crops and mulberry trees (the leaves of which were harvested to feed the silkworms) and rows of vines, many recently planted, that produced wine of decent quality, not solely for family consumption. The Vittuone lands were also irrigated artificially, for the cultivation of rice, a crop that was by now widespread around Milan, Novara and Vercelli (as it remains today) and much in demand in foreign markets.[212] At Merone, between Como and Lecco, the crops were maize, oats and pulses, milled in the family mill on the bank of the river Lambro. The count had not failed to put to use some beds of clay in the hills around Lecco, from which he made roof and flat tiles fired in his own kiln.

Despite their debts Carlo and his son managed to avoid ruin. To their aid came Carlo Francesco Carenna, who settled with their creditors. In his turn he needed to be seen to rights, and this was achieved by ceding him the rights to Merone and conditionally also Vittuone and, subject to the king's permission, the title of count of Merone.[213]

The *case da nobile* that consituted an integral part of each estate are of considerable interest.[214] The house at Vittuone had been left in excellent condition by count Annoni and was ready to live in. It was a fine house of more than twenty rooms, not including the cellars and attics, the factor's rooms, the stables and the poultry yards. Floors, ceilings, doors and windows were all in good repair. It had every convenience – a sink built into the kitchen wall, stoves and several fireplaces, glass in the windows. It had been kept very clean: there were several bathrooms and even the stable was paved. It was well provided – with water, having two wells and a cistern for rainwater – and with food: grains and vines grew around the house, destined not only for market but also for the houses's own oven and press, and there were animals in the yard and outbuildings.

The comforts enjoyed by the occupiers were extended to their guests in the reception rooms, over which the Annoni coat of arms held sway – its vivid colour contrast (a red castle on a gold field with a goose between its turrets) neutralized by the elegant white marble relief in which it was set.[215] More discreetly, in the votive shrine in the garden, saints watched over the estate in effigy – the Milanese Saint Carlo Borromeo protector of men, Saint Anthony protector of animals.

Saint Catherine protected the house at Merone, from her oratory beside it. Typical of the lower Alpine region, it consisted simply of nave and chapel. Over the altar stood an unremarkable altarpiece of the Madonna and saints, and more saints were painted on the walls. A balustrade, in accordance with Tridentine regulations, separated the altar from the faithful. The oratory was sparsely furnished. As was also required, there was an altar lamp burning by the tabernacle, indicating, when lit, the presence of the Holy Sacrament; there was a bell by the sacristy door to announce the beginning of the rite and the entrance of the celebrant, and a smaller one in the belfry to invite the faithful to show respect, for example by kneeling during the consecration. The only item of luxury in this ungarnished and indeed neglected place – for the floors and doors and windows were in poor repair, the sacred vestments were worn out and the dead flowers had not even been removed – was the silver chalice in which the wine was to turn into Christ's blood (in the Catholic creed).

The house itself was not in much better state. Once again the doors and windows needed attention and the floors had decayed in places. It was perhaps a hard task for a proprietor hounded by creditors to keep in good order this large house with its twenty-plus rooms and attics, cellars and stables in addition to the large establishment at Vittuone and the palace in Milan. However, if Carenna had wanted to stay there all that would have been necessary would have been repairs, not rebuilding, because all the conveniences of Vittuone were also there, from the kitchen sink to the baking oven, the well and cistern, and the plumbing.

After a certain amount of bargaining, Carlo Francesco took possession only of the estate of Merone and was invested as count in the early 1710s. He enjoyed it for a little more than fifteen years, dying without male issue in the 1720s; all his properties and his title passed to his sister Rosa.[216]

The only known personal document relating to this countess and landowner is her will, which may provide a graceful end to this story of two financier families and their moneymaking activities. In it she has a good word for everybody, even for her daughter-in-law.[217] Conventionally enough, Rosa stipulated that masses should be celebrated for her soul and alms given to the poor: according to the Catholic faith, to obtain redemption and eternal life one had to perform at least some good works as well as seek forgiveness of sins. But she wanted in particular that rations of rice (at a time when rice was the most prized cereal in Lombardy)[218] should be distributed in her memory to the hungry of Annone, Merone and Santo Stefano (Pieve di Corbetta). In the conviction of having given at least a moment of joy to the poor, equating this act of giving with the charity of her Saviour, she died on June 26, 1753.[219] With her the branch of the Carenna family descended from Giovanni Francesco and Giovanna Annoni died out, but not its pride in having climbed to a position of affluence and prestige far exceeding its beginnings in the Brianza hills. Two years before Rosa's death, her son-in-law, the marquess Giovanni Corrado De Olivera, had been honoured with the presidency of the Senate, the supreme ruling body of the State of Milan.[220] Four years after her death her son, count Gaetano Aliprandi, was appointed a Decurion and entered the close circle of the men of rank who governed Milan.[221]

Bibliography and notes to 'The Annoni and the Carenna in seventeenth-century Milan'

Archives and libraries

AGR	Archives générales du Royaume, Brussels
AGS	Archivo General de Simancas
AP	Archivio Plantin, Antwerp
APA	Archivio della Parrocchia di Santa Maria e San Giorgio, Annone di Brianza
APSE	Archivio della Parrocchia di Santa Eufemia, Milan
APSN	Archivio della parrocchia di San Nazaro, Milan
ARCV	Archivo de la Real Cancillería, Valladolid
ASCCM	Archivio storico della Camera di Commercio di Milano
ASCM	Archivio storico civico di Milano
ASDM	Archivio storico diocesano di Milano
ASM	Archivio di Stato di Milano
BNB	Biblioteca nazionale Braidense di Milano
FRM	Fondazione Raffaele Mattioli per la storia del pensiero economico, Milan
ÖNBW	Österreichische Nationalbibliothek, Vienna
SAA	Stadsarchief, Antwerp

Notaries

AGB	Giovanni Battista Aliprandi q. Luigi
BGC	Giulio Cesare Besozzi q. Giovanni Tommaso
BM	Massimiliano Bossi q. Ottavio
BO	Ottaviano Belingeri q. Tommaso
CA	Alessandro Canale q. Eleuterio
CB	Bartolomeo Carpani q. Francesco
CGA	Giovanni Ambrogio Caccia q. Alessandro
DF	Ferrando Dossena q. Francesco
FGA	Giacomo Antonio Fumagalli q. Giovanni Battista
FS	Stefano Fumagalli q. Giacomo Antonio
GBG	Giovanni Battista Ghezzi q. Giovanni Pietro
MGA	Giacomo Antonio Macherio q. Giovanni Andrea
MGB	Giovanni Battista Masnaghi q. Giovanni Antonio
OPA	Pietro Antonio Origo q. Francesco
PF	Francesco Pusterla q. Zanoto
RGF	Giovanni Francesco Rovelli q. Giovanni Antonio
RT	Tommaso Rondoni q. Cesare
SA	Ambrosio Sebilla
SGF	Giovanni Francesco Stellerio q. Agostino
TC	Cesare Tettamanzi q. Achille
VDCO	Orazio Vimercati De' Capitani q. Rinaldo

Abbreviations used in citations

cart.	*cartella* (folder)
ch., chs.	chapter, chapters
cod.	*codice* (bound volume)
f., ff.	folio, folios
fasc.	*fascicolo* (loose sheet)
p., pp.	pages, pages
q.	*quondam* (deceased)
r	recto
scat., scatt.	*scatola-e* (shelf, shelves)
s.v.	*sub voce*
v	verso
vol., vols.	volume, volumes

ANGIOLINI, ROCHE (eds.) 1995
Cultures et formations négociantes dans l'Europe moderne, sous la direction de F. Angiolini et D. Roche (Paris, 1995)

ANNONI 1970
A. Annoni, 'I rapporti tra lo Stato di Milano e i popoli della Confederazione Elvetica nei secoli XV e XVI', *Archivio storico lombardo, serie* IX, *anno* XI (1970), pp. 1–28

ARESE 1957
F. Arese, 'Elenchi dei Magistrati Patrizi di Milano dal 1535 al 1796', *Archivio storico lombardo, serie* VIII, *anno* LXXXIV (1957), pp. 149–99

ARESE 1980
F. Arese, 'Le supreme cariche del Ducato di Milano e della Lombardia austriaca 1706–1796', *Archivio storico lombardo, serie* X, *anno* CV–CVI (1979–80), pp. 535–98

AUREGGI 1962
O. Aureggi, 'I Lumaga di Piuro e di Chiavenna. Ricerche su patriziato e nobiltà nell'alta Lombardia', *Archivio storico lombardo, serie* IX, vol. II, *anno* LXXXIX (1962), pp. 222–89

BATTAGLIA 1961–2004
S. Battaglia, *Grande dizionario della lingua italiana*, 23 vols. (Turin, 1961–2004)

BATTISTINI 2003
F. Battistini, *L'industria della seta in Italia nell'età moderna* (Bologna, 2003)

BEDELL 2000
J. Bedell, 'Archaeology and probate inventories in the study of eighteenth-century life', *Journal of Interdisciplinary History*, XXXI, no. 2 (2000), pp. 223–45

BEDINI 2005
S.A. Bedini, 'L'orologio notturno. Un'invenzione italiana del XVII secolo', in *La misura del tempo. L'antico splendore dell'orologeria italiana dal XV al XVIII secolo*, ed. G. Brusa (Trent, 2005), pp. 201–19

BEDONI 1983
S. Bedoni, *Jan Brueghel in Italia e il collezionismo del Seicento* (Florence and Milan, 1983)

BEONIO-BROCCHIERI 1987
V.H. Beonio-Brocchieri, 'La manifattura rurale nella "pars alpestris" dello Stato di Milano tra XVI e XVII secolo', *Archivio storico lombardo, serie* XI, vol. IV, *anno* CXII (1987), pp. 9–28

BEONIO-BROCCHIERI 1997[1]
V.H. Beonio-Brocchieri, 'Artigiani, manifatture e protoindustrie fra città e campagna: la Lombardia del XVI secolo', *Studi di storia medioevale e di diplomatica*, no. 14, (1993), pp. 193–209

BEONIO-BROCCHIERI 1997[2]
V.H. Beonio-Brocchieri, 'Percorsi di ruralizzazione: la città e il contado fra mercato internazionale e mercato regionale', in Brambilla, Muto (eds.) 1997, pp. 123–37

BEONIO-BROCCHIERI 2000
V.H. Beonio-Brocchieri, *"Piazza universale di tutte le professioni". Famiglie e mestieri nel Ducato di Milano in età spagnola* (Milan, 2000)

BETTONI 2005
B. Bettoni, *I beni dell'agiatezza. Stili di vita nelle famiglie bresciane dell'età moderna* (Milan, 2005)

BIGATTI 1995
G. Bigatti, *La provincia delle acque. Ambiente, istituzioni e tecnici in Lombardia tra Sette e Ottocento* (Milan, 1995)

BILANCIO 1778
'Bilancio del commercio politico dello Stato di Milano per l'anno MDCCLXXVIII. vol. IV', ÖNBW, cod. SN 12326

BINAGHI OLIVARI, SÜSS, BAGATTI VALSECCHI 1989
M.T. Binaghi Olivari, F. Süss, P.F. Bagatti Valsecchi, *Le ville del territorio milanese. Aspetti decorativi, parchi e giardini, riuso* (Cinisello Balsamo, 1989)

BIZZOCCHI 2001
R. Bizzocchi, *In famiglia. Storie di interessi e affetti nell'Italia moderna* (Rome and Bari, 2001)

BOGNETTI, MOIOLI, PORTA, TONELLI (eds.) 2006–07
Edizione nazionale delle opere di Pietro Verri (prima serie, II): Scritti di economia, finanza e amministrazione, ed. G. Bognetti, A. Moioli, P.L. Porta, G. Tonelli, 2 vols. (Rome, 2006–07)

BORSIERI 1619
Il Supplimento della Nobiltà di Milano, compiled by Girolamo Borsieri (Milan, 1619), in *La Nobiltà di Milano descritta da R. P. F. Paolo Morigi . . . Aggiuntovi il supplimento in questa nova impressione del Sig. Girolamo Borsieri . . .* (Milan, 1619)

BRAMBILLA, MUTO (eds.) 1997
La Lombardia spagnola. Nuovi indirizzi di ricerca, ed. E. Brambilla and G. Muto (Milan, 1997)

BROGGI, MORANDI, POLETTI 1997
S. Broggi, G. Morandi and G. Poletti, *Sedie, poltrone, divani dal Rinascimento al Déco* (Novara, 1997)

BULLIO 1969
P. Bullio, 'Problemi e geografia della risicoltura in Piemonte nei secoli XVII e XVIII', *Annali della Fondazione Einaudi*, no. 3 (1969), pp. 37–93

CAIZZI 1999
B. Caizzi, *Dalla posta dei re alla posta di tutti. Territorio e comunicazioni in Italia dal XVI secolo all'Unità* (Milan, 1999)

CAPODICI 1994
S. Capodici, *Annone di Brianza. Ambiente, storia, arte* (Annone di Brianza, 1994)

CAVALLERA 2007
M. Cavallera, *Società e cultura del caffè e del cioccolato nella Milano del Settecento*, in Chiapparino, Romano (eds.) 2007, pp. 239–66

CHIAPPARINO, ROMANO (eds.) 2007
Il cioccolato. Industria, mercato e società in Italia e Svizzera (XVIII–XX sec.), ed. F. Chiapparino and R. Romano (Milan, 2007)

CIPOLLA 2002
C.M. Cipolla, *Storia economica dell'Europa pre-industriale* (Bologna, 2002)

COLOMBO 2004–05
G. Colombo, *La chiesa di S. Giorgio ad Annone Brianza*, tesi di laurea, Università degli Studi di Milano, Facoltà di Lettere e Filosofia, Corso di Laurea in Lettere (2004–05), *relatore* prof. G. Agosti

COPPOLA 1979
G. Coppola, *Il mais nell'economia agricola lombarda (dal secolo XVII all'Unità)* (Bologna, 1979)

COSMACINI 1999
G. Cosmacini, *La Ca' Granda dei Milanesi. Storia dell'Ospedale Maggiore* (Rome and Bari, 1999)

COVA 1995
A. Cova, *Banchi e monti pubblici a Milano tra interessi privati e pubbliche necessità*, in Pissavino, Signorotto (eds.) 1995, pp. 363–81

D'AMATO 2001
G. D'Amato, *L'arte di arredare. Storia di un millennio attraverso gusti, ambienti, atmosfere* (Milan, 2001)

D'AMICO 1997
S. D'Amico, *Immigrazione e ripresa economica a Milano dopo la peste del 1630*, in Brambilla, Muto (eds.) 1997, pp. 77–90

D'AMICO 2001
'Rebirth of a City: Immigration and Trade in Milan, 1630–59', *Sixteenth Century Journal*, vol. 32, no. 3 (Autumn, 2001), pp. 697–721

DE BERNARDI 1984
A. De Bernardi, *Il mal della rosa. Denutrizione e pellagra nelle campagne italiane tra '800 e '900* (Milan, 1984)

DE LUCA 1996
G. De Luca, *Commercio del denaro e crescita economica a Milano tra Cinque e Seicento* (Milan, 1996)

DE LUCA 2004
G. De Luca, 'Debito pubblico, sistema fiscale ed economia reale nella Lombardia spagnola: l'alienazione delle entrate. Prime direzioni di ricerca', in *Le forze del Principe. Recursos, intrumentos y limites en la práctica del poder soberano en los territorios de la Monarquía Hispánica. Actas del Seminario Internacional, Pavia 22–24 septiembre del 2000*, ed. M. Rizzo, J.J. Ruiz Ibáñez, G. Sabatini, 2 vols. (Murcia, 2004), I, pp. 179–210

DE MADDALENA 1964
A. De Maddalena, 'Il mondo rurale italiano nel Cinque e nel Seicento (Rassegna di studi recenti)', *Rivista storica italiana* (1964), pp. 349–426

DE MADDALENA 1974
A. De Maddalena, *Prezzi e mercedi a Milano dal 1701 al 1860* (Milan, 1974)

DE MADDALENA (ed.) 1989
"Millain the great". Milano nelle brume del Seicento, ed. A. De Maddalena (Milan, 1989)

DE MADDALENA 2000
A. De Maddalena, 'Nello Stato di Milano in tarda età spagnola (1636–1678). Cessioni e acquisizioni di beni feudali', *Storia economica, anno* III (2000), pp. 5–41

DESSUREAULT, DICKINSON, WIEN 1994
C. Dessureault, J.A. Dickinson and T. Wien, 'Living standards of Norman and Canadian peasants 1690–1835', in *Material Culture: Consumption, Life-style, Standard of Living 1500–1900 (B4 Proceedings Eleventh International Economic History Congress, Milan, 1994)*, ed. A.J. Schuuraman and L.S. Walsh (Milan, 1994), pp. 95–112

DE VRIES 1976
J. De Vries, *The Economy of Europe in an Age of Crisis, 1600–1750* (Cambridge, 1976)

DORIA 1986
G. Doria, 'Conoscenza del mercato e sistema informativo. Il know-how dei mercanti-finanzieri genovesi nei secc. XVI e XVII', in *La repubblica internazionale del denaro tra XV e XVII secolo*, ed. A. De Maddalena and H. Kellenbenz (Bologna, 1986), pp. 57–121

FAGIANI 1988
F. Fagiani, 'La pianura risicola piemontese nel primo sessantennio del secolo XIX. A – Il Vercellese (Parte prima)', *Rivista di storia dell'agricoltura*, vol. 28, no. 1 (1988), pp. 117–158, and 'La pianura risicola piemontese nel primo sessantennio del secolo XIX. B – Il Vercellese (Parte seconda) – Il Novarese – La Lomellina', *ibid.*, no. 2, pp. 23–67

FARINELLI, PACCAGNINI (eds.) 1988
Processo agli untori. Milano 1630: cronaca e atti giudiziari in edizione integrale, ed. G. Farinelli and E. Paccagnini (Milan, 1988)

FLANDRIN 1997
J.-L. Flandrin, *L'alimentazione contadina in un'economia di sostentamento*, in Flandrin, Montanari (eds.) 1997, pp. 465–89

FLANDRIN, MONTANARI (eds.) 1997
Storia dell'alimentazione, ed. J.-L. Flandrin and M. Montanari (Rome and Bari, 1997)

FRANGIONI 1983
L. Frangioni, *Milano e le sue strade. Costi di trasporto e vie di commercio dei prodotti milanesi alla fine del Trecento* (Bologna, 1983)

FUSCO 2004
R. Fusco, *Storia dell'arredamento. Dal '400 al '900* (Milan, 2004)

GEDDO 1998[1]
C. Geddo, *Collezionisti e pittori di genere nel Settecento a Milano e nel Lombado-Veneto*, in Porzio (ed.) 1998, pp. 104–13

GEDDO 1998[2]
C. Geddo, *Percentuali di dipinti di genere e di altri soggetti in collezioni lombardo-venete del Settecento*, in Porzio (ed.) 1998, pp. 114–18

GEDDO 2001
C. Geddo, 'Collezionisti e mecenati a Milano tra Sei e Settecento. I Durini conti di Monza', *Artes*, 9 (2001), pp. 41–124

GLAUSER 1979
F. Glauser, 'Der Gotthardtransit von 1500 bis 1660. Seine Stellung im Alpentransit', in *Histoire des Alpes. Perspectives nouvelles. Geschichte der Alpen in Neuersicht*, ed. J.F. Bergier (Basle and Stuttgart, 1979), pp. 16–51

GRAB 1986
A.I. Grab, *La politica del pane. Le riforme annonarie in Lombardia nell'età teresiana e giuseppina* (Milan, 1986)

GRENDI 1997
E. Grendi, *I Balbi. Una famiglia genovese fra Spagna e Impero* (Turin, 1997)

GRIDARIO ALBORNOZ
Libro delle gride, bandi et ordini fatti e pubblicati nella città e Stato di Milano nel governo dell'Eminentissimo Signor Cardinale don Filippo de Albornoz, in *Gridario Generale*, vol. I

GRIDARIO ALCALÀ
Gride dell'Eccellentissimo Signor Duca d'Alcalà Don Fernando Afon de Rivera Enriquez, Doque de Alcalà . . ., in *Gridario Generale*, vol. I

GRIDARIO GENERALE
Gridario generale delle gride, bandi, ordini, editti, provisioni, prematiche et altro fatti e pubblicati per ordine delli Eccellentissimi Signori Governatori che hanno governato lo Stato di Milano, 2 vols. (Milan, 1686)

GRIDARIO GUZMÁN
Libro delle gride, bandi, et ordini fatti e pubblicati nella città e Stato di Milano nel governo dell'Eccellentissimo Signor don Diego Filippez de Guzmán, Marchese di Leganes . . ., in *Gridario Generale*, vol. I

GRIDARIO SERMONETA
Gridario dell'Eccellentissimo Signor don Francesco Caetano, Duca di Sermoneta e di San Marco . . ., in *Gridario Generale*, vol. II

GRIDARIO SIRVELA
Gridario dell'Eccellentissimo Signor don Giovanni Velasco la Cueva, Conte de Sirvela, in *Gridario Generale*, vol. I

HOUSTON 1991
R. Houston, 'Alfabetismo e società in Occidente, 1500–1850', in *Istruzione, alfabetismo, scrittura. Saggi di storia dell'alfabetizzazione in Italia (sec. XV–XIX)*, ed. A. Bartoli Langeli and X. Toscani (Milan, 1991)

HUETZ DE LEMPS 1997
A. Huetz de Lemps, 'Bevande coloniali e diffusione dello zucchero', in Flandrin, Montanari (eds.) 1997, pp. 490–500

INVENTARIO 1620
'Inventario della casa di Milano di Francesco Ponga', attached to *Tutela et additio ereditatis* of November 20, 1620 (ASM, *Notarile*, *filza* 23090, GGB)

INVENTARIO 1624
'Inventario dei beni di Giovanni Pietro Carcano', deed of October 26, 1624 (ASM, *Notarile*, *filza* 22065, DF)

INVENTARIO ANNONE 1680
'Inventario della casa di Annone di Stefano Carenna', attached to the deed of *tutela* of November 16, 1680 (ASM, *Notarile*, *filza* 33291, FGA): see Documents B, no. 4

INVENTARIO MILANO 1627
'Inventario della casa di Milano di Giovanni Pietro Annoni', attached to the deed of *tutela* del December 27, 1627 (ASM, *Notarile*, *filza* 26485, BO): see Documents B, no. 1

INVENTARIO MILANO 1680
'Inventario della casa di Milano di Stefano Carenna', attached to the deed of *tutela* of November 16, 1680 (ASM, *Notarile*, *filza* 33291, FGA): see Documents B, no. 3

INVENTARIO VITTUONE 1627
'Inventario della casa di Vittuone di Giovanni Pietro Annoni', attached to the deed of *tutela* of December 27, 1627 (ASM, *Notarile*, *filza* 26485, BO): see Documents B, no. 2

JONES 1997
P. Jones, *Federico Borromeo e l'Ambrosiana. Arte e Riforma cattolica nel XVII secolo a Milano* (Milan, 1997)

KELLENBENZ 1987
H. Kellenbenz, 'Commercio tra la Lombardia e l'Europa centrale e orientale dal XV secolo alla metà del XVII secolo', in *Il commercio in Lombardia*, ed. G. Taborelli, 2 vols. (Milan and Cinisello Balsamo, 1986–87), II, pp. 95–100

LANGÉ 1972
S. Langé, *Ville della Provincia di Milano* (Milan, 1972)

LATUADA 1737–38
Descrizione di Milano ornata con molti disegni in rame delle fabbriche più cospicue che si trovano in questa metropoli, raccolta ed ordinata da Serviliano Latuada sacerdote milanese, 5 vols. (Milan, 1737–38)

LEVI PISETZKY 1957
R. Levi Pisetzky, 'La moda spagnola a Milano', in *Storia di Milano*, 18 vols. (Milan, 1953–96), X: *L'età della Riforma Cattolica (1559–1630)* (1957), pp. 879–927

LEYDI 2003
S. Leydi, 'Gli armaioli milanesi del secondo Cinquecento. Famiglie, botteghe, clienti attraverso i documenti', in *Armature da parata del Cinquecento. Un primato dell'arte lombarda*, ed. J.-A. Godoy and S. Leydi (Milan, 2003), pp. 29–59

LIBRETTO 1574–1619
'1574 al 1619. Libretto nel quale restano registrati dal foglio 3 sino al foglio 5 li SS.ri Mercanti descritti e dal foglio 6 sino al foglio 31 le nomine de' SS.ri Abbati della Camera di detti SS.ri Mercanti, come pure dal foglio 33 sino al foglio 40 li SS.ri Mercanti Utenti delle Strade, come diffusamente appare dal medesimo Libretto coperto di cartone bianco' (ASCCM, *Appendice*, *scatt*. 24, *fasc*. 6)

LITTA 1819–55
P. Litta, *Famiglie celebri Italiane* (Milan, 1819–55)

LUCCHINI 2004
E. Lucchini, *Giocattoli e bambini dall'antichità al 2000* (Lanciano, 2004)

LUDOVICO IL MORO 1983
Ludovico il Moro, la sua città, la sua corte (1480–1499) (Milan, 1983)

MACCARONELLO 2006–07
D. Maccarronello, *Il credito bancario nella corona spagnola durante il XVII e XVIII secolo. Gli Airoldi di Robbiate tra Lombardia e Sicilia*, tesi di Dottorato di ricerca, Università degli Studi di Catania, Dottorato di ricerca in Storia (Storia della Cultura, dell'Uomo e del Territorio in Età Moderna), 2006–07, *relatore* Prof. R. Tufano

MAFFI 2000
D. Maffi, 'Guerra ed economia: spese belliche e appaltatori militari nella Lombardia spagnola (1635–1660)', *Storia economica*, *anno* III, no. 3 (2000), pp. 489–527

MAFFI 2007
D. Maffi, *Il baluardo della corona. Guerra, esercito, finanze e società nella Lombardia seicentesca (1630–1660)* (Florence, 2007)

MAIFREDA 2000
G. Maifreda, *Gli ebrei e l'economia milanese. L'Ottocento* (Milan, 2000)

MARIACHER 1981
G. Mariacher, *Lampade e lampadari in Italia dal Quattrocento all'Ottocento* (Milan, 1981)

MARSILIO 2008[1]
C. Marsilio, 'Debito pubblico e operatori finanziari genovesi (1644–1656)', *Mediterranea. Ricerche storiche*, no. 12 (April 2008), pp. 149–72 (http://www.storiamediterranea.it/public/ md1_dir/ r999.pdf)

MARSILIO 2008[2]
C. Marsilio, 'Le fiere di cambio nel XVI e XVII secolo. Piacenza centro nevralgico del mercato del credito europeo', in *Storia economica e sociale di Piacenza e del suo territorio*, I: *L'età farnesiana 1545–1732* (Piacenza, 2008), pp. 255–308

MASPOLI, PALAZZI TRIVELLI (eds.) 2002
Stemmario Bosisio, ed. C. Maspoli and F. Palazzi Trivelli (Milan, 2002)

MAZZEI 1999
R. Mazzei, *Itinera mercatorum. Circolazione di uomini e beni nell'Europa centro-orientale 1550–1650* (Lucca, 1999)

MENNINGER 2007
A. Menninger, 'New beverages in early modern Europe: the rise of coffee, tea and chocolate (16th–18th century)', in Chiapparino, Romano (eds.) 2007, pp. 209–38

MOIOLI 1981
A. Moioli, *La gelsibachicoltura nelle campagne lombarde dal Seicento alla prima metà dell'Ottocento. Parte prima: La diffusione del gelso e la crescita produttiva della sericoltura* (Trent, 1981)

MOIOLI 1986
A. Moioli, 'La deindustrializzazione della Lombardia nel secolo XVII', *Archivio storico lombardo*, *serie* XI, vol. III, *anno* CXII (1986), pp. 167–203

MOIOLI 1988
A. Moioli, 'Assetti manifatturieri nella Lombardia politicamente divisa della seconda metà del Settecento', in *Storia dell'industria lombarda*, ed. S. Zaninelli, 3 vols. (Milan, 1988–92), I: *Dal Settecento all'unità politica* (1988), pp. 3–102

MOIOLI 1999
A. Moioli, 'Il mutato ruolo delle corporazioni nella riorganizzazione dell'economia milanese del XVII secolo', in *Corporazioni e gruppi professionali nell'Italia moderna*, ed. A. Guenzi, P. Massa and A. Moioli (Milan, 1999), pp. 44–78

MOLS 1979
R. Mols, 'La popolazione europea nei secoli XVI e XVII', in *Storia economica d'Europa*, ed. C.M. Cipolla, 5 vols. (Turin, 1979–80), II: *I secoli XVI e XVII* (1979), pp. 1–51

MONTANARI 2006
M. Montanari, *La fame e l'abbondanza. Storia dell'alimentazione in Europa* (Rome and Bari, 2006)

MULLER 1993
J.M. Muller, 'Private Collections in the Spanish Netherlands: Ownership and Display of Paintings in Domestic Interiors', in *The Age of Rubens*, ed. P.C. Sutton, (exhibition catalogue, Boston and Ghent, 1993), pp. 195–206

MUSITELLI, BOSSI, ALLEGRI 1999
S. Musitelli, M. Bossi and R. Allegri, *Storie dei costumi sessuali in Occidente* (Santarcangelo di Romagna, 1999)

MUTO 1995
G. Muto, *Il governo della Hacienda nella Lombardia spagnola*, in Pissavino, Signorotto (eds.) 1995, pp. 265–302

PAVARIN 2002–03
A. Pavarin, 'Hombres de Negocios, reti di relazione e "reciprocità" nella Milano di metà '600', tesi di laurea, Università degli Studi di Milano, Facoltà di Scienze Politiche, 2002–03, *relatore* prof. A. Moioli

PAVARIN 2006
A. Pavarin, 'L'evoluzione delle tecniche finanziarie a Milano a metà '600: la diffusione delle factorias', *relazione presentata al seminario del Centro interuniversitario di ricerca per la storia finanziaria italiana dedicato a 'Le forme del credito nell'Italia d'antico regime'*, Venice, Università Ca' Foscari, Dipartimento di Scienze economiche, April 7–8, 2006

PERI 1638
Il Negotiante di Gio. Domenico Peri genovese (Genoa, 1638)

PICCINELLI 2003
R. Piccinelli, *Le collezioni Gonzaga. Il carteggio tra Milano e Mantova (1563–1634)* (Cinisello Balsamo and Milan, 2003)

PISSAVINO, SIGNOROTTO (eds.) 1995
Lombardia borromaica – Lombardia spagnola. 1554–1659, ed. P. Pissavino and G. Signorotto, 2 vols. (Rome, 1995)

PONI 1976
R. Poni, 'All'origine del sistema di fabbrica: tecnologia e organizzazione produttiva dei mulini da seta nell'Italia settentrionale (sec. XVII-XVIII)', *Rivista storica italiana*, *anno* LXXXVIII, *fasc.* III (1976), pp. 444–97

PORZIO (ed.) 1998
Da Caravaggio a Ceruti. La scena di genere e l'immagine dei pitocchi nella pittura italiana, ed. F. Porzio (Milan, 1998)

RELAZIONE 1706
'Ecc.mo Senato. Relatione dell'Ingeg.re Colleg.to di Milano Carlo Franc.co Chiesa per la subrogatione de' beni de SS.ri Carlo et Gio. Pietro Padre, et filio Annoni sottoposti al fideicomisso transversale fatto dal fu S.r Alessandro Annone situati nel luogo e territorio di Merone, Pieve d'Incino, Ducato di Milano da detti SS.ri Conti alienati al S.r Carlo Fran.co Carena in luogo e scontro de' quali si è fatta la surogatione de' beni sit. nel luogo e territorio di Vituuone, Pieve di Corbetta di questo Ducato di Milano', April 27, 1706 (ASM, *Senato fedecommessi*, *cart.* 22, *fasc.* "1706. Annoni")

RENONCIAT 1993
A. Renonciat, 'La camera dei bambini', in *Luoghi quotidiani nella storia d'Europa*, ed. H.-G. Haupt (Bari, 1993), pp. 268–84

RIBOT GARCÍA 1989
L. Ribot García, 'Milano, piazza d'armi della monarchia spagnola', in De Maddalena (ed.) 1989, pp. 349–63

RIZZO 2001
M. Rizzo, *Alloggiamenti militari e riforme fiscali nella Lombardia spagnola fra Cinque e Seicento* (Milan, 2001)

ROSCI 1985
M. Rosci, *Ambienti del Seicento* (Novara, 1985)

SARTI 2006
R. Sarti, *Vita di casa. Abitare, mangiare, vestire nell'Europa moderna* (Bari, 2006)

SAVOJA 1995
M. Savoja, 'Aspetti del commercio nello Stato di Milano in epoca spagnola', in Archivio di Stato di Milano, *Aspetti della società lombarda in età spagnola*, 2 vols. (Como, 1985), II, pp. 51–93

SEGRE 1973
R. Segre, *Gli ebrei lombardi nell'età spagnola. Storia di un'espulsione* (Turin, 1973)

SELLA 1982
D. Sella, *L'economia lombarda durante la dominazione spagnola* (Bologna, 1982)

SIGNOROTTO 1996
G. Signorotto, *Milano spagnola. Guerra, istituzioni, uomini di governo (1635–1660)* (Milan, 1996)

SITONI DI SCOTIA 1705
'Theatrum genealogicum Familiarum Illustrium, Nobilium et Civium Inclijtae Urbis Mediolani . . . Johannes de Sitonis de Scotia J.C. Mediolanensis Anno Virginei Partum MDCCV' (ASM)

SOLDI RONDININI 1978
G. Soldi Rondinini, 'Le vie transalpine del commercio milanese dal sec. XIII al XV', in *Felix olim Lombardia. Studi di storia padana dedicati dagli allievi a Giuseppe Martini* (Milan, 1978), pp. 343–84

STATUS ANIMARUM 1610
'1610. Status Animarum Eclesiae Parochialis S.ti Nazarij in Brolio Mediolani' (ASDM, *Archivio Spirituale, sezione X, visita pastorale e documenti aggiunti, Luogo S. Stefano, anno 1610–31*, vol. 15)

SUBACCHI 1993
P. Subacchi, 'Patterns of Immigration: the Italian Community in Sixteenth-Century Antwerp', in *1st European Conference of International Commission of Historical Demography*, *Santiago de Compostela 22–25 septembro 1993* (Santiago de Compostela, 1993), pp. 505–15

SUBACCHI 1995
P. Subacchi, 'Italians in Antwerp in the Second Half of the Sixteenth Century', in *Minderheden in Westeuropese Steden (16de–20ste eeuw). Minorities in Western European Cities (sixteenth–twentieth century)*, ed. H. Soly and A.K.L. Thijs (Brussels and Rome, 1995), pp. 73–90

SUBACCHI 1999
P. Subacchi, 'Tra carestie ed epidemie: la demografia dell'area lombarda nel "lungo" seicento', in *La popolazione italiana nel Seicento*, ed. Società italiana di demografia storica (Bologna, 1999), pp. 243–59

SÜSS 1988
F. Süss, *Le ville del territorio milanese. Aspetti storici e architettonici* (Cinisello Balsamo, 1988)

TONELLI 1999
G. Tonelli, "Vendere, scuodere, comprare, sì per conto del negotio come per qualunque commissione di terza persona". I grandi operatori del commercio estero milanese nella Lombardia spagnola del XVII secolo (1600–1650)', tesi di Dottorato di ricerca, Università Commerciale 'L. Bocconi' di Milano, Dottorato di ricerca in Storia economica e sociale, 1999, *relatore* prof. A. Guenzi

TONELLI 2000
G. Tonelli, 'Il "Notarile" come fonte per la storia del commercio e della finanza a Milano (1615–1650)', in *Mélanges de l'École Française de Rome. Italie et Méditerranée*, vol. 112, no. 1 (2000), pp. 79–104

TONELLI 2002
G. Tonelli, 'Percorsi di integrazione commerciale e finanziaria fra Milano e i Paesi d'Oltralpe nel primo Seicento', in *Tra identità e integrazione. La Lombardia nella macroregione alpina dello sviluppo economico europeo (secoli XVII–XX). Atti del Convegno di Studio. Milano, 10–11 dicembre 1999*, ed. L. Mocarelli (Milan, 2002), pp. 151–94

TONELLI 2007[1]
G. Tonelli, 'Commercio di transito e dazi di confine nello Stato di Milano fra Sei e Settecento', in Torre (ed.) 2007, pp. 85–108

TONELLI 2007[2]
G. Tonelli, 'Ricchezza e consumo: il lusso di una famiglia nobile milanese nei primi anni dell'Ottocento', *Mediterranea. Ricerche storiche*, no. 11 (December 2007), pp. 491–516 (http://www.storiamediterranea.it/public/md1_dir/ r845.pdf)

TONELLI 2008[1]
G. Tonelli, *Materiali per lo studio di famiglie mercantili milanesi in età moderna* (Brescia, 2008) (http://www.giovannatonelli.it/en/doc.html)

TONELLI 2008[2]
G. Tonelli, *Materiali per lo studio delle relazioni commerciali e finanziarie fra Milano e i Paesi d'Oltralpe nella prima metà del XVII secolo* (Brescia, 2008) (http://www.giovannatonelli.it/en/doc.html)

TORRE (ed.) 2007
Per vie di terra. Movimenti di uomini e di cose nelle società di antico regime, ed. A. Torre (Milan, 2007)

TREZZI 1986
L. Trezzi, 'Un caso di deindustrializzazione della città: i molini da seta a Milano e nel Ducato (secoli XVII e XVIII)', *Archivio storico lombardo*, *serie* XI, vol. III, *anno* CXII (1986), pp. 205–14

VENTURELLI 1996
P. Venturelli, *Gioielli e gioiellieri milanesi. Storia, arte, moda (1450–1630)* (Cinisello Balsamo, 1996)

VENTURELLI 1999
P. Venturelli, *Vestire e apparire. Il sistema vestimentario femminile nella Milano spagnola (1539–1679)* (Rome, 1999)

VIGO 1976
G. Vigo, 'Manovre monetarie e crisi economica nello Stato di Milano (1619–1622)', *Studi storici*, *anno* 17, n. 4 (1976), pp. 100–26

VIGO 1994
G. Vigo, *Uno Stato nell'Impero. La difficile transizione al moderno nella Milano di età spagnola* (Milan, 1994)

WARREN 2008
J. Warren, 'The Annoni-Visconti Marriage Bowl', in *Art and Love in Renaisssance Italy* (exhibition catalogue, ed. A. Bayer, Metropolitan Museum of Art, New York, 2008), pp. 122–23, no. 50

ZUNCKEL 1997
J. Zunckel, *Rüstungsgeschäfte im Dreißigjährigen Krieg. Unternehmerkräfte, Militärgüter und Marktstrategien im Handel zwischen Genua, Amsterdam und Hamburg* (Berlin, 1997)

1 Subacchi 1999, p. 245, Mols 1979, p. 21.
2 Ludovico il Moro 1983.
3 'Della Città di Milano et sua edificatione', in *Discorso fatto sopra il sale* . . ., s. d. [1608], ff. 156ff. (FRM, *Archivio Verri*, *cart.* 435, *fasc.* 1; another copy in BNB, *Codici Morbio*, cod. 135).
4 *Ibid.*; see also the sources cited by contributors to De Maddalena (ed.) 1989.
5 On the Ospedale Maggiore di Milano as a charitable institution see Cosmacini 1999, pp. 77–133.
6 On the cultural initiatives of Cardinal Borromeo see Jones 1997, pp. 35–50; on the despatch of paintings from Flanders to Milan by the Annoni, Bedoni 1983, pp. 106–07.
7 De Maddalena 1964.
8 *Ibid.*, pp. 366–71, 378–83, 385–88; Annoni 1970, pp. 26–27; Sella 1982, pp. 21–22. One should bear in mind that until the end of the eighteenth century cereals could be exported from the State of Milan only with the permission of the authorities. On the grain supply of Milan in modern times see Grab 1986; Bognetti, Moioli, Porta, Tonelli (eds.) 2006–07, II, pp. 93–234, 247–371.
9 The State of Milan is also known as 'Spanish Lombardy' for the period from 1535 to the early eighteenth century. An imperial fief since 1395, it was autonomous until the extinction of the Sforza dynasty in 1535, when it passed to the Habsburgs of Spain and then, on the death of Charles II in the eighteenth century to the Habsburgs of Austria.
10 Sella 1982, pp. 16–18; Subacchi 1999, pp. 244–48.
11 D'Amico 1997, p. 78; Tonelli 1999, pp. 78, 196–216.
12 Sella 1982, pp. 38–42; Beonio Brocchieri 1987, 1997[1], 1997[2], 2000.
13 Moioli 1981, pp. 13–93, Battistini 2003, pp. 26–28. See the data given in the *Bilanci di commercio dello Stato di Milano* of 1752 (Bognetti, Moioli, Porta, Tonelli (ed.) 2006–07, I, p. 511); 1762 (pp. 592–93; 595); 1769 (pp. 633, 635–36); Bilancio 1778, *s.v.* One should bear in mind that the data given in the *Bilanci di commercio dello Stato di Milano* for the import and export of cereals are only partial.
14 Vigo 1994, pp. 63–78; Leydi 2003.
15 Soldi Rondinini 1978; Frangioni 1983; Caizzi 1999, pp. 71–161; Bigatti 1995; Torre (ed.) 2007.
16 An overview of Lombard exports is given in Tonelli 1999, pp. 18–19.
17 Moioli 1986; Moioli 1999, pp. 51–52.
18 De Vries 1976; with specific reference to the State of Milan, Vigo 1976.
19 The certificate of the Annoni's admission to the *utentes stratis* is held in ASCCM, *Appendice*, *scat.* 25, *fasc.* 4.
20 It was the duty of the *Universitas mercatorum* to fix one day in the week on which the financiers would meet to settle their bills; to select and monitor the *sensali*, the intermediaries in their contracts; to check weights and measures; to bring up to date the regulations of trade and, in their own court, administer justice in matters of commerce and finance and to hear appeals before reference to a higher court. Convicted persons who might expect expulsion or execution would appear before the Senate, the highest Milanese court (Tonelli 1999, pp. 84–97).
21 Certificates of admission to the *utentes stratis* are held in ASCCM, *Appendice*, *scatt.* 25-26.
22 The Libretto 1574–1619 (ff. 29–31) reveals that he had held the post of prior of the Camera dei Mercanti di Milano in 1615 (September and October), 1616 (June and July), 1617 (September to December), 1618 (December), 1619 (January).
23 Glauser 1979, pp. 23–30; Subbachi 1993, 1995. On the presence of Milanese merchants and financiers in Brabant and the Rhineland in the first half of the seventeenth century, see 'Mercanti, ditte e società milanesi o a partecipazione milanese presenti ad Anversa e a Bruxelles (prima metà del XVII secolo)' and 'Mercanti, ditte, società e case commerciali milanesi o a partecipazione milanese presenti nell'Europa centrale e orientale (prima metà del XVII secolo)', in Tonelli 2008[2]; these are supplements to the lists published and glossed in Tonelli 2002.
24 Kellenbenz 1987, pp. 98–100; Glauser 1979, p. 26; D'Amico 1997, p. 78; Zunckel 1997, pp. 320–21; Tonelli 2002; *Ratificatio et liberatio* of June 18, 1604 (ASM, *Notarile*, *filza* 23984, CGA) and 'A', attached company document of August 1, 1647 (*ibid.*, *filza* 26502, BO). On the presence of Milanese merchants and financiers in Lyons in the first half of the seventeenth century, see 'Mercanti, ditte, società e case commerciali milanesi o a partecipazione milanese presenti a Lione (prima metà del XVII secolo)', in Tonelli 2008[2]; this supplements the list published and glossed in Tonelli 2002.
25 The notarial files provide us with various examples of demands for compensation for goods that had not been received in a satisfactory state. One case is that of the dispute arising in 1620 between the shipper Giulio Volpi and Rinaldo Haeff, a Milanese merchant of Flemish origin, because his goods had arrived in Brussels in a very bad condition (documents of November 10, 1620 and December 22, 1620, in ASM, *Notarile*, *filza* 22057, DF). Regarding highway robbery, see the licences to carry arms granted to business-men and merchants in ASM, *Registri delle Cancellerie dello Stato*, *serie* XXI, nos. 30–36; and decrees of March 24, 1637 and July 10, 1637 (Gridario Guzmán), with which the governor of the State of Milan ordered his officials to prevent the garrisons under their command from molesting and using violence against forwarding agents. For the thefts and heists suffered by Milanese tradesmen and forwarding agents on various routes see the document of March 23, 1632 (ASM, *Registri delle Cancellerie dello Stato*, *serie* XXI, no. 31) and the decrees of March 31, 1636 (Gridario Guzmán), May 24, 1636 (Gridario Alcalà), April 24, 1639 (Gridario Guzmán) and November 28, 1661 (Gridario Sermoneta).
26 The flow of goods constituting imports into Lombardy is documented in Tonelli 1999, pp. 19–23. See further the account book of Giovanni Angelo Annoni (ASM, *Notarile*, *filza* 26487, BO); *Dato del datio della Mercantia* . . . (Milan, 1622; copies *ibid.*, *Finanze*, *parte antica*, *cart.* 5, and in BNB, ZN III.13).
27 There is a list of such fare in 'Ricapitolazione generale de' generi entrati e usciti nello Stato di Milano 1762 . . .', ff. 15v, 16v (FRM, *Archivio Verri*, *cart.* 384, *fasc.* 1). Lenten fare might be sold by specialist enterprises. On June 6, 1603, for example, one Gabriele q. Francesco Annoni formed a company for "the sale of salted fish, Lenten fare, fruit" (ASM, *Notarile*, *filza* 22376, MGA).
28 Tonelli 1999, pp. 14–15.
29 Procuratory of May 10, 1619 (ASM, *Notarile*, *filza* 26477, BO); attached to *confessio* of October 11, 1625 (*ibid.*, *filza* 23101, GGB); *protestatio* of August 2, 1631 (*ibid.*, *filza* 26489, OB); *conventiones* of September 9, 1654, regarding transport of goods to Leipzig between 1619 and 1627 (*ibid.*, *filza* 26505, BO); Mazzei 1999, p. 190.
30 Procuratories of June 6, 1617; May 30, 1618; August 28, 1618; January 25, 1622; April 28, 1623; January 30, 1625; March 4, 1628; July 7, 1628 (ASM, *Notarile*, *filze* 26475, 26476, 26479, 26480, 26482, 26486, BO); April 26, 1626 (*ibid.*, *filza* 27503, AGB); declaration in letters of exchange of February 19, 1621; July 4, 1623; February 27, 1625; July 23, 1625; May 18, 1629; June 10, 1629 (*ibid.*, *filze* 20993, 20995, 20997, VDCO).
31 Tonelli 2002, pp. 155–56.
32 Declaration in letter of exchange July 23, 1625 (ASM, *Notarile*, *filza* 20994, VDCO); account book of Giovanni Angelo Annoni (*ibid.*, *filza* 26487, BO). On the Annoni as suppliers of luxury goods to the Gonzaga, see the numerous letters published in Piccinelli 2003.
33 Many documents are preserved in the ASM in the files of the notary Ottaviano Belingeri q. Tommaso.
34 Procuratory of February 5, 1600 (ASM, *Notarile*, *filza* 16898, CB).
35 Declaration of Cristoforo Annoni in 1615 (ASCM, *Famiglie*, *cart.* 42); will of Cristoforo Annoni q. Stefano, March 28, 1630 (ASM, *Notarile*, *filza* 28503, TC); list of bequests in Capodici 1994, pp. 101–02. On the altarpiece see Colombo 2004–05, pp. 107–33.
36 Emilia Annoni, daughter of Giovanni Pietro, was born in Annone in early September 1612 (baptismal certificate of September 9, 1612, in APA, *Anagrafe – registri antichi. Registro dei battesimi 1604–1677*). On Milanese houses in the country and their architecture see Süss 1988; Binaghi Olivari, Süss, Bagatti Valsecchi 1989.
37 Many individuals declared to be natives of Annone appear as witnesses in notarial deeds drawn up for the Annoni in the ASM in the files of the notary Ottaviano Belingeri q. Tommaso. In these same files there are many cases of failure to repay mortgages: see also 'C' attached to the *Tutela et cura* of December 10, 1627 (ASM, *Notarile*, *filza* 26485, BO).
38 See the inventories marked 'B' and 'C' attached to the *tutela et cura* of December 10, 1627 (ASM, *Notarile*, *filza* 26485, BO). That mulberries, to feed silk worms, were growing on these lands is deducible from the existence of a balance with which to weigh silk in the Vittuone house (Inventario Vittuone 1627, f. [4r]).
39 Accounts attached to the *protestatio* of August 2, 1631 (ASM, Notarile, *filza* 26489, BO).
40 *Protestatio et confessio* of May 4, 1634 (ASM, *Notarile*, *filza* 26491, BO). On the Lumaga see Aureggi 1962.
41 *Liberatio* March 20, 1636 (ASM, *Notarile*, *filza* 26494, BO). The date Giovanni Pietro Annoni's partnership with Poquilin was established can be deduced from a deposition of 1651 (ASM, *Commercio*, *parte antica*, *cart.* 25). For the business partnership of Lodovico Mizzaferro and Cristoforo Annoni see the procuratory of June 10, 1619 (*ibid.*, *filza* 26477, BO). Like the Annoni, Mizzaferro had connections to Annone di Brianza: he got married there in 1604 (APA, *1. Matrimoni 1596–1637*, certificate of April 18, 1605).
42 The documentation is in ASM, *Commercio*, *parte antica*, *cart.* 28.
43 See the genealogical table in Colombo 2004–05.
44 Sitoni di Scotia 1705, f. 18 (in ASM). For the bowl and a possible date of the wedding see Warren 2008. Like their relations the Annoni with whom we are

immediately concerned, this couple also maintained close ties with their original *paese*: their son Luigi was baptized in Annone di Brianza (baptismal certificate of September 27, 1576, in APA, *Anagrafe-registri antichi. Registro dei battesimi dal 1575 al 1605* (1)).

45 Arese 1957, pp. 160, nos. 257–58, 184.

46 Document of 1604 attached to the *datium insolutum* of March 8, 1629 (ASM, *Notarile*, *filza* 26487, BO). The documentation of the sale by Enrique Pimentel, Bishop of Valladolid, brother of the deceased don Alonso, dated Madrid, January 16, 1623, is in AGS, Secretarías Provinciales, *legajo* 1801, document no. 489; that of the acquisition of the fiefs of Gussola and Martignana by Annoni is ASM, *Feudi camerali*, *parte antica*, *cart.* 277, *fasc.* 12.

47 See the marriage contract of July 21, 1626 (ASM, *Notarile*, *filza* 26484, BO) with the articles of association for the company of 1604, attached to the *datio insolutum* of March 8, 1629 (*ibid.*, *filza* 26487, BO).

48 Giovanni Visconti was the lord of Albusciago, Castano, Crenna, Cedrate (deed of July 26, 1627, in ASM, *Notarile*, *filza* 26484, BO; *ibid.*, *Feudi camerali*, *parte antica*, *cart.* 571, *fasc.* 'Albusciago'; Litta 1819–55, *Visconti di Milano*, *tavola* X).

49 Inventario Milano 1627. For the composition of the Annoni family in 1627 see the will of Giovanni Pietro Annoni q. Stefano of September 27, 1627 (ASM, *Notarile*, *filza* 26485, BO), the *tutela et cura* of December 10, 1627 (*ibid.*) and the genealogical table on p. 176. For the 'casa delli Annoni Banchieri' in the parish of San Nazaro: Status Animarum 1610, f. 8v.

50 Inventario Milano 1627, ff. [5r], [7r-v].

51 Musitelli, Bossi, Allegri 1999, pp. 170–74, 217–23, 230–34.

52 Bedell 2000, p. 145; Lucchini 2004, pp. 95–102. On dynastic strategies and the reactions of the next generation to the paths chosen for them by the head of the family see, definitively, Bizzocchi 2001, pp. 43–56.

53 Status Animarum 1610, f. 8v; testament of Cristoforo Annoni of May 28, 1630 (ASM, *Notarile*, *filza* 28503, TC).

54 See the indications of the residence of the Annoni brothers in 'Casa delli Annoni Banchieri' in Status Animarum 1610, f. 8v, and in the numerous deeds drawn up by them in the course of the 1610s and 1620s by the notary Ottaviano Belingeri.

55 Inventario Milano 1627, ff. [2v], [3v], [4v], [8v].

56 See for example Inventario 1624; Inventario Milano 1680, ff. 4[v]–17[r], [28r]–[33r].

57 Inventario Milano 1680, ff. 3[r]–[4v].

58 Inventario Milano 1627, f. [5v].

59 *Ibid.*, ff. [1r], [2v], [4r-v], [5v], [6r-v], [7r-v]. On the use of walnut in Lombardy see Broggi, Morandi, Poletti 1997, p. 17.

60 See, for questions of 'luxury' and 'comfort', the classifications of goods and products in Dessureault, Dickinson, Wien 1994 and in Bettoni 2005, pp. 23–34.

61 On the diet of the poorer classes in the modern era see Flandrin 1997.

62 Inventario Milano 1627, f. [8r]. On the consumption of meat from the second half of the sixteenth century onwards see Montanari 2006, p. 131; on self-sufficiency, Cipolla 2002, p. 44.

63 Inventario Milano 1627, ff. [1v], [2r], [8r].

64 *Ibid.*, ff. [2r-v]; Inventario Vittuone 1627, f. [1v].

65 Inventario Milano 1627, ff. [3r-v], [4r-v], [6r]; Inventario Vittuone 1627, ff. [1r-v], [2v], [3r-v], [4r-v].

66 Inventario Milano 1627, f. [4r]; Inventario Vittuone 1627, f. [3v].

67 Inventario Milano 1627, f. [6v].

68 Renonciat 1993, p. 269.

69 Inventario Milano 1627, ff. [3r-v], [6v]; Inventario Vittuone 1627, f. [1r], [4r-v]. On beds in the seventeenth century see Fusco 2004, pp. 112–14.

70 Inventario Milano 1627, ff. [2r-v], [3v], [4r], [6r-v].

71 Bettoni 2005, pp. 165–74.

72 Rosci 1985, pp. 21–23.

73 Inventario Milano 1627, ff. [4r], [5v], [6r].

74 *Ibid.*, ff. [4r-v], [5r]. On night clocks of the period see Bedini 2005.

75 Inventario Milano 1627, f. [5v].

76 *Ibid.*, f. [6v].

77 *Ibid.*, f. [8r], Inventario Vittuone 1627, ff. [1r], [5r]. On hygiene and linen in the modern era see Sarti 2006, pp. 247–55.

78 Inventario Milano 1627, ff. [3v], [4v], [5r-v], [6r-v], [7v].

79 *Ibid.*, f. [6r].

80 For a depiction of the feelings of girls forced by their families to enter convents see the episode of 'the nun of Monza' in Alessandro Manzoni's magnificent *I promessi sposi*, chs. IX–X.

81 Inventario Milano 1627, ff. [9r]–[10v]. On Milanese costume of the period, see Levi Pisetzky 1957, Venturelli 1999; on jewellery, Venturelli 1996.

82 Inventario 1620; Inventario 1624; Geddo 2001.

83 In the inventory of the estate of the Milanese financier Francesco Ponga there are noted, among other things, eight pictures of sacred subjects, crossed out because they were "all pledged as a caution for money" (Inventario 1620). From these same documents we learn the deceased's profession and his relation to Alberto Ponga, a *negoziante* admitted to the Camera dei Mercanti di Milano in 1622 (ASCCM, *Appendice*, *scat.* 25, *fasc.* 4).

84 Bedoni 1983, pp. 106–07.

85 See the will of Francesco Corenno q. Santino of March 5, 1595 (ASM, *Notarile*, *filza* 18551, MGB).

86 Deed of September 10, 1631 (ASM, *Notarile*, *filza* 26489, BO). The age at which Giacomo Antonio Carenna came to Brabant according to this document can be determined by reference to his baptismal certificate of March 8, 1591 (APA, *Anagrafe-registri antichi*, *Registro dei battesimi dal 1575 al 1605* (1)).

87 See the declaration in the letter of exchange of February 6, 1637 in ASM, *Notarile*, *filza* 28550, BM. Giovanni Battista Carenna's baptism is certified as January 6, 1596 in APA, *Anagrafe-registri antichi*, *Registro dei battesimi dal 1575 al 1605* (1).

88 *Liberatio* of September 9, 1616 (ASM, *Notarile*, *filza* 26475, BO); *attestatio* of March 26, 1620 (*ibid.*, *filza* 26478, BO), procuratory of January 12, 1625 (*ibid.*, *filza* 26482, BO).

89 See the *venditio*, with attached inventory, of May 23, 1615 (ASM, *Notarile*, *filza* 22049, DF) with the deeds for the constitution of the Annoni company as cited below.

90 Procuratory of October 8, 1627 (ASM, *Notarile*, *filza* 26485, BO).

91 Deed of September 10, 1631 (ASM, *Notarile*, *filza* 26489, BO).

92 The company was formed in 1604 and should have remained in being until 1609. It was instead quietly kept going until 1623 (*Datio insolutum* of March 8, 1629, with attached documents, in ASM, *Notarile*, *filza* 26487, BO).

93 *Ibid.*; deeds of June 18, 1604 (ASM, *Notarile*, *filza* 23984, CGA); procuratory of July 15, 1620 (*ibid.*, *filza* 26478, BO).

94 See for example the baptismal certificate of his daughter Theresa of July 29, 1631 (SAA, *St. Jacob*, *Dopen, 1627–37*, f. 51).

95 *Tutela* of February 4, 1631 (ASM, *Notarile*, *filza* 26489, BO); Tonelli 2000, p. 90.

96 Deeds of January 12, 1625 (ASM, *Notarile*, *filza* 26482, BO); accounts attached to deeds of October 11, 1625 (ASM, *Notarile*, *filza* 23101, GBG), March 8, 1629 (*ibid.*, *filza* 26487, BO), August 2, 1631 (*ibid.*, *filza* 26489, BO), March 20, 1635 (*ibid.*, *filza* 26494, BO).

97 See the company statutes attached to the *recognitio* of March 10, 1629 (ASM, *Notarile*, *filza* 26487, BO).

98 See the genealogical table of the Annoni family, p. 176.

99 See the contracts of employment in ASM, *Notarile*, *filza* 26146, RGF.

100 The documentation is in ASM, *Finanze*, *parte antica*, *cart.* 526; on the failure to obtain the Ferrarese grain see 'Relatione del Tribunale di Provisione . . . circa le diligenze usate per la penuria de grani del 1628' (ASCM, *Materie*, *cart.* 436).

101 See the document 'Quelle considerazioni, che mossero il passato Tribunale di Provvisione . . .' of February 16, 1623 (ASCM, *Materie*, *cart.* 571); Tonelli 2002. For the examples cited below in the text illustrating the indulgence of the authorities towards merchants from the sixteenth century to 1635 see Savoja 1995, pp. 53, 58; decree of July 20, 1611, in *Ordines Excellentissimi Senatus Mediolani (1490–1743)* (Milan, 1743), p. 204; G. Ferrandi, *Dato del datio della Mercantia* (Milan, 1696), p. 175; Frangioni 1983, pp. 126–27. A list of northern European merchants in Milan in the first half of the seventeenth century is in Tonelli 2002, pp. 185–89, recently enlarged from the research conducted for the present essay in Tonelli 2008[2]: 'Mercanti, ditte, società e case commerciali d'Oltralpe presenti a Milano (prima metà del XVII secolo)'. For the range of commercial and financial relations with Milan in the first half of the seventeenth century, see 'Traenti d'Oltralpe e trattari presenti a Milano (1610–1649)', *ibid.*, a supplement to the list published and annotated in Tonelli 2002.

102 On the use of a sea route as an alternative to that through Savoy see D'Amico 1997, p. 84. For the detour through the Sempione see documentation for the Piedmontese trader Petrino Gay in ASM, *Commercio*, *parte antica*, *cart.* 25.

103 See the decrees of September 24, 1635 (Gridario Albornoz), November 4, 1641 and June 11, 1642 (Gridario Sirvela).

104 Tonelli 2007[1], pp. 89–90.

105 Very probably the plague was brought into the State by a group of German soldiers hired to fight in the War of the Mantuan Succession.

106 The population of Milan declined from 115,000 at the end of the sixteenth century to about 75,000 in 1633 (Subacchi 1999, p. 245, D'Amico 1997, p. 77).

107 Farinelli, Paccagnini (eds.) 1988.

108 More specifically, Milan broke off commercial relations with the territories of Bergamo, Mantua and Turin, and then the Grisons, Locarno and

Mendrisio, the Valais, the Dauphinate, Provence, and all French ports (*Bando e sospensione d'alcuni luoghi dello Stato, e fuori di esso per causa di peste . . .* of December 29, 1629, repeating the ordinances of December 26, 1629, in the *Gridario* in BNB, Misc. 1089.43).

109 From Parma, Piacenza, Modena, Reggio Emilia, Ferrara and Bologna to Ancona, Florence, Lucca, Siena and Roma (Farinelli, Paccagnini (eds.) 1988, p. 40).

110 Moioli 1999, pp. 51–52.

111 Trezzi 1986.

112 D'Amico 1997, p. 77.

113 Deeds of June 7, 1630 (ASM, *Notarile, filza* 28546, BM), November 13, 1630 (*ibid., filza* 28440, BC), March 1, 1632 (*ibid., filza* 23108, GGB).

114 Deeds of June 20, 1629, June 26, 1630, October 11, 1631 (ASM, *Notarile, filza* 27506, AGB) and the numerous procuraties *ibid., filza* 23107, GGB. See further D'Amico 2001, and, on the Piacenza fairs, Marsilio 2008[2].

115 Accounts attached to the *protestatio* of August 2, 1631 (ASM, *Notarile, filza* 26489, BO).

116 *Ibid.*; procuratory of June 26, 1630 (ASM, *Notarile, filza* 27506, AGB); declarations in letters of exchange of January 13, 1635 (*ibid., filza* 28549, BM); April 11, 1635, June 20, 1635; November 20, 1635; November 27, 1635; March 26, 1636 (*ibid., filza* 28550, BM); August 19, 1636; December 10, 1636 (*ibid., filza* 28551, BM).

117 *Protestatio* of August 2, 1631 (ASM, *Notarile, filza* 26489, BO).

118 Deed of September 10, 1631 (ASM, *Notarile, filza* 28489, BO).

119 Procuratory of February 4, 1631 (ASM, *Notarile, filza* 26489, BO).

120 Procuratories of September 7, 1631 (ASM, *Notarile, filza* 26489, BO), December 4, 1637 (*ibid., filza* 26496, BO); mandate of June 3, 1643 (*ibid., filza* 26500, BO).

121 Procuratory of February 4, 1631 (ASM, *Notarile, filza* 26489, BO); *promissio* February 24, 1631 and *confessio* of March 27, 1632 (*ibid., filza* 26490, BO).

122 Not only the road through Basle but also that by Lindau, traversing the "Austrian provinces," led to the same destination, and went moreover directly to Nuremberg and Augsburg, where the Annoni exported silk (and silk with gold thread), sugar and spices (coming from distant lands, loaded high in vessels that docked in Venice and Genoa) and imported to Italy pearls, clocks and, probably, also skins and furs. See the procuratory of December 10, 1634 (ASM, *Notarile, filza* 26494, BO); the account book of Giovanni Angelo Annoni (*ibid., filza* 26487, BO); the accounts attached to the deed of August 2, 1631 (*ibid., filza* 26489, BO).

123 Agreement of October 4, 1631 between Paolo Annoni and Francesca Aliprandi q. Bonifacio attached to the *dos et promissio* of December 21, 1633 (ASM, *Notarile, filza* 26492, BO).

124 Procuratory of May 9, 1634 (ASM, *Notarile, filza* 26492, BO), *liberatio* of March 20, 1636 (*ibid., filza* 26494, BO).

125 Procuratory of December 4, 1637 (ASM, *Notarile*, 26496, BO); declarations of letters of exchange of these years in ASM in the *filze* of the notary Massimiliano Bossi q. Ottavio.

126 Procuratory of December 4, 1637 (ASM, *Notarile, filza* 26496, BO). For the collaboration of Giovanni Angelo Carenna with Paolo Annoni see the deed of May 12, 1633 (ASM, *Notarile, filza* 26548, BM); for the definition of *complimentario* or *complementario* see Battaglia 1961–2004 *s.v.*

127 Latuada 1737–38, pp. 270–71, and the plate entitled *Facciata del Palazzo del Sig. Conte Annone*.

128 Mandate of June 3, 1643 (ASM, *Notarile, filza* 26500, BO).

129 Maffi 2007, pp. 176–91.

130 *Ibid.*, pp. 194–200.

131 Signorotto 1996, p. 294.

132 'Relatione fatta da i Signori Delegati a S.E. a consultar il modo di proveder al sostenimento de i poveri operari . . .' of February 20, 1620 (ASCM, *Materie, cart.* 267).

133 Ribot García 1989, pp. 355–57. On the expense of maintainting contingents of soldiers in the State of Milan in the 1620s and from 1630 to 1659, see Muto 1995, p. 292; Maffi 2000.

134 Rizzo 2001; Maffi 2007, pp. 254–58.

135 Maffi 2007, pp. 312–13, 342–43.

136 *Ibid.*, pp. 344–45.

137 Pavarin 2006, pp. 3–5.

138 Pavarin 2002–03, pp. 99–100.

139 Maffi 2007, pp. 331–39.

140 Doria 1986.

141 Cova 1995; Grendi 1997, pp. 163–85; Marsilio 2008[1].

142 Pavarin 2004–05, pp. 1–78, 98–110.

143 *Confessio* of February 18, 1648 (ASM, *Notarile, filza* 27531, AGB).

144 ASCCM, *Appendice, scat.* 25, *fasc.* 7.

145 *Protestatio* of April 15, 1631 (ASM, *Notarile, filza* 23107, GGV), *assignatio* of October 10, 1631 (*ibid., filza* 23108, GGB). Filippo Del Conte held the post of prior of the Camera dei Mercanti di Milano in June and July 1615, in April 1616 and, with Giacomo Antonio Annoni, in the following month (Libretto 1574–1619, ff. 29–30).

146 De Luca 1996, pp. 207–08; Pavarin 2002–03, pp. 99–100.

147 The activity of Marcellino Airoldi from 1637 to 1644 has been traced from the following documents: various deeds of March 5, 1637 (ASM, *Notarile, filza* 28448, BC), *conventio et obligatio* of September 5, 1639 (*ibid., filza* 27517, AGB), procuratory of April 2, 1640 (*ibid., filza* 27518, AGB), *confessio et obligatio* of April 27, 1644 (*ibid., filza* 27525, AGB).

148 De Luca 1996, pp. 207–08; Signorotto 1996, p. 122. On Airoldi's activity, besides the overview presented here, see Maccaronello 2006–07.

149 *Obligatio et promissio* of July 15, 1644 (ASM, *Notarile, filza* 27526, AGB).

150 *Substitutio procuratoris* of June 23, 1648 (ASM, *Notarile, filza* 31480, RT); *procure* of November 24, 1650 (*ibid., filza* 27534, AGB) and of March 4, 1651 (*ibid., cart.* 27535, AGB). I am grateful to Alessandro Pavarin for having brought to my attention the first document cited in this note and for having helped me to understand the mechanisms underpinning the financial transactions in Milan in the period. My warm thanks also to Claudio Marsilio, who helped me verify the identity of the Corenno cited in these documents.

151 Procuratory of November 24, 1650 (ASM, *Notarile, filza* 27534, AGB); certificate of admission to the *utentes stratis* of 1619 (ASCCM, *Appendice, scat.* 25, *fasc.* 3).

152 Procuratory of March 4, 1651 (ASM, *Notarile, filza* 27535, AGB), deed of March 15, 1633 (*ibid., filza* 27509, AGB), *confessio* of May 27, 1642 (*ibid., filza* 28454, BC).

153 Maffi 2007, pp. 315–31, 344–45.

154 De Maddalena 2000; De Luca 2004.

155 ASM, *Feudi camerali, parte antica, cart.* 352, *fasc.* 'Merone'; *ibid., cart.* 396, *fasc.* 5-6 (fief of Monza); accounts attached to the *protestatio* of August 2, 1631 (ASM, *Notarile, filza* 26489, BO).

156 On Giacomo Antonio Carenna's loan to the Spanish Crown see the documents held in AGS, Contaduria de Mercedes, Juros del Reinado de Felipe IV, *legajo* 1157, *fasc.* 56. The deed conferring noble title, dated December 30, 1655 is *ibid.*, Secretarías Provinciales, 1435, ff. 297v–300v; a copy is in AGR, *Chambres des Comptes*, 146, ff. 241–42.

157 Procuratory of October 8, 1627 (ASM, *Notarile, filza* 26485, BO), deed of September 10, 1631 (*ibid., filza* 26489, BO).

158 Deed of May 12, 1633 (ASM, *Notarile, filza* 28548, BM), *protestatio* of October 24, 1635 (*ibid., filza* 27511, AGB), *protestatio* of June 4, 1638 (*ibid., filza* 27515, AGB), procuratory of July 6, 1641 (*ibid., filza* 26498, BO).

159 Inventario Milano 1680, f. 32r.

160 See for example the letters undersigned by Paolo Annoni between 1659 and 1665 in the AP.

161 Compare the sums indicated in the document drawn up in 1654 to grant a passport to Filippo Poquilin (ASM, *Commercio, parte antica, cart.* 25) with the deed of the constitution of the company of August 1, 1647 (*ibid., Notarile, filza* 26502, BO).

162 Inventario Milano 1680, ff. 14r–16r, 15v, 29r–v.

163 Deeds of September 21, 1640, October 2, 1640 (ASM, *Notarile, filza* 28023, CA), June 7, 1668 (*ibid., filza* 33288, FGA).

164 *Confessio* of May 13, 1653 (ASM, *Notarile, filza* 29771, PF). To set up a silk-working plant required considerable capital: a silk mill at second hand cost almost 1,000 *lire* (deed of April 26, 1664, *ibid., filza* 33288, FGA). On the various types of silk mills in northern Italy at the time and the different types of spun silk produced see Poni 1976; on the distribution of silk mills to the north of Milan in the second half of the seventeenth century see Trezzi 1986, p. 208.

165 *Confessio* of May 13, 1653 (ASM, *Notarile, filza* 29771, PF), *prorogatio* of July 15, 1665 (*ibid., filza* 33288, FGA), Inventario Milano 1680, ff. [29v]–[30r]. For the courts' views of the maximum permissible rate of interest see ASCCM, *Appendice, scat.* 2, *fasc.* 36.

166 *Confessio* of May 13, 1656 (ASM, *Notarile, filza* 29771, PF), *venditio iudicum* of September 6, 1661 (*ibid., filza* 33288, FGA). For the granting of extensions see the *prorogatio* of July 15, 1665 (ASM, *Notarile, filza* 33288, FGA).

167 Various deeds held in the files of the notary Giacomo Antonio Fumagalli q. Giovanni Battista; Inventario Milano 1680, f. 16[r]; *obligatio* of May 12, 1662 (ASM, *Notarile, filza* 33288, FGA).

168 Inventario Milano 1680, ff. [8v], [31v].

169 *Ibid.*, ff. 13[r]–[13v]. On the expulsion of the Jews from Milan at the end of the sixteenth century and their absence during Spanish rule of the State, with the exception of the Vitali family in Lodi, see Segre 1973 and Maifreda 2000, pp. 19, 37–42.

170 See the declarations in Inventario Milano 1680: "*mazzo d'instromenti et scritture concernenti al aquisto della presente casa comprata da Gio Batta Crespi, intitolati di mano del d.° fu Sig.r Bartholomeo*" (sheaf of instruments and documents concerning the acquisition of the present house bought from Giovanni Battista

Crespi, headed by the hand of Signor Bartolomeo, deceased), f. [10v]; "*Bartholomeo Carena ... morto il 6 febraio 1670*," f. [11v].

171 Pietro Verri wrote that the production of some Milanese silk weavers was sometimes below standard because they lived and worked in the same room: see Bognetti, Moioli, Porta, Tonelli (eds.) 2006–07, I, p. 260.

172 The sons of Giovanni Pietro Annoni exemplify this dynastic strategy. It was up to Paolo Annoni, the eldest surviving son after his brother Antonio's death, to ensure the continuance of the family. His brother Alessandro did not marry, but had a natural son whom he recognized, Francesco. In his will of September 12, 1663 Alessandro guaranteed Francesco an annuity for life of 3000 *lire*, which was not, however, to be continued for his own children. The bulk of Alessandro's estate passed to his brother Paolo's eldest son, Cristoforo Maria, entailed to the first born (that is, all subsequent beneficiaries were bound to pass on that portion of their estate to none other than the eldest legitimate male child) (ASM, *Notarile, filza* 32033, OPA).

173 Will of Stefano Carenna, September 6, 1680 (ASM, *Notarile, filza* 33291, FGA).

174 Inventario Milano 1680, ff. [25r]-[25v].

175 *Ibid.*, ff. 3[r], [4v], 21[r], 23[r], [26r]. For the education of Italian merchants of the time we possess the testimony of Giovanni Battista Peri regarding the situation in Genoa (Peri 1638, pp. 17–31); see, with reference to a wider context, chronologically and geographically, Angiolini, Roche (eds.) 1995, and on women's illiteracy Houston 1991, pp. 18, 21.

176 Inventario Milano 1680, f. 21[r].

177 *Ibid.*, f. [28r].

178 *Ibid.*, ff. [3r], [4v], 18[r], [20v], [26r], [28r].

179 *Ibid.*, ff. 2[r], [27v]; Inventario Annone 1680, f. 2[r].

180 Inventario Milano 1680, ff. 5[r], [21v], [27r]; Inventario Annone 1680, ff. [5v], [6r], [8v], 21[bis r],

181 Inventario Milano 1680, f. [21v]; Inventario Annone 1680, ff. [8v], [11r-v].

182 Inventario Annone 1680, f. [11v]. On the spread of maize see Coppola 1979.

183 De Bernardi 1984.

184 Inventario Milano 1680, ff. [1v], 2[r-v], 3[r]; Inventario Annone 1680, ff. 6[r-v].

185 Inventario Milano 1680, ff. 2[v], 3[r]; Inventario Annone 1680, ff. [3v], 5[v], [10v], [11r].

186 Inventario Milano 1680, ff. 2[r-v]; Inventario Annone 1680, f [10v].

187 Inventario Milano 1680, f. [27v].

188 On the rising popularity of chocolate in seventeenth-century Europe see Huetz de Lemps 1997, pp. 492–94; Menninger 2007, pp. 209–32; for Milan, Cavallera 2007, pp. 244–50. On the use of sugar and spices in the most prized form of it, even when consumed solid, see Tonelli 2007[2], pp. 502–03.

189 Inventario Annone 1680, f. [3v].

190 Borsieri 1619, p. 70.

191 Rosci 1985, pp. 8–9.

192 Inventario Milano 1680, f. 1[r].

193 *Ibid.*, f. [3v].

194 *Ibid.*, ff. [3v], [4r-v], [18v].

195 *Ibid.*, ff. [3v]-[4r]. On the importance of mirrors in seventeenth-century interior decoration see D'Amato 2001, pp. 176–77.

196 Inventario Milano 1680, f. [2v]. On lighting in the seventeenth century in Italy see Mariacher 1981, pp. 24–25. I do not have data on the maintenance of chandeliers in the seventeenth century, but to indicate the possible cost of the operation I note an example from the early nineteenth: in 1813 the Milanese noble Gian Mario Andreani spent 266 *lire* to have his chandelier cleaned, the equivalent of a labourer's pay for 160 days (payment order of December 31, 1813, no. 156, in ASM, *Sormani Andreani Verri Giussani, cart.* 690; De Maddalena 1974, p. 419, table 1).

197 Inventario Milano 1680, f. [4v]; see the genealogical table of the Milanese branch of the Carenna family, p. 175.

198 Inventario Milano 1680, f. [4v].

199 Muller 1993, p. 197.

200 Table 1: Subjects of paintings in Milanese patrician collections in the eighteenth century and in the houses of Stefano Carenna in 1680.

201 Inventario Milano 1680, ff. 5[r]-17[r]. On the confusing state of currency in Spanish and Austrian Lombardy and the measures adopted to improve it at the end of the eighteenth century see G. Bognetti, *Nota introduttiva* [to the third section, 'Tributi, Monete e Dazi'], in Bognetti, Moioli, Porta, Tonelli (eds.) 2006–07, I, pp. 681–91.

202 Inventario Annone 1680, ff. 3[r]-[5v], [7v], [10r-v].

203 Will of Stefano Carenna, September 6, 1680 (ASM, *Notarile, filza* 33291, FGA).

204 Marriage contract of September 12, 1689 (APSE, *Registro dei matrimoni dal 22-1-1632 al 17-6-1747*).

205 Will of Stefano Carenna, September 6, 1680 (ASM, *Notarile, filza* 33291, FGA).

206 *Protestatio* of September 2, 1638 (ASM, *Notarile, filza* 26496, BO); Signorotto 1996, p. 151.

207 In 1677 Antonio Annoni had formed a company for the transport of goods "produced in Flanders, Holland and Germany and other places" with Giovanni Battista Ponsampieri (whose place was later taken by Antonio Lauro). We know that in 1680 the company conducted business with traders in Amsterdam, Brussels, Basle, Friburg, Lucerne, Chur, Aldorf, Lugano and Lucca (*Conventiones* of September 7, 1780, in ASM, *Notarile, filza* 33204, BGC).

208 Tonelli 2002, pp. 177–78.

209 See the testimony given to the Milan Senate on March 8, 1706 (ASM, *Senato fedecommessi, cart.* 22); and the will of Alessandro Annoni, September 12, 1663 (*ibid.*, *Notarile, filza* 32022, OPA).

210 ASM, *Feudi camerali, parte antica, cart.* 201, *fasc.* 3.

211 Relazione 1706.

212 Bullio 1996; Fagiani 1998.

213 See the testimony given to the Milan Senate on March 8, 1706 by Giovanni Battista de Anni (ASM, *Senato fedecommessi, parte antica, cart.* 22). For the sale of the propeties of Vittuone and Merone see *Venditio et subrogatio* of July 3, 1706 (*ibid.*, *Notarile, filza* 39130, FS); copy of the despatch containing the conferment of noble title on Carenna *ibid.*, *Feudi camerali, parte antica, cart.* 352, *fasc.* 'Merone.'

214 See the description of both houses in Relazione 1706 and in Tonelli 2008[1]. The *casa da nobile* of Vittuone survives to this day (Langé 1972, pp. 560–61).

215 Or, in more detail, "*d'oro, al castello di rosso, merlato alla guelfa, aperto e finestrato del campo, sostenente, fra i due torrioni, un cigno d'argento, imbeccato del campo*" (Maspoli, Palazzi Trivelli 2002, pp. 84, 311).

216 ASM, *Feudi camerali, parte antica, cart.* 352, *fasc.* 'Merone.'

217 Will of Rosa Carenna Aliprandi, September 14, 1741 (ASM, *Notarile, filza* 39668, SGF).

218 On the price of cereals during these years in Milan see De Maddalena 1974, pp. 379–83.

219 Sitoni da Scotia 1705, f. 123. The Christian belief that charity to one's neighbour is the equivalent of charity to Christ is founded on Matthew 25: 31–40.

220 Arese 1980, p. 557.

221 Arese 1957, p. 181, note 73.

Subjects*	**Milanese patrician collections**	**Carenna collection in Milan**		**Carenna collection at Annone**	
	%	number of paintings	%	number of paintings	%
Portraits (and heads), [and figures]	10–15	4	4	4	8
Religious	35–40	42**	39	12	23
Secular (mythological, allegorical, history)	10–15	6	6	5	10
Landscapes	20–25	27	25	11	22
Still lifes, animals	5–15	24	22	18	35
Genre	3–5	0		0	
[other]		4	4	1	2
TOTALS		107	100	51	100

* These categories, except those in square brackets, are those of Geddo 1998[2].

** Not including the picture *"dove vi è l'imagine di un Crocifisso di ponti di setta et raggi adorati"* (with the image of Christ crucified embroidered and with golden rays (Inventario Milano 1680, f. [25v]); this was not a painting.

Sources: Inventario Milano 1680; Inventario Annone 1680; Geddo 1998[1], p. 105; Geddo 1998[2]

Translated by Paul Holberton

The Annoni family: a genealogical tree

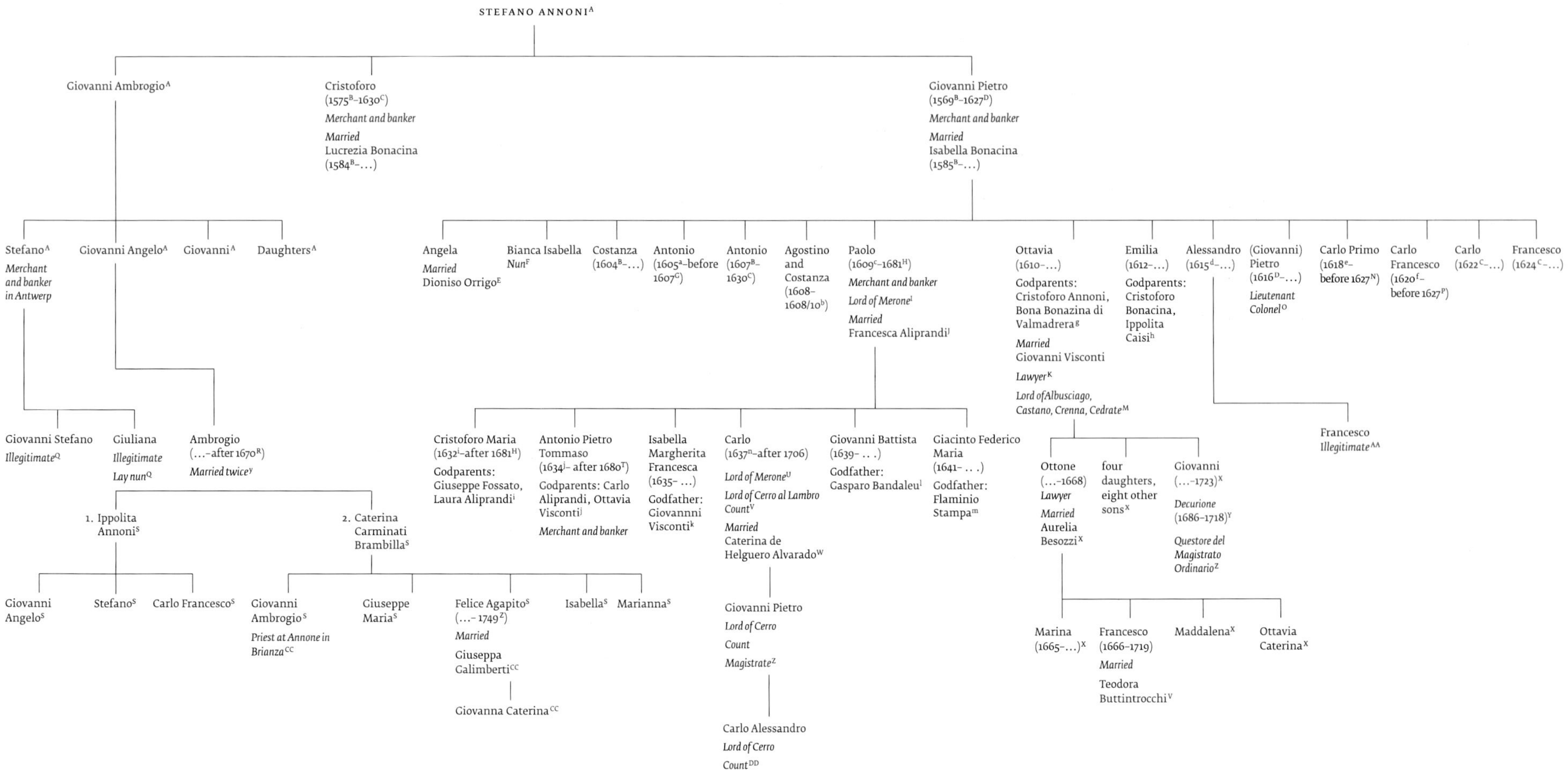

Notes in lower case: baptismal certificates of (a) December 2, 1605 (APSN, *Rubrica de'Battesimi 1600–1677*); b) February 19, 1608 (*ibid.*), dead by 1610, since they do not appear in the *Status Animarum* of 1610 (note B). Costanza probably had little hope of living when she was baptized, since she was given the name of her elder sister; c) March 16, 1609 (*ibid.*); d) July 2, 1615 (*ibid.*); e) January 1618 (*ibid.*); f) November 28, 1620 (*ibid.*); g) August 1, 1610 (APA, *Anagrafe–Registri antichi. Registro dei battesimi 1604–1677*); h) September 9, 1612 (*ibid.*); i) December 11, 1632 (APSN, *Libro de' Battezati nella Chiesa collegiata di S.to Nazaro in Broglio di Milano cominciato l'anno 1623 il p.mo Gen.o*); j) March 15, 1634 (*ibid.*); k) July 6, 1635 (*ibid.*); l) March 29, 1639 (*ibid.*); m) August 20, 1641 (*ibid.*); n) November 21, 1637, record of December 13, 1681, signed by the curate Baldassarre Cattaneo, priest at San Fermo, Milano (ASM, *Feudi camerali, parte antica, cart.* 352).
Notes in upper case: A) will of Cristoforo Annoni of May 28, 1630 (ASM, *Notarile, filza* 28503, TC); B) STATUS ANIMARUM 1610, p. 8v; C) *tutela* of February 4, 1631 (ASM, *Notarile, filza* 26489, BO); D) *tutela et cura* of December 10, 1627 (*ibid., filza* 26485, BO); E) marriage certificate of October 6, 1620 (APSN, *Libro dei matrimoni celebrati nella chiesa collegiata di S. Nazaro in Brolo dall'anno 1584 al 1631*); F) will of Giovanni Pietro Annoni q. Stefano of September 27, 1627 (ASM, *Notarile, filza* 26485, BO); G) another child, born in 1607 (note B), was given the same name; H) will of Paolo Annoni of September 18, 1681 (ASM, *Notarile, filza* 33204, BGC); I) oath by Paolo Annoni, lord of Merone, July 11, 1648 (ASM, *Feudi Camerali, parte antica, cart.* 352, *fasc.* 'Merone'); J) *conventio* of October 4, 1631, attached to the *dos et promissio* of December 21, 1633 (ASM, *Notarile, filza* 26492, BO); K) dowry contract of July 21, 1626 (*ibid., filza* 26484, BO); M) deed of June 27, 1627 (*ibid., filza* 26484, BO; ASM, *Feudi camerali, parte antica, cart.* 571, *fasc.* 'Albusciago'; LITTA 1819–55, Visconti di Milano, plate x); O) mandate of June 3, 1643 (ASM, *Notarile, filza* 26500, BO); P) because not named in her father's will (note F) nor in the wardships consequent on the deaths of Giovanni Pietro (note D) and Antonio (note C); Q) will of Stefano Annoni of February 12, 1664 (SAA, Notariaat (Ancien Régime), no. 3024, SA); R) request for transfer of a credit on salt granted December 18, 1680 (ASCM, *Famiglie, cart.* 49); S) 'Anno 1714 die 16 xmbrij …' (ASM, *Senato fedecommessi, cart.* 23, *fasc.* '11 Maij 1724. Isabella Annona minor nobis …'); T) *conventiones* of September 7, 1780 (ASM, *Notarile, filza* 33204, BGC); U) *venditio et subrogatio* of July 3, 1706 (*ibid., filza* 39130, FS); V) oath of Carlo Annone, lord of Cerro al Lambro, December 3, 1674 (ASM, *Feudi camerali, parte antica, cart.* 201, *fasc.* 3); W) ARCV, *PL Civiles, Masas* (OLV), *caja* 1160.3; X) F. Pavan, 'Giovanni Visconti († 1723)', in *La generosità e la memoria. I Luoghi Pii Elemosinieri di Milano e i loro benefattori attraverso i secoli*, ed. I. Riboli, M.G. Bascapè, S. Rebora (Milan, 1999), p. 155; Y) ARESE 1957, pp. 172 note 534, 176 note 636; Z) ARESE 1980, p. 567; AA) will of Alessandro Annoni of September 12, 1663 (ASM, *Notarile, filza* 32022, OPA); BB) ARESE 1957, p. 181 note 731; CC) *tutela* of December 13, 1749 (ASM, *Notarile, filza* 40211, GGB); DD) ARCV, *PL Civiles, quevedo* (F), *caja* 3600.6.
For the activities of the members of the Annoni family, see the citations in the essay.

The Carenna family: a genealogical tree

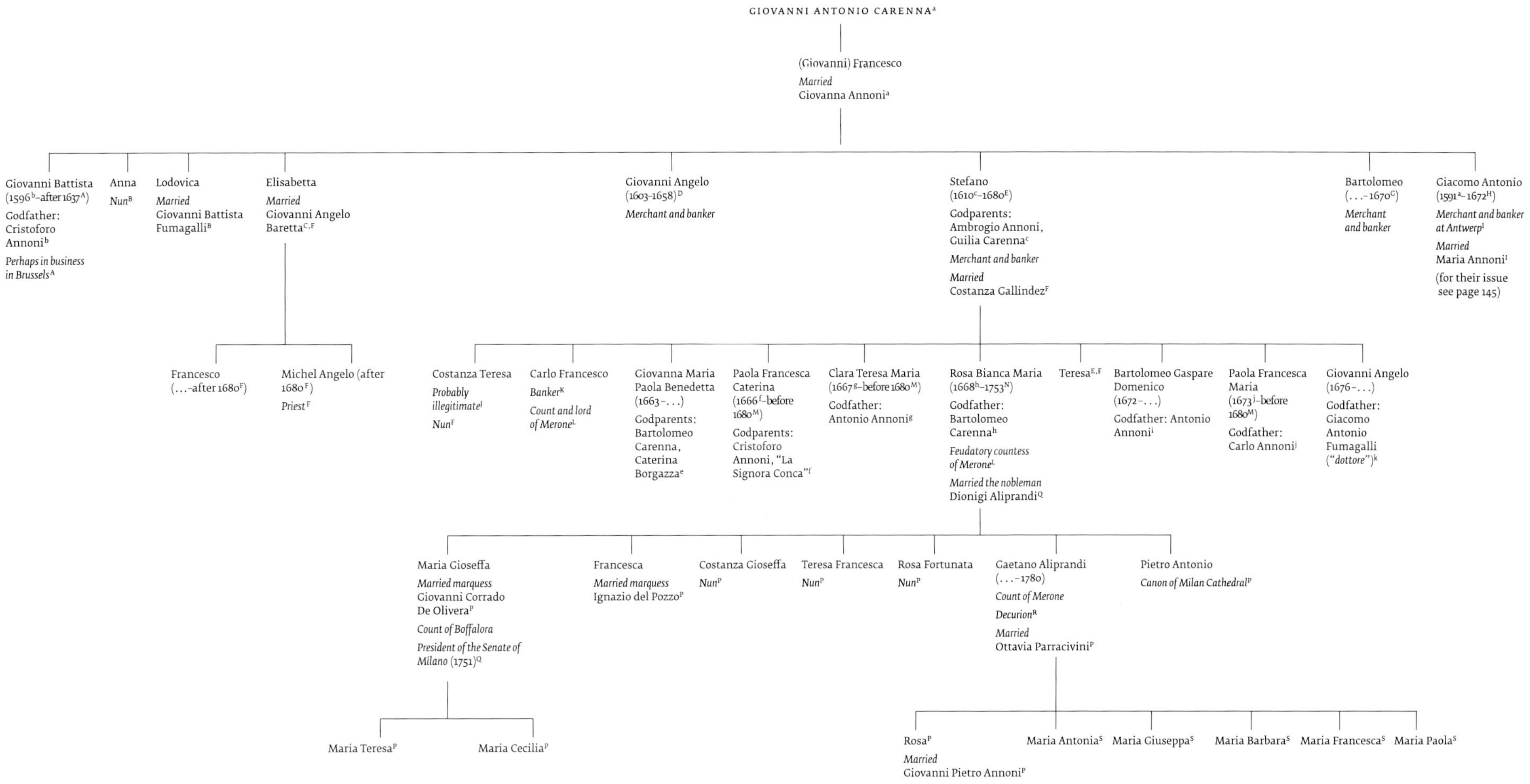

Notes in lower case: baptismal certificates of (a) March 8, 1591 (APA, *Anagrafe-registri antichi. Registro dei battesimi dal 1575 al 1605 (1)*); (b) January 6, 1596 (*ibid.*); c) October 18, 1610 (*ibid. Registro dei battesimi dal 1604–1677*); d) July 29, 1631 (SAA, *Sint-Jacob, Dopen, 1627–1637*, p. 51); e) March 24, 1663 (APSE, *Registro dei battesimi dal 12-9-1631 al 18-3-1713*); f) January 30, 1666 (*ibid., dal 17-8-1634 al 28-12-1717*); g) May 1, 1667 (*ibid., dal 12-9-1631 al 18-3-1713*); h) November 21, 1668 (*ibid.*); i) January 5, 1672 (*ibid.*); j) November 5, 1673 (*ibid.*); k) April 21, 1676 (*ibid., dal 17-8-1634 al 28-12-1717*).
Notes in upper case: (A) letter of exchange, February 6, 1637 (ASM, *Notarile, filza* 28550, BM); B) Giovanni Angelo's will of June 24, 1658 (*ibid., filza* 29773, PF); C) Elisabetta's will of April 5, 1661 (*ibid., filza* 33288, FGA); D) death certificate, 1658 (APSE, *Registro dei defunti dal 1635 al 1660*); E) *tutela*, November 16, 1680 (ASM, *Notarile, filza* 33291, FGA); F) Stefano's will of September 6, 1680 (*ibid.*); G) Stefano's *post mortem* inventory of November 16, 1680 (*ibid.*); H) here Documents B, no. 7, p. 181); I) here note 17, p. 144; J) probably illegitimate, because in his will (note F) Stefano calls her only "*mia figlia*", while he says of all his other children, "*havuti dalla Sig.ra Costanza Gallindez, mia moglie*"; K) *confessio* of February 2, 1706 (ASM, *Notarile, filza* 39130, FS); L) deeds held in ASM, *Feudi camerali, parte antica, cart.* 352, *fasc.* 'Merone', and *Finanze redditurari, cart.* 178; M) not being cited in her father's will (note F) or in the *tutela* (note E), yet not of marriageable age, she must have died; N) SITONI DI SCOTIA 1705, f. 123; O) marriage certificate of September 12, 1689 (APSE, *Registro dei matrimoni dal 22-1-1632 al 17-6-1747*, p. 94); P) will of Rosa Carenna Aliprandi of September 14, 1741 (ASM, Notarile, *filza* 39688, SGF); Q) ARESE 1980, pp. 556–57 (also for Corradi's public offices; R) ARESE 1957, p. 183; S) *consensus* of January 13, 1761 (ASM, *Senato fedecommessi, cart.* 17).
For the activities of the members of the Carenna family, see the citations in the essay.

Documents

A

Documents on the Antwerp branches of the Carenna and Annoni families

1.
Philip Rubens's letter, March 23, 1655, on behalf of the Burgomaster and Councillors of Antwerp certifying that Carenna was elected almoner in 1648. Philip, Peter Paul Rubens's nephew, was secretary to the council in 1648.
Archivo General de Simancas (Valladolid), Secretarías Provinciales, *libro* 1435, *legajo* 463

A todos quantos la presente Carta Vieren, o Leer oyeren = Nos los Burgomaestres Esclavines [regidores] y Consejo de la ciudad de Amberes hazemos saber y certificamos que Jacome Antonio Carenna Milanes hombre de negocios vezino desta dha ciudad, desde su mocedad vivio en ella y tubo domicilio fixo, como a ver de presente lo tiene con su muger hijos y familia en sus casas de morada situadas en la calle de la mera desta ciudad de Amberes, y como tal vezino y domiciliario fixo della por el año de mill y seiscientos y quarenta y ocho a sido por nos nombrado y cometido y sirvio el cargo de limosnero mayor desta dha ciudad y para que dello conste a su Ynstancia dimos la pr[ese]nte sellada del sello a las causas desta dha ciudad de Amberes y firmada por el licentiado Felipe Rubens n[uest]ro Secretario Jurado a veynte y tres de março de mill y seisçientos y çinquenta y cinco = Ph. Rubens

Transcribed by Dr Mercedes Ceron

2.
Ennoblement for Giacomo Antonio Carenna, December 30, 1655
Ibid.
Copies: Madrid, December 30, 1655, *ibid.*, *libro* 1435, *legajo* 2498; Brussels State Archives, Chambre des Comptes/Rekenkamer, Ms 146, ff. 241v–42r

Philippe par la grace de Dieu Roy de Castille [. . . .] salut. De la part du n[ost]re cher et bien amé Jacome Anthoine Carenna natif de l'Estat de Milan, resident en n[ost]re ville d'Anvers nous et esté tres humblem[en]t remonstré que la famille de Carenna, dont il seroit issu jouyroit au dict Estat et des preminences de Noblesse par privilige de l'Empereur qui avoit accordé le titre de noble a ses predecesseurs en recompense de leurs services rendues à n[ot]re tres auguste maison d'Austrice avec le port des armes qui s'ensuyvent a scavoir un escu tercé en pal de sinople d'argent et d'azur, celuy du millieu chargé d'un rameau d'olivier droit et arraché de synople, timbre une Aigle double nasissante au vol estendus de sables, couronnes et becquée d'or, languée de gueules, bourlet et hachaments d'azur et de sinople desquelles auroient usé ses d[ict]s predecess[eurs] audict Estat de Milan, comme aussy le remontrant en nos Pays Bas y ayant residé de[puis] sa jeunnesse, en qualité d'homme de negoces domicilié audict Anvers, sans y avoir exercé art merchanicque, ains esté employé par le Magistrat de lad[icte] ville en la charge d'aulmosnier d'icelle. Ce nonobstant comme depuis quelque temps aucuns officiers d'armes luy ont voulu disputer le port et l'usage desd[ictes] Armes en nostre Pays Bas, pour estre impetrees de l'Empereur et desirant le remontrant de les faire mettre en une Chappelle par luy fondée dans l'Eglise de Saint- Jacques audict Anvers, et dedicée a Saint Charles Borromeo et en continuer le port en nostre Pays Bas, affis qu'je le puisse faire sans empechement, les papiers et documents qu'il auroit eu du dict privilegé de l'Empereur ayant, esté bruslez au temps de la grande Contagion de Milan – il nous a tres humblement supplie de luy acccorder aussy le titre de noble avec le continuation du port des sud[ictes] armes. . .

3.
Will of Giacomo Antonio Carenna, March 9, 1669
Stadsarchief, Antwerp, notary archive Ambrosio Sebille, Ms 3031 (1669), previously published in part in P. Génard, 'Notices sur les riches tapisseries flamandes de Van Dyck dans la galerie de l'art de ce dernier' in sale catalogue, Rue Baeckelmans, Brussels (January 18, 1875); in Denucé 1932, pp. 189–90; and in Duverger, vol. 9 (1997), pp. 259–60

Ultima volontà che fin hora verbalmente, o, in servigio possa haver fatto in qualsivoglia maniera . . . . Prima raccomanda il detto sig.^{re} Testatore l'anima sua a Dio nostro Creatore et Salvatore, et alle preg[h]iere et intercessione della Santissima Vergine Maria, nostra Donna, et di tutta la Corte celestiale, et il suo corpo morto alla terra benedetta, eleggendo la sua sepoltura nella chiesa Parrocchiale di san Giacomo in questa città di Anversa, cioè nella sua capella di san Carlo Borromeo, ch'esso Testatore ha fatto fabricare et annesso una sacristia nella detta chiesa, dove fondò parimente un canonicato, con obligo di dire una messa quotidiana et il de profundis in detta sua capella, conforme le lettere di fondazione, a' quali si rapporta.
Item dà et lascia il detto sig.^{re} Testatore alla Camera de' poveri di questa città la somma di seicento fiorini una volta tantum.
Item dà et lascia alla Cappella del santissimo Rosario nella chiesa de' Padri Predicatori in questa città trecento fiorini, con obligo di dire cento et cinquanta messe di requiem speditivamente per solazzo del'anima sua.
Item alli Padri Capuccini anche somma di trecento fiorini con obligo di dire cento cinquanta messe come sopra.
Item simil somma di trecento fiornini alli Padri Carmelitani Scalzi con obligo di dire cento cinquanta messe come sopra.
Item alli Padri di San Francesco, alias Miure broders, la somma di cento et cinquanta fiorini con obligo di dire settanta cinque messe come sopra.
Item alli Padri Minimi la somma di ducento fiorini con obligo di dire cento messe come sopra.
Item dà et lascia il detto Testatore a' suoi servitori et alle sue serve, che gli serviranno al tempo della sua morte, a' cia[s]cheduno de essi un honorevole vestito di doglio a discretione de' suoi figlioli heredi, et a' più di lor salario oridinario.
Item dichiara il detto sig.^{re} Testatore d'haver dotato li suoi figlioli Gio. Francesco et Ignatio Carenna così con beni stabili come con denari contanti, nella qual dote sopravanza il detto sig.^{re} Gio. Francesco, suo figlio maggiore, il valore di quaranta quatro mille trecento novanta fiorini et otto piache moneta di Brabante, il qual sopraavanzo il detto sig.^{re} Testatore disce, che per certe considerationi che a ciò lo movino, dà et lascia per un prelegato al detto suo figlio maggiore Gio. Francesco Carenna, volendo et ordinando in questa conformità ch'esso sig.^{re} Gio. Francesco non sia obligato, in rispetto del detto sopraavanzo, a bonificare al sudetto sig.^{re}

Ignatio suo fratello cosa alcuna.
Et venendo il detto sig.^{re} testatore a disponere di tutti et qualsivoglia suoi altri beni, tanto mobili come stabili, et rendite, di qualunque natura che siano et in qualsivoglia parti che fossero trovati, senza alcuna riservatione, et compiti che saranno li sudetti legati et altre spese et debiti della sua casa mortuoria, di tutti questi beni esso sig.^{re} testatore dispone nella forma seguente, cioè, dà et lascia al detto suo figlio maggiore il sig^{re} Gio. Francesco Carenna la sua casa grande dove esso testatore habita de presente, situata nella Mera, et di più le sei case piccole che gli sono anesse alla detta casa grande et situate l'una apresso l'altra nella Eyckstrate.
Item anchora lascia al detto suo figlio maggiore li mobili seguenti, che si trovano al presente nella saletta maggiore di detta sua casa grande, cioè: le tapisserie fine di Brusselles, fatte a giusta misura, con le quali la detta saletta maggiore è adornata, rappresentando la Historia d'Achilles; item una pitura sopra la cheminea del infanticidio de Herodes, sendo originale et fatta dal quondam Cavagliere Pietro Pauolo Rubbens; item due pitture similmente fatte a misura, sopra li duoi portali in detta saletta, anche originali et fatta da Giacomo Jordaens, della historia di Cleopatra; item nella detta cheminea una pittura in forma di prospettiva, con duoi brandenari di lottone et duoi di ferro; item una tavola con il suo tapeto di Turquia; item vinti cadreg[h]e di pana rossa; item tre cortine di tela di cotton bianca, servendo alle finestre; item tutti li ornamenti che servono alla sua capella nella detta casa di sua habitatione, consistendo in un altare, sopra il quale è una pittura di Nostro Sig.^{re}, San Giuseppe et San Carlo Borromeo et tre altri piccoli quadri di devotione; item li cuori dorati de' quali la detta capella è adornata; item due cadreghe di detto cuoro dorato; item quattro candelieri et una croce d'argento argento di fattura come si usa in chiesa.
Item il detto sig.^{re} Testatore dà et lascia al detto suo figlio minore, il sig.^{re} Ignatio Carenna, la sua casa situata nella Langenieustrase, dove di presente habita il sudetto suo fratello Gio. Francesco; item la casa ch'esso Testatore tiene, situata nella Keyserstrase de rimpetto alla Coninckstrase; item
la casa di piacere, circondata d'acqua, chiamata l'Hoftervaeren, con tutti li mobili che vi sono dentro, et appartengono a essa casa, et di più tutte le sue terre, bosco, case di villano, stalla, appendenze et dependenze, il tutto situato sotto Mortsel.
Et tutti li suoi altri beni restanti, mobili et immobili, rendite, denari contanti, argenterie, gioie, accioni et crediti, il detto sig.^{re} Testatore dà et lascia a' detti suoi fugliuoli, li sig.^{ri} Gio Francesco et Ignatio Carenna, a ciascheduno di loro per la giusta metà, raccomandando il detto sig.^{re} Testatore a esso suoi figliuoli di voler osservare puntualmente questo suo testamento, et fare la divisione de' detti suoi beni restanti con ogni fraterno amore, guardando sempre la buona corrispondenza fra di loro, con che Iddio nostro Sig.^{re} darà loro la beneditione, come il Testatore desidera et spera dalla sua divina clementia.
Item il detto sig.^{re} Testatore vuole et ordina che de' suoi beni mobili non si venda niente in publico, ma in quanto alle pezze vecchie, che li suoi figliuoli non vorranno havere perse, le manderanno al mercato veccio, pigliando ciascheduno la metà del provenuto.
Et in caso che l'uno o l'altro de' detti suoi figliuoli non si conformasse con questo suo Testamento et ultima volontà in tutto et per tutto, il detto sig.^{re} Testatore vuole et ordina espressamente, che colui che mancherà di compirlo sarà et restarà escluso de' tutti et qualsivoglia li beni et casa mortuoria di esso testatore, come esso testatore in tal caso lo esclude con la sua simple portione legitima, senza poter [||] pretendere alcuna tre bellianica, o altra portione, et nella qual sua portione legitima si gli potrà imputare tutto quello che secondo il diritto e lecito et permesso, lasciando il detto Testatore in tal caso il residuo, a quello de' suoi figliuoli che in ogni punto osservare questa sua dispositione di ultima volonta.
Nella forma et maniera et sotto le conditioni sudette ha il detto sig.^{re} Testatore nominato et instituito, nomina et instituisce per suoi heredi pleno jure institutionis, li sudetti sig.^{ri} Gio. Fran.^{co} et Ignatio Carenna suoi figliuoli, et per mancamento, o per morte di alcuno di loro, li figliuoli legitimi di essi.
Tutto quello di sopra il detto sig.^{re} Testatore dichiaro esser suo testamento et ordinanza di ultima volontà, fatta del suo proprio motu senza persuasione alcuna; richiedendo da me notaro esserne fatto uno, o vero più instromenti publichi, che fu fatto et passato in questa citta d'Anversa nella casa di me notaro situata appresso la borsa de negotianti nella strada, detta de Israelstrete, in presenza di Gasparo Venstoct et Gio. Fran.^{co} Sebille come testimonij a ciò richiesta, et essendo il detto sig.^{re} Testatore et essi testimonij interrogati da me notaro se sapevano firmare risposero di sì et in cotesta conformità sottoscrissero di loro nomi meco notaro questa minuta.
[Signed] Jacomo Ant.^{o} Carenna
Gas.^{r} Vehstrudt
J. Sebille

4.
Will of Stefano Annoni, February 12, 1664
Stadsarchief, Antwerp, notary archive Ambrosio Sebille, Ms 3024

In nomine Domini nostri Ihesu Christi, Amen. L'anno Mille seicento sessanta quatro, adì dodici del mesa di febraro inanzi me Ambrosio Sebille notaro e tabellione publico in questa città d'Anversa, admeso nel suo Real Consiglio e Cancellaria di Brabante et in presenza de' testimony sottoscritti, comparse personalmente il sig.^{re} Steffano Annoni, figliuolo del quondam Gio. Ambrosio, nativo dello stato di Milano et residente in questa detta citta di Anversa, da me notaro ben conosciuto
....
[208] il suo corpo morto alla terra benedetta, eleggendo la sua sepoltur nella chiesa Parrochiale di san Giacomo in questa detta città d'Anversa.
Item lascia al Hospitale maggior di questa citta d'Anversa lire cento di grossi.
Item alla camera delli poveri di questa detta città lire ducento de grossi.
Item lascia alli Conventi di Carmelitani Scalzi, Minimi Franciscani, Capucini et Carmelitani calzati di questa detta città, a ciascun Convento cento pattaconi de piachi quarant'otto
[....]
[209] salute ... Item lascia la valuta de pattaconi cinquanta, per distribuirli a diversi poveri in questa città d'Anversa a discretione delli infranominati essecutori di questo suo testamento.
Item lascia alla detta chiesa Parrochiale di san Giacomo in questa detta città lire cento de grossi.
Item lascia et incarrica espressamente il detto testatore al infrascritto suo herede, et parimente a detti essecutori, di metter subito doppo la sua morte a rendita nel stato di Milano tanto capitale, che bsti per una mesa giornale e perpetua, la quale vuol et ordina sia fondata nella terra d'Annone in Monte di Brianza per la salute del anima sua.
Item lascia a Ferdinando van Pruysen suo cassiero lire cento de grossi a più del suo salario annuale [||] recognitione delli buoni et fedeli servity, ch'esso Ferdinando ha fatti al detto Testatore, con conditione però ch'habbia da render buon conto della cassa. Item lascia al suo servitore di casa, chiamato Henrico se resta servendo al detto Testatore fin alla sua morte, lire diecci de grossi, a più del suo salario ordinario.
Item lascia a Petronella sua serva di casa, con conditione di sopra, anche lire diecci de grossi, a più del suo salario.
Item lascia a Gio. Steffano Annone, suo figliulo naturale, la somma de lire mille de grossi.
Item dichiara il detto Testatore che vi sono liti pendenti tanto in questa citta d'Anversa, come a Spira, alla Haya et a Colonia, che vanno sotto nome suo, osia della sua compagnia intitulata Paulo Steffano Annone e Compagni, alla qual compagnia spettano tutte le dette liti in particulare, e perciò tocca anche a essa compagnia, di stare alle spese et sententie che ptrebbono esser date alla decisione de'dette liti.
Item lascia il detto Testatore a Guiliana Annone sua figlia naturale la somma de cinquanta pattaconi a più della dote de lire mille, che gli ha dato al tempo che detta Giuliana, s'ha messa Beghina, cioè lire ducento che sono impieghati in vita et in testa di essa Giuliana in questa detta città, et ottocento lire impiegate anche sopra questa città in rendita hereditaria et annuale con conditione che delle quatrocento lire de' dette ottocento lire la detta Giuliana possa disponere, et che le quatrocento [||] lire restanti debbino doppo la sua morte di essa Giuliana succedere al herede del detto Testatore, il tutto conforme le carte di rendita alle quali si rapporta.
Et compiti e sodisfatti che saranno li sudetti legati et altre spese et debiti della sua casa mortuoria, il detto Testatore ha dato e lasciato, dà et lascia in virtù di questa, tutti et qualsivoglia suoi beni restanti, mobili et stabili, denari, mercancie, plata, oro, joye, accioni, crediti et altri qualsivoglia effetti, in qualsivoglia parte che siano, o saranno ritrovati, tanto presenti, come futuri, nissuna cosa eccetuata nè riservata, a Gio. Ambrosio Annone suo nepote, figliuolo del quondam sig.^{re} Gio. Angelo Annone suo fratello pleno jure Institutionis, con conditione però, che in tutta questa heredità, il detto Gio. Ambrogio Annone ne goderà solamente l'usufrutto sua vita durante et che doppo la sua morte tutti li sudetti beni venghino a' suoi figliuoli legittimi di esso Gio. Ambrosio Annone goderene anche solamente l'usufrutto loro vita durante senza ch'il detto Gio. Ambrosio Annone, nè suoi figli legittimi possino in alcuna maniera carricare, vendere, cedere trasportare o altrimente alienare il capitale ch'essi haveranno hereditati dal detto testatore [....]
[218] et per mancamento de tali figliuoli de' figliuoli, al sig.^{re} Pauolo Annone suo cugino, et per mancamento di esso sig.^{re} Pauolo a' suoi figliuoli legitimi sostituendo il detto testatore al detto suo herede Gio. Ambrosio Annone et al'istessi suoi figliuoli legitimi di esso Gio.

Ambrosio Annone [...] Nomina et ordina per essecutori di esso suo testamento, al sig.[re] Gio. Francesco Carena suo cugino, figliuolo del sig.[re] Giacomo Antonio Carena, et al sig.[re] Francesco van Pruysen il Giovanne, residenti in questa detta città d'Anversa [...] lasciando il detto testatore per una recognitione, o memoria, al detto sig.[re] Gio. Francesco Carena una pittura a paesagio fatta da Pauolo Bril, et al detto sig.[re] Francesco van Pruysen lire cento de grossi in recompensa della fattica che haveranno nella causa sudetta.

5.
Inventory of Stefano Annoni, October 7, 1664
Stadsarchief, Antwerp, Notary archive Ambrosio Sebille, Ms 3024 (1664), as published by Duverger, vol. 8 (1995), pp. 380–83, doc. 1664, with some additions regarding furniture

Inventario de' beni mobili lasciati per la morte del quondam sig.[re] Steffano Annone, il quale morse adì ... del mese di maggio dell'anno mille seicento sessanta quatro in certa casa situata nella strata de Langenieustrate, in questa città d'Anversa havendo fatto il suo testamento inanzi me Ambrosio Sebille notaro publico in presenza de' certi testimony, adì dodici del mese di febraro prossimo passato, per il qual testam.[to] consta ch'il detto difunto ha lasciato tutti suoi beni restanti, a più di qualchi legati, spese et debiti della sua casa mortuoria al sig.[re] Gio. Ambrosio Annone suo nepote et doppo la suo morte a' figliuoli legitimi di esso Gio. Ambrosio, per goderne solam.[te] l'usufrutto loro vita durante, con dichiaratione che dopo la morte del detto Gio. Ambrosio Annone, et delli figliuoli legitimi di esso Gio. Ambrosi, succedano in proprietà assoluta alli figliuoli legitimi delli figliuoli legitimi del accenato Gio. Ambrosio Annone, et per mancam.[to] de tali figliuoli de figliuoli, al sig.[re] Pauolo Annone suo cugino, et per mancam.[to] di esso sig.[re] Pauolo, a' suoi figliuoli legitimi, sendo questo inventario fatto per me, il detto notaro Ambrosio Sebille, alla richiesta de' sig.[ri] Gio. Fran.[co] Carenna et Francesco Van Pruysen il giovane come essecutori del testam.[to] del detto difunto; adì cinque et altri giorni del mese di giugno del detto anno mille seicento sessanta quatro, in presenza di Ferdinando van Pruysen cassiero del detto defunto et Henrico Janssens servitore della detta casa mortuoria.
In detta casa mortuaria
Nella camera verso la strada:
quatro pitture li quatro elementi fatti da Maffeo Verone;
una pittura fatta d'Abraham Janseens, sendo una Diana;
una pittura fatta da Jordaens, triumpho di Venus; una pittura fatta da Snyers, caccia d'un singale; una pittura fatta da Luycx, fiori, con le figure fatte da Gonzael; duoi pitture fatte da Teniers;
un ritratto fatto da Van Dijcq;
un ritratto fatto da Tintoret;
una pittura, paesagio, fatta da Fockier[s] et le figure fatte dal Frouweelen Breugel;
una tavola col coperta turchesia;
duoi teste di pietra blanca;
duoi ferri di fuoco;
una partita di cuoro dorato rosso intorno alla detta camera.
Nel patio:
una calissa;
tre mappe veccie et una pittura di un marinaro;
otto pezze di ferro per pesare;
una pittura di un cane;
una pittura di un leone;
una pittura della regina Hester;
una altra pittura.
Nella camera sopra il patio:
una tavola con una coperta ordinaria;
quatro sedie di coro rosso di Prussia;
una piccola tavola con una coperta ordinaria;
un buffetto;
un coffre di servitio et una scabella da sedere;
una pittura, paesagio;
una pittura con fiori con una Madonna;
|un ritratto di uno della familia de Annone; una pittura con galere fatta da Naentchens;
duoi ferri di fuoco;
un mantice;
una cama di legno ordinario con le cortine di sayetta rossa;
un matrasso di lana con duoi coperte;
un letto di plume;
un speccio.
Nella camera grande verso il giardino:
una tavola con una coperta turquesca;
vinte una sedie di cuoro rosso di Prussia;
una pittura fatta da Rubens, sententia di Paris;
quatro scetsi fatti da Rubens;
un scetso del detto Rubens sopra carta;
una pittura, paesagio fatto da Pauolo Bril, la quale il difunto ha lasciato per il suo testam.[to] al Signor s.[r] Gio.v: Fran.[o] Carenna;
una pittura del Veccio Bassano rappresentando il corpo morto di Nostro Sig.[re];
duoi ritratti fatti da Holbien;
una quadra fatta da Vandycke con la Madonna et Santa Anna;
una quadra fatta da Quinten rappresentando la donna di Samaria;
una quadra fatta da Snijers con galline et paoni;
una pittura fatta dal detto Snyers di una volpe;
una quadra fatta da Luycx, fiori;
duoi piccole pitture, paesaggi fatte da Brouwer;
Un scribano di ebano, nel quale si trovarono:
un doppio ducatone d'argento, un doppio pattane d'argento, in moneta 36 piacche, un ducatone d'oro, una pezza quadra di oro, una croce d'oro, una piccola pietra rossa per mettere, et qualche soija;
una pittura paesagio;
una pittura de fiori con un cane, la quale stava nella cheminea;
duoi ferri di fuoco di ottone o cobre;
un speccio;
una partita di cuoro dorato intorno alla detta camera.
Nella piccola camera verso il giardino:
una tavola con una coperta ordinaria;
un'altra tavola;
un buffetto nel quale si ritrovano:
- tre pari di candelieri d'argento;
- un piato grande con un pote d'argento per lavare le mani;
- una saliera d'argento con un pimenteno;
- duoi mocchetti d'argento;
- una dozzena di cuchiari d'argento;
- una dozena di forchetti d'argento;
- duoi poti di porcellana con le coperte d'argento;
- cinque bicchiere di porcellana;
- quaranta sette piatti di porcellana grandi et piccoli;
- duoi tondi d'argento;
- duoi orinali di stanio;
- dodici piati grandi et piccoli di stanio;
- quaranta sette tondi di stanio;

dodici sedie di cuoro rosso di Prussia;
una pittura, poti di fiori di sei fogli, che si mette nelle camere per guardarsi dal vento; duoi ferri di fuoco et un mantice;
una pittura della festa di Cana Galilea fatta dal maestro Gio. di Bruges;
una pittura fatta da Snyers, caccia d'un zingale;
una pittura fatta dal detto Snyers con certi ucelli;
una pittura fatta dal detto Snyers con frutti;
una pittura, paesaggio, fatta da Momper con figure fatte dal fluweelen Breugel;
una pittura di Andromada fatta dal cavagliere Giosepino;
una pittura di Bacchus et altre figure;
una pittura con le Muse fatta da Frank;
una pittura della benedictione di Giacob fatta da Martino de Vos;
una pittura, paesaggio, fatta da Artois con le fugure di Van Balen;
una pittura, paesaggio, fatta da Grimmer con le piccole figure fatte da Martino van Cleeff o vero da Mostaert;
una pittura, paesaggio, fatta da Bruegel con una Susanna fatta da Gonzael;
una pittura piccola con la di testa San Giovanni;
un ritatto piccolo fatto da Brouwer;
sei pitture paesaggi fatte dal Giovane Momper;
un speccio.
Nella cucina:
una pittura de diversi ritratti;
un armario di legname bianco;
un escaparate con una pressa;
vinti quatro piati di stanio grandi et piccoli;
vinti quatro tondi di stanio;
dodici boccali di pietra con coperta di stanio;
dieci candelieri di ottone e cobre;
cenen cemen ecu visbecken di ottone o cobre;
un scaldaletto di ottone o cobre;
duoi cramilioni di ferro con un latto anche di ferro;
tre caffoiren di ferro;
cenendwellier di legno;
otto sedie di legno et paglia;
una tavola con una coperta ordinaria.
Nella piccola cucina:
un spiede per arrostare;
un mortiero di ottone o cobre;
duoi grily di ferro;
duoi orinali di stanio;
tre poti di ferro;
duoi chaudroni di ottone o cobre;
duoi panelli di ottone o cobre a cucinare;
un giuoco di verkeeren di legno ordinario;
quatro mochetti di ferro;
una lanterna.
[||]*Nella camera sopra la cucina:*
una cama di legno con una matrassa di paglia et una di lana, et anche un letto di plume et duoi coperte;
item un panilione di saijetta.
Nella camera sopra la camera piccola verso il giardino:
duoi sedie di cuoro rosso di Prussia;
una tavola senza coperta;
duoi coffri con vestiti vecci del difunto;
un buffetto;
una cama con uno letto di plumme, una matrassa di

lana, et una di paglia;
una coperta di lana et una coperta di sayetta con le sue cortine;
una scabella di legno;
una pittura di figure;
una pittura delle sette opere di misericordia;
una pittura del corpo morto di Nostro Signore, copia de quella pittura fatta da Bassano;[5]
un ritratto di un carretone;
un speccio;
una partita di cuoro dorato intorno alle detta camera.
Nella camera sopra la camera grande verso il giardino:
una cama di legno con le cortine di sayetta;
un letto di plume, una matrassa di paglia et una di lana;
duoi coperte di lana;
duoi tavole, l'una con una coperta di cuoro, et l'altra senza coperta;
quatro sedie di cuoro rosso di Prussia;
una pittura, ritratto del giardino di fuori del difunto;[6]
una pittura, paesagggio, fatta da Wildens;
duoi pitture, fatte da Naentkens, con barche et figure.
Nella camera sopra il contor:
una pittura grande, paesaggio;
una pittura di uccelli;
una pittura di un banchette;
tre pitture di diversi soggetti;
duoi pitture di fiori;
una pittura de soldati fatta da Van Eycke.
Nella camera sopra la camera verso la strada:
una tavola con uno coperta ordinaria;
sette sedie di cuoro rosso di Prussia;
duoi sedie di paglia et legno;
una pittura di >figura< Pallas et Venus;
una cama di legno con le sue cortine di sayetta;
un letto di plume con una matrassa di paglia et una di lana, et duoi coperte di lana;
un armario di legno;
duoi ferri di fuoco;
una cortina d'ormesino rosso per un letto;
duoi coperte di letto di seta fodrate di lana;
sei [...]
Nella camera della serva:
una cama di legno con un letto di plume, duoi coperte;
una piccola tavola;
quattro sedie di legno.
[|]*Nella camera del servitore:*
una cama di legno con un letto di plume;
matrassa di paglia et una coperta di lana;
duoi sedie di legno et una tavola;
una piccola pittura della Madonna.
Nella camera sopra il packuys:
una cama di legno con un letto di plume et una matrassa di lana, et una di paglia con una coperta di lana;
una fissicha con una pistoletta;
una pittura, paesaggio.
Nella camera del cassiero:
quatro pitture di poco valore;
una cama di legno con le cortine di sayetta;
un letto di plume, una matrassa di lana et una di paglia con duoi coperte di lana.
Nelli granari:
duoi tavole et alcune [...] per metterci la nappe;
alcuni fiaschi vuoti.
Nel packhuys:
una tavola;
un escaparate grande et vuoto;
un bilancio di ottone, o, cobre con cinque pezze di peso anche di cobre;
un altro esparate veccio et vuoto;
duoi pezze di piombo.
Nel giardino dietro la casa:
sette arbori d'orangi.
Nella stalla:
un cavallo con le redine et altre appertenenze;
un coffre per la havena.
Nelle cantine:
alcuna provisione di legno, carboni, biera, vino, oglio, butiero, vinagre, candele, et un poco di tabaco;
cinque vasi di legno per lavare.
Nel contor:
duoi pitture;
una tavola et una piccola cassa di legno;
due casse di legno con bande di ferro per metterci li denari.
Jan Steffano Annone signed Giov. Steffano annone

6.
Extract from the inventory of Francesco Carenna, April 2–4, 1691, Stadsarchief, Antwerp, Notary archive J. de Vos, Ms 1146 (1690–91), as published by Duverger, vol. 12 (2002), pp. 99–105, no. 3989, with some additions regarding the furniture

In de eersie Carner naer de voors. Saele:
De camer behangen met gouden leir witten gront
de notelwien schryff taffel acht hooge en int fluwede roode leunstoelen.
dry woitte catoene gordynen voorde gelasen
Een schoudoeck Blompot in de schouw
Twee Pourtraiten vuytbeeldende den heer Vader ende vrouwe Moeder des heere Afflyvigen
Een schoustuck voor de schouwe geschildert van Langen Jan vytbeeldende een Mariënbeelt ende Carolus Borromeus N° 6
Sesse stucken Landschappen vuytbeeldende de Tyden van't Jaer N° 7,8,9,10,11 en 12
In de Camer oft Salette daernaer:
Deselve camer behangen met tapyten representerende de Historie van Meliaser bestaende in sesse stucken
Een schilderye van Rubens voor de schouwe met eenige figuren Fruytagie ende Wilt N° 13
Een schilderye boven de deure wesende een Swaene, Ryger ende Hert etc. N° 14
Een schoudoeck in de schouwe met Blommen ende Dry Engeltkens
In de groote Salette aen den Hoff:
Twelff may fluweden [leun] stoden
[Twee] taffels met roode fluweel tafilcleeden dar oppe
12 velvet stool... [(two) tables with red velvet table cloths on them]
Een camer tapijten vuytbeeldende de Historie van Achilles bestaende in seven stucken Drye roode syde gordijnen voor de gelasen
Een groot schoustuck voor de schouwe vuytbeeldende Diana ende ander figueren geteeckent N° 15
Een stuck schilderye van Jordaens vuytbeeldende Cleopatra van't Serpent gebeden N° 16
Een ander van deselven meester oock vuytbeeldende Cleopatra met Marcus Anthonius N° 17
Een schoudoeck in de schouwe
Een roode syde gordinjne hangende voor de deure

Transcribed by Maria Juliet Marinus

7.
Jacques le Roy, *Notitia Marchionatus Sacri Romani Imperii, hoc est urbis et Antverpiensis* (Amsterdam, 1678), p. 386: Carenna's purchase of lordship, his chapel and death date

Hoves Burcht & Swyndrecht.
pagi invicem contermini sunt, Antverpiaeque vicini, sed in Flandria ad sinistram Schaldis ripam siti, quorum prior, insigni veteri castello ornatur, unde in Antwerpiam amoenissimus prospectus. Utriusque dominium tenuit praefatus Ioannes van Hove jure pignoratitio à Flandriae Comitatus Ordinibus, qui circa annum 1665 loca illa in perpetuum vendiderunt Iacobo Antonio Carenna, qui egregio ad posteros exemplo, filio suo natu majori per manus tradidit dominium Swyndrecht, minori Burcht. Obiit vero 25. Novembris anno 1672. Sepultus Antverpiae ad S Jacobum in chori ambitu boreali, in sacello S. Caroli Borromei quod fundaverat, ad cujus ingressum legitur humi, in sepulchrali lapide, insignibus ejus decorato
D.O.M.
Monumentum Jacobi Antoni Carenna Mediolanensis et suorum requiescant in pace.

Documents

B

Documents on the Milan branches of the Carenna and Annoni families

NOTES ON PROCEDURE

In transcribing these texts I have remained faithful to the orthography of the documents, except where some modernization was appropriate to help the reader. Variations reflecting linguistic usage have been preserved (single or double consonants, for example), but punctuation and accentuation have been introduced and capitalization has been adjusted to modern standards.

For an understanding of the many archaic or dialect terms contained in the inventories, there is an English glossary on the AGO website:
(http://www.ago.net/thomson-collection-publications/annoni-carenna-inventories-glossary).
For a modern Italian glossary, see Giovanna Tonelli, *Materiali per lo studio di famiglie mercantili milanesi in età moderna* (Brescia, 2008), available online at
http://www.giovannatonelli.it/en/doc.html.
This website will also feature any research updates on the Annoni and Carenna families. GT

1. Inventario Milano 1627

|[1r] **Inventario de' mobili ritrovati nella casa propria del q. sig.r Gio. Pietro Annone situata in P.R. P. s.to Nazaro in contrata di Postlaghetto et dove habitava al tempo della sua morte**

Prima in sala si sono travati gl'infrascritti mobili:
bofette n.° quatro di noce belle et bone;
cadreghe armate fatte di trippa bone n.° sette con la franza verde;
scagni di corame boni con la franza paiada n.° otto,
un par de brandenali grandi con li suoi pomi di lotono et suoi fornimenti da foco pesano in tutto lire vintisei grosse;
un bofetto da foco per sala.
In cusina:
un par de brandenali di ferro non molto boni con il suo fornimento di foco rotto |[1v] et frusti;
un vestero di noce frusto;
una cardenza con il suo cardencino di noce frusto;
una tavola di pobbia con sua banca da sedere;
un tavolinetto di noce frusto;
una stadera piciola di ferro;
candelieri di lotone boni n.° otto et pesano lire dece grosse;
un menarosto bono;
arame:
un parolo di rame di tenuta di due sechie;
duoi vasi grandi di rame;
un bacolono da comodar colarini;
lecarde n.° 2;
un padella et un padelino di torta;
un padelotto di anetra con suo coperto;
una caldara grande;
|[2r] una canevetta d'arame;
tre scaldaletti;
una padella da rostire;
sedellero due et un sedelino;
duoi caldari et un caldarino con suoi coperci;
pesa in tutto tutto questo arame lire n.° trecentosesantacinque picole;
lotono:
duoi bacili;
duoi cazuli;
una cazza et una cacetta;
un scaldino;
un cribietto;
un taier et la moschetta per le candele;
pesa in tutto d.° lotono lire otto et mezza grosse;
un cazul di ferro;
|[2v] una gradicella et un tripude di ferro di torta;
peltro:
orinali di peltro n.° sei pesano lire otto grosse;
capi di peltro tra grandi et picoli et tondi n.° ... et pesano libbre ... grosse;
un par de brandenaletti di camira con pomi di lotone che pesano lire sei grosse.
In una camera di s.ª:
tre casse di noce grande quasi nove;
un tavolino di noce;
duoi matarazzi di lana di peso de libre 40 grosse;
duoi letti di piuma con li suoi piumazzi pesano lire grosse ottanta;
coperte di lana bianche et bone quatro;
un moschetto quadro di dobletto quasi novo argentino in color d'oro et paiato con sua |[3r] coperta et tornaletto;
un altro moschetto quadro de filo et lana cremisole, verde et bianco con sua coperta et tornaletto;
due lettére di noce con sue colonne;
duoi paiarizzi;
un tapeto di Fiandra novo paiato et argentino.
In un'altra camera:
un moschetto di dobletto di Fiandra con sue franze di filisello di color rosso, bianco et moiello;
un altro moschetto di dobletto con sua coperta con le sue franze atorno di colore verde et bianco et suo tornaletto;
quadretti n.° dodeci tapezarie de Fiandra novi per far sei scagni;
una preponta di Venetia rossa et verde nova;
un'altra d.ª gialda et altro colore;
|[3v] brazza n.° trenta cinque tovaglie di Fiandra sotili;
brazza n.° centosette mantili sotili di Fiandra;
mantili casalenghi de lino in pezza n.° novantasei;
tovaglie casalenghe di lino in pezza brazza n.° vinti otto.
In un'altra camera:
un paramento di letto con sua coperta et tornaletto di dobletto di seta et filo argentino et color d'oro con le sue franze di seta del istesso colore;
un matarazzo di lana che pesa libre 20 grosse;
due catelonie bianche bone;
un letto di piuma de' peso de libre 40 grosse;
due catelonie bianche bone;
un letto di piuma de' peso de libre 40 grosse;
una lettéra con le sue colonne et paiarezzo;
|[4r] un tavolino di noce;
un scritorio di noce;
una cassa di noce grande;
duoi coffini picoli;
un coffine dipinto alla todesca;
un cassone et una cassa di noce;
un letto di piuma con il suo piumazzo de lire 42 grosse;
un matarazzo di lana di peso de libre 21 grosse;
due catelonie, cioè una rossa et una bianca, bone.
In un'altra camerra:
una lettéra di noce;
due casette dipinte fruste;
un'altra cassa di noce;
una culla di vimene;
doi vesteri di pezza frusti et rotti;
lenzoli para cinquantacinque tra boni et frusti;
|[4v] tovaglie tra bone et rotte n.° quara[n]t'una;
mantili tra boni et rotti numero trecento trenta sette;
serviette tra bone et fruste n.° cinquantanove;
altri lenzoli novi n.° 16;
ogiolate n.° quatro bianche;
tovaglie per la servitù n.° vinti;
sugamani de cusina n.° trenta;
filo tra di lino et stoppa cotto lire grosse n.° cinquanta;
fodrettoni para due;
fodrette para n.° vinti otto.
Nella camera dove dormiva il q. S.r Gio. Pietro:
casse di noce n.° tre bone et quasi nove;
una lettéra di noce con le sue colonne;
un balandrano di zambalotto nero, uno frusto;
|[5r] lenzoli n.° quatordeci novi;
un matarazzo di lana di peso de libre 20 grosse fodrato di tarliso quasi novo;
un letto di piuma con suo piumazzo con sua fodra quasi nova di peso de libre 40 grosse;
altri mantini n.° quarantadue.
In un'altra camera:
un vestero di pezza incornisato di larice bono;
duoi tapeti di filo di color diversi;
fazoletti n.° centocinquanta;
cavezzi di tela novi di lino n.° quatordeci;
tela di Fiandra, di renso, et de messachio brazza n.° 300;
fedretoni da paiola n.° due et tre fodrette;
una frutera de redesino;
un lenzoletto di paiola di redesino;
tre fasse con li lavorini di redesino;
panni di testa n.° quatro et una petenera;
|[5v] camise usate tra da homo et donna cento cinquanta;
scosali n.° trentacinque;
due tavole di noce con li piedi torniti;
un orologio da tavola;
un altro orologio da sono;
una tapezaria di corame frusta nera et oro per la sala di s.ª;
cadreghe armate di trippa n.° sei;
tapezaria di corame verde et oro per la sala da basso;
una tapezaria di Fiandra per la sala da basso;
un tavolino di noce;
un tapeto de filo argentino et bianco;
un coffenino picolo;
una boffetta di noce;
|[6r] un vestero di pechia incornisato di larice bono;
una veste in busto di tabì rosa scura di Venetia guarnita d'oro, con le maniche di tela d'argento che fu fatta per la monica Bianca Isabella;
una lettéra di noce con sue colonne;
un letto di piumma con suo piumazzo de' peso de libre 40 grosse;
un matarazzo di lana de' peso de libre 20 grosse;
due catelonie bianche;
una cadrega armata di trippa;
una copertina.
Nel camerino s.ª il portico:
un moschetto di rassa meschia con le franze di seta;
matarazzi n.° due di lana che pesa libre 40 grosse;
|[6v] una catelonia bianca bona;
una copertina di dobletto rigada;
un sforzero peloso meschio;
un tavolino piccolo di noce.
Nella camera da servitori:
duoi matarazzi di lana de' peso de libre 36 grosse;
una catelonia rossa et una bianca;
una lettéra di noce con il moschetto di dobletto di color morello et bianco;
un letto di penna con piumazzo de' peso de libre 36 grosse;
un paiarizzo;
due altre catelonie;
un tavolino di noce;
duoi archibucchij, un da foco et l'altro da rota;
un matarazzo frusto et una catelonia.
In dispensa:
un matarazzo de' peso de' libre 20 grosse, una lechietta et un cossino |[7r] da cunna;
due cunne di noce;
cossinini di piuma n.° tre;
cossini di lana n.° due;
un piumino per la cunna;
un piumino da letto prepontato;
un alto piumino non prepontato;
un pelotto vechio frusto;
duoi piumazzi coperti di tarliso di Fiandra;

un altro piumazzo di piuma;
un buratono di pechia;
catelonie di lana bianche n.° sette bone;
un tapeto avelutato grande;
un moschetto quadro di stamazzo cremisole con le sue franze di seta;
cossini di piuma n.° quindeci;
|[7v] una panera;
un tavolotto quadro di pieda nera con il contorno dipinto;
selle da cavallo usate n.° quatro;
una lettéra di noce;
un letto di piuma con suo piumazzo de' peso de libre 36 grosse;
un matarazzo di lana de' peso de libre 20 grosse;
una catelonia bianca;
una copertina de filo bianca et turchina;
scagni di noce n.° tre;
una cadrega armata rotta;
un servetial di peltro;
duodeci figure d'alabastro;
lavezzi tra grandi et picoli novi n.° quindeci.
In canepa:
|[8r] vaselli inchierciati di ferro n.° deciotto di tenuta de brente n.° cento otto;
una pidria;
una scala et un mastello;
brente n.° 14 vino vechio;
un salator di carne;
duoi segini grandi di lavar panni;
duoi altri picoli con le sue asse.
Sotto il portico:
due carozze, una quasi nova et un'altra frusta et un caretono da viaggio et carello.
In stalla:
tre cavalli di carozza di valuta de scuti n.° cento vinti cinque;
un muletto de' valore de scuti vinti cinque;
caponere n.° due;
selle per li cavalli con li suoi fornimenti |[8v] di carozza.
Argenti usati:
un cadino d'argento con suo bocale pesano onze n.° 78¼;
una bacila d'argento d'onze n.° 61½;
due tazze d'argento con li suoi piedi pesano onze n.° 54½;
una tazza d'argento indorata d'onze 24½;
due sotto coppe d'onze 24½;
quatro candelieri con la sua moschirola d'argento d'onze n.° 75;
duoi salini d'argento d'onze 23;
un salino indorato picolo d'onze n.° 4¼;
un bichiero grande d'argento indorato d'onze 16½;
cuchiali d'argento n.° 20;
forcine d'argento n.° 18.
|[9r] *Ori, zoie, et altre cose che restano presso la sig.ra Isabella, madre de' minori:*
duoi fili di bandina smaltati di bianco et nero d'onze n.° 6.6;
un orolugio con due granate et 24 diamantini e colanetta d'oro, in tutto onze n.° quatro;
un par de pendenti con sei diamantini et sei perle;
un para de brazadelli d'oro d'onze 2¼;
un para de brazadelli con diamantini n.° 7 d'onze n.° 1¾;
una crosetta d'oro con diamantini 17 et una perla; gli diamanti vagliono scudi tre l'uno et uno la perla;
un diamante in anello quadro con fondo |[9v] de circa grani sette, con il quale fu sposata la d.a Sig.ra Isabella;
un diamante et un anello de c.a grani n.° 3;
un diamante a facetto in anello de grani n.° 3 in c.a;
un anello a core entrovi diamanti tredeci et una foglia in mezzo de' prezzo de circa scudi vinti;
un anello a rosetta entrovi sette diam.ti per prezzo de scuti 18 in c.a;
un'altra rosetta entrovi nove diamanti de' valuta de scuti 12;
le su.te zoie restano presso d.a Sig.ra Isabella;
un diamante in annello a facetto in punta de grani otto in c.a;
una colanetta d'oro con un stecadenti d'onze |[10r] quatro.
Veste della sig.ra Isabella:
una veste di damasco de duoi colori verde et tanè c on lavori di seta;
una veste di fondo raso di color beretino et morello con lavori d'oro;
una sottana d'ormesimo solio cangiante con lavori di seta;
veste et sottana d'ormesino nero a opera con lavori di seta;
una veste d'ormesino beretino a opera con il suo gipone et sua sottana guarniti di seta;
una veste et sottana d'ormesino solio stratagliato;
|[10v] una veste et sottana et gipone di saglia di renso con guarnitioni nere quasi nove con sua sottana;
manti n.° 3 di donna colorati.

2. Inventario Vittuone 1627

|[1r] **Inventario de' mobili lasciati dal q. Gio. Pietro Annono nella casa da nobile situata nel loco di Vituone, pieve di Corbetta, Duc.to di Milano**

P.a un casamento di nobile con molti lochi, un giardino grande et un picolo.
Nella sala grande nova vi sono:
boffette di noce nove n.° tre;
cadreghe di corame bone n.° sei;
scagni di corame boni n.° quatro;
un trepiede di legno per le sidelle.
Nella camera avanti a detta sala:
una lettéra indorata nova.
In un'altra camera acanto ad essa:
una bofetta di noce bona;
item un scrittorio di noce;
una cadrega di corame frusta.
In un'altra camera acanto a d.a sala:
una lettéra indorata nova;
|[1v] una bofetta frusta;
doi matarazzi di lana coperti di tarliso novi di peso de libre quaranta grosse in c.a con suo paiazzo;
un piumazzo di piuma;
una cadrega di camera quasi nova.
In saletta:
una bofetta di noce et un scagno di corame quasi novo;
duoi brandenali frusti di ferro con li pomi di lotono con il suo ferro di foco.
Sotto il portico:
otto piante di naranzi grande.
Nel dispensino:
vaselli incierciato di ferro n.° quatro di tenuta di brente n.° venti quatro;
una panera, una marna;
un sigino de pagni di tenuta di mezza brenta.
Nella cusina:
duoi brandenali di ferro con suo fornimento de foco;
doi vaseletti d'aceto di tenuta d'una brenta tra tutti duoi;
una tavola di pecchia frusta;
un menarosto frusto;
|[2r] doi brandenali di ferro et suo ferro de foco rotto;
una graticella di ferro;
un scaldaletto di ramo frusto;
un tapeto di ferro;
un testo di azale;
una gratrola;
spedi di rosto, un grande et un picolo;
un armario di pechia frusto;
una padella di torta con suo coperto di ramo; sedelle di ramo due, una grande et una picola; un cribietto di ramo; duoi caldari di ramo con suoi coperti; una cazza di ramo; una caldirola di ramo; un paiolo di ramo et una padella di arame di peso ogni cosa de libre 45 grosse, et un vaso;
due caldaie da lavar li pagni che sono libre 40 grosse;
una lecarda d'azale;
un caldarino di far amido picolo;
una padeletta d'azale;
una cazirola d'azale;
lume n.° tre;
candelieri di lottone n.° quatro;
|[2v] una cardenza di noce frusta;
una peltrera frusta;
capi di peltro n.° deciotto de' peso de libre 15 grosse;
una banchetta di pobbia frusta et una scabella frusta.
In una camera acanto la cucina:
una bofetta di noce grande quasi nova;
due cardenze di noce usate et un cardenzino;
cadreghe di corame rotte n.° quatro;
un scagno di corame frusto;
un sbaraglino.
In un altro camerino annesso:
una lettéra di noce con sue colone picole;
duoi matarazzi di lana quasi novi di peso de lire quaranta in c.a et un paiazzo;
una cassa di pecchia dipinta frusta;
un tavolino di noce frusto.
In un altro camerino:
una lettéra picola con sue colonette di noce;
doi matarazzi et il loro piumazzo di lana di peso de lire quaranta in c.a et |[3r] una copertina ogiolata argentino et bianca;
un piumazzo di piuma quasi novo;
un paiarizzo;
una bofetta di noce;
un vaso di rame grande di tenuta di sei sechie di peso de lire . . . grosse;
una cadrega di legno.
In sala vechia:
una tavola di noce frusta;
un homo di ferarolo.
Nel solaro:
formento moggia n.° sesantacinque;
segla moggia n.° trenta;
avena somme n.° sette.
Nella camera grande di s.a:
un vestero di larice dipinto bello;
una lettéra di noce con sue colonette picole;
un matarazzo con suo piumazzo di lana di pelo de lire quindeci;

un piumazzo di piuma;
un paiarizzo;
una bofetta;
|[3v] una bofetta di noce;
una cadrega di corame frusta;
noce di rubbo stara n.° ducento.
Nella camera dove dorme la sig.ra:
una lettéra di noce con sue colonne grosse et suo paiarizzo;
matarazzi n.° tre quasi novi con un piumazzo di lana di peso de lire sesanta in tutto grosse;
un letto di piuma di peso de lire venti grosse;
due casse dipinte grande di pechia;
coperte di lana bianca n.° tre bone;
una coperta di lana rossa;
una oggiolata argentina;
una bofetta di noce grande bona et un tavolino picolo;
cossini di piuma con sue fodrette n.° cinque;
un'altra coperta di lana bianca;
un'altra lettéra con sue colonette picole;
un moschetto de filo rosso in color d'oro et bianco quasi novo.
In un'altra camera:
|[4r] un matarazzo di lana con suo piumazzo de' peso de lire vinti grosse;
una catelonia bianca quasi nova;
un par de lenzoli usati;
una cassa de noce bona;
una casa di pobbia di governare lane nova;
una cotta di pezza frusta;
una cunna di noce;
un piumazzo di lana;
una staderina di pesar seda.
In un'altra camera:
una lettéra indorata con suo paiarezzo;
un letto di piuma di peso de lire venti grosse con suo piumazzo;
un matarazzo di lana di peso de libre deciotto grosse;
catelonie n.° due bianche di lana;
un par de lenzoli;
due bofette;
formentono moggia n.° due;
miglio moggia n.° tre.
|[4v] *In un altro camerino:*
una lettéra indorata con sue colonne quasi nove et un paiarezzo;
una bofetta di noce.
In un altro camerino:
una lettéra di noce con sue colonne;
un tavolino di noce frusto;
una cadrega di corame frusta;
una bofetta di noce.
Nel torchio voi sono:
tine n.° diecesette inchierchiate di ferro sotto sopra di tenuta de brenta n.° vinti;
carere inchierchiate di ferro n.° quatro, cioè due grande et due picole, di tenuta de brente n.° trenta;
navazze per l'uva n.° tre;
un carello frusto.
Nella canevetta del vino bianco vi sono:
vaselli inchiercati di ferro n.° cinque di tenuta di |[5r] brente n.° quarantacinque;
un altro vasello di tenuta di brente n.° sette con duoi cerchij de ferro coli altri di legno;
duoi tignozi da pagni di tenuta de brente sei in c.ª;
tre scolapertiche.
In camera grande:
vaselli inchierciati di ferro n.° diecesette di tenuta de brente trecento in circa;
una scaletta per vaselli;
vino tra bianco et rosso brente n.° trecento settanta.

3. Inventario Milano 1680

|[1r] **Notta della mobilia, danari et altro ritrovati nella casa d'habitat.ne del fu d.° Sig.r Stephano Carena sit. in P.T. P.S. Euffemia di Mil.no**

Nel p.mo luogo nell'entrare in mano dritta nella porta della sod.ª casa:
n.° duoi quadri grandi, s.ª uno de' quali è dipinta la flagellat.ne di Nostro Sig.re, con cornice di noce nera, et l'altro dove sta di dipinto esso Sig.re Nostro con altre due figure, con cornice nera con un frisetto d'oro attorno;
una cassa di noce votta;
un paio de stivali di bulgaro;
una sella con suoi fornimenti per cavallo;
una gelosia grande, duoi cavaletti di pecchia;
due baste con suo ferro;
un tavolino ordinario.
Nel luogo superiore al sod.°:
una lettéra senza colone et testera, con matarazzo, piumazzo di lana, et paiazzo;
un tavolino di noce;
un archibuggio d'azalino di misura.
Sotto al portico:
banche n.° 3 di noce con sue spallere;
n.° 3 paesi sopra la carta;
|[1v] un'altra sella per cavallo con sua fornitura;
diverse asse di pecchia et diversi travetti di pecchia;
legna per abbrucciare, cioè schiene dolci, cara n.° quatro in c.ª;
due sassi, cioè scalini di marmo da porsi in opera;
due scalle a mano, una grande et l'altra piciola.
Nella stalla:
caponere n.° due;
un cavallo di pello morello grosso d'anni sei in circa;
un basto con coperta di vacchetta, et altri suoi fornimenti;
item tutti li suoi utensilij per servitio della stalla.
Nella cuccina:
un tavolino di noce mezzano;
altro tavolino di noce frusto;
una credenza di noce frusta con suoi scallini;
un vestaio di pecchia;
una mena rosto di ferro con sua cassa;
duoi brandanalli con cappia di ferro, bernazo, moglia, et guarda fuoco;
due cattenne;
duoi scaldini di ferro et due trepiedi di ferro;
un boffetto di noce;
|[2r] un vasselleto per accetto di tenuta d'una brenta in circa;
un trepiedi di legno per sidella;
cazze et ramponera di ferro;
un rastello di noce con suoi birolli;
una mesera;
lavezzi n.° 2 grami;
n.° 3 pallette di ferro con un cazuletto et graticola di ferro;
un mortaro di sasso;
diversi piatti di peltro, grandi et piccioli, pesano lire grosse d'once 28 novanta sei, dico libbre 96;
rame per servitio di cuccina di diverse sorti, cioè sidelle, caldari, lavamano, padelle, lecarde, coperti et altro di peso in tutto lire grosse come s.ª sessanta nove, dico libbre grosse n.° 69;
n.° cinque mantilli et una tovaglia per uso quotidiano de' padroni;
n.° 3 mantilli con una tovaglia per servitio della servitù, con duoi sugamani et una servietta;
diversi utensilij et vasi di vetro per servitio della tavola;
|[2v] n.° quatro scabelle di noce senza appoggio;
coltelli per servitio di cuccina n.° 6, et cucchiali per servitio della servitù n.° sei;
candiglieri d'ottone n.° sei di peso di lire grosse n.° sei da onze venti otto per lira;
una falce, un cribbio con altri utensilij di cuccina.
Nel dispensino vicino alla cuccina:
olle di terra grandi n.° otto, sei de' quali sono piene d'oglio grasso et buttiro respet.e;
diversa altra robba sopra due asse in d.° dispensino per servitio di d.ª cuccina.
Nella canepa sotto 'l portico all'ingresso della cuccina:
moggia n.° 18 in c.ª carbone;
legna, cioè fassine et schiochi, per il consumo del presente inverno per servitio della casa.
Nella saletta vicino alla cuccina:
una tavola di noce, giunta da due parti, con suo tapetto sopra;
altro tavolino di noce;
n.° 3 scagni et una cadregha di bulgaro |[3r] frusti;
un specchio con cornice nera in otto angoli;
quadri n.° sei paiesetti, senza cornice, ordinarij;
un quadro di S. Pietro, picciolo, con cornice nera ordinaria;
altro di S. Gerolamo, più grande, con cornice ordinaria;
altro quadretto con una figura d'un putto che tiene in mani un gallo con altre due animali;
due brandenali piccioli, con guarda fuoco, et suoi ferri per servitio del fuoco, tutti con suoi ornamenti di ottone;
un vestaro mezano di noce per servitio di ripor la robba delle figliuole minori.
Nel dispensinetto di d.ª saletta:
due mastelli piccioli per riporre le robbe commestive con diverse altre robbe di maiolica et vetro;
una portiera di pano turchino sopra la porta di detta saletta che responde in corte.
Nel dispensino s.ª d.ª saletta:
mezene n.° 3 di lardo, una marna, alcuni pezzi di carne salatta, et diverse asse, et altri utensilij per dispensa.
Nella salla grande di rimpetto alla porta:
cadreghe n.° sei et scagni n.° sei di bulgaro usati con chioderia tonda di ottone;
|[3v] n.° sei quadri grandi de' deserti, o siano heremi, s.ª uno de' quali è dipinto S. Antioco a cavallo con suo padre compagno, l'altro S. Giosaffatto in ginochione, altro un eremitto in estasi in una cappana, altro S. Idaco, et altro S.to Patroclo, et altro con altro s.to eremitto sedente con le mani giunte, tutti d'una med.ª grandeza et fattura, con cornici nere et frisetto bianco uguali;
un altro quadro con s.ª la favola d'Orfeo nella selva sonando, con cornice nera e frisetto bianco;
un altro quadro della med.ª grandezza dove vi è dipinto

il rapto di Proserpina, con cornice come s.ª;
un ritratto di mezza figura in grande del fu Sig.r Giacomo Antonio Carena;
altro quadro grande, senza cornice, s.ª il camino rapresentante una notte con diverse figure in diversi atti;
|[4r] paesini n.º quatro, bisquadri, con cornice nera ordinaria;
un quadro grande di S. Sabastiano in piedi con l'angelo che li leva le frezze, con cornice nera et frisetto bianco intagliato;
altro quadro di S.to Giuseppe con in braccio Nostro Sig.re di meza figura, con cornice nera et frisetto intagliato bianco;
tre specchij, uno grande, altro mezano et altro picciolo, con cornici nere;
n.º quatro tavole mezane di noce con suoi tappeti frusti di corame;
due boffettine di noce;
un utensilio per riporre li ferraioli, d.º «l'huomo»;
due brandinali grandi con pomi grossi d'ottone con tutti li suoi fornimenti per servitio del cammino della sala, guarniti del med.º;
una picca;
sopra uno de' tavolini descritti in detta sala vi sono n.º quatro pezzi di tappezzaria grandi di Fiandra con altri quatro pezzi piccioli di Fiandra frusti, coperti tutti con un tapetto fatto a fiori verde et nero frusto;
diversi ferraioli per huomo, duoi di baracano, |[4v] due di panno, et un balandrano, non compresi li vestimenti d'uso quotidiano per li minori.
Nel studio in testa entrando per d.ª salla:
pezzi n.º sei quadri mezani con vasi de fiori, con cornice nera et frisetto intagliato bianco, tutti d'una med.ª grandezza;
un ritratto del fu Sig.r Bartholomeo Carena, in meza figura, senza cornice;
due altri quadri paesi, mezani, con cornice nera et frisetto bianco intagliato, uguali;
un quadretto picciolo con una Madona che ha il bambino in braccio, con cornice al antica nera et duoi frisetti d'oro;
due altri quadretti, in ottangolo, de' frutti, con cornice nera;
altro quadro, senza cornice, con la figura di Baccho prostratta;
altro quadro con dipinta una sporta con d'entro di fusi, un'anitra, et peri, senza cornice;
un quadro d'una tigre legata alla cattena, che copre la bocca del camino;
|[5r] n.º tre tavolini di noce, uno de' quali è coperto d'un tappetto di corame frusto;
una cassetta di cipresso con d'entro diversi rottami per uso di casa;
un moggio di riso in un sacco;
altri n.º 3 sacchi votti;
mezza groppa di corame per solar le scarpe;
antiporti n.º 3, uno di noce, et altri duoi di pecchia frusti;
due pistole d'azalino di misura con sue fonde;
un vestaro di pecchia con d'entro due capelli; item n.º 10 processi de litti legati in due mazzi; item altro processo per la litte seguita s.ª la pezza di lago nel Comm.e d'Annone, dove si dice «la foppa rossa»; item un sacchetto d'altre scritture concernenti l'acquisto della possessione di Ronchetto fuori di P.T.; item un altro mazzo di scritture concernente la litte contra Anna Maria Campagnana; item altro processo concernente la litte contra Carlo Francesco Invernici;
item altro mazzo di scritture |[5v] concernente l'investitura della sod.ª possessione di Ronchetto; item altro mazzo di scritture di diversi confessi di spese et legati pagati, lasciati dal q.m Sig.r Gio. Angelo Carenna; item altro mazzo di scritture di cride et cedole concernenti l'interesse del datio del pane venale sopra diverse terre della Pieve d'Uggione; item altro mazzo di diversi instromenti di diversi acquisti; item altro mazzo d'instromenti, et scritture concernenti d.ª possessione di Ronchetto; item altro mazzo di scritture concernenti l'acquisto della possessione del Boscaccio et per li uttenti della roggia Cazanella che serve per adaquare d.ª possessione; item un libro in stampa intitolato *Relatione del Naviglio grande di Milano*; item un libro in ottavo manuscritto intitolato «Libro mastro di me |[6r] Gio. Angelo Carena seg.to B»; item altro libro in ottavo intitolato «Libro signato B di me Stephano Carena»; item altro «Libro» in ottavo longo che incomincia «1667 Cassa deve dare» et finisce a' fog. 13 «21 detto scosso da Carlo Pagano per frutto s.ª lire due milla, spirato per un anno a' 19 giugno 1680, a lire 4 soldi 10 per cento, lire 90», scritto tutto di mano del fu Sig.r Stephano Carena; item altro libro mastro signato «C» in ottavo attinente a Bartholomeo et Stephano Carena per mettà e commincia a' fog. n.º 1 «1661 sette torti e fillatti» e finisce a' foglio 24 «detto per sodetto Perlascha 21 lire 2.746.18»; item altro libro legato in foglie stese, dove sono diverse carte di diversi paesi e diverse città et mapamondi; item diversi altri libri da legere sopra il d.º vestaro |[6v] due mazzi di scritture di diversi confessi antichi, due bilanciette d'ottone senza pesi, n.º 3 spade;
sopra il tavolino sotto la finestra di d.º studio: un mazzo legato, cioè filza de' confessi concernenti la possessione del Boscaccio et di Ronchetto; item altro mazzo di scritture nel quale vi è un libretto dove sono notate dare et havere del fittabile della possess.ne de' Ronchetto con l'instrom.º del invest.ª fatta a Carlo Polito, fittabile d'essa possessione; item altro libretto intitolato «Libro della Possess.e del Roscaccio fuori di Porta Tic.e», dove è annotato il dare et havere del fittabile di detta possessione con l'instrum.º del investit.ª fatta a Carlo Ferrario, fittabile di d.ª possessione, con altri ricapiti concernenti a d.e possessioni; |[7r] item altri diversi instromenti attinenti all'acquisto della possess.e di Casoretto, fatto dal Sig.r Francesco Perlasca, con in specie l'istrom.to et sentenza graduatoria del credito che hanno il Sig.r Perlasca contra l'heredità Bellingera et l'istrom.º del credito che haveva il medemo contra Lorenzo Missaglia, ceduto al fu d.º S.r Stephano Carena a conto de' suoi crediti; item altro mazzo di scritture nel quale sono diversi pagamenti fatti a Dona Paula Fra.ca Gallindez monacha in S. Vincenzo novo Mil.º; item un libro intitolato «Libro de' diverse notte e memorie di me Stephano Carena del 1664»; item altro libro intitolato «Il perticato della Communità di Bonirola, pieve di Rosate»; item altro libro intitolato «1663 copia di lett.e», una casettina con suoi bilancini e pesi per pesar oro, et altro simile per pesar argenti; |[7v] altro scartapazzo dove sono diverse notte d'interessi di d.º Sig.r Stephano per la casa sig.º «n.º A»;
un cassone grande di noce frusto, entro del quale vi si è trovato libbre dieci once 6 setta sgreggia; item una pezza di copertine di roccadino et stoppa fatta a foggia di damasco rossa e gialla, et un feraiolo nero di scotto;
in detto cassone vi si sono trovatti: sacchetti n.º cinque di mille filippi d'argento per cadun sacchetto, che sono filippi n.º cinque milla;
item altro sacchetto con d'entro altri filippi n.º nove cento tre d'argento;
item n.º 28 scartozzi di parpaiole di lire cento per cadauno, che dano lire due milla otto cento imperiali;
item doble d'oro d'Italia, innoltre in diverse charte num.º nove cento ottantatre |[8r] parte di peso et parte correnti;
item vi si sono trovati in diverse carte involti ongari d'oro num.º sette cento sessanta uno, parte di peso et parte correnti;
item un altro cassone più picciolo, nel quale vi si sono trovati come siegue:
un mazzetto di confessi de' danari pagati al Sig.r dottor Antonio Maria Carboni;
item un mazzo di scritture dove sono diverse polize e confessi signato «B»;
altri due mazzi de scritture come s.ª signati «C» «D»;
diversi mazzi di lettere et notte di diverse spese;
un altro mazzo di scritture intitolato «In causa querelle coram eg.º D. Iudice Galli Mediolani», con altri più mazzetti di lettere;
item altro mazzo di scritture intitolato |[8v] «obligatione et ricognit.ne» fatta da Aurelio Carenna per alcuni beni sottoposti alla messa, che si va celebrando nella terra d'Annone fondata da un tal . . . Carenna sign.º «E»;
item un mazzetto di polize di cambio già pagate;
un altro mazzo dove sono diverse notte e memoriali datti al Magistratto rispetto al perticato rurale del Boscaccio;
contanti in d.º cassone come siegue:
sacchetti num.º due de filippi d'argento, cioè uno de filippi n.º ottocento cinquanta sette et l'altro di seicento ottanta sette con una charta nella quale vi sono involti altri filippi n.º venti et in un'altra carta vi sono involti filippi n.º trenta che in tutto fano filippi n.º |[9r] mille cinque cento novanta quatro;
item un sacchetto di quarti di Modona con d'entro n.º sette cento ottanta de sud. quarti;
item involti in più charte di monetta papalle, cioè giulij et pauli, n.º cinque cento venti;
item involti in un charta ducatoni di Milano n.º venti e mezo;
item involti in n.º venti due scartozzi parpaiole in somma de lire cento per ciascun scartozzo, che fanno lire due mille ducento;
item altro sacchetto d'altre parpaiole della somma di lire cento cinquanta imperiali;
item quatro soldi intieri involti in una charta n.º settanta quatro;
item in danari spezzi, involti in una carta, lire quant'una imperiali;
|[9v] item un sacchetto di genovine et diverse carte di genovine entro d.º sacchetto al numero de trecento venti due in tutto;
item un cassettino con d'entro una medaglia d'oro con l'effigie di Sisto quinto, altra di argento grande con l'effigie d'Innocentio X, un annello d'oro con pietra bianca, et un dobelone da quatro d'Italia;
item un altro cassone piccolo a mano dritta nel entrare della porta di d.º studio, nel quale vi si sono trovati come siegue, cioè:

cucchiali et forcine n.o 38 d'argento fino, n.o tre sottocoppe, una fruttera et un tondo, tre salini – uno de' quali è con sua pigna – et una peverina; quatro candeglieri compagni lavorati et due altri piccioli ordinarij con una mocchetta, tutti d'argento fino, et pesano tutti lirette venti et onze sei, dico libbre 20 once 6;

un collo di perle picciole di quatro fili pesano dinari sedeci;

altri due filli di perle picciole, pesano dinari tredeci;

una catenella d'oro di peso d'una onza;

duoi anelli d'oro, uno con gemma verde et l'altro rossa;

un orologgio con coperta d'ottone sopradorata;

mazzo di scritture che sono li instrumenti di vendita fatta da Sig.ri Federico et fratelli Carena a' SS. Bartholomeo et Stephano Carena di due case nella contrada di S. Euffemia in Porta Rom.a con le scritture concernenti al aquisto di d.e case, qual mazzo è intitolato di mano propria d'esso fu Sig.r Stephano Carena;

altro mazzo di diversi instromenti de' beni che si godono nel Commune d'Annone, liberi, intitolati di mano propria di d.o |[10r] fu Sig.r Stephano;

altro mazzo d'instromenti concernenti 'l credito de lire vent'una milla che deve il Sig.r Francesco Bicinetti assicurati sopra l'hostaria del Agnello in Porta Orientale, et della Croce Rossa in Porta Nova con annessi li ins.ti et recapiti per sicurezza di d.o credito;

altro mazzo d'instromenti concernenti l'acquisto della possessione di Molteno fatta l'anno 1662 dalla Regia Cam.a, intitolato di mano come sopra;

altro mazzo d'instromenti et altre scritture concernenti l'acquisto de' beni della villa di Vergano, pieve d'Uggione, notati di mano come s.a;

item altro mazzo d'instrom.ti et scritture concernenti l'aquisto del datio del pane venale comprato dal Magistratto per |[10v] le terre d'Uggione, Annone, Girone, Brongio et Molteno, intitolato di mano del fu Sig.r Bartholomeo Carena;

item altro mazzo d'instromenti et scritture concernenti al aquisto della presente casa comprata da Gio Batta Crespi, intitolati di mano del d.o fu Sig.r Bartholomeo Carena;

item altro instromento in stampa della liberatione dall'infeudatione per le terre delle Pievi d'Uggione et Garlatte;

item altro mazzo di scritture con diversi mazzetti involti con sopra un bollettino di mano propria del d.o fu S.r Stephano Carena che dice diversi instromenti et scritture appartenenti alli beni della |[11r] cassina, casa di Bagnolo, Molinatto et Rossa, ne' quali vi è anco un istrom.to de lire sette cento imperiali che resta debitrice la Comm.tà d'Imberido di soventione fattagli in magior somma;

item un volume d'instromenti num.o sedeci concernenti diversi crediti da squodersi contra diversi particolari et si pongano li infrascritti libri ne'quali sono notati d.i crediti per estenso;

item un altro mazzo d'instromenti al num.o di quaranta involti in una charta concernenti dive[r]si crediti da squodere et aquisti de' beni, come si descrivaranno più amplamente;

un altro mazzetto di scritture intitolato «Diverse scritture et gride concernenti alli beni aquistati da Ambrosio et parte Franceso fratelli de Tintori nel luogo di |[11v] Vergano», di mano propria d'esso Sig.r Stephano;

item un mazzo di diversi confessi di pagam.ti di tasse involti et legati in una charta et intitolati di mano propria d'esso S.r Stephano;

item un libro in quarto di charta pecora intitolato «Libro sig.to "A" di me Stephano Carena in Anversa»;

item altro mazzetto di scritture che si dice «Notta di diverse spese pagate per legati lasciati dal q.m Bartholomeo Carena mio fratello, morto il 6 febraio 1670» di mano d'esso fu Sig.r Stephano Carena;

item un mazzo di scritture, involte in una charta, che si è trovato esser num.o undeci chartelle del Banco di S.to Ambrosio della somma in tutto di lire novanta |[12r] nove mille e cinquanta e sono del tenor come siegue:

una di lire dieci milla in testa, de Stanco de Stanchi, pagabile anco a chi presenterà;

altra di lire nove mille ducento cinquanta, in testa di Giulio de Giulij, pagabile a qualsivoglia presentatore, a tergo della quale si vede esser state paghate lier mille sotto il 28 febraro 1673;

altra di lire quatro milla, in testa di Giacinta Tettamanzi, pagabile a qualsivoglia presentatore;

altra di lire otto mille nove cento, in testa della Capella di Nostra Sig.ra del Santiss.o Rosario, erretta nella chiesa parrochiale di S. Maria del luogo d'Annone, da pagarsi al cappellano che sarà elletto per tempi alla celebrat.ne della messa in d.a cappella, et d.a chartella |[12v] veniva posta dal d.o Sig.r Stephano come procuratore del R.do Prete Antonio Farina, cappellano titolare di d.a cappella;

altra di lire quarant'una mille cento, in testa del Sig.r Stephano Carena, sotto 'l dì 12 maggio 1670, che alias era in testa del Sig.r Bartholomeo Carena suo fratello;

altra chartella di lire due mille ottocento, in testa dello sod.o Sig.r Stephano Carena, che altre volte era in testa del Sig.r Gio. Angelo Carena suo fratello, datta alli 12 maggio 1670;

altra chartella di lire cinque mille cinque cento, in testa di Gio. Paolo Carena, nella quale si vede a tergo esser state riscosse lire cinque cento |[13r] l'anno 1655 14 ottobre, et di questa chartella se ne squode il frutto in virtù della procura fatta dal d.o Sig.r Gio. Paolo Carena a favore di Barth.o e Stephano Carena;

altra chartella di lire quatro mille, in testa di Giacintho Tettamanzo, pagabile a qualsiasi presentatore, del dì 9 genaro 1674, simile alla prima, in testa dello sod.o, che è di d.a somma;

altra chartella di lire sei milla, in testa di Josuè de Melchisedech q.m Abrhamo, con la conditione di pagarla a qualsivoglia presentatore;

altra di lire sei mille, in testa d'Isac d'Abram q.m Moisè, con la conditione al presentatore;

altra di lire sei milla, in testa di Mauritio |[13v] Scotto, pagabile a qualsivoglia presentatore, a tergo della quale si vede essere statte scosse a conto lire tre milla in tre partite;

item altro mazzo di scritture, nel quale si ritrovano li infrascritti ricapiti:

una fede del ragionato g[e]n.le Zucchelli in datta 17 sette[m]bre 1670, quale attesta che à libri di sua cura, e particolarmente à queli de' soventori de' cambij, tra li altri vi si trova il Sig.r Stephano Carena per creditore di lire trent'octo mille cento sessanta quatro soldi 3 denari 3 monetta di cambio, che prima si trovavano in testa del fu S.r Bartholomeo Carena suo fratello;

altra fede di Carlo Francesco Arrigone, rag.to g[e]n.le dell'imprese camerali |[14r] della Città di Milano in datta di 9 agosto 1658, con la quale attesta che li Sig.ri Bartholomeo e Stephano fratelli Careni vanno creditori in conto di capitale di lire venti due milla per un reddito di lire cinque cento quaranta annue s.a l'impresa della dogana;

altra fede simile fatta dal d.o Carlo Francesco Arrigone, partimenti sotto li 9 agosto 1658, nella quale appare che li Sig.ri Bartholomeo e Stephano fratelli Carena vanno creditori in conto di capitale de lire dieci milla, prezzo d'un annuo reddito de lire cinque cento assentato sopra l'impresa de' pristini;

|[14v] altra fede del medemo Sig.r Arrigone, in datta di 17 settembre 1664, nella quale appare che il Sig.r Bartholomeo e Stephano fratelli Carena sono creditori in conto di capitale di lire sette milla cinque cento assentato sopra l'impresa della dogana;

altra fede del med.o Arrigone, in datta 25 febraro 1671, nella quale appare che il Sig.r Stephano Carena è creditore di lire due milla quatrocento dieci soldi 12 denari 5 conto di capitale per annuo reddito de lire cento venti soldi 10 denari 6, in rag.ne del cinque per cento, assentato sopra l'impresa del sappone;

item altra fede del med.o Arigone, delli 21 giugno 1667, nella quale appare |[15r] che il Sig.r Bartholomeo e Stephano Carena sono creditori in conto capitale di lire sei mille, prezzo d'un annuo reddito de lire quatrocento venti, assentati sopra l'impesa del oglio e sapone;

altra fede, di 13 febraro 1669, fatta dal med.o Arrigone, nella quale appare che il Sig.r fu Stephano Carena v'è creditore in conto di capitale de lire otto mille seicento venticinque, prezzo d'un annuo reddito de lire cinque cento dieci sette e meza, assentato s.a il datio del bollino;

un pateat attestato dal S.r Giuseppe Annone, not.o et segretario della Città di Milano, nello quale appare esser statto |[15v] constituito et venduto un annuo reddito di lire trenta a favore del Sig.r Bartholomeo Carena per capitale di lire seicento sopra il Monte di S. Carlo;

item altra fede del d.o Sig.r Carlo Fran.co Arrigone, con la quale si vede che 'l Sig.r Stephano Carena va creditore in conto di capitale de lire sei mille cinque cento settanta quatro per un annuo reddito di lire trecento vent'otto in ragione del cinque per cento, assentato sopra la cava del sale di Varese, qual fede è sotto li 14 aprile 1677;

altra fede del med.o in datta delli 3 agosto 1678, con la quale si vede che 'l Sig.r Stephano Carena è creditore in conto di capitale de lire venti tre mille |[16r] cento settant'otto, prezzo d'un annuo reddito di lire mille cento cinquanta otto soldi 18, in ragione del cinque per cento, assentato s.a l'augumento del sale;

delle quali due chartuline che si sono contratate col Sig.r March.e Federico de Franchi, al quale se gli è fatto un riguardo che pagando fra determinato tempo il capitale in rag.ne del convenuto per publici instromenti rog.ti da me not.o infrascritto se gli habbia a fare la retrovendita delli sopra detti due effetti che dispongono le sod.e due cartuline;

una poliza di lire mille cento quaranta sette soldi 2 d'Antonio Langlois verso Carlo Ferrario o chi la presentarà, la quale è pervenuta in mano del d.o fu Sig.r Stephano Carena, quale si vede a tergo d'una poliza |[16v] haver scosso lire quattrocento trenta tre e meza, come si vede a tergo della d.a poliza di mano

propria d'esso Sr Stephano;
altra poliza di lire 100 contra Pietro Brambilla;
contanti ritrovati in d.[o] cassone:
philippi num.[o] cinque cento, di cui nove involti in diverse charte et sacchetti;
item un altro sacchetto de filippi n.[o] cento settanta;
item doppie di Spagna, fra di peso et correnti, num.[o] trecento cinquanta tre, involte in diverse charte;
item ongari n.[o] trecento undeci, parte di peso et parte correnti, involti in diverse carte;
item un sacchetto di genovine n.[o] cento otto;
item, involti in una carta, ducatoni di Milano n.[o] otto;
item reali di soldi 10 denari 6 l'uno n.[o] quaranta, involti in carta;
item scudini n.[o] dieci di Francia, involti in una charta;
item doppie d'Italia, parte di peso et parte correnti, involte in diverse charte in |[17[r]] un sacchetto, num.[o] ducento cinquanta quatro;
item lire ducento cinquanta imperiali in diverse monette spezze.

Salendo le scalle a mano dritta di d.[a] casa vi è una saletta nella quale vi sono come siegue, cioè:

cadreghe di bulgaro n.[o] quatro con chioderia d'ottone tonda doppia al antica;
item n.[o] quatro quadri de' paesi venuti da Fiandra, pinti a guazzo, con diverse figurine, con cornici nere et frisetto bianco intagliato;
altri due paesi più grandi rapresentanti uno un giardino con diverse figure, et altro una grotta con due eremitti, parim.[ti] dipinti a guazzo, con sue cornici solie et nere et frisetto bianco intagliato;
un altro quadro mezano rappresentante un paese con un molino, con sua cornice solia nera et frisetto bianco intagliato;
|[17v] un paio de brendenali piccoli, con suoi pomi d'ottone, con ferro guarda focco;
sopra d.[o] camino vi sono fruttere picciole n.[o] quatro, con cornice nera solia in ottavo;
una tavola di noce quasi nova sopra la quale vi è un quadro di terra, incorniciato di legno nero al antica, rappresentante una Maddalena;
due antiporti di pecchia con sua invetriata.

Nel camerino sopra l'andito della porta vi sono come siegue, cioè:

cadreghe num.[o] due et scagno, uno di bulgaro, usati, con chiodi d'ottone tondi;
item un tavolino di noce con suo tappetto di corame usato;
sopra d.[o] tavolino un quadro con sopra l'effigie di Nostra Sig.[ra] con figliolino in braccio et S.[to] Gioanni Battista a fianco sinestro, con conice nera al antica segnata di fiorami d'oro mordente;
item num.[o] quatro quadri mezani che rapresentano le |[18[r]] le quatro stagioni dell'anno, con cornice nera solia et frisetto intagliato miniato d'oro;
due quadri de' paesi, ordinarij, con cornice nera solia et frisetto intagliato bianco;
un quadro grande con una Maddona con il figliolo in braccio et altre tre figure a fianco dritto et a fianco sinistro et in capo due altre figurine, con cornice solia nera et frisetto bianco intagliato.

Nella camera nova vicina al sud.o camerino vi sono come siegue:

scagni di bulgaro novi n.[o] sei con chioderia d'ottone moderna;
tavole di noce num.[o] due nove;
sopra una di d.[e] tavole vi è un scrittorio di pero con otto casettini con d'entro diverse bagatelle per uso de' figliuoli, et d.[o] scrittorio |[18v] è con guarnitione d'alchimia;
item altro tavolinetto nero;
sopra d.[o] tavolino vi è un coffanino di veluto et altra guarnigione; di più vi è un quadro con l'effigie di S. Gioanni Battista fanciullo, con cornice nera al antica et frisetto dorato mordente;
item due quadri grandi, con cornici nere solie et frisetto bianco intagliato, s.[a] uno de' quali vi è dipinto il giuditio di Paride, et sopra l'altro il rapto d'Europpa da Giove formato in un bue;
item altri due quadri dei paesi mezani con diverse figurine, con cornici nere solie et frisetto bianco intagliato;
item n.[o] dieci quadretti piccioli di frutteria et paesini, con cornice intagliata et indorata;
|[19[r]] item quadro grande di Tobbia con l'angelo che gli addita la gloria del cielo, con quatro altri angioli, con cornice solia nera et frisetto bianco intagliato;
un specchio picciolo in quadro, con cornice tutta dorata.

Nella camera annessa nova vi sono come siegue, cioè:

scagni n.[o] quatro drappo di filisello giallo et cremisile fatti a fiore s.[a] la fatura di damasco con chioderia d'ottone tonda al anticha;
una tavola grande di noce, sopra la quale vi è un tappetto di filisello gialo et cremesile sopra la fattura di damasco come sopra, con una trabbacca di letto piegata con sua coperta del med.[o] drappo del tappetto di s.[a] descritto, fornito |[19v] con franza di setta del med.[o] colore;
un quadro s.[a] d.[a] tavola con l'effiggie del Cardinal Federico Borromeo, con cornice solia nera et frisetto bianco intagliato;
item altro quadro grande con sopra dipinto una Madona che ha il figliolo in bracci dormente con a fianco sinestro S.[to] Giuseppe et la culla del bambino coperta di una veste nera, incorniciato di cornice nera solia con frisetto bianco intagliato;
item un altro quadro con l'effigie di S. Pietro apostolo, di grandezza simile al sod.[o], che sta chino orando, con cornice nera solia et frisetto bianco intagliato;
item un altro quadro di grandezza ordinaria |[20[r]] con sopra l'effiggie di S.[ta] Anna, con in braccio la Maddonna, et S. Elisabetta, con cornice nera solia et frisetto bianco intagliato;
item due paesi mezani con qualche puoche figure, con cornice solia nera et frisetto bianco intagliato;
item un tavolino picciolo nero, sopra quale vi sono doi quadretti piccioli del Sig.[re] et della Madona della parolla, con cornici nere solie et frisetto bianco intagliato;
una letttéra con mezze colone intagliate a scacchi adorati et rossi, con sua testera con duoi leoni et un cimiere in mezzo, rossa et adorata, sopra la quale vi è un matarazzo, et duoi cossinoni, et duoi cossini piccioli di lana novi, con coperta di rasetto celeste, et paiado a rigadone.

|[20v] *Nella altra camera poi annessa alla nova che resta sopra il portico vi sono come siegue, cioè:*

scagni piccoli et una cadrega di bulgaro con chioderia nova doppia d'ottone;
una tavola di noce con sopra un tappetto di corame buono;
sopra detta tavola vi è una Maddonna che allatta il bambino, con cornice nera all'antica et frisetto dorato;
item quadri grandi num.[o] quatro, tutti d'una misura, uno de' quali vi è sopra dipinto S. Agostino, l'altro S.[to] Ambroggio, l'altro S.[to] Gregorio, et l'altro S. Gerolamo, con cornice solia nera et frisetto bianco intagliato;
item un altro quadro mezzano con s.[a] un apostolo, cioè St Tadeo, |[21[r]] con cornice nera solia et frisetto bianco intagliato;
item una tavola di noce nova con sopra una cassetta di pobbia votta;
item altro tavolinetto picciolo con suo cassetto sotto, coperto con un tapetto di corame et di sopra di d.[o] tavolino vi è un coffanino picciolo delle figliuole;
una lettéra di noce con meze colone con un puoco d'intaglio, quale ha sopra matarazzo di lana, letto di piuma, et paiazzo con piumazzo di pena, et una coperta s.[a] di roccadino fatta et lavorata s.[a] la fattura di damasco di colore morello et giallo;
item un quadrettino con sopra un aquasantino d'argento con cornice di pero nera;
item una cadregha di camera di noce;
|[21v] item un sforziero guarnito di tolla indorata usato con d'entro diverse camiscie da huomo.

Nel transito del portico al apartamento retro vi sono come siegue, cioè:

una cassa di pecchia grande, entro della quale vi sono duoi cavezzi di stoppa, cioè uno da far siugamani et l'altro mantilli per la servitù, item quatro lire di stoppa in azza filata;
un baullo usato con sopra una copertina di rocadino verde et giallo a scachi usata;
item una valisia di corame con sua fonitura di ferro;
item un cassone mezano di pecchia frusto con d'entro diverse tattare;
un schioppo di rotta da due cani, et una spada frusta et antica;
|[21[bis r]] item una borsa lavorata grande usata;
item due pertiche cariche di biancheria che si descriverà.

Nel med.[o] coridore stramezzato vi sono come siegue:

un burattone grande di pecchia tutto fornito;
item tre barilli per riporre farina o crusca cerchiati di legno;
item una rampinera di cinque rampini doppij di ferro.

Sopra il solaro del appartamento retro vi sono come siegue, cioè:

moggia due di formento in circa;
una panera per fare pane usata;
un sacco con d'entro circa stara 3 farina di formento;
una stadera grossa di ferro;
un trepiedi di ferro grande da caldara;
item una cocchietta usata.

Nella camera annessa al d.[o] solaro vi sono |[22 bis v] *come siegue, cioè:*

un tavola di noce con sopra un tappetto di rocadino rosso et paiado fatto a fiori su l'opera di damasco;
item un quadro con l'effigie d'una Madona de' sette dolori, con cornice solia nera et frisetto bianco intagliato;
item altro simile della Madona con S.[to] Giuseppe quando va in Egitto, con cornice come sopra;
item altro quadro simile di S. Philippo Neri che vien rapito in estasi celebrando messa, con cornice nel modo et forma di sopra descritti;
un quadretto picciolo dove sta dipinta S.[ta] Maria Madalena penitente, con corniceto con due fregi d'oro attorno;
item un quadro con s.[a] un aquasantino d'argento che ha

un Christo nel mezo, tutto d'argento, |[22r] con quatro fioretti all'angoli di d.º quadretto, tutti d'argento con cornice nera;
un vestaro non molto grande di pecchia tutto dipinto a fiori con d'entro diverse biancherie che si descriveranno;
item altre due casse di noce grandi quasi nove con d'entro diverse biancherie, che assieme con tutta l'altra biancheria qui si descriverà;
item un'altra cassa di pecchia dipinta con entro robba di puoco valore;
una lettéra con mezze colone intagliate a rebbesco, meza dorata et meza dipinta, di color di bronzo, con sua testera indorata et inargentata;
sopra d.ª lettéra vi è il suo letto fornito, cioè matarazzi di lana, piumazzo di piuma, et piazzo, cossini di lana, fodrette, lenzuoli di lino et una |[22v] coperta di roccadino paiado et turchino lavorata a fiori;
una cuna con lecietta et cossino;
una cadrega di bulgaro con chioderia d'ottone tonda;
qual camera tappezzata tutta di tappezzaria usata di corame rosso et verde miniata ad oro con sue collone;
seguita tutta la biancheria che si ritrova in casa:
lenzuoli num.º sessanta mettà di lino et mettà di stoppa et stoppina, compresi buoni et grami;
mantilli, parte di stoppa et parte di lino, numero ducento et tra buoni et grami;
tovaglie num.º trenta sottili et grosse;
serviette num.º venti otto;
sciugamani per la cuccina num.º venti quatro;
fodrette per cossini n.º trenta di lino;
|[23r] camise da huomo di lino num.º venti quatro tra buone et grame;
biancharia per li figliuoli, cioè camise di lino num.º quaranta fra buone et grame; scossali per le figliuole num.º dodeci;
cavezzi intieri di lino numero sette;
cavezzi di stoppina n.º quatro;
cavezzi num.º due per tovaglie di brazza 24 per cavezzo;
item cavezzi n.º due per far mantini, uno di lino et l'altro di stoppina;
fazzoletti num.º trenta sei sottili;
sottocalzoni di tella di lino, paia num.º otto;
sottocalzette paia n.º 20, et scalfini paia numero venti.
Nella camera annessa alla sodetta, chiamata la camera dipinta, vi sono come siegue, cioè:
|[23v] una lettéra con colone longhe al antica et suoi pomi, tutte adorate, nella quale vi si deve metter la trabbaca di filliselo paiado et rosso già descritti, che era s.ª un tavolino in una delle camere nove, qual lettéra è fornita di due matarazzi di lana et paiazzo, piumazzo di pena, et due cossini di lana con sue fodrette et lenzuoli et coperta di rocchadino rosso et paiado, fatta a fiore sopra l'opera di damasco;
altra lettéra, cioè banca e tavola con s.ª paiazzo, et un letto di piuma con piumazzo della med.ª et lenzuoli duoi con coperta di oggiolata di roccadino paiado usata;
due tavolini di noce, sopra uno de' quali vi sè la tappezzaria per due camere |[24r] di rasetto a listone paiado et celeste, coperta con un altro tappetto di roccadino novo morello et giallo, fatta a fiori sopra l'opera di damasco. L'altro tavolino resta coperto con un tappetto di lana a listone con s.ª un quadro d'una Maddona che ha il bambino che sposa S.ta Cattharina, con cornice nera solia et frisetto intagliato bianco;

item una cuna con sopra sei coperte di lana, una nova et l'altre usate, et un piumino da letto;
item due cadreghe armate di bulgaro usate, con franza verde et gialla et chioderia |[24v] di ottone;
item due belle casse di noce grandi, in una de' quali vi è della biancharia già descritta, et nell'altra vi si è trovato un paro di pistolle d'azalino, una banda bianca di vello, o sia buratto, con diversi frissi gialli et rossi;
contanti nella sodetta cassa:
sacchetti numero quatro de filippi mille per ciascuno sacchetto;
item un altro sacchetto de filippi num.º sette cento cinquanta, che sono in tutto d.i cinque sacchetti filippi num.º quatro mille sette cento cinquanta;
|[25r] item in d.ª camera due quadretti piccioli, uno con s.ª l'imagine della B.V. con il figliuolino in braccio, et altro con s.ª S. Francesco orando ad un crocifisso, ambidue con cornicette neri et frisetto nero.
Nella camera vicina al appartamento retro, et p.ma sopra l'altro coridore si sono trovate le seguenti cose:
una lettéra di mezze colone intornite di noce dove dorme la serva, con fornimento di mattarazzo di lana, letto di piuma, piumazzo del med.º pararizzo et duoi lenzuoli con sua coperta di oggiolata paiada fruste;
una cassa di noce usata et altra di pecchia, |[25v] quali casse sono proprie della serva;
un scabello et una cunetta di legno frusti.
Nella camera sopra la cuccina vi sono le seguenti robbe:
quadri mezani num.º tre, uno di Santo Antonio, l'altro di S.ta Lucia, l'altro di S. Carlo, con cornici nere et frisetti intagliati bianchi attorno;
altro quadro di Nostro Sig.re con un calice in mano picciolo, con cornice doppia nera all'antica;
altro quadro dove vi è l'imagine di un Crocifisso di ponti di setta et raggi adorati, con cornice doppia di pero al antica;
|[26r] item altro quadro grande con s.ª il ritratto del fu Sig.r Gio. Angelo Carena in piedi, senza cornice;
due tavole di noce, sopra una de' quali vi è un tappetto di corame frusto indorato con sopra diversi libri in stampa per li minori, et sopra tappeto frusto di fisellata gialda e celeste; sopra l'altra tavola vi è un scrittorio di pero intagliato di roncagine et inverniciato, con diversi cassettini voti con pometti di ottone adorati;
item una cassettina di pecchia con una chiavetta;
item un cesto grande di vimini;
item due sforzieri frusti con dentro diversa biancharia delli figliuoli già descritta;
item una lettéra di noce con mezze collone |[26v] lavorata d'oro et suoi pomi a foggia di pomi granati adorati;
sopra detta lettéra vi è un mattarazzo di lana, letto di piuma frusto, et suo piumazzo del medemo suo paiazzo, duoi lenzuoli di lino et coperta oggiolata di roccadino usata;
una cadrega armata di bulgaro con franza turchina et gialla, et chioderia d'ottone tonda all'antica;
una cassa grande di noce, nella quale vi si è trovato due cavezzi di tella già descritti;
contanti ritrovati in d.ª cassa:
un sacchetto di filippi numero mille;
item altro sacchetto di philippi n.º nove cento;
scartozzi num.º sedeci di parpaiole di |[27r] lire cento per ciaschun scartozzo, che tutti d.i danari di d.ª cassa constituiscono la somma di lire quatordeci mille novecento imperiali.

Nel solaro poi superiore a d.ª camera vi si è ritrovato come segue:
moggia dieci sette formento in grana;
item somme quindeci di avena in circa.
Nel camerino vicino al detto solaro vi è:
una lettéra, banca, e tavola, con sopra un paiazzo et una cassa di pecchia votta.
Nel solaro sopra le stanze nove verso strada si è trovato:
carbonina moggia due in circa
et più pezzi num.º quatro d'asse di larice.
Nella cassina sopra la salla si è trovato esservi:
un caro di fieno |[27v] maggiengo.
Nella canepa sotterranea a d.ª stalla et studio si sono trovati come siegue:
numero undeci vasselli, cerchiati tutti di ferro, tra grossi et piccioli, di diverse tenute, di tenuta in tutto di brente n.º sessanta quatro, de' quali ve ne sono ripieni di vino bianco et rosso di brente trenta incirca;
item quatro barilli, uno serchiato di ferro et li altri tre di legno;
due secchioni da lavar pani grandi, tutti cerchiati di ferro, cioè di tre cerchij per cadauno;
item tutte le calastre di legno per tutti detti vassellami, scalla, martelli, raspa, pidria, mastelli, et altri utensilij di canepa.
|[28r] Nella descrittione delle robbe, ricapiti et scritture ritrovate nello studio della sodetta casa si sono tralasciati li seguenti due libri, quali contengono diversi crediti, cambiali et altri con dare et havere, ad effetto di poscia riconoscerli per vedere se si poteva ponere una notta distinta di tutti li crediti, ma essendo hora riconosciuti et ritrovatili haver corrispondenza et relatione a diversi altri ricapiti anco delli di sopra descritti in d.º studio, onde non si può ponere per certo la notta distinta de' detti crediti dare et havere. Perciò si descrivono li med.mi libri che, con la vista d'altri recapiti, s'haverà dalla d.ª Sig.ra tutrice la perfetta cognitione, et questo anco così mandando la sod.ª Sig.ra tutrice et sono come sieguono, cioè:
|[28v] il p.mo è un libro bislongo con cartone di cartha pecorina, intitolato sopra il sod.º carthone di mano propria del detto fu Sig.r Steffano Carena con le seguenti parolle «Libro de' diverse notte e raccordi segnato n.º A», di foglij n.º 92, che comincia nel p.mo foglio di mano del fu Sig.r Bartholomeo Carenna, fratello del d.º fu Sig.r Stephano Carena, come siegue:
«Notta delle partite che noi Batholomeo et Gio. Angelo Carenna habbiamo d'havere da diversi», come siegue:
il Banco di S. Ambrogio di Milano deve dare a me Bartholomeo Carenna q. Francesco lire 50·000 moneta di cambio posta in d.º banco de' contanti, cioè lire 18·000 sotto il 12 9bre 1629, lire 6·000 sotto il dì |[29r] 30 ottobre 1631; lire 6·000 sotto il dì 20 settembre 1632; lire 2·474 sotto il dì 14 febraro 1634 et lire 17·525 sotto il dì 6 marzo 1634, come appare cinque chartelle del d.º Banco che si ritrovano presso di me, il qual banco paga per il frutto di d.ª partita a ragione di lire 4 soldi 10 per cento l'anno ogni tre mesi, dico lire 50·000»;
et detto libro è di foglij 92 come s.ª, qual siegue esser scritto di mano del d.º fu S.r Stephano Carenna sino a' fog. 49 con partita che finisce così:
«1680 haver scosso per contanti, et datogli ricevuta sotto li 10 maggio 1680, per lire 52.10 per contra l'anno 1679, lire 52.10»

siegue in d.° libro un foglio piegato con sopra un bigliettino cuccito di fillo rosso con inscritione |[29v] di mano propria del fu Sig.r Stephano Carenna come siegue: «siegue qua avanti a' fog. n.° 51 altre notte de' debitori diversi»

et d.° fog. 51 commincia «Notta de' diversi debitori 1671: Sebastiano Spreciofiggi di Eglo q. Antonio deve dare a me Stephano Carenna lire 600 imperiali per la quale m'ha vendute pertiche otto roncho et campo di pezze di magior perticato appellatto "alla Roccha" in commune di Eglo, et ciò con patto di gratia a riscuoterlo tempo anni sette, che spiraranno ultimo 8bre 1678, havendogline fatto successiva invest.ra d'affitto per detto tempo da pagarsi lire trenta all'anno netti, pagando |[30r] lui ogni carichi et per la manutentione fattaci ancor sigortà in solidum il Sig.r Carlo Spreiafiggi suo fratello, il tutto come per instromento rogato dal not.° Pietro Francesco Isaccho il dì 31 ottobre 1671, che si ritrova presso di me segnato n.° lire 600»,

qual libro resta scritto da d.° foglio 51 sino al fog.° 62 di mano propria del fu S.r Stephano Carenna, che si finisce come siegue:
«e più d.° Rizzi deve dare altre lire 5·000 simili, parimente obligato la sod.a casa con li patti, modi, conditioni et sigortà per lire 4·000 del Sig.r Enrico de Lorenzi q.m Andrea da pagare l'interessi |[30v] in rag.ne di lire 4.10 per cento come s.a et il tempo caderà a' 2 luglio 1681, come amplamente vedesi adietro in questo libro a' fog. 55 per altri due instromenti lire 5·000, in tutto lire 6·200»

qual libro da detto foglio 62 sino al fog.° 86 resta in bianco, nè vi resta scritta cosa alcuna;

dal foglio poi 86 sino al fog. 89 resta detto libro scritto di mano del fu Sig.r Bartholomeo Carenna et commincia come siegue: «1658»

siegue la notta delli danari che alla giornata vanno entrando per il frutto delli |[31r] dannari che alla giornata vanno entrando de' conto de noi fratelli Carenna

et finisce sopra il "pristino delle scansie" per un anno spirato a' 30 dicembre 1665 a' 5 per cento fanno lire 500, [in tutto] 25·900.5.6;

alla fine dal foglio 89 sino all'ultimo foglio 92 si trova a' fog. 91 scritto di mano del fu S.r Barth.° Carena come siegue: «adì 30 giugno 1662 pagati lire 100 per il livello della Sig.ra Livia Giovanna Carenna, monaca in S. Maria Maddalena in Milano, et sono per sei mesi finiti come sopra lire 100».

et finisce l'ultima partita: «adi . . . febraro pagato il livello di Livia Gioanna Carenna per sei mesi finiti a' 30 dicembre 1665 lire 100»,

|[31v] item l'altro libro in quadro coperto di carta pecora intitolato sopra il med.° coperto con le seg.ti notte: «1660 libro segnato "B" di me Steffano Carenna»,

qual libro è scritto tutto di mano propria del d.° fu Sig.r Stephano Carenna, et è di foglij n.° 58 postilati, la p.ma partita de' quali commincia a' fog. 1 et è del tenore come siegue:

«1660
Simone Giorgalli et Giug.mo Samuelli di Venetia conto mio devono adì 24 marzo a' libro "A" lire 16·781.4, assegnatomeli debitori il d.° libro v.ta di fiorini 3·641 19/24 a' loro remessi per detto mio conto Paolo Steffano Annoni d'Anversa, cioè fiorini 528.14, fiorini 675 per li 9 et 23 marzo co' fiorini 600 per li 27 aprile e fiorini 1·841 3/8 per li 5 maggio prossimo fiorini 3·645.192. 16·781.4»

|[32r] et finisce a' fog. 41 come siegue:
«1677
Il Sig.r Paolo Annone, conto de' tempi a sè med.mo, conto ecc. deposito lire quatordeci milla, quali sono in saldo di d.° conto vecchio de' deposito, come in questo a' fog. 39 con obligat.e di pagarmi dette lire 14·000 fra anni quattordeci, cioè lire milla cadun'anno senza alcun interesse, comminciando il p.mo pagamento la festa di S. Martino del corrente anno 1677 et così successivamente cadun'anno d.e lire 1·000, cioè lire quattro cento sessanta cinque assegnatemi squodere da Carlo Gerosa, fittabile delli beni a Lusciana in Monte Brianza, et il rimanente a compimento delle d.e lire |[32v] milla l'anno dal Sig.r Conte Carlo Annone figliuolo del sod.° Sig.r Paolo, con patto et conditione che non pagando li d.i termini doppo duoi mesi habbia a buonifficarmi l'interesse in ragione de' cinque per cento l'anno, come il tutto più amplam.e appare per instrom.to rog.to sotto li 18 giugno 1677 dalli notari Sig.r Giulio Cesare Besozzo et Giacomo Ant.° Fumagallo, con risserva che tanto delli effetti entrati et che in appresso potranno entrare nelli libri della compagnia de' negotij segnati n.° "C" et "D" sotto nome di Paolo et Stephano Annoni compagni, ne' quali io ho havuto participatione, nè debba io anchora partecipare la mia contingente portione, conforme dispongono le capitulat.ni |[33r] d'essa compagnia, et vedesi in sodetti suoi libri signati "C" et "D" 39 lire 14·000».

Notta delle case situate in Milano:

p.ma la sodetta casa da nobile situata in P.T. P. di S.ta Euffemia di d'entro di Milano, cioè sopra il corso che va a S.to Celso et per contro il monastero delle monache di S.to Agostino, quale consiste nelli luog[h]i corte come sopra descritti nel formare l'inventario della sod.a mobilia, alla quale vi è coherenza da una parte d.a strada che va a S.to Celso, dall'altra il Sig.r Francesco Ferrandi, dal altra Giuseppe Azzio, et dall'altra Ottavio Homati, salvo errore delle |[33v] coherenze;

item altra casa da nobile con giardino et altro casino annesso posti nelle sod.e Porta et P.a, nella contrada detta di S.ta Euffemia, a' quali case et casino vi è coherenza da una parte la strada detta la contrada di S.ta Euffemia sod.a, dal altra la strada detta il Terragio, dal altra il S.r Phisico Gioanni Battista Sittone, et dal altra Giuseppe Vadabelli,

salvo l'errore delle coherenze;

item altra casa posta in P.T. P. S.to Alessandro di Milano nella contrada d.a di S.to Alessandro, quale è stata venduta dal d.° Sig.r Stephano Carena al Sig.r Benedetto Zucchelli, rag.to della Città di Milano, per il prezzo de lire tredeci mille trenta cinque imperiali et detto Sig.r Zucchelli anchora deve pagare tutto |[34r] detto prezzo di d.e lire tredeci mille trenta cinque imperiali con tutti li suoi ingressi dal giorno della vendita in avanti.

4. Inventario Annone 1680

|[1r] **Notta de' beni posti nella terra et territorio d'Annone, pieve d'Uggione, Ducato di Milano**

Una casa grande da nobile, situata come s.a, qual consiste in diversi et più luoghi, cioè in sei luoghi in terra tutti in un piano, con suoi superiori et baltresca sino al tetto, inclusive stalla, cassina, pozzo, giardino tutto murato; legnera grande dove altre volte v'era un torchio; corte circondatta di muro con portico grande con suoi superiori sino al tetto; altro portico con fornelli num.° tre piantati con sue caldare di rame et molini per trar la setta; porta grande et altra porta che esce nella corte delli massari et altre sue ragioni et pertinenze sotto le sue notorie coherenze.

Nella salla a' piano di terra in d.a casa, qual riesce |[1v] nel mezo de' luoghi in terra, vi si è trovato la seguente mobiglia, cioè:

un tavolino di noce con suo tapetto di corame usato;

cadreghe numero quatro, et scagni n.° parimente quatro di bulgaro usati, con chioderia di ottone all'antica;

altra tavola di noce;

una rastellera di noce lavorata con suoi cornici da metter arme longhe et corti, con una cassa a proportione di noce con diversi cassettini d'entro in un sol tenente con d.a rastellera et s.a detta rastellera, cioè di presente, una schioppetta;

n.° cinque pezzetti di quadri, cioè il ritratto d'un Salvatore con cornice di legno, altre due ritratti et due paesini;

una credenza di noce nova con sua seratura |[2r] et chiave per g[...]amar robba, con d'entro diversi piatti grandi et piccioli di maiolicha per servitio della tavola;

due brandenali con l'haste grosse di ottone bene lavorati et altri suoi ferramenti per fornimento del camino di d.a sala;

un tripiedi di ferro lavorato per mettervi il cadino per lavar le mani;

un specchio mezano con cornice di pero nera lavorata.

Nel'altra sala contingua a mano sinestra entrando vi sono come siegue, cioè:

n.° quatro tavole di noce, due granti et due mezane;

una cassa di noce nova votta;

due cadreghe armate di bulgaro con franze assai buone;

una banca con spaletta di noce;

|[2v] n.° quatro pezzi di quadri grandi senza cornice, s.a uno de' quali vi è la cenna de' Re Baldassare et altri tre baccanali;

altro quadro di S. Antonio da Padova, con cornice nera et frisetto bianco;

un armario nel muro di d.a sala vicino alla porta della canepa con d'entro diversi vasi di vetro.

Nella canepa annessa a detta sala vi sono come siegue, cioè:

num.° due tine cerchiate di due cerchij di ferro per cadauna, et un tinotto con un cerchio di ferro solo, et altri di legno di tenuta di b.e n.° trenta cinque per cadauna;

n.° sette vascelli tra grandi e mezani, tutti cerchiati di ferro, di tenuta di brente cinquanta due in circa;

|[3r] n.° quatro altri vasselli, cioè tre di tenuta di due brente per caduno, et uno di una brenta cerchiato di ferro;

nelli sod.i vasselli, che parte sono voti et parte sono pieni, vi sono brente n.° trent'una di vino in circa tra bianco e rosso;

item tutti li calastri et altri suoi utiensilij per servitio della canepa sod.a et una moschirola.

Nella dispensa vicino alla canepa, che riesce in testa del portico di d.a casa, vi sono come siegue, cioè:

n.° otto quadri piccioli, cioè due con figure di duoi imperatori romani, altri due di due famine, et altri quatro con paesini, tutti senza cornice;

un cassone di noce frusto con d'entro diversa quantità di maiolica per servitio della tavola;

altro cassone di noce all'antica pieno di stoppa |[3v] e lino;

altro cassone di pobbia con d'entro diverse tattare di puoco valore;
una tavola di noce grande frusta;
un secchione grande di tenuta di b.^{e} 4 novo con due serchij di ferro;
un altro secchione di tenuta di b.^{e} 2 novo serchiato di legno;
un avello di sasso con suo coperto di noce di tenuta d'una brenta in circa, votto;
una olla grande ricolma meza d'oglio di linosa;
un vestaro mezano di pecchia, entro al quale vi si è ritrovato:
p.^{ma} lire n.° dieci imperiali contanti et una doppia d'Italia intiera;
una gavetta di corda per tirare a siugare panni;
una tazza di porcellana fina custodita in una scattola;
diversi baslottini di legno con d'entro molti chiodi;
un mazzo di polize, cioè:
una poliza di lire 1.050 contra li SS. Antonio |[4r] et Gaspare padre et figliolo Ferrarij d'Annone, detta sotto 'l dì 5 agosto 1679 passato;
altra polize contra Andrea Carena di d.° luogo d'Annone di lire 300 in datta delli 2 maggio 1679;
altra polize contra Francesco Frigerio del med.° luogo d Annone di lire 105 sotto 'l dì 9 marzo 1679;
ristretto de' conti et obligo fatto da Francesco Spreciafigo della villa di Vergano a favore delli furono SS. Stephano et Bartholomeo fratelli Carena di lire 121 soldi 7 denari 9 in datta di 18 9bre 1669;
obbligo per scrittura privata di Gio. Angelo Annone, d.° Albrigo, di pagare stara otto di formento et stara 20 mistura ogni anno di due termini con appenditij, datto sotto 'l dì 25 ottobre 1677, che anco dura;
un mazzo de diversi instromenti, fra quali vi è |[4v] l'ins.^{to} d'acquisto fatto da Stephano Carpano q.^{m} Pietro Martire di diversi pezzi di terra delli heredi di Ambrogio Carena per il prezzo de lire mille trenta nove soldi 4 per persona da nominarsi, quale ha poi nominato la persona esser il d.° fu Sr Stephano Carena, come per d.° instrom.^{to} rogato il dì 22 giugno 1680 dal not.° Pietro Maria Delfinone;
altro instromento di detto in paga fatto dalli fratelli Tentori di Vergano a d.^{i} q.^{m} Sig.^{ri} Bartholomeo e Stephano fratelli Carena de pertiche 160 tavole sette piedi 10 terreno nel d.° comune di Vergano, rogato dal notaro Christophoro Hortali il dì 11 maggio 1663, con annesso duoi altri instromenti d'acquisto di puoco spatio di terra fatto dal fu Sig.^{r} Stephano Carena da Carlo Franc.° Spreiafigo et Battista Spreiaficco, rogato da Hermes Delphinone li 20 ottobre 1674 et 26 giugno 1676;
|[5r] altro instromento di cessione fatta da Altobello et fratelli Cassina a favore di d.° Bartholomeo et Stephano fratelli Carena d'un credito di lire sei cento che havevano sopra la communità d'Uggione, come per instrom.^{to} rogato dal fu notaro Giacomo Antonio Fumagalli il dì 21 luglio 1662;
item altri instromenti di diverse investiture et altri crediti che ci vedono hora sodisfatti;
diversi mazetti de' confessi per scritture private;
item un carni[e]re pieno di diverse scritture, cioè istromenti antichi, una filza de confessi de pagamenti fatti alli esatori per li carichi ordinarij et straordinarij;
due bilancini, uno per pesar l'oro, l'altro argento, con suoi pesi et cassette;
due bilancette con suoi pesi;
un rastelletto con sopra diverse lett.^{e} piegate;
|[5v] una stadera tutta di ferro che leva lire cinquanta da trenta oncie per lira;
in esso camerino: un scagno di bulgaro et due altri scagni di legno;
un tavolino sotto alla finestra.

Nel dispensino sotto alla scalla:

vi sono n.° 3 olle grandi per mettervi oglio, et alcune asse per riporvi robbe commestive.

Nella cucina contigua alla sala p.^{mo} loco descritta, nella quale vi è il forno, vi si è trovato come siegue:

una credenza di noce con sue scalinate frusta con d'entro diversi vasi et utensilij per servitio di cucina;
una tavola di noce usata;
n.° tre scagni di bulgaro grami;
item un tavolino di noce con suo cassetto frusto;
una banca di noce con sua spalletta;
un banco per riporvi le zaine;
|[6r] duoi brandenalli con gabbia di ferro con tre cattene da fuoco, bernazzo, moglia, guarda fuoco, trepiedi per scaldini et boffetto;
sopra la bocca del forno in d.^{a} cuccina vi è il suo coperto di ferro nuovo, sì come alla bocca del seratore di d.° forno;
peltro capi n.° 19 pesano lire dieci sette grosse da onze trenta per lira.

Nella dispensa annessa a detta cucina vi sono come siegue, cioè:

una credenza usata con sua scalinata di noce con sopra diversi tondi di maiolica, d'entra della quale credenza vi sono diversi utensilij di cucina di puoco momento;
una capponera;
n.° tre lavezzi, duoi grandi col altro mezano;
una lecarda di ferro;
pallette di ferro n.° cinque, una craticola di ferro;
|[6v] diverse asse per riporre s.^{a} robba;
tre piedi, un menarosto;
diversi pezzi di rame per servitio di cuccina consistenti in caldari, padellini et altri, in tutto lire grosse da once 30 l'una n.° venti otto;
una caldara grande di tenuta d'una brenta e mezza in circa;
n.° quatro candeglieri d'ottone con un bacille, parimenti d'ottone, di peso di lire otto in circa da once 30 per caduna lira;
cucchiali et forzine d'argento para n.° quatro, coltelli con manico d'osso n.° quatro;
un cesto con d'entro 6 mantini et 2 tovaglie per uso della tavola.

Nella legnera annessa al giardino di d.^{a} casa, dove altre volte vi era il torchio, vi è come sigeue:

p.^{ma} una quantità di molte asse nove, molti |[7r] fassi di lino in pianta;
cara n.° quatro in circa legna d'abbrucciare;
molti travi et travetti per uso di fabricare.

Nella corte di d.^{a} casa vi sono anco:

copi novi num.° quatrocentro in c.^{a};
item sotto il portico una tavola grande di noce usata et duoi scagni di veralle.

Nella camera poi ascendendo per la scalla in testa del portico a mano sinistra, che è sopra la dispensa, vi sono come siegue, cioè:

duoi tavolini di noce, sopra quali vi è il suo tapetto di corame dipinto usato;
n.° tre quadri, cioè uno con il ritratto della Madona con le mani in croce, con cornice nera; altro con S. Giuseppe che ha il bambino in bracio, con cornice nera et friseto bianco; altro con l'Annonciata, con cornice nera;
item n.° 6 quadretti picciole di cesto de fiori, con cornice nera et frisetto bianco;
item un specchio piccolo, con cornice nera;
|[7v] una cadrega di bulgaro con chiodi all'antica et franza verde et un scabellino di noce;
item una lettéra di noce con sue collone intornite et testera di noce; sopra detta lettiera vi è un paiazzo, due buoni mattarazzi, coperta di lana romana, altra d'oggiolata di roccadino color verde et giallo, lenzoli n.° 2, piumazzo et cossini di lana;
una cassa di noce grande quasi nuova, entro alla quale vi sono n.° quatro lenzuoli di stoppina et lino buoni:
item tovaglie ordinarie buone n.° 4;
item mantini n.° 53 buoni;
item serviette n.° dieci buone;
item sciugamani n.° cinque;
item camiscie da huomo n.° 3;
item fodrette n.° 14 di lino buone;
item un colletto di dante grande;
item un mazzetto di setta di lire quatro in circa per la Sig.^{ra} tutrice;
item quatro cucchiali et quatro forcine d'argento con quatro colteli con manico d'osso;
item la sedia di camera con l'orinario di stagno.

Nella camera contigua alla sod.^{a} et in fronte di d.^{a} |[8r] scalla, qual è sopra la canepa per metà vi si è trovato come siegue:

una lettéra di noce con sue collone longhe all'antica, sopra quale vi è un paiazzo et una coperta di lana piegata assai bona;
altra lettéra con mezze colone di noce intornite et sua testera, et sopra quale vi è il pagliazzo, letto di piuma, matarazzo, lenzuoli duoi di lino, et piumazzo di lana con due coperte, una di lana assai buona, altra di rocchadino et fillo color bianco et turchino usata, et un cossino di lana;
un scagno da varalle;
item due sforzieri coperti di corame frusto e rotto, entro quali non vi è cosa alcuna;
item un quadretto d'una Maddona, frusto, con cornice nera.

Nel dispensino sopra la cantina per un'altra mettà |[8v] vi si è trovato come siegue, cioè:

una marna di pecchia con sopra un assa di noce;
una stadera grossa tutta di ferro, un sedazzo;
un'altra marnetta;
una cassa di pobbia frusta, una concha nova;
cesti n.° tre di vimini grandi;
stara due farra vestita; stara uno faggioli;
una cassa di pecchia senza coperto con sopra un secchio; in un guarnerio vi sono n.° duoi candiglieri di peltro et altre tattare di poco valore.

Nella camera a mano dritta sopra la scalla, quale per esser di transito non v'è d'entro cosa alcuna, andando avanti a drittura vi è una altra camera grande, nella quale vi sono l'infrascritte robbe:

p.^{ma} una lettéra nova di noce con sue collone intornite et testera di noce, sopra la quale vi è paiazzo, duoi mattarazzi buoni |[9r] di lana fina, piumazzo di piuma bono, tre coscini con sue fodrette, due coperte di lana di Roma, et un paio di lenzuoli;
un scrittorijno quadro coperto di rasetto frusto;
duoi tavolini di noce buoni;
una cadregha di camerra con orinale di peltro;
duoi quadri, uno con l'effiggie di S. Carlo et l'altro d'una Madona, con cornici nere;

un quadrettino in ottangolo, con guarnitione d'ottone, venuto da Roma;
n.º sei quadretti di cesti de fiori, con cornici nere soglie et frisetto adorati;
una candella benedetta di lire 2 in circa;
altri quadri n.º 6 di cesti de fiori un poco più grandi delli s.ª descritti, con cornici nere soglie et frisetti bianchi;
altro quadrettino di paese, con cornice nera et frisetto bianco;
una cassa di noce mezana con d'entro un piumazzo di piuma con duoi cossini, uno di piuma et l'altro di lana, un tappetto di corame novo per |[9v] tavola; una coperta di rocadino per il letto di colore turchino et d'oro;
un paio di calzette di setta verde usate et altro paro di reffo bianco et turchino;
un bavulo picciolo coperto di pello di camuccia, d'entro del quale vi si è trovato un velte, cioè una revoltana nova con tutti i suoi fornimenti;
item una cassa di noce grande nova, entro la quale vi si è trovato come siegue:
lenzuoli n.º 15 di stoppina e lino;
camiscie n.º 5 da huomo di lino;
mantini n.º16;
tovaglie n.º quatro;
fodrette per coscini n.º otto di lino;
serviete n.º 2;
sotto calzoni para n.º tre;
giupponi di bombacina bianca n.º 2;
una copertina per letto di rocchadino color giallo e roso fatta a fiorami.
Nella camera superiore alla salla vicina alla canepa non vi è cosa alcuna perchè serve di transito all'altra camera |[10r] superiore, alla sala di mezzo, et in questa vi si è trovato come siegue, cioè:
una tavola di noce nova con sopra un tapetto di corame usatto;
una lettéra di noce con sue colone intornite et testera di noce;
quadri n.º cinque, cioè tre paesini et due altre figure;
un quadro grande con l'effiggie di meza figura del Beato Federico Borromeo;
una cadregha di bulgaro frusta con franza verde et chioderia d'ottone all'antica;
un vestaro molto grande di noce bellissimo, entro al quale vi è come segue:
una coperta di letto nuova;
un tappetto et una coperta di filo et rochadino nove color di turchino et d'oro a fiorami sop.ª l'opra di damasco;
una coperta d'oggiolata bianca;
un piumazzo di piuma;
n.º 20 lirette di rocchadino filato;
setta cruda da lavorare lirette n.º cento trenta cinque onze otto, dico libre 135 once 8;
|[10v] item guarda robba nel muro di d.ª camera, quale ha sopra le sue ante et chiavi vi è un baslotto con d'entro lire grosse n.º 6 in circa sale; item rocchadino lirette n.º 20 in circa già spinatto;
di più in d.ª camera vi è un barile con d'entro un staro in c.ª di sale;
noci moggia n.º quatro.
Nella camera poi superiore alla cucina vi si è trovato come siegue, cioè:
p.ma un tavolino di noce con sopra il suo tappetto di corame;
quadri n.º tre, uno con l'effigie di S.to Fran.co stigmatizato, l'altro con l'effigie della Madona orante al bambino Giesù, altro con s.ª un paesino, tutti con cornice nera et un puoco di frisetto nero;
una lettéra di noce con sue colone et testera intornite con sopra un paiazzo et di sotto di d.ª lettéra vi è un boccale di stagno;
altro tavolino con sopra un tappetto di corame et quale ha sopra due azze di doppione et un paio di maniche di dante;
|[11r] una cassa di noce tutta piena di setta da lavorare, che sono lirette n.º cento quaranta tre onze otto, dico libbre 143 once 8;
item altra cassa di noce nova grande, nella quale vi si è trovato l'infrascritta biancheria:
lenzuoli num.º trenta, mettà tutto lino et mettà stoppa et lino assieme;
nel cassettino di d.ª cassa vi si è trovata una borsa con d'entro filippi n.º diecisette.
Nelli solari di sopra a detti luoghi, et unitmente in tutti d.i solari, fatto il calcolo si è ritrovato esservi come siegue:
p.ma moggia n.º ventij formento;
segale moggia cinque e stara tre;
scandella moggia n.º cinque et stara sei;
linosa stara n.º cinque;
|[11v] avena stara n.º quatro;
formentone moggia n.º. . .;
miglio moggia n.º dodeci.

PETER PAUL RUBENS
(1577–1640)
The Massacre of the Innocents
c. 1610
Oil on panel
142 × 182 cm
The Thomson Collection,
Art Gallery of Ontario, Toronto

AUTHORS

DAVID JAFFÉ is Senior Curator at the National Gallery, London.

GIOVANNA TONELLI is Senior Researcher in Modern History, University of Milan.

ACKNOWLEDGEMENTS

Since my earlier studies of the picture I have tried to push the interpretation of the *Massacre* further, especially in pursuing Rubens's use of sculptural models, and to discover more about the first known owner of the painting, originally identified by George Gordon. Carenna proved to be an elusive figure and it was only visits to the archives with Giovanna Tonelli that made it possible to reconstruct him from legal papers that had remained silent for so long.

This project was begun with the research assistance of Ben Hunting, Jessica Cerasi and Amanda Bradley. Amanda Bradley provided both invaluable organization in expanding notes into text and further research material, especially in the first and third chapters. Elizabeth Stephen edited the text at an early stage, and it has greatly benefited from being read by three Rubens scholars, Ben van Beneden, Gregory Martin and Elizabeth McGrath. I am further grateful to Giovanni Agosti, Joost van der Auwera, Sophie Azzola, Rachel Billinge, Dorrit van Camp, Lorne Campbell, Mercedes Ceron, Gia Colombia, José Luis Colomer, Alain Crookham, Ingrid Demeuter, Rembrandt Duits, John Elliott, Paolo Galemberti, George Gordon, Fiona Healey, Dirk Imhof, Jo Kirby, Veronika Kopecky, Silvio Leydi, Emilia Maggio, Maria Juliet Marinus, Jeffrey Muller, Caroline Oates, Joe Padfield, Jeroen Puttevils, Paul Taylor, Alejandro Vergara, Diana Widmaer Picasso, Marjorie E. Wieseman and not least the staff at the Milan, Antwerp, Brussels, Simancas, Valladolid and Annone di Brianza archives. DJ

First published September 2009 by
Skylet Publishing
in association with the Art Gallery of Ontario

ISBN 9781903470 81 7
9781903470 86 2 (5 volume boxed set)

FRONT COVER

Peter Paul Rubens (1577–1640), *The Massacre of the Innocents*, *c*. 1610, oil on panel, 142 × 182 cm

Distributed in Canada by University of British Columbia Press
www.ubcpress.ca
and in the United States by the University of Washington Press
www.washington.edu/uwpress/
and in Europe and elsewhere by Paul Holberton publishing
www.paul-holberton.net

Produced by Paul Holberton publishing, London
www.paul-holberton.net

Designed by Philip Lewis

Origination and printing by e-graphic, Verona, Italy

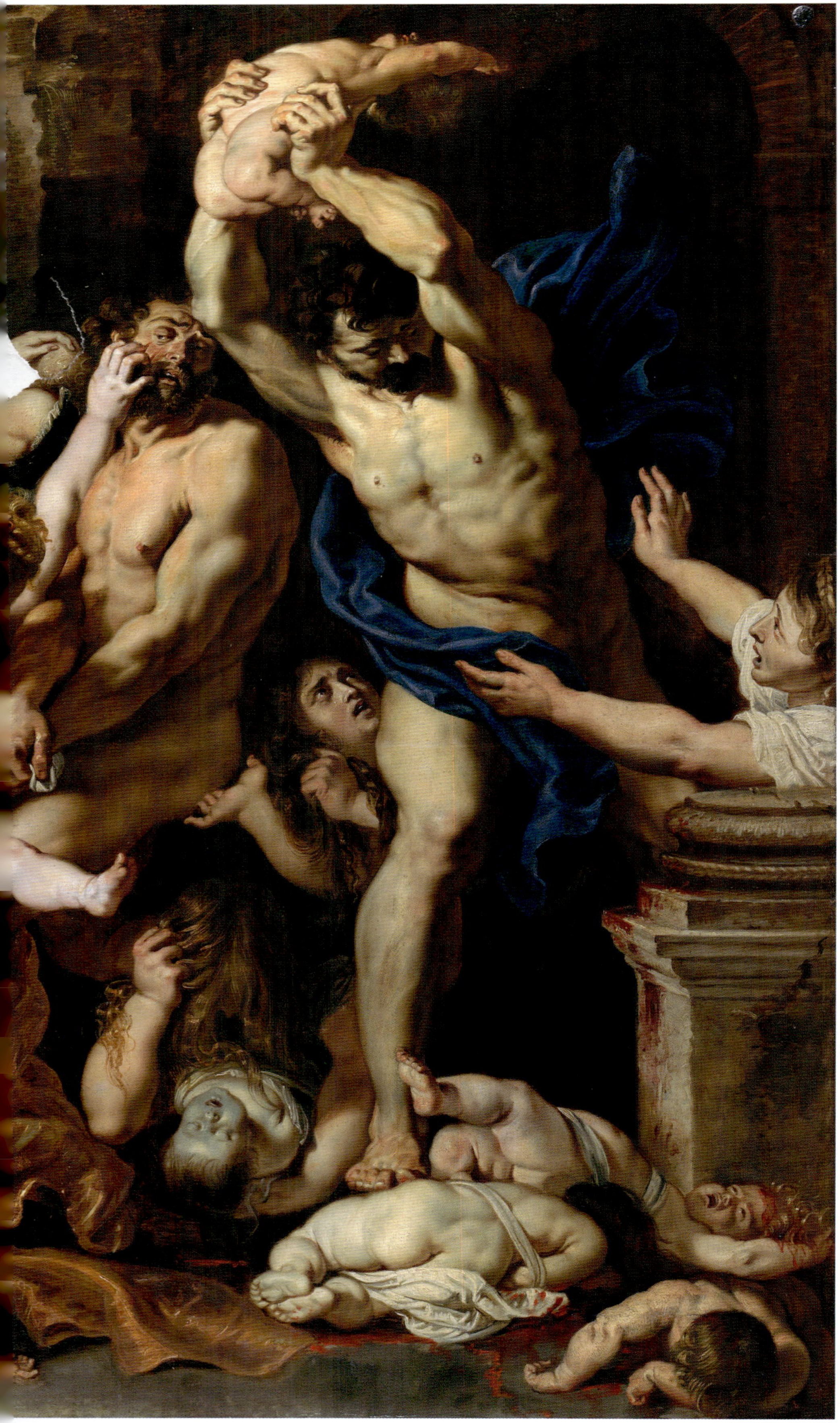

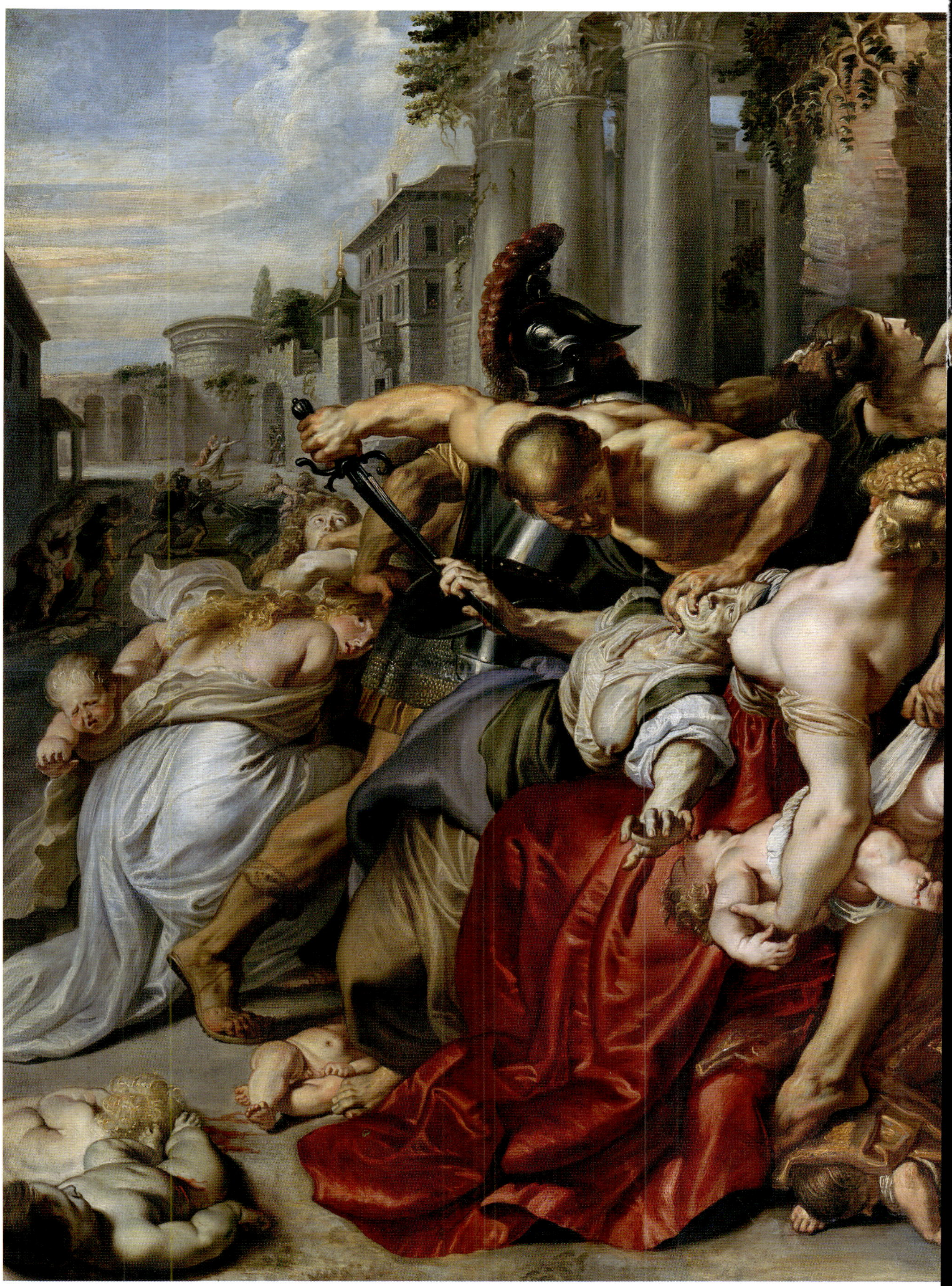